MW01141836

Physical Education for Exceptional Students: Theory to Practice

Douglas C. Wiseman
Plymouth State College

DELMAR PUBLISHERS INC.™

I(T)P™

NOTICE TO THE READER

Publisher does not warrant or guarantee any of the products herein or perform any independent analysis in connection with any of the product information contained herein. Publisher does not assume, and expressly disclaims, any obligation to obtain and include information other than that provided to it by the manufacturer.

The reader is expressly warned to consider and adopt all safety precautions that might be indicated by the activities described herein and to avoid all potential hazards. By following the instructions contained herein, the reader willingly assumes all risks in connection with such instructions.

The publisher makes no representations or warranties of any kind, including but not limited to, the warranties of fitness for particular purpose or merchantability, nor are any such representations implied with respect to the material set forth herein, and the publisher takes no responsibility with respect to such material. The publisher shall not be liable for any special, consequential, or exemplary damages resulting, in whole or in part, from the reader's use of, or reliance upon, this material.

Cover design by Spiral Design Studio

Delmar Staff
  Associate Editor: Erin J. O'Connor
  Project Editor: Andrea Edwards Myers
  Production Coordinator: Sandra Woods
  Art and Design Coordinator: Karen Kunz Kemp

For information, address Delmar Publishers Inc.
3 Columbia Circle, Box 15-015
Albany, New York 12212-5015

Copyright © 1994
by Delmar Publishers Inc.

(The trademark ITP is used under license.)

All rights reserved. No part of this work covered by the copyright hereon may be reproduced or used in any form or by any means— graphic, electronic, or mechanical, including photocopying, recording, taping, or information storage and retrieval systems— without written permission of the publisher.

Printed in the United States of America
Published simultaneously in Canada by Nelson Canada,
a division of The Thomson Corporation

  2 3 4 5 6 7 8 9 10 XXX 00 99 98 97 96 95 94

Library of Congress Cataloging-in-Publication Data
Wiseman, Douglas C.
  Physical education for exceptional students: theory to practice / Douglas C. Wiseman.
    p. cm.
  Includes bibliographical references (p.) and indexes.
  ISBN 0-8273-5296-4
    1. Physical education for handicapped children—Study and teaching—United States. 2. Physical education for exceptional children—Study and teaching—United States. I. Title.
  GV445.W56 1994
  371.9'04486—dc20   93-8387
                                                                CIP

Contents

Preface

Physical Education for Exceptional Children has evolved from over thirty years of visitations, observations, discussion, research, teaching, and my own course evaluations within the fields of physical and special education. The result is a book that approaches the topic from the practitioner's point of view and addresses those with special needs in a way that makes sense to students who are beginning their study. The enthusiastic endorsements from students and colleagues who have used many of the elements contained in this text have been a source of stimulation for me, and I am grateful.

What do we mean by the term *exceptional*? What is *inclusionary education*? Upon what basis should students with disabilities be mainstreamed in regular physical education classes or have special classes of their own? What is meant by the expression, *least restrictive environment*? How can support for our programs be procured from parents, physicians, administrators, and the general public? How can we determine the extent of adjustment a child has made to his or her disability? What are the practical implications of Public Law 94-142 (the Education for All Handicapped Children Act) and subsequent legislation? What kinds of developmental activities should be included in an adapted physical education program? Need all members of a class be assigned the same activity at the same time? What criteria should be used for evaluating and grading students with disabilities within regular or special classes? Is contract teaching appropriate?

To these and other equally important questions we must find answers if the teaching profession is to be responsive to the needs of all students.

This text has been written with the understanding that physical education for exceptional students can be taught as a single course, a course with a laboratory, or a two-semester course; that both undergraduate and graduate students will be reading it; and that some will already have had significant exposure to special education, while others will have had none. With this understanding of the diversity of the programs and students enrolled therein, this book has been organized so that should an instructor want to omit a chapter, or its portion, this can be done without loss of continuity. Each chapter stands alone.

While this book has been prepared primarily for students in physical education who are in the midst of their studies, practitioners of therapy, nursing, and other health-related and teaching fields will find its contents useful as they study and prescribe in their respective arts.

This text is divided into three sections. Section I, Foundations of Adapted Physical Education, contains three chapters: Defining the Problem, Physical and Motor Growth, and Principles of Program Organization.

Section II, Introduction to Exceptionalities, includes ten chapters: Physical, Motor, and Postural Fitness Disorders; Sensory Disabilities (specifically visual and auditory impairments); Cardiovascular Disorders; Musculoskeletal Disorders (acquired and congenital); Neurological Disorders; Mental Disabilities; Behavioral and Emotional Disorders; The Gifted; Learning Disabilities; and Other Health Conditions (including AIDS, allergies, child abuse, diabetes mellitus, dysmenorrhea, infectious diseases, Marfan's syndrome, and panic attack).

Section III, Programs in Action, has seven chapters: Adapted Games and Sports; Outings, Camping, and Aquatics; Special Olympics and Wheelchair Athletic Programs; Making Your Own Supplies and Equipment; Evaluation (product and process); Record Keeping and Public Relations, and Epilogue.

At the beginning of each chapter are lists of learning objectives and key terms. Recommended laboratory assignments have been provided at the end of Chapters 2 through 20. You will also find developmental activities placed within pertinent sections of the chapters. These have been provided in response to the complaints that I have heard (and had) about other texts that neglect to address the necessary linkages between theory and practice. Recommended readings are also available.

Appendix materials include a roster of commonly referenced agencies and organizations, a checklist for braces and wheelchairs, developmental exercises without and with apparatus, suggested exercises for relaxation, architectural barrier-free design codes, and author as well as subject indexes. Accompanying the text is an instructor's guide. Included one will find recall- and recognition-type items selected to measure the attainment of the learning objectives and other topics of significance within the chapters. Each item has been validated through jury review, and internal consistency and stability coefficients greater than .90 have been obtained for the entire battery.

From the era of the one-room school to a time when colleges and universities are commonplace, we have become increasingly aware that the uniqueness of the individual is a paramount consideration in planning and conducting a curriculum. We have realized that society can best be served when this premise is followed. At the same time, however, we have not successfully met the needs of the atypical student. Under the present system, students with disabilities are often excused from certain classes for an assortment of superfluous reasons. The physical education class is no exception. Many misguided theorists have felt that programs of physical education are too athlete-dominated, too structured to include lifetime sports skills, and—at best—no place for youngsters with less than maximum physical endowments.

It is paradoxical that these misguided theories may not be misguided at all. All too many programs are geared to the athlete, and in short very little is done to classify students according to physiological-psychological structure and function. The administrators either cannot procure support from physicians or do not choose to; instructors are too busy with other priorities to create variant lesson plans for one class; or teachers in the schools lack the skill necessary to offer programs that will meet the needs of all enrolled so that youngsters with disabilities will not have to be sent to a study hall or given a menial assignment.

If the premise that education is for all is correct, it should follow that we must give everyone the opportunity to develop skills. Because of the number of children in the schools who have assorted disabilities, we must be prepared to modify, moderately restrict, or perhaps adapt programs so that everyone has a chance to become physically educated. Toward this end this text has been written.

Acknowledgments _____

Its completion, however, would not have been possible without the thoughtful input of colleagues and students alike. To all of them I offer my heartfelt gratitude. I also want to extend my appreciation to the corps of professionals at Delmar Publishers Inc. Their guidance and support helped make this task a labor of love. Specifically I want to mention James DeWolf, Vice President of Publishing; Susan Simpfenderfer, Publisher; Erin O'Connor, Associate Editor; and Megan Terry, Editorial Assistant. I am convinced that the most important task they had was to make this text the best available.

The author and staff at Delmar Publishers wish to express their appreciation to the reviewers of this manuscript who contributed many constructive comments and suggestions.

Steve Grineski
Moorhead State University
Moorhead, MN

Doug Perry
Concordia College
Moorhead, MN

Monica Lepore
West Chester University
West Chester, PA

Richard A. Shade
University of Wyoming
Laramie, WY

Mary S. Owens
Texas Tech University
Lubbock, TX

Katharine K. Sheng
CUNY
New York, NY

Dedication _____

This book is dedicated to my grandchildren

Rebecca Catherine
Stephen Mark
Trystan Leigh
...and others who may follow.

SECTION I

Foundations of Adapted Physical Education

CHAPTER 1

Defining the Problem

Objectives
After reading this chapter, you should be able to

- **Discuss major historical eras in the development of physical education for exceptional children.**
- **Differentiate among the various labels given to adapted physical education.**
- **Identify general classifications of disabilities.**
- **Discuss the process relative to the educational placement of children with disabilities**
- **Discuss characteristics of special schools relative to physical education for children with disabilities.**
- **Describe problems and issues related to the mainstreaming of children with disabilities.**
- **Identify some commonalities and/or trends relative to the education of exceptional children, with particular emphasis on adapted physical education.**

INTRODUCTION

The study of exceptional children must begin with an awareness of what makes them different from the **norm**. As the reader would expect, however, *normal* is a relative term that can only be defined when it is referenced against what is usual (or ordinary). What may be normal in one setting can be markedly at odds with what is normal in another setting. A blind child who is in residence at a school for the visually impaired would not be considered unusual. On the other hand, should a blind child with a heart ailment be enrolled in that same school, special (or adapted) programming may be required beyond what would ordinarily be prescribed.

Within public schools, children may be found who have certain characteristics that are unlike what would ordinarily be expected. This does not mean that these children are

---

KEY TERMS

adapted physical education	least restrictive environment
Amateur Sports Act	mainstreaming
anomalies	modified physical education
Child-Find	musculoskeletal
corrective physical education	neurological*
developmental physical education	norm
disabled	orthopedic physical education
disorder	preventative physical education
due process	psychological disturbances
entitlements	Public Law (PL) 94–142
exceptional children	Rehabilitation Act
gifted and talented	resource rooms
group homes	sensory disorders
individual educaton plan (IEP)	special classes
intellectual disorders	special physical education
labels (labeling)	special schools
learning disabled	trauma

---

in the wrong setting. Rather it means that a modification in their curriculum or in the way that the curriculum is delivered is likely to be necessary. The point is that all children have the right to expect the best of what an educational establishment has to offer, and they have the right to expect it in an environment that is least restrictive to their learning.

Exceptional children are those who exhibit physical, intellectual, and/or behavioral traits that differ from those generally viewed as the norm. Within the context of special education, I am not using *deviation from the norm* to mean a blond-haired child who might be sitting amongst a class full of brunettes. Obviously such a child would not be in need of special services. Simply said, the variance to which I am referring is one for which it is necessary to modify the education program. Such deviation may be a mild, temporary **disorder**; or it could be one that is totally debilitating and, in some instances, life threatening.

When working with exceptional children, it is not uncommon for **labels** to be attached to disabilities, e.g., specific learning disability, mentally retarded, or hard-of-hearing. The reader should not be unduly concerned with what might appear to sanction insensitivity. Instead it is important for you to know that by federal and state law a student must be assessed, then described as having a specific disability before he/she qualifies for special services as a **disabled** child. (See Chapter 3 for discussion pertinent to individual education plans and funding.) Hence labels can be thought of as enabling strategies—strategies that set the stage for **entitlements**.

The physical education program has significant contributions to make to the quality of life of these individuals—contributions not possible through other avenues in the curriculum of the school or clinic. To this end, the methods and materials of physical education may have to be adapted in a way that will foster optimum learning.

WHAT IS ADAPTED PHYSICAL EDUCATION?

Many titles have been given to programs that deal with the atypical student. Although there are emphases inherent in each of these titles, we will see in the following list the characteristics that commonly prevail.

- **Corrective physical education** indicates the rehabilitative effect of activity. The implication here is that activity and exercise are remedial in nature.
- **Developmental physical education** reflects the notion that programs of activity will help a person improve basic body structure and function.
- **Modified physical education** denotes that programs are adjusted to make possible a learning situation for all regardless of **anomalies** (abnormalities) existing within the class membership.
- **Orthopedic physical education** pertains to the **musculoskeletal** system and its proper grooming through appropriate body mechanics programs.
- **Preventative physical education** gives the impression that carefully selected activity can help to forestall the occurrence of certain disease conditions.
- **Special physical education** focuses on the specific anomalies themselves, indicating that special things need to be done in special cases.

One can see that each of these program designations indicates a particular area of emphasis. Yet each is concerned with the student and improving upon his or her "set for learning." A term with broader connotations—suggested by the United States Office of Education and endorsed by the American Alliance for Health, Physical Education, Recreation and Dance—is **adapted physical education**. By definition it is

> ...a diversified program of developmental activities, games, sports, (and) rhythms suited to the interests, capacities, and limitations of students with disabilities who may not safely or successfully engage in unrestricted participation in the vigorous activities of the general education program (Committee on Adapted Physical Education, American Association for Health, Physical Education, and Recreation 1952).

Physical education should be for all, whether they are partially sighted, hard of hearing, subject to convulsions, amputees, **learning disabled**, or have a functional heart disorder (to cite a few examples). These students can be mainstreamed in the regular class and, if necessary, be assigned to a resource room or special class for therapy. Programs can be individualized, corrective, developmental, modified, orthopedic, preventative, or special, but each should be adapted to accommodate all students. A quality program is one in which rhythmics, fitness, individual and team sports, camping, and aquatics are offered to teach skills and knowledge not just for today, but for a lifetime. Mueller (1990) said it well:

> Being physically educated involves knowing the joy and exhilaration of moving well, and experiencing the fun and freedom of any movement, even if not done so well. It involves feeling whole, able, and competent as a person. Being physically

educated is not a point one arrives at but is a continuous process; it is one aspect of becoming whole and progressing toward one's full potential.

Programming for those with special needs is not a recent phenomenon. There is evidence of varying treatment of the disabled well before the birth of Christ. However, the promise of success for the atypical was largely a product of the attitudes people had toward disability. As Daniels and Davies (1975) stated,

> ...attitudes have ranged from viewing the disabled person as a pariah to considering him an economic liability; permitting modest utilization of his limited abilities; allowing restricted participation in the social life of the group; and finally adopting a laissez-faire attitude, according to which the disabled gets along as well as he could, depending on certain factors. These factors may be personal and family resources, charitable assistance, the type and level of social organization, and nonofficial and official organized efforts on behalf of the disabled.

For primitive human beings, fitness was the key to survival. They had to have sufficient strength and endurance to fish and to hunt for food and clothing, as well as to fight to protect their lives and the lives of their families. That the meek or weak perished was of concern to our primitive ancestors. Thus physical education had as its inauguration the development of fitness for hunting and combat.

Existing records indicate that corrective gymnastics were used by the Chinese in approximately 3000–2600 B.C. Massage and hydrotherapy were used by the early Greeks and Romans. The positive effects of exercise on psychological behavior appear to have been well recognized during certain periods of early civilization—effects acknowledged in some quarters to be valid as we contemplate the twenty-first century. The Greeks in particular recognized the virtue of an appropriate balance between physical, mental, and social training.

Unfortunately the concern of those in early civilization for the 'body beautiful' left little place for those less endowed. The physically disabled were subjected to mockery, while those endowed with strong and attractive bodies were selected for participation in advanced training programs. The weak were allowed to weaken even more. (This is not unlike the pattern of many school physical education curricula today. Those who are getting the quality programs in physical education are often the ones who need it least. Until the enactment of the Education for All Handicapped Children Act, [**Public Law 94-142**] students with disabilities were assigned to study halls, or if allowed to remain in the physical education class, were expected to keep score for contests, hand out towels at the end of class, or some such alternative.) Can you think of any schools today where this practice is still in place (in spite of the law)?

Although several earlier programs of a more positive nature can be documented, the main impetus for identifying total needs of the physically disabled did not begin until the early 1900s and, for those who are mentally retarded, as late as the 1960s, Table 1.1. Humanism did begin to replace an apparent lack of concern. More and more disabled persons were beginning to be identified as needing services, and structures were established to address these needs. In 1973 the **Rehabilitation Act** (Public Law 93-112) provided for nondiscrimination on the basis of disability:

...including reasonable accommodation, accessibility and equal opportunity, in physical education, intramurals, recreation, and sport (DePauw 1990).

The Education Amendment of 1974 (Public Law 93-380) provided impetus for the development of individualized education plans (IEPs) in physical education classes and, in a broader sense, the entire school curriculum. And in 1978 the **Amateur Sports Act** (Public Law 95-606) was passed which requires that the United States Olympic Committee (USOC) encourage and promote sport for disabled athletes including where feasible their participation with able-bodied athletes (DePauw and Clarke 1986).

TABLE 1.1.

A Continuum of Events: When, Who, and What as They Relate to the Evolution of Physical Education for the Exceptional Individual, 3000 B.C. to Present.

When	Who	What
B.C.		
3000	Chinese	Performed corrective (crude) gymnastics, therapeutic exercises
2600	Egyptians Hindus Greeks Romans	Advocated exercise, massage, baths
776	Greeks	Held games and contests (Olympics)
460	Hippocrates	Recognized value of exercise for strengthening muscle tissue, aiding rehabilitation, and improving mental attitude
	Herodicus	Advocated medical gymnastics
	Diocles	Advocated walking exercises
	Themison	Advocated passive and active exercises
A.D.		
30	Galen	Classified exercise by vigor, duration, frequency, use of apparatus and body part involved; advocated specific exercises for muscle tonus, exercises in rapid repetition, and resistive exercises
200	Praxagoras Philotinus Theon	Recommended specific movement patterns to help combat illness
476	Christians	Emphasized development of the mind; exercise sanctioned for elite only
900	Rhazes	Spoke of value of exercise for body enrichment
	Avicenna	Thought proper exercise could replace physicians and remedies
1000	Judaeus	Indicated that idleness was harmful to one's health

TABLE 1.1

When	Who	What
A.D.		
1200	Actuarius	Prescribed exercises and diet to combat mental disease
	Aquinas	Praised effects of exercise on body development
1300	Catalan	Related value of exercise to medical treatment
	Petrarch	Supported the use of exercise rather than drugs for rehabilitation
1450	Licht	Reported on the development of hospitals and nursing
	da Vinci	Reported principles of biomechanics as subject for study
1500	Rabelais	Wrote that the aim of education is training of the intellect and nurturing of the body
	Borelli	Classified muscle tone and contractions; identified body's center of gravity
1600	Willis	Accumulated microscopic data on muscular motion
	Sydenham	Recommended horseback riding for tuberculosis patients
1700	Locke	Believed good health is essential to child development
	Andry	First to relate exercise to musculoskeletal system; recommended corrective exercise techniques for: reducing weight, increasing flexibility, strengthening spine, and correcting postural deformities (orthopedics)
	Galvani Von Haller	Studied excitability of muscle tissue
	Hoffman	Spoke about the importance of exercise in medical treatment
	Guts Muths	Classified individuals into groups according to skill development (for games and contests)
	Jahn	Aimed toward the development of the body and mind through gymnastics apparatus, mass drills, and games or skill
1800	Tissot	Wrote *Medical and Surgical Gymnastics*, which contained description of exercise use in the cure of disease
	Ling	Addressed attention to the educational benefits of exercise
	Bampfield	Recommended specific exercises for scoliosis
	Delpech	Established a school for girls with scoliosis
	Zander	Developed weight machinery for resistive exercise
	Sherrington	Announced laws of reciprocal innervation and reciprocal inhibition of reflex stimuli, and the "all or none law"

TABLE 1.1

When	Who	What
A.D.		
	Bowditch	Indentified "staircase" phenomenon
1915	State of Ohio	Conducted census of physically disabled persons as first move toward providing more adequate rehabilitation services
	Lowman	Used Hubbard tank for hydrogymnastics
	Klapp	Experimented with creeping exercise for spinal deformities
	Hitchcock	Measured students to show physical development
	Sargent	Assessed body proportions
	Wright	Developed ambulation techniques for paraplegics
	MCCloy	Authored motor ability testing instruments
1935	U.S. Government	Passed Social Security Act, which authorized the government to match state money for the care of physically handicapped children
	Stafford	Proposed that physically handicapped individuals compete in athletics. This led to wheelchair athletic competition
	F.D. Roosevelt	Influenced the country to provide additional programs for persons with disabilities
	American Association for Health, Physical Education, and Recreation	Published physical fitness testing instruments
	Eisenhower	Established President's Council on Youth Fitness
	J.F. Kennedy	Gave impetus to national effort regarding programs for the mentally retarded
	E. Shriver	Initiated Special Olympics for the mentally retarded
1970	Public Law 91-230	Elementary and Secondary Education Act (ESEA) authorized support for **gifted and talented** as well as learning disabled children and youth
1970	Public Law 91-517	Developmental Disabilities Assistance Act gave impetus to research, rural service delivery models, and more
1972	Public Law 92-424	Mandated that at least ten percent of Head Start enrollment opportunities be available to handicapped children
1972		Social Security Act (1935) was amended to include provision which directed financial support for the disabled

TABLE 1.1

When	Who	What
1973	Public Law 93-112	Section 504 of the Rehabilitation Act (actually adopted in 1977) stated that one cannot be denied access to any program or activity receiving federal funds on the sole basis of handicap.
1974	Public Law 93-380	Stated that handicapped children must be placed in least restrictive environments, and that an individualized program be prepared and available for each such student. It protected the rights of children (and parents) in placement decisions. Further it mandated that states establish goal of providing educational benefits for all handicapped children from birth to age twenty-one.
1975	Public Law 94-142	Education for All Handicapped Children Act (EHA) was passed. It mandated that by September 1, 1978, all states provide a free and appropriate education for all handicapped children between the ages of three and twenty-one. Although Congress passed this law in 1975, it was not fully implemented until 1980 (see Chapter 3)
1977	Public Law 95-49	Amended the Education for All Handicapped Children Act (EHA) by providing an approved federal definition of learning disabilities
1978	Public Law 95-561	The Gifted and Talented Children's Education Act was passed which offers incentives to local and state education agencies to identify and educate gifted and talented students. It includes inservice training for teachers, and research
1978	Public Law 95-606	The Amateur Sports Act was passed which promotes the integration of disabled athletes with those who are able-bodied in sports competition.
1984	Public Law 98-199	Amendments to the Education for All Handicapped Children Act (EHA) were approved that require states to collect data on the number of handicapped youth exiting their systems and to address their anticipated service needs. The amendments also provide incentives to states for them to offer services to handicapped preschool children.
1986	Public Law 99-372	Handicapped Children's Protection Act gave authority for parents to be reimbursed legal fees attendant to their going to court to secure an appropriate education for their children.
1986	Public Law 99-457	Part H amended the Education for All Handicapped Children Act (EHA). It legislated comprehensive services for children (birth through age two) and their families.
1990	Public Law 101-336	The Americans with Disabilities Act provides civil rights protection to individuals with disabilities in private-sector employment, public accommodations, public services, transportation, and telecommunications

TABLE 1.1

When	Who	What
1990	Public Law 101-476	Individuals with Disabilities Education Act (IDEA) replaces the term *handicapped* used in Public Law 99-457 (the Education of the Handicapped Amendments of 1986) with *individuals with disabilities*.

If we consider, however, that (1) approximately 10 percent of the potential work force is handicapped by some form of chronically disabling condition and (2) approximately 12 percent of the school-aged population is disabled, it is apparent that there is a great deal more work to do.

TYPES AND INCIDENCE OF EXCEPTIONALITIES

It is important to put into perspective the proportion of disabilities that exist among the school-aged population. For convenience to the reader these disabilities are classified into the following ten categories:

1. Physical fitness and body mechanic disorders include overweight (Figure 1.1) and underweight conditions, and postural, strength, endurance, and flexibility deficiencies.

Figure 1.1. An overweight condition is very often an impedance to efficient general and specific movement patterms.

2. Organic disorders include acute or chronic cardiovascular diseases, functional and structural heart murmurs.

3. **Sensory disorders** include hearing and vision disabilities. Physical education and other teaching practitioners must be aware that receptive and/or expressive communication skills may be retarded or nonexistent in students with sensory disorders.

4. Musculoskeletal disorders include muscular and/or orthopedic impairments—congenital or acquired, temporary or permanent. Examples of musculoskeletal disorders are joint injuries, spina bifida, amputations (Figure 1.2), and muscular dystrophy.

Figure 1.2. Amputee

5. Neurological disorders include such conditions as cerebral palsy (Figure 1.3), multiple sclerosis, epilepsy, and poliomyelitis (polio). (Polio is reappearing because of what appears to be complacency on the part of those responsible for seeing to it that children are immunized.)

6. **Psychological distrubances** are abnormal behaviors as defind by a group norm. Neurosis and psychosis are psychological disturbances.

7. **Intellectual disorders** are present in individuals whose scores on appropriately selected intelligence tests are below the standard deviation of mean intelligence scores. The arithmetic average of intelligence scores is 100, and the standard deviation is 15 or 16 (depending upon the assessment instrument selected for

Figure 1.3. Cerebral palsy is a neurological disorder.

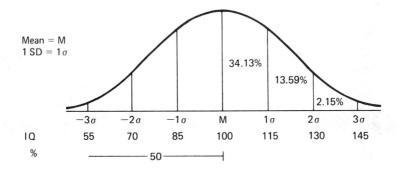

Figure 1.4. A curve of normal probability representing standard deviation ordinate points from the mean of the distribution, and the expected percentage of students earning scores to those points.

administration). In general, one who earns a score at or below two standard deviations below the mean (arithmetic average) would be considered mentally retarded or, as more and more professionals are saying, developmentally disabled, Figure 1.4.

8. Learning-disabled children are those who, for assorted **neurological** and/or psychological reasons, have deficiencies in understanding or transmitting language. Learning disabilities can be caused by brain **trauma** and perceptual dysfunction. (Of the various exceptionalities to be found within public school

settings, learning disabilities are among those creating the greatest challenges. This is not because of a child's lack of academic interest, but rather the inability of school practitioners, with all the sophisticated software and hardware available, to be able to characterize in an objective way one's existing knowledge and learning style[s].)

9. The gifted and talented are individuals whose knowledge, physical fitness, or neuromuscular skills are at any point above one standard deviation of what would be considered average (see Figure 1.4).

10. Other health conditions include AIDS, allergies, anemia, or child abuse—each of which could require an adapted physical education program.*

Table 1.2 lists the relative incidence of common disabilities within the school-aged population. Table 1.3 relates the extent to which these disabilities are being serviced within regular classes, **resource rooms**, or separate classes.

TABLE 1.2.

Estimates of Prevalences (by Percentages) of Common Disabilities within the School-Aged Population

Disability Types	Percentage Estimates
Speech disorders	4.000
Learning disabilities	3.000
Mental retardation (Developmental disabilities)	2.500
Seriously Emotionally disturbed	2.000
Orthopedic/neurological impairments	0.500
Hearing impairments	0.100
Visual impairments	0.100
Deafness	0.075
Deafness and blindness	0.060

If 12–15 percent of the school-aged population are disabled to the extent that special education services are needed, it is essential that every teacher, administrator, and for that matter every school employee be prepared to deal with these conditions. There is no escaping the need to provide meaningful programs for these children. It should be unnecessary to say that each and every child, regardless of ability or disability, has the right to an appropriate education. Nonetheless, the disabled have all too often been denied this right. We must do everything in our power to assure that this denial does not continue.

AN OVERVIEW OF SPECIAL SCHOOLS

Under certain conditions disabled children may be assigned to programs housed within **special schools** in order to help them achieve optimum growth and development.

---

* See Chapters 4–13 for a thorough discussion of disabilities and their adapted physical education activity considerations.

TABLE 1.3

Estimates (by Percentages) of Exceptional Children Receiving Special Services

Disability Types	Percentage Estimates		
	Regular Class	Resource Room	Separate Class
Mental retardation (Developmental disabilities)	5.8	23.5	57.9
Speech disorders	74.9	19.7	3.8
Orthopedic impairments	27.7	18.0	32.0
Hard of hearing and deaf	30.5	1.9	43.4
Visual impairments	37.9	25.2	21.0
Deafness and blindness	8.9	6.3	36.8
Seriously Emotionally disturbed	12.6	32.9	34.5
Learning disabilities	17.6	59.0	21.8
Other health impaired	30.6	20.8	18.7

Source: U.S. Department of Education, Office of Special Education and Rehabilitation Services. Twelfth Annual Report to Congress on the Implementation of the Education of the Handicapped Act, 1989.

Such a placement would provide the **least restrictive environment**. The following are the more common types of special education settings currently in operation:

1. Residential schools are designed to provide twenty-four-hour comprehensive home, medical, and instructional care. Some residential schools offer program options on an out-patient basis. The out-patient lives at home with his/her family and is transported to the school for instruction during normal school hours. (Although the number of residential centers appears to be diminishing throughout the country, the placement of certain disability types in such a setting is still considered by some to be a viable option.)
2. Hospital instruction provides educational opportunities for persons who are confined temporarily or permanently to hospitals or other health facilities.
3. Homebound instruction is designed to accommodate those who are bedridden because of a chronic illness or during a postoperative convalescence.
4. Day schools include special schools, **special classes** within a public school, and cooperative programs in which students spend a portion of their time in both special classes and regular classes.

Each plan provides for special needs, and as with any plan each has relative strengths and weaknesses. A program that is successful for one child may not be appropriate for another. Each student should be evaluated and a plan prepared that provides for an environment least restrictive to his/her learning. To place the child appropriately, one must be familiar with the options available and the advantages of each. The child must be the focal point of any consideration in this regard.

Among the factors to be considered in the educational placement of a child are

1. Description of the exceptionality (or exceptionalities)
2. Medical diagnosis and prognosis

3. Whether the condition is acquired or congenital
4. Age of the youngster
5. Educational diagnosis
6. Aptitudes: scholastic, physical, and social
7. Vocational goals (if pertinent)
8. Previous reports by educators, social workers, and others
9. Parent, guardian, sibling, and/or peer attitudes
10. Educational alternatives: types and locations of schools
11. Cost of total service: funding options
12. Unusual factors peculiar to the child in question

PROBLEMS AND ISSUES RELATED TO ADAPTED PROGRAMS IN PUBLIC SCHOOLS

In addition to special schools of the types described, most disabled children will attend regular schools in which one will find regular or adapted physical education programs in operation. When considering least-restrictive options therein, the local education agency (school district), local school officials, the parent(s) (guardians or surrogate parents), along with various consulting individuals/groups must address a number of factors. Included among the issues for their individual and collective deliberations are the following.

1. The school district has the responsibility to:
   a) develop and administer a **Child-Find** program that will identify all educationally disabled persons between birth and the age of twenty-one.
   b) see that a proper evaluation of the identified child is carried out in accordance with federal and state regulations.
   c) ensure that any child who is coded as having a disability (e.g., deaf, emotionally handicapped, orthopedically impaired, etc.), as a consequence of a comprehensive evaluation, has his/her individual education plan filed with the state Department of Education.
   d) see that a policy of confidentiality is enforced in accordance with federal and state statutes.
   e) arrange for special education staff development opportunities to be available for faculty and administrators.
   f) publish policies and procedures that
      (1) describe the local processes for referring, evaluating, developing individual education plans, and placement of educationally disabled students.
      (2) ensure that coordination occurs with other local and state agencies in addressing their needs.
   g) see that the programs for which it has responsibility are in all respects in compliance with federal and state laws.
   h) replace and hire new personnel who have been trained and are knowledgeable in areas related to the successful integration of exceptional children in fields for which they are seeking employment.

      i)   provide parents of educationally disabled students with information regarding their rights and responsibilities as they pertain to special education.

2. The local school officials have the responsibility to
   a) carry out the policies of the federal and state governments and the local school district as they relate to the development, maintenance, and evaluation of programs for educationally disabled children.
   b) establish a favorable school climate for the child by providing an administration and faculty who support the principles of integrative placements.
   c) ensure that exceptional children have architectural access to their school programs. This includes access to a toilet facility, classrooms, lunchroom, special subject areas, and the library.
   d) offer recommendations to the school district as they relate to improving structural impediments. For example, the individual education plan may include a suggestion that a space not previously used by a disabled child be incorporated into one's program. Access to the space would be necessary and thus could require modifications in the entrance to and/or layout of the room.
   e) encourage employees (teachers and other clinicians) to be thoughtful in their day-to-day assessments of children in order to establish base data should referral or additional analyses become necessary.
   f) monitor the progress of individual education plans to see that all matters pertaining to their implementation are being carried out in an appropriate and orderly way, and that all pertinent records are maintained and secure.
   g) provide additional assistance to those responsible for carrying out individualized plans, if necessary, in the way of volunteers or paid aides. Student teachers can also provide very useful assistance.
   h) encourage teachers and clinicians to participate in in-service training dealing with the educationally disabled child. (Compensation for such training is encouraged should the scheduling of these sessions occur beyond the usual school day.)
   i) cooperate with parents (guardians or surrogate parents) in ways that will reinforce their understanding of their legal rights and responsibilities.

3. The parents (guardians or surrogate parents) have the responsibility to
   a) familiarize themselves with their legal rights and responsibilities as they pertain to federal and state laws governing special education.
   b) visit the placement site in order to gain firsthand knowledge as to the disposition of free access routes for their child.
   c) actively participate in meetings as they are scheduled to address their child's individual education plan needs.
   d) meet with teaching, administrative, and consulting practitioners who will be responsible for carrying out the provisions of the individual education plan. Among other reasons, it is helpful to be able to match names with faces. Once a child is coded, the law states that an individual education plan (IEP) must be prepared. Meeting those who will be responsible for the implementation of the plan is very important. It may be necessary to be in communication with these persons for extended periods of time.

e) share their insights with pertinent school authorities as to how they might best deal with the personal and social idiosyncrasies of the child. After all, who knows more about these things than the parent (or guardian, as the case may be).

f) prepare strategies to be carried out in the home that will help reinforce those skills being addressed within the approved individual education plan.

g) to access **due process** procedures should that parent (guardian or surrogate parent) disagree with the Special Education Evaluation/Placement Team's disposition of their child's referral, assessment procedures, or findings.

h) actively engage in dialogue with all available resources in ways that will prepare that parent (guardian or surrogate parent) to actively contribute to their child's physical, mental, and emotional growth.

i) prepare the child emotionally for the transition into what might be a brand new experience. All children need a strong support system when encountering new opportunities.

The value of your visiting institutions of the type discussed in this chapter cannot be overstated. Students of adapted physical education and other special education topics are encouraged to arrange for visits in order to observe many of the successful practices in the field. Even one new idea gained can help you cope with the diversified issues related to programming activities for exceptional populations.

RECENT TRENDS IN ADAPTED PHYSICAL AND RECREATIONAL EDUCATION

There are virtually as many opinions on programming for students with disabilities as there are people charged with their education. Several commonalities are emerging, however, and are offered here as trends. Many exciting changes are occurring. What can you add to this list?

1. Greater attention is being focused on the interdisciplinary approach to working with persons with disabilities. No longer is it considered defensible for a teacher to disregard the expertise of the school nurse, family and/or school physician, psychologist, social worker, special education teacher or consultant, or parents when planning teaching/learning modules for an exceptional child. It is not a weakness to ask questions of these specialists. It is a weakness not to.

2. There has been a significant increase in the amount of research being done pertaining to exceptional children.

3. Parents (guardians and surrogate parents) are becoming more aware of their rights insofar as the responsibility of the district to finance the education of their children.

4. More and more disabled students are being integrated with their school-aged peers in the public schools.

5. There are an increasing number of **group homes** providing services for persons with disabilities.

6. More and more students with disabilities are living in communities with their families and friends and going to school during the day.

7. Facilities are being developed and improved to make them **barrier-free**.

8. Computer hardware and software are being designed for use by students with disabilities in order to enhance their learning opportunities. More software options are available for assistance in developing individual education plans.

9. Teachers of students with disabilities are relying less on the results of *single* testing instruments.

10. The disabled child's self-image is being improved. This is due in part to the greater understanding being demonstrated by family, friends, and the community at large.

11. Teachers are becoming better prepared to work with students with disabilities in integrated physical education class settings.

12. Students with disabilities are being exposed to a wider variety of physical education, interscholastic, and recreation activities—including aquatics (e.g., diving, power boating, sailing, scuba diving, snorkeling, swimming, water skiing), dual sports (e.g., badminton, handball, paddleball, racketball, squash, tennis), individual/self-testing (e.g., archery, bowling, golf, gymnastics, quoit, shuffleboard, skiing, skydiving, track, weight lifting), rhythmics (e.g., clog dancing, folk dancing, round dancing, square dancing), and team sports (e.g., basketball, field hockey, lacrosse, soccer, softball, volleyball).

13. Management-level educators are demonstrating increasing appreciation of the value of physical education in the development of the 'whole' child.

14. There has been an increase in the number of children with multiple rather than single disabilities. This has affected the perceived missions of special-purpose institutions, i.e., schools for the deaf, the blind, and so forth. With advances in medicine, more and more children with disabilities are surviving infancy for entrance into the public schools.

15. Children with special needs are being identified earlier in their lives, e.g., Child-Find (New Hampshire Standards for the Education of Handicapped Students 1988).

16. A reappraisal is being made as to what constitutes a handicap. How would you distinguish between a handicap and a disability?

17. Individuals with disabilities are becoming increasingly independent.

18. Day and residential camps for persons with disabilities are increasing in number, as are opportunities for extracurricular activities such as baseball, basketball, cheerleading, field hockey, soccer, track and field, volleyball, and wrestling.

19. An increasing number of colleges and universities are offering undergraduate, graduate, and/or postgraduate professional preparation programs in adapted physical and recreational education.

20. More and more of those who serve persons with disabilities are becoming aware of federal and state grants for studies relating to persons with disabilities (e.g., Field Initiated Research, Handicapped Children's Early Education Program Research, Handicapped Student Research).

SUMMARY

Education for exceptional children has evolved through a series of milestones—legislative and otherwise. Adapted physical education has emerged as a major contributor to the successes enjoyed by exceptional children in schools and clinics. Depending upon the nature of the disability, the program of physical education is modified in ways that will encourage optimum benefits. To provide for these gains, exceptional children are placed in environments least restrictive to their learning. **Mainstreaming** provides exceptional children with the opportunity to enjoy the physical and social benefits made possible when children with differing abilities participate together. A review of the literature reveals trends that are promising.

REFERENCES

Committee on Adapted Physical Education. 1952. Guiding principles for adapted physical education. *Journal of the American Association for Health, Physical Education, and Recreation* 23(4): 15.

Daniels, A. S., and E.A. Davies. 1975. *Adapted physical education.* New York: Harper and Row.

DePauw, K. P. 1990. PE and sport for disabled individuals in the United States. *Journal of Physical Education, Recreation and Dance* 61(2): 53–57.

DePauw, K. P., and K.C. Clarke. 1986. Sports for disabled U.S. citizens: Influence of amateur sports act. In *Sport and Disabled Athletes,* edited by C. Sherrill. Champaign, IL: Human Kinetics.

Mueller, L. M. 1990. What it means to be physically educated, *Journal of Physical Education, Recreation and Dance* 61(3): 100–1.

New Hampshire State Board of Education. 1988. *New Hampshire standards for the education of handicapped students.* Concord, NH: New Hampshire State Board of Education.

RECOMMENDED READINGS

Bedini, L. A. 1990. Separate but equal? Segregated programming for people with disabilities. *Journal of Physical Education, Recreation and Dance* 61(8): 40–44.

Brown, L., B. Wilcox, E. Sontab, B. Vincent, N. Dodd, and L. Gruenwald. 1980. Toward realization of the least restrictive educational environments for severely handicapped students. In *Normalization, Social Integration and Community Services,* edited by R. J. Flynn and K. E. Nitsch. Baltimore: University Park Press.

Churton, M. W. 1988. Federal law and adapted physical education. *Adapted Physical Activity Quarterly* 5:278–84.

Deiner, P. L. 1983). Mainstreaming. In *Resources for Teaching Young Children with Special Needs.* New York: Harcourt Brace Jovanovich, Inc.

Goodwin, J., and D. Flatt. 1991. Teaching lifetime sports to at-risk students. *Journal of Physical Education, Recreation and Dance* 62(5): 26–27.

Greer, J. V. 1991. A child is a child is a child. *Exceptional Children* 57(3): 198–99.

Kaufman, M. J., E.J. Kameenui, B. Birman, and L. Danielson. 1990. Special education and the process of change: Victim or master of educational reform? *Exceptional Children* 57(2): 109–15.

Moucha, S. A. 1991. The disabled female athlete as a role model. *Journal of Physical Education, Recreation and Dance* 62(3): 37–38.

Richey, D. L. 1991. The process and politics of advocacy. *Journal of Physical Education, Recreation and Dance* 62(3): 35–36.

CHAPTER 2

Physical and Motor Growth _____

Objectives

After reading this chapter, you should be able to

- Identify and discuss the various classifications of bones found within the human skeletal system.
- Describe the ways in which bones articulate with other bones.
- Identify and discuss the various types of diarthrodial joints and the movements possible as a result of these articulations.
- Identify and discuss the planes and axes of the body.
- Know the types of muscle tissue and functions of each type.
- Identify and discuss the various types of muscle contractions.
- Know the classifications and principles of levers and their applications in the human body.
- Differentiate between the functions of the central and peripheral nervous systems.
- Discuss motivational and other psychological principles related to growth and development and their possible implications for teaching and learning.

INTRODUCTION

Before one can understand fully the depth and breadth of movement patterns and their anomalies, it is necessary to study human structural and neural anatomy. Students and practitioners of adapted physical education place considerable emphasis on the analysis of the **skeletal system** and the **muscular system**. A good working knowledge of basic anatomical structure and function helps them to prescribe appropriate activities for children in selected standard and developmental programs of physical education, kindergarten through high school. A knowledge of pertinent concepts helps to provide a sound basis upon which to make intelligent choices of activities appropriate to a student's needs (Buck, Harrison, Fronske, and Bayles 1990). To be physically educated, one needs a cognitive understanding of how individuals move (Lambert and Trimble 1987).

KEY TERMS

abduction	isotonic contraction
adduction	joints
agonists	levers
antagonists	medulla oblongata
articulations	motor unit
atrophy	muscular hypertrophy
autonomic nervous system	muscular system
axes (sagittal, frontal, vertical)	neuromuscular
central nervous system	neurons
cerebellum	peripheral nervous system
cerebrum	planes (sagittal, frontal, transverse)
circumduction	pons
concentric contraction	readiness
eccentric contraction	rotation
extension	reflex arc
flexion	skeletal system
homeostasis	synergists
isometric (static) contraction	

Beuter, Duda, and Widule (1989), among others, have studied various factors contributing to movement efficiency. In this chapter I will not present anatomical landmarks or kinesiological principles in detail; this is done in books dedicated to that purpose. (See Recommended Readings at the end of this chapter.) Instead we will examine structures that are influenced most by congenital and acquired disabilities. We will discuss topics that are particularly pertinent to those responsible for working with persons with disabilities:

1. The skeletal system, including **articulations**, movements in **joints**, and **planes** and **axes**
2. The muscular system, including classifications of muscles and types of muscle contractions
3. The body as a system of **levers**
4. The nervous system
5. Principles of growth

THE SKELETAL SYSTEM

The basic structure of support and protection in human beings is the skeleton, Figure 2.1. It is composed of 206 bones (excluding the small sesamoid bones, which vary in number). A larger number is found in the newborn, but during growth some of these bones merge to form one bone from what previously had been two or more. These are generally classified into one of the following four groups:

1. Long bones, found in the extremities and comparatively long, have a cylindrical shaft; their ends, or the two extremities, appear larger than the remaining

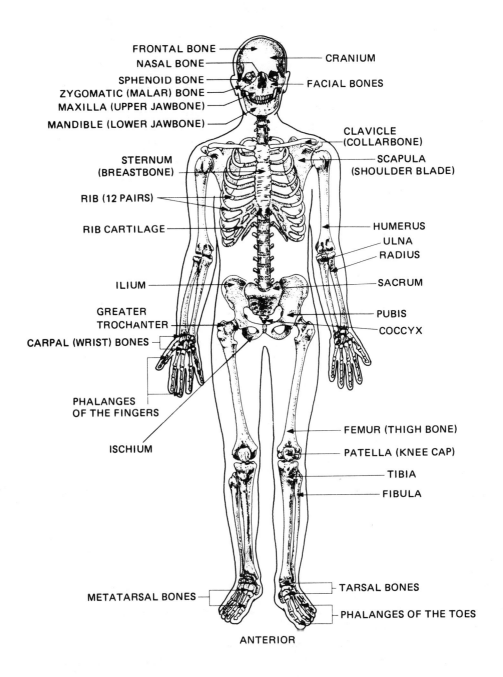

FRONTAL BONE
NASAL BONE
SPHENOID BONE
ZYGOMATIC (MALAR) BONE
MAXILLA (UPPER JAWBONE)
MANDIBLE (LOWER JAWBONE)

CRANIUM
FACIAL BONES

STERNUM
(BREASTBONE)

CLAVICLE
(COLLARBONE)
SCAPULA
(SHOULDER BLADE)

RIB (12 PAIRS)

RIB CARTILAGE

HUMERUS
ULNA
RADIUS

ILIUM

GREATER
TROCHANTER
CARPAL (WRIST) BONES

SACRUM

PUBIS
COCCYX

PHALANGES
OF THE FINGERS

ISCHIUM

FEMUR (THIGH BONE)
PATELLA (KNEE CAP)
TIBIA
FIBULA

METATARSAL BONES

TARSAL BONES
PHALANGES OF THE TOES

ANTERIOR

Figure 2.1. The human skeleton

portions of their lengths. They increase in length at the epiphysial cartilage. As the cartilage extends in both directions, ossification will normally occur, and an extension in length will result. When the period of growth concludes around the thirtieth year of life, the shaft and its extremities are united. Such activities as walking, jumping, and throwing require long-bone function. The long bones of the lower extremities also serve to support the weight of the body. Among the long bones are the humerus in the upper arm, the radius (thumb side) and the ulna in the lower arm, the femur in the upper leg, and the tibia (weight-bearing bone) and the fibula (lateral side bone) in the lower leg.

2. Short bones are found in the wrist (carpals) and the ankle (tarsals). Rather oblong in shape, they are relatively compact and solid and provide reasonable strength for their size. Another example of a short bone is the kneecap (patella).
3. Flat bones provide protection for internal organs and provide sites on their broad surfaces for muscle attachment. Examples of flat bones are the pelvis, ribs, scapulae, skull, and sternum.
4. Irregular bones are so named because they cannot be classified easily by length or shape. Examples of irregular bones are those in the spinal column, Figure 2.2, and certain bones that give shape to the face.

There are contours, depressions, perforations, and projections on the surfaces of all bones. Often used as reference points by anatomists and kinesiologists, these bone irregularities provide sites for articulations (connections at joints), as well as ligamental, muscular, and tendonal attachments. They also provide channels for blood vessels and nerves.

Articulations

Articulations are sites where bones connect to form joints. Most bones are connected at sites of articulation that, along with muscle, provide the basis for movement. At junctures where bones unite to form movable joints, their lubricated bony surfaces are protected with fibrous tissue capsules. These joints are ordinarily classified as one of two types.

1. Amphiarthrodial joints are articulations in which bony surfaces are united by intervening fibrous or cartilaginous material so as to allow slight movement. The vertebral column represents a site for amphiarthrodial joints.
2. Diarthrodial joints are articulations in which a separation (cavity) exists between the ends of the adjoining bones. Characteristically a diarthrodial joint is protected within a capsule. Within this ligamentous capsule lies a synovial membrane that secretes a fluid that provides for nearly frictionless motion (unless the capsule is damaged).

Diarthrodial articulations are important to the physical education practitioner who is considering activity prescriptions (e.g., developmental activities). The potential for body movement is predicated in large part upon the soundness of joints with diarthrodial articulations. The various types of diarthrodial articulations are listed here.*

---

*A third classification is synarthrodial articulation. An example is the sutures in the skull. Because it is a fixed joint wherein no movement is possible, I will not deal with it here.

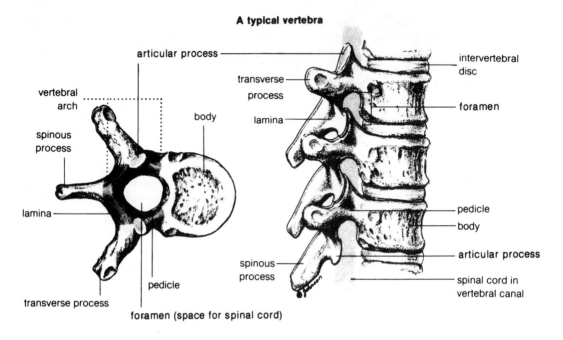

A typical vertebra

articular process

vertebral arch

spinous process

body

lamina

transverse process

pedicle

foramen (space for spinal cord)

intervertebral disc

transverse process

lamina

foramen

pedicle

body

spinous process

articular process

spinal cord in vertebral canal

a. Superior view

b. Right lateral view

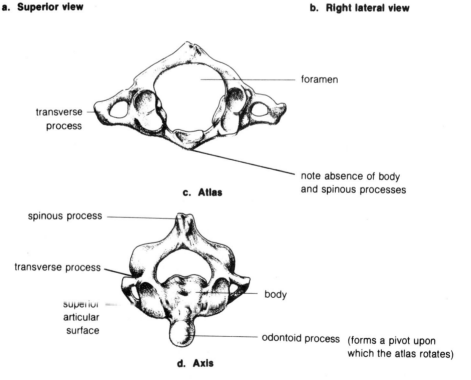

transverse process

foramen

note absence of body and spinous processes

c. Atlas

spinous process

transverse process

superior articular surface

body

odontoid process (forms a pivot upon which the atlas rotates)

d. Axis

Figure 2.2. Vertebrae comparison

1. In arthrodial (gliding joint) articulations the articulating surfaces, although irregular in shape, are ordinarily flat or slightly curved. Examples of arthrodial joints are the carpals (wrists) and tarsals (ankles). Arthrodial articulations are non- axial; the only movement possible is gliding.

2. In enarthrodial or spheroidal (ball and socket) articulation the ball-shaped head of one bone fits into the socket (cup, cavity) of a second bone. It is a triaxial joint as it allows for **flexion** and **extension, abduction** and **adduction,** and **circumduction.** Examples of ball and socket joints are the shoulders and the hips.

3. In ginglymoid (hinge) articulation the spoollike surface of one bone fits into the concave surface of a second bone. As a consequence the bone with the concave surface is able to glide partially around the 'spool' in a hinge-type movement. Only flexion and extension movements are possible in this type of joint. The movement is in one plane around a single axis (uniaxial). The elbow and the knee are examples of ginglymoid joints.

4. In condyloid (ellipsoidal or ovoid) articulation an oval, convex surface unites with a concave surface. This class of joint is biaxial in that movement around two axes in two planes is possible (flexion and extension, abduction and adduction). An example of such a joint is at the wrist (radiocarpal joint). When the movement in the two planes is achieved sequentially, circumduction occurs.

5. In saddle articulation (a subclassification of condyloid articulation) the ends of the convex surfaces of the joining bones are tipped up, making, as Wells (1971) points out,

    ...the surface (is) concave in the other direction, like a western saddle.

    Where the reciprocally concave and convex surfaces come together, they are biaxial. An example of a saddle articulation is the carpometacarpal joint of the thumb.

6. In trochoid (pivot) articulation a small convex surface of one bone fits within a concave notch of a second bone, allowing for a rotation (pivoting) to occur. The movement is uniaxial. Examples are the radioulnar joint of the arm and the atlantoaxial joint of the neck.

Movements in Joints

During the description of diarthrodial articulations, I briefly referred to abduction, adduction, flexion, extension, and circumduction. These terms, and **rotation**, will be described briefly in this section.

1. Abduction is a lateral movement of a limb in a direction away from the midline of the body, Figure 2.3. Examples of such movement include lateral elevation of the arms or legs. Adduction is the opposite of abduction; movement of the arms or legs is toward the midline of the body.

2. Flexion is a bending that decreases the angle at a joint. Flexion occurs when, for example, the elbow or knee are bent. Extension is the opposite of flexion, and increases the angle at the joint, Figure 2.4. Lateral flexion is applied when the head (or torso) bends laterally, Figure 2.5.

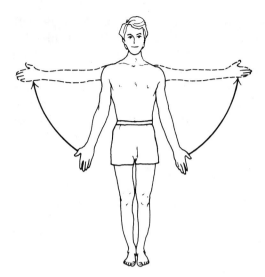

Figure 2.3. Abduction

Figure 2.4. Flexion: The left arm and forearm and right thigh are drawn forward in sagittal planes. The right knee is also flexed. Extension: The left thigh and knee are extended. Hyperextension: The right arm is hyperextended at the shoulder.

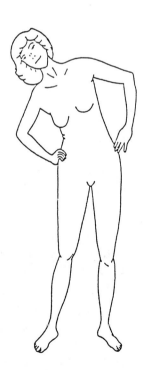

Figure 2.5. Lateral flexion: The head and torso are bending laterally in the frontal plane.

3. Circumduction includes a sequence of flexion, abduction, extension, and adduction movements. Circumduction occurs when the arms are swung in a circle (with the shoulder joint serving as the apex of movement). Circumduction is also possible in a properly functioning hip joint.
4. Rotation is movement around the longitudinal axis of a bone. For example, pronating the hand (placing the palm face down) is a rotation originating at the radioulnar joint. Supinating the hand (placing the palm face up) is also rotation.

Planes and Axes

When describing diarthrosis, I referred to movements occurring in planes or around axes. Relating movements in this way provides one with valuable reference points for motion analysis.

There are three planes, each of which is perpendicular to the other two. Likewise there are three axes, each of which is perpendicular to the reference plane. In other words the axis around which a movement occurs is always at right angles to the plane in which that movement takes place, Figure 2.6.

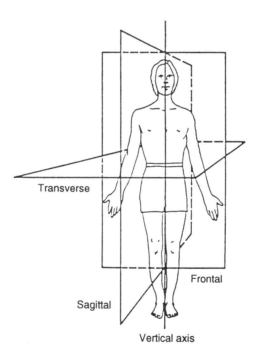

Figure 2.6. Planes and axes of the human body.

The planes of the human body are as follows:

1. The *sagittal plane* divides the body into right and left halves. A limb movement forward or backward is movement in the sagittal plane.
2. The *frontal plane* divides the body into front and back halves. Lateral movement of the arm (abduction) is movement in the frontal plane.

3. The *transverse plane* divides the body into upper and lower segments. A rotation of the head or hips would be examples of movement in the transverse plane.

The axes of the human body are as follows:

1. The *sagittal axis* passes through the body horizontally from front to back (anterior to posterior).
2. The *frontal axis* passes through the body horizontally from side to side.
3. The *vertical axis* is perpendicular to the ground.

Examples of movement around axes that are perpendicular to the planes in which the movements occur are as follows:

1. Rotation of the head in rotary breathing while swimming the crawl stroke is in the transverse plane and around the vertical axis.
2. Arm curls in barbell lifting are in the sagittal plane and around the frontal axis.
3. Movement of the arms and legs during side straddle hops (jumping jacks) is in the frontal plane and around the sagittal axis.

THE MUSCULAR SYSTEM

A muscle is contractile tissue consisting of bundles of elongated cells (muscle fibers) that function to produce body movements. Muscles, along with selected portions of the skeleton (e.g., rib cage) help to protect vital organs. In addition they assist with posture and locomotion. Movement would not be possible without the muscular system, Figure 2.7.

As a consequence of origins and insertions the muscles, working in pairs (prime movers and antagonists), provide for movements in joints (e.g., abduction, adduction, flexion, extension, circumduction, and rotation). Unlike the smooth muscle found, for example, in the walls of the intestines, and cardiac muscle, located in the walls of the heart, skeletal (striated) muscle is responsible for posture and locomotion. There are 277 paired and 3 unpaired striated muscles comprising the muscular system, Table 2.1.

TABLE 2.1.

Paired and Unpaired Muscles: Number per Body Area

Body Area	Number Paired	Number Unpaired
Head	26	1
Neck, nape, back	106	0
Chest, abdomen	34	2
Upper limbs	49	0
Lower limbs	62	0
Total:	277	3

Source: Adapted from Schade (1970). *Introduction to functional human anatomy.* Philadelphia: W. B. Saunders.

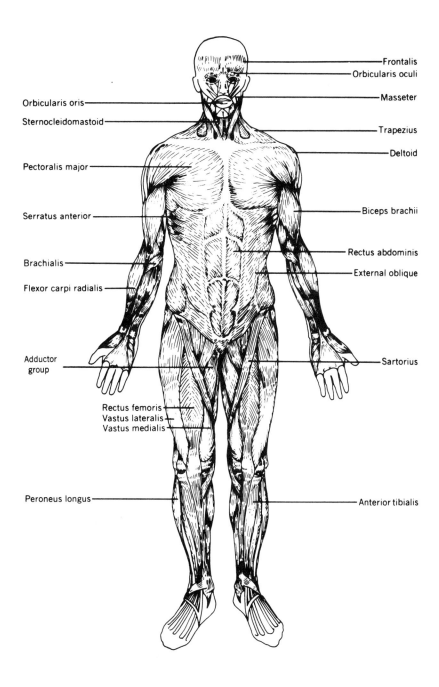

Figure 2.7. Superficial skeletal muscles of the human body

It is interesting to note that the shape and size of muscles are influenced largely by their functions. For example, long and slender muscles are related to agility and speed of movement, while short and broad muscles are located where significant strength is necessary. Each muscle—long or short, slender or broad—has a belly (the prominent, thick, contractile elements of the muscle) and two or more tendons that connect the belly to the skeleton. One of the connections, or attachments, is referred to as the origin (head) of the muscle. The connection on the other end of the muscle is called the insertion. A given muscle may be able to move more than one joint depending on its origin and insertion; that is, its attachment, Table 2.2.

TABLE 2.2.

Selected Skeletal (Striated) Muscles (Musculi): Origin, Insertion, Action

Musculi	Origin	Insertion	Action
Musculus biceps brachii (short head)	Tip of coracoid process	Bicipital tuberosity of radius; apo-neurosis of biceps; fascia of ulnar side of forearm	Flexion of elbow; adduction at shoulder joint
Musculus biceps brachii (long head)	Supraglenoidal tuberosity; posterior part of glenoid labrum	Bicipital tuberosity of radius; fascia of ulnar side of forearm	Flexion of elbow and shoulder; supination of forearm: fixation of shoulder joint
Musculus triceps brachii (long head)	Intraglenoid tuberosity of scapula	Olecranon; dorsal fascia of forearm	Extension of elbow joint: adduction of arm (long head); maintenance of elbow in extended position
Musculus triceps brachii (lateral head)	Posterior surface of humerus; lateral intermuscular septum	Olecranon; dorsal fascia of forearm	Extension of elbow joint; adduction of arm (long head); maintenance of elbow in extended position
Musculus triceps brachii (medial head)	Posterior surface of humerus below radial groove; medial and lateral intermuscular septa	Olecranon; dorsal fascia of forearm	Extension of elbow joint; adduction of arm (long head); maintenance of elbow in extended position
Musculus brachialis	Anterolateral and anteromedial surface of humerus; medial and lateral inter-muscular septum	Ulnar tuberosity; coronoid process	Flexion of forearm; flexion of arm against resistance

TABLE 2.2.

Musculi	Origin	Insertion	Action
Musculus deltoideus	Lateral third of clavicle; acromion; spine of scapula	Deltoid tuberosity of humerus	Abduction, flexion, extension of arm internal and external rotation
Musculus pectoralis major	Anterior aspect of clavicle; side and front of sternum; front of cartilage of ribs 2-6; apo-neurosis of external oblique muscle	Greater tubercle of humerus	Flexion and adduction of arm; internal rotation of arm; raising of ribs during forced inspiration
Musculus latissimus dorsi	Thoracolumbar fascia, spinous and interspinous ligaments-T6-L3; crest of ilium; last 3-4 ribs	Crest of lesser tubercle of humerus; intertubercular groove	Adduction and internal rotation of arm; drawing down of scapula (inferior fibers); drawing back of scapula (superior fibers)
Musculus rectus aidominis	Xiphoid process; costoxiphoid ligament; cartilage of ribs 5-7	Ventral surface of symphysis; linea alba above symphysis; su-perior ramus of pubis	Flexion of vertebral column; depression of thorax
Musculus psoas major	Intervertebral discs of lowest thoracic and all lumbar ver-tebrae; bodies and transverse processes of lumbar vertebrae	Lesser trochanter	Rotation of femur; tilting of thigh at hip joint;flexion of spine and pelvis; abduction of lumbar spine
Musculus gluteus maximus	Lateral portions of lower sacral and coccygeal vertebrae; back of sacrotuberous ligament; outer surface of ilium; thoracolumbar fascia	Gleuteal tuberosity of femur; iliotibial tract	Extension and external rotation of femur; tension of fascia lata and iliotibial band; stabilize knee joint when extended
Musculus rectus femoris	Anterior inferior spine of ilium (long head); poster-osuperior surface of rim of acetabulum (short head)	Proximal border of patella; tibial tuberosity	Flexion of femur at hip joint; extension of leg

TABLE 2.2.

Musculi	Origin	Insertion	Action
Musculus biceps femoris (short head)	Lateral lip of linea aspera; supra-condylar ridge; lateral intermuscular spectum	Head of fibula; lateral condyle of tibia	Flexion of leg; extension and adduction of femur
Musculus biceps femoris (long head)	Ischial tuberosity sacrotuberous ligament	Head of fibula; lateral condyle of tibia	Same as short head plus external rotation of leg
Musculus gastrocnemius	Medial condyle of femur, femoral margin of capsule of knee joint; small area on back of femur (medial head); lateral condyle of femur, small area above lateral condyle (lateral head)	Calcaneal tendon	Plantar flexion and supination of foot; raising of heel; flexion of knee

Source: Adapted from Wells (1971); Schade (1970); Pick, Pickering, and Howden (1977).

Muscles having primary action on a joint are known as **agonists**. Muscles offering opposing action to the agonists are known as **antagonists**. Muscles that assist the agonists are referred to as **synergists**. In short, movement is made possible through the interaction of the striated muscles, the skeleton, and the joints.

As one would expect, muscles are very responsive to use and disuse. Those that are subjected to highly resistive exercise tend to enlarge. This is called **muscular hypertrophy**. **Atrophy**, on the other hand, tends to arise in muscles that are not used. This results in decreased size and strength. Can you think of any categories of handicapping conditions in which decreased muscle size and strength would be expected? What about the size of one's leg after it has been in a cast as treatment for a fracture? Can this be classified as atrophy? Are children with cerebral palsy likely to have smaller and weaker muscles in those areas affected by the condition?

Classifications of Muscles

As implied previously, the method of attachment can vary considerably from muscle to muscle. The arrangement of the fibers comprising the muscle itself can also be different. The classification of striated muscle is based upon these variations, Figure 2.8.

1. A longitudinal muscle has fibers that lie parallel to its vertical axis. The *musculus rectus abdominis*, located on the abdomen, is a longitudinal muscle.
2. A fusiform muscle is ordinarily spindle-shaped and tapers at each end. It may be long or short, slender or broad. The *musculus brachialis*, located in the arms, is a fusiform muscle.

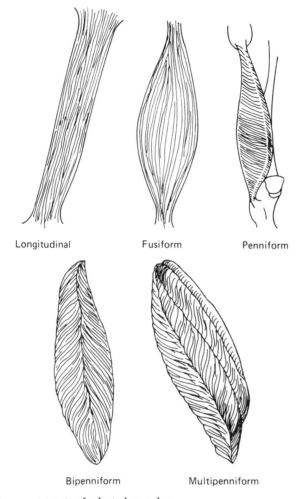

Figure 2.8. Fibral arrangements of selected muscles

3. A penniform muscle has a featherlike fiber arrangement, in which a series of parallel fibers extend diagonally from the side of a tendon. The *musculus tibialis posterior*, located in the leg, is a penniform muscle.
4. A bipenniform muscle has fibers that extend diagonally from each side of the tendon (as opposed to penniform, in which the fibers emerge from one side of the tendon). The *musculus rectus femoris* in the front of the thigh is a bipenniform muscle.
5. A multipenniform muscle is attached to more than one tendon: the muscle fibers extend diagonally between the tendons. The medial portion of the *musculus deltoideus* in the shoulder is multipenniform.
6. A triangular muscle is fan-shaped and flat. The fibers emerge from a slim attachment and end with a broad attachment opposite. The *musculus pectoralis major* in the chest is triangular.

7. A quadrate muscle is flat and consists of four sides. The fibers run parallel to each other. The *musculi rhomboideus major* and *minor*, located between the scapulae and the spine, are quadrate muscles.

Types of Muscle Contractions

There are four basic types of muscle contractions with which you should be familiar. These types (classifications) depend on whether the muscle shortens, lengthens, or remains the same during the contraction process.

1. In the **isotonic contraction** the work performed is a product of force and distance, i.e., the amount of force necessary to move a resistant load over a distance. Tension remains virtually constant as the muscle shortens.
2. In the **concentric contraction** the distance is reduced between the point of origin and the point of insertion of the muscle. The muscle shortens regardless of tension level. Most physical activities use this type of contraction.
3. In the **eccentric contraction** there is a gradual reduction of the contraction as the body (a) yields to a force that is stronger than that of the contracting muscle, or (b) slowly lowers a weight. In most cases the muscle does not increase in length but returns to its normal preexercise (resting) length.
4. In the **isometric contraction** the amount of work performed is a product of force and time, i.e., the amount of work necessary to apply sufficient force to a resistance over time. There is no appreciable change in muscle length. Isometric contractions are also called *static* contractions.

THE BODY AS A SYSTEM OF LEVERS

Now that I have described the various movements possible within the joints of the body, one can readily appreciate the fact that the body is a system of levers. Although we cannot alter these levers, we can make more efficient use of the entire body system if an understanding of how levers work is in place.

A lever is a rigid structure (bone) pivoting about a fixed support or fulcrum (joint). The lever serves to impart pressure or motion from a force or effort applied at one point (muscle contraction) to a resisting force at another point. Within the human body are first-, second-, and third-class levers.

The First-class lever

A crowbar is used as a first-class lever. In the body a first-class lever action exists during extension of the elbow. As is shown in Figure 2.9, force F is applied by the tricep at the olecranon process. The fulcrum A is at the joint of the elbow, and the resistance R is located in the forearm. As force is applied at the elbow from above, the olecranon process is pulled up and the arm descends.

The Second-class lever

When we lift a wheelbarrow, we are using a second-class lever. For a second-class lever, the resistance is located between the fulcrum and the force. There is conflicting opinion as to whether there is a second-class lever in the human body. There are some anatomists and kinesiologists who claim that when the foot is plantar-flexed (extended)

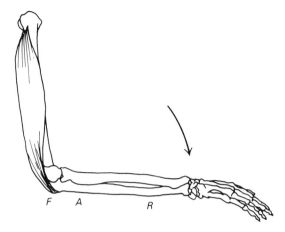

Figure 2.9. The first-class lever

in a weight-bearing position, a second-class lever exists. The resistance is believed to be at the ankle joint where the body weight is transferred to the foot, the fulcrum is the contact point of the foot with the ground, and the force is at the site where the Achilles tendon attaches to the heel. Others believe that the forearm during flexion would be a second-class lever if all flexors except the *musculus brachioradialis* were paralyzed.

The Third-class lever

Figure 2.10 reveals a third-class lever in the arm. Here the fulcrum *A* is at the joint of the elbow, the force *F* is applied by the bicep at the point where it attaches to the radius, and the resistance *R* is the weight of the forearm.

THE NERVOUS SYSTEM

All body functions are governed by the nervous system. A muscle cannot contract, the heart cannot beat, and a gland cannot secrete substances if stimulation does not occur first.

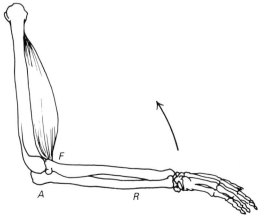

Figure 2.10. The third-class lever

Components

The nervous system can be divided into two structural components. One of these is the **central nervous system** (CNS), which consists of the brain and the spinal cord, Figure 2.11. The second component is the **peripheral nervous system** (PNS), which consists of twelve pairs of cranial nerves and thirty-one pairs of spinal nerves that provide the medium for stimulation throughout the body.*

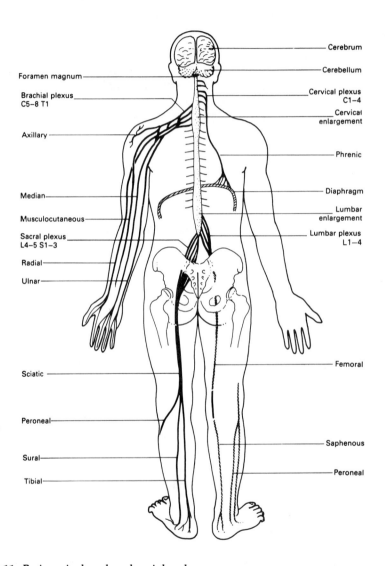

Figure 2.11. Brain, spinal cord, and peripheral nerves

---

* The **autonomic nervous system** (ANS) is more of a functional than a structural system. Since as such it overlaps the brain, spinal cord, and peripheral system, it is not a structural entity. Using the central nervous system and the peripheral nervous system, it supplies stimulation to smooth and cardiac muscles.

Loofbourrow (1960) summarized **neuromuscular** integration very well when he wrote:

> The forces which move the supporting framework of the body are unleashed within skeletal muscles on receipt of signals by way of their motor nerves. In the absence of such signals, the muscles normally are relaxed. Movement is almost always the result of the combined action of a group of muscles which pull in somewhat different directions, so the control of movement involves a distribution of signals within the central nervous system (CNS) to appropriate motor nerves with precise timing and in appropriate number. In order for movements to be useful in making adjustments to external situations, it is necessary for the central nervous system to be appraised [*sic*] of these situations, which are continually changing. A means of providing this information promptly exists in a variety of receptors sensitive to changes in temperature, light, pressure, etc. These receptors are signal generators which dispatch signals (nerve impulses) to the CNS over afferent nerve fibers. The CNS receives these signals together with identical ones from within the muscles, joints, tendons, and other body structures and is led thereby to generate and distribute in fantastically orderly array myriads of signals to various muscles. This, despite the enormous complexity of the machinery involved, enables the individuals to do one main thing at a time. This is integration. It is what Sir Charles Sherrington meant by "the integrative action of the nervous system."

The **neuron** (nerve cell) is the structural and functional unit of the nervous system. Each neuron has dendrites that relay impulses toward the cell body. Each neuron also has an axon that relays impulses away from the cell body. Neurons and muscle fibers form what is referred to as the neuromuscular system. Should an injury or illness cause a disruption in the impulses between the central nervous system and the muscle itself, paralysis can result.

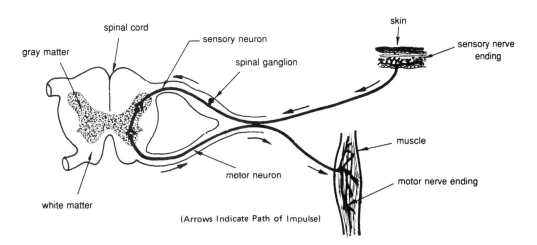

Figure 2.12. The knee-jerk reflex involves two neurons—sensory and motor

The **motor unit** is the functional organ of the neuromuscular system. Each motor unit consists of a single motor neuron and all the muscle fibers that its axon supplies. A complete **reflex arc** would include a receptor (a sensory nerve terminal that can pick up and transmit sensory stimuli), an afferent (sensory) neuron, a synapse, an efferent (motor) neuron, and an effector, which could be a muscle (an organ of response). See Figure 2.12 to examine the knee jerk reflex arc.

Where a muscle has a large number of motor units supplying relatively few muscle fibers, more precise movement patterns are possible.

Neurons that transmit impulses from the brain and the spinal cord to muscle tissue and glands are known as efferent (motor) neurons. Afferent (sensory) neurons are those that receive stimuli and relay them to the spinal cord and the brain.

The brain consists of four main divisions, Figure 2.13.

1. The **cerebrum**, the largest part of the brain, is located above and anterior to the cerebellum and the pons. It consists of two hemispherical masses enclosed within the cortex (external layer of gray matter). It serves as the seat of conscious processes within human beings. The neurons of the cerebral cortex have specific control of sensorimotor functions and special senses.

2. The **pons** serves to connect the cerebral cortex with the medulla oblongata and the cerebellum. In addition to its service as a conduction pathway, neurons in the lower portion of the pons assist in the regulation of respiration.

3. The **medulla oblongata**, actually a continuation of the spinal cord to the pons, serves to connect nerve fibers to those higher centers of the brain that control cardiac, respiratory, and vasomotor functions.

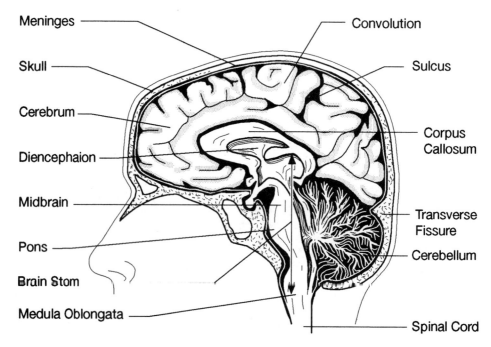

Figure 2.13. Display of the brain with the four major divisions: cerebrum, pons, medulla oblongata, and cerebellum

4. The **cerebellum**, often referred to as the 'small brain,' is located below the cerebrum and to the rear of the skull. The function of the cerebellum is especially important to the physical education practitioner because it controls (a) balance, through maintenance of muscle tonus and control; (b) coordination; and (c) kinesthesis, that is, knowing where the body and/or its parts are in relation to space.

Muscular activity is controlled by an integrated circuit consisting of motor and sensory impulses. With practice one can improve performance. Movements that are at first uncoordinated and frustrating can become enjoyable and a basis for new skills. One of the essential components of physical and motor growth is the proper integration of the neuromuscular system.

If we who are interested in the optimum growth and development of children understand the concepts of structural and neural anatomy, we can choose appropriate developmental and general activities more intelligently. We must also understand patterns of normal growth and development, for our primary responsibility as physical educators is in the psychomotor domain.

PRINCIPLES OF GROWTH AND PLANNING FOR TEACHING

Growth and development begin at the time of conception and continue until one reaches full physiological maturity in adulthood. Through millions of microscopic cells we emerge into human form. If growth continues unimpeded, the systems of the body reach an optimum level—structurally and functionally—in a rather predictable sequence, Figures 2.14 and 2.15.

By the time children enter school, much of their basic structure is established. How they function beyond that point largely depends on the ability of the physical education practitioner to monitor changes and individualize instruction. While the accommodation of individual differences is certainly not a new concept, it has received increased emphasis in recent years under the rubric of teaching and learning style analysis. The attention many teachers and clinicians give to preparing individualized education plans (IEPs) shows that this concept is being put into practice.

Regardless of the curriculum plan used, there are certain principles to which one should subscribe when planning for teaching.

1. Consider the effect of the experiences we provide. Students are more likely to repeat experiences that satisfy their needs. If an initial experience, e.g., going into the water for the first time, is negative, the individual will probably not be interested in going into the water again. I can recall that in my third and final week of paratrooper training school we were expected to make our first parachute jump. Needless to say, the experience of that first jump had everything to do with whether or not one would be willing to take another jump. One must reduce stress and anxiety as much as possible. I did complete my fifth training jump that week and was a proud graduate of airborne training school. Yes, to the extent that stress and anxiety can be kept to a minimum, experiences are more likely to be repeated—and enjoyed.

2. Plan for frequent practice. Drill and practice are necessary for meaningful achievement in a selected skill area. Can you imagine the amount of training

Figure 2.14. Expected development sequence: One to fifteen months. From *G. H. Sage, Introduction to Motor Behavior,* © 1971 by Addison-Wesley Publishing Company, Inc. Reprinted with permission of the publisher.

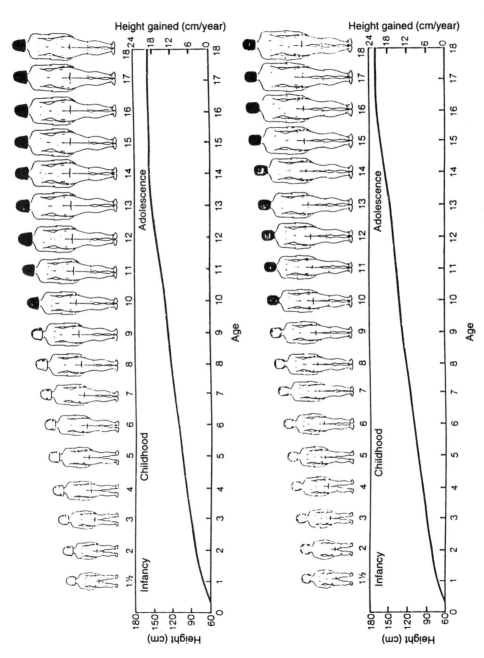

Figure 2.15. *Average changes in height that occur between infancy and adolescence. Adapted from Growing Up, J. M. Tanner. Copyright (1973) by Scientific American, Inc.*

that goes into preparing one's self for a wheelchair marathon event? Not only is muscular and cardiovascular endurance involved, but so is technique. Improving one's technique requires practice. Contrary to an often held opinion, however, practice does not make perfect unless that practice is performed correctly. If you happen to teach swimming classes, you know how hard it is to have someone change from a flawed, outdated frog kick to a more efficient whip kick. When teaching the breaststroke, I would much rather work with beginning swimmers, i.e., those who have been uncontaminated with inappropriate yet rehearsed skills.

3. Be aware of student **readiness**. Children are more likely to profit from instruction if they are physiologically, mentally, and psychologically ready for it. We should assess neuromuscular skill and physical fitness levels when determining readiness. Student readiness has to be established before proper progression can be encouraged, let alone achieved.

4. Be aware that learning is an active process. To learn, the student must be aroused to learn and find some value in learning. Motivation is a vital force in learning, and its source should shift from extrinsic (the teacher) to intrinsic (the student). According to Frost (1975) there are nine categories of motivation. Although proposed a number of years ago, these factors still demand attention today.

    a) **Homeostasis**. Human beings tend to maintain constant internal environments. The tendency to return to a state of equilibrium is known as homeostasis. Any stress (e.g., trauma, heat, fright, anger, fatigue) upsets the state of homeostasis and stimulates people to act. Fright may cause people to flee, anger may cause people to fight, and trauma may cause people to move away from the source of danger. The need to reduce tension and return to the state of equilibrium can be, and often is, an important motivator.

    b) *Satisfaction of needs.* Under conditions of danger or threat to life, the desire to survive takes precedence over most other needs. People who are starving have little interest in old-age pensions. The individual about to be run over by a car has little thought of anything but to get out of the way.

    c.) *Self-concept.* The way people see themselves and the way they believe they are looked upon by others influence their personalities and behavior. People who think of themselves as kind and helpful try to assist others in trouble. Those who perceive themselves as fighters will try to establish that image. People who think of themselves as intellectuals will no doubt give careful, thoughtful answers to questions.

    d) *Expectations.* Closely related to the notion of self- concept is that of expectations. People who believe others expect them to be helpful in civic organizations will probably try to play that role. Trying to live up to an established reputation can be quite motivating. The roles people feel they are expected to play often determine how they act.

    e) *Level of aspiration.* Levels of aspiration are related to the concept of expectations and involve setting goals. Aspiring to achieve a worthwhile objective, striving toward an ideal, and trying to accomplish a difficult task are marks of a highly motivated individual. They generally lead to success in a particular endeavor. Goals should be challenging but achievable. They should be worthy of intense effort and commitment. Goals so high that failure results lead to lower levels of aspiration and cause drops in performance. A level of aspiration that is too low does not lead to great accomplishments. Success generally leads to a higher level of aspiration; repeated failure leads to a lower level of aspiration.

f) *Frustration, challenge, and self-discovery.* For optimum development of the individual, tasks should be difficult enough to require effort and hard work but not so difficult that they result in frustration and a sense of failure. A gradual increase in difficulty constantly challenges the individual to practice and improve and results in the greatest learning and the best performance. When task difficulty is increased suddenly and to such an extent that a person is not ready either physiologically or psychologically, his or her attempts to succeed will result in failure. Too many failures and goals that are persistently blocked can lead to aggression, regression, fixation, apathy, and dependency.

g) *Social determinants.* All people are motivated to a greater or lesser degree by the opinions of their peers, the customs of the people with whom they associate, and the socioeconomic status of the group to which they belong. Behavior is often motivated by a desire to achieve socially, by the expectations of those to whom people look for approval, and by the cultural milieu in which they move.

h) *Propriate striving.* The *proprium* may be defined as that which is intimately and peculiarly ours. It is related to the ego and the self and is central to our sense of uniqueness. It includes those aspects that "make for a sense of inward unity" (Frost 1974). Propriate striving is reaching outward and upward for something greater than self. It is maintaining a commitment to a goal that is high. It is the attempt to maintain a state in which there is a constant drive to action, a continual effort to reach the goal. It is resistance to homeostasis until the goal is reached. Illustrative of propriate striving are examples upon examples of those who went beyond normal limits in reaching goals motivated by the desire to excell. Four such examples are:

(1) Olga Korbut who in the 1970s became an inspiration to many young women by her assorted feats in women's gymnastics at the Olympic Games.

(2) David Kiley who from the 1970s into the 1990s earned worldwide recognition through his accomplishments by winning five gold medals in the 1976 Paralympic Games in Canada, played on five United States Men's Wheelchair Basketball Teams, and has climbed the tallest mountain peak in the state of Texas.

(3) Jim Knaub who in the 1980s won several wheelchair marathon events.

(4) Susan Ann Moucha who in 1986 and 1988 competed in the United States Olympic Sports Festival as a disabled cyclist and placed second and first respectively; in 1988 ran in the Paralympics in Seoul, Korea, and received a gold medal in the 800-meter track event; and, in 1989, was honored nationally as a Healthy American Fitness Leader.

(Can you add to this list the names of those who have reached goals far beyond what would normally be expected? What contributes to the success these individuals enjoy? Among other factors, it is propriate striving.)

i)   *Arousal.* There are untold numbers of instances where human beings have performed unbelievable feats under the influence of strong emotion. Lifting heavy objects to free a loved one, running great distances when frightened, struggling to be free when a life is at stake, and acting more explosively under the influence of anger are examples. Although there is a difference between the arousal that permits performance of high-level athletic skills and the arousal that facilitates learning basic motor skills, in each instance learning takes place best when individuals are relaxed yet attentive. Too much arousal interferes with the learning of complex motor tasks. Too little arousal causes the learner to be careless and inattentive. There is an optimal state of arousal for each individual and for each set of circumstances.

Susan Ann Moucha (1991), referred to earlier, has enjoyed the many benefits of local, regional, and national competition. Factors contributing to her motivation to succeed are well established in the records she has acquired.

> Sport has enabled me to grow physically, mentally, and socially. If it were not for sport, I might, as a hemiplegic (right side of body affected), cerebral palsy athlete, still be 'within my shell.' Swimming, cycling, and running have been my pathways to great opportunities— opportunities which others only envision.

In addition to 'reaching for the stars,' we must encourage our students to strive toward immediate and intermediate objectives. We should employ reinforcement to increase students' receptiveness to learning new skills. Evaluation enables students to establish impressions of their present status and/or achievement levels. In addition to videotape playbacks and formal testing techniques, planned and casual praise can be vital sources of positive reinforcement.

Of significant concern to disabled children and their parents or guardians is our ability to relate to them those cognitive, physiological, and psychological growth factors that influence optimum performance. One of the purposes of this text is to enhance your awareness of underlying physical and motor behavior patterns of students with whom you may work.

SUMMARY

An understanding of the skeletal, muscular, neurological, and motivational factors contributing to the proper planning and execution of physical education programs is critical to all who are concerned about being effective teachers. The skeletal system provides protection and the base of support for muscular activity. The movement that occurs in response to reflex or choice is prompted by a highly sophisticated nervous system. Given the motivation to survive or to excell, an individual is capable of more than what was previously thought possible. Acknowledging that interruptions within and between these systems can impact upon desired achievement, a thoughtful integration of these systems is what makes for teaching that is in keeping with the best of what a caring professional has to offer. In Chapter 3, Principles of Program Organization, you will learn of the factors important to the administration of programs taught by these knowledgeable practitioners.

RECOMMENDED LABORATORY ASSIGNMENTS

1. Successfully complete undergraduate courses in anatomy, physiology, and kinesiology.
2. Arrange to audit advanced anatomy and kinesiology classes in order to better understand the mechanisms underlying anatomical structure and function.
3. Participate in laboratory sessions where kinesiological principles are practiced.
4. Arrange to interview scholars of anatomy to learn their perceptions of important anatomical principles and concepts.
5. Arrange to interview those presently working with persons with disabilities. Ask what aspects of structural and neural anatomy are most important to their planning for teaching and learning.
6. Film and study the growth patterns of children, birth to eighteen years of age.
7. Examine factors that impede normal growth and development (see Section II).
8. Confer with teachers who have reputations for being successful in motivating learners with disabilities.
9. Meet with students with disabilities in order to gain insights as to their views of factors contributing to their various degrees of success.
10. Review the recommended readings.

REFERENCES

Beuter, A., J. L. Duda, and C. J. Widule. 1989. The effect of arousal on joint kinematics and kinetics in children. *Research Quarterly for Exercise and Sport* 60(2): 109–16.

Buck, M. M., J. M. Harrison, J. Fronske, and G. W. Baules. 1990. Teaching biomechanics concepts in junior high physical education classes. *Journal of Physical Education, Recreation and Dance* 61(6): 91–93.

Frost, R. B. 1974. Motivation and arousal. In *The Winning Edge*. Washington, DC: American Association for Health, Physical Education and Recreation.

———. 1975. *Physical education foundations—practices—principles*. Reading, MA: Addison-Wesley.

Lambert, L. T., and R. T. Trimble. 1987. *The basic stuff in action for grades 4–8*. Reston, VA: American Alliance for Health, Physical Education, Recreation and Dance.

Loofbourrow, G. N. 1960. Neuromuscular integration. In *Science and Medicine of Exercise and Sports*. New York: Harper and Brothers.

Moucha, S. A. 1991. The disabled female athlete as a role model. *Journal of Physical Education, Recreation and Dance* 63(3): 37–38.

Pick, T., T. Pickering, and R. Howden, eds. 1977. *Gray's anatomy*. New York: Bounty Books.

Sage, G. H. 1971. *Introduction to motor behavior*. Reading, MA: Addison-Wesley.

Schade, J. 1970. *Introduction to functional human anatomy*. Philadelphia: W. B. Saunders.

Tanner, J.M. 1973. *Growing Up*. Scientific American, Inc.

Wells, K. F. 1971. *Kinesiology: The scientific basis of human motion*. Philadelphia: W. B. Saunders.

RECOMMENDED READINGS

Annett, J. 1959. *Feedback and human behavior.* Middlesex, England: Penguin.

Beuter, A., L. Carriere, and J. P. Boucher. 1987. Relationships between electromyography and kinematics in human stepping strategies. *Neuroscience Letters, 77:* 119–23.

Bjork, R. A. 1979. *Retrieval practice.* Unpublished manuscript. Los Angeles: University of California.

Brooks, V. B. 1986. *The neural basis of motor control.* New York: Oxford University Press.

Close, J. R. 1964. *Motor function in the lower extremity: Analyses by electronic instrumentation.* Springfield, IL: Charles C. Thomas.

————. 1973. *Functional anatomy of the extremities.* Springfield, IL: Charles C. Thomas.

Cormier, S. M., and J. D. Hagman, eds. 1987. *Transfer of learning.* New York: Academic Press.

Dewhurst, D. J. 1967. Neuromuscular control system. *IEEE Transactions on Biomedical Enqineering,* 14: 167–71.

Grillner, S. 1975. Locomotion in vertebrates: Central mechanisms and reflex interaction. *Physiological Reviews* 55: 247-304.

Herschler, C., and M. Milner. 1980. Angle-angle diagrams in above-knee amputee and cerebral palsy gait. *American Journal of Physical Medicine* 59(4): 175–83.

Heyward, V. H. 1991. *Advanced fitness assessment and exercise prescription.* Champaign, IL: Human Kinetics.

Keele, S. W. 1986. Motor control. In *Handbook of perception and human performance. Vol. 2, Cognitive processes and performance. Section V, Information processing,* edited by K. Boff, L. Kaufman, and J. P. Thomas. New York: Wiley.

Lawson, H. A., and J. H. Placek. 1981. *Physical education in the secondary schools: Curricular alternatives.* Boston: Allyn and Bacon.

Orlick, T. 1990. *In pursuit of excellence.* 2d ed. Champaign, IL: Leisure Press.

Powers, S. K., and E. T. Howley. 1990. *Exercise physiology: Theory and application to fitness and performance.* Dubuque, IA: William C. Brown.

Prentice, W. E. 1990. *Rehabilitation techniques in sports medicine.* St. Louis, MO: Times Mirror/Mosby.

Rasch, P. J., and R. K. Burke. 1978. *Kinesiology and applied anatomy.* Philadelphia: Lea and Febiger.

Sanders, A. F. 1990. Issues and trends in the debate on discrete vs. continuous processing of information. *Acta Psychologica* 74: 123–67.

Schmidt, R. A., C. A. Lange, and D. E. Young. 1990. Optimizing summary knowledge of results for skill learning. *Human Movement Science* 9: 325–48.

Swinnen, S., R. A. Schmidt, D. E. Nicholson, and D. C. Shapiro. 1990. Information feedback for skill acquisition: Instantaneous knowledge of results degrades learning. *Journal of Experimental Psychology: Learning, Memory, and Cognition* 16: 706–16.

Thompson, C. W. 1977. *Kranz manual of kinesiology.* St. Louis, MO: C. V. Mosby.

Wickstrom, R. L. 1977. *Fundamental motor patterns.* Philadelphia: Lea and Febiger.

Widule, C., R. E. Lindseth, and G. P. DeRosa. 1986. *The use of kinematic energy ratio to evaluate the gait of cerebral palsy, myelomeningocele, and "normal" children.* Unpublished document. West Lafayette, IN: Purdue University.

Winter, D. 1983. Biomechanical patterns in normal walking. *Journal of Motor Behavior* 15: 302–30.

CHAPTER 3

Principles of Program Organization

Objectives

After reading this chapter, you should be able to

- Discuss factors to be considered by those engaged in curriculum evaluation and revision.

- Describe various assessment mechanisms that can be used in the identification of those individuals who are in need of special accommodation.

- Identify and discuss the sequence of events as they transpire from the point of referral to the development of an individual education plan (IEP) for an educationally handicapped child.

- Describe the composition of the Evaluation and Placement Team, and the roles each member can play in the development and administration of individualized programs.

- Discuss the procedures for preparing an individual education plan (IEP), while taking into account Public Law 94-142 and related amendments.

- Describe ways in which students can be identified for placement into developmental physical education programs.

- Discuss the ingredients of the individual education plan (IEP) with respect to total service and implementation options.

INTRODUCTION

School systems do not experience easy, comfortable, and untroubled growth. They are subjected to both well-founded and capricious criticism. Sometimes curricula are changed to reflect an emphasis thought at the time to be appropriate. Unfortunately these changes are too frequently based upon opinion, not upon research. Curricula preparation should not be governed entirely by what people think is appropriate. One illustration is in regard to some of the nationwide testing programs. In a given year a

---

KEY TERMS

approval form	hidden curriculum
assessments	intelligence
behavior	medical examination
behavioral objective	medical excuse form
computer-assisted instruction	medical referral form
computerized curriculum	occupational therapist
congenital	parent conference
curriculum	pathology
curriculum management	physical health
dysfunction	procedural safeguards
early intervention	progress form
evaluation	referral service
Evaluation and Placement Team	related services
federal mandate	special education services
free appropriate public education (FAPE)	student evaluation form
functional	videodisk
handicap	

---

school system may not appear to have done as well as it has in prior years. As a consequence, teachers begin to incorporate within their programs those concepts about which students are now being tested. In short the test writers become the curriculum builders for the schools. New is not necessarily better. On the other hand, procedures that have been followed for years are not automatically better either. New approaches to meeting the needs of all students should be researched and field tested before they are declared to be the best answers.

To a great extent, arriving at solutions that will best serve the exceptional child is predicated upon asking the right questions. For example, Dunst (1986) commented that researchers should explore "How much variance does early intervention account for beyond that attributed to other formal or informal treatments?" not "Does early intervention work?" Since 1976–1977, nearly 4.5 million students between birth and age twenty-one have received **special education services**, which is an increase of approximately 20 percent since Public Law 94–142 was enacted (Gerber and Levine-Donnerstein 1989). Over 43 percent of this increase can be attributed to those students who are coded as learning disabled. It is apparent that these children and those coded in other categories have profited in some measurable way as a result of having been identified earlier in their lives. However, whatever number contemporary studies reveal, a relatively small percentage of those in need of service are being accommodated. Will (1986) states that pursuant to the current regular education initiative, school districts are challenged to uncover ways to serve as many children with disabilities as possible within the regular classroom.

The popularity of **early intervention** is suggested by a recent survey of forty-nine state directors of special education (Carter and Sugai 1989). Thirty-four claimed that they either required (n = 23) or recommended (n = 11) their respective local education agencies to establish such interventions.

As referenced in Chapter 1, Section 504 of the Rehabilitation Act of 1973 provides that no handicapped child, for that reason, be denied the benefits of or be subjected to discrimination under any program or activity receiving federal financial assistance. It is important for the reader to acknowledge, however, that teachers should be seeking to accommodate the needs of students with disabilities because it is right, not just because it is the law. The programs should be based upon the premise that children with various skills and potentialities will be accessing them. The better teachers will account for many factors as they contemplate curriculum and delivery options. Those who teach adapted physical education

> ...need competencies in assessment prescription, instructional techniques, content knowledge, and curriculum planning (DePauw 1990).

In this regard, Dauer and Pangrazi (1979) suggest a number of principles that should be addressed by those who are engaged in curriculum evaluation and revision.

1. The major purpose of writing a **curriculum** is to give direction and continuity to the physical education program. If, for example, some activities are found to be inappropriate for a certain age group of children, these activities might be deleted from the next year's program. On the other hand, if youngsters are found to be exceptionally able in one of the objective areas, it might mean that less emphasis should be placed there and more time spent in areas where children are below par in performance. In all cases, the curriculum guide should be written with enough detail to provide direction and still retain a reasonable degree of flexibility.

2. The activities selected for the curriculum should be based on their potential to help teachers and students reach expected objectives. For example, selection should consider vigorous physical activity that promotes growth and physical fitness as well as instructional sequences that lead to a broad range of movement competencies and skill development. To further emphasize this point, it could be stated that the number-one program guideline should be developing a curriculum that ultimately provides for physical fitness and fundamental motor skills.

3. Teachers and administrators also should be aware of the **hidden curriculum** when they write guides. The hidden curriculum contains a wide range of learnings that occur in the affective domain. For example, many attitudes, emotions, and social mores can be learned by students from what they perceive about the ways in which the school environment is organized. An attempt should be made to arrange the learning environment so that both the hidden and the formal, written curricula facilitate the purposes of the program.

4. Planning should be done on a districtwide basis, with attendance by a representative sample of the population the guide is to serve. Teachers and supervisors from all levels should be included so the scope and sequence can be carried out and the various program levels can be integrated. The program should be under the direction of a competent staff member, since the director

coordinates the group's efforts as well as the implementation of the program. The curriculum committee should be ongoing in its function, meeting periodically to review and upgrade the programs.

One procedures that can facilitate this process is using computer data bases. As Minor (1989) states,

> The utilization of this computerized information management program (provides an alternative to) traditional curriculum guides. Teachers will be able to use their own computer, located in a planning room or in the classroom, to retrieve intended learning outcomes at a moment's notice. A series of instructional suggestions can be coordinated with the outcomes, developed by experienced teachers, and captured in the computerized curriculum data base for teaching and assessing the learning outcomes on the various cognitive levels identified by Bloom and associates.

Minor (1989) goes further to describe the national significance of a **computerized curriculum** data base by stating,

> A computerized, curriculum management program will provide a powerful tool for helping teachers address local and national curriculum and instructional needs. More important, however, since all the information is housed in a data base, it can also be shared with colleagues and school districts electronically.... The results of this type of information sharing would assist all participating school districts in organizing the curriculum and instruction needed to prepare their youth for survival in a rapidly moving, competitive world, while also giving schools an up-to-date curriculum data base.

The technology that makes this type of curriculum development possible is due not only to advances in microcomputer knowledge, but also to the development of the optical disc. As Bosco (1984) states, a 12-inch **videodisk** can store up to 30 minutes of motion pictures or 54,000 still frames on one side. Any frame can be displayed within a maximum of five seconds. Special authoring software systems allow an instructional designer to write complex scripts for interactive branching lessons (Jarvis, 1984).*

5. The curriculum should be broad and balanced. It should include a wide variety of activities and experiences to be taught through different approaches. The elementary school years, for example, are a time for experimentation, practice, and decision making about activities that are personally enjoyable for the children. The more activities a youngster can experience, the greater chance he or she has to experience success. It should be a premise of the program that it offer something for everyone.

6. The program should be of such a nature that it can be enjoyed by all youngsters, regardless of their individual skill levels. Activities that require a high level of

---

*Commonly used authorizing languages are *Pascal* and *Basic*. Depending upon the sophistication of the program, costs for an authoring system generally run between $400 and $ 3,000.

skill are likely to be inappropriate for a large group of students. Along the same lines, consideration for exceptional children and others with special needs should be included in the planning of the program.

7. Program activities should be selected to make possible the achievement of desirable behavioral changes, associated educational values, and personal benefits. It is true that behavioral changes in children and the values they receive from participation are determined more by instructional procedures than by the programs per se. However, the selection of activities should be such that the aforementioned changes and values can be achieved with appropriate methodology. For example, a program relying chiefly on exercises, games, sports, and relays would do little for the individual child in terms of self-direction, creativity, and self-reliance.

8. Program content should rest on a foundation of efficient body management and fundamental movement skills geared to the developmental needs of the child. This implies an instructionally oriented program that leads toward a goal of reasonable movement competency and concept acquisition. The program should set aside sufficient time for skill instruction and practice. Practice must be systematically organized and based on good concepts of motor learning. The emphasis on instruction can be intense enough to lead to a reasonable mastery of skills.

9. Activities should be organized so that they can be presented to youngsters in a sequential fashion, arranged in meaningful progression beginning with easy experiences and proceeding to the more difficult.

   Computer-assisted instruction is surfacing as a valid method for developing concept awareness. However, as Malouf et al. (1991) state,

   > "To be effective, computer-assisted instruction must be carefully integrated into the overall program of instruction. The teacher must play an active role, and the computer must be used in a manner appropriate to the content and stage of learning" (see Figure 3.1).

   The curriculum should reflect progression from grade to grade, within each grade, and within activities. It should ensure that the activities are taught in an orderly manner.

10. It is desirable to offer extended opportunities for children who are interested and skilled in particular areas. Intramural programs, sport days, play days, special interest clubs, and recreational opportunities after school should be implemented and considered from the viewpoint of a total program for youngsters. Obviously if these experiences are available for children who are interested and capable, the program could place more emphasis on developing skills and offering successful experiences for all children.

11. Activities in the program should be scheduled in line with the seasons of the year. Sports in particular are more readily accepted when they are offered during the time of the year when high schools, colleges, and professional teams are actively involved in the same sports.

12. Specialized interests can affect the development of a curriculum. For example, winter games might be inappropriate in the South and Southwest; year-round

Figure 3.1. Integrated program planning on a computer

swimming programs might be impossible in the North. Certain popular activities should be considered when adults in the area participate in them regularly.

13. Climate is a factor that determines the extent of outdoor play. Some traditional outdoor activities may need to be modified to provide for a broad program of instruction indoors. Extremely hot weather and sunshine along the southern borders of the country have a marked effect on what activities can be scheduled and how they can be taught.

14. The physical education program must have a climate of positive administrative support if it is to achieve its educational goals for all children. The administration has an obligation to provide competent direction; efficient instruction; adequate indoor and outdoor facilities, including outdoor covered areas, hard-surfaced areas, and well-drained playing fields as needed; adequate budget for equipment and supplies; suitable storage space for supplies and equipment; dressing rooms and facilities for showers; and office or other space for the specialist(s). The degree of administrative support has a profound effect on the program.

15. Changes and trends in junior and senior high school physical education programs can have a significant effect on the makeup of the elementary school program. For example, at the present time high school programs have limited requirements and place much emphasis on offering a broad spectrum of elective activities to students. The elementary school program needs to provide

students with a background of activity, so they have the knowledge and experience to select activities later in their educational careers (Dauer and Pangrazi 1979).

The schools should provide a balance of success and failure for all children. A curriculum that does not take into account the uniqueness of each individual enrolled is destined to provide abnormally high failure rates for many children. Goodlad (1963) addressed this issue when he wrote,

A steady diet of failure for even hardy personalities is destructive of self-esteem.

Our mission, then, is to consider the needs, interests, and capabilities of each student before we prescribe the program of activities deemed most likely to elicit his or her cognitive, psychomotor, and affective development.

In keeping with this premise, the American Alliance for Health, Physical Education, Recreation and Dance, and the Joint Committee on Health Problems in Education of the American Medical Association and the National Education Association have provided a list of principles that has been a valuable source of guidance for those who organize and administer programs of physical education for persons with disabilities.

1. There is a need for common understanding regarding the nature of adapted physical education. (For a definition of adapted physical education, the reader is referred to Chapter 1.)
2. Adapted physical education has much to offer the individual who faces the combined problem of seeking an education and living most effectively with a handicap.* Through adapted physical education the individual can
   a) be observed and referred when the need of medical or other services is suspected.
   b) be guided in avoidance of situations that would aggravate the condition or subject him to unnecessary risks or injury.
   c) improve neuromuscular skills, general strength, and endurance following convalescence from acute illness or injury.
   d) be provided with opportunities for improved psychological adjustment and social development.
3. The direct services and the **related services** essential for the proper conduct of adapted physical education should be available to our schools. These services should include
   a) adequate and periodic health examinations.
   b) classification for physical education based on the health examination and other pertinent tests and observations. (See "Selection of Students for Adapted Physical Education," in this chapter.)
   c) guidance of individuals needing special consideration with respect to physical activity, general health practices, recreational pursuits, vocational planning, psychological adjustment, and social development.
   d) arrangement of appropriate adapted (or developmental) physical education programs.

*See Chapter 1 and all of Section II where developmental activities are presented for selected disabilities.

e) evaluation and recording of progress through observations, appropriate measurements, and consultations.

f) integrated relationships with other school personnel, medical and its auxiliary services, and the family to assure continuous guidance and supervisory services.

g) cumulative records for each individual, which should be transferred from school to school (while in keeping with the Family Education Rights and Privacy Act of 1974, more frequently referred to as the Buckley Amendment).

4. It is essential that adequate medical guidance be available for teachers of adapted physical education. The possibility of serious **pathology** requires that programs of adapted physical education should not be attempted without diagnosis, written recommendation, and supervision of a physician. The planned program of activities must be predicated upon medical findings and accomplished by competent teachers working with medical supervision and guidance. There should be an effective **referral service** between physicians, physical educators, and parents aimed at proper safeguards and maximum student benefits. School administrators, alert to the special needs of children with disabilities, should make every effort to provide adequate staff and facilities necessary for a program of adapted physical education.

5. Teachers of adapted physical education have a great responsibility as well as an unusual opportunity. Physical educators engaged in teaching adapted physical education should

a) have adequate professional education to implement the recommendations provided by medical personnel.

b) be motivated by the highest ideals with respect to the importance of total student development and satisfactory human relationships.

c) develop the ability to establish rapport with students who may exhibit social maladjustment as a result of the disability.

d) be aware of a student's attitude toward his/her disability

e) be objective in relationships with students.

f) be prepared to give the time and effort necessary to help a student overcome a difficulty.

g) consider as strictly confidential information related to personal problems of the student.

h) stress similarities rather than deviations, and abilities instead of disabilities.

6. Adapted physical education is necessary at all school levels.

The student with a disability faces the dual problem of overcoming a **handicap** and acquiring an education that will enable him/her to take his/her place in society as a respected citizen. Failure to assist a student with his/her problems may retard the growth and development process.

Offering adapted physical education in preschool programs, the elementary grades, and continuing through the secondary school and college will assist the individual to improve function and make adequate psychological and social adjustments. It will be a factor in attaining maximum growth and development within the limits of the disability. It will minimize attitudes of defect and fears of insecurity. It will help him/her face the future with confidence. (Presented with permission of the American Alliance for Health, Physical Education, Recreation and Dance.)

ADAPTED AND DEVELOPMENTAL PHYSICAL EDUCATION

While it may be necessary to assign some students to a comprehensive adapted physical education program, others may profit by receiving a general program supplemented by developmental activities. In this regard, students will be assigned to one and/or the other on the basis of their performance in selected affective, cognitive and/or psycho-motor test batteries. Most will be in the mainstream. If, however, a student has a sensory, motor, and/or structural **dysfunction** that impedes his or her optimum functioning within the general physical education class, a developmental program may be appropriate. For example, all students may be required to take a screening test in order to help the instructor make an appropriate activity prescription. One such test is presented in Figure 3.2. Students who earn a score of forty or less are assigned to a developmental physical education class with attention being paid to those areas of relative weakness.

CONFIDENTIAL STUDENT SELECTION SHEET FOR DEVELOPMENTAL PHYSICAL EDUCATION

Examination Date: _____

STUDENT'S NAME: _____ AGE: _____ SEX: _____

BIRTHDATE: _____ SCHOOL: _____ GRADE: _____

ADDRESS: _____ PHONE: _____

1. *AGILITY JUMP*

    Have the child watch you demonstrate the agility jump and say: "On the word go, can you jump with your feet together across one line and then the next and back again as fast as possible until I say stop?" (3 lines, 1 foot distance between them)
    Time for 15 seconds.

Score 5 points if jumped smoothly without landing on lines.
Score 4 points if jumped smoothly but lands on lines.
Score 3 points if lands with feet apart.
Score 2 points if child lands on the line more than 3 times regardless of number of passes.
Score 1 point if child can't jump over any line.

2. *HOP IN PLACE* (Dynamic Balance)

    Determine the child's non-preferred foot by asking him/her to gently kick the bottom of your foot, and say: "Can you hop 10 times on your (non-preferred) foot on the X?"

Score 5 points for 9-10 hops.
Score 4 points for 7-8 hops.
Score 3 points for 5-6 hops.
Score 2 points for 3-4 hops.
Score 1 point for 0-2 hops.

    NOTE: Hops must be continuous in order to be counted.

---

3. *STORK STAND* (Static Balance)

Say to the child: "Can you stand like a stork on your (preferred) foot until I say stop?" Time for 10 seconds or until other foot hits the floor, foot shuffles, hands come off the hips, or eyes open. (The bottom of the foot of the nonsupporting leg is placed on the medial side of the knee of the supporting leg.)

Score 5 points for 9–10 seconds.
Score 4 points for 7–8 seconds.
Score 3 points for 5–6 seconds.
Score 2 points for 3–4 seconds.
Score 1 point for under 3 seconds.

4. *SIT-UPS* (Abdominal Strength)

Have the child lie on his/her back on a mat and say: "Can you clasp your hands behind your head, bend your knees, and do 5 sit-ups?" (Hold the child's ankles; his/her knees should be touched by his/her elbows on each sit-up.)

Score 5 points for 5 correct sit-ups.
Score 4 points for 4 correct sit-ups.
Score 3 points for 3 correct sit-ups.
Score 2 points for 2 correct sit-ups.
Score 1 point for 1 correct sit-up.

5. *BALANCE BEAM* (Dynamic Balance)

Say to the child: "Can you walk across the beam using the heel-toe walk?" The teacher should demonstrate the walk. (The student is to walk forward along the beam as far as possible by placing the heel of the foot which is taking the step against the toe of the supporting foot on each step. Both feet must point forward, not toe out. The last foot of the beam on which the student is able to place his/her toe becomes the score. Allow two trials and take the better score. Mark beam with tape in one foot intervals.)

Score 5 points if 8 or more feet of the board are successfully covered using specific walk.
Score 4 points for 6–7 feet.
Score 3 points for 4–5 feet.
Score 2 points for 2–3 feet.
Score 1 point for under 2 feet.

6. *ANGELS IN THE SNOW* (Bilaterality)

Say to the child: 'Will you lie on your back with your feet together and your arms at your sided Can you move the part of your body which I say?" (Demonstrate if necessary.)

A. Make an angel in the snow.Go!
B. Move only your arms. Go!
C. Move only your legs. Go!
D. Move only the arm and leg that I touch (left arm, right leg).
E. Move only the arm and leg that I touch (right arm, left leg).

Score 1 point if all movements reach their maximum extension, are smooth, and if there are no false starts or overflow into other limbs.

7. *DIRECTIONS IN SPACE*

Say to the child: "Please sit, close your eyes, and follow my directions."

A. Move into the space behind you. Go!

B. Move into the space beside you. Go!

C. Point to the space between your feet. Go!

D. Point to the space above your head. Go!

E. Touch the bottom of your feet. Go!

Score 1 point for each correct response that is made within 3 seconds.

8. *IDENTIFICATION OF BODY PARTS*

Have the child sit, and say: "Keep your eyes closed and touch the part of your body that I say."

A. Touch your ankles. Go !

B. Touch your wrist. Go!

C. Touch your hips. Go!

D. Touch your chest. Go!

E. Touch your elbows. Go!

Score one point for each correct response that is made within 3 seconds. (Score 0 points if the child touches another body part before touching the correct one.)

9. *BEND AND REACH*

Have the child sit, and say: "With your legs straight, grasp your toes and hold for 5 seconds." (Demonstrate)

Score 5 points if child touches toes and holds for 5 seconds.

Score 4 points if child touches ankles and holds for 5 seconds.

Score 3 points if child touches calves and holds for 5 seconds.

Score 2 points if child touches knees and holds for 5 seconds.

Score 1 point if child touches thighs and holds for 5 seconds.

10. *OCULAR TRACKING*

Have the child sit, and say: "l am going to hold my thumbs in front of you. Without moving your head, see how fast that you can look from one thumb to the other." (Hold your thumbs 1 foot apart and 1 foot from the student's eyes.)

Score 5 points if the eyes travel from one thumb to the other in a straight line without hesitation. Score 0 if the eyes hesitate or wander.

11. *VISUAL-MOTOR PURSUIT*

Have the child stand in front of a ball attached to a string, and say: "See if you can touch the swinging ball with one finger, like this, as it passes you by." (Demonstrate)

NOTE: Attach the ball and string to a chinning bar so that it hangs, when motionless, to the level of the student's chin (top of ball just under the chin).

Have the child stand at arms distance from the ball, his/her fist should be clenched.

Tester should: A. Grasp the ball with the right hand.

B. Bring it to a position which makes the string horizontal.

C. Release it so that it swings from the child's left to right.

Student should: A. Start with his/her arms at the side.

B. Make the touch directly in front of his/her body.

NOTE: The teacher should start the ball five (5) times allowing it to swing past the child three (3) times after each release. As soon as the child touches the ball or attempts to, or the ball comes back and stops, the tester should begin again.

Score 1 point each time the child touches the ball. *No point* is given if the ball touches the hand; i.e., if it swings back to the extended hand after a "miss" has occurred.

12. *CATCHING THE BALL*

Say to the child: "Can you catch the ball as I throw it to you?" (Use a ball 6" in diameter.)

NOTE: Stand 8 feet from the child. Use a soft underhand motion designed to bring the ball to the student at chest level. At no time during the flight of the ball should it rise higher than the student's head. Throw five (5) times.

Score 1 point for each ball caught with the *hands* only.

13. *THROWING THE BALL*

Say to the child: "Can you throw the ball to me using an overhand throw?"

Score 5 points if the child throws with a weight shift at the time the ball is released, and proceeds to step forward with the opposite foot.
Score 4 points if weight shifts forward, but the child steps forward unilaterally.
Score 3 points if the ball is thrown with one arm and no body shift.
Score 2 points if the child throws either overhand or underhand using both arms at the same time.
Score 1 point if the child pushes the ball with hands and feet.

14. FLEXED-ARM HANG (Upper-Arm Strength)

Say to the child: "Can you hold yourself on the bar for 5 seconds keeping your chin above the bar and gripping it with your palms facing away from your body?" (Demonstrate)

NOTE: Lift the child to the bar.

Score 1 point for each second the child holds the position. His/her chin should be above the bar (not touching it). Stop scoring once the elbows begin to "unlock," or if the chin touches the bar.

Figure 3.2. Confidential Student Selection Sheet for Developmental Physical Education. *Courtesy of the Department of Health and Physical Education, Ridgewood Public Schools, Ridgewood, New Jersey.*

To plan intelligently to meet the needs of students enrolled in physical education classes, we must gather information from various sources as a critical first step. Data indicating special placement may be obtained from referral, diagnostic testing, and/or medical examination. In the section that follows, we will examine these and various other information sources.

SELECTION OF STUDENTS FOR SPECIAL EDUCATION SERVICES

The success of any program of developmental physical education depends on accurate identification and placement. To succeed in this mission, however, we must acquire reliable information from various sources. If a child is suspected of having an educational handicap, the following sequence of events should occur:*

1. A referral form is completed by the parent, teacher, physician, or other referral source and is presented to the principal of the local school.
2. The parents are notified that a referral has been made to the special education **Evaluation and Placement Team.**

---

* Courtesy of School Administrative Unit #48, Plymouth, New Hampshire.

3. The Evaluation and Placement Team requests permission from the parent to review the student's file, collect information and—if necessary—conduct a classroom or home observation.

4. The Evaluation and Placement Team (including parents) meet to review the information that has been collected. On the basis of that information the team decides that the child is not educationally handicapped or the team requests permission from the parent for the child to be evaluated for the referring problem.

5. The evaluation is conducted at the school district's expense, and a written report of the results is made to the Evaluation and Placement Team and the parents.

6. The Evaluation and Placement Team (including parents) meet to review the results of the evaluation and determine if the student is educationally handicapped. The team then determines that the child is not educationally handicapped, or the child is determined to be educationally handicapped.

7. An individual education plan (IEP) is written by the Evaluation and Placement Team. If it is accepted by the parents and the school district, a placement is made; or if the individual education plan is not accepted, an appeal procedure is begun.

8. Placement is made in the least restrictive environment (program) that can implement the individual education plan.* The placement is at no cost to the parent and may include educationally related services, such as speech and language therapy, counseling, or occupational therapy.

9. The individual education plan is reviewed at least annually. Determination of the handicapping condition is reviewed at least every three years.

10. If a child is determined by the Evaluation and Placement Team to no longer require special education he/she may be discharged from oversight by that committee.

Let us now examine these steps (events) with a view toward their processing and implications.

Referral

As indicated earlier, there are many sources of referrals, not the least of which are parents. Recognition of the importance of parental involvement in special education arose out of a **federal mandate** that schools and families cooperate in the planning of individual education programs for disabled children. This entire process begins with referrals. Parents, teachers, guidance counselors, nurses/physicians, and other professional practitioners can play a significant role in identifying children who are potentially in need of accommodation. To that end, a number of examples of referral forms have emerged. One such form is presented in Figure 3.3.

Once a referral is made, the school will need to request permission to access pertinent records, Figure 3.4.

---

* See Chapter 14, for a review of least restrictive environment alternatives (The Cascade System).

SCHOOL ADMINISTRATIVE UNIT #48 REFERRAL

Directions: In order for this referral to be effective, it must be filled out <u>completely</u> and submitted to the principal.

Student's Name _____ Birth Date _____

Chronological Age _____ Sex _____ Grade_____

School _____ Teacher/Counselor _____

Name of Parent/Guardian _____ Telephone _____

Address_____

Referred by: _____ Date_____
               Name   Position   Title

   I. Specify reasons for referral:_____

   II. Actions taken thus far to deal with problem: (Parent conference, classroom adjustments, counseling, previous special services,...)

_____

_____

_____

   III. Known significant health problems: _____

_____

_____

   IV. Other agencies involved with student: _____

_____   _____
          Agency   Contact

_____   _____
          Agency   Contact

V. Who has discussed the problem with the parents? What was their reaction?

_____

Classroom teacher or counselor should complete the following:

  I. Number in priority order only those areas of concern.

Speech and Verbal Communication	____	Work Habits	____
Visual Behavior	____	General Motor Behavior	____
Auditory Behavior	____	Discrepancy Classwork and Tests	____
In-class Social Behavior	____	Attentional Behaviors	____
Out-of-class Social Behavior	____	Absenteeism/Tardiness	____

  II. Indicate specific observed behaviors for above areas checked:

_____

_____

_____

  III. Describe program and materials used with student:

_____

_____

_____

_____

  IV. Estimated grade level at which student is functioning:

    Reading:_____ Math: _____

  V. Current test information:

_____

_____

_____

_____

  VI. Areas of strength and/or interest observed in student:

_____

_____

_____

_____

_____

Signature	School/District

Figure 3.3. Referral form. *Courtesy of School Administrative Unit #48, Plymouth, New Hampshire.*

SCHOOL ADMINISTRATIVE UNIT #48 PERMISSION TO EXCHANGE INFORMATION

Name of Child

Date of Birth

I hereby give my permission for the following exchange of information for the purpose of evaluation and/or placement9 of my child in a Special Education program:

☐   Gather pertinent educational, psychological, and/or medical records from

_____

_____

_____

(list agencies being requested to release information)

to the Special Education Evaluation /Placement Team of _____

_____.

(Name of School)

☐   Release the following information:

_____

_____

_____

(list items released)

to _____

(Name of agency or person to be sent information)

_____   _____
            Signature   Date

_____
(Relationship of person to child)

Figure 3.4. Permission to access records form. *Courtesy of School Administrative Unit #48, Plymouth, New Hampshire.*

Evaluation and Placement Team/Parent Conference I

In recent history very few pieces of legislation have had as great an impact on programs of physical education as the Education for All Handicapped Children Act of 1975 (Public Law 94–142), as revealed in Chapter 1. The underlying principle of this law, which appears to be the source of much anxiety among practitioners, is related to mainstreaming in general and individualized instruction in particular. With regard to these two components the law reads as follows:

> The term "special education" means specially designed instruction, at no cost to parents or guardians to meet the unique needs of a handicapped child (individuals with disabilities), including classroom instruction, instruction in physical education, home instruction, and instruction in hospitals and institutions.

> The term "individualized education program (plan)" means a written statement for each handicapped child (individuals with disabilities) developed in any meeting by a representative of the local education agency or an intermediate educational unit who shall be qualified to provide or supervise the provision of special "designed" instruction to meet the unique needs of handicapped children (individuals with disabilities), the teacher, the parents or guardian of such a child, and, whenever appropriate, such child.

Representing the school administrative unit on the Evaluation and Placement Team should be those persons who, among other things, will be directly responsible for overseeing and/or implementing an individual education plan (should it be deemed appropriate for development). You are referred to Table 3.1 for a roster of suggested team members.

Upon examining reasons for the referral and discussing the results of what was found in the student's educational, psychological, and/or medical records, a decision may be made to proceed further to gather additional evaluatory information. Assuming parental permission is granted, arrangements are made at the school district's expense for pertinent **assessments** to be carried out. (See Figure 3.5 for an example of a Permission to Test form.) These assessments may include such areas as

1. **Intelligence**, as measured by such tests as the
   a) *Stanford-Binet Intelligence Scale*—an instrument used for those two years of age and older. It is a 142-item verbal and non-verbal test designed to measure mental abilities in the following categories: conceptual thinking, language, memory, numerical reasoning, reasoning, social reasoning, and visual motor skills. Administered by professionally trained, certified examiners, its results help to identify children and adults who would benefit from specialized learning experiences.*
   b) *Wechsler Intelligence Scale for Children—Revised*—an instrument appropriate for those between the ages of six and sixteen. It consists of twelve subtests divided into two major divisions: verbal and performance. The verbal portion of the test consists of arithmetic, digit span, general comprehension,

---

* Available through The Riverside Publishing Company, P.O. Box 1970, Iowa City, Iowa 52244

School Administrative Unit # 48

PERMISSION TO TEST FORM

Date: _____

Dear: _____

The Special Education Evaluation and Placement Team is recommending an evaluation of your child to_____

_____

_____

The Team is writing to ask your permission for your child,_____,
to receive the following evaluation by qualified examiners:

Evaluations: Examiners:

_____   _____

_____   _____

_____   _____

_____   _____

You have the right to request a meeting with a school district representative to discuss this proposed action. The school district will arrange the evaluation, pay for the testing, make the results available to you, and not change the program of your child without prior knowledge and written approval (or until all due process procedures have been exhausted). If you disagree with the evaluation results or a decision based on those results, you have a right to an independent evaluation.

You may refuse to permit the evaluation with the understanding that the district may request a hearing to present its reasons and try to obtain approval to conduct the evaluation(s).

We hope that you will contact the school with any questions you may have.

Sincerely,

_____   _____
            Signature   Title

PARENTAL PERMISSION FOR EVALUATION OF_____

____ *I give* my permission for the _____ School District to
        arrange for and conduct the above-described evaluation of my child.
____ *I do not give* my permission for my child to receive the above-described evaluation.

_____   _____
            Signature   Date

Relationship to child: _____

NOTE: This permission will expire 45 days from the date of signature.

Figure 3.5. Permission to test form. *Courtesy of School Administrative Unit #48, Plymouth, New Hampshire.*

TABLE 3.1

Suggested Members for an Evaluation and Placement Team

Position	Permanent Members	Consulting Members
School administrator	X	
Special education administrator	X	
Developmental physical education teacher	X	
Teacher making referral	X	
Parent (or guardian)	X	
Director of physical education		X
School nurse		X
School psychologist		X
Physical therapist		X
Speech pathologist		X
Occupational therapist		X
Audiologist		X
Social worker		X
Guidance counselor		X
Physician		X
Ophthalmologist/optometrist		X
Vocational rehabilitation counselor		X
Other consultants (as deemed necessary)		X

Source: Adapted from Walker (1976).

general information, similarities, and vocabulary. The performance section consists of block design, coding and mazes, picture arrangement, picture completion, and object assembly. Like the Stanford-Binet Intelligence Scale, a professionally trained examiner is required. Further it is designed to assist those charged with individualizing a curriculum for persons identified by the test as needing assistance.*

2. **Behavior**, as measured by such tests as the:

   a) *American Association on Mental Deficiency (AAMD) Adaptive Behavior Scale*—an instrument for those between the ages of three and sixteen. It is a 95-item paper-pencil scale designed to assess those whose adapted behavior indicates possible emotional disturbance, mental retardation, or other learning disabilities. Acknowledging that no instrument yet devised can measure for the many and complex variables in social maladaptation, this instrument appears to be the best available (MacMillan, 1982).**

   b) *The ABC Inventory*—an instrument for those between the ages of 3 1/2 and 6 1/2 years of age. It is designed to assess the readiness of preschool-age children for school and provides an index of his/her maturity. The inven-

---

* Available through The Psychological Corporation, a subsidiary of Harcourt Brace Jovanovich, Inc., 7500 Old Oak Boulevard, Cleveland, Ohio 44130
** Available through CTB/McGraw-Hill, Del Monte Research Park, Monterey, California 93940

tory consists of four sections requiring the performance of each of the following tasks, respectively: (1) drawing a man, (2) answering language questions, (3) answering cognitive questions, and (4) performing motor activities. The scores generated by this test will help to identify those in need of further evaluation.*

3. **Physical health**, as measured by a comprehensive **medical examination**, Figure 3.6. Although some impairments requiring developmental activities are obvious, others are not. The medical examination, conducted by a skilled physician, will provide valuable information to the members of the Evaluation and Placement Team as they contemplate decisions about the referred child. A complete medical examination should consist of the following components:

   a) Medical history—which, as Vickery, Donald, and Fries (1976) point out, "...is the most important communication between the patient and the physician". Past illnesses, accidents, surgical procedures, and the immunization record are examples of items appropriate for inclusion in one's medical history.

   b) Family health history—including a record of family-acquired and **congenital** diseases and/or conditions, as well as the current health status of siblings and parents.

   c) Height and weight.

   d) Heart rate and blood pressure.

   e) Blood sample test (for anemia or other diseases of the blood).

   f) Lung test (including report of X-ray analysis).

   g) Vision test (including acuity, depth perception, color blindness, and general eye condition, such as conjunctivitis).

   h) Hearing test (including results of acuity as measured on an audiometer, and other otological findings such as chronic discharges, excessive ear wax, and ruptured eardrum).

   i) Nasal passages (adenoids, septum deviation, and/or growths).

   j) Glands (including lymph nodes and thyroid).

   k) Tonsils (size, inflammation, and general condition or absence).

   l) Abdomen (unusual shape, size, tenderness, possible hernia).

   m) Condition of the hands and fingers (unusual joint alignment, flexion, and extension).

   n) Condition of the feet and toes (unusual joint alignment, arch, bunions, or callouses).

   o) Standard testing of reflexes and other neural characteristics.

   p) Muscular and skeletal anomalies.

   q) Skin condition (boils, impetigo, eczema).

   r) General posture (body lean, head tilt, scoliosis, kyphosis, lordosis, and other conditions discoverable by gravity-line analysis).

Upon receipt of the results of the various assessments, the Chair of the Evaluation and Placement Team will arrange for a meeting of the group (including the parents) in order

---

* Available through Educational Studies and Development, 1357 Forest Park Road, Muskegon, Michigan 49441

HEALTH EXAMINATION

To be filled in by parent or guardian before the time of the examination.
(please print plainly with ink)

Pupil's Name _____ Birth _____ Sex M___ F ___
         (Last)   (First)   (Middle)   (Month) (Day) (Year)

Address _____ Phone _____ Parent or Guardian_____
      (Street or Route)   (City)

Family Physician's Name_____ Phone _____
            (Last)   (First)   (Initial)

Infancy and Preschool History: Record unusual problems, e.g., convulsions, accidents, operations, exposure to tuberculosis, behavior difficulties _____

Past History of Illness: State the year in which the child had any of the following:

Communicable Diseases		Other Diseases		Other Conditions	
Chickenpox	19__	Asthma	19__	Constant cough	19__
Diphtheria	19__	Diabetes	19__	Fainting spells	19__
German measles	19__	Hay fever	19__	Frequent colds	19__
Measles	19__	Heart trouble	19__	Frequent sore throat	19__
Mumps	19__	Kidney trouble	19__	Frequent urination	19__
Poliomyelitis	19__	Pneumonia	19__	Hearing difficulty	19__
Scarlet fever	19__	Rheumatic fever	19__	Tire easily	19__
Whooping cough	19__	Tonsilitis	19__	Vision difficulty	19__

History of Immunization and Tests

Completed Booster Dose			Completed Booster Dose			Completed Booster Dose		
Diphtheria	19__	19__	Whooping cough	19__	19__	Smallpox	19__	19__
Tetanus	19__	19__	Poliomyelitis	19__	19__	Other	19__	19__

	Date	Result		Date	Result			
Chest x-ray	19__	___	Other test	19__	___			

Other information of value to the teacher _____

HEALTH EXAMINATION

To be completed by examining physician
Vision, without glasses,   right eye 20/_____, left eye 20/_____
            with glasses,   right eye 20/_____, left eye 20/_____
            Color vision _____ test used _____

Hearing, right ear _____, left ear _____

Eyes	_____	Normal	_____	Defect	_____
Ears	_____	Normal	_____	Defect	_____
Nose	_____	Normal	_____	Defect	_____
Throat	_____	Normal	_____	Defect	_____
Thyroid	_____	Normal	_____	Defect	_____
Lymph nodes	_____	Normal	_____	Defect	_____
Heart	_____	Normal	_____	Defect	_____
Lungs	_____	Normal	_____	Defect	_____
Blood pressure	_____	Systolic	_____	Diastolic	_____
Abdomen	_____	Normal	_____	Defect	_____
Genitals	_____	Normal	_____	Defect	_____
Posture	_____	Normal	_____	Defect	_____
Extremities	_____	Normal	_____	Defect	_____
Nervous system	_____	Normal	_____	Defect	_____
Skin	_____	Normal	_____	Defect	_____
Nutrition	_____	Normal	_____	Defect	_____
Musculature	_____	Normal	_____	Defect	_____
Other	_____	Normal	_____	Defect	_____

Laboratory test _____
_____
_____

Findings and Recommendations _____
_____
_____
_____

Immediate medical referral   yes ____ no ____   Dental referral   yes ____ no ____

Unlimited activity _____ Limited activity _____

Parent present   yes ____ no ____

                                        _____ M.D. _____
                                              Examining Physician   Date

Figure 3.6. Example of a generally accepted medical examination form.

to discuss findings with a view toward determining whether the student is or is not deemed educationally handicapped (according to the criteria established by the federal and state governments).* For an example of a form announcing such a meeting, you are referred to Figure 3.7.

Evaluation and Placement Team/Parent Conference II

In anticipation of questions that might arise during the **parent conference**, the team chair may want to invite those persons who were directly involved in administering the

---

SCHOOL ADMINISTRATIVE UNIT #48

PRIOR NOTICE OF
SPECIAL EDUCATION EVALUATION PLACEMENT TEAM (SEEPT) MEETING

Dear _____   Date _____

We are planning a meeting of the Special Education Evaluation and Placement Team concerning your child _____. You are encouraged to attend and participate in this meeting. The meeting is scheduled for:

    Date: _____   Time: _____

    Place: _____

The purpose(s) of the meeting is (are): _____
_____
_____

Participants at the meeting will be: _____
_____
_____
_____

The school district would like to ensure parental participation at this meeting. If you are unable to attend and would like to reschedule at a mutually agreed-upon time, please call _____ at phone # _____ as soon as possible. If you do not respond, we will assume that you will attend.

We look forward to your participation.

                                        _____

Note: This meeting was arranged at a mutually agreeable time on _____.
                                                        Date

Figure 3.7. Meeting announcement form. *Courtesy of School Administrative Unit #48, Plymouth, New Hampshire.*

---

* In most cases, the Chair will be the special education administrator for the school or district.

various tests. As consultants their clarification of reported findings could aid the team as it examines the reports available. From these reports, Figure 3.8, general conclusions are drawn.

SAU #48

EVALUATION REPORT

Student: _____   Date: _____

District: _____   Grade: _____

Case Manager: _____

Evaluation Team:

Member: Position
_____   Teacher in area of disability
_____   Qualified examiner in disability
_____   Individual knowledgeable of student
_____   Representative from district
_____   _____
_____   _____
_____   _____
_____   _____

Academic Assessment: _____
Examiner: _____
Date(s) Administered _____   Age: _____
Summary of Results: _____
_____
_____
_____
_____
_____
_____
_____

Type of Evaluation: _____
Examiner: _____
Date(s) Administered _____   Age: _____
Summary of Results: _____
_____
_____
_____
_____
_____

* * *

Type of Evaluation: _____

Examiner: _____

Date(s) Administered _____ Age: _____

Summary of Results: _____

_____

_____

_____

_____

_____

* * *

Type of Evaluation: _____

Examiner: _____

Date(s) Administered _____ Age: _____

Summary of Results: _____

_____

_____

_____

_____

_____

* * *

Type of Evaluation: _____

Examiner: _____

Date(s) Administered _____ Age: _____

Summary of Results: _____

_____

_____

_____

_____

_____

_____

GENERAL CONCLUSIONS

It is the determination of the _____

School District Special Education Evaluation and Placement

Team that this student ☐ is not educationally handicapped.

☐ is educationally handicapped.

Primary Handicap _____

Secondary Handicap _____

Additional Secondary Handicap _____

Additional Secondary Handicap _____

If a specific learning disability was considered by the team as a possible educational handicapping condition or if LD is the primary handicap, complete and attach a Written Summary for Students with Specific Learning Disabilities.

Parents' Rights: For information regarding the rights of appeal or to an independent evaluation, please refer to the document <u>Parental Rights in Special Education</u> that

_____ is attached   _____ was provided to parents, date _____

SAU #48

WRITTEN SUMMARY

for Students with Specific Learning Disabilities

Note: This summary must be attached to a completed Evaluation Report.

Student: _____

The consideration of a specific learning disability is based upon the evaluations, including an observation and vision and hearing screening, summarized in the Evalutaion Report.

Observation: relevant behavior noted and relationship to academic functioning

_____

_____

Medical Findings: educationally relevant medical findings

_____

_____

Severe Discrepancy between achievement and ability that is not correctable without special education or special education and educationally related services

_____

_____

Effects of Environmental, Cultural, or Economic Disadvantage

_____

_____

CONCLUSION

The Special Education Evaluation and Placement Team determined that this student

☐ has a specific learning disability

☐ does not have a specific learning disability

This decision reflects my conclusion. Signature below

_____ / _____

_____ / _____

_____ / _____

This decision does not reflect my conclusion. A separate statement is attached presenting my conclusion.

_____ / _____

Figure 3.8. Evaluation report form. *Courtesy of School Administrative Unit #48, Plymouth, New Hampshire.*

The reader should note that reference is made to parental rights, under "General Conclusion." It is critical that procedural safeguards are in place to ensure that parents (guardians or surrogate parents) are apprised of and/or engaged in each and every phase of the Evaluation and Placement Team's activity (as it pertains to their child). In summary, Public Law 94–142 provides that parents have the right to

1. consent in writing before the child is initially evaluated.
2. consent in writing before the child is initially placed in a special education program.
3. request an independent education **evaluation** if they feel the school's evaluation is inappropriate.
4. request an evaluation at public expense if a due-process hearing decision is that the public agency's evaluation was inappropriate.
5. participate on the committee that considers the evaluation, placement, and programming of the child.
6. inspect and review educational records and challenge information believed to be inaccurate, misleading, or in violation of the privacy or other rights of the child.
7. request a copy of information from their child's educational record.
8. request a hearing concerning the school's proposal or refusal to initiate or change the identification, evaluation, or placement of the child, or the provision of a **free appropriate public education** (**FAPE**).

Hardman et al. (1990) spoke clearly about **procedural safeguards** when they wrote,

These safeguards protect the child and family from decisions that could adversely affect their lives. In addition, families can be more secure in the knowledge that every reasonable attempt is being made to educate their child appropriately.

Individual Education Plans (IEPs)

If it is determined that the child is educationally handicapped, an individual education plan—Figure 3.9—would be prepared that is in keeping with all pertinent elements of the law. In brief, this plan must include

1. a statement of the child's present level of educational performance, including academic achievement, behavioral, and psychomotor performance data generated by the formal evaluation process.
2. a statement of annual goals that describes the educational performance to be achieved by the end of the school year under the child's IEP.
3. a statement of short-term instructional objectives, which must be measurable intermediate steps between the present level of educational performance and the annual goals. These objectives, stated in behavioral terms, should each include three elements: (a) a statement of conditions, (b) a statement of performance, and (c) a statement of accuracy (or standards by which attainment of the objective will be judged) (Mager 1962).
   An example of a **behavioral objective** containing these three elements is: In a stationary position and using the pads of the fingers of the dominant hand (element *a*), the student will bounce a basketball (element *b*) eight times

consecutively (element *c*). The conditions (element *a*) refer to the fact that the learner is expected to be in a static position and use the pads of the fingers of the preferred hand in order to perform the skill in question. The performance (element *b*) refers to the fact that the student will bounce a basketball. The standards of accuracy (element *c*) for judging whether the student has reached the behavioral objective state that he/she must perform the skill eight times consecutively.

4. The date when the services will begin and the length of time that the services will be given. For example: Speech therapy will begin October 1 and continue for a period of six weeks. At the end of the six weeks an evaluation will be conducted in order to determine whether there is a need to continue the therapy. All other services will begin September 5 and will continue throughout the school year.

5. A statement of specific educational services needed by the child (determined without regard to the immediate availability of those services), including a description of

    a) all special education and related services that are needed to meet the unique needs of the child (including the type of physical education program — standard, developmental, or combined—in which the child will participate). Related services might include, for example, two twenty-minute sessions per week with the specific learning disabilities specialist; one half-hour session per week with the **occupational therapist**; three half-hour sessions per week with the guidance counselor; 50 percent of classroom time in a resource room (for reading skills).

    b) any special instructional materials that will be needed to implement the IEP.

6. A description of the extent to which the child will participate in regular educational programs.

7. A justification for the type of educational placement that the child will have.

8. Objective criteria, evaluation procedures, and schedules for determining—on at least an annual basis—whether the short-term instructional objectives are being achieved.

9. A list of the individuals who are responsible for implementation of the IEP.

10. A signature of the parent (guardian or surrogate parent) or student (if he/she is eighteen years of age or older) indicating approval of the individual education program contents.

Evaluation

The program of physical education arising out of planning meetings will require continuous review and adjustment. Children mature, resulting in numerous changes from what may have been observed during initial observational and testing sessions. Strategies may be employed that do not appear to be generating expected outcomes. As a consequence of these factors the teacher will want to continue to gather information.

In addition to the forms described heretofore in this chapter and to the discussion provided as to their use(s) it may be useful for the physical educator to consider additional procedures in order to help refine the program of activities suitable for the

School Administrative Unit #48

INDIVIDUAL EDUCATIONAL PROGRAM

_____ School District

Start Date _____   End Date _____   SPEDIS # _____

STUDENT _____ DOB _____ CA _____

GRADE _____ HANDICAP(S) _____ CODE _____

_____ _____

PARENT(S) OR GUARDIAN _____

ADDRESS _____

_____ PHONE _____

CASE MANAGER _____ PHONE _____

ASSESSMENT INFORMATION

Date of last evaluation meeting _____

Assessment(s)	Examiner(s)	Date(s)
_____	_____	_____
_____	_____	_____
_____	_____	_____
_____	_____	_____
_____	_____	_____
_____	_____	_____

PRESENT LEVEL OF EDUCATIONAL PERFORMANCE

Strengths: _____

_____

_____

_____

Copies: White—Parent
         Yellow—District File
         Pink/Gold—Service Provider

Student Name _____

Weaknesses: _____

_____

_____

_____

RECOMMENDED SPECIAL ED. AND RELATED SERVICES	AMOUNT OF TIME	SERVICE PROVIDER

_____

TIME SPENT IN REGULAR CLASSROOM _____

DURATION OF TOTAL EDUCATION PROGRAM:
(If other than regular school calendar, please note below)
_____ school days per year   _____ length of school day in hours
       covered by IEP

INSTRUCTIONAL AREA:
STUDENT'S PRESENT LEVEL OF PERFORMANCE: _____

_____

_____

_____

ANNUAL GOAL: _____

_____

_____

Student Name _____

SHORT-TERM OBJECTIVE(S),
EXPECTED COMPLETION DATE(S) AND CRITERIA OF SUCCESSFUL PERFORMANCE:

CLASSROOM MODIFICATIONS

Expectations for the student when participating in the regular class or program.

DISCIPLINE: Does the student's handicapping condition(s) require a modification of rules and regulations outlined in the students' handbook? No _____ Yes _____
If yes, describe modifications_____

Student Name _____

STATE MANDATED TESTS: Is it appropriate for this student to participate in state mandated group testing? Yes _____ No _____
Modifications required _____
_____

GRADUATION DIPLOMA: (To be addressed for students entering or enrolled in high school programs.) The Team has determined that the student:
_____ is expected to graduate in _____ (month/year)
_____ is not expected to graduate with a regular diploma but is expected to receive
    (a) diploma of completion _____.
    (b) certificate of completion _____.

THIS PROGRAM WAS WRITTEN ON _____ AND WILL BE IN EFFECT FROM _____ TO _____. IT WILL BE MONITORED REGULARLY BY THE CASE MANAGER, _____. AN ANNUAL REVIEW MEETING WILL DETERMINE THE EFFECTIVENESS OF THE PROGRAM.

FINANCIAL RESPONSIBILITY FOR THIS PLACEMENT WILL BE THE _____ _____ SCHOOL DISTRICT'S AS PRESCRIBED BY STATE LAW AND STATE BOARD OF EDUCATION REGULATIONS.

_____
Signature of Authorized Representative
of the School District

ACCEPTANCE

_____ I/We do accept this Individual Education Program

_____ I/We do not accept this Individual Educational Program

_____   _____
Date   Parent/Guardian/Student over age
                                                    18 Signature

Figure 3.9. Example of a generally accepted format for an individual education program (plan). *Courtesy of School Administrative Unit #48, Plymouth, New Hampshire.*

child in question. These strategies may also be employed if the child is not coded as educationally handicapped—they can be referred to as enabling enhancement procedures.

Medical examinations, for example, should be supplemented by persons in a position to make day-by-day observations of students' structural and **functional** behavior. In instances where deviations are suspected by the teacher, students should be referred to the proper medical authority in accordance with school policy. Figure 3.10 is an example of a developmental physical education referral form which, when completed by any of the teachers within the school, would be sent to the principal, special education teacher (coordinator), director of physical education, and the Evaluation and Placement Team (if pertinent). Upon receiving the form, the group would meet in order to discuss its disposition. If parental approval and medical opinion are necessary—as in cases of suspected sensory, musculoskeletal, neurological, or behavioral dysfunctions—a **medical excuse form** is forwarded, via the parent, to the family physician, Figure 3.11.

DEVELOPMENTAL PHYSICAL EDUCATION REFERRAL FORM

Date: _____

Teacher making referral:_____

School in which student is registered: _____

Student's name: _____ Sex: _____ Grade: _____
           Last   First   MI

Suspected reason for referral (please check)

    Physical fitness problem:

        Strength   _____   Specific location: _____

        C/V Endurance _____

        Flexibility   _____   Specific location: _____

    Motor fitness problem:

        Agility   _____

        Balance   _____

        Coordination _____

    Other:

        Postural   _____

        Sensory   _____

        Musculoskeletal _____

        Neurological _____

        Behavioral   _____

        _____ _____

        _____ _____

Additional remarks (Please explain): _____

_____

_____

Figure 3.10. Example of a referral form for developmental physical education.

TOWNSHIP OF OCEAN SCHOOL DISTRICT
DEPARTMENT OF HEALTH, PHYSICAL EDUCATION, AND DRIVER EDUCATION

MEDICAL EXCUSE FORM

Date: _____

Dear Parent:

Recognizing the fact that students with varied physical limitations evidence different needs, the Department of Physical Education has designed a program to afford students (postoperative, convalescent, and the physically limited) an opportunity to participate in a developmental activities program.

It would be beneficial to your child if he or she were enrolled in one of the classes. If you concur, please sign this form, submit to the proper medical authority, and forward to the appropriate building principal at your earliest convenience. If you have any additional questions, please contact your child's physical education teacher.

Sincerely,

_____

Principal

TO BE COMPLETED BY THE PARENT

I would like to have my son/daughter _____ assigned to the
                                                              (Pupil's name)
appropriate developmental physical education class.

_____

(Parent's signature)

_____

(Date: Month, Day, Year)

TO BE COMPLETED BY THE FAMILY OR SCHOOL PHYSICIAN

Nature of the illness or physical limitation:_____

_____

_____

Approximate duration of the excuse: _____

Please indicate the activities you recommend for the student by checking the appropriate category (or categories) indicated below. Only those activities that are appropriate to the categories checked will be included in the student's developmental and/or general physical education program.

____   Calisthenics (including stretching, progressive resistance, and repetition)

____   Postural exercises (geared to address specific or general deviations)

_____   Weight training

_____   Cardiovascular endurance activities (including rope jumping, interval, Fartlek, and marathon training)

_____   Modified games (including basketball, volleyball, soccer)

_____   Recreational activities (including archery, bowling, quoit, shuffleboard, table tennis)

_____   Gymnastic apparatus and tumbling (selected according to physical abilities)

_____   Rehabilitative exercises (please list)

1. _____

2. _____

3. _____

4. _____

5. _____

General comments (including identification of contraindicated activities, if any):

PLEASE PRINT

Name: _____

Address: _____

Telephone: _____

Signed: _____

Figure 3.11. Example of a medical excuse form. *Courtesy of Township of Ocean School District, Ocean Township, New Jersey.*

A variety of **medical referral forms** and medical excuse forms are used by practitioners of physical education. You should consider modifying whatever forms offered to best suit your situation. Figure 3.12 is another example of a physical education referral form. This one has the approval and endorsement of the Committee on the Medical Aspects of Sports of the American Medical Association.

Upon the basis of medical, parental, and staff-member opinion and deliberation, the child could be scheduled for developmental and/or general physical education classes. However, on occasions developmental physical education classes must be scheduled in conflict with the student's other classes. The school administrator who recognizes the importance of the developmental physical education program may grant permission for the youngster to be excused from certain classes on a rotating basis. An **approval form** used to enlist parental or guardian approval for such a plan is shown in Figure 3.13.

PHYSICAL EDUCATION DIVISION

Physical Education Medical Referral Form
ASAW #1313-1975

Dear Dr. _____:

(This space can be used for information about state/local physical education requirement, rationale of adapted physical education, objectives and benefits of local programs, organization and administration of local classes, purposes and uses of this form and related areas to improve understanding and communication among physicians, physical educators, parents, and others concerned with and involved in the education, health, and welfare of the student. Procedures for returning the form can be included in this section or at the end of the form.)

John J. Jones, M.D.   George T. Smith, Supervisor
Director, School Health Department   Division of Health, Physical
                                       Education and Athletics

Student Information

Name: _____ School: _____
Home address: _____ City _____State_____Zip _____
Home telephone: (___) _____ Grade and Section_____

Condition

Brief description of condition:

Condition is   ☐ permanent   ☐ temporary

Comments: _____

If appropriate, comments about student's medication and its effects on participation in physical activities:

_____

Student may return to unrestructed activity _____, 19____
Student should return for reexamination _____, 19____

Functional capacity

☐ *Unrestricted:* No restrictions are placed relative to vigorousness or type of activities.

☐ *Restricted:* Condition is such that intensity and type of activities need to be limited. *(Check one category below.)*
   ☐ *Mild:* Ordinary physical activities need not be restricted, but usually vigorous efforts need to be avoided.
   ☐ *Moderate:* Ordinary physical activities need to be moderately restricted and sustained strenuous efforts avoided.
   ☐ *Limited:* Ordinary physical activities need to be markedly restricted.

Activity Recommendations

Indicate body areas for which physical activities should be minimized, eliminated, or maximized.

	Comments, including any medical contraindications to physical activities
Neck	
Shoulder girdle	
Arms	
Elbows	
Hands and wrists	
Abdomen	
Back	
Pelvic girdle	
Legs	
Knees	
Feet and ankles	
Toes	
Fingers	
Other (specify)	

Remedial

☐ Condition is such that defects or deviations can be improved or prevented from becoming worse through use of carefully selected exercise and/or activities. The following are remedial exercises and/or activities recommended for this student: (Please be specific.)

_____

_____

_____

_____

_____

_____

_____

_____

Signed _____ M.D.

Address _____

_____ Zip _____

Telephone No. (   ) _____

Date _____ 19 ___

Figure 3.12. Medical referral form. *Recommended by the Committee on Medical Aspects of Sports of the American Medical Association, 1975.*

TOWNSHIP OF OCEAN SCHOOL DISTRICT

Dear Parent:

Your child, _____. has been recommended for involvement in the developmental physical education class because of

    _____   Low physical vitality

    _____   Low motor ability

    _____   Posture

    _____   Medical problems

With your permission, your child will be scheduled for individualized enrichment activities _____ days per week in addition to the regular physical education program (as appropriate).

THE ENRICHMENT PROGRAM HAS BEEN PLANNED ON A ROTATIONAL BASIS SO THAT STUDENTS DO NOT MISS THE SAME CLASSROOM ACTIVITIES EACH WEEK. Further testing is repeated at nine-week intervals in order to assess individual progress. Upon achievement of minimal performance levels, students are released from the program. (You will be kept apprised of your child's progress.)

Thank you very much for your cooperation.

Sincerely,

_____

Principal

P.S. If you desire any additional information, call the teacher named below on

_____ between _____ at _____.
       Days   Time   Telephone

Please return this form to: _____
                                    Teacher's name

_____   _____
        School   Address

I do/do not (circle one) wish to have my child_____
                                      First/Last name
scheduled in the developmental physical education program.

_____   _____
     Parent's name   Date

Figure 3.13. Example of a parent/guardian approval form. *Courtesy of Township of Ocean School District, Ocean Township, New Jersey.*

As a result of observing performances while students participate in team, individual, dual, rhythmic, and other general physical education activities, certain deficiencies may become apparent to you. You might notice postural problems in students who are waiting for their chance to play volleyball. You may notice deficiencies in perception as students attempt to play quoit or weaknesses in arm strength as students attempt to complete cross-rest swings on the parallel bars. These are but a few of the dysfunctions you may recognize during a general physical education class. I will discuss other examples in Section II, Introduction to Exceptionalities.

An example of a **progress form** used to apprise parents or guardians of a child's progress in the developmental physical education program is shown in Figure 3.14.

Another way to gather information as to the appropriateness of the individual education plan you are using or updating is to ask the student involved. An example of a **student evaluation form** used to procure information from the student is shown in Figure 3.15. The student's input is invaluable as his/her perceptions of program effectiveness will influence a mindset for learning.

SUMMARY

The organization of quality programs depends upon many factors. In relation to these factors, we have an obligation to keep up to date with the information technology available if we hope to translate current practices into our curricula.

TOWNSHIP OF OCEAN SCHOOL DISTRICT

Dear Parents:

Your child, _____ has been participating in our developmental physical education program. After careful review, it has been determined that he/she may benefit from continuation in the program. If you agree, please check the appropriate space below and sign you name, your child's name, and his/her grade.

Thank you.

_____   _____
           Principal   Date

(Detach and return to school)

_____   Please continue my child in the developmental class.
_____   Do not continue my child in the program at this time. (My reasons are indicated on the back of this form.)

_____   _____
      Student's name   Parent/Guardian signature
      Grade: _____   Telephone: _____

Figure 3.14. Example of a parent/guardian developmental physical education progress form. *Courtesy of Township of Ocean School District, Ocean Township, New Jersey.*

STUDENT EVALUATION FORM

Name: _____ Grade: _____ Date: _____

Why were you placed in the developmental program? _____

How long have you been enrolled in the program?_____

How many days per week do you follow your prescribed program? _____

What specific improvements have you made?

    Physical fitness: _____

    Motor fitness: _____

    Posture: _____

    Physical disability:_____

    Other: (improved relations with classmates, better performance in other subjects, ability to perform activities of daily living without tiring, etc.

    _____

    _____

    _____

    _____

    _____

In the space below, please add any other comments which you believe would assist the physical education staff and/or the individualized education plan committee in making your particular developmental program more meaningful.

Figure 3.15. Example of student evalation form. *Courtesy of Township of Ocean School District, Ocean Township, New Jersey.*

In Chapter 3 you learned about the importance of thoughtful curriculum development. The improvement of sensorimotor skills depends upon the prescription and administration of activities that are in keeping with students' needs and capabilities. If we are mindful of the affective, cognitive, and psychomotor characteristics of the students in our care, as revealed through valid assessment procedures, we will find that more growth and development than was deemed possible will occur.

To that end, there are legal considerations that must be taken into account. These procedural safeguards help ensure that all pertinent parties are involved in the development of appropriate programs and strategies. Parents, teachers, and other school practitioners have the power to produce insightful and significant changes. The use of an IEP and other documents appropriate to 'advice and consent' will assist them immeasurably in this endeavor.

In Section II, I will present developmental activities designed to help us prescribe programs for exceptional children. These developmental activities are bases we use to prepare appropriate behavioral objectives and strategies and to establish attainable standards consistent with student capabilities.

RECOMMENDED LABORATORY ASSIGNMENTS

1. Interview curriculum specialists within public and/or private schools and colleges in order to review the guidelines they use when embarking upon curriculum revision.
2. Develop a scorecard that could be used to assess the general and developmental physical education curriculum from kindergarten to twelfth grade.
3. Perform the test activities in the Confidential Student Selection Sheet for Developmental Physical Education yourself to gain further insight into the nature of the difficulty of each requirement.
4. Administer the test activities in the Confidential Student Selection Sheet for Developmental Physical Education to students in an elementary school.
5. If you have completed Recommended Laboratory Assignment #4, prepare a list of developmental activities that would address the suspected deficiencies of the students you tested.
6. Examine various standardized tests, including those presented within the chapter, with reference to validity, reliability, standard error of measurement (estimate), and ease of administration as revealed in such documents as Buros' *Mental Measurements Yearbook* (by Buros; Mitchell; or Conoley and Kramer— depending upon the edition) and *Test Critiques* (by Keyser and Sweetland).
7. Interview school physicians in order to determine the scope of the medical examination typically administered to school-age children.
8. Obtain and review medical excuse forms being used within various public and private schools. Design a form that would incorporate what you believe to be the most important features.
9. Obtain and evaluate various public and private grade school physical education curricula with regard to the existence and scope of general and developmental physical education classes.
10. Interview practitioners of physical education to learn what methods and materials they use for prescribing and conducting programs of activities for exceptional students.
11. Work with various software programs in order to gain insights as to their relative strengths and weaknesses regarding total curriculum and IEP development.
12. Arrange to sit in on some of the meetings of an Evaluation and Placement Team. At the conclusion of each session you attend, meet with the physical education teacher to review findings and rationale.
13. Obtain or design appropriate forms of the type described in this chapter and draw up an IEP in physical education for a hypothetical student with a selected deficiency. Review your recommendations with successful practitioners.
14. Review the recommended readings.

REFERENCES

Bosco, J. J. 1984. Interactive video: Educational tool or toy? *Educational Technology*, 24(4):13.

Carter, J., and G. Sugai. 1989. Survey on prereferral practices: Responses from state departments of education. *Exceptional Children*, 55:198–302.

Committee on Adapted Physical Education. 1952. Guiding principles for adapted physical education. *Journal of the American Association for Health, Physical Education, and Recreation* 23(4):15, 28.

Dauer, V. P., and R. P. Pangrazi. 1979. *Dynamic physical education for elementary school children.* Minneapolis: Burgess Publishing Company.

DePauw, K. P. 1990. PE and sport for disabled individuals in the United States. *Journal of Physical Education Recreation and Dance* 61(2):53–57.

Dunst, C. J. 1986. Overview of the efficacy of early intervention programs. In *Evaluating early intervention programs for severely handicapped children and their families,* edited by L. Bickman and D. L. Weatherford. Austin, TX: PRO-ED.

Education for all handicapped children act of 1975, PL 94–142. In *Weekly Compilation of Presidential Documents* 11(49).

Gerber, M. M., and D. Levine-Donnerstein. 1989. Educating all children: Ten years later. *Exceptional Children,* 56(1):17–27.

Goodlad, J. I., ed. 1963. *Planning and organizing for teaching.* Washington, DC: National Education Association.

Hardman, M. L., C. J. Drew, M. W. Egan, and B. Wolf. 1990. *Human exceptionality.* 3d ed. Boston, MA: Allyn and Bacon.

Jarvis, S. 1984. Videodiscs and computers. *BYTE* (July): 187–203.

MacMillan, D. L. 1982. *Mental retardation in school and society.* 2d ed. Boston, MA: Little, Brown, and Company.

Mager, R. F. 1962. *Preparing instructional objectives.* Belmont, CA: Fearon Publishers.

Malouf, D. B., P. J. Jamison, M. H. Kercher, and C. M. Carlucci. 1991. Integrating computer software into effective instruction. *Teaching Exceptional Children* 23(4):57–60.

Minor, R. O. 1989. Computer technology can manage curriculum, link learning to instruction. *NASSP Bulletin* 73(521): 75–79.

Vickery, D. M., and J. F. Fries. 1976. *Take care of yourself: A consumer's guide to medical care.* Reading, MA: Addison-Wesley.

Walker, J., ed. 1976. *Functions of the placement committee in special education: A resource manual.* Washington, DC: National Association of State Directors of Special Education.

Will, M. 1986. *Educating students with learning problems: A shared responsibility.* Washington, DC: U.S. Department of Education, Office of Special Education and Rehabilitative Services.

RECOMMENDED READINGS

Bedini, L. A. 1990. Separate but equal? Segregated programming for people with disabilities. *Journal of Physical Education, Recreation and Dance* 61(8):40–44.

Benton, S. 1968. *Intensive programming for slow learners.* Columbus, OH: Charles E. Merrill.

Bilken, D., S. Lehr, S. J. Searl, and S. J. Taylor. 1987. *Purposeful integration…inherently equal.* New York: The Center on Human Policy, Syracuse University.

Byrnes, M. 1990. The regular education initiative debate: A view from the field. *Exceptional Children* 56(1): 345–49

Carter, M. J., C. M. Foret, D. D. McLean, and W. P. Callahan. 1991. Using computers to link social service providers. *Journal of Physical Education, Recreation and Dance* 61(4): 34–36.

Cone, J. D., D.D. Delawyer, and V. V. Wolfe. 1985. Assessing parent participation: The parent/family involvement index. *Exceptional Children* 51: 417–24.

Freiberg, K. L. 1992. *Annual editions: Educating exceptional children.* Guilford, CT: The Dushkin Publishing Group, Inc.

Haggerty, T. R. 1990. Coping with information overload: A strategy for busy professionals. *Journal of Physical Education, Recreation and Dance* 61(9): 47–51.

Kephart, N. C. 1961. *The slow learner in the classroom.* Columbus, OH: Charles E. Merrill.

McCubbin, J., and L. Zittel. 1991. PL 99–457: What the law is all about. *Journal of Physical Education, Recreation and Dance* 62(6): 35–37, 47.

Macera, C. A., K. L. Jackson, G. W. Hagenmaier, J. J. Kroenfeld, H. W. Kohl, and S. N. Blair. 1989. Age, physical activity, physical fitness, body composition, and incidence of orthopedic problems. *Research Quarterly for Exercise and Sport* 60(3): 225–233.

McDaniel, E. A., and H. DiBella-MCCarthy. 1989. Enhancing teacher efficacy in special education. *Teaching Exceptional Children* 21(4): 34–38.

Morris, P. R., and H. T. Whiting. 1971. *Motor impairment and compensatory education.* Philadelphia: Lea and Febiger.

Nirje, B. 1969. The normalization principle and its human management implications. In *Changing Patterns in Residential Services for the Mentally Retarded,* edited by R. Kugel and W. Wolfensberger. Washington, DC: The President's Committee on Mental Retardation.

Pianta, R. C. 1990. Widening the debate on educational reform: Prevention as a viable alternative. *Exceptional Children* 56(4): 306–13.

Ruiz, N. T. 1989. An optimal learning environment for Rosemary. *Exceptional Children* 56(2): 130–44.

Semmel, M. I., T. V. Abernathy, G. Butera, and S. Lesar. 1991. Teacher perceptions of the regular education initiative. *Exceptional Children* 58(1): 9–24.

Smith, S. W. 1990. Individualized education programs (IEPs) in special education—from intent to acquiescence. *Exceptional Children* 57(1): 6–14.

Taylor, M. S., and D. P. Saverance. 1990. Computers, physical education, and the year 2000. *Journal of Physical Education, Recreation and Dance* 62(7): 18–39.

Taylor, W., and T. Baranowski. 1991. Physical activity, cardiovascular fitness, and adiposity. *Research Quarterly for Exercise and Sport* 62(2): 157–63.

Turnbull, A. P. 1983. Parent-professional interactions. In *Systematic instruction of the moderately and severely handicapped,* 2d ed., edited by M. E. Snell. Columbus, OH: Charles E. Merrill.

Wolfensberger, W. 1972. *Normalization: The principle of normalization in human services.* Toronto: National Institute on Mental Retardation.

Yell, M. L., and C. A. Espin. 1990. The Handicapped Children's Protection Act of 1986: Time to pay the piper? *Exceptional Children* 56(5): 396–407.

SECTION II

Introduction to Exceptionalities

CHAPTER 4

Physical, Motor, and Postural Fitness Disorders _____

Objectives

After reading this chapter, you should be able to

- Discuss the attention given to postural deviations throughout various periods of history.
- Differentiate between physical and motor fitness and define the components of each.
- Discuss the importance of nutrition to one's overall health.
- Describe techniques available for assessing physical and motor fitness.
- Discuss formal and informal postural screening procedures.
- Discuss appropriate remedial exercises for common functional postural malalignments.
- Demonstrate developmental activities appropriate to the acquisition of physical and motor fitness.

INTRODUCTION

Concern about physical fitness is not a recent phenomenon. A review of history indicates that prior to the turn of the century much attention was paid to researching and publishing the effects of internal and external stimuli on what was perceived as normal patterns of human growth. Those who were motivated to assess the quality of human growth attended to the development and refinement of test and measurement methods and materials, Table 4.1. As data were gathered and analyzed, attempts were made to prescribe developmental exercises to remedy low functional levels.

KEY TERMS

agility	nutrition
ankle (foot) pronation	objective evaluation
balance	pelvic tilt
baseline (assessment)	pes planus
bilateral	physical fitness
cardiovascular endurance	postural fitness
coordination	practitioner-made tests
dynamic posture	prone position
flat back	repetitions
flexibility	round shoulders
formal posture evaluation	scoliosis
general slump	screening
genu valgum	skinfold measurements
genu varum	standardized tests
informal posture evaluation	static posture
kyphosis	strength
lordosis	subjective evaluation
lumbar	supine position
motor fitness	torticollis
muscular endurance	winged scapulae

TABLE 4.1

Overview of Selected Topics Pertaining to the Assessment and Development of Physical, Motor, and Postural Fitness: 1851–1900

Date(s)	Author(s)	Topic(s)
1851	Roth, Matthias	*The Prevention and Cure of Many Chronic Diseases by Movements*
1852	Hare, Samuel	*Facts and Observations on the Physical Education of Children, Expecially as Regards the Prevention of Spinal and Other Deformities*
1859	Hutchinson, Jonathan	"The Thorax"
1876	Sayre, Lewis	*Orthopedic Surgery and Diseases of the Joints*
1879	Lister, Sir J.	"An Address on the Influence of Position upon Local Circulation"
1883	Bradford, E. H.	"The Effect of Recumbency on the Length of the Spine"
1884	Clevenger, S. V.	"Disadvantages of the Upright Position"
1886	Cunningham, D. J.	"Lumbar Curve in Man and the Apes"

TABLE 4.1

Date(s)	Author(s)	Topic(s)
1887	Allis, Oscar H.	"Man's Aptitude for Labor in the Erect Position"
1888	Bullard, W. M., Bracket, E. G.	"Observations on the Steadiness of the Hand and on Static Equilibrium"
1889	Stilman, Charles	"Round Shoulders"
1890	Lagrange, Fernand	*Physiology of Bodily Exercise*
1891	Lane, W. Arbuthnot	Some of the Laws Which Influence the Growth of Children
1892	Kellogg, J. H.	"The Relation of Static Disturbances of the Abdominal Viscera to Displacement of the Pelvic Organs"
1893	Mosher, Eliza	"Habits of Posture a Cause of Deformity and Displacement"
1894	Schafer and Thane, editors	*Quain's Anatomy*
1896	Hall, Winfield S.	"The Changes in the Proportions of the Human Body during the Period of Growth"
1897	Hutchinson, Woods	"Some Deformities of the Chest in Light of Its Ancestry and Growth"
1898	Burke, Frederick	"Growth of Children in Height and Weight"
1899	Roth, Bernard	Treatment of Lateral Curvature of the Spine
1900	Trettien, August	"Creeping and Walking"

Yet in spite of much work accomplished by our colleagues of years past, low levels of physical, motor, and postural fitness constitute the greatest number of anomalies to be found among our school-age population today. The reasons are numerous. Among those most frequently sited are

1. Insufficient number of **screening** programs in existence throughout the public schools, grades kindergarten to twelfth
2. Apparent lack of concern for the eventual outcomes related to undiagnosed or untreated fitness problems
3. Too few physical education curricula that include developmental fitness programs
4. Poor postural habits on the part of students
5. Weak musculature, particularly in the arms and abdominal areas
6. Lack of understanding as to what constitutes appropriate physical, motor, and postural fitness

PHYSICAL FITNESS

Physical fitness refers to one's present capacity to engage successfully in activities requiring varying degrees of muscular strength, **muscular endurance**, **cardiovascular endurance**, and **flexibility**. And, as you might expect, research abounds as to the benefits of different training techniques upon these components (Wyness 1990). Something with which researchers tend to agree, however, is that deficiency in either or all of these factors is likely to have some negative effect on one's success in activities requiring these physical fitness components. For example, we need arm strength to perform well on the horizontal bar in gymnastics, Figure 4.1. Trunk flexibility is more important than arm strength to success in many of the ingredients of floor exercise routines, Figure 4.2. Body structure often seems to dictate physical activity. For example, individuals who are endowed with heavy muscular and endomorphic (broad, large) frames are more inclined to participate in such sports as football and selected field events (shot put, hammer throw).

Figure 4.1. Gymnastic exercise on the horizontal bar

Figure 4.2. Gymnastic floor exercise

Individuals with ectomorphic (slender, small) frames might be more likely to participate in badminton, tennis, track, or swimming, where a great deal of muscle bulk is not necessary and in fact may hinder efficient performance.

MOTOR FITNESS

Motor fitness, for the purposes of this text, refers to our capacity to perform tasks that require **agility**, **balance**, and **coordination**. While most—if not all—physical education activities require more or less of the components comprising motor fitness, some activities place an emphasis on balance, Figure 4.3; others require coordination, Figure 4.4; still others seem to demand more in the way of agility, Figure 4.5. In short an activity that demands agility, balance, coordination, endurance, flexibility, and **strength** will be performed most successfully by those who demonstrate these elements of motor fitness, Table 4.2.

Figure 4.3. These activities require balance.

POSTURAL FITNESS

Postural fitness is the efficiency we incorporate into the static (without motion) or dynamic (with motion) positioning of our bodies. Although there is little evidence as to what effect postural problems, other than those related to the vertebral column, have on functional and structural anomalies in later life, they do appear to influence imagery— how we perceive ourselves and how others perceive us. Our self-image is reflected in how we act and move. The better our posture, the more positive the image we radiate while we move.

To perform a variety of activities successfully—that is, with enjoyment, with efficiency, and without undue stress—we need minimal levels of physical, motor, and

Figure 4.4. Field hockey requires coordination. *Courtesy of Office of News Service, Plymouth State College, Plymouth, New Hampshire.*

Figure 4.5. Basketball requires agility. *Courtesy of Office of News Service, Plymouth, State College, Plymouth, New Hampshire.*

TABLE 4.2

Components and Definitions of Physical and Motor Fitness

Components	Definitions
Agility	Dexterity and ease of physical action; ability to change direction quickly and with control.
Balance	Stability produced by even distribution of weight on each side of body's vertical axis. Static balance is retention of equilibrium while stationary; dynamic balance is maintenance of control while in motion.
Coordination	Ability to integrate movement patterns to include hand-eye, foot-eye, both hands, both feet, arm-trunk, leg-trunk.
Endurance, cardiovascular	Ability of circulatory system to adjust to and recover from physical stress without negative side effects.
Endurance, muscular	Ability of muscles to contract and relax, repetitively, against moderate resistance.
Flexibility*	Ability to extend and flex articulated segments of the body about a joint. Flexion decreases the angle at a joint; extension increases the angle at a joint.

TABLE 4.2

Components	Definitions
Strength*	Amount of force that can be exerted against resistance in one maximum effort. Dynamic strength (S_D) means force being applied over a distance ($S_D = F \times D$). Static strength (S_S) means force versus resistance—in a continuous muscular contraction—for a period of time ($S_S = F \times T$).

Note: S = strength, D = distance, F = force, T = time

*Certain body segments may be stronger and more or less flexible than other body segments. Each segment therefore must be assessed according to its own present capacity.

postural fitness. Although body structure has a great deal to do with how we function, we can improve both provided we have will and motivation. Whether we wish to become recreational golfers, hikers, or professional basketball players, there are developmental activities appropriate for us.

SCREENING

There are two general types of evaluatory instruments (tests) that can be used to evaluate physical, motor, and postural fitness levels: **practitioner-made tests** and **standardized tests**.

Practitioner-made tests are ordinarily prepared by classroom teachers to assess students' present status and achievement levels. Specific directions regarding test-item administration are followed, and grading procedures appropriate to the purpose are employed, Table 4.3.

It is important to keep in mind that grades generated by students on issues portrayed in Table 4.3 would not necessarily be used as bases upon which to assign grades at the conclusion of a marking period. Rather they help identify a student's present status with respect to the variables under consideration. Utilizing objective grading systems helps you recognize relative weaknesses that should be addressed right away and provides baseline data for the future.

Standardized test are those prepared by individuals or agencies who specialize in the development of formal testing instruments. They come with manuals that prescribe specific administrative procedures to be followed during testing. Use of standardized tests enables you to compare your students' scores with norms that were established during the developmental phases of the tests (Johnson and Nelson 1979).*

Each type of testing instrument (practitioner-made or standardized) has its advantages and disadvantages. The most important component of any test is its validity. Unless a test measures what it purports to measure, it will be virtually impossible to assess accurately your students' comformity to a given competency. It is important to use the best test possible, whether practitioner-made or standardized, to measure the quality

---

*Norms are usually given in percentile form, based upon age, gender, and/or grade level. You may develop your own norms over a period of time for your particular setting. If you plan to compare your students' scores to norms, be sure to follow the test directions exactly.

TABLE 4.3

Selected Test-Grading Techniques for Appraising Physical, Motor, and Postural Fitness

Techniques	Procedures	Examples
Pass/No pass	Before administering the test, establish a standard for a "pass" based upon the diffiiculty of the test and your previous experience with the test.	To "pass," a sixth-grade child must be able to complete twenty sit-ups in one minute.
Maintenance of standards	Before administering the test, establish standards of achievement within the "pass" category.	To earn an "A" in posture, student (while laterally placed to a plumb line), must demonstrate alignment through tragus of ear, tip of shoulder, tip of iliac crest, lateral border of knee, external malleolus. Sudents earns a "B" if any one body segment is out of line; a "C" if two body segments are out of line; a "D" if any three body segments are out of line.
Range of scores	After administering and scoring the test, find the arithmetic difference between the high and low scores, then divide by the number of letter grades you desire to give.	If, in a timed zigzag test for agility, the best score is ten seconds and the worst score is forty seconds, the range is thirty. When you divide this by five (for the five letter grades "A" to "F"), the letter grade breakdown is as follows: A—10–15 seconds B—16–21 seconds C—22–27 seconds D—28–33 seconds F—34— seconds
Standard deviation	After administering and scoring the test, compute the mean and the standard deviation.	If the mean (arithmetic average) of a distribution of push-up scores is 25, and the standard deviation is 2, the grades would be: A—30– B—28–29 C—23–27 D—21–22 F— 20

TABLE 4.3

Techniques	Procedures	Examples
Split standard deviation	After administering and scoring the test, if the middle range of scores is rather small, compute the mean and the standard deviation.	If the mean of a distribution of wall volley scores is 15 volleys in 30 seconds, and the standard deviation is 2, the grades would be: A—18– B—16–17 C—14–15 D—12–13 F— –11

and quantity of student growth. (Further discussion of evaluatory strategies is presented in Chapter 18.)

NUTRITIONAL STATUS

In no small way are self-efficacy expectancies important determinants of eating habits (Kingery 1990). Nutritional status contributes a great deal to the level of performance students demonstrate in physical, motor, or postural fitness screening tests. Body type must also be taken into account; if it is not, resulting scores can be meaningless. Therefore it is important to appraise a student's nutritional status and body type so that your judgments will be in keeping with his or her limitations. For example, medically fragile students may require specialized health care beyond what would normally be provided during the school day (The Council for Exceptional Children 1992).

Subjective Evaluation

Subjective evaluation of students' nutritional status should be made regularly by physical education teachers and/or nurses. It can be done in the first-aid room, gymnasium, locker or shower rooms. Subjective evaluation will help you recognize potential problems as symptoms become obvious, so that corrective measures can be taken. Among the more common symptoms of good and poor **nutrition** are:

Good nutrition	*Poor nutrition*
Well-developed and muscular body	Muscle tonus lacking; overweight or underweight
Facial expression alert; skin and eyes clear	Facial expression weary; skin blemished, eyes lackluster
Good-natured, pleasant to talk with, slow to fatigue	Irritable, overreacts, tires quickly

Objective Evaluation

Although hydrostatic weighing and water displacement are considered by many to be among the most accurate methods to use when evaluating body fat content, lack of access to necessary equipment precludes further consideration of these methods in most schools. Therefore we will discuss three objective measurement techniques that can be used in most school settings: measuring body circumferences; referring to gender, age, height, and weight tables; taking **skinfold measurements**.

Measurement of body circumferences Using the student as his or her own frame of reference, take repeated measurements of selected segments, usually at intervals of three to six months. These measurements will reflect changes that, if deemed unusual, can be evaluated by a physician, Figure 4.6.

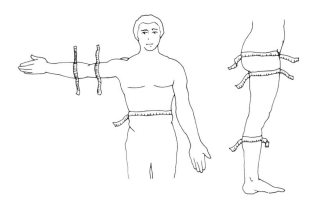

Figure 4.6. Sites for taking body-circumference measurements

Gender, age, height, and weight tables Using standardized tables allows you to compare a student's status with standards published by various agencies, including insurance companies. The more reliable tables take into account such factors as small, medium, or large body frames, Table 4.4.

Skinfold measurements By calculating the thickness of a fold of tissue (measured in millimeters), you can estimate the amount of fat under the skin. Skinfold measurements are made with calipers. Of the various types of calipers available, the Lange calipers are considered to be the most practical because they are easy to handle and reasonably priced, Figure 4.7.

The usual sites for caliper measurements are the biceps, triceps, subscapular, abdominal, and waist areas, Figure 4.8. Since high correlations exist between fat levels at various landmarks, Montoye (1978) suggests that to measure skinfolds at more than three or four sites is not worth the additional time or effort.

A variety of procedures can be used to analyze skinfold measurements. One acceptable method is to take measurements at the triceps and subscapular areas. If, for example, a nine-year-old girl earned a score of 19.0000 (triceps fatfold in millimeters), it would be possible—referring to Table 4.5—to see that the norm equivalent is at the eighty-fifth percentile. This can be interpreted to mean that she earned a score greater than approximately 85 percent of the girls her age.

TABLE 4.4

Height-Weight Table

MEN			
Height (With Shoes On)		**Weight in Pounds as Ordinarily Dressed, Including Shoes**	
Feet	*Inches*	*Small Frame*	*Medium Frame*	*Large Frame*
5	2	112–120	118–129	126–141
5	3	115–123	121–133	129–144
5	4	118–126	124–136	132–148
5	5	121–129	127–139	135–152
5	6	124–133	130–143	138–156
5	7	128–137	134–147	142–161
5	8	132–141	138–152	147–166
5	9	136–145	142–156	151–170
5	10	140–150	146–160	155–174
5	11	144–154	150–165	159–179
6	0	148–158	154–170	164–184
6	1	152–162	158–175	168–189
6	2	156–167	162–180	173–194
6	3	160–171	167–185	178–199
6	4	164–175	172–190	182–204

WOMEN			
Height (With Shoes On)		**Weight in Pounds as Ordinarily Dressed, Including Shoes**	
Feet	*Inches*	*Small Frame*	*Medium Frame*	*Large Frame*
4	10	92–98	96–107	104–119
4	11	94–101	98–110	106–122
5	0	96–104	101–113	109–125
5	1	99–107	104–116	112–128
5	2	102–110	107–119	115–131
5	3	105–113	110–122	118–134
5	4	108–116	113–126	121–138
5	5	111–119	116–130	125–142
5	6	114–123	120–135	129–146
5	7	118–127	124–139	133–150
5	8	122–131	128–143	137–154
5	9	126–135	132–147	141–158
5	10	130–140	136–151	145–163
5	11	134–144	140–155	149–168
6	0	138–148	144–159	153–173

Source: Metropolitan Life Insurance company (1992)

Note: The moderately active young adult requires about 15 calories per pound of desired body weight each day. The very active individual requires more calories.

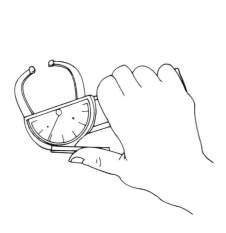

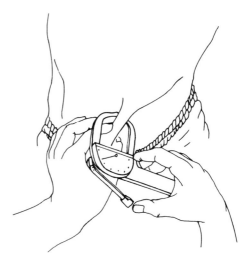

Figure 4.7. Skinfold Calipers. *Courtesy of J.A. Preston Corporation, 71 Fifth Avenue, New York, New York.*

Figure 4.8. Measuring waist area using Lange Skinfold Calipers

TABLE 4.5

Skinfold (Fatfold) Measurement Made with Calipers

TRICEPS FATFOLD (MALES) IN MILLIMETERS					
Age Midpoint N		PERCENTILES			
(Years)		5	15	50	85	95
0	4	13.0000	13.0000	15.0000	15.0000	15.0000
1	28	8.0000	9.0000	11.0000	16.0000	18.0000
2	61	7.0000	8.0000	10.0000	13.0000	15.0000
3	100	7.0000	8.0000	11.0000	13.0000	15.0000
4	112	7.0000	8.0000	11.0000	13.0000	15.0000
5	110	6.0000	7.0000	10.0000	13.0000	15.0000
6	129	6.0000	7.0000	9.0000	12.0000	14.0000
7	130	6.0000	7.0000	10.0000	13.0000	17.0000
8	126	6.0000	7.0000	9.0000	13.0000	16.0000
9	125	6.0000	7.0000	10.0000	16.0000	23.0000
10	121	6.0000	7.0000	11.0000	15.0000	23.0000
11	124	7.0000	8.0000	12.0000	21.0000	26.0000
12	125	7.0000	9.0000	12.0000	22.0000	29.0000
13	114	7.0000	9.0000	12.0000	22.0000	27.0000
14	111	6.0000	8.0000	11.0000	17.0000	24.0000
15	95	6.0000	8.0000	12.0000	20.0000	25.0000
16	116	6.0000	8.0000	13.0000	20.0000	28.0000
17	91	6.0000	8.0000	14.0000	23.0000	31.0000
18	70	6.0000	7.0000	12.0000	17.0000	28.0000
20	349	6.0000	7.0000	13.0000	22.0000	28.0000

TABLE 4.5

TRICEPS FATFOLD (MALES) IN MILLIMENTERS

Age Midpoint (Years)	N	PERCENTILES				
		5	15	50	85	95
30	538	6.0000	8.0000	15.0000	22.0000	29.0000
40	635	6.0000	10.0000	15.0000	22.0000	28.0000
50	413	7.0000	9.0000	15.0000	22.0000	27.0000
60	243	7.0000	10.0000	15.0000	23.0000	30.0000
70	125	6.0000	9.0000	13.0000	22.0000	27.0000
80	41	6.0000	7.0000	12.0000	20.0000	23.0000
90	6	3.0000	3.0000	7.0000	20.0000	20.0000

TRICEPS FATFOLD (FEMALES) IN MILLIMEIERS

Age Midpoint (Years)	N	PERCENTILES				
		5	15	50	85	95
0	1	8.0000	8.0000	8.0000	8.0000	8.0000
1	34	6.0000	8.0000	10.0000	14.0000	16.0000
2	74	7.0000	9.0000	12.0000	15.0000	16.0000
3	104	8.0000	9.0000	11.0000	14.0000	16.0000
4	106	7.0000	9.0000	11.0000	14.0000	16.0000
5	127	7.0000	9.0000	11.0000	14.0000	18.0000
6	138	8.0000	9.0000	11.0000	15.0000	19.0000
7	126	7.0000	8.0000	12.0000	15.0000	19.0000
8	132	7.0000	8.0000	11.0000	16.0000	20.0000
9	119	8.0000	10.0000	3.0000	19.0000	26.0000
10	111	7.0000	9.0000	14.0000	19.0000	26.0000
11	101	8.0000	10.0000	14.0000	22.0000	29.0000
12	115	8.0000	10.0000	14.0000	21.0000	27.0000
13	117	9.0000	11.0000	16.0000	26.0000	31.0000
14	98	10.0000	11.0000	17.0000	24.0000	30.0000
15	97	11.0000	13.0000	18.0000	30.0000	43.0000
16	107	12.0000	14.0000	21.0000	27.0000	35.0000
17	89	12.0000	14.0000	20.0000	26.0000	36.0000
18	70	11.0000	14.0000	18.0000	29.0000	35.0000
20	412	11.0000	14.0000	21.0000	30.0000	37.0000
30	630	12.0000	15.0000	23.0000	33.0000	42.0000
40	688	13.0000	16.0000	24.0000	31.0000	42.0000
50	400	15.0000	18.0000	27.0000	36.0000	44.0000
60	270	15.0000	19.0000	28.0000	36.0000	45.0000
70	168	14.0000	19.0000	27.0000	36.0000	43.0000
80	66	10.0000	14.0000	24.0000	33.0000	43.0000
90	10	4.0000	7.0000	16.0000	30.0000	30.0000

TABLE 4.5

SUBSCAPULAR FATFOLD (FEMALES) IN MILLIMETERS

Age Midpont N		PERCENTILES				
(Years)		5	25	50	85	95
0	1	5.0000	5.0000	5.0000	5.0000	5.0000
1	33	4.0000	5.0000	7.0000	9.0000	11.0000
2	74	5.0000	5.0000	7.0000	10.0000	12.0000
3	103	4.0000	5.0000	6.0000	8.0000	10.0000
4	106	4.0000	5.0000	6.0000	8.0000	10.0000
5	126	4.0000	4.0000	5.0000	7.0000	9.0000
6	138	4.0000	5.0000	6.0000	8.0000	12.0000
7	126	4.0000	4.0000	5.0000	8.0000	11.0000
8	132	4.0000	4.0000	6.0000	8.0000	13.0000
9	119	4.0000	5.0000	6.0000	12.0000	15.0000
10	111	5.0000	5.0000	7.0000	12.0000	21.0000
11	101	4.0000	5.0000	8.0000	19.0000	27.0000
12	115	5.0000	6.0000	8.0000	15.0000	26.0000
13	117	6.0000	6.0000	9.0000	20.0000	30.0000
14	98	6.0000	7.0000	11.0000	18.0000	24.0000
15	97	7.0000	8.0000	11.0000	24.0000	43.0000
16	107	8.0000	8.0000	13.0000	24.0000	35.0000
17	89	7.0000	8.0000	12.0000	20.0000	30.0000
18	70	7.0000	9.0000	12.0000	23.0000	40.000
20	412	7.0000	8.0000	13.0000	25.0000	35.0000
30	630	7.0000	8.0000	14.0000	28.0000	41.0000
40	688	7.0000	10.0000	16.0000	31.0000	41.0000
50	400	8.0000	11.0000	21.0000	36.0000	47.0000
60	270	9.0000	13.0000	22.0000	36.0000	46.0000
70	168	8.0000	12.0000	23.0000	35.0000	42.0000
80	66	6.0000	8.0000	17.0000	30.0000	37.0000
90	10	5.0000	6.0000	10.0000	24.0000	32.0000

SUBSCAPULAR FATFOLD (MALES) IN MILLIMETERS

Age Midpoint N		PERCENTILES				
(Years)		5	15	50	85	95
0	4	6.0000	6.0000	7.0000	10.0000	10.0000
1	28	4.0000	5.0000	6.0000	9.0000	11.0000
2	61	4.0000	5.0000	6.0000	8.0000	9.0000
3	99	4.0000	5.0000	6.0000	8.0000	9.0000
4	112	4.0000	4.0000	5.0000	7.0000	8.0000
5	109	4.0000	4.0000	5.0000	7.0000	8.0000
6	129	4.0000	4.0000	5.0000	6.0000	8.0000
7	130	3.0000	4.0000	5.0000	7.0000	10.0000

TABLE 4.5

Age Midpoint N		PERCENTILES				
(Years)		5	15	50	85	95
8	126	4.0000	4.0000	5.0000	7.0000	9.0000
9	125	4.0000	4.0000	5.0000	8.0000	14.0000
10	121	4.0000	4.0000	5.0000	9.0000	12.0000
11	124	4.0000	5.0000	6.0000	12.0000	17.0000
12	125	4.0000	5.0000	7.0000	15.0000	23.0000
13	114	5.0000	6.0000	7.0000	14.0000	28.0000
14	111	4.0000	5.0000	7.0000	12.0000	18.0000
15	95	5.0000	6.0000	8.0000	15.0000	25.0000
16	116	6.0000	7.0000	9.0000	14.0000	22.0000
17	91	7.0000	8.0000	11.0000	22.0000	31.0000
18	70	6.0000	7.0000	11.0000	15.0000	23.0000
20	349	7.0000	8.0000	11.0000	20.0000	30.0000
30	539	7.0000	9.0000	14.0000	25.0000	32.0000
40	635	8.0000	10.0000	16.0000	25.0000	32.0000
50	413	8.0000	10.0000	17.0000	27.0000	35.0000
60	243	8.0000	11.0000	19.0000	30.0000	35.0000
70	125	7.0000	10.0000	15.0000	25.0000	32.0000
80	41	6.0000	9.0000	15.0000	23.0000	28.0000
90	6	4.0000	4.0000	7.0000	18.0000	18.0000

SUBSCAPULAR FATFOLD (MALES) IN MILLIMETERS

Source: The Tecumseh (Michigan) Community Health Study

Consider consulting with other physical education instructors and developing a set of norms for your school system. This can be done rather readily for both boys and girls throughout an entire school-age range. An accumulation of scores that have been gathered over a period of time would help ensure the validity of the norm standards for the population being considered for eventual assessment.

MEASURING ISOLATED COMPONENTS OF FITNESS

Few test activities in physical education can measure isolated components of physical, motor, and postural fitness. For example, a substantial number of experts have recommended using the softball throw as a test activity for measuring explosive arm strength. If two individuals with an equal amount of arm strength threw the ball, however, the one who knows how to throw the ball will get the better score. Therefore the softball throw should be considered to be a test of something besides explosive arm strength—perhaps coordination. If on the other hand a medicine ball is thrown (put) with two hands from a sitting position, neither coordination nor the individual's height

Figure 4.9. Sitting medicine ball put. (Note the pelvis is behind the restraining line).

would have an influence upon the distance the ball would travel. If we assume that leg length among individuals of the same age is more variable than torso length, we can expect to obtain more reliable explosive arm strength scores if the students are sitting down when the test is taken, Figure 4.9.

If you are as aware as possible of factors that contribute to performance, the scores earned by your students will reflect their fitness accurately. Like the softball throw, many tests measure an ability besides the one being addressed. I will attempt to consider such issues in the sections to come.

DEVELOPMENTAL ACTIVITIES

The major components of physical and motor fitness, along with a selection of tests that measure such qualities, are included in the developmental activities that follow. I have chosen to describe activities that require little or no special measuring equipment.

I. Goal: Physical Fitness

Major Objective

1. Extensor arm strength and endurance

Figure 4.10. Push-up: Extended-arm position

Figure 4.11. Parallel-bar dip

2. Flexor arm strength and endurance

Figure 4.12. Straddle Pullup

Interim Performance Objective

1.1 Perform as many push-ups as possible, Figure 4.10.

    1.1A Starting from straight-arm front-leaning rest position, lower the body until chest touches the floor or mat.

    1.1B During **repetitions** do not let the body sag or pike.
        1.1Ba Timed
        1.1Bb Until exhaustion

1.2 To perform as many parallel-bar dips as possible, Figure 4.11.

    1.2A Starting from straight-arm support position at one end of parallel bars, lower the body until the elbows form right angles; Return to starting position.

    1.2B During repetitions do not swing or kick.
        1.2Ba Timed
        1.2Bb Until exhaustion

2.1 Perform as many modified (straddle) pull-ups as possible, Figure 4.12.

    2.1A Lie on back with arms extended up, palms facing away, fingers interlaced with partner's fingers (partner of equal size stands, straddling body at chest).

    2.1B Pull self up until lateral borders of chest contact medial portions of partner's thighs.

    2.1C During repetitions, keep the body in straight line from heel contact on floor to head.
        2.1Ca Timed
        2.1Cb Until exhaustion

Major Objective	*InterimPerformance Objective*

Figure 4.13. Pullup

2.2 Perform as many pull-ups (palms away) or chin-ups (palms facing body) as possible, Figure 4.13.

2.2A Starting from straight-arm hanging position on a horizontal bar (feet off floor), raise (pull) the body until the chin comes above bar. Return to starting position.

2.2B During repetitions do not swing or kick.
2.2Ba Timed
2.2Bb Until exhaustion

3. Abdominal strength and endurance*

Figure 4.14. Flexed-knee lift

3.1 Perform as many flexed-knee lifts as possible, Figure 4.14.

3.1A Starting from **supine position**, bring knees toward the chest; hold for eight seconds. Return to starting position

3.1B Continue each repetition deliberately; keep knees together.

3.2 Perform as many flexed-knee curl-ups (sit-ups) as possible, Figure 4.15.

3.2A Starting from **supine position** with knees flexed and together, fingers interlaced behind the neck, raise trunk until elbows touch knees. Return to starting position (elbows touching floor or mat).

3.2B Perform repetitions while keeping heels as close to buttocks as possible.
3.2Ba Timed
3.2Bb Until exhaustion

Figure 4.15. Flexed-knee curlup

* Trunk flexibility is included in the developmental activities described.

Major Objective	*Interim Performance Objective*

4. Leg explosive strength

Figure 4.16. Standing long (broad) jump

Figure 4.17. Vertical jump

5. Elevation of the shoulders

Figure 4.18. Shoulder elevation

4.1 Jump as great a distance forward as possible, Figure 4.16.

    4.1A Starting from a standing position, jump as far as possible.

    4.1B Continue trials as long as improvement is demonstrated.

4.2 Jump as high as possible, Figure 4.17.

    4.2A Facing a wall, reach up as far as possible and make a chalk mark.

    4.2B Turning preferred side to wall and from a squat no greater than forty-five degrees, jump as high as possible while extending arm (that is nearest to the wall). Make chalk mark on wall

    4.2C Continue trials as long as improvement is demonstraed.

5.1 Improve upon the extent of shoulder elevation, Figure 4.18.

    5.1A From **prone position**, arms straight, hold two-foot stick at its ends and raise it as high as possible.

    5.1B Hold position for three seconds. Return to starting position.

    5.1C Following rest period, repeat effort.
        5.1Ca Do not bounce.
        5.1Cb Keep chin on floor.
        5.1Cc Keep wrists and elbows straight.

Major Objective

Interim Performance Objective

6. Flexion of the hips, back; elasticity of the hamstring muscles

Figure 4.19. Sit and reach

6.1 Improve upon the extent of reach, Figure 4.19.

    6.1A From sitting position on the floor or mat, legs extended, and feet no farther than two inches apart, reach with the fingertips as far as possible.

    6.1B Following rest period, repeat effort.
        6.1Ba Do not bounce.
        6.1Bb Do not bend knees.

7. Flexion and extension of the ankles

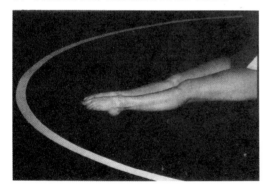

Figure 4.20. Ankle extension (plantar flexion)

7.1 Improve upon the extent of flexibility in the ankles, Figure 4.20.

    7.1A While sitting on floor or mat with legs extended, flex the ankles dorsally as far as possible.

    7.1B Hold position for three seconds. Return to starting position.
        7.1Ba Keep backs of knees on floor or mat.
        7.1Bb Keep heels on floor or mat and stationary.

    7.1C While sitting on the floor or mat with legs extended, plantarflex (extend) the ankles as far as possible

    7.1D Hold position for three seconds. Return to starting position.
        7.1Da Keep back of knees on floor or mat.
        7.1Db Keep heels on floor or mat and stationary.

II. Goal: Motor Fitness

Major Objective	*Interim Performance Objective*

1. Agility

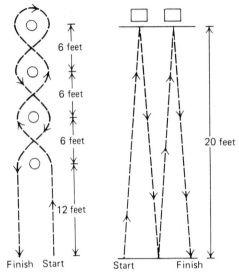

Figure 4.21. Zigzag run

Figure 4.22 Shuttle run

1.1 To reduce the amount of time it takes to complete change-of-direction tasks successfully

    1.1A Zigzag run, Figure 4.21
        1.1Aa From upright position follow prescribed pattern as quickly as possible.
        1.1Ab Repeat as instructed.

    1.1B Shuttle run, Figure 4.22
        1.1Ba From standing position run designated distance; pick up object; return, place object on floor.
        1.1Bb Repeat task once with second object.
            1.1Bb*a* Perform task as quickly as possible.
            1.1Bb*b* Do not throw object.

    1.1C Right and left boomerang run, Figure 4.23
        1.1Ca From standing position follow prescribed pattern as quickly as possible.
        1.1Cb Repeat as instructed.

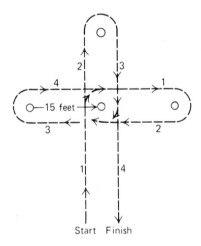

Figure 4.23 Right and left boomerang run

Figure 4.24. Air volley

Major Objective Interim	*Performance Objective*

2. Hand-eye coordination

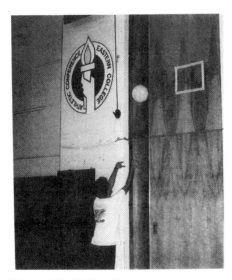

Figure 4.25. Wall volley

2.1 Hit a volleyball with the hands through a series of repetitions for a predetermined period of time, Figure 4.24.

    2.1A Floor volley (waist high)
        2.1Aa Both hands
        2.1Ab Preferred hand
        2.1Ac Other hand

    2.1B Air volley (selected height)
        2.1Ba Both hands
        2.1Bb Preferred hand
        2.1Bc Other hand

    2.1C Wall volley, Figure 4.25
        2.1Ca Place feet behind line three to six feet from wall

3. Foot-eye coordination

3.1 Hit a soccer ball with the feet through a series of repetitions for a predetermined period of time.

    3.1A Wall volley
        3.1Aa Place feet behind restraining line three to six feet from wall.
        3.1Ab Volley the ball continuously.
            3.1Ab*a* Either foot
            3.1Ab*b* Preferred foot
            3.1Ab*c* Other foot

    3.1B Air volley (selected height)
        3.1Ba Either foot
        3.1Bb Preferred foot
        3.1Bc Other foot

Developmental activities related to static and dynamic balance are in Chapter 5; those related to cardiovascular endurance are in Chapter 6.

Each of the developmental activities may be administered individually, as a cluster, or as a complete battery. There are other test activities and, collectively, test batteries that are available for assessing physical and motor fitness, Table 4.6.

TABLE 4.6

Selected Physical and Motor Fitness Test Batteries

Title /Source	Age/Grade	Activities
FITNESSGRAM Institute for Aerobic Research 12330 Preston Road Dallas, TX 75230	Ages 5–16+	One-mile run/walk Percent fat estimated from calf and triceps skinfolds Sit and reach Sit-up Pull-up for flexed arm hang

Fit Youth Today
American Health and
  Fitness Foundation
6225 U.S. Highway 290 East
Suite 114
Austin, TX 78723
	Grades 4–12	Twenty-minute steady state jog
		Bent-knee curl-up
		Sit and reach
		Percent fat estimated from
		  calf and triceps skinfolds

Physical Best Program
American Alliance for
  Health, Physical Education,
Recreation and Dance
1900 Association Drive
Reston, VA 22091
	Ages 5–18	One-mile run/walk
		Sum of calf and triceps skinfold
		  measurements*
		Sit and reach
		Modified sit-ups (sixty seconds)
		Pull-ups
		
		*Optional measures include:
		The sum of triceps and
		  subscapular skinfold measures
		The tricep thickness only
		The body mass index

Note: Instructional guides and norms (per ages and/or grade levels) for each of the test batteries are available from the publishers.

POSTURE

There are two general ways a student's posture can be assessed: informally and formally.

Informal Posture Evaluation

Informal posture evaluation occurs when the students are unaware that you are observing their posture. This can be done during any physical education activity. For example, posture can be observed and evaluated while students play volleyball, Figure 4.26. If a student appears to need a more formal appraisal, you can schedule a formal screening session.

Formal Posture Evaluation

Formal posture evaluation is ordinarily conducted in the privacy of a nurse's office, teacher's office, or behind a partition in a locker room. In this way the student's modesty and privacy are respected and the anomaly (one might find) remains confidential.

Figure 4.26. Informal postural screening can be done during a volleyball game.

Assess the student's posture in three dimensions: anteriorly, Figure 4.27; posteriorly, Figure 4.28; and laterally, Figure 4.29. If a student cannot align his or her body in a manner corresponding to a prescribed norm, there may be a structural problem—in which case you should refer the student to a physician. If on the other hand the student

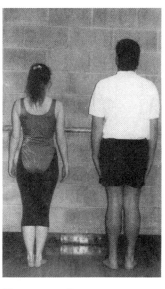

Figure 4.27. Anterior posture   **Figure 4.28**. Posterior posture   **Figure 4.29**. Lateral posture

can align his or her body correctly, the problem you have noticed is probably functional, i.e., a result of weak musculature, lack of motivation, or both. In this instance you should provide appropriately designed developmental activities that will help the student attain normal posture.

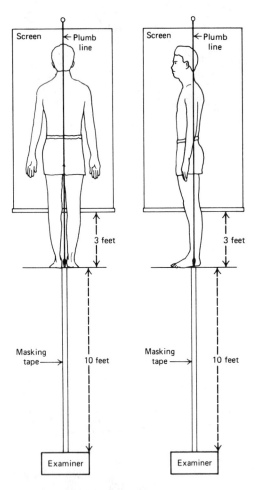

Figure 4.30. New York State Posture Test: Rating position. *Courtesy of Bureau of Physical Education, State Department of Education, Albany, New York.*

Although there are a number of posture assessment devices on the market, the one most available for, and easily used by, school or other health practitioners is one similar to that found within the New York State Posture Test. It incorporates a suspended plumb line that must be placed three feet in front of a screen. The examiner should sit (or stand) ten feet in front of the line. The thirteen feet between the examiner and the screen should be marked off with tape, Figure 4.30.

The student faces the screen and straddles the tape behind the plumb line, with the external ankle malleoli no farther apart than the width of the shoulders. Once you have made a posterior assessment, the student turns sideways, with the left external ankle malleolus in line with the plumb bob. In this position, lateral posture is evaluated.* Consider making yearly, objective ratings in accordance with the student's conformity to the norms indicated on the New York State Posture Rating Chart, Figure 4.31. Further, photographing the students while ratings (observations) are being made will provide pictorial documentation for future reference (and discussion with the student involved).

As a consequence of formal postural appraisal you may recognize a number of anomalies. Where a question exists as to the origin and extent of the problem, refer the student to a physician. Sometimes braces or surgery are needed to correct the problem. Only a physician can make those determinations.

In most cases you should include therapeutic exercise in a student's regimen of prescribed activity. It is therefore necessary to be aware of the nature of some of the more

---

* The student should not wear bulky clothing. Bathing suits or leotards are suitable. No shoes or socks should be worn.

A:

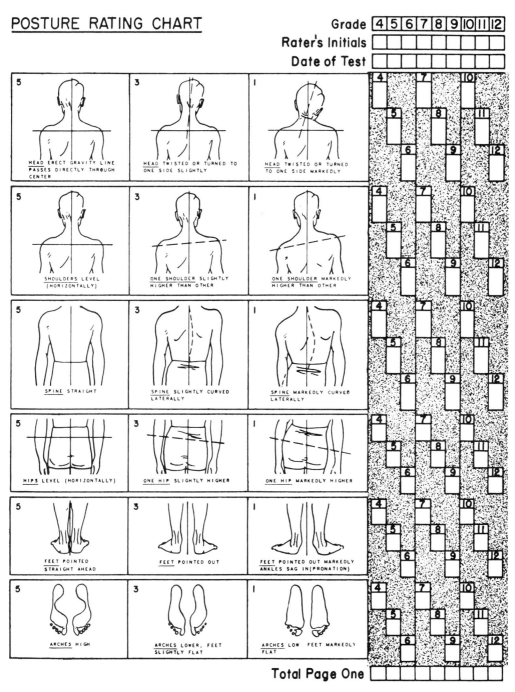

Figure 4.31. A: New York State Posture Rating Chart: Posterior view; B: New York State Posture Rating Chart: Lateral view. *Courtesy of Bureau of Physical Education, State Department of Education, Albany, New York.*

B:

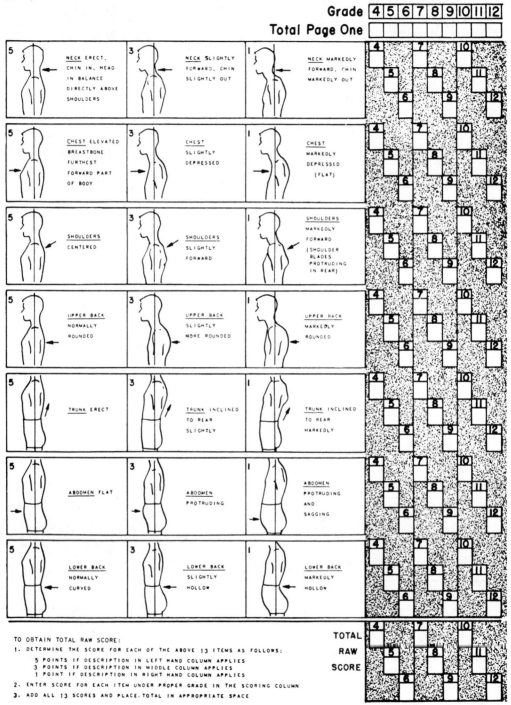

To obtain total raw score:

1. Determine the score for each of the above 13 items as follows:

   5 points if description in left hand column applies
   3 points if description in middle column applies
   1 point if description in right hand column applies

2. Enter score for each item under proper grade in the scoring column

3. Add all 13 scores and place total in appropriate space

common anomalies found among the school-age population. You should likewise be familiar with developmental activities that advance the treatment process.

The earlier in a child's life that a dysfunction is recognized, the greater the probability of successful treatment. Unless discovered early, a functional problem may have become structural. Once a postural problem has become structural, very little can be gained with exercise and motivation alone.

DEVELOPMENTAL ACTIVITIES

I. Goal: Postural Fitness

Major Objective	*Interim Performance Objective*
1. Correction of **general slump** (Figure 4.32), often related to muscle laziness, insufficient motivation, and/or poor self-image	1.1 Alleviate deficiency by doing exercises similar to supine stretch, Figure 4.33.

1.1A Lie on back with feet, legs, arms, and fingers extended.

1.1B Pressing lower back to floor or mat, stretch and hold eight seconds, relax for ten seconds.
    1.1Ba Repeat sequence two more times

Figure 4.32. General slump

Figure 4.33. Supine stretch

2. Correction of body lean, which may be related to student's lack of awareness of postural alignment with respect to a vertical frame of reference

2.1 Duplicate appropriate posture stance through mirror imagery.

    2.1A Stand in front of body-length mirror
        2.1Aa Align anterior view correctly.

Major Objective	*InterimPerformance Objective*

2.1Ab Align lateral
view correctly

2.1B Repeat without looking in
a mirror

Note: A plumb line may be hung against
the mirror to assist with alignment.

3. Correction of excessive forward
head lean, often found in conjunc--
tion with kyphotic conditions;-
sometimes related to auditory
or visual dysfunction

3.1 Improve head-trunk linearity by
doing exercises similar to resistive
neck flattener, Figure 4.34.

3.1A From sitting or standing
position interlock hands and
place them behind the neck.

3.1B Pull forward with hands while
resisting with neck muscles.
3.1Ba Hold eight seconds.
3.1Bb Relax ten seconds.
3.1Bc Repeat sequence two or
more times.

Figure 4.34. Resistive neck flattener

4. Correction of **torticollis** (wryneck),
a contraction—often spasmodic—
of the muscles of the neck, in
which the head is drawn to one
side and rotated so that the chin
points to the opposite side

4.1 Reduce deficiency by doing
exercises similar to lateral neck
flexion—opposite side

4.1A Stretch neck to shoulder on
opposite side of contracture.
4.1Aa Touch chin to clavicle;
hold three seconds; relax
ten seconds.
4.1Ab Repeat sequence two
more times.

5. Correction of **round shoulders**, a
condition in which the tips of the
shoulders are turned in toward the
chest; usually caused by strong pectoralis muscles and weak antagonists

5.1 Alleviate deficiency by doing
exercises similar to two-arm
isometric press against doorjamb,
Figure 4.35.

Major Objective   *Interim Performance Objective*

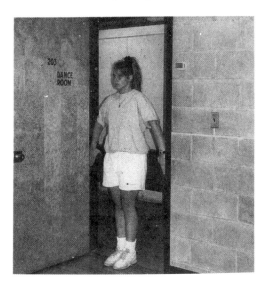

Figure 4.35. Two-arm isometric press

6. Correction of **kyphosis** (Pott's curvature), an abnormal concave forward curvature of the spine usually found in the thoracic area. Unless there is disease of the spinal column, the condition is often a result of general upper torso slump.

Figure 4.36. Breaking chains

7. Correction of **winged scapulae**, often equated with poor muscle

5.1A Stand an equal distance before and between doorjambs and place both hands so that force is applied in a backward direction.

    5.1Aa While throwing chest forward and keeping arms straight, pull against resistance for eight seconds.

    5.1Ab Relax ten seconds.

    5.1Ac Repeat sequence two more times.

6.1 Alleviate deficiency by doing exercises similar to breaking chains, Figure 4.36.

6.1A Standing with back against corner of wall, feet no farther than shoulder-width apart, fists together in front of chest, slowly pull arms back as far as possible

    6.1Aa Inhale to maximum capacity during pulling phase.

    6.1Ab Hold position eight seconds; exhale.

    6.1Ac Relax ten seconds.

    6.1Ad Repeat sequence two more times.

7.1 Alleviate deficiency by doing exercises similar to hanging by

Major Objective	*Interim Performance Objective*
definition in the thoracic area of the back	hands from horizontal bar (or ladder).

Major Objective | *Interim Performance Objective*

definition in the thoracic area of the back

hands from horizontal bar (or ladder).

7.1A Timed

7.1B Until exhaustion

8. Correction of functional C-curve **scoliosis**, Figure 4.37, a roto-lateral curvature of the spinal column usually located in the thoracic area and frequently caused by an imbalance of strength on either side of spine that pulls spine to one side; compensatory S-curve may develop

8.1 Alleviate deficiency by doing-exercises similar to **bilateral** stretching, Figure 4.38.

8.1A From standing position, raise arm on concave side of C-curve.

8.1B Supinate hand of opposite arm and press it into outside of leg (same side).

8.1Ba Hold position eight seconds.

8.1Bb Relax ten seconds.

8.1Bc Repeat sequence two more times.

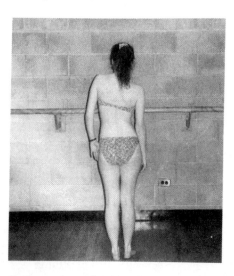

Figure 4.37. Scoliotic curve: Beginning stages

Figure 4.38. Bilateral stretch

9. Correction of **lordosis**, an abnormal convex forward curvature of the spine usually found in the **lumbar**

9.1 Alleviate deficiency doing exercises similar to the "mad cat," Figure 4.39.

Major Objective

area and related to weak abdominal musculature

Figure 4.39. The "mad cat"

10. Correction of **flat back**, an absence (or decrease) in normal convex forward lumbar spinal curve

Figure 4.40. Prone leg lift

11. Correction of **pelvic tilt** caused by a downward rotation of the anterior iliac spine by unusually taut hip flexors. Taut lumbar extensors rotate the posterior sacrum upward.

Interim Performance Objective

9.1A From a position on the hands and knees, round and flatten the back alternately.

10.1 Alleviate deficiency by doing exercises similar to trunk and leg lifts from the prone position, Figure 4.40.

    10.1A Raise trunk; hold eight seconds; relax ten seconds.

    10.1B Raise legs; hold eight seconds; relax ten seconds.

    10.1C Repeat sequence two more times.

11.1 Alleviate deficiency by doing exercises similar to back flattener and pelvic lift, Figure 4.41.

    11.1A From standing position, reduce curve in lumbar spine and lift pelvis
        11.1Aa Hold position eight seconds

Major Objective

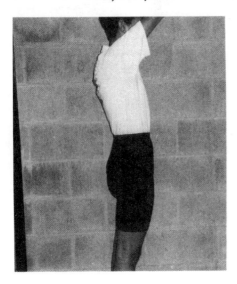

Figure 4.41. Back flattener and pelvic tilt

Interim Perfomance Objective

11.1Ab Relax ten seconds.
11.1Ac Repeat sequence
         two more times.

12. Correction of **genu valgum** (knock-knee), often caused by excessive body weight pressing down upon the medial portion of the knee, placing unusual stress upon the medial collateral ligament

Figure 4.42. Lateral knee rotation

12.1 Alleviate deficiency by doing exercises similar to knee rotation, Figure 4.42.

  12.1A From standing position, big toes touching, heels to three inches apart, hold on to back of chair or rail.

  12.1B Keep feet flat on floor, flex knees slightly, rotate knees to the outside.

    12.1Ba Hold position forcefully eight seconds.
    12.1Bb Relax ten seconds.
    12.1Bc Repeat sequence two more times.

Major Objective

13. Correction of **genu varum** (bowleg), often related to an imbalance in strength between the peroneal and tibial muscle groups

Figure 4.43. Medial knee rotation

14. Correction of **ankle (foot) pronation**, in which ankles roll in; often associated with foot eversion (toeing out). Body weight places unusual stress upon medial portion of the ankle.

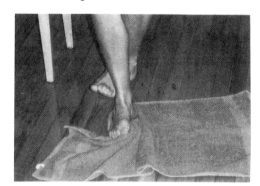

Figure 4.44. Lateral-to-medial ankle rotation

Interim Performance Objective

13.1 Alleviate deficiency by doing exercises similar to medial knee rotation, Figure 4.43.

    13.1A From standing position, heels touching, toes at forty-five-degree angle, hold on to back of chair or rail.

    13.1B Keep feet flat on floor, flex knees slightly, rotate knees to the inside, try to put them together.
        13.1Ba Hold position forcefully eight seconds.
        13.1Bb Relax ten seconds.
        13.1Bc Repeat sequence two more times.

14.1 Alleviate deficiency by doing exercises similar to lateral-to-medial rotation of the affected ankle, Figure 4.44.

    14.1A Sit on chair, place bottom of affected foot on towel.

    14.1B Place instep of opposite foot under and outside affected foot (apply pressure with instep to external malleolus area).

    14.1C Rotate ball of affected foot laterally and drag towel medially.
        14.1Ca Continue until towel can no longer be moved.
        14.1Cb Repeat procedure with other foot if affected.

Major Objective	*Interim Performance Objective*
15. Correction for **pes planus** (flatfoot), related to insufficient strength in musculature supporting-longitudinal arch of the foot	15.1 Alleviate deficiency by doing exercises similar to picking up marbles, Figure 4.45.

15.1A Sit on chair, pick up a marble with toes of the affected foot, place marble in a receptacle.

15.1B Continue until you have placed a selected number of marbles in the receptacle.

Figure 4.45. Picking up marbles

Many of these developmental activities can be used to remedy other conditions related to those specified. It is also likely that more than one exercise can reduce a specific problem.* The prescriptions included in the activities are designed to help the student achieve desirable gains in areas deemed deficient. If modified, these activities are still useful provided that normal orientation planes are adhered to.

Whatever exercise you select, be sure that it is valid to purpose. If one's goal is to develop muscular endurance, one should not place emphasis on increasing resistance loads. Increasing repetitions while maintaining resistance loads will elicit gains in endurance. Doing isometric contractions at one angle will not likely develop strength or flexibility through a limb's full range of motion. As Kuntzleman (1978) points out,

A [technique] that claims to increase flexibility should allow the muscles, tendons, and ligaments to go through their full range of motion.

In short, *stress equals adaptation:* the body adapts to the stress imposed upon it by the prescribed exercises. You must apply this principle to ensure that your physical, motor, and postural fitness programs are designed to improve the strength, endurance, agility, balance, coordination, and flexibility of your students.

SUMMARY

There are many factors that contribute to one's physical, motor, nutritional, and postural fitness. Although these areas are problematic in that they comprise the greatest sources of anomalies within the schools, there is reason for shared optimism if the focus is on developing reasonable goals—goals that are within the capabilities of our students.

---

* See Appendices C, D, and E for a description of additional exercises that are useful for achievement of general physical, motor, and postural fitness.

The role of school and other health practitioners is essentially fourfold:

1. Identify procedures appropriate to the valid assessment of physical, motor, nutritional, and/or postural fitness.
2. Administer these instruments (procedures) with a view toward identifying those in need of developmental programs.
3. Prescribe activities suitable for reducing—to the greatest extent possible—selected problem areas.
4. Re-evaluate and monitor gains toward and maintenance of optimal status.

Programs designed to address topics presented in this chapter are an important part of the overall education process and should be given increased emphasis in the schools (American College of Sports Medicine 1987). The development and maintenance of lifelong exercise habits are critical to enriched living. Read further to examine other issues affecting one's overall health.

RECOMMENDED LABORATORY ASSIGNMENTS

1. Obtain and become familiar with various standardized tests that are designed to measure physical, motor, and postural fitness levels.
2. Perform the developmental activities described in this chapter. List other activities that the student could perform to meet the intended educational goal(s).
3. Using various formal and informal assessment techniques, practice screening students with respect to their **static posture**.
4. Construct a test that would measure **dynamic posture** (while contrasting the principles of static osture with the various dimensions of movement).
5. Practice using skinfold calipers and pertinent norm tables.
6. Visit a school and observe the physical, motor, and postural characteristics of students in various grades, kindergarten to twelfth. Create a list of features that appear to characterize those in various grade levels.
7. Administer a physical and/or motor fitness test battery to a group of public school students. Interpret the findings with a view toward activity prescription.
8. Review the recommended readings.

REFERENCES

American College of Sports Medicine. 1987. Physical fitness in children and youth. *Pediatrics* 80(3): 422–23.

The Council for Exceptional Children. 1992. In *Educating Exceptional Children*, edited by K. Freiberg. Guilford, CT: The Dushkin Publishing Group, Inc.

Johnson, B. L., and J. K. Nelson. 1979. *Practical measurements for evaluation in physical education.* Minneapolis: Burgess.

Kingery, P. M. 1990. Self-efficacy and the self-monitoring of selected exercise and eating behaviors of college students. *Health Education* 21(1): 26–29.

Kuntzleman, C. T. 1978. *Rating the exercises.* New York: William Morrow.

Montoye, H. J. 1978. *An introduction to measurement in physical education.* Boston: Allyn and Bacon.

Wyness, G. B. 1990. Participation in a twelve-week moderate exercise program: Selected physiological effects. *Journal of Physical Education, Recreation and Dance,* 61(2): 65–68.

RECOMMENDED READINGS

American Academy of Orthopaedic Surgeons. 1965. *Joint motion: Method of measuring and recording.* Chicago: The American Academy of Orthopaedic Surgeons.

Barney, V. S., C. Hirst, and C. R. Jensen. 1972. *Conditioning exercises.* St. Louis: C. V. Mosby.

Boone, T. 1990. Obsessive exercise: Some reflections. *Journal of Physical Education, Recreation and Dance* 62(7): 45–49.

Dahlgren, W. J., S. Boreskie, M. Dowds, J. B. Mactavish, and E. J. Watkinson. 1991. The medallion program: Using the generic sport model to train athletes with mental disabilities. *Journal of Physical Education, Recreation and Dance* 62(9): 67–73.

Dunlap, P., and L. A. Berne. 1991. Addressing competitive stress in junior tennis players. *Journal of Physical Education, Recreation and Dance* 62(1): 59–63.

Elias, B. A., K. E. Berg, R. W. Latin, M. B. Mellion, and P. J. Jofschire. 1991. Cardiac structure and function in weight trainers, runners, and runner/weight trainers. *Research Quarterly for Exercise and Sport* 62(3): 326–32.

Engelman, M. E., and J. R. Morrow. 1991. Reliability and skinfold correlates for traditional and modified pull-ups in children grades 3–5. *Research Quarterly for Exercise and Sport* 62:(1): 88–91.

Fox, K. 1991. Motivating children for physical activity: Towards a healthier future. *Journal of Physical Education, Recreation and Dance* 62(7): 34–38.

Girandola, R. N., R. A. Wiswell, and G. Romero. 1977. Body composition changes resulting from fluid ingestion and dehydration. *Research Quarterly* 48(2): 299–303.

Going, S. B., and T. G. Lohman. 1990. The skinfold test—A response. *Journal of Physical Education, Recreation and Dance* 61(8): 74–78.

Gottlieb, G. L., and G. C. Agarwal. 1973. Postural adaptation: The nature of adaptive mechanisms in the human motor system. In *Control of Posture and Locomotion.* New York: Plenum Press.

Heusner, W. W., and W. D. Van Huss. 1978. Strength, power, and muscular endurance. In *An Introduction to Measurement in Physical Education.* Boston: Allyn and Bacon.

High, D. M., E. T. Howley, and B. D. Franks. 1989. The effects of static stretching and warm-up on prevention of delayed-onset muscle soreness. *Research Quarterly for Exercise and Sport* 60(4): 357–61.

Hutchinson, G. E., P. S. Freedson, A. Ward, and J. Rippe. 1990. Ideal to real—Implementing a youth fitness program. *Journal of Physical education, Recreation and Dance* 61(6): 52–58.

Katch, F. I., T. Hortobagyi, and T. Denahan. 1989. Reliability and validity of a new method for the measurement of total body volume. *Research Quarterly for Exercise and Sport* 60(3): 286–91.

Katch, F. I., and W. D. McArdle. 1977. *Nutrition, weight control, and exercise.* Boston: Houghton Mifflin.

Krause, J. V., and J. N. Barham. 1975. *The mechanical foundations of human motion: A programmed text.* St. Louis: C. V. Mosby.

Lang, D. A., and W. J. Stinson. 1991. The young child: Stress management strategies to use. *Journal of Physical Education, Recreation and Dance* 62(2): 59–60, 69–70.

Lavay, B., and M. Horvat. 1991. Jump rope for heart: and special populations. *Journal of Physical Education, Recreation and Dance* 62(3): 74–78.

Looney, M. A., and S. A. Plowman. 1990. Passing rates of American children and youth on the FITNESSGRAM criterion-referenced physical fitness standards. *Research Quarterly for Exercise and Sport* 61(3): 215–223.

Morrow, J. R. 1991. Research on teaching in physical education: Review and commentary. *Research Quarterly for Exercise and Sport* 62(4): 351.

Park, R. J. 1990. 1989 C. H. McCloy research lecture: Health, exercise, and the biomedical impulse, 1870–1914. *Research Quarterly for Exercise and Sport* 61(2): 126–40.

Pate, R. R., C. A. Slentz, and D. P. Katz. 1989. Relationships between skinfold thickness and performance of health related fitness test items. *Research Quarterly for Exercise and Sport* 60(2): 183–89.

Reiken, G. B. 1991. Negative effects of alcohol on physical fitness and athletic performance. *Journal of Physical Education, Recreation and Dance* 62(8): 64–66.

Riley, D. P. 1976. *Strength training*. West Point: United States Military Academy.

Santschi, W. R., J. DuBois, and C. Omoto. 1963. *Moments of inertia and centers of gravity of the living human body*. Wright-Patterson Air Force Base, Ohio: Behavioral Sciences Laboratory.

Sedlock, D. A. 1991. Postexercise energy expenditure following upper body exercise. *Research Quarterly for Exercise and Sport* 62(2): 213–16.

Simons-Morton, B. G., N. M. O'Hara, G. S. Parcel, I. Wei Huang, T. Baranowski, and B. Wilson. 1990. C hildren's frequency of participation in moderate to vigorous physical activities. *Research Quarterly for Exercise and Sport* 61 (4): 307–14.

Wilson, B. R., H. W. Olson, H. A. Sprague, W. D. Van Huss, and H. J. Montoye. 1990. Somatotype and longevity of former university athletes and nonathletes. *Research Quarterly for Exercise and Sport* 61(1): 1–6.

CHAPTER 5

Sensory Disabilities: Vision and Hearing

Objectives
After reading this chapter, you should be able to

- Know the gross anatomical structures of the eye and the ear.
- Distinguish blindness from partial vision, and deafness from severe hearing impairments.
- Describe the general incidence of vision and hearing impairments likely to be found among the school-age population.
- Describe the various screening instruments used for assessing potential sensory impairments.
- Describe the signs and symptoms associated with those who are likely candidates for referral to specialists.
- Know the major congenital and acquired causes of loss of vision and hearing.
- Discuss the characteristics of persons with audiovisual impairments as they relate to physical education.
- Discuss program modifications normally required in working with the audiovisually impaired.
- Discuss appropriate activities for the audiovisually impaired and the remedial values of each activity.

INTRODUCTION

Visual acuity and **auditory acuity** is something many of us take for granted. This is not the case for individuals who have been deprived of sight or hearing because of congenital or **acquired** (**adventitious**) reasons. We can help children who have to live without light

```
┌─────────────────────────────────────────────────────────────────────┐
│                            KEY TERMS                                  │
│                                                                       │
│   acquired                          legal blindness                   │
│   adventitious                      lesion                            │
│   amblyopia                         malignant                         │
│   astigmatism                       myopia                            │
│   audiometer                        nystagmus                         │
│   auditory acuity                   ophthalmologist (oculist)         │
│   auditory aphasia                  optician                          │
│   baseline (sports)                 optometrist                       │
│   blindism                          partial vision                    │
│   blindness                         perceptual-motor                  │
│   braille                           peripheral vision                 │
│   central deafness                  pitch                             │
│   coin click test                   psychogenic deafness              │
│   conversation test                 retinoblastoma                    │
│   deafness                          sensorineural deafness            │
│   deficit                           signing                           │
│   diabetic retinopathy              sign language                     │
│   educationally blind               Snellen chart                     │
│   etiology                          sounding devices                  │
│   hard of hearing                   strabismus                        │
│   hearing impaired                  visual acuity                     │
│   hyperopia                         visually impaired                 │
│   incidence                         watch tick test                   │
│   intensity                         whisper test                      │
│   kinesthetic                                                         │
└─────────────────────────────────────────────────────────────────────┘
```

or sound to bridge the gap between their perceptions of ideas or objects and the perceptions of their school-age colleagues. I doubt that a more intriguing challenge exists anywhere in the field of special and physical education.

How do we plan programs for children with visual or auditory impairments? What is the major mission of our program? How does impaired vision and/or hearing influence a child's ability to learn? What should the interim objectives be? Will the attainment of the interim objectives set the stage for achieving the major objective(s)? How much time should each session take? How large will the class be? What abilities do the class members have? Are we familiar with the individualized education plans (IEPs) for the coded youngsters in the class? Will we have to modify any of the available supplies and equipment? Will there be any professional or volunteer assistance for the class? Will we know when optimum student performance has been achieved?

To answer these and other questions, school practitioners will have to devote a significant portion of their available planning time to studying the students' needs and characteristics. This chapter will describe these needs and characteristics.

ANATOMY OF THE EYE

One of the most sensitive body structures is the eye. Although the eye is a very important part of the human body, its anatomy is relatively uncomplicated, Figure 5.1. Some important structures are defined in the following list:

1. Sclera—the white outer coat of the eye; tough opaque tissue that covers the eyeball except for the area of the cornea
2. Cornea—the clear, transparent, and glasslike portion of the eye that completes the covering of the eyeball
3. Retina—the expansion of the optic nerve that receives the image formed by the lens; the structure upon which light rays focus
4. Lens—the portion of the eye structure that lies just behind the iris and the pupil
5. Iris—the colored portion of the eye; contains the pupil at its middle point

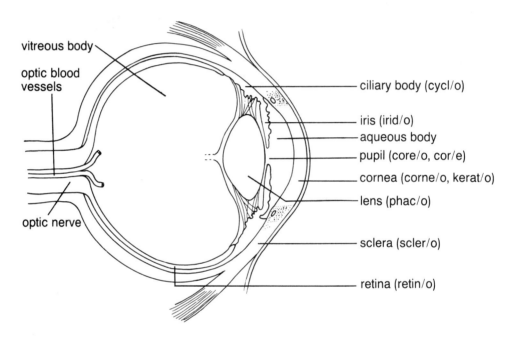

Figure 5.1. The human eye

BLINDNESS AND PARTIAL VISION

Concern for blind and partially sighted persons has been documented in this country for 165 years.* Yet medical and educational practitioners are still scrutinizing the literature and conducting research to find better ways to cope with deficiencies that hinder the optimum growth and development of the visually disabled. Why? Because the challenge of dealing with each child's disabilities seems to obscure the main concern, which should be the whole child. Instead of attending solely to a person's disabilities, we should address his/her abilities.

Definitions and Categories of Visual Anomalies

Individuals with sight deficiencies are distinguished from those with normal sight primarily by the degree of useful vision that they have. Visual senses develop in a rather

---

* The Perkins Institution and Massachusetts Asylum for the Blind was incorporated in 1829.

predictable way. Acknowledging that there may be some variance in its development, the expected sequence is presented in Figure 5.2.

The traditional definition of **blindness**, which is used for educational and legal purposes, is 20/200 or less in the better eye with a corrective lens, or **peripheral vision** of

Developmental Age	Visual Responses and Capabilities
0–1 month	Attends to light and possible forms: weak ciliary muscles and limited fixation ability.
1–2 months	Follows moving objects and lights; attends to novelty and complex patterns; stares at laces; begins binocular coordination.
2–3 months	Eyes fixate, converge, and focus; discriminates faces and yellow, orange, and red color waves.
3–4 months	Eye movements smoother and acuity improving; manipulates and looks at objects.
4–5 months	Eyes shift focus from objects to body parts; attempts to reach for and move to objects; visually explores environment; recognizes familiar faces and objects: tracks objects across entire field of vision.
5–6 months	Reaches and grasps objects indicating eye-hand coordination.
6–7 months	Shifts visual attention from object to object; reaches and rescues dropped objects; fluid eye movements.
7–8 months	Manipulates objects looking at results; watches movements and scribbling.
9–10 months	Visual acuity very good, accommodation smooth; looks for hidden objects even around corners; imitates facial expressions; plays looking games.
11 months to $1\frac{1}{2}$ years	All optical skills refined and acuity sharp; fits objects together and marks spontaneously.
$1\frac{1}{2}$ to 2 years	Matches objects, points to objects in book; imitates strokes and actions.
2 to $2\frac{1}{2}$ years	Visually inspects objects in distance; imitates movements of others; matches colors and like forms; increased visual memory span; orders objects by color; regards and reaches.
$2\frac{1}{2}$ to 3 years	Matches geometric forms; draws crude circle; inserts circle, square and triangle; puts pegs in holes and two puzzle pieces together.
3–4 years	Matches identical shaped objects by size; good depth perception; discriminates line lengths and most basic forms.
4–5 years	Refined eyehand coordination; colors, cuts and pastes; draws square; perceives detail in objects and pictures.
5-6 years	Perceives relationships in pictures, abstract figures, and symbols; copies symbols; matches lelters and words.
6–7 years	Identifies and reproduces abstract symbols; perceives constancy of letter/word styles; associates words with pictures; reads words on sight.

Figure 5.2. Sequence of visual development. *Courtesy of Barraga (1983). Visual handicaps and learning, Austin, TX: Exceptional Resources.*

twenty degrees or less (United States Code, Title 20 Education, Paragraph 107e Definitions, 1976). For the purposes of this text, partial sight is considered to be a visual range of from 20/70 to 20/200 in the better eye. (An individual with 20/70 acuity in the better eye sees at twenty feet what a person with normal vision sees at seventy feet.)

Other than **legal blindness**, there are various kinds of defects that may underlie loss of optimal vision. The more common of these dysfunctions are presented in the list that follows.

1. Refractive errors, including **myopia** (nearsightedness) in which the eyeball is too long from front to back. In this instance the light rays focus in front of the retina instead of on the retina, Figure 5.3. **Hyperopia** is a condition in which the eyeball is too short from front to back, causing farsightedness. With this condition, the light rays focus behind the retina, Figure 5.4. The third of the more common refractive-type errors is **astigmatism**, a condition in which there is blurred vision caused by a defective curvature of the refractive surfaces of the eye. As a consequence light rays are not sharply focused on the retina.

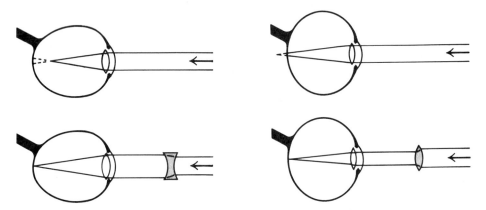

Figure 5.3. Myopia and correction with concave lens

Figure 5.4. Hyperopia and correction with convex lens

2. Developmental anomalies affecting the structure of the eye, including cataracts (a condition in which the normally transparent lens of the eye becomes cloudy or opaque).
3. Impaired muscle function of the eye. **Nystagmus** is a constant involuntary rapid movement of the eyeballs from side to side, up and down, in a rotary motion, or a combination of these. **Strabismus** is a condition of malalignment due to a lack of equal pull from the lateral and medial ocular muscles of the two eyes. When the two eyes do not align, the result is double vision. **Amblyopia**, often referred to as 'lazy' eye, is one of the leading causes of visual impairment in young children. Early treatment by patching or surgery is critical.
4. Color vision problems, in which certain conditions affecting the cones in the retina result in reduced ability to distinguish certain colors, most often reds, blues, and greens (Haring and McCormick 1990). Although not totally color

blind, I am unable to distinguish between these colors. I remember the difficulty I had in elementary school geography classes whenever we were expected to match colors on a map with a 'key' representing land elevation, population density, and rainfall. Neither the teachers nor I knew at that time that I was color blind. When using crayons, I could select the correct color because of the label on its wrapping. Thus my problem did not become apparent as one might guess that it would...or could. (As you might expect, my grades in geography map quizzes left much to be desired.) First of all, an early diagnosis would have been, and is, essential. Assuming that a diagnosis had been made, can you think of methods and materials that these teachers could have employed in order to assist me in overcoming this 'handicap'?

5. Defects or diseases of the eye, including infections and injuries. Examples of these conditions are: diabetic retinopathy (in which the retina is damaged by diabetes mellitus*), retinoblastoma (a **malignant** tumor of the eye), missiles (e.g., pencil/pen points, noses of paper planes, points of arrows, BBs) striking the eye, or damage from ultraviolent light from the sun. Both visible and invisible light waves can travel through the cornea to the translucent lens. When these waves converge on the retina for an extended period of time or in high doses, damage can be extensive.

Incidence

If a visual anomaly can be fully corrected by glasses or other means, the defect is not considered a visual handicap in an educational sense. Likewise many **visually impaired** children and adults are not reported (Kirchner 1983). For these and other reasons, the prevalence of visually impaired individuals among the school-age population is quite difficult to determine. We do know, however, that this number is significantly less than the number of children who are developmentally or learning disabled (Kirk and Gallagher 1989).

Although there are contradictions as one surveys the data generated by studies of the American Foundation for the Blind, the American Printing House for the Blind, and the U.S. Department of Education, it is generally believed that approximately 0.1 percent of school-age children are visually disabled (Livingston 1986).

Etiology

There are five known causes of blindness. These causes and their percentages of **incidence** are listed by Ward (1986) and shown in Table 5.1.

Although these rates indicate the relative and probable frequencies of visual impairment **etiologies**, what is likely to be more important information is the extent to which these children are accommodated within public school settings. In Figure 5.5 the reader will find evidence of the ranked changes in the percentages of visually impaired children being serviced within public school versus residential settings since 1949. It is apparent that increased attention is being paid to these children within local schools.

---

* The reader is referred to Chapter 13, for a review of diabetes mellitus.

TABLE 5.1

Causes of Legal Blindness, Ages 0–5

Etiology	Percent	
Prenatal influence	55.0	
Hereditary		37.2
Other congenital		17.8
Infectious diseases (rubella, syphilis)	14.0	
Injuries, poisonings (excess oxygen)	9.3	
Neoplasms (retinoblastoma)	5.4	
General diseases (diabetes mellitus, vascular)	3.1	
Undetermined	13.2	

Source: Adapted from Ward (1986)

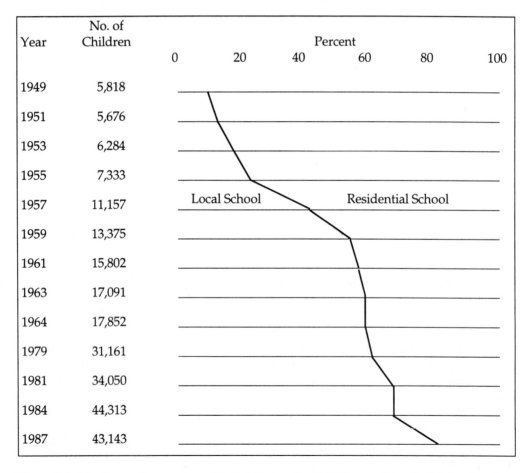

Figure 5.5. Number and percentage of United States school children registered with the American printing House for the Blind, by type of school, 1949–1987. *Courtesy of the American Printing House for the Blind.*

Screening

The term most people equate with visual ability is acuity. Visual acuity is often measured with a **Snellen chart** containing block-letter *E*s that face up, down, right, or left, Figure 5.6. The individual being screened stands twenty feet from the chart and is asked to read the symbols (often with either eye covered). The twenty-foot distance becomes the top number in the visual acuity index; the bottom number stands for the size of the line of *E*s (or other letters, as the case may be) that can be read successfully.

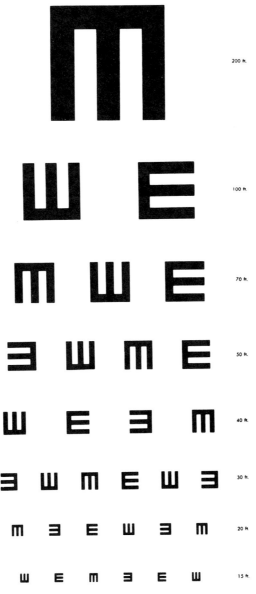

Figure 5.6. Snellen Symbol Chart. *Copyrighted by the National Society to Prevent Blindness. Reprinted by permission.*

To be tested for peripheral vision, the individual stands approximately forty inches from a black background—often a chalkboard—upon which a visual stimulus is placed. If the person with eyes fixed upon the center of the visual stimulus can see only twenty degrees or less of the periphery with the better eye (with correction), he/she is considered to be **educationally blind**.

These tests are general screening procedures. For reasonably accurate results, strict standards of distance and lighting must be enforced. The scope of visual ability, however, must be evaluated by persons professionally trained to use instruments of greater sophistication. Who are the professionals who work with the visually handicapped?*

1. **Ophthalmologist**—a physician (M.D.) who specializes in the diagnosis and treatment of all defects and diseases of the eye. He/she can prescribe drugs and glasses and is qualified to perform surgery. These specialists are also known as **oculists** (a less-preferred term).
2. **Optometrist**—a licensed, nonmedical practitioner who measures refractive errors (irregularities in the size or shape of the eyeball or surface of the cornea) and eye muscle disturbances. The optometrist's treatment is limited to the prescribing and fitting of glasses.
3. **Optician**—a maker of glasses; grinds lenses to prescriptions, fits them into frames, and adjusts frames to the wearer.

The physical educator or school nurse should make referrals through the student's parents or guardians to optometric specialists. Our mission in visual screening therefore is:

1. Identification of those with apparent visual deficiencies
2. Referral to optometrists or medically trained specialists
3. Follow-up of the outcome of the formal visual examination
4. Implementation of appropriate physical education activities to meet identified needs

The following conditions should be followed as a guide to recognizing possible vision problems:

1. Appearance of eyes
   _____ Reddened eyes or lids.
   _____ Encrusted lids.
   _____ Excessive eye watering (tears).
   _____ One eye turns in or out.
   _____ Eyes do not appear directed at the same point.
   _____ Eyes flutter back and forth or wander.
2. Observable behaviors
   _____ Excessive rubbing of the eyes.
   _____ Frequent blinking, squinting, or frowning.
   _____ Eyes do not easily follow moving objects.
   _____ Holds book or object closely.

---

* *Source*: American Foundation for the Blind

_____ Poor eye-hand coordination.
_____ Walks hesitantly, bumping or tripping on things.
_____ Acts afraid when others are moving about.
_____ Does not reach directly for objects.
_____ Easily disoriented within familiar area(s).
_____ Tilting or turning head to favor one eye.
_____ Shutting or covering one eye.
_____ Avoids close work.
_____ Examines objects tactually rather than visually.
_____ Has difficulty adjusting to bright or dim light.
_____ Slides foot forward to locate a step or curb.
_____ Does not make eye contact with person speaking.
_____ Shading or cupping eyes in bright light.

3. Complaints
_____ Burning, itching eyes.
_____ Painful eyes.
_____ Headaches.
_____ Blurred vision.
_____ Dizziness, nausea.

PRINCIPLES OF EDUCATION

Whether a person is blind or has **partial vision,** he/she may require some special programming. Children with these conditions may require slightly modified games, supplies, and equipment. Often, however, activities can be conducted just as they would be for anyone. In this chapter's "Developmental Activities" I will present special activities for visually impaired children. In Section III, Chaper 14, you will see how to adapt activities to meet the unique abilities of all class members.

Opinions vary regarding the intellectual and behavioral traits of visually disabled children. In 1930, Villey stated:

> No mental faculty of the blind is affected in any way, and all of them, under favorable circumstances, are susceptible of blossoming out to the highest degree of development to which a normal being can aspire.

Yet it has also been reported by at least one writer that mental activity is distorted by the absence of sight (Cutsforth 1951).

It appears that, although certain communication skills are deficient due to a depressed reception of visual stimuli, visually disabled individuals can achieve at a rate commensurate with their cognitive potential, the ability of their instructor(s) to communicate ideas, and their motivation for learning.

Researchers have studied the attitudes formed by people who have been told that they are losing their sight. Barron (1975) addressed the fear of being identified with stereotypes of blind people. She states that many of those with good intentions overprotect visually disabled individuals, leading to increased difficulty for those responsible for care and treatment. Cohen (1977) and Keegan, Greenough, and Ash (1976) also examined the effects of others' indulgence upon rehabilitation of blind individuals.

The following list of principles can help us assist visually disabled individuals with their adjustments:

1. Recognize that blind individuals are not necessarily totally blind. Some have limited degrees of vision that may vary in intensity from time to time.

2. Speak normally. If you use gestures, continue to express yourself in this way. Do not alter your vocabulary in deference to those who are blind. It is reasonable to use the word *see*. Seeing is a verbal image that communicates itself as effectively to blind as to sighted people. The words *blind* and **blindness** are likewise appropriate to use with blind people. Do not confuse lack of vision with the inability to communicate. Maintain normal **pitch** and **intensity** in your voice. When addressing a blind person, preface your remarks by using his or her name or by lightly touching him or her on the arm.

3. Describe surroundings as they change. This helps to sharpen a blind person's ability to identify sounds with objects and to become familiar with the environment. Describe where everyone is sitting so that the blind person can direct speech to the appropriate individual.

4. When you enter the presence of a blind person, speak promptly and identify other persons for him or her. When you leave the room, say that you are leaving. It can be awkward for everyone if the blind person continues to address you after you have left.

5. Blind people memorize the positions of equipment such as tables, bleachers, and other furnishings. Never change the arrangement of a familiar room without explaining the new arrangement. Accompany the blind person on an orientational walk around the room.

6. Provide large print documents for required and elective reading, Figure 5.7.

7. When walking with a blind person, offer your arm rather than taking his or hers. Guide the person simply and directly to the destination. You should stop when you are to ascend or descend stairs, bleachers, curbs, and so forth so that he/she will be prepared for the change. An explanation of the intended change may be necessary.*

8. When guiding a blind person to a seat, place his or her hand on the back of the chair to use as a guide in sitting down. (If you help a blind person know his or her position in relation to objects through the sense of touch, usually he/she is capable of doing the rest.)

9. If you hand a blind individual a ball, paddle, or any item, speak before you place it in his or her hand. This helps to eliminate mishandling of the item.

10. Describe sounds, physical landmarks, smells, and wind currents when relating them to the movement of objects and people.

11. Blind people like to know about the beauty that surrounds them. They enjoy hearing detailed descriptions of flowers, colors, and what people are wearing. They appreciate your comments about their appearance as would any friend.

12. Oral and tactile stimulation are the main media of communication for the blind. Keep this principle in mind when you prepare your lessons.

---

* In describing the position of equipment in a gymnasium, it might be helpful for the blind person to visualize the floor as a clock and the positions of the various items in relation to one, three, five, seven, nine, and eleven o'clock.

That ıʖ
rookie on the Knıcʚʟ
onship team became a folk hero ın
New York. There were more cele-
brated teammates: Walt Frazier,
Earl Monroe, Bill Bradley, Willis
Reed, Dave DeBusschere. But
ᶠrom 1972 to 1976, there was no
˥ıt to how high the decibels
rise in Madison Square
ᵂingo stepped
˙ɔwn

Figure 5.7. Sample of large print material. *Adapted from Reader's Digest, Large-type Edition.*

PRINCIPLES OF PHYSICAL EDUCATION

It is estimated that better than 80 percent of visually disabled children are currently attending local schools. It is likely that this percentage will increase. Consequently teachers of physical education must be prepared to present lessons not only for special classes but for mainstreamed or inclusionary settings as well. (See Figure 5.8 for a partial list of materials suitable for classroom use by students and/or teachers.)

Regardless of the arena in which the lesson is to be taught (special or mainstreamed), there are fundamental principles that should be followed with regard to play areas, supplies and equipment, and activities.

Play Areas
The following fundamental principles apply to play areas:

1. Play areas should be large, uncluttered, and free of equipment not needed for the lesson.
2. The boundaries of outdoor play areas should be hedges or shrubbery, not walls or fences. Solid obstacles are unreasonable hazards for the visually disabled. Mats can be placed on fences where necessary.
3. A boundary for an outdoor game can be a change in the composition of the playing surface. For example, the playing area might be grass and the out-of-bounds area might be sand. Textural differences enable visually disabled players to know when they are out of bounds.

Partially Sighted	Blind

PAPER

____	Regular notebook paper	____	Braille transcription paper
____	Bold line paper	____	Graph paper
____	Raised line paper	____	Raised line paper
____	Non-glare paper		

BOOKS

____	Regular print	____	Braille books
____	Recorded books	____	Recorded books
	____ Cassette		____ Cassette
	____ Reel		____ Reel
	____ Disks/Records		____ Disks/Records
____	Large print	____	
____		____	

EQUIPMENT

____	Tape recorder	____	Tape recorder
	____ Cassette		____ Cassette
	____ Reel-to-reel		____ Reel-to-reel
____	Typewriter (large type)	____	Typewriter
____	Adjustable-top desk	____	Braillewriter
____	Magnification devices	____	Slate and stylus
____	Lamps	____	Abacus
____	Closed-circuit television	____	Braille rulers
____		____	Braille erasers
____		____	Talking calculator
____		____	Kurzweil reading machine
____		____	

OTHER

____	Large-print maps	____	Braille labeler
____	Relief models	____	Swail dot inverter (for making raised dot drawings)
____	Raised line drawing kit		
____	Black felt-tip pens	____	Raised-line drawing kit
____	Large, soft lead pencils	____	Braille maps and globes
____	Yellow acetate (place over dittos to increase contrast)	____	Relief models
____	Writing guides (helps person write on lines)	____	Optacon (electronic device that enables blind person to read print)
____		____	Raised print and braille clocks
____		____	Writing guides (helps person write on lines)
____		____	
____		____	
____			

Figure 5.8. Materials/equipment checklist

4. Boundaries for indoor playing areas should be painted yellow or orange so that the lines can be more easily detected by those who have residual vision.

5. Playing areas should be well lighted to help those who can perceive reflection.

6. Though more expensive than using guide wires or sighted partners when walking or running track, an *electronic guidance system* (EGS) has been field tested and found to be very effective to the blind as they navigate track or other athletic field areas.

7. **Baselines**, base areas, and field positions can be made of different substances than other areas of the field. Be sure that abrupt elevations or declines do not exist where visually disabled children will be running.

Supplies and Equipment

1. Portable aluminum rails are available for use in such activities as bowling. They are easily moved from station to station and assembled.

2. Sounding devices are valuable aids. Electronic balls with beepers are gradually replacing balls with bells. Metronomes placed behind the backboard of a basketball goal will help to orient blind children as to placement of the basket. A bell, beeper, or metronome can be placed on the deck of the shallow end of the swimming pool for proper orientation while swimming. A whistle can alert the blind student to where the instructor or leader is or if a game/playing violation has occurred. A meaningful set of signals can be worked out for a multitude of conditions.

3. A megaphone or microphone can be used to describe the progress of the game—progress that can be observed naturally by those with normal vision.

4. Balls of a bright color—yellow or orange—can be seen more easily by those with partial vision.

5. Students who are wearing glasses should cover them with protective devices during activities.

6. The history, rules, terminology, and strategy governing various games can be prepared in **braille** and given to the blind student before the class presentation. Braille can also be used on the walls of swimming pools to designate water depths and on gymnasium floors and walls to identify shapes, sizes, and colors. Large-print materials can also be provided as alternatives for partially sighted individuals.

7. Stationary bicycles help develop the cardiovascular systems of the visually disabled.*

Activities

In order to assist the visually disabled toward eventual participation in team, individual, rhythmic, or aquatic activities, readiness skills must be emphasized at the outset.

Many blind persons have idiosyncrasies in common. One of the motions—**blindisms**—most prevalent in blind people is rocking forward and backward. This

---

* Information concerning the purchase of special equipment for the blind can be obtained by contacting: American Foundation for the Blind, Inc., Aids and Appliances Division, 15 West Sixteenth Street, New York, New York 10011. [Telephone: (212) 620-2000]

appears to be a consequence of movement repression. Children have an innate desire to move through their environment. Being without sight inhibits the opportunity to make that expression a reality. Thus we should provide as many opportunities for progressive movement as possible. Movement is comprised of many dimensions. The essential components of movement orientation for the visually disabled are described in the next section.

DEVELOPMENTAL ACTIVITIES

I. Goal: Body Awareness

Major Objective	*Interim Performance Objective*
1. Image, Figure 5.9	1.1 Identify body parts.

Figure 5.9. Body part identification

> 1.1A Touch head.
> 1.1B Touch neck.
> 1.1C Touch shoulders.
> 1.1D Touch back.
> 1.1E Touch chest.
> 1.1F Touch stomach.
> 1.1G Touch hips.
> 1.1H Touch arms.
> 1.1I Touch legs.

2. Body alignment

2.1 Assume appropriate posture in accordance with standard posture tests (See Chapter 4 for information related to the evaluation of static and dynamic posture.)

> 2.1A Stand
> 2.1B Sit
> 2.1C Stoop
> 2.1D Walk

3. Movement of body parts

3.1 Move a selected body part through a prescribed pattern.

4. Movement integration

4.1 Move two or more body parts at the same time.

> 4.1A Move right arm and left arm.
> 4.1B Move right arm and left leg.
> 4.1C Move left arm and right leg.
> 4.1D Move head, an arm, a leg.

II. Goal: Orientation to Space

Major Objective	*Interim Performance Objective*
1. Static balance	1.1 Remain still for a predetermined period of time.

        1.1A Assume supine position.

        1.1B Assume prone position.

        1.1C Sit.

        1.1D Kneel.

        1.1E Stand.

2. Dynamic balance — 2.1 Maintain constant motion for a period of time in a prescribed space.

3. Laterality — 3.1 Move to the right or left within a prescribed area.

4. Directionality — 4.1 Move to a specified position in relation to an object.

        4.1A Move in front of object.

        4.1B Move behind object.

        4.1C Move to the left of object.

        4.1D Move to the right of object.

        4.1E Move between objects.

5. Levels, Figure 5.10 — 5.1 Sense varying points of elevation.

        5.1A Move up and down from floor.

        5.1B Move on top of and under objects.

Figure 5.10. Levels: Climbing up a ladder

Major Objective	*Interim Performance Objective*
6. Form perception, Figure 5.11	6.1 Perform movements through specific geometric patterns.

Figure 5.11. Movement through a geometric pattern

6.1A Move around a square.

6.1B Move around a triangle.

6.1C Move around a circle.

7. **Kinesthetic**/sound integration	7.1 Face origin of sound while in prone, sitting, kneeling, standing positions.

7.1A Make quarter turns.

7.1B Make half turns.

7.1C Make three-quarter turns.

7.1D Make full turns.

III. Goal: Weight Transfer and Force

Major Objective	*Interim Performance Objective*
1. Shifting weight	1.1 Maintain balance following weight transfer from one balance point to another.

1.1A Transfer weight from all fours to kneeling position.

1.1B Transfer weight from right foot to left foot.

1.1C Transfer weight from left foot to right foot.

2. Creating and absorbing force, Figure 5.12	2.1 Vary muscle tension in accordance with demands of specified motor activity.

Major Objective Interim

Performance Objective

Figure 5.12. Absorbing force

2.1A Jump.

2.1B Turn selected weight.*

2.1C Twist rope.

2.1D Push selected weight.

2.1E Pull selected weight.

IV. Goal: Movement in Planes

Major Objective

1. Transverse plane (movement around axis)

2. Sagittal plane (movement forward and backward)

3. Frontal plane (movement in lateral direction)

Interim Performance Objective

1.1 Move around the body's longitudinal axis.

    1.1A Turn in prone position.

    1.1B Turn in standing position.

2.1 Move specific body parts in accordance with given directions.

    2.1A From standing position bend forward at waist.

    2.1B From anatomical position (standing, arms at sides, palms facing forward) flex right elbow forward.

    2.1C From anatomical position flex left knee backward.

    2.1D From supine position, sit up.

3.1 Move specific body parts in accordance with given directions

    3.1A From anatomical position, elevate right arm to the side. Origin of movement is from the shoulder (do not flex elbow).

---

* For items 2.1B, 2.1D, and 2.1E it may be desirable for a partner to serve as the weight. Under supervised conditions, the performer and the partner will gain greater insight into what constitutes force absorption.

Major Objective	*Interim Performance Objective*
	3.1B From anatomical position flex trunk to the left (do not flex knees).

V. Goal: Rhythms

Major Objective	*Interim Performance Objective*

1. Movement to a tempo	1.1 Display rhythm appropriate to prescribed tempo.
	
	1.1A Clap hands; take steps.
	    1.1Aa 4/4 time
	    1.1Ab 3/4 time
	    1.1Ac 2/4 time
	    1.1Ad 6/8 time

2. Movement to changes in tempo	2.1 Speed up and slow down movement in accordance with prescribed tempi. 2.1A Clap hands to changing tempo. 2.1B Take steps to changing tempo.

VI. Goal: Movement Integration

Major Objective	*Interim Performance Objective*
1. Explore ways to move from place to place.	1.1 Perform assorted movements. 1.1A Run. 1.1B Hop. 1.1C Skip. 1.1D Slide. 1.1E Gallop.
2. Create ways to integrate mobility tasks.	2.1 Move as instructed. 2.1A Move to right (or left). 2.1B Move to a specified position in relation to an object. 2.1C Move through geometric patterns. 2.1D Move to changing tempi.

DEAFNESS AND PARTIAL LOSS OF HEARING

The anatomy of the ear is presented in Figure 5.13. As reported in Chapter 1, visual and auditory disabilities constitute a clear proportion of disabilities among school-age

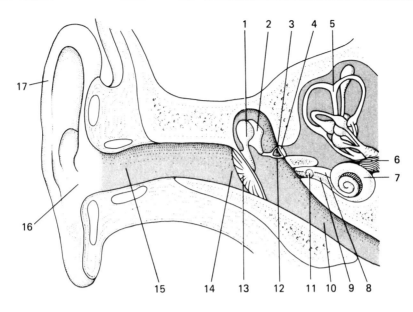

Figure 5.13. The human ear. *Courtesy of Schade (1970).*

1. Hammer (malleus)
2. Anvil (incus)
3. Musculus stapedius
4. Oval window
5. Verticalis
6. Vestibulocochlear nerve
7. Cochlea
8. Scala vestibuli
9. Scala tympani
10. Eustachian tube
11. Round window
12. Stirrup (stapes)
13. Tympanic membrane
14. Musculus tensor tympani
15. External auditory meatus
16. Conch of auricle (external ear)
17. Helix of auricle (external ear)

children. Because of the impact these conditions have on communication and adjustment skills, it is critical that you understand the principles that should be applied in the education of children with hearing impairments.

Deafness can be as much a handicap to learning as is lack of vision, especially if the problem is not discovered early. All too often, hearing deficiencies go unnoticed until other potential reasons for lack of scholastic achievement are dismissed. Consequently the impatience of a teacher or peer may aggravate an already frustrated learner.

Children who are deaf and **hard of hearing** want to do well in physical education activities, however, and will not be discouraged unless we fail to provide an appropriate learning environment.

Definitions and Categories of Auditory Anomalies

Two measurements are used to describe auditory levels: pitch (highness or lowness of sound) and intensity (loudness or softness of sound) as measured in decibels. Pitch and intensity are evaluated formally on an **audiometer**. Correct use of an audiometer requires special training ordinarily not given to undergraduates preparing to become teaching practitioners. Priliminary screening procedures on the other hand are used by physical education and other teachers. Because of their importance these procedures are described in the section about auditory screening.

The Conference of Executives of American Schools for the Deaf (1938) established classifications that make possible a universal nomenclature for use by persons responsible for diagnosis and program prescription. These classifications are

1. *Deaf*—those in whom the sense of hearing is nonfunctional for the ordinary purposes of life. This general group is made up of two distinct classes, based entirely on the time the loss of hearing occurred.
   a) The congenitally deaf: Those who were born deaf
   b) The adventitious deaf: Those who were born with normal hearing but in whom the sense of hearing became nonfunctional later through illness or accident
2. Hard of Hearing—those in whom the sense of hearing, although deficient, is functional with (or without) a hearing aid.

Within these broad classifications Davis and Silverman (1978) suggest further definitions of auditory acuity. These refinements are accepted by most special education practitioners.

1. Slight hearing loss is a twenty-six- to forty-decibel loss in the better ear. A child in this category may be overlooked unless his or her behaviors appear symptomatic of a hearing deficit (see "Screening"). The student may have difficulty with distant sounds and may need preferential seating and speech therapy.
2. Mild hearing loss is a forty-one- to fifty-five-decibel loss in the better ear. In this instance the student can understand conversational speech, may miss class discussion, may require hearing aids and speech therapy.
3. Marked hearing loss is a fifty-six- to seventy-decibel loss in the better ear. With this degree of impairment the student will require the use of hearing aids, auditory training, and intensive speech and language training.
4. Severe losses are those in which there is a seventy-one- to ninety-decibel loss in the better ear. The student can only hear loud sounds close up and is sometimes considered deaf. He/she needs intensive special education, hearing aids, and speech and language training.
5. Extreme losses are those that equal or exceed a ninety-one-decibel loss in the better ear. Although the student may be aware of loud sounds and vibrations, he/she relies on vision rather than hearing for information processing. This student is considered deaf.

The acquisition of speech depends in large part on whether individuals are congenitally or adventitiously deaf. A person who has never heard sounds will have difficulty simulating normal voice patterns. Nevertheless, great strides are being made. Those with auditory dysfunctions are communicating at a level never before thought possible.

Incidence

A review of the literature leads to confusion as to the total number of persons in the United States who have hearing deficiencies. At best the numbers represent gross estimates because many cases go unreported. On the other hand, figures representing the number of children who have hearing anomalies are relatively accurate because auditory screening is increasingly commonplace in today's schools. These data have made it possible for the United States Department of Education (1987) to report that nearly seventy thousand children are receiving special education services under the PL 94-142 classifications of hard-of-hearing and deaf. This figure represents 0.175 percent of the school-age population, preschool through grade 12. Approximately three-quarters of this group receive their education within the local schools (Craig and Craig 1987).

Etiology

It has been estimated that approximately 60 percent of hearing losses are congenital—hereditary or prenatal—in origin. Of the 40 percent of adventitious losses the most common types are:

1. **Central deafness**—a condition whereby the auditory pathways within the central nervous system (CNS) are affected by
   a) diseases such as arteriosclerosis, cerebral hemorrhage, multiple sclerosis, or a tumor
   b) a **lesion** in the cortex affecting auditory symbolizalization, commonly referred to as **auditory aphasia**.
2. **Psychogenic deafness**—a condition that is related to maladaptive affective behavior such as that exhibited by neurotics or psychotics.
3. **Sensorineural deafness**—a condition caused by a defect in Corti's Organ (the terminal acoustic apparatus in the cochlea, Figure 5.13.), the auditory nerve, or both. Diseases that can provoke the condition are influenza, measles, meningitis, mumps, scarlet fever, and whooping cough.*

Screening

Besides the audiometer—which is considered to be the most formal and refined instrument of measurement for assessing auditory acuity, Figure 5.14—there are a number of informal techniques that can be used by the physical educator or other classroom teacher. Although they are subjective, informal techniques provide a basis for reasonable judgment as to whether a student should be referred to a specialist for a complete audiometric examination.

A selection of screening techniques is described here in order of reliability.

1. To perform the **watch tick test**, place a watch at the orifice of the student's ear. Move the watch progressively farther away until the student gives a sign that the sound of ticking is no longer heard. Judge this distance in relation to what students with normal hearing are able to hear.

---

* In addition to being an adventitious disorder, sensorineural deafness is the most common type of congenital auditory dysfunction. Influenza, measles, and mumps can all cause deafness in infants whose mothers were afflicted during the first trimester of pregnancy. The majority of acquired (adventitious) hearing losses are of the conductive type.

A conductive loss prohibits conduction of sound waves to the inner ear—often because of a physical obstruction. In this case residual hearing is likely to exist. On the other hand a hearing disorder caused by the inability of the nerve fibers to carry sound impulses may result in total deafness. In this case a standard hearing aid would be of no value. Implantations of microcircuits and electrodes in the inner ear may help.

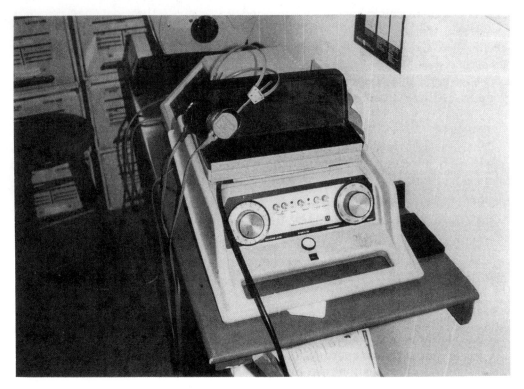

Figure 5.14. Audiometer

2. To perform the **coin click test**, tap a coin on a hard surface at an intensity the student can hear. Progressively decrease the intensity until the student signals that no further sound is heard. Compare the student's acuity to a person with normal hearing.
3. To perform the **conversation test**, converse normally with the student while you move away. If the child has difficulty hearing you beyond a distance of ten feet, he/she should be referred to a specialist.
4. To perform the **whisper test**, whisper to the student at a volume that could be heard by a person with normal hearing. If the student cannot understand the words being whispered, he/she should be referred to a specialist.

According to Knobloch and Pasamanick (1974) and Mollick and Etra (1981) other general indicators of hearing loss might be

1. Hearing and comprehension of speech
    a) general indifference to sound
    b) lack of response to the spoken word
    c) response to noises as opposed to words
2. Vocalization and sound production
    a) monotonal quality
    b) indistinct speech

    c) lessened laughter

    d) meager experimental play

    e) vocal play for vibratory sensation

    f) distorted or immature speech—By the age of six a youngster should be able to pronounce clearly such blends as *th, tl, gr, br,* and *pr*. More difficult sounds, e.g., *thr, sk, st, shr, z, sh, ch,* and *j*, may not be mastered until age seven or eight.

    g) head banging, foot stamping for vibratory sensation

    h) yelling or screeching to express pleasure or need

    i) speaking louder than what would ordinarily be considered normal

3. Visual attention

    a) augmented visual vigilance and attentiveness

    b) alertness to gesture and movement

    c) marked imitativeness in play

    d) vehemence of gestures

4. Social rapport and adaptation

    a) subnormal rapport in vocal games

    b) intensified preoccupation with things rather than persons

    c) puzzled and unhappy episodes in social situations

    d) suspiciousness and alertness, alternating with cooperation

    e) marked reaction to praise and affection

5. Emotional behavior

    a) antrums to call attention to self or need

    b) tensions, tantrums, resistance—due to lack of comprehension

    c) frequent obstinacies or irritability at not making self understood

Many of these symptoms could underlie a variety of cognitive, psychomotor, and affective conditions unrelated to hearing **deficits**. Nonetheless, they are highly predictive of a hearing deficiency.

PRINCIPLES OF EDUCATION

Hearing disorders do not affect intelligence scores except to the extent that verbal language skills are inhibited. As Dunn (1963) points out,

> ...deaf children who incur their losses early show weakness in the verbal aspects of mental operations—an educational rather than an intellectual characteristic.

Since auditory dysfunctions appear to cause less impairment in intellectual acumen than has been thought, teachers and administrators should provide educational opportunities commensurate with the highest of expectations. The intelligence scores of deaf and hard-of-hearing students fall well within a normal probability curve. If we use appropriate methods and materials, the actualization of cognitive, social, and motor skills is within reach for such students.

When relating to hearing-impaired students, keep the following principles in mind.

1. Become familiar with **signing** skills. Many deaf and **hard-of-hearing** individuals know hand language. For increasing communication competence, signing skills are requisite, Figure 5.15.

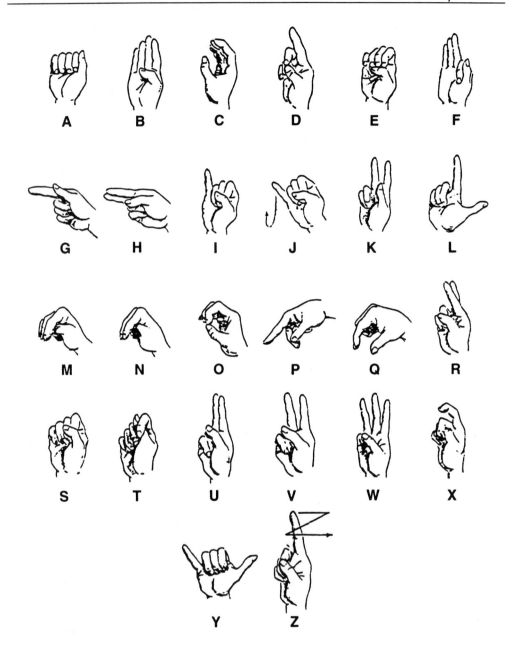

Figure 5.15. American manual alphabet. *Illustration from American Sign Language: A Comprehensive Dictionary by Martin Sternberg. © 1987 by Martin Sternberg. Reprinted by permission of HarperCollins Publishers.*

2. Help other children understand what a hearing loss is to help them empathize (more than would ordinarily be expected of peers) with those so afflicted.

3. Before starting a lesson, be sure you have the attention of all youngsters. They should be where they can see you easily. Always turn and face the class when you have something to say. Do not teach or talk to the chalkboard. At the same time keep in mind that activity going on behind you will be visually distracting; in other words consider the background. Further, do not stand with your back to a window. The glare in the background makes it difficult to see your lips.

4. Be sure that the child can see your lips in order to read them. (Being clean shaven may be helpful). Do not exaggerate lip movement when speaking, however. Try to speak naturally.

5. Do not hasten to blame a **hearing-impaired** child who does not appear attentive. It may be that his or her hearing aid is not functioning properly. Further there is evidence that many children can hear with greater acuity on some days than they can on others.

6. Remember that hearing-disabled children must expend more effort to hear than do their classmates. Consequently they are prone to mental and emotional fatigue.

7. Be sure that the hard-of-hearing child is encouraged to speak clearly. Over a period of time, hearing loss leads to improper diction and tone. It may be necessary to schedule remedial sessions with the speech pathologist.

8. Foster the hearing-disabled child's social skills. Emotions may be expressed intensely because of insufficient speech development. Help hearing-impaired youngsters realize that aggressive physical gestures are not always the best way to get someone's attention.

9. Use preferential seating. Seat the children with hearing losses near the front of the classroom, close to your desk/instruction area. A student with a bad left ear should be seated on your right as you face the class, whereas a student with a bad right ear should be on your left.

10. Teach by demonstrating whenever possible. Visual stimulation is the main medium of communication for deaf and hard-of-hearing students. Establish signals such as raising a hand, swinging an arm, or blinking a light.

11. Emphasize the use of written handout materials and overhead projections. Where students may have difficulty in understanding what is said, they would still receive the message through vision.

12. Vibrations picked up through the floor, chair, table, or other object also provide stimuli for hearing-impaired students. Use floor stamping, a record player, or drum beating as sources of vibrations during rhythmic and other related activities.

PRINCIPLES OF PHYSICAL EDUCATION

As a result of Public Law 94-142 many disabled children are enrolled in the public schools. This is particularly true for the deaf and hard of hearing. Hence the teacher of physical education should be abreast of contemporary principles governing education in general as well as those needed to program suitable activities for the physical education classroom or clinic.

Because hearing impairment has many causes, expressions of motor and sensory behavior may be quite varied. Youngsters who have been born deaf will have little speech development. Children who have acquired auditory dysfunctions because of illness or injury usually have verbal skills comparable to those of their peers. Some have learned to read speech, lip-read, and use **sign language**, while others have not. Skill development may also have been affected by lack of auditory stimulation.

DEVELOPMENTAL ACTIVITIES

Approaches to the physical education of hearing-impaired children can be as varied as the etiologies of the impairments. In most cases, however, we should provide curricula that will develop perceptual and motor skills, body awareness, spatial orientation, balance, and hand-eye and foot-eye coordination. Since hearing-impaired children have some vestibular dysfunction and generally have problems with equilibrium, balance orientation is fundamental to their progress and should be taught first.

Balance should be developed in the static (stationary), dynamic (moving), and rotational (in flight) states. Developmental tasks that are related to activities of daily living provide students with the opportunity to associate what we teach them with their lives out of class. This makes the experience students share in the adapted physical education class more valuable.

The recommended sequence for the **perceptual-motor** aspect of total motor and sensory development is as follows.

I. Goal: Orientation in Space

Major objective	*Interim Performance Objective*
1. Static balance	1.1 Remain still for a predetermined period of time.
	1.1A Sit on chair.
	1.1B Sit on floor.
	1.1C Kneel.
	1.1D Stand.
	1.1Da Feet apart
	1.1Db Feet together
	1.1E Stand on toes, feet together.
	1.1F Stand on two low balance beams, twelve inches apart, one foot on each beam.
	1.1G Stand on low balance beam.
	1.1H Stand on high balance beam.
2. Dynamic balance	2.1 Maintain control while in motion.
	2.1A Walk on line taped to floor.
	2.1Aa Forward
	2.1Ab Sideways
	2.1Ac Backward

Major Objective	*Interim Performance Objective*
	2.1B Walk on low balance beam while holding hands with partner who walks on another beam placed parallel and twelve inches away.
	2.1Ba Forward (join inside hands)
	2.1Bb Sideways (join both hands)
	2.1Bc Backward (join inside hands)
	2.1C Walk on two low balance beams, twelve inches apart, one foot on each beam.
	2.1Ca Forward
	2.1Cb Backward
	2.1D Walk on low balance beam.
	2.1Da Forward
	2.1Db Sideways
	2.1Dc Backward
	2.1E Walk on high balance beam.
	2.1Ea Forward
	2.1Eb Sideways
	2.1Ec Backward
	2.1F Walk on high balance beam while reducing support base.
	2.1Fa Forward, heel-to-toe
	2.1Fb Backward, toe-to-heel
3. Rotational balance	3.1 Maintain kinesthetic awareness of body position while maintaining balance.
	3.1A Stand on floor, feet shoulder-width apart. Execute controlled turns within prescribed space.
	3.1Aa 90°
	3.1Ab 180°
	3.1Ac 270°
	3.1Ad 360°

Major Objective	*Interim Performance Objective*
	3.1B While standing on preferred foot, execute controlled turns within prescribed space. 3.1Ba 90° 3.1Bb 180°
	3.1C While standing sideways on low balance beam, feet shoulder-width apart, execute controlled turns to floor. 3.1Ca Forward 180° 3.1Cb Backward 180°

SUMMARY

Vision- and hearing-impaired children are to be found in increasing numbers within our local schools. As a consequence it is essential that teachers and other school practitioners understand the nature of these conditions.

In Chapter 5 you learned about the anatomy of the eye and ear, the pertinent definitions and various categories comprising these anomalies, relative incidences among the school-age population, etiologies, screening strategies, principles of successful social interaction skills, as well as developmental activities. In no small way is your attention to these issues important to optimizing the opportunities for success. Please take this information with you as you proceed with the recommended laboratory assignments and readings offered in the sections that follow.

RECOMMENDED LABORATORY ASSIGNMENTS

1. Arrange to visit special and regular schools that accommodate blind and/or deaf children to discuss methods and materials with physical education teachers there. Much can be learned by observing programs in action.
2. Complete a physical education field experience with students who are blind or deaf.
3. Simulate a blind or hard-of-hearing condition for a day or for a physical education class period. Tape-record your reactions to stressful conditions as they occur. (It may be necessary to have another student serve as your guide for the selected time span.)
4. Perform the progression of developmental activities described in this chapter. List other tasks that could help an impaired child meet the intended educational goals and objectives.*

---

* Deaf and blind children constitute another classification of disability that is emerging in increasing proportions. The unique characteristics of children who are deaf and blind call for a multidisciplinary educational approach. In any setting—special or public school—physical education is an important part of that approach.

5. Obtain and practice using various sensory screening instruments in order to become more proficient in their use.
6. Learn American or other sign language methodologies.
7. List the ways supplies, equipment, and facilities might be adapted to enhance the teaching of blind or deaf children.*
8. Review the recommended readings.

REFERENCES

Barraga, N. 1983. *Visual handicaps and learning.* Austin, TX: Exceptional Resources.

Barron, S. 1975. *Psychological problems of retinitis pigmentosa.* Mimeographed. Dallas: South Central Regional Center for Services to Deaf-Blind Child, c/o Callier Center for Communication Disorders.

Cohen, B. 1977. *Study to explore the affective response of a young adult to a sensory loss of blindness.* Mimeographed. Boston: Perkins School for the Blind.

Conference of Executives of American Schools for the Deaf, Committee on Nomenclature. 1938. Report of the Conference Committee. *American Annals of the Deaf* 83: 1–3.

Craig, W., and H. Craig. 1987. Director of services for the deaf. *American Annals of the Deaf* 83:1–3.

Cutsforth, T. D. 1951. *The blind in school and society.* New York: American Foundation for the Blind.

Davis, H., and R. Silverman. 1970. *Hearing and Deafness.* 4th ed. New York: Holt, Rinehart and Winston, Inc.

Dunn, L. M., ed. 1963. *Exceptional children in the schools.* Fort Worth, TX: Holt, Rinehart and Winston, Inc.

Haring, N. G., and L. McCormick. 1990. *Exceptional children and youth.* 5th ed. Columbus, OH: Merrill Publishing Company

Keegan, D. L., T.J. Greenough, and D. G. Ash. 1976. Ajustment to blindness. *Journal of Ophthalmology* 11: 22–29.

Kirchner, C. 1983. Statistical brief No. 23. Special education for visually handicapped children: A critique of numbers and costs. *Journal of Visual Impairment and Blindness* 77(1): 219–223.

Kirk, S. A., and J.J. Gallagher. 1989. *Educating exceptional children.* 6th ed. Boston: Houghton Mifflin Company.

Knobloch, H., and B. Pasamanick. 1974. *Developmental diagnosis.* 3d ed. New York: Harper and Row.

Livingston, R. 1986. Visual impairments. In *Exceptional Children and Youth,* 4th ed., edited by N. G. Haring and L. McCormick. Columbus, OH: Merrill Publishing Company.

Mollick, L. W., and K.S. Etra. 1981. Poor learning ability...or poor hearing. In *Educating Exceptional Children,* edited by K. Freibert. Guilford, Ct: The Dushkin Publishing Group, Inc.

Schade, J. 1970. *Introduction to functional human anatomy.* Philadelphia: W. B. Saunders.

Sternberg, M. L. 1981. *American sign language: A comprehensive dictionary.* New York: Harper and Row.

United States Code. 1976. *Title 20 education, Paragraph 107e definitions.* Washington DC: U.S. Government Printing Office.

United States Department of Education. 1987. *Ninth annual report to Congress on the implementation of the Education of the Handicapped Act.* Washington, DC: Author.

Villey, P. 1930. *The world of the blind.* London: Duckworth.

* A new service has emerged that enables telephone communication between hearing telephone customers and those who are deaf, hard-of-hearing (or speech impaired), without special equipment. To access the service, contact AT&T for instructional information.

Ward, M. 1986. The visual system. *In Foundations of Education for Blind and Visually Handicapped Children and Youth*, edited by G. Scholl. New York: American Foundation for the Blind.

RECOMMENDED READINGS

Adams, R. D., A. N. Daniel, and L. Rullman. 1972. *Games sports and exercises for the physically handicapped.* Philadelphia: Lea and Febiger.

Adelson, E., and S. Frailberg. 1974. Gross motor development in infants blind from birth. *Child Development* 45: 114–26.

American Alliance for Health, Physical Education, Recreation and Dance 1971. *The best of challenge.* Washington, DC: Author.

California Leadership Action Team for the Visually Impaired. 1985. *Statement of educational needs of visually impaired students in California.* San Francisco, CA: American Foundation for the Blind.

Buell, C. 1974. *Physical education for blind children.* Sprintfield, IL: Charles C. Thomas.

Corn, A. L., and I. Martinez. 1983. *When you have a visually handicapped child in your classroom: Suggestions for teachers.* New York: American Foundation for the Blind.

Cox, R. L. 1978. A program for able pre-college students who are blind. *Kappa Delta Pi Record* 15: 101, 108.

Cratty, B., and T. Sams. 1968. *Body image of blind children.* New York: American Foundation for the Blind.

Eichstaedt, C. B. 1978. Signing. *Journal of Physical Education, Recreation and Dance* 49: 19–21.

Falls, J. 1977. Scouting report: Bad eyes, good legs, strong heart. *The Boston Marathon.* New York: Macmillan.

Flexor, C., and L. A. Wood. 1984. The hearing aid: Facilitator or inhibitor of auditory interaction? *Volta Review* 86: 354–55.

Guttman, L. 1976. Sports for the blind and partially sighted. *Textbook of sports for the disabled.* Aylesbury, England: H, M and M Publishers.

Hawkins, D. B. 1984. Comparisons of speech recognition in noise by mildly-to-moderately hearing-impaired children using hearing aids and FM systems. *Journal of Speech and Hearing Disorders* 49: 409–18.

Jeffers, J., and M. Barley. 1971. *Speechreading (lipreading).* Springfield, IL: Charles C. Thomas.

Kleeman, M. L., and J. H. Rimmer. 1993. Relationship between physical fitness levels and attitudes toward physical education in a visually impaired population. *Research Quarterly for Exercise and Sport: Supplement* 64(1): A–16.

Kooyman, W. J. 1970. Physical education of pupils with defective vision and problems of orientation. *Teacher of the Blind* 58: 99–105.

Leavitt, R. 1985. Counseling to encourage use of SNR enhancing systems. *Hearing Instruments* 36: 8–9.

Ling, D. 1976. *Speech and the hearing-impaired child: Theory and practice.* Washington, DC: The Alexander Graham Bell Association for the Deaf.

Lydon, W. T., and M. L. McGraw. 1973. *Concept development for visually handicapped children: A resource guide for the teachers and other professionals working in educational settings.* New York: American Foundation for the Blind.

Mykelbust, H. R. 1964. *The psychology of deafness.* New York: Grune and Stratton

Pate, G. S. 1981. Research on prejudice reduction. *Education Leadership.*

Ports, M. 1988. 20/20 does not always mean perfect. *Teaching K–8.*

Rey, P. D., and S. Steiner. 1976. Pursuit-motor performance of deaf and hearing girls. *Research Quarterly* 47: 184–87.

Ross, M., D. Brackett, and A. Maxon. 1982. *Hard-of-hearing children in regular schools.* Englewood Cliffs, NJ: Prentice-Hall.

Scholl, G. T., ed. 1986. *Foundations of education for blind and visually handicapped children and youth.* New York: American Foundation for the Blind.

Spungin, S. J., ed. 1975. *Precollege programs for blind and visually handicapped students.* New York: American Foundation for the Blind.

Stevens, S. S., and F. Warshofsky. 1975. *Sound and hearing.* New York: Time-Life Books.

Swallow, R. M., ed. 1977. *Assessment for visually handicapped children and youth.* New York: American Foundation for the Blind.

Swallow, R. M. 1981. Fifty assessment instruments commonly used with blind and partially seeing individuals. *Journal of Visual Impairment and Blindness* 75: 65–72.

Tanabe, K. 1972. Use of Gesell Scale of gross motor development as it relates to deaf-blind children. In *Role of Physical and Occupational Therapy in Meeting the Needs of the Deaf-Blind Child: Workshop Proceedings*, edited by June Horsley. Omaha, Nebraska.

Taylor, C. 1974. *Rhythm: A guide for creative movement.* Palo Alto: Peek Publications.

Telesensory Systems, Inc. 1978. Efficient optacon reading. In *Optacon Teacher Seminar.* Palo Alto, CA: Author.

Whitaker, S., M. Stevens, K. C. Moore, and E. Kiernan. 1991. Communication therapy: It's not all talk. *Cotting Update* 1(3): 5.

Workman, S. 1988. Developing visual skills. *Teaching K–8.*

Zelski, R. F., and T. Zelski. 1985. What are assistive devices? *Hearing Instruments* 36: 12.

CHAPTER 6

Cardiovascular Disorders

Objectives
After reading this chapter, you should be able to

- Identify the major structures and functions of the heart and the vascular system.

- Describe the various screening techniques available for assessing cardiovascular efficiency.

- Discuss the etiology and incidence of major cardiovascular disorders.

- State the classifications of heart functions as defined in accordance with expected capability levels.

- State the underlying principles that guide the prescription of physical education activities.

- Explain the value of appropriately selected and medically approved developmental activities for those with cardiac disorders.

INTRODUCTION

Of all the anomalies found within the school-age population, **heart disease** evokes the most interest and controversy. One explanation is that an inappropriate activity prescription could affect the student's capacity for rehabilitation. In addition, heart disease continues to lead the causes of death each year. We therefore have good reason to exercise extreme care when considering the direction that a cardiac management program should take, Figure 6.1.

Whereas research has revealed rather consistent relationships between cardiovascular response and physical activity among adults (Taylor and Baranowski 1991), there appears to be inconsistency in findings as they relate to studies carried out among school-age children. Some studies have demonstrated relationships (Saris et al. 1980; Watson and O'Donovan 1977; Weymans et al. 1986), while others have not (Ilmarinen and Rutenfranz, 1980; Kobayashi et al. 1978; Mirwald and Bailey 1986; and Mirwald et al. 1981). Factors

```
                              KEY TERMS
```

acquired (disorders)	heart disease
aerobic (fitness)	heart murmur
aorta	heart muscle
aortic artery	hypertensive heart
arteriocardiogram	myocardial infarction
atrial septal defect	patent ductus arteriosus
atrium	physical education screening
ballistocardiogram	prognosis
blood pressure	prosthesis
cardiac cycle	pulmonary artery
cardiovascular disorders	pulmonary stenosis
coarctation of the aorta	pulmonary vein
coronary heart disease	pulse rate
diagnosis	rheumatic heart disease
diastolic pressure	stethoscope
dorsiflexion	systolic pressure
electrocardiogram	therapeutic classes
exercise prescriptions	transposition of great vessels
Fallot's tetralogy	ventricular septal defect
formal medical screening	ventricle

Condition	Percentage of Total
Major cardiovascular	37.65%
Cancer	20.03%
Accidents	3.82%
Chronic Pulmonary	3.40%
Diabetes	1.88%
Suicide	1.26%
Others	31.97%

Figure 6.1. Leading causes of death in the United States. *From National Office of Vital Statistics, Washington, D. C.*

contributing to this discrepancy, however, may not be as much a function of intersubject variability (e.g., anthropometrics, baseline fitness levels, age ranges, and gender), but rather the design of the research (e.g., sample size and threats to internal validity, including history, instrumentation, regression, and expectancy) and the integrity of using self-reports as a basis for drawing inferences. Something to which everyone seems to agree, however, is that appropriate exercise and a healthy heart muscle go hand in hand.

Located between the lungs and the upper chest, the **heart muscle** is a machine far less complex in structure than we might imagine, Figure 6.2. The right and left **ventricles** of the heart are the pumping chambers. They pump the blood into the body through two large arteries: the **pulmonary artery** and the **aorta**. The pulmonary artery supplies blood to the lungs, and the aorta—through its numerous branches—carries blood to the other organs of the body. The two chambers of the heart that accept blood that has circulated through the body are the right **atrium** (*aay-tree-um*), which receives the venous (dark) blood through the vena cava, and the left atrium, which receives the arterial (red) blood from the lungs through the **pulmonary veins**. The atria respond to the heart's own system of stimulation which, comprised of specialized muscles, generates and regulates the electrical impulses that keep the heart beating. Every complete beat of the heart requires the atria to contract while the ventricles (the lower chambers) relax. While the ventricles contract, there is relaxation of the atria. This pumping action, called the **cardiac cycle**, creates the 'lub dub' sounds that are heard through a **stethoscope**.

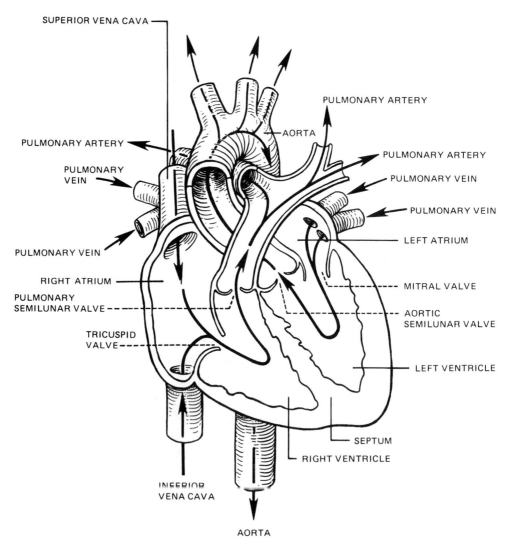

Figure 6.2. The normal heart. *Reproduced with permission. "If Your Child Has a Congenital Heart Defect," 1991. Copyright American Heart Association.*

In sequence the blood flows through the right heart to the lungs, back to the left heart, and then to the rest of the body.

It is inappropriate to generalize about **cardiovascular disorders** for the purposes of predicting a student's functional limitations. In this regard, the *Encyclopedia of Sports Sciences and Medicine* of the American College of Sports Medicine (1971) reports that

> The discovery of a systolic murmur...in a young adult does not per se permit definitive evaluation of his ability to perform physical activity. Likewise, the finding of an abnormal electrocardiogram or changes in heart size or configuration by X-ray may not be sufficient to estimate physical fitness of the heart and blood vessel system.

We must make an appropriate activity prescription after considering the idiosyncrasies of each student's heart structure. Every child should be given the opportunity to participate in activities that have been selected in accordance with his/her capacity. During the 1960s, two to three weeks of bed rest were recommended for a person who acquired a **myocardial infarction.*** Today, the dangers of prolonged bed rest are well documented. Those with uncomplicated conditions [no evidence of absence of rhythm (arrhythmia), congestive heart failure, or shock] progress rapidly with a supervised program of increased activity (Phipps, Long, and Wood, 1983). With modernization of therapeutic, medicinal, and surgical cardiovascular techniques, individuals who formerly may have participated minimally may find that higher levels of activity are possible and in fact encouraged.

Although the reaction of the heart to selected stress gradients can be assessed through the use of an **electrocardiogram** (Figure 6.3), additional screening procedures provide a more complete basis upon which to prescribe levels of activity.

SCREENING

Formal Medical Screening
Formal medical procedures, usually performed by health care professionals, include **arteriocardiograms, ballistocardiograms, blood pressure** measurements, and **pulse rate** measurements.

If a student has a history of a heart problem or experiences shortness of breath, cyanosis, dizziness, irregular and accentuated heartbeat, or increased sensitivity to temperature changes, **formal medical screening** procedures are appropriate.

Arteriocardiogram The arteriocardiogram (angiogram) is performed by injecting the arteries with a radiopaque substance in order to make them visible on X-ray film. This procedure helps to demonstrate whether there is a narrowing of the space (lumen) within the artery (Thompson 1971).

Ballistocardiogram The ballistocardiogram records the body's reaction (recoil) to the contraction of the heart and subsequent ejection of blood into the aorta. Exceedingly small movements are amplified and recorded by an electrocardiographic machine after

---

* Development of tissue damage in the heart muscle (myocardium) usually due to local or temporary obstruction in a coronary artery

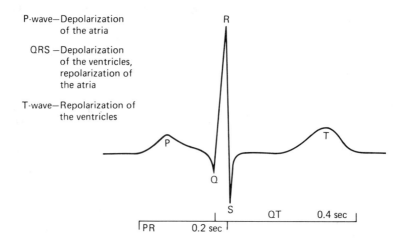

Figure 6.3. The pattern of one normal heartbeat

Note: An atrial flutter that is abnormal refers to a situation in which its rhythm accelerated to between 240 and 360 beats per minute. When atrial contractions become too rapid and irregular, they are called atrial fibrillations. This occurs when a person is having a heart attack. Fibrillations can also occur in the ventricles (ventricular fibrillations).

being translated by a pickup device into an electrical potential. This technique is used as a basis for calculating cardiac output (Stedman's Medical Dictionary 1972).

Blood Pressure Blood pressure is the amount of force that exists in selected larger arteries at the height of the pulse wave. It is the pressure exerted by the blood on the wall of the vessel. A sphygmomanometer is used to measure the ratio between the **systolic** (action phase) **pressure** and the **diastolic** (resting phase) **pressure**, Figure 6.4.

Upon transcription the systolic pressure is the numerator in the ratio. This number is influenced by the age, gender, muscular development, and degree of emotional and physical stress of the person and by the altitude at which the measurement is taken. As a general rule, blood pressure is lower in women than in men and lower in childhood than in old age. According to Thomas (1989) the following three findings would be considered atypical:

1. Systolic pressure persistently above 140
2. Diastolic pressure persistently above 100
3. Pulse pressure constantly greater than 50 (B-43)

See Table 6.1 for estimated normal blood pressures.

Pulse Rate Pulse rate is the regular contraction and alternate expansion of an artery as a result of heartbeat. This rate is usually between sixty-eight and seventy-two beats per minute. Younger children's pulse rates are a bit higher than that because stroke volumes are not yet at mature levels. The rates of conditioned athletes are generally lower as a result of greater stroke volume. In a properly nourished person the stronger the heart is, the more blood can be pumped with each beat, and consequently the less frequently the heart has to beat.

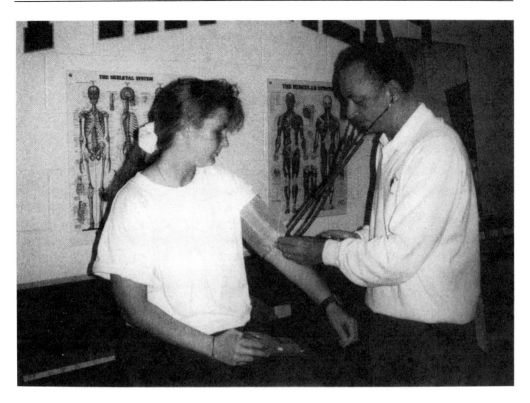

Figure 6.4. The sphygmomanometer is used to measure the ratio between the systolic and the diastolic pressure.

TABLE 6.1

Normal Blood Pressures (Estimates)

Age	Systolic Range			Diastolic Range		
	Minimum	*Average*	*Maximum*	*Minimum*	*Average*	*Maximum*
15–19	105	117	129	73	77	81
20–24	108	120	132	75	79	83
25–29	109	121	133	76	80	84
30–34	110	122	134	77	81	85
35–39	110	123	135	78	82	86
40–44	112	125	137	79	83	87
45–49	115	127	139	80	84	88
50–54	116	129		81	85	89
55–59	118	131		82	86	90
60–64	121	134		83	87	91

TABLE 6.1

Age	Average Systolic Blood Pressure	
---	Boys	Girls
5	80	85
6	85	86
7	89	89
8	92	92
9	95	93
10	95+	96
11	96	100
12	98	102
13	101	103
14	106	104
15	110	106
16	112	107
17	112	103
18	113	101
19	117	105

The pulse is ordinarily measured in the radial artery. In correct pulse assessments,

1. The subject's arm should be parallel to the floor, perhaps resting on a table/ counter top, as an elevated or lowered limb is likely to affect the reading.
2. The examiner's index and second fingers of one hand should be used when taking the pulse (the thumb should not be used).
3. Pressure of the fingers on the artery should not be so great as to impede circulation.
4. The pulse should be counted for fifteen seconds and multiplied by four, or thirty seconds and multiplied by two in order to calculate the heart rate per minute, Figure 6.5.

Exercise Prescriptions

Once the student has undergone formal screening and his or her physician has had the opportunity to collect, review, and analyze the data, rest, rehabilitative, instructional, or recreational activities can be prescribed. Specific activities are then prescribed by the physican in consort with the physical education specialist. The following outline contains guidelines for **exercise prescriptions**:

I. Assessment
    A. Cardiovascular capacity
        1. Steady state
        2. Non-steady state
    B. Strength and endurance
        1. Arms
        2. Legs
        3. Torso

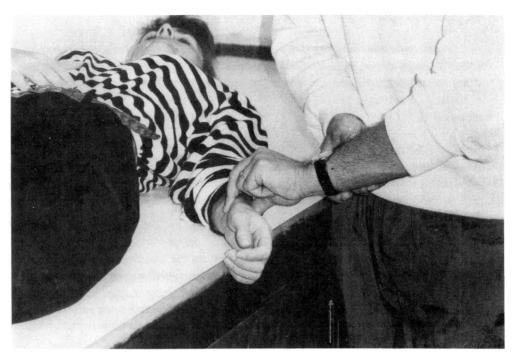

Figure 6.5. Taking pulse counts

      C. Flexibility
      D. Medical history
      E. Motivation
      F. Prognosis
  II. Prescription criteria
      A. Heart rate
      B. Blood pressure
      C. Electrocardiogram changes
      D. Caloric demands
      E. Clinical observations
      F. Potential for change
      G. Availability of trained personnel
      H. Pleasurableness
 III. Program
      A. Supervision
      B. Safety
      C. Format
         1. Warm-up
         2. Activities (content)
         3. Tapering-off period
      D. Reevaluation
      E. Revision

As Naughton and Hellerstein (1973) point out:

> Physical reconditioning should be part of a comprehensive treatment program which includes supervision; periodic reevaluation; diet to improve nutrition and attain normal body weight and serum lipids; abstinence from the use of tobacco, ...medication when indicated,...as well as attention to psychologic and social adjustment.

Physical Education Screening

Many screening procedures can be administered by physical education practitioners to assess the cardiovascular efficiency of students with normal, healthy hearts. Three of the most widely used **physical education screening** strategies are the **aerobic** step dance, the distance run, and the Harvard Step Test.

Aerobic step dance Using the aerobic step dance, the pulse rates are monitored on a regular basis in order to ascertain changes prompted by the cardiovascular requirements of the movements. As subjects increase their experiences with the movements over time, pulse rates will decrease as stroke volumes increase. Screening enables the instructor to establish target heart rates based upon stress levels observed during prior performance.

Although many aerobics programs assess heart rates in a very informal, random way, the refinement of exercise requirements and regular assessments of heart rates will increase the reliability of the findings. From these determinations, target stress levels can be modified in order to meet the needs of the subjects.

The distance run According to Cooper (1977) the distance run is very reliable for assessing the efficiency of the heart. Although criteria for judging fitness levels pursuant to performance on a nine-minute run are available, the reader will find reliability of placements to be at least as high when students are subjected to a twelve-minute run. In Table 6.2 you can find the aerobic fitness classifications of students by noting the distances they can run in twelve minutes.

The Harvard Step Test The Harvard Step test was developed at the Harvard Fatigue Laboratory by David Dill and his associates. With attention to prescribed techniques it is possible to administer the five-minute test in a school setting with no special equipment other than a bench twenty inches high and a stopwatch.* (For testing a group, a large wall clock with a sweep second hand will suffice.) Scoring is based upon duration of effort (measured to the nearest thirty seconds) and total pulse beat one and one-half minutes following cessation of the test, Table 6.3. The following norms have been established to allow for the relative placement of the students being examined:

Good— above 80
Average— 50-80
Poor— below 50

---

* The bench may be sixteen inches high for girls between the ages of 12 and 18; fourteen inches high for boys and girls under 12.

TABLE 6.2

Twelve-minute Walking/Running Test: Distance (Miles) Covered in Twelve Minutes

Fitness Category		Age (Years)					
		13–19	*20–29*	*30–39*	*40–49*	*50–59*	*60+*
I. Very	(Men)	<1.30	<1.22	<1.18	<1.14	<1.03	< .87
poor	(Women)	<1.0	< .96	< .94	< .88	< .84	< .78
II. Poor	(Men)	1.30–1.37	1.22–1.31	1.18–1.30	1.14–1.24	1.03–1.16	.87–1.02
	(Women)	1.00–1.18	.96–1.11	.95–1.05	.88–.98	.84–.93	.78–.86
III. Fair	(Men)	1.38-1.56	1.32-1.49	1.31–1.45	1.25–1.39	1.17–1.30	1.03–1.20
	(Women)	1.19–1.29	1.12–1.22	1.06–1.18	.99–1.11	.94–1.05	.87–.98
IV. Good	(Men)	1.57–1.72	1.50–1.64	1.46–1.56	1.40–1.53	1.31–1.41	1.21–1.32
	(Women)	1.30–1.43	1.23–1.34	1.19–1.29	1.12–1.24	1.06–1.18	.99–1.09
V. Excellent	(Men)	1.73–1.86	1.65–1.76	1.57–1.69	1.54–1.65	1.45–1.58	1.33–1.55
	(Women)	1.44–1.51	1.35–1.45	1.30–1.39	1.25–1.34	1.19–1.30	1.10–1.18
VI. Superior	(Men)	>1.87	>1.77	>1.70	>1.66	>1.59	>1.56
	(Women)	>1.52	>1.46	>1.40	>1.35	>1.31	>1.19

Source: From the *Aerobics Way* by Kenneth H. Cooper. © 1977 by Kenneth H. Cooper. Used by permission of Bantam Books, a division of Bantam Doubleday Dell Publishing Group, Inc.

TABLE 6.3

Scoring for the Harvard Step Test

	Heartbeats 1 1/2 Minutes Into Recovery											
	40–44	45–49	50–54	55–59	60–64	65–69	70–74	75–79	80–84	85–89	90–94	95–99
Duration of effort (minutes)					Score (Arbitrary Units)							
0–1/2	6	6	5	5	4	4	4	4	3	3	3	3
1/2–1	19	17	16	14	13	12	11	11	10	9	9	8
1–1 1/2	32	29	26	24	22	20	19	18	17	16	15	14
1 1/2–2	45	41	38	34	31	29	27	25	23	22	21	20
2–2 1/2	58	52	47	43	40	36	34	32	30	28	27	25
2 1/2–3	71	64	58	53	48	45	42	39	37	34	33	31
3–3 1/2	84	75	68	62	57	53	49	46	43	41	39	37
3 1/2–4	97	87	79	72	66	61	57	53	50	47	45	42
4–4 1/2	110	98	89	82	75	70	65	61	57	54	51	48
4 1/2–5	123	110	100	91	84	77	72	68	63	60	57	54
5	129	116	105	96	88	82	76	71	67	63	60	56

Source: From Conzolazio, Johnson, and Pecora (1963).

To take the step test, the student stands in front of a bench and on command steps up to the bench with one foot then the other. On count three the student steps down with the lead foot and on count four with the trailing foot. This exercise is repeated at a rate of thirty four-count routines per minute for up to five minutes. Oral cadence may be counted by the testing supervisor or by a pretaped recording.

ETIOLOGY AND INCIDENCE OF CARDIOVASCULAR DISORDERS

At one time it was thought that an enlarged heart was automatically pathological, i.e., caused by a disease. Cardiovascular-type exercise was therefore contraindicated. Subsequently, however, it was learned that the heart, because it is a muscle, can enlarge as a result of exercise. Marathon runners have been found to have larger than normal hearts. Runners are considered by many to have healthier hearts and greater cardio-vascular efficiency levels than most other trained athletes, Figure 6.6. Heart enlargement, then, is not necessarily pathological. But there are anomalies that can affect heart size, structure, and function.

Figure 6.6. Endurance-type activity

Congenital Disorders

Heart diseases may be congenital or acquired. It is has been estimated that of every one thousand live births, one has a defective cardiovascular system (Hardman et al. 1990). Although an examination of trends will reveal improvement, a large number of these children die within the first year of life. Of those who survive the first year of life it is believed that one in thirty thousand has a heart anomaly. More than 90 percent of these congenital disorders are among those discussed in the following sections.

Ventricular Septal Defect Ventricular septal defects occur in the wall that separates the ventricles of the heart. The anomaly is a result of the failure of the lower embryonic septum to merge with the upper embryonic septum. Although a small opening may not significantly affect normal pumping action, too large an opening can do so.

Pulmonary Stenosis Pulmonary stenosis is an obstruction of flow between the right ventricle and the pulmonary artery. If the obstruction occurs within the right ventricle below the valve, the resulting malformation is often classified as a ventricular septal defect. According to Selzer (1966) the obstruction is often an isolated lesion resulting from an error in fetal development that occurs after the septum is closed.

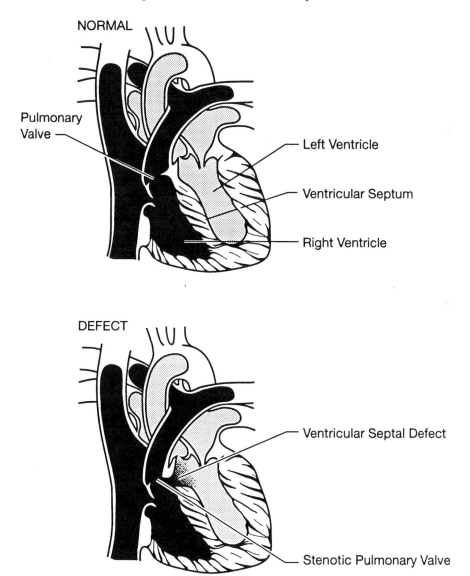

Figure 6.7. Fallot's tetralogy. *Reproduced with permission. "If Your Child Has a Congenital Heart Defect," 1991. Copyright American Heart Association.*

Fallot's Tetralogy   **Fallot's tetraolgy** is considered to be the most common congenital heart dysfunction. It is a result of four disorders:

1. Ventricular septal defect
2. Pulmonary stenosis
3. Inappropriate positioning of the **aortic artery**—it overrides the left and right ventricles instead of just the left ventricle
4. Enlarged right ventricle

The **diagnosis** and **prognosis** depend on the severity of the disorders contributing to the tetralogy, separately or in combination, Figure 6.7. A label commonly applied to a newborn with Fallot's tetralogy is *blue baby*.

Atrial Septal Defect   An **atrial septal defect** is a condition caused by improper closure of the septum during the formative stage of heart development. Its location may vary, and its severity depends on the amount of blood passing (shunted) through the space, Figure 6.8.

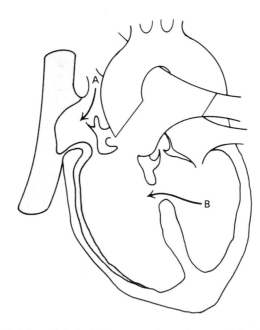

Figure 6.8. Atrial septal defect. A hole (*A*) between the atria causes blood to shunt to the right side of the heart. (*B*) indicates site of ventricular septal defect, a hole in the septum that separates the two ventricles (pumping chambers).

In general, it is thought that consequences of an atrial septal defect are twofold:

1. In children, increase in blood flow through the lungs is associated with chance of respiratory infections.
2. Extended overfilling of the pulmonary vessels may increase pressure within the pulmonary artery.

More research is needed before definitive claims can be made with respect to these theories.

Patent Ductus Arteriosus All children are born with the ductus arteriosus open. **Patent ductus arteriosus** results from the failure of this path (channel) to close normally during further heart development, Figure 6.9.

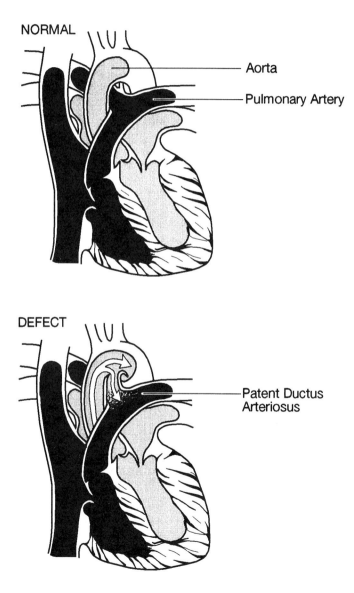

Figure 6.9. Patent ductus arteriosus. *Reproduced with permission. "If Your Child Has a Congenital Heart Defect," 1991. Copyright American Heart Association.*

This defect is common in infants whose mothers had German measles (rubella) early in pregnancy. If not diagnosed, patent ductus arteriosus can result in serious consequences, even death. If recognized and surgically treated, patients can expect to lead normal, active lives.

Coarctation of the Aorta **Coarctation of the aorta** is a constriction (narrowing) of the aorta at a point where in the fetus the ductus arteriosus enters the aorta. Consequently there is an increase in blood pressure, particularly in the upper extremities. The result is a **hypertensive heart**. Corrective surgery consists of removing the narrowed portion of the aorta and suturing the healthy ends. When suturing is contraindicated, a **prosthesis** is used to connect the two ends of the aorta.

Transposition of Great Vessels Because of the seriousness of **transposition of the great vessels**, few individuals survive it beyond the first year of life. The pulmonary artery may be located to the rear of the aorta instead of the other way around. Transposition of the great vessels also occurs if

1. the aorta originates from the right ventricle and the pulmonary artery originates from both ventricles.
2. both the aorta and the pulmonary artery originate from the right ventricle.

Acquired Disorders

The most common of the various **acquired** heart conditions are

1. **rheumatic heart disease**
2. hypertensive heart
3. **coronary heart disease** (New York Heart Association 1970).

Rheumatic Heart Disease Rheumatic heart disease is a consequence of damage caused by a hemolytic streptococcal infection. One or more valves may be affected to the extent that they contain scar tissue and as a result do not open and close normally. Rheumatic fever is one of the major causes of chronic heart disease in children.

Rheumatic fever does not always result in rheumatic heart disease. In fact it has been estimated that approximately one-third of rheumatic fever patients will develop heart disease. According to Silber (1987) this accounts for between 0.7 and 2.0 youngsters per 1,000 of those with normal heart function. Rheumatic fever can, however, affect many other tissues and organs of the body. Some of these effects are

1. Swelling of the larger joints of the body: knees, elbows, ankles, and hips
2. Small lumps or rashes under the epidermis (the outer layer of skin)
3. Involuntary and uncoordinated movements of the face and the extremities (often referred to as chorea or Saint Vitus' dance).
4. Respiratory tissue involvement to the extent that pneumonia may develop

Hypertensive Heart Hypertensive heart is not necessarily associated with high blood pressure. If untreated, however, high blood pressure may lead to dysfunction within the circulatory system. The left ventricle may have to work harder to pump blood through the body, and the arterial system in general becomes subject to increased stress. Whenever the walls of a vessel are forced to resist unusual pressure, there is the probability that weaknesses may develop.

Coronary Heart Disease Coronary heart disease is hardening of the inner walls of an artery (arteriosclerosis) or hardening of the arteries accompanied by the deposit of fat (lipids) in the inner arterial walls (atherosclerosis).*

Conditions that increase susceptibility to coronary heart disease include

1. Aging, because of the increased potential for bearing physical and emotional stress as the years progress
2. Diabetes mellitus, associated with deficient insulin secretion leading to excess sugar in the blood
3. Excessive cigarette smoking
4. High blood pressure
5. Increased levels of cholesterol and/or triglycerides (blood lipids)

Of the various cardiovascular disorders that have been described, congenital and rheumatic heart defects are the two most prevalent conditions to be found among the school-age population. Hypertension and coronary heart disease are most often a feature of aging and are more likely to be found among individuals over forty-five.

Heart Murmurs

Heart murmurs can be congenital or acquired, functional or structural. Functional heart murmurs are sounds apparently caused by rapid circulation of blood across normal heart valves. This condition is not particularly unusual. It can be distinguished from the structural murmur in which, because of a leaking or too-narrow valve, the heart must force a small stream of blood across that valve at great speeds. A physician can determine whether a murmur is functional or structural by assessing the timing of each murmur within the heartbeat. If a structural murmur is present, surgery, medication, or therapeutic exercise will probably be recommended.

CLASSIFICATION OF CARDIAC DISEASE

The New York Heart Association (1970) has classified cardiac disease patients according to symptoms they experience during various intensities of exercise. These classifications are as follows:

Class I— Patients with cardiac disease but with no limitations of physical activity. Ordinary physical activity causes no anginal pain, dyspnea, fatigue, or palpitation.

Class II— Patients with slight limitation of physical activity. Although physical activity results in anginal pain, dyspnea, fatigue, and palpitation, patients are comfortable at rest.

Class III— Patients with marked limitation of physical activity. They are comfortable at rest, but even mild activity yields negative symptoms.

Class IV— Patients who are unable to carry on any physical activity without discomfort. Symptoms of cardiac insufficiency or anginal syndrome are likely to be present even during periods of rest. Negative symptoms would be increased if physical activity were undertaken.

---

* When the arteries supplying blood to the brain are involved, a stroke may result. When the involvement is in the coronary arteries, angina pectoris (chest pain) may result—symptom of a heart attack.

In the 7th edition of *Nomenclature and Criteria for Diagnosis of Diseases of the Heart and Great Vessels*, a further classification—relevant to therapeutic exercise—was described. These **therapeutic classes** are:

Class A— Patients with a cardiac disease whose ordinary physical activity need not be restricted

Class B— Patients with cardiac disease whose ordinary physical activity need not be restricted, but who should be advised against severe or competitive physical activity

Class C— Patients with cardiac disease whose ordinary physical activity should be moderately restricted and whose more strenuous efforts should be discontinued

Class D— Patients with cardiac disease whose ordinary physical activity should be considerably restricted

Class E— Patients with cardiac disease who should be at complete rest

All physical education prescriptions for cardiac patients must be approved by the attending physician in advance of their implementation. Additional principles we should consider when choosing appropriate activities are as follows

1. No single exercise is appropriate for all individuals. Consider each person's unique needs.
2. The frequency and duration of the exercise should be governed by the individual's current status. If a student has a low endurance threshold at first, include some form of jogging or low-impact aerobic step dancing in his/her prescription.
3. The intensity of the exercise should be between 50 percent and 80 percent of the student's endurance capacity. Endurance capacity can be determined by assessing pulse rate at various workout intensities. For example, if a physician determines that a student's optimal heart rate endurance capacity is 150 beats per minute (BPM), the training heart rate (THR) should not exceed 120 BPM (75–120 BPM range).
4. For individuals in therapeutic classes C, D, or E, it may be necessary to limit exercises to those that can be performed standing (class C), sitting (class D), or lying down (class E).
5. How well the individual's heart reacts to an exercise prescription will help you determine the alterations to be made and the progression to be followed.

DEVELOPMENTAL ACTIVITIES

Before a student with a cardiovascular disorder begins a physical education program, he/she must undergo a thorough medical examination—including a graded exercise stress test,—and must have a physician's referral. (See Chapter 3 for a review of pertinent medical forms.) Only then may the student participate in physician-approved activities. In all instances the selection, frequency, intensity, and duration of developmental exercises must be compatible with the structural and functional characteristics of the individual's current cardiac capacity.

The developmental activities that follow are appropriate as specified for those with selected cardiovascular disorders.

I. Cardiovascular Development (Therapeutic Class E)

Major Objective	*Interim Performance Objective*

1. Deep breathing

    1.1 Control rate and extent of inhalation and exhalation (lying/supine position).

        1.1A Inhale one-half perceived maximum capacity.

        1.1B Exhale.

        1.1C Inhale three-quarters perceived maximum capacity.

        1.1D Exhale.

        1.1E Inhale perceived maximum capacity.

        1.1F Exhale.

        1.1G Relax.

        1.1H Repeat progressive inhalations.
            1.1Ha Hold each inhalation three seconds.
            1.1Hb Hold each inhalation five seconds.

        1.1I Relax.

2. Relaxation

    2.1 Relax selected body parts progressively (lying/supine position).

        2.1A Ankles and feet
            2.1Aa Point toes downward (plantar flexion).
            2.1Ab Point toes upward (**dorsiflexion**).
            2.1Ac Relax.

        2.1B Knees
            2.1Ba Flex moderately.
            2.1Bb Relax.

        2.1C Hips and abdomen
            2.1Ca Press small of back against support.
            2.1Cb Relax.

        2.1D Chest
            2.1Da Inhale one-half perceived maximum capacity; exhale.
            2.1Db Relax.

Major Objective	*Interim Performance Objective*
	2.1E Neck
	2.1Ea Tighten neck muscles.
	2.1Eb Relax.
	2.1F Shoulders
	2.1Fa Elevate (shrug) shoulders.
	2.1Fb Relax.
	2.1G Elbows
	2.1Ga Flex moderately.
	2.1Gb Relax.
	2.1H Wrists and hands
	2.1Ha Flex; relax.
	2.1Hb Extend; relax.

II. Goal: Cardiovascular Development (Therapeutic Class D)

Major Objective	*Interim Performance Objective*
1. Deep breathing	1.1 Control rate and extent of inhalation and exhalation with progressive abduction of the arms (sitting position).
	1.1A Inhale one-half perceived maximum capacity with arms elevated 90° from sides.
	1.1B Exhale; return arms to original position.
	1.1C Inhale three-quarters perceived maximum capacity with arms elevated 130°–140° from sides.
	1.1D Exhale, return arms to original position.
	1.1E Inhale perceived maximum capacity with arms elevated 180° from sides (above head).
	1.1F Exhale; return arms to original position.
	1.1G Relax.
	1.1H Repeat progressive inhalations and arm elevations
	1.1Ha Hold each inhalation three seconds.
	1.1Hb Hold each inhalation five seconds.
	1.1I Relax.

Major Objective	*Interim Performance Objective*

2. Relaxation

2.1 Relax selected body parts progressively (sitting on a chair), knees bent at 90°, feet flat on floor, elbows and forearms on armrest.

    2.1A Ankles and feet
        2.1Aa Elevate heels.
        2.1Ab Elevate toes.
        2.1Ac Relax.

    2.1B Knees
        2.1Ba Slide away from chair to increase joint angle.
        2.1Bb Return; relax.

    2.1C Hips and abdomen
        2.1Ca Press small of back against chair back.
        2.1Cb Relax.

    2.1D Chest
        2.1Da Inhale perceived maximum capacity while hyperextending back.
        2.1Db Exhale; relax.

    2.1E Neck
        2.1Ea Rotate.
        2.1Eb Relax.

    2.1F Shoulders
        2.1Fa Elevate.
        2.1Fb Relax.

    2.1G Elbows
        2.1Ga Flex; bring hands to shoulder.
        2.1Gb Return; relax.

    2.1H Wrists and hands
        2.1Ha Hyperextend wrist; form fist.
        2.1Hb Relax.

III. Goal: Cardiovascular Development (Therapeutic Class C)

Major Objective	*Interim Performance Objective*

1. Elevate heart rate to appropriate conditioning level.

1.1 Control heart rate by controlling extent of work performed.

    1.1A Ride stationary bicycle.
        1.1Aa Monitor speed.
        1.1Ab Monitor heart rate.

Major Objective	*Interim Performance Objective*
	1.1B Walk on treadmill.
	1.1Ba Monitor inclination and speed.
	1.1Bb Monitor heart rate.
	1.1C Jog (Treadmill or track).
	1.1Ca Control own distance and speed.
	1.1Cb Monitor heart rate.

IV. Goal: Cardiovascular Development (Therapeutic Class B)

Major Objective	*Interim Performance Objective*
1. Applied Fartlek (speed play) training	1.1 Alternate jogging with sprinting while controlling pulse level and physiological fatigue, Figure 6.10.

                                       1.1A Job selected distance/time.

1.1B Sprint selected distance/time.

1.1C Walk and record pulse.

1.1D Jog shorter distance/time.

1.1E Sprint longer distance/time.

1.1F Walk and record pulse.

1.1G Repeat sequence.

Figure 6.10. Aerobic step dance as an alternative to jogging and sprinting

V. Goal: Cardiovascular Development (Therapeutic Class A)

Major Objective	*Interim Performance Objective*
1. Applied interval training	1.1 Discover distance and running time necessary to elevate heart rate to 180 BPM.

1.1A Select distance and time.

1.1B Jog to warm up, then run to selected point.

1.1C Walk and record pulse.
    1.1Ca Allow pulse to drop to 120 BPM.
    1.1Cb Select new target distance if necessary.

Major Objective	*Interim Performance Objective*
	1.1D Alternate run (to 180 BPM) and walk (to 120 BPM) for four trials.
	1.1E Increase distance to elicit 180 BPM heart-rate response with instructor's permission.

Note: Under ordinary circumstances, students in Class A could perform activities suitable for therapeutic Classes A through E; students in Class B could perform activities suitable for therapeutic Classes B through E; students in Class C could perform activities suitable for therapeutic Classes C through E; students in Class D could perform activities suitable for therapeutic Classes D through E

SUMMARY

In order to understand the role of exercise in cardiovascular health, it is necessary to familiarize oneself with the various factors contributing to optimum heart structure and function. In Chapter 6 you were presented with information on the anatomy of the heart; normal blood flow, pressure, and rate; assessment procedures; and common acquired and congenital disorders.

The New York Heart Association has suggested criteria by which individuals with heart dysfunction can be classified according to the symptoms they express. Utilizing these guidelines, physician-approved developmental activities can be prescribed. A sample of these activities is presented for the various therapeutic classifications. Carefully examine these options with a view toward their implementation, as appropriate.

I once heard it said that just the thought of exercise can cause one's heart rate to increase. Although this may be the case for some, it is not the preferred way to generate optimum heart function and response. A knowledge of this chapter's contents will go a long way to facilitate the acquisition of pertinent goals and objectives for those needing and wanting improved health.

RECOMMENDED LABORATORY ASSIGNMENTS

1. Arrange to visit hospitals and school agencies that accommodate persons with cardiovascular dysfunctions in order to discuss successful methods and materials used by instructors who work there.
2. Interview physicians, teachers, and patients to ascertain their respective perceptions as to successful care, treatment, and rehabilitative methods and materials being used.
3. Perform Cooper's nine- and/or twelve-minute runs and the Harvard Step Test. Record and analyze related data.
4. Participate in low-, moderate- and/or high-impact aerobic exercise programs in order to gain insights as to their value in cardiovascular conditioning.

5. Perform the developmental activities described in this chapter. Identify other developmental activities that could be used by those in need of cardiovascular development or maintenance.

6. Arrange to observe the administration of an electrocardiogram. Observe and record testing procedures.

7. Complete a course in cardiopulmonary resuscitation (CPR).

8. Arrange to be put on the mailing list of local, regional, and national heart associations in order to keep abreast of current developments in cardiac rehabilitation and care.

9. Become certified to administer and/or assist with cardiovascular stress tests.

10. Review the recommended readings.

REFERENCES

The American College of Sports Medicine. 1971. *Encyclopedia of sport sciences and medicine.* New York: Macmillan.

American Heart Association. 1991. *If your child has a congenital heart defect.* Dallas, TX: Author.

Conzolazio, C. F.,R. E. Johnson, and L. J. Pecora. 1963. *Physiological measurements of metabolic function in man.* New York: MCGraw Hill.

Cooper, K. H. 1977. *The aerobics way.* New York: M. Evans.

Hardman, M. L., C. J. Drew, M. W. Egan, and B. Wolf. 1990. *Human exceptionality.* 3d ed. Boston: Allyn and Bacon.

Ilmarinen, I., and J. Rutenfranz. 1980. Longitudinal studies of the changes in habitual physical activity of school children and working adolescents. *In Children and Exercise IX,* edited by K. Berg and B. Eriksson. Baltimore, MD: University Park Press.

Kobayashi, K., K. Kitamura, M, Miura, H. Sodeyama, Y Murase, M. Miyashita, and H. Matsui. 1978. Aerobic power as related to body growth and training in Japanese boys: A longitudinal study. *Journal of Applied Physiology* 44: 666–72.

Mirwald, R. L., and D. A. Bailey. 1986. *Maximal aerobic power.* London, Ontario: Sports Dynamics.

Mirwald, R. L., D. A. Bailey, N. Cameron, and R. L. Rasmussen. 1981. Longitudinal comparison of aerobic power in active and inactive boys aged 7.0 to 17.0 years. *Annals of Human Biology* 8: 405–14.

Naughton, J. P., and H. K. Hellerstein, ed. 1973. *Exercise testing and exercise training in coronary heart disease.* New York: Academic Press.

Nomenclature and criteria for diagnosis of diseases of the heart and great vessels. 7th ed. New York: New York Heart Association.

Phipps, W. J., B. C. Long, and N. F. Woods, eds. 1983. *Medical-surgical nursing: Concepts and clinical practice.* 2d ed. St. Louis: C. V. Mosby Company.

Saris, W. H., R. A. Binkhorst, A. B. Cramwinchel, F. van Waesberghe, and A. M. van der Veen-Hezemans. 1980. The relationship between working performance, daily physical activity, fatness, blood lipids, and nutrition in school-children. *In Children and Exercise IX,* edited by K. Berg and B. Ericksson. Baltimore, MD: University Park Press.

Selzer, A. 1966. *The heart: Its function in health and disease.* Berkeley: University of California Press.

Silber, E. N. 1987. *Heart disease.* New York: Macmillan Publishing Company.

Stedman's medical dictionary. 22nd ed. 1972. Baltimore: Williams and Wilkins.

Taylor, W., and T. Baranowski. 1991. Physical activity, cardiovascular fitness, and adiposity in children. *Research Quarterly for Exercise and Sport* 62(2): 157–63.

Thomas, C. L., ed. 1989. *Taber's cyclopedic medical dictionary*. 16th ed. Philadelphia: F. A. Davis Company.

Thompson, W. A. 1971. *Black's medical dictionary*. 29th ed. London: Adam and Charles Black.

Watson, A. W., and D. J. O'Donovan. 1977. Influence of level of habitual activity on physical working capacity and body composition of post-pubertal school boys. *Quarterly Journal of Experimental Psysiology* 62: 325–32.

Weymans, M. L., T. M/ Reybrouck, H. J. Stijns, and J. Knops. 1986. Influence of habitual levels of physical activity on the cardiorespiratory endurance capacity of children. In *Children and Exercise XII*, edited by J. Rutenfranz, R. Mocellin, and F. Flint. Champaign, 1L: Human Kinetics.

RECOMMENDED READINGS

Amsterdam, E. A., J. H. Wilmore, and A. N. DeMaria, eds. 1977. *Exercise in cardiovascular health and disease*. New York: Yorke Medical.

Astrand, P. O., and K. Rodahl. 1977. *Textbook of work physiology*. 2d ed. New York: McGraw-Hill.

Ballor, D. L., L. M. Burke, D. V. Knudson, J. R. Olson, and H. J. Montoye. 1989. Comparison of three methods of estimating energy expenditure: Caltrac, heart rate, and video analysis. *Research Quarterly for Exercise and Sport* 60:(4): 362–68.

Bonbright, J. M. 1990. Physiological and nutritional concerns in dance. *Journal of Physical Education, Recreation and Dance* 61(9): 35–37.

Brill, P. A., H. E. Burkhalter, H. W. Kohl, S. N. Blair, and N. N. Goodyear. 1989. The impact of previous athleticism on exercise habits, physical fitness, and coronary heart disease risk factors in middle-aged men. *Research Quarterly for Exercise and Sport* 60:(3): 209–15.

Cunningham, L. N. 1990. Relationship of running economy, ventilatory threshold, and maximal oxygen consumption to running performance in high school females. *Research Quarterly for Exercise and Sport* 61(4): 369–74.

Davis, R. 1991. Teaching stress management in an elementary classroom. Journal of Physical Education, Recreation and Dance 62(2): 65–66, 70.

deGruchy, G. C. 1978. Disorders of hemoglobin structure and synthesis. In *Clinical hematology in medical practice*, edited by D. Penington, B. Rush, and P. Castaldi. Oxford: Blackwell Scientific Publications.

Dinucci, J., D. McCune, and D. Shows. 1990. Reliability of a modification of the health-related physical fitness test for use with physical education majors. *Research Quarterly for Exercise and Sport* 61:(1): 20–25.

Draper, D. O., and G. L. Jones. 1990. The 1.5 mile run revisited—an update in women's times. Journal of Physical Education, Recreation and Dance 62(7): 78–80.

Elias, B. A., K. E. Berg, R. W. Latin, M. B. Mellion, and P. J. Hofschire. 1991. Cardiac structure and function in weight trainers, runners, and runner/weight trainers. Research Quarterly for Exercise and Sport 62(3): 326–32.

Evans, B., K. J. Cureton, and J. W. Purvis. 1978. Metabolic and circulatory responses to walking and jogging in water. *Research Quarterly* 49: 442–49.

Fletcher, G. F., and J. D. Cantwell. 1974. *Exercise and coronary heart disease*. Springfield, IL: Charles C. Thomas.

Gutgesell, H. P. 1978. Echocardiographic estimation of pulmonary artery pressure in transposition of the great arteries. *Circulation* 57: 1151–53.

Haskel, W. L. 1978. Cardiovascular complications during exercise training of cardiac patients. *Circulation* 57: 920–24.

Jackson, A., K. Der Weduwe, R. Schick, and R. Sanchez. 1990. An analysis of the validity of the three-mile run as a field test of aerobic capacity in college males. *Research Quarterly for Exercise and Sport* 61(3): 233–37.

Jokl, E., and J. T. McClellan, eds. 1971. *Exercise and cardiac death.* Baltimore: University Park Press.

Katch, B. L., T. Gilliam, and A. Weltman. 1978. Active versus passive recovery from short-term supramaximal exercise. *Research Quarterly* 49: 153–61.

Kremenitzer, J. P. 1990. Aerobic fitness dancing in the elementary schools. *Journal of Physical Education, Recreation and Dance* 61(6): 89–90.

Lavay, B., and M. Horvat. 1991. Jump rope for heart for special populations. *Journal of Physical Education, Recreation and Dance* 62(3): 74–78.

McKay, E. R., and J. A. Lucas. 1977. *Survey of need for an educational program for cardiac exercise technicians and leaders.* Palatine, IL: Office of Planning and Research, William Rainey Harper College.

Midtlyng, J. 1990. Aquatic fitness—waves of the future. *Journal of Physical Education, Recreation and Dance* 61(5): 41–43.

Mueller, L. M. 1990. What it means to be physically educated. *Journal of Physical Education, Recreation and Dance* 61(3): 100–1.

Noland, M., F. Danner, K. Dewalt, M. McFadden, and J. M. Kotchen. 1990. The measurement of physical activity in young children. *Research Quarterly for Exercise and Sport* 61(2): 146–53.

Reid, G. S. 1974. *A group therapy approach to the treatment of coronary heart patients.* Master's thesis. University of Saskatchewan.

Ross, J., and R. A. O'Rourke. 1976. *Understanding the heart and its diseases.* New York: McGraw-Hill.

Seaward, B. L., and A. M. Snelling. 1990. A marketing strategy for a campus wellness program. *Health Education* 21(5): 4–8.

Wilson, P. K., ed. 1975. *Adult fitness and cardiac rehabilitation.* Baltimore: University Park Press.

Wyness, G. B. 1990. Participation in a twelve-week moderate exercise program—selected physiological effects. *Journal of Physical Education, Recreation and Dance* 61(2): 65–68.

Zwiren, L. D., P. S. Freedson, A. Ward, S. Wilke, and J. M. Rippe. 1991. Estimation of VO_2 Max: A comparative analysis of five exercise tests. *Research Quarterly for Exercise and Sport* 62(1): 73–78.

CHAPTER 7

Musculoskeletal Disorders Acquired and Congenital

Objectives

After reading this chapter, you should be able to

- Know the common movements associated with the major joints of the body.
- Identify some structural congenital anomalies and discuss some possible causal factors.
- Describe temporary injuries common to muscles and bones.
- Describe various mechanical aids one can employ in order to enhance mobility.
- Discuss crutch techniques for mobility training.
- Describe activity-prescription principles for those with muscular disorders.

INTRODUCTION

The ability to run and participate vigorously in activities of our choice without restraint is one many of us take for granted. To the nearly sixty thousand **orthopedically impaired** individuals in the United States under the age of twenty-one who are served in special education programs, however, this is a luxury seldom enjoyed (U.S. Department of Education 1987).

Bones have three major functions:

1. *Protection*—e.g., the skull, which protects the brain; the ribs, which protect the lungs
2. *Support*—as made possible by the nature of the skeletal framework holding the body in an erect position

---

KEY TERMS

ambulation (ambulatory)	muscular dystrophy
amputations	musculoskeletal disorders
aplasia	myasthenia gravis
autosomal recessive trait	orthopedically impaired
bone disorders	ossification
braces	osteoarthritis
bursitis	osteochondrosis
clubfoot	osteomyelitis
congenital amputation	paralysis
congenital dislocation of the hip	plantar flexion
contraindicated	prosthetist
dislocation	range-of-motion activities
distal	rheumatoid arthritis
Erb's palsy	rhythmic patterning
fractures	rickets
gaits	self-care skills
habilitation	soft-sign tests
hypotonic	spina bifida
joint inflammation	spondylolisthesis
luxation	sprain
mobility	strain
mobility aids	subluxation
muscular atrophy	temporary acquired injuries
muscular disorders	

---

3. *Movement*—generated by muscles contracting and pulling bones as levers through various ranges of motion (see Chapter 2).

The muscles, bones, joints, supportive structure, and sensory and motor nerves all work in unison to provide controlled movement. Should a lesion or other anomaly arise that impacts upon either or all of these processes, optimum function of the musculoskeletal system is compromised (Phipps, Long, and Woods 1983).

Musculoskeletal disorders can range from a minor **sprain** to a quadruple **amputation**; from **bursitis** to **muscular dystrophy**. It is the responsibility of the physical education practitioner to know the common physical and behavioral characteristics, probable prognoses, and suggested activity prescriptions for children with various kinds of musculoskeletal disorders.

These disorders may be congenital or acquired. A congenital anomaly is one with which an individual is born. Acquired anomalies are conditions arising after birth from disease or injury. An amputation due to an accident is an example of an acquired disorder.

In this chapter, we will discuss disorders—congenital and acquired—most likely to be found among the school-age population.

CLASSIFICATION OF JOINTS

It is essential to understand the nature of various bone articulations, particularly at weight-bearing sites, before we can comprehend the ramifications of joint injury. Since the shape of a joint is the prime determiner of its function, a review of such joints as the ankle, knee, hip, shoulder, elbow, wrist, and fingers will aid in recognizing injury potential, Table 7.1.

TABLE 7.1

Joint Classification and Normal Movement

Joint	Classification	Expected Movement
Ankle	Hinge	Flexion, extension
Knee	Hinge*	Flexion, extension
Hip	Ball and socket	Flexion, extension, abduction, adduction, rotation, circumduction
Shoulder	Ball and socket	Flexion, extension, abduction, adduction, rotation, circumduction
Elbow	Hinge	Flexion, extension
Wrist	Condyloid	Flexion, extension, abduction (ulnar flexion), adduction (radial flexion)
Fingers	Hinge	Flexion, extension

*The knee, because of its skeletal structure, resembles two condyloid joints lying side by side. The knee joint is the largest single articulation within the body.

The area of the knee constitutes a prime site for injury because of weak bone stability. Sprains, for example, are relatively common during athletic competition because the joint's strength is in its ligaments. Although the ligaments are strong, rigorous contact upon the medial or lateral portions of the knee while the foot is set firmly on the ground is likely to stretch or tear them. This kind of injury is very painful and should be attended to by a physician.

Soft-Sign Evaluation

There are several **soft-sign tests** that can help you determine the nature of a joint injury, Figure 7.1.

1. The anteroposterior test is designed to evaluate the anterior and posterior stability of the knee. With the student in the supine position and the injured knee flexed, place your thumbs in a side-by-side position directly over the tibial tubercle. Pull the tibia gently forward and backward. If movement exceeds approximately one-fourth inch, there may be a looseness of the cruciate ligaments (drawer sign).

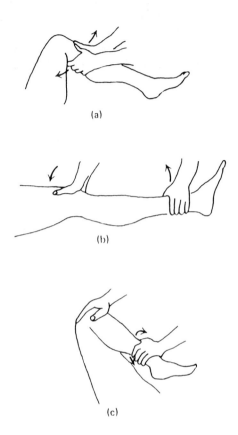

(a)

(b)

(c)

Figure 7.1. Soft-sign tests for joint injury: *A*, anteroposterior test; *B*, collateral ligament test; *C*, tibial rotation test

2. The collateral ligament test is designed to test the lateral mobility of the medial and lateral collateral ligaments. With the student in the supine position, injured leg extended, hold the ankle of the injured leg with one hand and the side of the knee with the other hand. Ligaments that are intact will offer little lateral movement. Medial ligament test: Gently push knee inward with one hand while gently pushing ankle outward with the other hand. Lateral ligament test: Gently push knee outward with one hand while gently pushing ankle inward with the other hand.

3. The tibial rotation test is designed to identify loose tissue within the knee. The student lies in the supine position and flexes the injured knee. Cover the surface of the patella with one hand. Hold the ankle with the other hand and move it in a small circle while attempting to feel unusual grating or clicking vibrations with the hand you have placed on the knee.

TEMPORARY ACQUIRED INJURIES

When a joint exceeds its normal range of motion, when articulating surfaces are jammed (as when an individual attempts to break a fall with a fully extended arm), or when the joint receives a blow, an injury is likely to occur.

Joint injuries are classified as sprains, **strains**, **dislocations**, or **fractures**. A sprain results when a joint is twisted beyond its normal range of motion, stretching the connective tissue. Damage is to the ligaments, tendons, or joint capsule, Figure 7.2. Of the various temporary acquired injuries, the sprain is the most common.

Strain results if the muscle or adjacent tissue is stretched beyond normal limits. A strain is often referred to as a muscle pull. According to Klafs and Arnheim (1973) a strain may vary in magnitude between a minute separation of connective tissue and muscle fiber to a complete avulsion of tendons or a rupture of the muscle, Figure 7.3.

A dislocation is classified according to whether there is a complete separation (**luxation**) or incomplete separation (**subluxation**) between articulating bone surfaces. The most common sites of dislocation are the phalanges—particularly the thumb or fingers—and the shoulder joint, Figure 7.4.

A fracture is an injury in which a bone is broken or cracked. A fracture may be simple or compound. In a simple fracture, the bone tissue does not penetrate the skin. In a compound fracture, the bone does penetrate the outer skin layer, Figure 7.5.

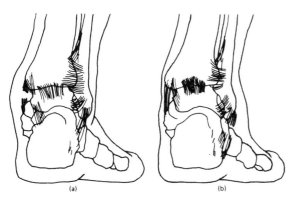

Figure 7.2. Right ankle sprain: *A*, medial; *B*, lateral

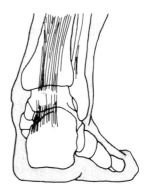

Figure 7.3. Strain: Achilles tendon

Figure 7.4. Dislocation: thumb

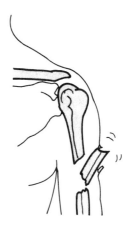

Figure 7.5. Compound fracture

Simple fractures may be subclassified into five basic groups:

1. Comminuted fracture, in which there are several bone fragments at the site of the break, Figure 7.6.
2. Depressed fracture, in which a flat-bone is pushed in—usually the skull, Figure 7.7.
3. Green-stick fracture, in which the break is incomplete, Figure 7.8. (The term *green-stick* is used because the fracture is similar to that of a fresh twig bent to the degree that the bark is split on one side.)
4. Transverse fracture, in which the bone is broken perpendicularly to its long axis, Figure 7.9.
5. Longitudinal fracture, in which the bone is split along its length, Figure 7.10. The significant difference between the longitudinal fracture and the transverse fracture is that in the former there is a greater chance that the break will also be compound; the bone is more likely to penetrate the skin.

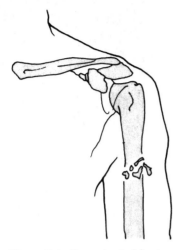

Figure 7.6. Comminuted fracture

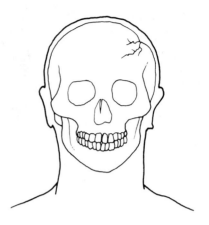

Figure 7.7. Depressed fracture

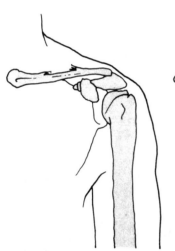

Figure 7.8. Green-stick
fracture: clavicle

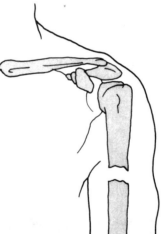

Figure 7.9. Transverse fracture

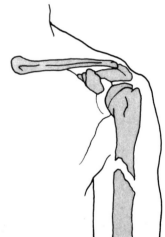

Figure 7.10. Longitudinal
fracture

There is little need to excuse a student from class during the period of conva-lescence. In addition to developmental tasks of the type described in Chapter 4, there are many aquatic, rhythmic, individual, and team activities appropriate for students with musculoskeletal injuries. (See Chapter 14 for games and sports adapted for children with injuries.)

JOINT INFLAMMATION

Inflammation is the body's defensive reaction to some form of system irritant. Inflammation may be caused by

1. blows and the entrance of foreign bodies
2. chemicals
3. heat and cold
4. microorganisms
5. surgery

When **joint inflammation** occurs, movement can be painful or impossible. Bursitis, **osteoarthritis**, and **rheumatoid arthritis** are the three common types of joint inflammation.

Bursitis is inflammation of the bursa around a joint. The bursa is pouchlike connective tissue usually lined with a synovial membrane that reduces friction at the site of the joint.

Osteoarthritis is an inflammation of the bones and joints with accompanying formation of bone spurs (projecting slivers of bone) around the joints.

Rheumatoid arthritis is a severe inflammatory condition often involving several joints at the same time. Frequently accompanying this condition are stiffness, swelling, sensitivity, and cartilaginous hypertrophy. The etiologies and treatments for these three inflammatory conditions are shown in Table 7.2.

TABLE 7.2

Bursitis, Osteoarthritis, Rheumatoid Arthritis: Etiology and Treatment

Disorder	Etiology	Treatment
Bursitis	An inflammation caused by trauma or overuse, often occurring at the bursa of the shoulder or elbow joints.	May react positively to heat or cold; mobilization exercise; corticosteroid injections as prescribed by attending physician.
Osteoarthritis	The exact cause of this bone and joint disease is not certain, although several principles appear common. It is likely to develop in a joint that has been subjected to injury, strain, or stress, or where a hidden birth defect exists. Heredity is thought to be a major factor when small joints in the fingers and toes (leading to Heberden's nodes) are involved.	No specific cure, but heat, rest, special exercises, surgery, and prescribed medication may slow down and control the disease process. In advanced cases, artificial joints (particularly at the hip) have relieved pain and restored function.
Rheumatoid arthritis	Precise etiology is not known, although evidence points to a latent virus or similar organism. Emotional stress, depression, and shock precede emergence of symptoms. Emotional or psychological factors do not cause the condition, but they appear to contribute to the problem in some manner.	Treatment includes the use of heat, rest, exercise, posture training, splints, walking aids, surgery, and prescribed medication in order to relieve pain, reduce inflammation, prevent or correct deformities, and assist in keeping the joints functional.

BONE DISORDERS

Although any of the previously described conditions could in a general sense be classified as **bone disorders**, in this section I will present those that cause bone degeneration at sites other than joints. These disorders are **osteochondrosis, osteomyelitis, rickets,** and **spondylolisthesis.***

Osteochondrosis

Osteochondrosis is a bone anomaly in which there is apparent degeneration at one or more centers of bone **ossification.** In children, bone should replace cartilage at the juncture of the diaphysis and epiphysis as normal physical growth takes place. For a youngster with osteochondrosis this growth pattern is impaired. The parts of the bone that contribute to the ossification process are described in Table 7.3.

As ossification is disturbed, often a consequence of malnutrition and trauma, a number of osteochondrosic diseases may emerge. Among the most prevalent are Legg-Calve-Perthes disease, Figure 7.11, and Osgood-Schlatter disease, Figure 7.12.

Individuals who have osteochondrosis must refrain from weight-bearing activities and, in the case of Osgood-Schlatter disease, deep knee bends or duck walks. For reasons not completely understood, normal blood supply is diminished to the extent that previously healthy tissue begins to soften. Bearing weight restricts blood supply to the affected area, and as softening occurs, points of articulation may become deformed. Sites of articulation will recover as normal circulation replaces dead tissue with healthy bone cells, Figure 7.13.

Osteomyelitis

Osteomyelitis is an inflammation of a bone and its medullary (marrow) cavity. This condition is occasionally referred to as *myelitis*. The symptoms are fever, pain, and rigid musculature over the affected area.

TABLE 7.3

Structures That Affect Linear Growth in Bone Tissue

Structure	Function
Hyaline cartilage	Embryonic skeleton is slowly transformed into endochondral bones through process of ossification.
Epiphyses (2) and diaphysis	Epiphyseal cartilage, located between the ends of long bone (epiphyses) and its shaft (diaphysis), continues to thicken and ossify.
	When the cartilage cells cease to multiply, and when the remaining cartilage is completely ossified, growth is complete (around twenty-fifth year).

---

* Scoliosis, a structural bone disorder, is discussed in Chapter 4.

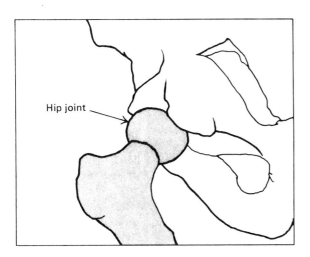

Figure 7.11. Site of Legg-Calve-Perthes disease

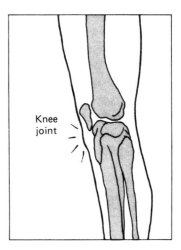

Figure 7.12. Site of Osgood-Schlatter disease

Figure 7.13. Sam Brown belt: Recommended for those with Legg-Calve-Perthes disease

The youngster with osteomyelitis can participate in virtually any developmental or recreational activity that allows the affected limb to be immobilized. When rehabilitation is complete, resumption of all normal activity is possible with approval of the child's physician.

Rickets

Rickets, usually equated with a diet deficient in vitamin D, is a metabolic disease that primarily affects children. Although various symptoms can be detected by a physician, the common obvious characteristic is that the long bones (e.g., tibia, femur) are curved (concave toward medial side).

Among the physical education activities approved for children with rickets, aquatic programs usually prove to be the most beneficial. Since sunshine promotes the acquisition of vitamin D within the body, swimming in the warm out-of-doors is ideal.

While weight-bearing activities are not recommended for those with demonstrable long-bone rickets syndrome, many developmental activities can be performed in prone, supine, and sitting positions.

Spondylolisthesis

Spondylolisthesis is a condition in which the body of one of the lumbar vertebrae, usually the fifth, slips forward beyond its normal alignment with the next lowest spinal segment, the sacrum. Since an extreme lordotic condition may be an exacerbation to the malaligned vertebrae, we should gear developmental activities to strengthening abdominal muscles and stretching muscles of the lower back. Attention should also be given to improving body alignment.

Painful nerve pressure in the lumbar spine is likely, and it is possible that inordinate stress will aggravate an already existing malalignment. Consequently the following activities are usually **contraindicated** for students with spondylolisthesis:

1. Contact sports
2. Weight lifting where resistant loads are great
3. Highly fatiguing activities
4. Activities likely to induce twisting of the spinal column (e.g., some floor exercise routines in gymnastics)

AMPUTATIONS

An amputation is an extremely traumatic experience, particularly for someone who has actively participated in athletics. The success of any therapeutic program, therefore, depends upon our ability to integrate psychological with physiological know-how. The best approach is to draw upon expertise from diversified yet related disciplines. This multidisciplinary team should include

1. the attending physician who is familiar with the medical aspects of the case and who is attuned to appropriate care and treatment that takes the prognosis into account.
2. a nurse who is trained to provide prescribed care.
3. a physical therapist who is trained in the use of various therapeutic modalities.
4. a **prosthetist** who can prepare an appropriately designed prosthesis (artificial limb).
5. a mobility instructor who can train the amputee in the use of the prosthesis and assorted **mobility aids**, as movement is attempted.
6. a physical education instructor who is versed in the selection of developmental activities appropriate to the maintenance and/or improvement of physical and motor fitness—general and specific—as well as appropriate recreational modalities.
7. a social worker who can address problems in social interaction as the amputee prepares to return to the community.
8. an occupational therapist who can help the amputee acquire **self-care skills** that may be diminished as a result of limb loss.
9. a vocational therapist who can help the amputee select educational experiences geared toward job training.
10. the amputee's family who knows the basic needs, moods, interests, aspirations, and original capabilities of the amputee.

Etiology

Although there are those who have **congenital amputations**, the general causes of acquired amputations are revealed in Table 7.4.

TABLE 7.4

Amputations: Ranked by Cause

Rank	Etiology	Possible Sources
1	Trauma	Power tool and farm accidents
		Vehicle accidents
		Gunshot or dynamite explosions
2	Cancer	
3	Infections	
4	Vascular conditions	Gangrene (e.g., from diabetes mellitus)
		Clotting

Amputation Sites

Amputation is usually performed at a site that will leave a good support (stump) to which a prosthesis can be attached.* Appendage (limb) amputations occur

1. below the knee (BK)
2. above the knee (AK)
3. below the elbow (BE)
4. above the elbow (AE).

Each site results in unique problems for the amputee and members of the multi-disciplinary team. The most difficult cases involve the loss of a leg—not only the physical loss itself, but the emotional stress experienced by the patient who must deal with the ramifications of the loss. "How will I ever be able to get around as I once could?" "I will never be able to walk, run, dance, or move freely again." These worries, of course, are not completely true. With a prosthesis the amputee will be able to walk, dance, drive a car, and so forth. If the prosthesis can be fitted as soon as possible following the amputation, psychological rehabilitation can begin more quickly. (It may be possible for prosthesis measurements to be taken before surgery. This will expedite the construction of a properly fitting device.)

Types of Prostheses

A prosthesis is an artificial part used to assist in the performance of a natural function. It may be in the form of an artificial eye, dentures, or a limb. In this section attention will be paid to prostheses used as limbs or parts of limbs. Accordingly they may or may not look like the limbs they are designed to replace.

---

*On occasions those with congenital amputations will require surgery on their stumps in order to create a firm base of support for prosthetic devices.

Much research has been done with respect to the structure and function of prosthetic devices, and there have been many advances. It is a mixed blessing that we can attribute these advances to the fact that an increasing number of individuals are in need of their use.

There are three general classifications of prosthetic devices.

1. The practical prosthesis enables the amputee to pick up and deliver objects, write, type, drive a car, and attend to activities of daily living. Many of the prostheses falling in this category may not be very aesthetic, but they do serve a useful function, Figure 7.14.

Figure 7.14. Example of a practical prosthetic device

2. The cosmetic prosthesis looks like a real limb (the hand in particular) but has no practical purpose. The shape and texture are matched to the existing limb. Many amputees would choose this prosthetic device over that portrayed in Figure 7.14 in social settings. Normally the practical prosthesis is used when specific jobs or tasks requiring a holding or pinching function are necessary.

3. The combination prosthesis has the appearance of an actual limb while serving a function. Some are computer-driven; some require the surgical implantation of a mechanical and/or electronic device. The Utah Artificial Arm was developed for those with amputations above the elbow (AE). Its major feature is that it has the capacity to respond to electrical signals provided by the muscles of the arm and/or shoulder of the wearer, Figure 7.15. The elbow can be locked at varying angles allowing a variety of activities to be carried out. Research is currently underway that will extend the device's current elbow flexion and extension ability to rotation of the wrist.

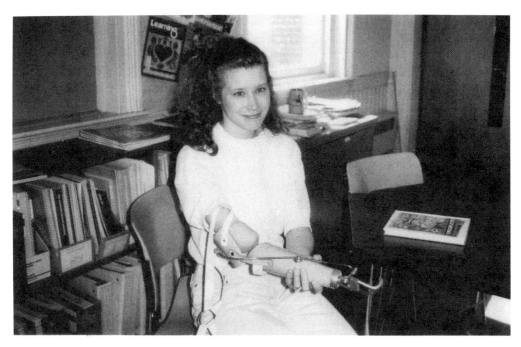

Figure 7.15. The Utah Artificial Arm. *From The Center for Engineering Design, University of Utah, and Motion Control, Inc.*

Mobility Aids and Braces

Regardless of the etiology underlying a musculoskeletal disorder, it is likely that the patient's mobility can be enhanced through the use of **mobility aids** and/or **braces**. Among the most popular devices are canes; orthocanes,* Figure 7.16; crutches; ortho-crutches, Figure 7.17; walkers, Figure 7.18; wheelchairs; short-leg braces, Figure 7.19; and long-leg braces**, Figure 7.20.

As the reader should expect, aids and braces come in many shapes, sizes, and weights. The type that is selected for use is dependent upon the unique requirements of the individual. For example, should the student need support at the knee joint in addition to the ankle joint, he/she would want a brace similar to that shown in Figure 7.20, a long-leg brace. These braces come in frames of metal or plastic designed to be strapped above and below pertinent joints. This support aids in **ambulation** but can also reduce or prevent deformities.

Speaking of ambulation, many individuals have difficulty learning to use crutches whether or not they are wearing braces. Walking, sitting down, getting up, ascending and descending stairs, and other activities are not easy. The developmental activities in the next section are intended to help a person learn these and other skills. It is important

---

* Users often find that orthocanes provide more security—less slippage than regular canes because one's weight is over the long axis of the cane instead of to its rear.

** The reader is referred to Appendix B for a review of factors contributing to the appropriate fit and use of braces and wheelchairs.

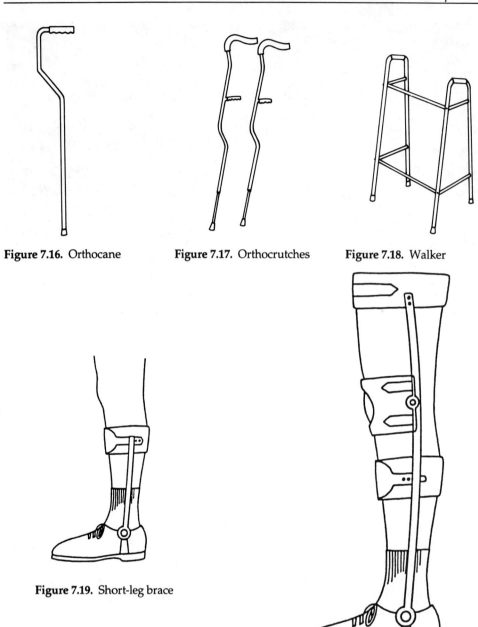

Figure 7.16. Orthocane   **Figure 7.17.** Orthocrutches   **Figure 7.18.** Walker

Figure 7.19. Short-leg brace

Figure 7.20. Long-leg brace

to support the individual during the learning process to prevent falling. The person who is learning to use crutches should wear a heavy belt around his/her waist. Stand behind the person and grip the belt firmly with your hand, palm up. Should the person begin to lose balance, exert pressure forward while your other hand pulls backward on the person's shoulder, Figure 7.21.

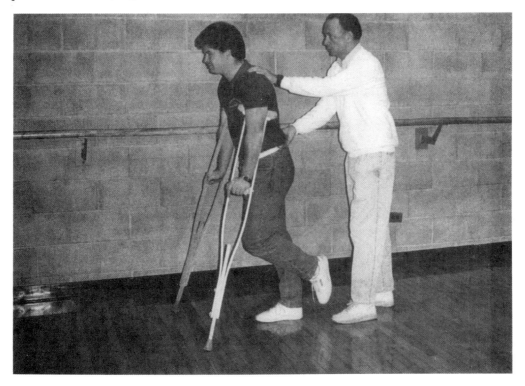

Figure 7.21. Crutch walking with assistance

DEVELOPMENTAL ACTIVITIES

Physical education practitioners often find themselves in positions of observing children placing themselves at risk because of poor crutch management. The following seven developmental activities provide a basic orientation to the correct use of crutches. Be sure that rubber stoppers are securely fastened to the bottom of each crutch leg to help prevent slipping when use is attempted.

I. Goal: Use of Crutches*

Major Objective	*Interim Performance Objective*
1. Fitting crutches	1.1 Select properly fitting crutches.
	1.1A Measure from under the arm to a distance six inches anterior and lateral to the shoe.

---

* Adapted from Lumex, Incorporated.

Major Objective	*Interim Performance Objective*
	1.1B Elbow should be able to flex between twenty-five and thirty degrees when the hand grasps crutch grip.
	1.1C When advancing the crutch to take a step, it should be possible to extend the elbow fully.
2. Crutch walking	**2.1** Demonstrate swing-to **gait**.
	2.1A Raise both crutches and place them in front of the body.
	2.1B Lean into crutches and push the body off floor while straightening the elbows (flex neck slightly).
	2.1C Land between crutches heel first.
	2.1D When feet touch floor, shift weight to the feet and repeat.
	2.2 Demonstrate swing-through gait, Figure 7.22.
	2.2A Raise both crutches and place them in front of the body.
	2.2B Lean into crutches and push the body off floor while straightening elbows (flex neck slightly). To increase height, pike (jacknife) the body.
	2.2C As feet clear floor, swing through crutches to point where heels contact floor.
	2.2D When feet touch floor, lean forward from ankles and repeat.

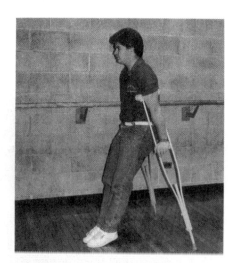

Figure 7.22. Swing-through gait

Note: Too vigorous a swing will diminish control.

Major Objective

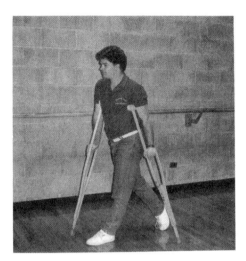

Figure 7.23. Two-point gait

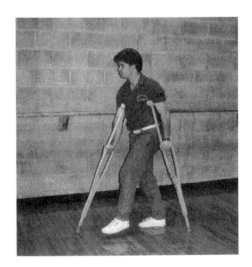

Figure 7.24. Four-point gait

3. Managing doors

Interim Performance Objective

2.3 Demonstrate two-point gait, Figure 7.23.

   2.3A Advance right crutch and left foot.

   2.3B Advance left crutch and right foot.

   2.3C Repeat.

> *Note*: The three-point gait is used if only one leg can bear weight. The weight-bearing leg swings through the crutches while the other leg is held in knee-flex position.

2.4 Demonstrate four-point gait, Figure 7.24.

   2.4A Advance right crutch.

   2.4B Advance left foot.

   2.4C Advance left crutch.

   2.4D Advance right foot.

   2.4E Repeat.

3.1 Open door and pass through unrestrained.

   3.1A Face door at an angle sufficient to allow it to pass by feet as it opens.

Major Objective	*Interim Performance Objective*
	3.1B Turn doorknob with left hand while supporting the body on crutches with right hand.
Note: Procedure may be adjusted in accordance with direction door swings.	3.1C As door opens to point beyond feet, place tip of left crutch against it to keep it open.
	3.1D Proceed through door opening.
4. Sitting in a chair	4.1 Seat body safely in a chair.
	4.1A Turn and back into chair until chair's edge is felt against backs of the legs.
	4.1B With weak leg raised slightly from the floor, remove crutches from under arms and, grasping them at a point close to the grips, place crutches in front of the body.
	4.1C Holding crutches in one hand, bend knee of the stronger leg until a sitting position is assumed. Free hand may be used as a guide.
5. Getting up from a chair	5.1 Rise safely from a chair.
	5.1A Keeping the head well forward and placing the stronger leg at a point of stability, reverse the procedure described in Interim Performance Objective 4.1.
6. Ascending stairs	6.1 Climb stairs safely.
	6.1A Facing stairs, place crutches close to first step.
	6.1B Push on crutches, straighten the elbows, flex neck slightly, and place stronger leg on first step.
	6.1C While straightening the back, lift both crutches and the weaker leg up onto the first step.

Major Objective	*Interim Performance Objective*

6.1D Repeat procedure for succeeding steps: when staircase has handrail, place both crutches under the arm farthest from the handrail and proceed as described.

7. Descending stairs

7.1 Climb down stairs safely.

7.1A Stand with the toes of the stronger leg close to edge of step.

7.1B Lower both crutches and the weaker leg onto next step while bending the knee of the stronger leg to a point where stability is assured.

7.1C Lean on crutches and lower the body, placing the stronger leg on same step as crutches and weaker leg.

MUSCULAR DISORDERS

There are many causes of muscular dysfunction. Sprains and strains have been discussed previously. Although debilitating, sprains and strains are ordinarily temporary. The more severe and permanent **muscular disorders** are such conditions as **muscular atrophy**, muscular dystrophy, and **myasthenia gravis**. We will discuss each of these three conditions in the sections that follow. There are many other disorders of the muscular system (Gilroy and Meyer 1975), but it is beyond the scope of this text to elaborate on the etiology, diagnosis, and prognosis of each, Table 7.5.*

Muscular Atrophy

Although often confused with muscular dystrophy by laypersons because of the general muscular characteristics visible in those so affected, muscular atrophy is caused by the degeneration of motor neurons within the cell bodies. As a consequence muscle fibers are not innerved, and action does not occur. Disused muscle tissue atrophies; hence muscular atrophy.

According to Sherrill (1976), lesions within the lower motor neurons are likely to result in the following observable musculocharacteristics:

1. Atrophy, the extent of which will depend on the number of cell bodies that have been destroyed.

---

* See the recommended readings for further information about muscle disorders.

TABLE 7.5

Some Disorders of the Muscular System

Disorder	Description
Myalgia	Tenderness or pain in the muscles: muscular rheumatism
Myatonia	Deficiency or loss of muscular power
Myectopia	Muscular dislocation
Myesthesia	Muscular sensitivity
Myocele	Muscular protrusion through the sheath of a muscle
Myocelialgia	Abdominal muscular pain
Myodemia	Fatty degeneration of muscle tissue
Myodiastasis	Muscular rupture
Myofascitis	Inflamed condition of a muscle and its fascia
Myogelosis	Hardening of a portion of muscle tissue
Myoedema	Unusual concentration of fluid in muscle tissue
Myomalacia	Softening of muscle tissue
Myonacrosis	Numbness of muscle tissue
Myosclerosis	Hardening of muscle tissue
Myositis	Inflamed muscular condition

2. Fasciculations, which are fine or coarse irregular twitchings of muscle parts. They appear irregularly and are unassociated with movement of the affected muscle at the joint. These fasciculations can be seen through the skin with the naked eye.
3. Fibrillations, irregular twitches that are similar to fasciculations but cannot be seen through the skin. Instead they are recorded electromyographically.
4. Loss of reflexes due to the interruption of the reflex arc.
5. Paralysis and absence of sensory disturbances, in which the muscles are flaccid and **hypotonic**. The extent of the disturbance, however, will depend on the number of cell bodies that are unable to function.

The etiology of muscular atrophy is not completely understood. Additional research is needed before this disease can be described without qualification. There is some evidence, however, that the condition is more likely to occur in males than females and more prevalent in middle and old age than in childhood. Regardless of gender or age, appropriately prescribed **range-of-motion activities** and hydrotherapy will enhance circulation and help to keep joints pliable.

Muscular Dystrophy

Muscular dystrophy is a progressive degeneration of muscle fibers. There is no involvement of the central or peripheral nervous systems. Of the various classifications of dystrophy the most prevalent and most severe is the Duchenne's muscular dystrophy

TABLE 7.6

Classifications of Muscular Dystrophy

Type	General Description
Becker	Although progression is slower, the symptoms are much like those of Duchenne's muscular dystrophy. (The patient may not lose his or her ability to walk for two decades or more following the onset of the disease.)
Distal form	Relatively rare, characterized by a progressive deterioration of the **distal** muscles of the four limbs.
Limb-girdle muscular dystrophy	Characterized by general weakness in either the pelvic or shoulder girdle. In advanced stages, paraspinal muscles may be involved.
Ocular form	Characterized by weak eye movements. Partial involvement of the facial muscles is likely.
Scapuloperoneal form	Involves proximal muscles of the upper limbs and shoulder girdle and distal muscles of the lower limbs.

(childhood muscular dystrophy). Some other kinds of muscular dystrophy are described in Table 7.6.

Duchenne's muscular dystrophy is usually undetected until children (usually male) begin to walk, when a general clumsiness becomes apparent. The child will be prone to falling with little cause. Progressive deterioration becomes manifest as follows:

1. Weakness develops in muscles of the pelvic girdle. The child develops a waddling gait and, in attempts to rise from the prone position, tends to "climb up upon" himself/herself.
2. Arm muscles are affected. There is severe retardation of muscle development.
3. Eighty percent of patients have pseudohypertrophy of muscles, particularly in the calves. The youngster will often be confined to a wheelchair by the age of ten.
4. Facial muscles are affected. Lack of control becomes apparent.
5. There is cardiorespiratory involvement. Sudden death occurs in 80 percent of those afflicted with muscular dystrophy by the age of twenty (Emery and Walton 1972). The remaining twenty percent usually die in their twenties.

The evolving weakness progresses from the proximal, limb-girdle muscles to the distal muscles. The frequency of Duchenne's muscular dystrophy in young males supports the theory that its inheritance is sex-linked and recessive. According to Gilroy and Meyer (1975), a number of sporadic cases suggests that cell mutation can also occur.

There are nearly fifty individuals per one million population with diagnosed muscular dystrophy. Approximately one-third of these arise within families where there are other male children with muscular dystrophy.

The prognosis is anything but optimistic. Retention of strength, respiratory efficiency, general fitness, and **mobility** skills are the goals of any physical education program for children with muscular dystrophy. Keep the following in mind when prescribing activities:

1. Keep the student ambulatory as long as possible.
2. Watch the child's diet. Wheelchair inactivity makes it easier to gain weight.
3. Braces and orthopedic procedures may have been prescribed by the student's physician to help prevent deformities.
4. Respiratory exercises will help the child retain residual breathing ability.
5. Provide for success in recreation-type activities within a class to foster favorable social interaction.*

Myasthenia Gravis

Unrelated to the two previously described diseases, **myasthenia gravis** is a condition manifested by an inordinate weakness of the voluntary muscles following activity. Subsequent to a prescribed rest period, which may vary in length from individual to individual, recovery of normal strength levels can be expected.

Myasthenia gravis is more frequent in females than in males by a ratio of two to one. The incidence level is approximately one in ten thousand persons (Schwab 1963). Its etiology is unknown, and medical examinations indicate that the abnormality is confined to muscle tissue.

Since myasthenia gravis can be fatal if unchecked,** the physical education practitioner should communicate with the attending physician before preparing activity prescriptions. In most cases the patient will be able to participate in the regular program. This assumption should not be made, however, without corroboration by a physician.

CONGENITAL DISORDERS

By definition, *congenital* means existing prior to or at birth, but not inherited. Congenital anomalies are structural or functional disabilities with which one is born. There are numerous reasons why such conditions arise. Among the most prevalent are prenatal infections, drug ingestion, radiation, and chromosomal anomalies. Predisposition to most congenital anomalies arises during the first trimescer of pregnancy.

Various congenital deficiencies have been described by Smith (1970) and others. I will discuss five: **clubfoot** (talipes), **congenital dislocation of the hip**, **Erb's palsy**, **spina bifida**, and appendage disfiguration.

Clubfoot

Clubfoot (talipes) is among the most common of the foot defects. Although cerebral palsy can cause a clubfootlike condition, the most prevalent etiology of clubfoot is congenital. The deformity may involve one or both feet, and may be one of the following types:

1. Talipes calcaneus is a permanent dorsal flexion of the foot. The individual is forced to walk on the inner side of the heel because it is the only portion of the foot in contact with the ground.

---

* For further information regarding the nature of muscular dystrophy, write to: Muscular Dystrophy Association of America, Inc., 1790 Broadway, New York, NY 10019.

** Depending on the strain, drug therapy will ordinarily accompany any form of activity prescription.

2. Talipes equinus is a **plantar flexion** of the foot. The individual is forced to walk on his/her toes.

3. Talipes equinovarus is an adduction and inversion at the anterior midtarsal joints and the subtalar joint, Figure 7.25. Muscle tissue is contracted to the extent that it pulls the foot into an extended (plantar flexed) position. As a consequence, the individual is forced to walk on the outside of the foot and ankle.

The following treatment is recommended for talipes equinovarus:

a) Plaster cast to keep foot in overcorrected position

b) Special shoes with steel rods to assist the feet to become aligned

c) Passive and active-assistive exercise to help maintain muscle tonus and flexibility

The most prevalent of the various types of clubfoot, talipes equinovarus accounts for approximately sixty to seventy percent of the cases.

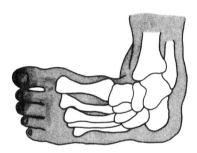

Clubfoot accounts for 25 percent of the congenital anomalies seen in crippled children's clinics. If diagnosed at birth, most talipes conditions can be improved by surgery. Surgery, coupled with therapeutic exercise geared to stretch and strengthen appropriate muscle groups, results in a favorable prognosis.

Figure 7.25. Talipes equinovarus: Schematic representation

Congenital Dislocation of the Hip

The hip joint is formed where the ball-shaped head of the femur articulates with the cup-shaped acetabulum of the pelvis. When the head is partially separated (sublaxated) or completely separated (luxated) from normal placement in the acetabulum, the joint is dislocated. If a youngster is born with this anomaly, it is referred to as congenital dislocation of the hip.

Of the various skeletal deformities this condition ranks second in prevalence after clubfoot. If it is not treated, irreversible alterations to normal bone growth will be the likely result. It has been illustrated by Boyd (1956) and others that early identification and correction of this impairment (and of clubfoot) have been successful to the extent that these conditions are rarely observed among school-age children.

Erb's Palsy

The condition known as Erb's palsy (paralysis) is **paralysis** of the muscles of the shoulder and upper arm. It results from damage to the cervical roots of the fifth and sixth spinal nerves at the time of delivery.

The absence of flaccidity of muscular reflexes reveals the loss of tonus. If the upper and lower neurons are paralyzed, the individual is unable to move the affected limb. If the lower neuron remains intact, some motor responses are possible even though a flaccid appearance exists. The affected arm hangs limp, and the wrist is flexed. If the condition exists at the time the child enters school, a reversal in muscle tonus is unlikely.

Spina Bifida

Although the exact causes of all spina bifida cases are unknown, there is a slight tendency for the condition to run in families. (It has been found that one form—myelomeningocele—appears to be transmitted genetically through an **autosomal recessive trait**.) In the United States, estimates of prevalence range from 0.3 to 0.9 in 1,000 live births (Shurtleff, Lemire, and Warkany 1986), and it represents the most common congenital disorder that affects the spine.

The condition results from failure of a posterior portion of the vertebral arch to close. As a consequence spinal cord tissue is likely to protrude through the gap, and to the extent that it is damaged, neurological problems can surface. However, it should also be noted that it is difficult to predict whether pathological changes will take place in the spinal cord if the condition is not treated (Swinyard 1966). Although surgical procedures may effect realignment of nerve tissue and artificial closure of the bony canal, varying degrees of paralysis in the lower limbs and organs of the lower abdomen may still remain, Figure 7.26.

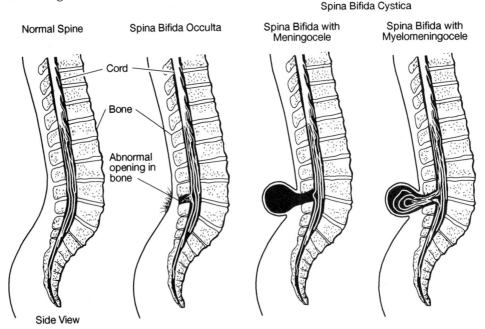

Figure 7.26. Side views of a normal spine, spina bifida occulta, and spina bifida cystica. *From Hardman, Drew, Egan, and Wolf (1990). Human exceptionality, Boston, MA: Allyn and Bacon.*

Of the various classifications of spina bifida, myelomeningocele is the most severe, followed by meningocele and spina bifida occulta. Myelomeningocele is a protrusion of a portion of meninges (protective covering of the spinal cord) through the skin, usually around the lumbar area of the vertebral column. If feasible, surgery is performed immediately following birth in order to close the myelocele. It is a risky operation at best, and few children with myelomeningocele live beyond childhood with or without surgery.

Meningocele is a rather uncommon form of spina bifida. The meningocele is also a protrusion of the meninges, but unlike myelomeningocele the spinal cord and nerve roots remain in a normal position. Surgical efforts are usually made to remove the meningocele sac. Should paralysis occur, the condition is permanent and entails total loss of sensation from the point of the meningocele to the feet.

Spina bifida occulta is a minor form of spina bifida in that there is often no more than a mole in the lower lumbar area of the skin. Some muscle tonus may be lacking due to assorted anomalies of the spinal cord itself.

For spina bifida patients who are paraplegic, moving about is possible with the use of braces and crutches. The major problem for a child enrolled in school is the inability to control the bladder. This problem can be solved using various devices that collect the urine externally. Two such devices are the external urinary device and the ileal conduit. The external urinary device is a soft rubber tube that is placed over the penis and carries urine to a collection bag. The ileal conduit is a surgically implanted ureter that transports the urine through a stoma (opening). A collection bag is worn over the opening.

When working with children who have congenital disorders, think in terms of what they can do, not in terms of what they cannot do. There are many developmental physical fitness and motor skills that can be developed in and out of the classroom. The youngster with spina bifida will be receptive to such a program if it is geared to his/her capabilities and interests.

Appendage Disfigurement (Congenital Amputation)

The failure of a body part to grow normally is called **aplasia**. This congenital appendage disfigurement occurs during embryonic and fetal growth; the unborn child develops without normal limbs. For example, a condition in which the forearm did not develop as expected would be referred to as radial aplasia, Figure 7.27 Although lower limb disfigurement is possible, the upper limbs are most commonly affected. An infant may be born without arms, hands, and/or fingers, or these limbs may be disfigured.

Sometimes surgical amputation of existing tissue is performed to provide a stump for a properly fitted prosthesis. In other instances the appendage is left as is. In speaking with students and others who have congenital amputations, it has been revealed by several that they prefer to go without prosthetics in that the artificial devices seem to call the attention of others to the handicapping condition. How do you feel about this?

Simple adaptations of activities, supplies, and/or equipment enable a student with a congenital amputation to add to his/her options of games to play. (See Chapter 17 for construction ideas.)

Range of motion exercises, including those that are of the passive variety, can go a long way to enhance neural and cardiac circulation in those who are unable to initiate their own movements because of musculoskeletal disorders. Those administering the exercises should be mindful of the need to include movements in and around various planes and axes (see Chapter 2). Using **rhythmic patterning** through music (and its assorted tempi) will stimulate the student cognitively and establish a mind set for the rate and intensity of the exercise to be undertaken. This can help to create cooperative efforts between student and mentor.

SUMMARY

There are many and varied anomalies that can arise within the musculoskeletal system. They can be rather minor and perhaps temporary, or they can be profound to

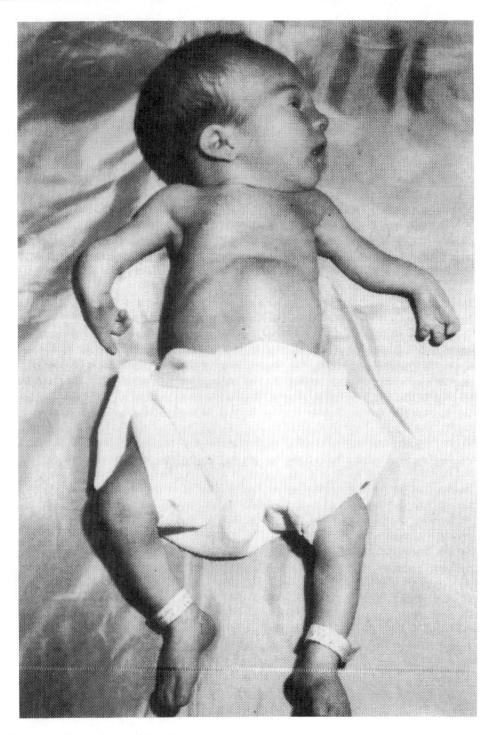

Figure 7.27. Example of radial aplasia

the extent that one's life is threatened. In all instances early identification and intervention can lead to the most productive outcomes. The role of the physical education practitioner is to provide a systematic response to the needs of those requiring special accommodation. This can range from teaching the proper use of crutches to carrying out passive exercise routines with those unable to initiate movement of their own. Within that range, the reader will want to consider the employment of activities described in previous chapters and those presented in sections to follow. Read on and learn more about the various options available.

RECOMMENDED LABORATORY ASSIGNMENTS

1. Arrange to visit special and regular schools to observe physical education programs adapted to students with various musculoskeletal disorders.
2. Interview those charged with the organization and administration of these programs to find out what curricular components are most successful.
3. Become proficient in the use of crutches.
4. Work with students while employing passive, active-assistive, and active exercise routines to music with various tempi.
5. Interview selected members of a multidisciplinary team to find out how each views his or her role in the **habilitation** of the amputee.
6. Learn how to provide hygienic care for a limb stump.
7. View and study visual aids such as filmstrips, slides, films, posters, and other video media related to the care and treatment of temporary acquired injuries.
8. Successfully complete American National Red Cross courses in first aid and advanced first aid.
9. Study the function and placement of cosmetic and/or practical prosthetic devices.
10. Make a list of procedures that could be followed in order to construct and/or adapt supplies and equipment to enhance the teaching plan for students with conditions described in this chapter.
11. Review the recommended reading.

REFERENCES

Boyd, H. B. 1956. Advances in conquering crippling. *Crippled Child* 35: 4-7.

Emery, A. E., and J. N. Walton. 1972. Abnormalities of the electrocardiogram in hereditary myopathies. *Journal of Medical Genetics* 9: 8–12.

Gilroy, J., and J. S. Meyer. 1975. *Medical neurology.* New York: Macmillan.

Klafs, C. E., and D. D. Arnheim. 1973. *Modern principles of athletic training.* St. Louis: C. V. Mosby Company.

Lumex, Incorporated. 1964. *Crutch training manual.* Bay Shore, New York: Lumex, Incorporated.

Phipps, W. J., B. C. Long, and N. F. Woods, eds. 1983. *Medical-surgical nursing: Concepts and clinical practice.* 2d ed. St. Louis: C. V. Mosby Company.

Schwab, R. S. 1963. Problems in the diagnosis and treatment of myasthenia gravis. *Medical Clinics of North America* 47: 1511–24.

Sherrill, C. 1976. *Adapted physical education and recreation.* Dubuque: William C. Brown.

Shurtleff, D., R. Lemire, and J. Warkany. 1986. Embryology, etiology, and epidemiology. In *Myelodysplasias and extrophies*, edited by D. B. Shurtleff. Orlando, FL: Grune and Stratton.

Smith, D. W. 1970. *Recognizable patterns of human malformation*. Philadelphia: W. B. Saunders Company.

Swinyard, C. A., ed. 1966. Comprehensive care of the child with spina bifida manifesta. In *Rehabilitation Monograph No. 31*. New York: New York University.

U.S. Department of Education. (1987). *Ninth annual report to Congress on the implementation of the Education of the Handicapped Act*. Washington, DC: GPO.

RECOMMENDED READINGS

Armstrong, R. W., P. L. Rosenbaum, and S. M. King. 1987. A randomized, controlled trial of a "buddy" programme to improve children''s attitudes toward the disabled. *Developmental Medicine and Child Neurology* 29(3): 327–36.

Batshaw, M. L., and Y. M. Perret. 1986. *Children with handicaps: A medical primer*. 2d ed. Baltimore, MD: P.H. Brookes.

Bigge, J. L. 1982. *Teaching individuals with physical and multiple disabilities*. 2d ed. Columbus, OH: Merrill Publishing Company.

Bleck, E. E. 1982. Muscular dystrophy—Duchenne type. In *Physically handicapped children: A medical atlas for teachers*. 2d ed., edited by E. E. Bleck and D. A. Nagel. New York: Grune and Stratton.

Bleck, E. E., and D. A. Nagel, eds. 1982. *Physically handicapped children: A medical atlas for teachers*. 2d ed. New York: Grune and Stratton.

Christensen, C., and D. C. Wiseman. 1972. Strength, the common variable in hamstring strains. *Athletic Training* 7(2): 36.

Connor, F. P., J. Scandary, and D. Tulloch. 1988. Education of physically handicapped and health impaired individuals: A commitment to the future. *Division of the Physically Handicapped Journal*, 10(1): 5–24.

Crain, D. C. 1971. *The arthritis handbook*. New York: Exposition Press.

Cunningham, P., and J. Gose. 1986. Telecommunication for the physically handicapped. Proceedings of the Conference on Computer Technology and Persons with Disabilitie0s. Northridge, CA.

Dobling, J. 1983. *Prevention of spina bifida and other neural tube disorders*. London: Academic Press.

Dutton, D. H. 1986. Strategies to promote integration and acceptance of students with disabilities among their nondisabled peers, using microcomputers. Proceedings of the Conference on Computer Technology and Persons with Disabilities. Northridge, CA.

Esposito, B. G., and T. M. Reed. 1986. The effects of contact with handicapped persons on young children's attitude. *Exceptional Children* 53: 224–29.

Evans, F. G. 1966. *Studies on the anatomy and function of bones and joints*. New York: Springer-Verlag.

Foulds, R. 1986. *Interactive robotic aids—One option for independent living: An international perspective, 37* (Monograph). New York: World Rehabilitation Fund, Inc.

Friedman, L. W. 1978. *The surgical rehabilitation of the amputee*. Springfield, IL: Charles C. Thomas.

Gayle, G. W., G. M. Davis, R. L. Pohlman, and R. M. Glaser. 1990. Cardiorespiratory and perceptual responses to arm crank and wheelchair exercise using various handrims in male paraplegics. *Research Quarterly for Exercise and Sport* 61(3); 224–32.

Geddes, D. 1978. *Physical activities for individuals with handicapping conditions*. St. Louis: C. V. Mosby Company.

Jones, L. E. 1988. The free limb scheme and the limb-deficient child in Australia. *Australain Paediatric Journal* 24(5): 290–94.

Kamenetz, H. L. 1986. Wheelchairs and other indoor vehicles for the disabled. In *Orthotics et cetera*, edited by J. B. Reford. Baltimore: Williams and Wilkins.

Macera, C. A., K. L. Jackson, G. W. Hagenmaier, J. J. Kronenfeld, H. W. Kohl, and S. N. Blair. 1989. Age, physical activity, physical fitness, body composition, and incidence of orthopedic problems. *Research Quarterly for Exercise and Sport* 60(3): 225–33.

Mensch, G., and P. M. Ellis. 1986. *Physical therapy management of lower extremity amputations*. Rockville, MD: Aspen Publishers, Inc.

Pollingue, A. 1987. Adaptive behavior and low-incidence handicaps: Use of adaptive behavior instruments for persons with physical handicaps. *Journal of Special Education* 21(12): 170–81.

Raynes, M., M. Snell, and W. Sailor. 1991. A fresh look at categorical programs for children with special needs. *Phi Delta Kanran* 73(4): 326–31.

Sanders, G. 1986. *Lower limb amputations: A guide to rehabilitation*. Philadelphia: F. A. Davis Company.

Schock, N. 1985. *The child with muscular dystrophy in school*. Lexington, MA: Appalachian Satellite Program Resource Center.

Turek, S. L. 1984. *Orthopaedics: Principles and their application*. Philadelphia: J. B. Lippincott Company.

Umbreit, J., ed. 1983. *Physical disabilities and health impairments: An introduction*. Columbus, OH: Merrill Publishing Company.

Wesson, C. L., and M. Keefe. 1989. Teaching library skills to students with mild and moderate handicaps. Teaching Exceptional Children 21(3): 28–31.

Williamson, G. G., and M. Szczepanshi. 1987. *Children with spina bifida: Early intervention and preschool programming*. Baltimore, MD: P. H. Brookes.

Winnick, J., and F. Short. 1985 *Physical fitness testing of the disabled, Project UNIQUE*. Champaign, IL: Human Kinetics Publishers.

Wright, B. 1983. *Physical disability—A psychological approach*. 2d ed. New York: Harper and Row.

York, J.,T. Vandercook, C. MacDonald, C. Heise-Neff, and E. Caughey. 1992. Feedback about integrating middle-school students with severe disabilities in general education classes. *Exceptional Children* 58(3): 244–58.

Zohar, J. 1973. Preventive conditioning for maximum safety and performance. *Scholastic Coach* 42(65): 113–15.

CHAPTER 8

Neurological Disorders _____

Objectives

After reading this chapter, you should be able to

- **Describe the relative incidences of selected neurological disorders.**
- **Know common symptoms indicative of neurological impairment.**
- **Know the factors to be reviewed in a neurological examination.**
- **Describe various test batteries available for evaluating perceptual ability.**
- **State the differences between spastic and athetotic cerebral palsy; between grand mal, petit mal, and Jacksonian forms of epilepsy; between abortive, nonparalytic, and paralytic poliomyelitis.**
- **Describe hypotheses as to the etiology of multiple sclerosis.**
- **Know a sampling of developmental activities appropriate for persons with selected neurological disorders.**

INTRODUCTION

The exact origin of many **neurological impairments** escapes description. Because of the complexity inherent in the structure and function of the human brain (see "The Nervous System" in Chapter 2), much of the data upon which educational decisions have been based has been rather speculative. Neurology, a relatively new discipline, has only recently become oriented toward therapeutic rather than descriptive study. As a consequence of this reversal in emphasis, we can make more intelligent decisions with respect to the **modeling** of prescriptive activities for the classroom.

As a prelude to the selection of any medical, therapeutic, or educational program design, an analysis of the student's neurological status must be made. During this examination the family physician or **pediatrician** may recognize a syndrome typical of a particular neurological anomaly. Gilroy and Meyer (1979) describe a number of elements that should be included in a comprehensive **neurological examination**.

KEY TERMS

active-assistive motion	multiple sclerosis
active motion	neurological examination
active-resistive motion	neurological impairment
ataxia	non-locomotor skills
athetosis	passive motion
cerebral palsy	pediatrician
epilepsy	perceptial disorders (anomalies)
fine motor (development)	petit mal seizure
grand mal seizure	poliomyelitis
gross motor (development)	prevalence
hyperactivity	psychosocial development
hyperextension	reflexive behavior
Jacksonian seizure	rigidity
locomotor skills	sensory integration
mobility maintenance	soft signs
modeling	spasticity
Moro's reflex	tremor
motor development	

---

1. Medical history—including such things as previous head injuries associated with loss of consciousness, convulsions, visual and hearing disorders, and medications.
2. Family history—including the educational background of the parents, age and sex of siblings, and familial medical and psychiatric disorders.
3. Developmental profile—including when the individual being examined was able to sit, stand, and walk unsupported; speak single words and phrases.
4. Reason for referral—why the individual was thought to be in need of a neurological examination.
5. General physical examination that takes into account age, height, weight, blood pressure, heart rate, urinalysis, and cranial circumference.
6. Awareness assessment—the individual's consciousness with respect to where he/she is, the time of day, and the identity of particular individuals as they are pointed to.
7. Speech—including assessment of the student's ability to speak coherently and to hear and understand the spoken words of others.
8. Mood—including elation, irritability, and fear.
9. Perception—including recent and unusual thoughts and tastes, sounds, and smells the student has experienced.
10. General knowledge—including the student's awareness of current events and his/her vocabulary compared with age and grade-level expectations.
11. Memory—as it relates to the student's ability to remember events that have occurred during various periods of his history.
12. Reasoning—including an assessment of the student's judgment as to what to say or do under certain circumstances. For example, "What would you say if

someone came into the room and said that there was a fire in the hall?" The reply of "Run for the window!" may be considered to be poor judgment under the circumstances.

13. Object recognition—which refers to the student's ability to identify items as they are pointed to.

14. General mathematics—referring to the student's ability to solve simple addition and subtraction problems.

15. Gait—assessment of how the student moves; general posture, arm-leg opposition, shuffle while walking.

16. Static posture—the student's ability to sit and stand without undue twitching, squirming; head tilts and body leans.

17. Muscle tonus and strength—compared with that of "normal" individuals of the same gender, age, and body somatotype.

18. Coordination—including the student's ability to button a shirt, tie a shoe, catch a ball.

19. Reflexes—including tendon reflexes (knee jerk, etc.), abdominal and plantar responses.

20. Sensations—including assessment of senses of touch, smell, and taste.

21. Status of head and neck—tenderness or deformity.

22. Status of arms and legs—limb symmetry, limb and digit deformity.

23. Status of vertebrae—shape and tenderness.

24. Status of skin—pallor, temperature, wetness or dryness, presence of lesions.

25. Retention and recall—including measurement of the individual's ability to recall specific discussions or events that have taken place during earlier segments of the examination.

After the neurological examination the attending physician contrasts the findings with available norms. A decision is then made as to the diagnosis and follow-up required. Are further evaluative procedures necessary? Can the child be expected to profit from school attendance? Is a mainstreamed setting the least restrictive environment, or should a special class be recommended? These and other questions must be answered before we can hope to set any short- or long-range goals. The prognosis for successful medical, therapeutic, and educational treatment depends on diagnosis of the type and extent of the neurological dysfunction.

PERCEPTUAL DISORDERS

Of the various neurological disabilities that can be observed and identified through the examination process, the ones that elude classic definition are related to **perceptual disorders**. The reason is that there are many views as to what comprises perceptual ability. Some definitions of perceptual ability include auditory perception; others may include such things as kinesthetic, tactile, or visual perception, Table 8.1.

However we define perception, it is likely that discriminatory behavior will be included to some degree. A descriptive model can be attached to children's neurological development as they grow. If there is a flaw in conformance to the expected pattern, less-than-optimum neurological organization is likely. With some children, deficiencies are not evident except in performance of tasks requiring fine motor skills. For others, how-

TABLE 8.1

Perception: Selected Components and Definitions

Components	Definitions
Auditory perception	Determine origins of sounds (directionality). Discriminate between ranges of pitch and intensity. Distinguish important sounds from background noise (relevant-peripheral discrimination). Distinguish between accent and beat (e.g., 2/4, 3/4, 4/4, 6/8).
Kinesthetic perception	Be cognizant of dynamic movements. Be cognizant of static body and limb posture. Integrate movement with awareness. Distinguish degrees of resistance. Distinguish relative weights of objects.
Tactile perception	Differentiate between temperature levels. Distinguish between textures and shapes. Register sensitivity to touch and pain. Register presence of pressure. Distinguish direction in which objects are moving when in contact with the skin.
Visual perception	Discriminate between colors, distances, heights, shapes, and speeds of objects. Focus attention on a selected object when it is among other objects having similar or different colors, shapes (relevant-peripheral discrimination). Distinguish distance of objects (depth perception).

ever, disorganization in general perceptual patterns is definitive and recognizable. The teaching practitioner should know some of the major symptoms and circumstances indicative of neurological deficiencies.

1. Continuous involuntary muscle action
2. Deficits of sequential organization and short-term memory
3. Developmental language disabilities
4. Diminished self-esteem
5. Discrepant perceptions of the youngster by adults
6. Early onset of temperamental dysfunction
7. Emotional disturbance in relatives
8. Family problems
9. Fine motor incoordination
10. Inability to differentiate between pitch and/or intensity of sounds
11. Inability to distinguish between various forms and colors
12. Inability to follow simple directions
13. Inattention in multiple settings where distractions are imminent
14. Nonspecific awkwardness
15. Introversion or extroversion

16. Primary depression and anxiety
17. Rhythmic motion patterns during movement (intention tremor) or continuously (non-intention tremor)
18. Severe problems with balance and coordination
19. Signs of neuromaturational delay
20. Sleep disorders
21. Emotional instability; person thoroughly likes or dislikes people without obvious basis for attitude
22. Stretch reflex resulting in flexion at many joints
23. Strong involuntary muscle contractions and hypertonicity

In addition to screening for the specific items listed, one may administer standardized tests. Among the various test batteries that successfully assess components of perceptual ability and sensory processing deficits are the Ayres Sensory Integration and Praxis Tests (SIPT) (1989), the Cratty Gross Motor Test (1969), the Frostig Developmental Test of Visual Perception (1964), the Roach-Kephart Purdue Perceptual-Motor Survey (1966), and the Lincoln-Oseretsky Motor Development Scale (Sloan 1955). The evaluative components of each of these tests are outlined in the sections that follow.*

Ayres Sensory Integration and Praxis Tests (SIPT)

     I. Space Visualization (SV)
    II. Figure-Ground Perception (FG)
   III. Manual Form Perception (MFP)
   IV. Kinesthesia (KIN)
    V. Finger Identification (FI)
   VI. Graphesthesia (GRA)
  VII. Localization of Tactile Stimuli (LTS)
 VIII. Praxis on Verbal Command (PrVC)
   IX. Design Copying (DC)
    X. Constructional Praxis (CPr)
   XI. Postural Praxis (PPr)
  XII. Oral Praxis (OPr)
 XIII. Sequencing Praxis (SPr)
 XIV. Bilateral Motor Coordination (BMC)
  XV. Standing and Walking Balance (SWB)
 XVI. Motor Accuracy (MAc)
XVII. Postrotary Nystagmus (PRN)

Cratty Gross Motor Test

    I. Level I
       A. Body perception
          1. Stomach-front
          2. Back
          3. Stomach-legs

---

* For information on scoring and other procedural matters, contact source(s) provided in the References section of this chapter.

       4. Right side
       5. Left side
   B. Gross agility
       1. Quick get-up
   C. Balance
       1. Eyes open
   D. Locomotor agility
       1. Crawl-hop
   E. Ball throwing
       1. Form
   F. Ball tracking
       1. Swinging ball

II. Level II
   A. Body perception
       1. Left arm
       2. Left leg
       3. Right arm
       4. Left elbow
       5. Left knee
   B. Gross agility
       1. Kneel and rise
   C. Balance
       1. Arms folded, eyes closed
   D. Locomotor agility
       1. Pattern jump-hop
   E. Ball throwing
       1. At target
   F. Ball tracking
       1. Catching

Frostig Developmental Test of Visual Perception

  I. Eye-motor coordination
   A. Drawing pencil line between two parallel horizontal or curved lines
   B. Connecting dots or figures
 II. Figure-ground
   A. Overlapping outlines
   B. Embedding figures
III. Form constancy
   A. Overlapping forms
   B. Embedding forms
 IV. Position in space
   A. Placing objects such as chairs, ladders, and stars into position
  V. Spatial relations
   A. Reproducing designs or figures by connecting dots

Roach-Kephart Purdue Perceptual-Motor Survey

I. Balance and postural flexibility
   A. Walking
   B. Jumping
   C. Skipping
   D. Hopping
II. Body image and differentiation
   A. Identifying body parts
   B. Imitating movement
   C. Moving about obstacles
   D. Testing back strength
      1. Elevating upper back (timed)
      2. Elevating legs from prone position
   E. Coordinating movements
III. Perceptual-motor match
   A. Drawing on chalkboard
      1. Single circle
      2. Double circle
      3. Horizontal lines
      4. Vertical lines
   B. Rhythmic writing
IV. Ocular ability
   A. Controlling eye movements
   B. Pursuing target visually
V. Form perception
   A. Drawing geometric figures on blank pieces of paper

Lincoln-Oseretsky Motor Development Scale

I. Walking backward
   A. Heel-toe on line six feet long
II. Crouching on tiptoes
   A. Timed for ten seconds
III. Stork stand (modified)
   A. Eyes open: timed for ten seconds
IV. Touching the nose
   A. Eyes open (three trials), eyes closed (three trials), using right and left index fingers alternately
V. Touching fingertips with the thumb
   A. From little finger of preferred hand to other fingers and reverse
   B. Repeating with little finger of other hand to other fingers and reverse
VI. Tapping rhythmically with feet and index fingers
   A. While seated in chair, tapping index fingers and feet simultaneously for ten seconds
VII. Jumping over a rope
   A. After two-foot take-off, jumping over rope sixteen inches high and landing on both feet

VIII. Describing arcs
    A. Eyes open (ten seconds); eyes closed (ten seconds); left index finger on right thumb, right index finger on left thumb

IX. Standing heel-to-toe
    A. Timed for fifteen seconds (eyes closed)

X. Closing and opening hands
    A. Timed for ten seconds: arms extended and pronated (palms down); closing and opening hands alternately

XI. Making dots
    A. Timed for fifteen seconds; making dots on paper with one pencil in each hand

XII. Catching tennis ball
    A. Five trials with each hand from a distance of ten feet

XIII. Making a ball
    A. Wadding cigarette paper (or gum wrapper) with thumb and fingers; two trials with each hand; timed in seconds taken to complete task

XIV. Winding thread
    A. Winding a six-and-one-half-foot piece of thread onto an empty spool; one trial with each hand; timed in seconds

XV. Balancing a rod horizontally
    A. Balancing rod on index finger; two trials with each hand; timed for ten seconds

XVI. Describing circles in the air
    A. Arms abducted to ninety degrees; making circles with index fingers; timed for ten seconds

XVII. Tapping with each hand
    A. Tapping each hand independently; timed for ten seconds

XVIII. Placing coins and matchsticks into a box
    A. Placing pennies with left hand and matchsticks with right hand; timed in seconds taken to complete task

XIX. Turning 180 degrees
    A. Jumping while making a one-half turn; landing on balls of the feet; holding three seconds

XX. Putting matchsticks into a box
    A. Using left and right hands simultaneously to place ten matchsticks with each hand into respective sides of box

XXI. Winding thread
    A. While walking, winding thread around index finger; one trial with each hand; timed in seconds taken to complete task

XXII. Throwing tennis ball
    A. From a distance of eight feet, shot putting a tennis ball at a ten-inch-square target; five trials with each hand

XXIII. Sorting forty matchsticks
    A. Sorting matchsticks into four equal piles in corners of box; one trial with each hand; timed in seconds taken to complete task

XXIV. Drawing horizontal lines
    A. Drawing as many parallel lines as possible between two parallel vertical lines; timed for fifteen seconds (preferred hand) and twenty seconds (other hand)

XXV.   Cutting out a paper circle with scissors
    A. Timed in seconds taken to complete task with each hand

XXVI.   Putting coins into two boxes
    A. Placing ten coins into a box one at a time; one trial with each hand; timed in seconds taken to complete task

XXVII.   Tracing a maze
    A. Tracing a maze with each hand; timed in seconds taken to complete task

XXVIII.   Balancing on tiptoes
    A. Balancing with eyes closed; timed in seconds

XXIX.   Tapping with feet and fingers
    A. Tapping right index finger and right foot simultaneously, then tapping left foot alone

XXX.   Jumping, touching heels
    A. Jumping into the air, touching heels, and landing without losing balance

XXXI.   Tapping feet and describing circles
    A. Tapping each foot alternately while describing circles in the air with index fingers

XXXII.   Standing on one foot
    A. Timed for ten seconds on each foot

XXXIII.   Jumping and clapping
    A. Clapping hands three times while in the air

XXXIV.   Balancing on tiptoes
    A. Balancing for ten seconds on each foot; eyes open

XXXV.   Opening and closing hands
    A. Opening and closing hands for ten seconds while sitting with forearms supinated (palm up) and arms flexed ninety degrees from body at the shoulder

XXXVI.   Balancing a rod vertically
    A. Balancing an eighteen-inch-long rod on index finger while sitting in chair; three trials with each finger; timed for five seconds

DEVELOPMENTAL ACTIVITIES

Each test battery administered provides information as to the extent of selected neurological dysfunctions. Where gross deficiencies exist, it may be necessary to consult a physician. In many cases a carefully selected prescription of developmental activities will provide the basis for addressing the disorder.

I. Goal: Perception

Major Objective	*Interim Performance Objective*
1. **Non-locomotor skills**	1.1 Imitate selected tasks during and following their demonstration.
	1.1A Stretch selected body parts.
	1.1B Bend selected body parts.

Major Objective

Figure 8.1. Standing on preferred foot and two hands

Figure 8.2. Balancing on preferred knee

Figure 8.3. Balancing on preferred foot

Interim Performance Objective

1.1C Twist selected body parts.

1.1D Raise and lower the body and selected body parts.

1.1E Stand on preferred foot while supporting self with two hands, Figure 8.1.
    1.1Ea Lower head to floor.
    1.1Eb Return to starting position.

> *Note*: Encourage students to emphasize bi- and cross-lateral movements while performing Interim Performance Objectives 1.1A through 1.1D. This will help improve body awareness and laterality.

1.1F Maintain balance on preferred knee, Figure 8.2.

1.1G Maintain balance on preferred knee.
    1.1Ga Lower head to floor.
    1.1G Return to starting position.

1.1H Stand on preferred foot with hands on hips.
    1.1Ha Raise bottom of other foot and place on inside of knee (preferred leg).
    1.1Hb Maintain balance, Figure 8.3.
        1.1HB*a* Eyes open.
        1.1Hb*b* Eyes closed.

1.1I Stand with feet no wider than shoulder-width apart.
    1.1Ia Turn 180°; retain balance.
    1.1Ib Turn 360°; retain balance.

1.1J Stand with feet no wider than shoulder-width apart.
    1.1Ja Click heels together once; return to starting position.
    1.1Jb Click heels together twice; return to starting position.

Major Objective	*Interim Performance Objective*
2. Locomotor skills	2.1 Perform selected tasks appropriately within a given space as instructed.

          2. lA Walk with typical arm-leg opposition.

          2.1B Run.
               2.lBa   Heel-toe; repeat.
               2.1Bb   Ball of foot; repeat.

          2.1C Slide.
               2.lCa   Right-left-together.
               2.lCb   Left-right-together.

          2.1D Hop.
               2.1Da   Right foot only.
               2.1Db   Left foot only.
               2.1Dc   Right-left; repeat

          2.1E Jump.
               2.lEa   Both feet.
               2.lEb   One foot to both feet.
               2.lEc   Both feet to one foot.

| 3. Manipulative skills | 3.1 Perform selected manipulative tasks appropriately as instructed. |

          3.1A Throw with expected arm-leg opposition.

          3.1B Catch.

          3.1C Implement control.
               3.lCa   Trace straight line.
               3.lCb   Trace curved line.

          3.1D Hit and kick.
               3.lDa   Stationary ball.
               3.1Db   Moving ball.

| 4. Patterning skills | 4.1 Trace selected patterns with and without drawing implement. |

          4.1A Draw a circle.
               4.1Aa   Preferred hand.
               4.lAb   Other hand.
               4.lAc   Both hands simultaneously.

          4.lB Draw a square.
               4.1Ba   Preferred hand.
               4.1Bb   Other hand.
               4.1Bc   Both hands simultaneously.

Major Objective	*Interim Performance Objective*

4.1C Draw a triangle.
    4.1Ca Preferred hand.
    4.1Cb Other hand.
    4.1Cc Both hands
           simultaneously.

5. Integration skills

5.1 Integrate selected tasks.

5.1A If answer to question is yes, hop on right foot.

5.1B If answer to question is no, hop on left foot.

5.1C If hair is not blond, hop on right foot.

5.1D If hair is blond, hop on left foot.

5.1E If you like to play basketball, slide in circle going to the right.

5.1F Distinguish colors.
    5.1Fa If color held up is red, draw a circle with right hand.
    5.1Fb If color held up is blue, draw a square with left hand.

5.1G Walk and catch.

5.1H Walk and kick.
    5.1Ha Stationary ball.
    5.1Hb Moving ball.

5.1I Run and catch.

5.1J Run and kick.
    5.1Ja Stationary ball.
    5.1Jb Moving ball.

Many variations of the Interim Performance Objectives are suitable for use with students who demonstrate atypical perceptual behavior. The tasks as presented are meant to stimulate your thinking as to the multiplicity of options waiting to be created. It is important to remember that favorable responses are most often gained when specific symptoms are addressed via direct practice.

CEREBRAL PALSY

According to Keats (1965), **cerebral palsy** is a

> ...general term used to designate any paralysis, weakness, incoordination, or functional deviation of the motor system resulting from an intracranial lesion.

Harryman (1986) goes on to say that the alteration or interruption of motor function is its distinguishing characteristic. Because the brain has control of total body function, the ramifications of such a lesion are multiple, depending on its location and severity. Cerebral palsy should not be considered a disease. Cerebral palsy is a condition—a condition that may arise before, during, or after birth, Table 8.2.

TABLE 8.2

Cerebral Palsy: Origin, Percentage of Relative Incidence, and Selected Causes

Origin	Percentage of Incidence	Selected Causes
Natal	60	Anoxia (oxygen starvation). Pressure change sudden enough to cause brain hemorrhage. Vitamin K deficiency in newborn, leading to hemorrhage. Weakness in vessels due to premature birth.
Prenatal	30	Anoxia. Cerebral hemorrhage. Failure of brain to develop. Infection of mother, first trimester. Metabolic disturbance in mother, Rh factor.
Postnatal	10	Accidents. Anoxia of brain. Infections of central nervous system (e.g., encephalitis, meningitis).

Incidence and Symptoms

Although estimates vary as to the incidence of cerebral palsy among children, the range is generally reported to be between 1.5 and 5 per 1,000 live births (Anderson 1986; Whaley and Wong 1985). It should be added, however, that its diagnosis may occur between infancy and older childhood, leading to numbers in the upper range. Russ and Soboloff (1958) cite a number of symptoms as indications of cerebral palsy.

1. Infant
   a) Poor neck control after four weeks
   b) Unable to resist a slow pull from supine to a sitting position
   c) Refusal to suckle
   d) Difficulty in swallowing or suckling
   e) Excessive crying
   f) Excessive vomiting
   g) Fisted hands after four months
   h) Presence of tonic neck reflex after six months

2. The young child
    a) Convulsions
    b) **Hyperactivity**, hyperirritability
    c) Retarded developmental progress—especially noted when the child fails to sit up, crawl, and walk by one year
    d) Hypotonicity of muscle
3. The older child
    a) Convulsions, hyperactivity, hyperirritability
    b) Short attention span
    c) Marked retarded developmental progress
    d) Speech defects
    e) Auditory difficulties
    f) Ophthalmic defects
    g) Flaccidity

Given the limitations of traditional observation methods, data must be sought from individuals representing assorted categories of professional preparation. These multi-disciplinary team members can offer invaluable information concerning the true capabilities of individuals not revealed through commonly-designed screening sessions. According to Meyen (1990), information relative to the following areas should be collected and shared by the multidisciplinary team prior to developing programs for individuals with cerebral palsy or other neurological impairments:

1. Physical/motor abilities—the impact of physical disability relative to its effect upon
    a) Fine motor control
    b) Gross motor control
    c) Abnormal postures
    d) Need for orthotic devices
2. Medical information
    a) Chronic illness (such as seizures)
    b) Acute illness
    c) Medications (and their side effects)
    d) General health (such as stamina)
    e) Medical contraindications (activities that should be avoided)
3. Sensory abilities
    a) Visual
    b) Hearing
    c) Tactile
4. Academic skills
    a) Reading
    b) Mathematics
    c) Writing
5. Communication abilities
    a) Language
        (1) Receptive
        (2) Expressive

b) Speech
c) Need for an augmentative system
6. Social skills
7. Positioning necessary for optimal functioning
8. Adaptive equipment necessary

Reflexive Behavior

As a child grows, predictable reflexes appear. Some reflexes serve important functions from infancy to adulthood (e.g., equilibrium reactions that allow us to respond to a shifting center of gravity). Other reflexes, however, should be discouraged because they can impede motor development. Those with cerebral palsy tend to retain reflexive idiosyncrasies longer than would ordinarily be expected in a developing child. As a consequence a number of these **reflexive behaviors** are clinical signs that assist in the diagnosis of motor dysfunction. Examples of these reflexive **soft signs** are

1. Asymmetrical tonic neck reflex, extension of limbs on the side toward which the face is turned while there is flexion of the limbs (fencing stance) on the other side of the body. When this reflex persists, hand-eye coordination and controlled rolling around the body's vertical axis are impeded.

2. Symmetrical tonic neck reflex, extension of the upper limbs and flexion of the lower limbs when the head is placed in a hyperextended position; flexion of the upper limbs and extension of the lower limbs when the head is brought forward during neck flexion. Although muscle tonus is aided to some degree by such reflexive activity, its persistence will ordinarily impede normal creeping and crawling behavior.

3. Babinski's sign, in which the big toe extends upward when the sole of the foot is stimulated. By the twentieth month of life this reflex is ordinarily replaced by curling of the toes upon similar stimulation.

4. Grasp reflex, in which the fingers flex to grasp when the palm of the hand is stroked. Around the fourth month of life this reflex is generally replaced by voluntary grasping (and releasing). The youngster with cerebral palsy will usually find grasping to be simple, though releasing remains difficult. (Attention should be paid to addressing skills related to releasing, e.g., throwing a ball.)

5. **Moro's reflex**, in which **hyperextension** of the head, abduction and extension of the upper limbs, and extension and spreading of the fingers occur if the child's head is dropped backward when he/she is in a reclining or partially reclining position. Persistence of Moro's reflex may impede hand-eye coordination.

6. Startle reaction—a rapid flexion of the limbs and fisting of the hands when noise, light, or quick movements toward the child's face occur. Normally this reflex disappears by the eighth month of life.

7. Rooting reflex—movement of the face in the direction of stimulation such as a touch on the cheeks or lips. If the reflex persists, normal development of eating behavior may be affected.

8. Tonic labyrinthine reflex, in which general body flexion occurs when the child is placed in the prone position and general body extension occurs when the child is placed in the supine position. This reflex inhibits ability to lift the head when the child is on his/her stomach or back. There is difficulty adducting the upper

limbs toward the midline of the body, and it is virtually impossible for the child to creep or crawl. The tonic labyrinthine reflex has not been observed in infants who are developing normally.

In physical education class we should attempt to reduce activities that stimulate these eight involuntary reflexes unless the reflexes can be incorporated into meaningful movements.

Classifications

There are five classifications of cerebral palsy based upon specific symptoms exhibited by individuals being considered for treatment. According to Andrews (1978), **spasticity** and **athetosis** are the most common classifications and, therefore, most likely to be found among children attending school. Spasticity and athetosis occur in approximately 60 percent and 22 percent of diagnosed cases respectively.

Other classification types, with percentages of frequency, are **ataxia** (8 percent), **rigidity** (3 percent), and **tremor** (2 percent). The remaining 5 percent is made up of those individuals who do not portray specific characteristics that allow placement into one of the five categories. The American Academy for Cerebral Palsy refers to this group as *mixed*—consisting of individuals who exhibit behavior typical of two or more classifications, none of which appears to be dominant. The five classifications and motorial characteristics of each are described in Table 8.3.

The various modalities of surgical and therapeutic treatments are beyond the scope of this text. There are, however, activities that we should consider incorporating into any short- and long-range physical education goal models. In this regard, Moucha (1991) related,

Physical activity has enabled me to function as a 'normal' person. I grew up unable to do many things with my right hand: hold pots and pans, grasp things, balance a cup filled with liquid, and write. However, through physical activity, I have acquired the motor skills necessary for these tasks. The crossover from sport into daily life is strengthened by my efforts to maintain an excellent fitness level.

DEVELOPMENTAL ACTIVITIES

Two basic principles are employed in these developmental activities.

1. Sherrington's law of reciprocal innervation leading to reciprocal motions
2. the Pavlov method of condition and response

I. Goal: Reciprocal Innervation and Condition Response

Major Objective	*Interim Performance Objective*
1. Passive motion, Figure 8.4	1.1 Increase awareness of movement potential of
	1.1A Elbows.
	1.1B Shoulders.

TABLE 8.3

Cerebral Palsy: Classifications, Brain Area Involvement, and Motorial Characteristics

Classification	Brain Area Involved	Motorial Characteristics
Spasticity	Motor cortex and pyramidal tracts	Involuntary contractions of involved muscles (usually antigravity) when they are stretched. This results in tenseness, exaggerated stretch reflexes, and purposeless motion. Scissors gait (resulting from inward rotation of legs, hip flexion, knee adduction, and contracted musculus gastrocnemius, which lifts the heel off the floor) is common. Upper limb involvement results in elbow, wrist and finger flexion; forearm pronation.
Athetosis	Basal ganglia and extrapyramidal tracts	Marked incoordination and constant motion of extremities and, to a lesser extent, trunk and neck muscles. Speech is impaired. Posture is unpredictable and the affected person must be secured to prevent falling.
Ataxia	Subcortical, likely in cerebellum	Impairment of balance and orientation in space. Muscle tonus lacking, as is coordination of movement.
Rigidity	Diffuse	Muscle tension giving a 'lead pipe' stiffness in trunk and limbs. Severe mental retardation is common.
Tremor	Basal ganglia	Rhythmic and involuntary contractions of some flexor and extensor muscle groups.

Major Objective

Interim Performance Objective

1.1C Knees.

1.1D Hips.

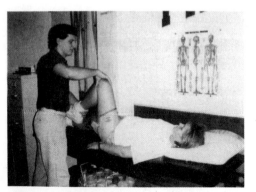

Figure 8.4. Passive motion

Note: Exercise caution when muscles are tense. Do not attempt to extend limbs through full range of motion when tenseness is evident. Synchronizing movements to selected music tempi may help the student mentally 'walk through' the patterns.

Major Objective	*Interim Performance Objective*

2. **Active-assistive motion**

> *Note*: Activity if appropriate for all cerebral palsy classifications.

2.1 Perform selected movements with assistance.

   2.1A Flex limbs.

   2.1B Extend limbs.

   2.1C Abduct and adduct limbs.

   2.1D Circumduct limbs.

3. **Active motion**

> *Note*: Activity is appropriate for all classification types who are capable of performing same.

3.1 Perform selected movements without assistance.

   3.1A Flex limbs.

   3.1B Extend limbs.

   3.1C Abduct and adduct limbs.

   3.1D Circumduct limbs.

4. **Active-resistive motion**

> *Note*: Activity is appropriate for students with spastic and athetoid classification types.

4.1 Perform selected movements against resistance.

   4.1A Flex limbs.

   4.1B Extend limbs.

   4.1C Abduct and adduct limbs.

EPILEPSY

There is much confusion as to the cause of **epilepsy** and its associated convulsions. Some have referred to it as a disease. Others have thought it to be a symptom of some other underlying problem. It is known that viral infection of some types of brain tissue can stimulate convulsion. It is also known that brain concussions are sometimes a trigger to convulsive activity. It appears that epilepsy is a condition of multifaceted origin fostering disturbance of the electrochemical activity of the brain.

Every individual has physiopsychic tolerance levels. For some these limits are low. In such instances individuals appear to be more susceptible to convulsing when the electrochemical balance is affected. When this occurs, loss of consciousness is likely.

The term epilepsy is of Greek origin and literally means *seizure*. Although seizure (convulsion) is the major characteristic of epilepsy, there is a minor form in which a momentary loss of consciousness occurs without convulsion. This form is known as petit mal.

Incidence

Since many individuals with tendencies toward convulsion do not report or have not reported on their behalf this fact, the reliability of **prevalence** statistics is debatable. On the basis of the data available, it would appear that there are over 1 million persons in the United States with characteristics identified with an epileptic syndrome. If this statistic is correct, approximately one of every two hundred to three hundred persons is subject to seizure (Phipps, Long, and Woods, 1983).

Classifications

There are three main types of epilepsy: grand mal, petit mal, and Jacksonian.

Grand mal epilepsy Grand mal is the most prevalent and dramatic type of epilepsy and constitutes between 60 percent and 70 percent of the reported cases. The following characteristics are prevalent in a **grand mal seizure**:

1. A sensation (aura) comes to the victim, indicating an impending convulsive attack.
2. The victim falls to the floor in semi- or unconscious (comatose) state.
3. The victim utters sounds and may emit saliva from the mouth.
4. The victim's muscles undergo strong contractions, usually rhythmic.
5. Incontinence.

Do not attempt to restrain an individual who is experiencing a grand mal seizure. Loosen constricting clothing, particularly around the neck, and turn the head to the side to allow the tongue to fall forward so that it does not block the airway. Move furniture away if the victim is likely to hit it during the convulsion (particularly with his/her head). Following convulsive activity, be sure that the victim rests. Finally, *never leave the victim alone; file a report.*

Petit mal epilepsy Petit mal epilepsy ranks second in prevalence and accounts for approximately 20–30 percent of reported cases. It is often difficult for even the most experienced observer to detect the occurrence of a **petit mal seizure**. Symptoms vary but are ordinarily nothing more than a day-dreaming facial expression or a twitching of the eyelids. Although they are brief, attacks may occur as frequently as fifteen to twenty times in a single day.

Jacksonian epilepsy Jacksonian epilepsy comprises approximately 10 percent of the known cases. This condition is characterized by convulsions occurring on one side of the body. In the initial phase of the seizure, there usually is no loss of consciousness. As the attack progresses up the side of the body from the foot, for example, a slight tingling and twitching sensation leads to gross spasm of major muscle tissue. At this juncture, the victim may lose consciousness.

First aid for a **Jacksonian seizure** is the same as for a grand mal seizure.

Principles of Physical Education

A number of principles are basic to the programming of activities for students subject to epileptic convulsion.

1. Avoid highly competitive activities where stress may exceed the epileptic student's convulsive-tolerance level.
2. Closely supervise students who are participating in gymnastics or swimming. It is imperative that a trained spotter be close enough to the student to keep him/her from injury should a seizure occur. (A different color headband or bathing cap worn by epileptics while in the water can help an instructor or lifeguard to maintain constant vigilance.)
3. Avoid contact sports. Head injuries resulting from contact in football or boxing, for example, could be extremely dangerous.

4. Provide rest periods when anxiety appears likely. Give the student the opportunity to slow down.
5. Familiarize yourself with the student's medical history, as well as the medicine being taken, e.g., phenytoin (Dilantin), mephenytoin (Mesantoin), or phenobarbital. Schedule visits to the nurse, if appropriate, so that the student's medication can be taken according to a medically approved timetable.
6. Schedule developmental activities that include opportunities for psychological and sociological satisfaction. Individuals with epilepsy are often subjected to cruel encounters with peers who do not understand the condition. Give the epileptic students the opportunity to gain a feeling of adequacy and acceptance through planned experiences in physical education. Opportunities of this nature should not be left to chance.

DEVELOPMENTAL ACTIVITIES

I. Goal: Psychosocial Development

Major Objective	*Interim Performance Objective*
1. Adequacy	1.1 Recognize oneself as being equal to others when participating in selected physical education activities. 1.1A Identify strengths through diagnostic screening instruments. 1.1B Attempt to succeed in activities appropriate to strengths.
2. Comradeship	2.1 Experience acceptance by individuals within the class and the class as a whole. 2.1A As a squad/group member. 2.1B As a squad/group leader.
3. Satisfaction	3.1 Experience gratification through participation in successful experiences (see Interim Performance Objective 1.1B).
4. Security	4.1 Reduce apprehension of entering into class activities. 4.1A Recognize strengths. 4.1B Recognize and accept weaknesses.

As epileptic students recognize their strengths, they should learn that all of us have relative strengths and weaknesses, and that everyone has contributions to make to the enrichment of their own lives and the lives of others. Our challenge is to educate epileptic children to think of what they can do, rather than of what they cannot do (a principle to keep in mind when working with all children).

POLIOMYELITIS

For twenty-five years Richard Chaput was completely paralyzed, unable to function except to speak and move his head, existing on a flat stretcher, a bed, and in an iron lung. (Chaput 1972.)

This was the physical life of Richard Chaput. Yet, as Representative Cleveland of the second congressional district of New Hampshire stated,

He [Richard] has no power to move and yet has moved men (1971).

Poignant yet incomplete testimony to a man who, stricken with poliomyelitis at the age of nine, contributed more in his life than many even think of contributing.* So it is with many individuals impaired by the disease known as poliomyelitis (infantile paralysis, polio).

Complacency on the part of many is leading to a re-emergence of polio. Vaccines virtually eradicated the disease prior to 1962, Table 8.4. But an increasing number of children are being afflicted. Why? Because many children are not being inoculated. We must again emphasize prevention rather than cure. As was pointed out some years ago,

"The long term effective elimination of poliomyelitis depends upon the organization in every community of systematic programs for the immunization of infants during their first year of life" (Langmuir 1961).

TABLE 8.4

Poliomyelitis: Prevalence, Statistics, 1946–1961

Year	Number of Reported Cases
1946	25,000
1952	57,000
1955	28,000
1956	15,000
1957	5,000
1960	3,000
1961	1,300

Source: Adapted from Daniels and Davies (1965)

---

* Mr. Chaput participated in over one hundred scheduled speaking engagements a year; addressed over 350,000 people; frequently appeared on radio programs; actively engaged in counseling activities; received the Jaycees' "Ten Outstanding Young Men in America" award in 1975.

Although there are various types of poliomyelitis, it is generally agreed that each is caused by a filterable virus. The disease causes central nervous system damage, particularly in the motor cells found within the gray matter (anterior horn) of the spinal cord. (The medulla and the cerebrum may also be involved.) Muscles that are denied innervation become paralyzed.

The three known classifications of poliomyelitis are abortive, nonparalytic, and paralytic. The symptoms of abortive poliomyelitis are similar to those of influenza or a common cold. Among the discomforts are headache, fever, and nausea. Minor symptoms of this sort could be easily overlooked as being caused by a poliomyelitis virus. Following this distressful period, the symptoms disappear—abort, if you will; thus the name, abortive poliomyelitis.

Nonparalytic poliomyelitis is a classification that involves the central nervous system but does not damage the motor cells permanently. In addition to the symptoms of abortive poliomyelitis, the victim might experience general and specific pain and acute contractions of one or more muscle groups located in the upper and lower extremities, neck, and back.

Paralytic poliomyelitis includes three possible afflictions.

1. Spinal, which involves upper limbs, lower limbs, respiratory muscles, and trunk muscles.
2. Bulbar, which affects the muscles of the respiratory center.
3. Spinal-bulbar, which involves a combination of voluntary and involuntary muscles. This is the most serious of the three paralytic forms, and the one that causes most fatalities.

We can best help the student who is convalescing from poliomyelitis by focusing on physical and motor fitness tasks that foster strength, endurance, and coordination. These appear to be the physical abilities usually affected by the virus.

DEVELOPMENTAL ACTIVITIES

I. Goal: Muscular Strength and Endurance

Major Objective

1. Grip strength and endurance

Interim Performance Objective

1.1 Demonstrate improved grip strength and endurance.

   1.1A Flex rubber ball.
      1.1Aa Three sets of ten repetitions.
      1.1Ab Three sets of fifteen repetitions.

   1.1B Flex hand dynamometer.
      1.1Ba Record score.
      1.1Bb Retest following training bouts with rubber ball.

Major Objective

Interim Performance Objective

2. Arm strength and endurance

Figure 8.5. Prone push-ups with knees on floor

2.1 Demonstrate improved flexor and extensor arm strength and endurance.

   2.1A Curl selected weights.
      2.1Aa Three sets of ten repetitions.
      2.1Ab Three sets of fifteen repetitions.

   2.1B Perform prone pushups, knees on floor, Figure 8.5.
      2.1Ba Three sets of ten repetitions.
      2.1Bb Three sets of fifteen repetitions.

3. Leg strength and endurance, Figure 8.6

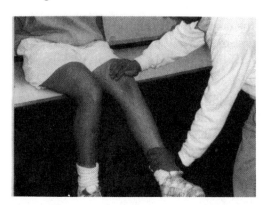

Figure 8.6. Leg extensions

3.1 Demonstrate improved flexor and extensor leg strength and endurance.

   3.1A With variable resistance placed on lower leg(s), perform leg extensions from sitting position.
      3.1Aa Three sets of ten repetitions.
      3.lAb Three sets of fifteen repetitions.

   3.1B With variable resistance placed behind ankle(s), attempt to flex knee from prone position.
      3.lBa Three sets of eight seconds at 135°.
      3.1Bb Three sets of eight seconds at 90°.
      3.1Bc Three sets of eight seconds at 45°, Figure 8.7.

> *Note*: Length of rest period between isotonic and isometric exercise sets should be determined on the basis of performer's readiness to proceed.

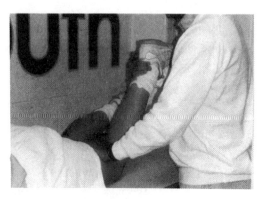

Figure 8.7. Leg flexions

II. Goal: Coordination

Major Objective	*Interim Performance Objective*
1. Hand-eye coordination	1.1 Hit an airborne balloon with the hand repeatedly for a predetermined period of time.

      1.1A Contact balloon tossed by second individual.
          1.1Aa Both hands.
          1.1Ab Preferred hand.
          1.1Ac Other hand.

      1.1B Air volley balloon.
          1.1Ba Both hands.
          1.1Bb Preferred hand.

    1.2 Hit an airborne volleyball with the hand repeatedly for a predetermined period of time (see Chapter 4).

Activities that promote cardiovascular development are also beneficial to children convalescing from poliomyelitis. These activities are described in Chapter 6.

MULTIPLE SCLEROSIS

Many misconceptions exist about **multiple sclerosis** (often called MS) and its associated ramifications. Although the term *sclerosis* means *hardening* (as it does in the term *arteriosclerosis*, hardening of the arteries) multiple sclerosis is not related to arteriosclerosis. Multiple sclerosis, named by the French neurologist Charcot, refers to the scarring (often seen in microscopic analysis as an accumulation of plaque) that is a consequence of damage done to the nervous system. As Matthews (1978) points out,

> "MS (Multiple Sclerosis) is often referred to as a primary demyelinating disease, by which is meant that the initial damage produced by the disease is to the myelin sheaths, leaving the axons intact."

The replacement of myelin with plaque appears to be the prime factor contributing to the symptoms of multiple sclerosis (Table 8.5).

Multiple sclerosis involves afflictions at more than a single site. Where plaque forms in more than one area, a syndrome emerges and the diagnosis is made.

Incidence

The likelihood of multiple sclerosis onset increases during the latter teen years and peaks in the early thirties. Although symptoms may emerge after age sixty, this occurrence is rare. The same holds true for youngsters under age ten, although some cases have been documented. Several studies have demonstrated that there seems to be an increased incidence of MS within families. Although the exact prevalence of this disease is not known—since in many cases the diagnosis is not known—Phipps, Long, and Woods (1983) point out that the incidence is likely to be greater than five hundred thousand.

TABLE 8.5

Symptoms Associated with Multiple Sclerosis

Category	Symptom
Muscles	Loss of smooth muscle action. Progressive weakness in lower extremities.
Nerves	Sensation of numbness in feet that progresses to waist.
Vision	Eye pain. Blurriness in one eye. Declining vision in one eye.
Bladder	Inability to pass urine under control.
Balance	Unsteadiness (vertigo) when walking.

It is virtually impossible to generalize about the prognosis for multiple sclerosis patients. It is extremely variable in its course and severity. Because MS can influence various components of the nervous system and is often characterized by exacerbations and remissions, it is very difficult to make a specific diagnosis. In short, there is no specific diagnosic test for multiple sclerosis.

Etiology
Although many theories have been submitted as to the cause of multiple sclerosis, no one cause has emerged. Among the possible causes under investigation are

1. A latent measles virus existing within the central nervous system
2. A high consumption of animal fat
3. Climate
4. Geography
5. Familial incidence
6. Age
7. A disturbance of blood-clotting mechanisms
8. A virus not necessarily related to measles
9. Autoimmunity

Taken separately, each of the nine options might relate to the acquisition of virtually any disease; together, the factors appear to comprise a syndrome. More research is needed, however, before specific answers are possible. At present, viruses and auto-immunity appear to be the preferred hypotheses as to cause.

DEVELOPMENTAL ACTIVITIES

I. Goal: Mobility Maintenance

Major Objective	*Interim Performance Objective*
1. Reduce high levels of spasticity.	1.1 Demonstrate postural realignment resulting in a reduction of leg extensor spasms.

Major Objective	*Interim Performance Objective*

1.1A Bend chin down toward the chest (Matthews 1978).

2. Prolong existing strength levels.

2.1 Maintain repetition and set exercise levels.

    2.1A Arms
        2.1Aa Flex elbows.
        2.1Ab Extend elbows.

    2.1B Legs
        2.1Ba Flex hips and knees.
        2.1Bb Extend hips and knees.

    2.1C Trunk
        2.1Ca Flex trunk toward legs.
        2.1Cb Extend trunk.

3. Acquire ability to use mobility aids.

3.1 Demonstrate competence in the use of selected mobility aids.

    3.1A Walking sticks

    3.1B Crutches

    3.1C Walkers

    3.1D Wheelchairs

SUMMARY

In Chapter 8 you were introduced to a variety of conditions and diseases having a bearing upon optimal functioning of the nervous system. It is clear from my experience that students afflicted with these anomalies can pose problems unique to themselves. Good general health, hygiene, and appropriate exercise, however, are needs that they share with all individuals.

The role of the physical education practitioner is to establish a process by which students with neurological disorders can sustain and, to whatever extent possible, improve functioning levels. To do so requires an understanding of factors contributing to the students' present state. Valid and comprehensive examinations administered by multidisciplinary specialists will go a long way to identify the breadth and depth of the dysfunction. This holds true for those with symptoms of perceptual disorders, cerebral palsy, epilepsy, poliomyelitis, or multiple sclerosis. Although prevention is possible in some instances, many problems are a feature of family, geography, viruses, or chance.

Given that many of these individuals—irrespective of condition or disease etiology—will be under your supervision, it is critical that you thoughtfully select developmental and other activities appropriate to their individual needs and capacities. Samples of activities have been presented in the chapter. Others, are described in sources to be found in the recommended readings. To develop additional insights, complete the recommended laboratory assignments.

RECOMMENDED LABORATORY ASSIGNMENTS

1. Arrange to visit special and regular schools that accommodate persons with perceptual disorders, cerebral palsy, epilepsy, poliomyelitis, and multiple sclerosis, in order to discuss methods and materials with practitioners who work there.

2. Complete a physical education practicum with students who have demonstrable characteristics related to any or all of the conditions described in this chapter.

3. Perform the progression of developmental activities described in this chapter. List other tasks that could be performed by a student to meet the stated educational goals.

4. Become proficient in the use of mobility devices (see Chapter 7 and Appendix B).

5. Interview physicians and physical therapists to learn about additional physical education objectives for students with neurological impairments.

6. Make a list of adaptations you could make in supplies, equipment, and facilities to enhance the teaching plan for those with conditions described in this chapter. (For ideas to stimulate your thinking, refer to Chapter 17).

7. Review the recommended readings

REFERENCES

Anderson, K. M. 1986. The nervous system. In *Comprehensive Pediatric Nursing*, edited by G. M. Scipien, M. U. Barnard, M. A. Chard, J. Howe, and P. J. Phillips. New York: McGraw-Hill Book Company.

Andrews, P. A. 1978. *Cerebral palsy—the wastebasket overturned*. Paper presented at conference entitled The School-Aged Handicapped Child, at Dartmouth-Hitchcock Medical Center. Continuing Medical Education Course. Lebanon, NH.

Ayres, A. J. 1989. *Sensory Integration and Praxis Tests*. Los Angeles: Western Psychological Services.

Chaput, R. 1972. *All I can give*. Canfield, OH: Alba House Commur:icaticns.

Cleveland, J. D. 1971. *Congressional Record—House*, April 17 Washir:gton, DC.

Cratty, B. J. 1969. *Perceptual-motor behavior and educational processes*. Springfield, IL: Charles C. Thomas.

Daniels, A. S., and E. A. Davies. 1965. *Adapted physical education*. New York: Harper and Row.

Frostig, M. 1964. *Administration and scoring manual for the Marianne Frostig Developmental Test of Visual Perception*. Palo Alto: Consulting Psychologists Press.

Gilroy, J., and J. S. Meyer. 1979. *Medical neurology*. 3rd ed. New York: Macmillan Publishing Company.

Harryman, S. E. 1986. Cerebral palsy. In *Children with Handicaps: A Medical Primer*, 2d ed., by M. L. Bartshaw and Y. M. Perret. Baltimore, MD: Brookes.

Keats, S. 1965. *Cerebral palsy*. Springfield, IL. Charles C. Thomas.

Langmuir, A. D. 1961. Next steps in poliomyelitis control. *Children* 8:206.

Matthews, W. B. 1978. *Multiple sclerosis: The facts*. New York: Oxford University Press.

Meyen, E. L. 1990. *Exceptional children in today's schools*. 2nd ed. Denver, CO: Love Publishing Company.

Moucha, S. A. 1991. The disabled female athlete as a role model. *Journal of Physical Education, Recreation and Dance* 62(3): 37–38.

Phipps, W. J., B. C. Long, and N. F. Woods, eds. 1983. *Medical-surgical nursing: Concepts and clinical practice*. 2d ed. St. Louis: C. V. Msoby Company.

Roach, E. G., and N. Kephart. 1966. *The Purdue Perceptual-Motor Survey*. Columbus, OH: Charles E. Merrill.

Russ, J. D., and H. R. Soboloff. 1958. *A primer of cerebral palsy*. Springfield, IL: Charles C. Thomas.

Sloan, W. 1955. *The Lincoln-Oseretsky Motor Development Scale*. Chicago: C. H. Stoelting.

Whaley, F. F., and D. L. Wong. 1985. *Essentials of pediatric nursing*. St. Louis, MO: C. V. Mosby Company.

RECOMMENDED READINGS

Adams, R. C., A. N. Daniel, and L. Rullman. 1972. *Games, sports and exercises for the physically handicapped*. Philadelphia: Lea and Febiger.

Adams, R. D., and M. Victor. 1977. *Principles of neurology*. New York: McGraw-Hill Book Company.

Bailey, D. B., R. J. Simeonsson, D. E. Yoder, and G. S. Huntington. 1990. Preparing professionals to serve infants and toddlers with handicaps and their families: An integrative analysis across eight disciplines. *Exceptional Children* 57(1): 26–35.

Bowers, L. 1971. A program for neurological organization. *The Best of Challenge*. Washington, DC: American Alliance for Health, Physical Education, and Recreation.

Cole, K. N., P. E. Mills, P. S. Dale, and J. R. Jenkins. 1991. Effects of preschool integration for children with disabilities. *Exceptional Children* 58(1): 36–45.

Compton, D., P. Goode, B. S. Towns, and L. Motheral. 1988. Project PAIRS: A peer-assisted swimming program for the severely handicapped. In *Educating Exceptional Children*, edited by K. Freiberg. Guilford, CT: The Dushkin Publishing Group, Inc.

Cruickshank, W. M. 1976. The problem and its scope. In *Cerebral Palsy: A Developmental Disability*, 3d ed., edited by W. M. Cruickshank. Syracuse, NY: Syracuse University Press.

Cunningham, P., and J. Gose. 1986. Telecommunications: A new horizon for the handicapped. *Proceedings of the Computer Technology/Special Education Rehabilitation*. Northridge, CA.

Education Daily. November 30, 1984. New keyboard allows disabled to type with their eyes.

Frenay, M. A. 1964. *Understanding medical technology*. St. Louis: The Catholic Hospital Association.

Haeussermann, E. 1952. *Evaluating the developmental level of preschool children handicapped by cerebral palsy*. New York: United Cerebral Palsy Association.

Heilman, A. 1952. Intelligence in cerebral palsy. *The Crippled Child* 30: 11–13.

Lotz, H. W. 1986. *Cerebral palsy not necessary: Maxi-move. Do-it-yourself for parents with movement-delayed children under eight*. Linthicum Heights, MD: Willyshe Publishing Company.

Magill, J., and N. Hurlbut. 1986. The self-esteem of adolescents with cerebral palsy. *American Journal of Occupational Therapy* 40(6): 402–7.

Mysak, E. D. 1968. *Neuroevolutional approach to cerebral palsy and speech*. Columbia University, NY: Teachers College Press.

Ottenberg, M. 1978. *The pursuit of hope*. New York: Rawons, Wade.

Patel, H. S. 1977. Physical developmental therapy technique for severely multiply handicapped children. *The Best of Challenge*. Washington, DC: American Alliance for Health, Physical Education, and Recreation.

Peters, D. M. 1964. Developmental and conceptual components of the normal child: A comparative study with the cerebral palsy child. *Cerebral Palsy Review*, 25: 3–7.

Picado, M. E. 1978. Coincidence-anticipation apparatus for a gross motor task. *Research Quarterly* 49: 240–45.

Rocklin, R. 1971. The Guillain-Barre syndrome and multiple sclerosis. *New England Journal of Medicine* 284: 803–8.

Romich, B. A., and C. B. Vagnini. 1985. *Integrating communications, computer access, environmental control and mobility.* Paper presented at the Technology for Disabled Persons, Discovery '84. Chicago, IL.

Rose, T. L., M. L. Calhoun, and L. Ladage. 1989. Helping young children respond to caregivers. *Teaching Exceptional Children* 21(4): 48–51.

Sherrill, C. and C. A. Mushett. 1984. Fourth national cerebral palsy games: Sports by ability...not disability. *Palaestra* 1: 24–27.

Tarnowski, K. J., and R. S. Drabman. 1986. Increasing the communicator usage skills of a cerebral palsied adolescent. *Journal of Pediatric Psychology* 11(4): 573–81.

CHAPTER 9

Mental
Disabilities _____

Objectives

After reading this chapter, you should be able to

- Discuss the definition of mental retardation and its essential components.
- Know the relative incidence and medical classifications of mental disabilities and their associated intellectual and behavioral characteristics.
- Describe the multidimensional model as it relates to identifying and servicing those with mental retardation.
- Identify prenatal, perinatal, and postnatal causes of mental retardation.
- Relate selected research findings to the selection of curricula, methods, and materials.
- Discuss adaptations to the teaching environment for a student with a mental disability.
- Discuss various evaluation instruments and criterion-referenced materials recommended for use with the mentally disabled.
- Know some developmental activities appropriate for those with mental retardation.
- Describe factors contributing to the effective utilization of concepts and cooperative learning strategies in classrooms and clinics.

INTRODUCTION

Mental retardation is a condition in which subaverage intellectual functioning is exhibited. Likewise, Warkany (1977) has reported that it is not unusual to observe physical disabilities in those who are found to be severely retarded. As a consequence, their ability to respond to cognitive challenges may be inhibited by musculoskeletal impairments.

KEY TERMS

abstract application	*I Can* program
adaptive behavior	informal assessments
chromosomal abnormality (anomaly)	intelligence tests
clinical types of retardation	locomotor patterning
coding	medical classifications
concept production	mental retardation
concrete and represented application	microcephalus
Down syndrome	motor fitness
educable	perinatal
educational classifications	phenylketonuria (PKU)
elevation of awareness	postnatal
environmental influences	prenatal
fetus	sensorimotor development
fine motor competencies	shunt
formal assessments	social relationships
gestational disorder	specialists
gross motor competencies	subaverage intellectual functioning
hydrocephalus	transfer (of training)

Emotional disturbances may exist as well. Many mentally impaired individuals portray clinical signs of neuroses or psychoses that may inhibit their ability to cope with frustrations imposed by the demands of a class. Successful learning can occur only if the teacher understands the underlying deficiencies associated with the intellectual disorders of the students. As Baroff (1974) points out,

> For individuals with relatively mild deficits, the impact may be largely confined to academic achievement during the school years and to the level of job aspiration in adulthood. At more severe levels of deficit, virtually every aspect of living is involved with the paramount effect being to render the person incapable of assuming the normal degree of independence expected of an adult in our culture.

DEFINITION

To better appreciate the underlying complexity of a mental disability, carefully review the components of mental retardation as defined by the American Association on Mental Retardation (AAMR).* According to the AAMR (1992), the definition of mental retardation is as follows:

> Mental retardation refers to substantial limitations in present functioning. It is characterized by significantly subaverage intellectual functioning, existing concurrently with related limitations in two or more of the following applicable adaptive skill areas: communication, self-care, home living, social skills, com-

---

* The AAMR was formerly known as the American Association on Mental Deficiency (AAMD).

munity use, self-direction, health and safety, functional academics, leisure and work. Mental retardation manifests before age 18.

To explain this definition, the Association offers the following phrase-by-phrase clarification.

- *Mental retardation refers to substantial limitations in present functioning*—Mental retardation is defined as fundamental difficulty in learning and performing certain daily life skills. There must be a substantial limitation in conceptual, practical, and social intelligence. These personal capabilities are specifically affected while others (e.g., health and temperament) may not be.
- *It is characterized by significantly subaverage intellectual functioning*—This is defined as an IQ score of approximately 70–75 or below, based on assessment that includes one or more individually administered general **intelligence tests**. (See Figure 9.1.) It can be seen that an intelligence score of 70 is at a point two standard deviations below the arithmetic average (mean) of intelligence scores. While it should be noted that a recorded intelligence quotient (IQ) of 70 is intended as a guideline only for the determination of retardation, MacMillan (1982) agrees that it

...could be extended upward to IQ 75, especially in school settings, if according to clinical judgment the child exhibits impaired adaptive behavior assumed to be caused by deficits in reasoning and judgment.

Where measurable responses are possible, intelligence may be assessed by any of several standardized tests, Table 9.1. Typical of the examinations used most often for such purposes are the Wechsler Scale (standard deviation = 15) and the Stanford-Binet Scale (standard deviation = 16), Table 9.2. Although some individuals think that persons whose scores are slightly below the mean are mentally retarded, the key phrase in the AAMR's definition—*significantly subaverage intellectual functioning*—argues against one making such judgements. Individually administered general intelligence tests, along with other available test scores and information, should be reviewed by a multidisciplinary team.

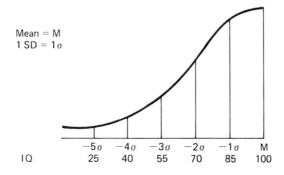

Figure 9.1. A normal probability curve of subaverage intelligence: The mean is seen as 100, the standard deviation as 15.

TABLE 9.1

Sample Listing of Intelligence Tests

Title
California Short-Form Test of Mental Maturity
California Test of Mental Maturity
Cattell Infant Intelligence Scale
Columbia Mental Maturity Scale
Kuhlmann-Anderson Test
Otis-Lennon Mental Ability Test
Peabody Individual Achievement Test
Ross Test of Higher Cognitive Processes
Science Research Associates Tests of Educational Ability
Slosson Intelligence Test
Stanford Binet Scale
Test of Nonverbal Intelligence
Thurstone Test of Mental Alertness
Wechsler Adult Intelligence Scale
Wechsler Intelligence Scale for Children—Revised
Wechsler Preschool and Primary Scale of Intelligence
Wide Range Intelligence-Personality Test

TABLE 9.2

Classification of Levels of Mental Retardation by Intellectual and Adaptive Criteria

Standard Deviations below Mean IQ of 100	Binet IQ: SD of 16	Wechsler IQ SD of 15	Designation	Adaptive Behavior
1–2	68–84	70–85	Borderline	Slow learner, may be emotionally normal
2–3	52–67	55–69	Mild	Educable to perhaps grades 4–5
3–4	36–51	40–54	Moderate	Trainable to routine tasks and self-help skills
4–5	20–35	25–39	Severe	May learn minimal self-help skills; group home ordinarily
5+	≤19	≤24	Profound	With few exceptions, vegetative state

- *Existing concurrently*—means that intellectual limitations are occurring at the same time as adaptive skill limitations.
- *With related limitations*—The limitations in adaptive skills are more closely related to the intellectual limitations than to some other circumstances such as cultural or linguistic diversity or sensory limitation.
- *In two or more of the following adaptive skills areas*—Evidence of adaptive skill limitations is necessary since intellectual functioning alone is insufficient for a diagnosis of mental retardation. Functional limitations must exist in at least two adaptive skill areas, showing a generalized limitation and reducing the probability of measurement error. **Adaptive behavior** refers to the degree to which one complies with the criteria for social responsibility as generally imposed by the group to which she belongs. Kirk and Gallagher (1989) suggest that deficits reflect a failure to meet standards of independence and social responsibility expected of the person given his/her age and cultural group. In short it appears to be a matter of age and social expectations.
- *Communication, self-care, home living, social skills, community use, self-direction, health and safety, functional academics, leisure, and work*—These skill areas are central to successful life functioning and frequently relate to the need for supports for people with mental retardation. Assessment of functioning must be referenced to the individual's chronological age.
- *Mental retardation manifests before age 18*—The 18th birthday approximates the age when individuals in this society typically assume adult roles. Although we would all hope that development does not cease when one arrives at 18 years of age, for purposes of defining mental retardation, an upper limit is accepted generally. That limit·is 18.

There are many problems intrinsic to attempting to label individuals in accordance with their performance on intelligence tests. Many factors influence ability to succeed at an assigned task. Although a person scores relatively low on a standardized test, she might adapt to the requirements of her environment (i.e., social expectations). Should such an individual be classified as retarded? Many of my colleagues believe that doing so would be inappropriate. It is now believed that retardation is a very relative phenomenon. Given that alternative forms of intelligence tests do not appear to have consistent levels of predictive validity, it will be found that scores from test to test and from session to session often vary.

INCIDENCE

Since classification depends on demonstrable intellectual as well as adaptive behavior competencies, the exact number of retarded citizens is far lower than was once perceived. At present between 2 percent and 3 percent of the population is considered to be mentally retarded. Although preventive and early intervention strategies are having an influence on reducing the number of mentally disabled children in the public schools, another factor may be that these children are being more accurately diagnosed. Thus they are being identified for services under a different rubric. At one time it was suggested that thirty out of every one thousand school-age children are retarded to the extent that special services are needed (Gilroy and Meyer 1979). This number is subject to fluctuation depending upon how one uses the statistics.

For purposes of educational description those who are deemed mentally retarded can be placed into three general groups. These groups, their relative intelligence quotients, and percentage of each group within a given population of retarded persons are shown in Table 9.3.

TABLE 9.3

Educational Classification of Mentally Retarded Persons

Classification	Relative IQ*	Percentage among Retarded
Educable	50–75	83
Trainable	25–49	14
Custodial	≤24	3

*Numerical delineations should be viewed with extreme caution. Consider the IQ ranges as variable limits. The same holds true for percentages indicated.

Whatever the exact number of **educable** and trainable children will be within our own educational settings, it is for certain that we should be prepared to provide suitable educational experiences for them.

MEDICAL CLASSIFICATIONS AND CLINICAL TYPES OF RETARDATION

Gross anomalies within the central nervous system are more likely to arise during the first three months of pregnancy (first trimester) than during any other period of fetal development. By the end of this time, the spinal cord—including ganglia and nerves, the cerebellum, cerebral hemispheres, thalamus, and basal ganglia—have all virtually reached structural completion.

The greatest contributors to structural deficiences within the central nervous system appear to be German measles (rubella) and irradiation. Other causes include drug ingestion, poor nutrition, and transmission of subnormal genes.*

Not all mental retardation arises as a result of **prenatal** structural disturbances. Isaacson and Van Hartesveldt (1978), for example, cite internal and external environmental factors as retarding development, perhaps through the second year of life. Others have said that environment contributes to intelligence throughout life. A great deal more investigation will be necessary before we will know to what extent mental retardation can be prevented.

Various prenatal, **perinatal** (natal), and **postnatal** causes of mental retardation are presented in the following outline:

1. Prenatal causes
   a) Infections
      (1) German measles (rubella)
      (2) Malaria

---

* An analysis of fluid surrounding the **fetus**, aspirated between the fifteenth and eighteenth weeks of pregnancy, will often reveal defects not observed by other procedures.

(3) Mumps
(4) Syphilis
b) Irradiation
c) Drug ingestion
d) Chromosomal anomalies
e) Genetically determined metabolic anomalies that effect
(1) Nutrition
(2) Hypoglycemias (carbohydrates)
(3) Lipidoses (fats)
(4) Aminoacidurias (proteins)
2. Perinatal (natal) causes
a) Anoxia
b) Hypoxia
c) Prematurity
d) Trauma
3. Postnatal causes
a) Environmental deprivation
(1) Maternal deprivation
(2) Familial deprivation
(3) Social deprivation
(4) Cultural deprivation
(5) Institutional deprivation
b) Hormonal anonalies
c) Infections
d) Toxins
e) Trauma

As a consequence of these and other as yet undetermined causes of mental retardation, the AAMR (Grossman 1973) prepared medical classifications to assist those charged with the care and treatment of the mentally retarded. The ten categories of causation—with descriptions—are reviewed in the following list:

1. Infections and intoxicants include prenatal infections (e.g., rubella, syphilis) and postnatal encephalitic infections resulting from such diseases as measles and mumps.
2. Trauma includes prenatal injuries such as irradiation and hypoxia, perinatal conditions resulting from prolonged anoxia during a difficult delivery, and postnatal hypoxia (anoxia) or injury of the brain.
3. Metabolic or nutritional deficiencies include such conditions as galactosemia (an abnormally high level of blood galactose), hypoglycemia (an abnormally low level of blood glucose), and **phenylketonuria (PKU),** which may reflect the inability of the body to metabolize protein properly.*
4. Postnatal gross brain disease includes neoplasms and a large number of heredodegenerative disorders of undertermined etiology. Among the symptoms are somatic abnormalities, skin lesions, skin and nerve tremors (neurofibromas), bone cysts and erosion, and brain tumors.

---

* A protein-free diet is available through Mead Johnson & Company.

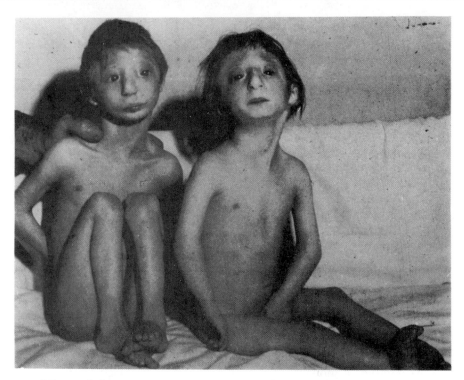

Figure 9.2. Microcephalus

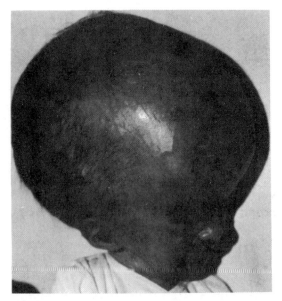

Figure 9.3. Hydrocephalus

5. Unknown prenatal causes is a classification reserved for conditions for which the etiology cannot now be established. Common examples of cranial anomalies found in this category are **microcephalus** (Figure 9.2) and **hydrocephalus** (Figure 9.3).*

6. **Chromosomal abnormality** is apparently the result of gene mutation, radiation, and drug ingestion. Occurring in approximately 20 percent to 30 percent of those diagnosed as severely disabled (Haring and McCormick 1990), Down syndrome is one of the most common examples of mental

---

* If a hydrocephalic syndrome is identified in a timely fashion, a **shunt** implanted at a point behind one ear will release fluid pressure from the skull. This procedure can reduce the potential for mental retardation.

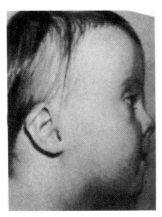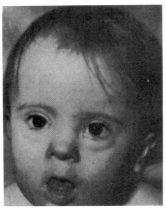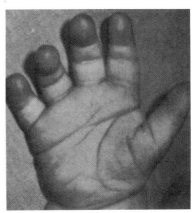

Figure 9.4. Some characteristics of Down's syndrome

disorders to be found in this category, Figure 9.4. Although few children with Down's syndrome have all the characteristics typical of the condition, the more frequently observed traits include:

a) Presence of forty-seventh chromosome in each cell (as opposed to the ordinary twenty-three pairs)*

b) epicanthic folds (skin folds located between the root of the nose and eyebrows)

c) broad nose bridge

d) oblique palpebral fissures (openings between the eyelids)

e) open mouth

f) protruding tongue

g) square-shaped ears

h) lack of cilia in nose (causative of some respiratory ailments)

i) reduced forward convex curve in nape of the neck

j) stocky build

k) dry skin

l) appearance similar to that of others with Down syndrome

7. **Gestational disorders** are a consequence of premature birth (delivery before thirty-seven weeks have lapsed since the first day of the mother's last menstrual period); low birth weight (five pounds, eight ounces or less); and postmaturity (gestation exceeds normal prenatal period by seven days or more).

8. Psychiatric disorders is a category reserved for individuals who become retarded following psychosis or other psychiatric disorders. No preexisting cerebral pathology is present.

9. Environmental influences include sensory deprivations such as blindness or deafness, and instances in which the person is deprived of maternal, familial, social, or cultural stimulation.

---

* A significant factor in the formation of the extra chromosome is maternal age. The average age of mothers with babies having Down syndrome is forty years. It is important to note that some instances of Down syndrome are due to defective sperm as opposed to mother's age (Holmes 1987). In this instance an additional chromosome would not exist.

10. Another category includes cases in which there is no evidence of physical cause or structural defect, there is no history of subnormal functioning in parents or siblings, or there is no evidence of an associated psychosocial factor.

While these categories of causation are helpful for purposes of identifying possible sources of a suspected anomaly, it is equally important that one acquire a knowledge of an individual's capabilities and an understanding of the structure and expectations of his/her social and personal environment. According to AAMR (1992) this is now considered prerequisite to describing a state of functioning and making an educational diagnosis. The exact medical etiology of a condition may not be as important as having an understanding of the multidimensional aspects of any given condition. This approach allows for an accurate description of change over time in an individual's responses to growth opportunities, environmental changes, educational activities, and therapeutic interventions. In short the intent of the multidimensional diagnostic, classification, and support system is to

1. broaden the concept of mental retardation.
2. avoid reliance solely on IQ scores to assign a level of disability.
3. relate the individual's needs to the levels of supports necessary to enhance his/her independence/interdependence, productivity, and community integration (AAMR 1992).

PRINCIPLES OF PHYSICAL EDUCATION

When reviewing program options for those who are mentally disabled, an awareness of factors contributing to their syndromes may be of significant worth to the planning and delivery of activities. As with all children, programs for the mentally disabled should be based upon an assessment of physical, mental, and behavioral competencies. Likewise as with all children, one can expect to find great variability in skill levels. It is critical for physical education practitioners to keep abreast of the literature as it relates to the principles and practices of successful teaching. What may be an effective strategy for one individual could frustrate learning in others. The important thing is to be 'tuned in' to 'what works.' As Nelson, Cummings, and Boltman (1991) point out,

> ...teachers must not assume that certain concepts are understood when they are not. If children misunderstand the concepts presented in the teacher's written or oral directions, the instructions will confuse rather than orient them to the task demands.

In short, we might find that a child could perform the skill if she understood the directions.

In addition to establishing procedures by which directions are understood, there are other principles that underscore the planning of activities. Through the years, the American Alliance for Health, Physical Education, Recreation and Dance (1977) and others have suggested what have shown to be effective guidelines. The following items appear in the literature most frequently:

1. Physical fitness, motor ability, and physical proficiency levels of mentally retarded persons can be improved. Increasingly, mildly (educable) disabled persons are achieving physical and motor tasks in the same distribution found in the general population.
2. Mentally disabled persons can learn most of the motor skills that their non-retarded contemporaries learn. There is a great deal of overlap in performances of mentally retarded and nonretarded individuals.
3. Physical education and recreation activities must be broken down into small components and the basic-to-simple principle of teaching fully used.
4. Motivation and individual success are cornerstones for a successful overall program. Success breeds success and often leads to a reversal of the failure-frustration cycle in which so many retarded persons have been locked.
5. Mentally disabled persons of all ages can accomplish worthwhile objectives when provided with appropriate, sequential, and progressive programs and opportunities within the scope of their individual abilities and interests.
6. Little **transfer** of skill has been shown from one activity to another. Conversely there is great specificity in motor activity and learning, as transfer appears to occur only under specific conditions.
7. Substantial correlation between motor performance, physical proficiency, and intelligence has been noted in mentally retarded subjects, especially those at lower functional levels—i.e., severely, profoundly, and some moderately retarded persons.
8. Novelty activities, motivational devices, unusual programs, and a variety of methods contribute to successful performance and in stimulating mentally disabled individuals to achieve.
9. Fine motor skills appear to be an important attribute in developing vocational skills that can be used in sheltered workshops or in general employment.
10. **Social relationships**, peer acceptance, and other indicators of true group interaction and integration do not automatically result for retarded children through active participation in physical education, recreation, and related activities. Although some studies have shown positive relationships among a variety of physical/motor and social characteristics, several others have shown retarded youngsters in both regular and special physical education programs less accepted and more rejected at the end of such experiences than at the beginning.
11. Today, information and generalizations about physical fitness, motor ability, and physical proficiency levels of moderately (trainable) mentally retarded persons are made in the same ways they were made about mildly (educable) retarded persons; some years ago. Research and empirical and practical experiences gained from extensive work with mildly retarded persons are being shown applicable and appropriate to moderately retarded populations.
12. Specific contributions of active participation in physical activity programs to other facets of a mentally disabled child's education and development have been reported. These activities have served as bases for art projects, English assignments, oral expression, safety lessons, and arithmetic manipulations. Self-concept has increased; greater vocational productivity has resulted; and a

variety of speech impairments have improved in the stressfree, noncompetitive, and accepting environment of these programs that were helpful to the individual in building confidence and becoming better able to deal with the stresses of everyday life. (Adapted from *The Best of Challenge*, Volume III, American Alliance for Health, Physical Education, Recreation and Dance; Washington, DC.)

Assuming that the practitioner has considered all relevant factors in arriving at a decision as to an appropriate curricular offering, he/she will now be faced with determining the present functioning levels of those for whom the activities are being designed.* To arrive at a determination of status, the teacher may choose to use informal observations and task analyses or may want to employ formal assessment instruments.

Informal Assessments

According to Payne, Polloway, Smith, and Payne (1977) the following competencies can be used as targets for a checklist or rating scale as **informal assessments** of gross and motor competencies.**

Gross Motor Competencies

1. Walks without stumbling or falling.
2. Runs without falling.
3. Runs without bumping into objects.
4. Hops with both feet.
5. Hops with one foot.
6. Skips using each foot alternately.
7. Pushes or pulls large objects.
8. Grasps, holds, and releases large objects.
9. Throws objects.
10. Catches thrown objects.

Fine Motor Competencies

1. Grasps, holds, and releases small objects.
2. Traces objects and forms.
3. Copies objects and forms.
4. Draws objects with brush or large pencil.
5. Writes letters.
6. Laces shoes and ties shoelaces.
7. Zips zippers, buttons buttons, and fastens fasteners.
8. Holds and uses appropriate eating utensils.
9. Cuts with appropriate instruments.

---

* You will remember from Chapter 3 that one of the requirements of individual education plans is knowing the student's present functioning levels.
** A checklist provides for 'yes' or 'no' responses; a rating scale allows the rater to record the quality of the performance (e.g., excellent, very good, average, fair, poor).

Not only will the data generated from checking/rating these items assist the teacher in determining the areas in which the student has deficiencies, but can also be used in lessons to develop the areas in which he/she revealed these deficits.

Formal Assessments

The more formal evaluative tools available to help us develop individualized program prescriptions for these youngsters with mental disabilities include

1. Ness revision of the University of Connecticut and Mansfield Training School Motor Skills Test, the Assessment Instrument—Basic Movement Performance Profile (1974)
2. American Alliance for Health, Physical Education, Recreation and Dance Motor Fitness Test for the Moderately Mentally Retarded (1976)

Assessment Instrument—Basic Movement Performance Profile*
Items Listed in Order of Difficulty

BASIC MOVEMENT PERFORMANCE PROFILE
SCORE SHEET: Perfect Score is 80

Name: _____ School: _____

Age:_____ Gender:_____ Date: _____

Mental Retardation Classification: _____ Score: _____

Circle appropriate basic movement response.

1. Walking
   0—makes no attempt at walking
   1—walks while being pulled
   2—walks with toe-heel placement
   3—walks with shuffle
   4—walks with heel-toe placement and opposite arm-foot swing
2. Pushing (wheelchair)
   0—makes no attempt to push wheelchair
   1—makes some attempt to push wheelchair
   2—rushes wheelchair once with arms only
   3—pushes wheelchair with continuous motion for ten feet
   4—pushes wheelchair carrying adult occupant continuously for ten feet
3. Ascending Stairs (up four stair steps)
   0—makes no attempt to walk up stairs
   1—walks up one step with assistance
   2—walks up four steps with assistance
   3—walks up four steps: two feet on each step
   4—walks up foursteps; alternating one foot on each step

---

* Originally developed by Hollis F. Fait and colleagues at the Mansfield Training School; subsequently revised by Richard Ness using residents at the Denton State School, Denton, Texas.

4. Descending Stairs (down four stair steps)
   0—makes no attempt to walk down stairs
   1—steps down one step with assistance
   2—walks down four steps with assistance
   3— walks down four steps; two feet on each step
   4—walks down four steps; alternating one foot on each step
5. Climbing (four rungs; first choice ladder of slide, second choice step ladder)
   0—makes no attempt to climb ladder
   1—climbs at least one rung with assistance
   2—climbs 4 rungs with assistance
   3—climbs 4 rungs, two feet on each rung
   4—climbs 4 rungs, alternating one foot on each rung
6. Carrying (folded folding chair)
   0—makes no attempt to lift chair from floor
   1—attempts but not able to lift chair from floor
   2—lifts chair from floor
   3—carries chair by dragging on the floor
   4—carries chair ten feet
7. Pulling (wheelchair)
   0—makes no attempt to pull wheelchair
   1—makes some attempt to pull wheelchair
   2—pulls wheelchair once with arms only
   3—pulls wheelchair with continuous motion for 10 feet
   4—pulls wheelchair carrying adult occupant continuously for ten feet
8. Running
   0—makes no attempt to run
   1—takes long walking steps while being pulled
   2—takes running steps while being pulled
   3—jogs (using toe or flat surface of foot)
   4—runs for twenty-five yards with both feet off the ground when body weight shifts from the rear to the front foot
9. Catching (bean bag tossed from five feet away)
   0—makes no attempt to catch bean bag
   1—holds both arms out to catch bean bag
   2—catches bean bag fewer than five of ten attempts
   3—catches bean bag at least five of ten attempts
   4—catches bean bag at least eight of ten attempts
10. Creeping
    0—makes no attempt to creep
    1—will assume hands and knees position
    2 creeps with a shuffle
    3—creeps alternating hands and knees
    4—creeps in a cross-lateral pattern with head up
11. Jumping Down (two-foot take-off and landing from eighteen-inch folding chair or bench)
    0—makes no attempt

1—steps down from chair with assistance
2—steps down from chair
3—jumps off chair with two-foot take-off and landing with assistance
4—jumps off chair with two-foot take-off and landing while maintaining balance

12. Throwing (overhand softball, three attempts)
0—makes no attempt to throw
1—grasps ball and releases in attempt to throw
2—throws or tosses a ball a few feet in any direction
3—throws ball at least fifteen feet in air in intended direction
4—throws ball at least 30 feet in the air in intended direction

13. Hitting (volleyball with plastic bat)
0—makes no attempt to hit ball
1—hits stationary ball fewer than three of five attempts
2—hits stationary ball at least three of five attempts
3—hits ball rolled from fifteen feet away fewer than three of five attempts
4—hits ball rolled from fifteen feet away at least three of five attempts

14. Forward Roll
0—makes no attempt to do forward roll
1—puts hands and head on mat
2—puts hands and head on mat and pushes with feet and/or knees in an attempt to do roll
3—performs roll but turns shoulder and rolls to side
4—performs forward roll

15. Kicking (soccer ball)
0—makes no attempt to kick stationary ball
1—pushes stationary ball with foot in an attempt to kick it
2—kicks stationary ball several feet in any direction
3—kicks stationary ball several feet in intended direction
4—kicks ball rolled from fifteen feet away in direction of roller

16. Dynamic Balance (four-inch beam with shoes on)
0—makes no attempt to stand on beam
1—stands on beam with assistance
2—walks at least five steps with assistance
3—walks at least five feet without stepping off beam
4—walks at least ten feet without stepping off beam

17. Hanging (two hands on horizontal bar)
0—makes no attempt to grasp bar
1—makes some attempt to hang from bar
2—hangs from bar with assistance
3—hangs from bar for at least five seconds
4—hangs from bar for at least ten seconds

18. Dodging (a large cage ball rolled from fifteen feet away)
0—makes no attempt to dodge ball
1—holds up hands or foot to stop ball
2—turns body to avoid ball

3—dodges ball at least five of ten attempts
4—dodges ball at least eight of ten attempts
19. Static Balance (standing on one foot with shoes on)
    0—makes no attempt to stand on one foot
    1—makes some attempt to stand on one foot
    2—stands on one foot with assistance
    3—stands on one foot for at least five seconds
    4—stands on one foot for at least five seconds with five-pound weight in the same hand as elevated foot
20. Jumping (standing long jump, threeattempts)
    0—makes no attempt to jump
    1—jumps with one-foot stepping motion
    2—jumps from crouch with two-foot take-off and landing at least one foot
    3—jumps from crouch with two-foot take-off and landing at least two feet
    4—jumps from crouch with two-foot take-off and landing at least three feet

(Ness, Richard, "Assessment Instrument - Basic Movement Performance Profile," Revised. Reprinted by permission.)

Although the aforementioned test is valid in its entirety for identifiable groups of children, it is not necessary for a teacher to employ the 'all-or-none' law for all children. If, for example, observations have revealed that the student can already perform the tasks required in items 1-11, the teacher may want to begin the **formal assessment** with item #12. Similarly the teacher might want to consider modifying that item to allow for a student to first demonstrate an underhand rather than overhand throw. What can surface as a major problem when diagnosing readiness levels is to administer a test item just because its there. Thoughtful selection of tasks to be demonstrated will enable the practitioner to know exactly where to begin in his/her teaching.

AAHPERD
Motor Fitness Test for the Moderately Mentally Retarded*

Item   Description

1. Flexed-arm Hang, Figure 9.5   Adjust the bar to approximately standing height. The student grabs the bar with an overhand grip (palms facing away from the body) and with the aid of a spotter (who lifts the performer at the waist) jumps to the flexed-arm position. Proper position is one in which the chin is level and above the bar; elbows are close to the sides, and the chest is close to the bar. Object of the test is to hold the proper position as long as possible.

Figure 9.5. Flexed-arm hang

* Norms according to age and gender are available in percentile form from AAHPERD Publication Sales, PO Box 704, Waldorf, MD 20604.

Item   Description

2. Sit-ups in thirty seconds   The student lies on back on the mat with knees flexed to less than ninety degrees, feet on the mat, and heels not more than twelve inches from the buttocks. Hands are placed behind neck with fingers interlaced; elbows should be resting on the mat. A partner holds the feet so that they remain in contact with the mat. On the command, 'Go', the student should curl up into a sit-up position and touch one elbow to the opposite knee; recline; repeat the sit-up and touch the other elbow and knee. Continue in this alternating manner until the command, 'Stop.' The purpose is to perform as many sit-ups as possible in thirty seconds.

3. Standing long jump   From a crouch position behind a restraining line, the student jumps as far as possible. Both feet must land at the same time, and the score is the distance between the restraining line and the body part landing closest to that line. The best jump of three trials is scored (measured to the nearest inch).

4. Softball throw for distance   Approaching but not crossing the restraining line, the student throws a softball overhand as far as possible. The best of three throws is recorded to the nearest foot.

5. Fifty-yard dash   Two students take standing positions behind the starting line. When both runners are ready, indicate the 'set' position (from the finish line) by raising arms sideways with a stop watch in each hand. Make the 'go' signal by briskly bringing the arms down and starting watches at the same time. Stop each watch as respective runners cross the finish line with the body. One trial is recorded and measured to the nearest tenth of a second.

6. Three hundred-yard run/walk   Five to ten students should prepare to run at the same time following the standard start. On the signal, 'Ready—Go,' the

Item	Description
	students run the three hundred-yard distance as quickly as possible. The timer reads the times aloud as each runner finishes, while a recorder marks times to the nearest second. (Walking is permitted but should be kept to a minimum, since the purpose is to finish in the shortest possible time.)
7. Height	Attach a tape measure vertically upon a wall. The student removes shoes and stands erect with back against the wall. Heels, calves, buttocks, shoulder blades, and head should be against the wall. Align head so that the student is looking straight ahead. Then place a square piece of wood against the wall above head and gently lower block until it just touches student's head. Take a reading to the nearest one-quarter inch.
8. Weight	Student removes shoes, any excessive clothing, and heavy objects from pockets. Student steps squarely onto scale. Take a reading to the nearest pound.
9. Sitting bob and reach	Student removes shoes and lies down on back with feet against box. Hold knees on the floor if necessary. The student sits up and reaches as far as possible along the measuring stick with both hands, Figure 9.6. Thumb of one hand should be grasped by the second hand to ensure that both hands extend equally far. The student holds reach for three seconds while the score is recorded to the nearest one-half inch. (As only one trial is permitted, a warm-up period may be provided.)
10. Hopping	The student tries to hop three times in succession on one foot. This should be done first on one foot and then the other. The student may have three trials on each foot. Scoring is as follows: 0—unable to jump off the floor on one foot and land on the same foot

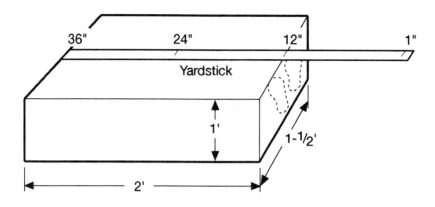

Figure 9.6. Bob and reach board

Item	Description
	1—able to hop once
	2—able to hop twice in succession
	3—able to hop three times in succession
	The final score is the sum of the best trial with each foot.
11. Skipping	Student performs a series of at least three consecutive skips (step-hops on one foot then the other). Scoring is as follows:
	0—unable to take a step and hop
	1—able to take one step and hop
	2—able to take three steps and hop on alternate feet
	3—same as above but well-coordinated skipping
	The final score is the best of three trials.
12. Tumbling progression	The student demonstrates the log roll (four consecutive rolls), forward roll, and backward roll. In the long roll, arms should be extended overhead, and waistline should be on the centerline of the mat. Scoring is as follows:
	0—unable to perform
	1—able to perform four consecutive rolls

Item	Description

Description

2—able to perform four consecutive rolls deviating less than one foot from a straight line

In the forward roll, the student starts from a squatting position. During the start of the roll, weight should be mostly on the hands with the head tucked under (student should land on the back of the neck—*softly*). On the roll-up, hands should be placed on the shins and the student should rise to a standing position. Scoring is as follows:

0—unable to perform
1—able to roll over with poor form
2—good form in getting over but unable to rise to feet without use of hands
3—good form throughout

On the backward roll, the student starts from a squatting position. During the roll, weight should be supported on the hands and the head should not turn to the side. Then hands and arms should push hard to ensure landing on the feet. Good form requires a tucked position throughout the roll. Scoring is as follows:

0—unable to perform
1—able to roll over with poor form
2—able to roll over and land on feet
3—good form throughout

The final score is the sum of the best of two trials for each type of roll.

13. Target Throw

The student stands behind a fifteen-foot restraining line (for nine-year-olds or younger) or twenty-foot line (others) and is permitted five practice throws with a twelve-inch softball at a target. Five official throws are then made. The sum of these throws represents the final score. (Adapted by permission of the American Alliance for Health, Physical Education, Recreation and Dance, 1900 Association Drive, Reston, VA 22091)

There is evidence that a positive relationship exists between improved physical and/or motor skills and classroom achievement.* As a child increases his/her level of performance in tasks requiring tactility, kinesthesia, vision, hearing, and sensorimotor integration, it is more likely that achievement in cognitive-behavioral skills will occur.

A student who is knocking over the paints, bumping into things and bothering other students is less likely to have his/her mind on the task at hand. Bumping into things, tripping, and general awkwardness can be reduced by learning to move well through space. As Gamache (1978) points out,

> This is a 'motor world'. The infant kicks and moves his body. He 'practices' eye-hand movements. All of these activities should precede the talking, reading and writing stages. Motor activities form the foundations for other learning activities. If we ignore the motor aspect, then we are ignoring the most significant avenue of learning. It must be remembered that the learning (or other) disabled child will not learn with most of the conventional methods. Through motor training, many of these children can learn and achieve success. Learning is sequential—motor (learning) should be a significant first step in the sequence.

In order to supplement the tasks to which you were introduced in the preceding sections, you might want to consider administering activities designed to emphasize sensorimotor integration—i.e., environmental awareness, kinesthesis, and locomotive patterning. Examples of such activities are presented next.

DEVELOPMENTAL ACTIVITIES

I. Goal: Sensorimotor Development**

Major Objective	*Interim Performance Objective*
1. Elevation of awareness	1.1 Improve tactile sense.
	1.1A Brush
	1.1B Stroke
	1.1C Tap
	1.1D Touch textures
	1.2 Improve kinesthesia.
	1.2A Being cuddled
	1.2B Being held tightly

---

*The reader is referred to Chapter 4 for additional examples of test items and test batteries appropriate for integration within a program for mentally disabled students.

**Adapted from Webb, R. C., Sensory-motor training of the profoundly retarded, *American Journal of Mental Deficiency* 74: 287.

Major Objective   *Interim Performance Objective*

1.3 Improve visual sense.

    1.3A Observe ball
        1.3Aa Suspended and still
        1.3Ab Suspended and moving
        1.3Ac Bouncing
        1.3Ad In flight to target

    1.3B Observe ray of flashlight.
        1.3Ba Still against wall
        1.3Bb Moving against wall

1.4 Improve auditory sense.

    1.4A Respond to own name.

    1.4B Respond to naming of things.
        1.4Ba Toys
        1.4Bb Furniture

1.5 Improve sense of taste.

    1.5A Experience extremes.
        1.5Aa Sweet (honey)
        1.5Ab Sour (lemon)
        1.5Ac Bitter (alum)
        1.5Ad Salt (salt)

1.6 Improve olfactory sense.

    1.6A Experience strong odors.
        1.6Aa Coffee
        1.6Ab Vinegar
        1.6Ac Cinnamon

1.7 Improve detection of temperature differences.

    1.7A Warm water

    1.7B Cold water

1.8 Integrate sensory behavior

    1.8A Perform mirror play, Figure 9.7.

Figure 9.7. Mirror play

2. Kinesthesis

2.1 Lift head while in prone position.

2.2 Rock under control.

2.3 Swing under control.

    2.3A Swing in hammock.

    2.3B Swing in suspended seat.

Major Objective Interim   *Preformance Objective*

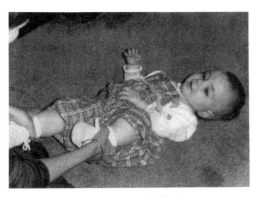

Figure 9.8. Passive channeled limb movement

2.4 Channel limb movement

    2.4A Move passively, Figure 9.8.

    2.4B Move actively with assistance.

    2.4C Move actively.

2.5 Reach with control.

2.6 Grasp and experience feel of various textures.

    2.6A Water

    2.6B Sand

    2.6C Smooth substances

    2.6D Sticky substances

2.7 Throw small balls (objects) with control.

3. Locomotive patterning

3.1 Control rolling movements.

3.2 Crawl according to directions.

3.3 Walk according to directions.

3.4 Ascend and descend stairs.

3.5 Control intensity and frequency of bouncing movements.

    3.5A Bounce on air mattress.

    3.5B Bounce on inner tube.

    3.5C Bounce on trampoline.

Note: Students must be closely supervised (provide hand contact), particularly during the use of the trampoline.

An alternative to processing the tasks described in "Developmental Activities" *according to a teacher's plan* is an instructional system that employs a contract between the mentally disabled student and her teacher. One such program is *I Can* (Swanson, 1992). In short, the *I Can* system involves contracting with a student for achievement in the four areas represented by *I Can*.

I—independence — where a student contracts to demonstrate that he/she can work by himself/herself for a specific period of time while engaged in an agreed-upon task

C—completion — where a student contracts to demonstrate that he/she can finish a task within an agreed-upon time limit or with equipment/materials available

A—accuracy — in which a student contracts to demonstrate that he/she can satisfy the criteria for success (e.g., archery, basketball, foul shooting, golf putting, for three periods in a row)

N—neatness   — where a student contracts to demonstrate that he/she can put all of her equipment away in its proper place after satisfying agreed-upon standards for time and accuracy.

Prior to a lesson the instructor will meet with the student in order to discuss goals and prior accomplishments and, as the term progresses, adjustments are made; contracts are rewritten. With the *I Can* program system, the student, her parents, and the instructor all know of what pertinent parties have agreed. Further, goals are likely to be met in that the student himself/herself has contributed to their development. As one would surmise, contracts of some sort can be prepared for most if not all physical education activities.

The mentally retarded can benefit significantly from participation in carefully planned adapted and developmental physical education programs. Like other children they need the opportunity to succeed. With this opportunity more growth than ever believed possible is becoming a reality. The expectation of success, however, must be based upon fair play on the part of the teacher, who should not attempt to set objectives beyond the grasp of the learner.

One way to assist students in their acquisition of skills of the type described in previous sections, or those to be found in Chapters 14, 15, and 16, is to focus upon the development of concepts. As indicated previously, a student must first understand what is to be done before she can be expected to perform at optimum levels. To that end it is suggested that the physical education practitioner consider the employment of learning processes of the type described by Nelson, Cummings, and Boltman (1991). Simply stated, these processes include using concrete examples, **concept production**, and application.

1. **Concrete and Represented Application**—When preparing students for drills, games, or testing, the teacher will use such terms as *over, under, behind, on top,* and *beneath*; or expressions such as *pick it up* or *put it down*. When presenting concepts at a concrete level, the students themselves—or objects to be employed in the event—should be used so that they will not be distracted by a need to first learn about objects with which they are yet unfamiliar. For example, have the students put their hands on top of their heads, on top of their feet, on top of a tumbling mat, on top of a vaulting box; when sitting, under their knees, etc. Ask them to pick up and put down a pencil. You might demonstrate the tasks when introducing them for the first time. Use repetition for emphasis. Remember, developmentally disabled students often have problems with short-term memory. As a consequence it will be necessary to repeat the concepts daily and provide opportunities for review one or two weeks later.

2. Concept Production in Everyday Speech—Ask the students to arrange an activity space using concepts they have already learned. For example, turn *on* the light, put chairs *behind* each other (a column), place a block of wood *on* top of each chair, put a towel *under* each chair. Then ask the students to describe to others in the class what they did to arrange the room. (Be sure that the students are first familiar with light, chairs, blocks of wood, and towels.)

3. Abstract Application—Provide opportunities for children to reverse the concept idea. That is, from the previous example place the chairs *side-by-side* (a row), a block of wood *under* each chair, a towel on *top* of each chair, turn *off* the light (at

Figure 9.9. Dealing with concepts

the end of the class period). Ask the students to describe what they did and what they will do at the *end* of the class period. From carrying out one concept at a time per a single directive, the students can combine concepts through a sequence without intervening directions. Since mentally disabled children have difficulty in transferring information from one setting to another, it would be useful for you to talk with other teachers about integrating concepts that you have introduced. For example, they can have a student sit on the second seat in the first column; place his/her pencil and paper on the desk; put his/her books under the seat. Then generate examples for students where they will be requested to stand on the floor and write on the chalkboard. The more integration and "transference by design" that are done, the easier it will be for the students to grasp the "true" meaning(s) of concepts. Give the system a chance. It does work! (See Figure 9.9)

SUMMARY

Throughout the chapter, various terms have been used to identify those who have deficits in cognitive functioning. They include *mentally disabled*, *mentally retarded*, and *developmentally disabled*. For purposes of this section of the book, these are meant to be used interchangeably. I have chosen to approach the topic in this way in order to familiarize the reader with nomenclature typically used in the profession.

The definition of mental retardation encompasses three basic elements: intellectual functioning, adaptive behavior, and manifestation. Each of these contributes—to a greater or lesser degree—to the syndrome and must satisfy various classification criteria before **coding** can occur. Contributing to the data base would be a score from an intelligence test. Several examples of such tests were offered. Coupled with behavior that is below norm expectations and the fact that the deficits arose during the period between conception and age 18, the child can be educationally diagnosed with some assurance of accuracy.

From reading the chapter it should have become apparent that there are many causes of retardation, and that these causes serve to provide a basis upon which children can be classified. Given medical diagnostic advances and early intervention, the exact incidence of retarded children is decreasing. Nevertheless there are a sufficient number in our schools and clinics to warrant thoughtful consideration of integration methodology. In this regard, a variety of educational principles and developmental activities were presented. Similarly samples of formal and informal assessment and delivery systems were described.

I have found from discussing the matter with **specialists** in the field, examining related literature, and reflecting on my own personal experiences, that proper planning can and does lead to student performances far above what one might expect. Cooperative learning can contribute to this growth in that all pertinent parties have played a role in establishing the goals and objectives.

Finally, arguments and strategies were posed for employing concepts in one's teaching. Opportunities for success need to be available. The integration of concepts within and between classes has been found to be a very workable alternative in one's overall efforts.

RECOMMENDED LABORATORY ASSIGNMENTS

1. Arrange to visit integrated classes and resource centers that accommodate the mentally retarded in order to discuss methods and materials with practitioners who work there. Much can be learned by observing programs in action.

2. Complete a physical education practicum with students with different levels of mental retardation.

3. Seek opportunities to assist in the coaching of mentally disabled children and adults as they prepare for Special Olympics competition (see Chapter 16).

4. Perform the progression of developmental activities described in this chapter. List other tasks that could help mentally retarded children to acquire intended educational goals.

5. Become proficient in the administration of the Basic Movement Performance Profile (Ness) and the Motor Fitness Test (AAHPERD) designed for the moderately mentally retarded.

6. Interview physicians and classroom teachers to gain additional insight into their perceptions of the relationship between motor skills and class achievement. Discuss integrated curricula option possibilities.

7. Make a list of adaptations of supplies, equipment, or facilities that would enhance teaching plans for those with different levels of mental retardation.
8. Prepare sample lessons that would reveal the utilization of concepts and other cooperative planning models.
9. Review the recommended readings.

REFERENCES

American Alliance for Health, Physical Education, Recreation and Dance. 1976. *Motor fitness testing manual for the moderately mentally retarded.* Washington, DC: The Alliance.

American Alliance for Health, Physical Education, Recreation and Dance. 1977. *The best of challenge.* Washington, DC: The Alliance.

American Association on Mental Retardation. 1992. *Mental retardation: Definition, classification, and systems of supports. A workbook.* Washington, DC: Author.

Baroff, G., S. 1974). *Mental retardation: Nature, cause, and management.* New York: John Wiley.

Gamache, P. 1978. *Curriculum guide.* Laconia, NH: Laconia State School and Training Center.

Gilroy, J., and J. S. Meyer. 1979. *Medical neurology.* 3d ed. New York: Macmillan.

Grossman, H. J., ed. 1973. *Manual on terminology and classification in mental retardation.* Washington, DC: American Association on Mental Deficiency.

Haring, N. G., and L. McCormick. 1990. *Exceptional children and youth.* 5th ed. Columbus, OH: Merrill Publishing Company

Holmes, L. 1987. Epidemiology of Down syndrome. In *New Perspectives on Down Syndrome,* edited by S. M. Pueschel, C. Tingey, I. E. Rynders, A. C. Crocker, and D. M. Crutcher. Baltimore: Paul H. Brookes.

Isaacson, R. L., and C. Van Hartesveldt. 1978. The biological basis of an ethic for mental retardation. *International Review of Research in Mental Retardation.* New York: Academic Press.

Kirk, S. A., and J. J. Gallagher. 1989. *Educating exceptional children.* 6th ed. Boston: Houghton Mifflin Company.

MacMillan, D. L. 1982. *Mental retardation in school and society.* 2d ed. Boston: Little, Brown and Company.

Nelson, R. B., J. A. Cummings, and H. Boltman. 1991. Teaching basic concepts to students who are educable mentally handicapped. *Teaching Exceptional Children* 23(2): 12–15.

Ness, R. 1974. *The Standardization of the Basic Movement Performance Profile for Profoundly Retarded Institutionalized Residents.* Doctoral dissertation. North Texas State University.

Payne, J. S., E. A. Polloway, J. E. Smith, and R. A. Payne. 1977. *Strategies for teaching the mentally retarded.* Columbus, OH: Merrill Publishing Company.

Swanson, D. P. 1992. I can: An acronym for success. *Teaching Exceptional Children* 24(2); 22–26.

Warkany, J. 1977. Congenital malformations of the central nervous system and mental retardation. *Research to Practice in Mental Retardation.* Baltimore: University Park Press.

Webb, R. C. 1969. Sensory-motor training of the profoundly retarded. *American Journal of Mental Deficiency* 74:287.

RECOMMENDED READINGS

Alter, M., and J. Gottlieb. 1987. Educating for social skills. In *Advances in Special Education: A Research Annual,* Vol. 6, edited by J. Gottlieb and B. W. Gottlieb. Greenwich, CT: JAI Press.

Balthazar, E. E. 1976. *Balthazar scales of adaptive behavior.* Palo Alto, CA: Consulting Psychologists Press.

Bennett, R. E., and C. A. Maher. eds. 1984. Microcomputers and exceptional children. *Special Services in the Schools* 1(1): 1–113.

Boyer, E. L. 1990. *The basic school.* New York: Harper and Row.

Bracken, B. A. 1984. *Bracken basic concept scale.* Columbus, OH: Merrill Publishing Company.

Carter, C. H. 1966. *Handbook of mental retardation syndromes.* Springfield, IL: Charles C. Thomas.

Croce, R., M. Horvat, and G. Roswal. 1993. Effects of exercise duration and fitness level on speed and accuracy of problem solving in individuals with mental retardation. *Research Quarterly for Exercise and Sport* 64(1): A–114.

Dahlgren, W. J., S. Boreskie, M. Dowds, J. B. Mactavish, and E. J. Watkinson. 1991. The medallion program: Using the generic sport model to train athletes with mental disabilities. *Journal of Physical Education, Recreation and Dance* 62(9): 67–73.

Dever, R. B. 1989. A taxonomy of community living skills. *Exceptional Children* 55: 395–404.

Dunn, L. M. 1968. Special education for the mildly retarded: Is much of it justifiable? *Exceptional Children* 35: 5–22.

Eckert, H. M., and G. L. Rarick. 1976. Stabilometer performance of educable mentally retarded and normal children. *Research Quarterly* 47: 619–623.

Edwards, V. D., and J. Hofmeier. 1991. A stress management program for elementary and special-population children. *Journal of Physical Education, Recreation and Dance* 62:(2): 61–64.

Forness, S. R., and E. A. Polloway. 1987. Physical and psychiatric diagnoses of pupils with mild mental retardation currently being referred for related services. *Education and Training in Mental Retardation* 22: 221–28.

Jordan, T. E. 1972. *The mentally retarded.* Columbus, OH: Merrill Publishing Company.

Kochanek, T. T., R. I. Kabacoff, and L. P. Lipsitt. 1990. Early identification of developmentally disabled and at-risk preschool children. *Exceptional Children* 56(6): 528–38.

Lambert, N., M. Windmiller, D. Tharinger, and L. Cole. 1981. *ABS: AAMD adaptive behavior scale, school edition: Administration and instructional planning manual.* Monterey, CA: Publishers Test Service.

Lehr, D. H., and E. L. Meyen. 1982. Mental retardation. In *Exceptional Children in Today's Schools: An Alternative Resource Book,* edited by E. L. Meyen. Denver, CO: Love.

MacMillan, D. L. 1988. Issues in mild mental retardation. *Education and Training in Mental Retardation* 23: 273–84.

McCormick, P. K., J. W. Campbell, R. Pasnak, and P. Perry. 1990. Instruction of Piagetian concepts for children with mental retardation. *Mental Retardation* 28:(6): 359–66.

Meichenbaum, D. 1980. Cognitive behavior modification with exceptional children: A promise yet unfulfilled. *Exceptional Education Quarterly* 1: 83–88.

Moran, J. M., and L. H. Kalakian. 1977. *Movement experiences for the mentally retarded or emotionally disturbed child.* Minneapolis, MN: Burgess Publishing Company.

Nelson, R. B., and J. A. Cummings. 1981. Basic concept attainment of educable mentally handicapped children: Implications for teaching concepts. *Education and Training of the Mentally Retarded* 16: 303–6.

Porretta, D. L., and K. O'Brien. 1991. The use of contextual interference trials by mildly mentally handicapped children. *Research Quarterly for Exercise and Sport* 62(2): 244–48.

President's Committee on Mental Retardation. 1976. *Mental retardation: Century of decision.* Washington, DC: U.S. Government Printing Office.

Raynes, M., M. Snell, and W. Sailor. 1991. A fresh look and categorical programs for children with special needs. *Phi Delta Kappan* 73(4): 326–31.

Repp, A. C. 1983. *Teaching the mentally retarded.* Englewood Cliffs, NJ: Prentice-Hall.

Simeonsson, R. J., D. B. Bailey, G. S. Huntington, and M. Comfort. 1986. Testing the concept of goodness of fit in early intervention. *Infant Mental Health Journal* 7: 81–94.

Smith, D. W. 1979. *Recognizable patterns of human malformation.* Philadelphia: W. B. Saunders.

Surburg, P. R., and V. Sutlive. 1993. Use of imagery practice for improving a motor skill of students with mental retardation. *Research Quarterly for Exercise and Sport: Supplement* 64(1): A–118.

Terman, L. M., and M. A. Merrill. 1960. *Stanford-Binet Intelligence Scale.* Boston, MA: Houghton Mifflin.

Thorndike, R. L., E. P. Hagen, and J. M. Sattler. 1986. *The Stanford-Binet Intelligence Scale, fourth edition.* Chicago: Riverside.

Turkington, C. 1992. Special talents. In *Educating Exceptional Children,* edited by K. Freiberg. Guilford, CT: The Dushkin Publishing Group, Inc.

Vaughn, S., C. S. Bos, and A. R. Lund. 1986. But they can do it in my classroom: Strategies for promoting generalization. *Teaching Exceptional Children* 18: 176–80.

Wechsler, D. 1974. *Wechsler intelligence scale for children—revised.* New York: Psychological Corporation.

Weisz, J. R. 1981. Effects of the "mentally retarded label" on adult judgements about child failure. *Journal of Abnormal Psychology* 90(4): 371–74.

CHAPTER 10

Behavioral and
Emotional Disorders

Objectives

After reading this chapter, you should be able to

- Describe the relative incidence of behavioral disorders among school-age children.
- Identify common and characteristic behaviors of children with psychological impediments.
- Discuss selected screening procedures.
- Discuss the probable causes and the classifications of common behavioral disorders.
- Discuss autism and some remedial strategies.
- Identify defense mechanisms commonly employed by those with emotional problems.
- Relate how the environment might increase negative behaviors in children.
- Discuss the role of the teacher in establishing a stress-reduced environment.
- Discuss some recommended techniques for dealing with disciplinary problems.
- Describe the underlying principles of behavior modification, and techniques related to the application of these principles.

INTRODUCTION

Maladaptive behavior constitutes a major source of anxiety for many public school teachers. One reason is that the actions of children with emotional problems are often unpredictable. On one occasion a youngster may behave in a manner consistent with the best that a teacher may expect of anyone. At another time, however, the child may act in an unrestrained manner, pushing others, using profanity, throwing things, or running away.

KEY TERMS

anxiety reaction	programmatic procedures
autism	projection
behavior modification	psychological/environmental factors
biological factors	psychoses
compensation	rationalization
defense mechanisms	reaction formation
depressive reaction	regression
disassociative reaction	reinforcement
evaluation	repression
fixation	schizophrenia
identification	seriously emotionally disturbed
management	shaping
manic-depressive psychosis	stimulus control
neurosis	sublimation
obsessive-compulsive reaction	substitution
phobia	suicide
phobic reaction	

When attempting to describe these or other behaviors, a variety of terms often surface. Among the more common are such expressions as aggressive, delinquent, disruptive, immature, overactive, and shy. Using these terms in itself often provokes controversy. Who decides what constitutes delinquency? What is immaturity? By what standard? When does shyness become an inhibitor to attaining educational and social responsibility? Given that the objectivity of some evaluations would have to be considered suspect, it should not be surprising that problems abound when attempting to legitimize data generated by observations. Unfortunately there are no simple answers. As a consequence it is not difficult to understand why behavior disorders are universally recognized as significant social problems.

When categorizing behavioral and emotional disorders, many professional organizations advocate use of the term *behavior disorders* (Gearheart, Weishahn, and Gearheart 1992). On the other hand, the reader should note that federal regulations governing the implementation of PL 94-142 use the term **seriously emotional disturbed**, defined as follows:

> The term means a condition exhibiting one or more of the following characteristics over a long period of time and to a marked degree, which adversely affects educational performance:
>
> 1. an inability to learn which cannot be explained by intellectual, sensory, or health factors;
> 2. an inability to build or maintain satisfactory interpersonal relationships with peers and teachers;
> 3. inappropriate behavior or feelings under normal circumstances;
> 4. a general pervasive mode of unhappiness or depression; or
> 5. a tendency to develop physical symptoms or fears associated with personal or school problems.

The term includes children who are schizophrenic or autistic.* The term does not include children who are socially maladjusted unless it is determined that they are seriously emotionally disturbed (*Federal Register*, August 23, 1977. p. 42478).

Regardless of the name applied to the condition, there is evidence of problem behavior. This and how the physical education practitioner can best address the problem represent my concerns and underscore the rationale for the sections that follow.

INCIDENCE

Tara was a bright, fifteen-year old who was raped by her stepfather. Her performance in school was well above average at the time of the attack. Be reminded that while you are reading this chapter, she is now out of school attempting to support her new baby. *Tom* learned that he is HIV-positive. Embarrassed and perceiving himself as unable to communicate with his parents or teachers, he decided that **suicide** was "the only way out". *Martha* and *Eddie* quit school, ran away from their respective homes, and are now sharing a pad in Greenwich Village in New York. Being unskilled and therefore unable to find suitable employment, *Eddie* is now soliciting for his girlfriend who is prostituting in order to meet expenses. Remember *Tara*? Her seventeen-year old boyfriend assaulted her stepfather and is now serving time in prison. Both his and *Tara's* parents are in the process of a divorce.

Do you think that these incidences are contrived? Made up? Read on. In 1989 the Children's Defense Fund reported the following in *One Day in the Lives of American Children, 1987*: 1,293 teenagers will give birth; 1,849 children will be abused; 3,288 children will choose to run away from home; 1,629 children will be incarcerated in adult jails; 2,989 children will see their parents divorce; and 6 teenagers will commit suicide.

It is any wonder that our schools are plagued with problems arising from troubled youths? And what is disturbing in particular is that most of these conditions are preventable. With the exception of those few with specific genetic predispositions, children are not born with emotional anomalies. These problems are acquired within the homes, within the neighborhoods, and/or within the schools.

An examination of reports pertaining to the prevalence of behavioral disorders reveals conflicting findings. This will probably hold true as long as there is inconsistency in assessing and defining behavior. The estimates have varied from less than 1 percent to greater than 30 percent of the school-age population (Haring and McCormick 1990), depending upon the design of the data-gathering instruments and the population tested. The federal accounting of handicapped students (U.S. Department of Education 1988) indicates that approximately 1 percent of the school population are severely emotionally disturbed. However, Kauffman and Kneedler (1981) point out that this seemingly conservative value may be due to the fact that, because PL 94-142 requires that special education be provided to all students who are found to be handicapped, many districts may be finding only as many behaviorally disordered students as can be accommodated within the limitations of budget and personnel.

---

* In Public Law 101-476 (1990) **autism** was listed as a separate disability

Considering input from assorted sources, it would seem wise to assume that one out of every ten to twelve students will demonstrate behaviors of a nature that require intervention...by someone.

ETIOLOGY AND CLASSIFICATIONS

The issues involving the identification of causes for aberrant behavior are a microcosm of the questions faced by the entire field of adapted physical education. One reason is that few authorities agree as to the cause of behavioral disorders in young people. Nevertheless it is important to examine such factors in order to avoid circumstances that may aggravate existing conditions. Even knowing probable causes can lead to the selection of meaningful intervention strategies. Although it would take numerous listings to identify every condition that has been suggested as a cause of behavioral disorders, it is possible to classify three general categories: **biological factors, psychological/environmental factors**, and a combination of the two.

Biological

There is increasing evidence that behavioral characteristics can be influenced by genetic and other biological factors. Since genes influence chemical responses in our bodies, many events operating before, during, and after birth can lead to brain dysfunction. Longitudinal research programs are revealing the effects of both nature and nurture on human adjustment. The results increasingly point to heredity as a contributory condition in some behavioral disorders (Achenbach 1982). Yet, given the fact that many assessment procedures for studying brain disorders lack significant levels of validity, the issue continues to intrigue and baffle research and teaching practitioners (Werry 1986). Among the organic influences that underlie behavioral disorders are

1. Brain involvement resuting from chemical imbalance, disease, trauma and drugs
2. Glandular dysfunction

Psychological/Environmental

The family unit is universally recognized as the primary contributor to social (behavioral) development in children and adolescents (Haring and McCormick 1990). Secondary factors relate to the interaction between the family and its environment, including the school and community. Additional influences having a bearing on behavior include such things as illness, peer pressure, sense of self, fear of failure, and other stress-related issues. In short, psychological/environmental influences that may cause behavioral disorders are:

1. Child abuse
2. Urbanization
3. Poverty
4. Residence in a slum area
5. Discrimination
6. Stress
7. Peer pressure
8. Image of law enforcement

9. Loss of identity
10. Breakdown of family unit
11. Untreated maladies
12. Perception of self as not being cared for or loved

Combination

Although biological and psychological/environmental conditions have been presented separately, few theorists are of the belief that they operate in total independence (Garrison and Earls 1987). The research of Thomas and Chess (1977) shows that an individual's temperament (perhaps caused by chemical interactions) often influences the rearing practices adopted by his/her parents or the methods and mannerisms (M & Ms) his/her teacher will employ. This in turn has a bearing upon his/her behavioral development. There appears to be little doubt that interaction of the organism and its environment will play a major role in behavior and its modification.

When examining the literature regarding behavioral and emotional disorders, it is not uncommon to find reference to such terms as **neuroses** and **psychoses**. These are considered to be major classifications of mental disorders. Given the frequency with which these expressions are used, the following descriptions are offered.

Neurotic Disorders The neurotic individual retains contact with reality, and his/her personality is not essentially different from that of a normally functioning person. The neurotic's conduct may be inefficient and inadequate, but generally it is not antisocial. Also referred to as *psychoneurosis*, neurosis is characterized by manifestations of apprehension that are directly felt and expressed. Among the more common neurotic behaviors are

1. **Anxiety reaction**—which is marked by anxiety that is out of proportion to any obvious cause
2. **Depressive reaction**—which is a state resulting from a real or imagined loss and may progress to psychotic depths
3. **Disassociative reaction**—characterized by such conditions as amnesia or sleep walking
4. **Obsessive-compulsive reaction**—characterized by anxiety associated with persistent repetitive impulses, e.g., desires to carry out certain acts such as handwashing, counting, or touching repeatedly
5. **Phobic reaction**—which is characterized by abnormal fears (**phobias**) of existing stimuli such as water, heights, confined places, and fire

Psychotic Disorders A person suffering from a psychotic disorder loses touch with reality. He/she may react erroneously to it or build up false concepts regarding it. The person's behavioral responses are deemed peculiar, abnormal, and antisocial. Of the various types of psychotic disorders, two have received the most attention.

1. **Manic-depressive psychosis**—characterized by alternating moods of depression and exaltation
2. **Schizophrenia** (dementia praecox)—the most common and serious of the functional disorders. A number of the symptoms related to schizophrenia are listed in Table 10.1.

TABLE 10.1

Schizophrenia: Selected Symptoms

Symptom	Description
Moodiness	Individual is given to sudden gloom (moroseness) with little or no provocation.
Delusions	Individual subscribes to persistent erroneous beliefs.
Hallucinations	Individual reacts to any of numerous auditory, visual, or tactile perceptions having no external cause or stimulus.
Solitariness	Individual prefers to be secluded, remote from others.
Stupor	Individual portrays a mental attitude in which the senses and faculties are extremely dull.

Autism In 1943 Kanner described the composition of autistic behavior in children. *Early infantile autism*—a type of schizophrenia—has received increased attention in recent years. That this condition is diagnosed is due in part to the sensitivity training many practitioners are receiving in their undergraduate and graduate professional preparation programs. Many children who in the past were referred to as "just plain naughty" are being properly diagnosed as autistic and provided with appropriately-developed individual education plans (IEPs).

Characteristics. An autistic child is one who is compelled to satisfy the ego in ways that violate common codes of behavior. In addition to being emotionally disturbed, the child often exhibits characteristics common to those who are classified as mentally retarded. Receptive and expressive language skills are often diminished to the extent that radical behavior is likely when demands fall short of realization.

The autistic child may demonstrate the following social characteristics:

1. Bizarre behavior
2. Inflexible behavior
3. Repetitive behavior
4. Self-injuring behavior, including biting and hitting self
5. The wish to be away from other people

In addition to the social characteristics just identified, the following motor characteristics may be expressed:

1. Lack of gross and fine motor coordination essential to the performance of activities of daily living, e.g.,
   a) walking, running, skipping, hopping.
   b) bathing, brushing, dressing, feeding oneself.
   c) using writing or other implements.
2. Low levels of audiomotor and visuomotor ability, as seen in:
   a) failure to clap hands or stamp feet in rhythmical cadence (to music).
   b) failure to move objects in prescribed patterns or pursuits.
   c) failure to imitate selected movement patterns.

Misconduct can be expected of any normal youngster. When isolated incidents begin to merge, however, referral to a specialist should be considered. Similarly if we know how children feel about each other or the activities in which they are engaged, we can identify trends that might indicate an underlying problem or symptoms of one to come. A review of the data generated through observations or more formal assessment procedures will help one establish proper intervention strategies. Following years of research and field testing, the American Psychiatric Association (1987) identified nine major groups of behavior disorders*—disorders that may be exhibited by children of various ages.

I. Developmental disorders
   A. Mental retardation
      1. Mild mental retardation
      2. Moderate mental retardation
      3. Severe mental retardation
      4. Profound mental retardation
      5. Unspecified mental retardation
   B. Pervasive developmental disorders
      1. Autistic disorder
      2. Pervasive developmental disorder not otherwise specified
   C. Specific developmental disorders
      1. Academic skill disorders
      2. Language and speech disorders
      3. Motor skills disorder
II. Disruptive behavior disorders
   A. Attention-deficit hyperactivity disorder
   B. Conduct disorder
   C. Oppositional-defiant disorder
III. Anxiety disorders of childhood or adolescence
   A. Separation anxiety disorder
   B. Avoidant disorder of childhood or adolescence
   C. Overanxious disorder
IV. Eating disorders
   A. Anorexia nervosa
   B. Bulimia nervosa
   C. Pica
   D. Rumination disorder of infancy
V. Gender identity disorders
   A. Gender identity disorder of childhood
   B. Transsexualism
   C. Gender identity disorder of adolescence or adulthood, nontranssexual type
VI. Tic disorders
   A. Tourette's disorder

---

* The reader will note, pursuant to reading other chapters in Section II, that a number of these categories may overlap with those of other exceptionalities. For example, children who express developmental disabilities may also be identified as autistic, learning disabled, or retarded.

    B. Chronic motor or vocal tic disorder
    C. Transient tic disorder
VII. Elimination disorders
    A. Functional encopresis
    B. Functional enuresis
VIII. Speech disorders not elsewhere classified
    A. Cluttering
    B. Stuttering
IX. Other disorders of infancy, childhood, or adolescence
    A. Elective mutism
    B. Identity disorder
    C. Reactive attachment disorder of infancy or early childhood
    D. Stereotypy/habit disorder
    E. Undifferentiated attention-deficit disorder

DEFENSE MECHANISMS

When a individual is confronted with the notion that his/her actions are unacceptable to others, **defense mechanisms** may emerge. Within reasonable limits such mechanisms may be quite normal. Extremely defensive behavior, however, can be a symptom of an underlying emotional anomaly. The ten more prevalent defense mechanisms are presented in the following list.

1. **Compensation** is an attempt to make up for lack of ability by attaining substitute goals. A youngster who is poorly skilled in a particular activity may demonstrate maladaptive behavior to gain the desired attention (a substitute goal).

2. **Fixation** exists when expected and normal personality development is altered to the extent that the individual may continue to react as a child when confronted with certain dilemmas. An example of fixation is overdependence on a parent in such circumstances.

3. **Identification** is imitation of the actions of someone else. Ordinarily the person imitated is an object of hero worship, but an underdog might be imitated also.

4. **Projection** is a mechanism by which unacceptable desires or actions are disowned and often attributed to someone else. An example is to blame the teacher for a poor or failing test grade.

5. **Rationalization** is a process whereby an individual offers excuses for his/her thoughts or actions. An example is blaming a basketball teammate for a poor lead pass when the individual misses an easy lay-up shot.

6. **Reaction formation** refers to the development of character traits, attitudes, and forms of behavior that are in direct opposition to the person's inner feelings. An example is the school bully who fears that he/she is a coward.

7. **Regression** is an anxiety-evading mechanism often manifested by the readoption of immature patterns of thought, behavior, and emotional responses. Tattling and temper tantrums are examples of regressive behavior.

8. **Repression** excludes unacceptable desires, impulses, and thoughts from conscious awareness. It is important to note, however, that these repressed

thoughts (or feelings) may surface when provocative incidents similar to those that caused the original thoughts repeat themselves.

9. **Sublimation** is the channeling of undesirable impulses and drives away from their primitive objectives into activities of a higher order. *Sublimation* is a Freudian term used to explain unconscious mental processes wherein sexual instinct that cannot be satisfied at the moment finds an outlet through creative cognitive activity.

10. **Substitution** is often equated with compensation. Substitution refers to situations in which activities that require less skill or practice are selected over those that require more commitment.

SCREENING PROCEDURES

At some point, educators need to turn their considerable talents to the tasks of convincing the voting members of society that it is far more efficient to identify and attend to those who present unacceptable behavior when they are children than to house, feed, and fear them when they become adults (Maag and Howell 1991). Further, as Meyen (1990) points out, comprehensive assessment of students with emotional problems is critical to establishing an effective learning environment. Informal and formal procedures designed to assess academic, motor, sensory, and social functioning are crucial to an understanding of the various forces influencing behavior.

Since a person's decision to visit a psychologist or psychiatrist is likely to result from external rather than internal prompting, it is critical that school-based educational personnel be familiar with symptoms that can be identified with a psychological anomaly. Typical reasons to recommend that a child receive further assessment are indicated by the following circumstances:

1. When a student is virtually never selected by other children for involvement in the activity of the group, an underlying socio-peer problem may exist.
2. When a student is overly jealous of the successes of others.
3. When a student is tardy or frequently absent from class.
4. When a student bullies other children.
5. When a student makes little or no effort to achieve or is inattentive or lazy.
6. When a student is prone to quickness of temper.
7. When a student frequently appears sad or depressed.
8. When a student is overly competitive.
9. When a student exhibits nervous reactions such as restlessness, twitching, stuttering, and nail biting.
10. When a student does not appear to care whether he is liked.

We can also use more formal and objective evaluation instruments to measure the social qualities of students. Among these are the Blanchard Behavior Rating Scale (1936) (Table 10.2) and the Cowell's Social Adjustment Index (1958) (Table 10.3).

In regard to scores generated by these instruments, it may be of prime importance to make special note of individual rather than total values. A total score may obscure a specific deficit or inter-item trend that would need attention.

While the two aforementioned instruments represent examples of those to be completed by teachers or supervisors, there are other scales which provide opportunities for

TABLE 10.2

Blanchard Behavior Rating Scale (Modified)

	No opportunity to observe	Never	Seldom	Fairly often	Frequently	Extremely often	Score
1. Is popular with classmates	____	1	2	3	4	5	____
2. Seeks responsibility in the classroom	____	1	2	3	4	5	____
3. Shows intellectual leadership in class	____	1	2	3	4	5	____
4. Shows initiative in assuming responsibility in unfamiliar situations	____	1	2	3	4	5	____
5. Is alert to new opportunities	____	1	2	3	4	5	____
6. Shows keenness of mind	____	1	2	3	4	5	____
7. Volunteers ideas	____	1	2	3	4	5	____
8. Grumbles over decisions of classmates	____	5	4	3	2	1	____
9. Takes justified criticism by others without showing anger or pouting	____	1	2	3	4	5	____
10. Is loyal to the group	____	1	2	3	4	5	____
11. Discharges assigned responsibilities well	____	1	2	3	4	5	____
12. Has favorable attitude toward cooperation with the teacher	____	1	2	3	4	5	____
13. Makes loud criticism and comments	____	5	4	3	2	1	____
14. Respects the rights of others	____	1	2	3	4	5	____
15. Is truthful	____	1	2	3	4	5	____
16. Is dependable and trustworthy	____	1	2	3	4	5	____
17. Has good study habits	____	1	2	3	4	5	____
18. Is liked by others	____	1	2	3	4	5	____
19. Makes a friendly approach to others in the group	____	1	2	3	4	5	____
20. Willing to try new activities	____	1	2	3	4	5	____

Source: B. E. Blanchard (1936). Presented with permission of the American Alliance for Health, Physical education, Recreation and Dance.

TABLE 10.3

Cowell's Social Adjustment Index (Modified)

Positive Behavior Trends (Form A)	Markedly (+3)	Somewhat (+2)	Only Slightly (+1)	Not at All (+0)
1. Enters heartily and with enjoyment into the spirit of social exchange	____	____	____	____
2. Frank, talkative and sociable, does not stand on ceremony	____	____	____	____
3. Self-confident and self-reliant, tends to take success for granted, strong initiative, prefers to lead	____	____	____	____
4. Quick and decisive in movement, pronounced or excessive energy output	____	____	____	____
5. Prefers group activities, work, or play; not easily satisfied with individual projects	____	____	____	____
6. Adaptable to new situations, makes adjustments readily, welcomes change	____	____	____	____
7. Is self-composed, seldom shows signs of embarrassment	____	____	____	____
8. Tends to elation of spirits, seldom gloomy or moody	____	____	____	____
9. Seeks a broad range of friendships, not selective or exclusive in games and the like	____	____	____	____
10. Hearty and cordial, even to unfamiliar persons, forms acquaintanceships very easily	____	____	____	____

Source: Charles C. Cowell (1958). Presented with permission of the American Alliance for Health, Physical Education, Recreation and Dance.

students to rate each other. Provided that the students are able to remain anonymous, actual attitudes toward peers may be revealed. We have to expect, however, that the reliability of student ratings may be suspect because the way children feel toward each other may vary from day to day, or episode to episode. This is particularly true of younger children.* Nevertheless these ratings do provide another source of information.

---

* Reliability refers to the degree to which an assessment instrument measures a trait in a consistent way.

Keep in mind that it is the trend one might uncover between and within individual ratings that can be very useful in establishing a data base important to classroom management strategies or referrals. Two testing instruments that allow for student ratings of peers are the Cowell Personal Distance Scale (1958) (Table 10.4) and the Nelson (Modified) Sports Leadership Questionnaire (1966) (Table 10.5).

TABLE 10.4

Cowell Personal Distance Scale (Modified)

What to Do	I would be willing to accept him/her						
If you had full power to treat each student on this list as you feel, just how would you consider him/her? How near would you like to have him/her to your family? Check each student in *one* column as to your feeling toward him/her (circle your own name).**	Into my family as a brother	As a very close pal	As a member of my club	On my street as a 'next-door' neigh-bor	Into my class at school	Into my school	Into my city
	7	6	5	4	3	2	1
1._____							
2._____							
3._____							
4. etc. _____							

**Given the fact that trends may be more important than a single rating, the student could include himself/herself in the ratings, thus providing for complete anonymity.

TABLE 10.5

Nelson (Modified) Sports Leadership Questionnaire

A. _____ B. _____	1. If you were on a trip and had a choice of the players you would share a dormitory room with, who would they be?
A. _____ B. _____	2. Who are the most popular members of the team?
A. _____ B. _____	3. Who are the best scholars on the team?
A. _____ B. _____	4. Which players know the most about the sport in terms of strategy, rules, etc.

Table 10.5 *continued*

A. _____ B. _____	5. If the coach was not present for a workout, which athletes would be the most likely to take charge of the practice?
A. _____ B. _____	6. Which players would you listen to first if the team appeared to be disorganized during a crucial game?
A. _____ B. _____	7. When the team is behind in a close contest and there is still a chance to win, who is the most likely teammate to score the winning points?
A. _____ B. _____	8. Of all of your teammates, who exhibits the most poise during crucial parts of the contest?
A. _____ B. _____	9. Who are the most valuable players on the team?
A. _____ B. _____	10. Who are the players who play "most for the team"?
A. _____ B. _____	11. Who are the most consistent point makers for the team?
A. _____ B. _____	12. Who are the most respected performers on the team?
A. _____ B. _____	13. Which teammates have the most overall ability?
A. _____ B. _____	14. Which teammates train the hardest to improve their performance off season?
A. _____ B. _____	15. Who are the most likeable players on the team?
A. _____ B. _____	16. Which players have most favorably influenced you?
A. _____ B. _____	17. Which players have actually helped you the most?
A. _____ B. _____	18. Which teammates do you think would make the best coaches?
A. _____ B. _____	19. Which teammates do you most often look to for leadership?
A. _____ B. _____	20. Who are the hardest workers during regular practice hours?

Source: Dale O. Nelson (1966). Presented with permission of the American Alliance for Health, Physical Education, Recreation and Dance.

Upon examining the responses of the students, it will become clear who is favored in areas referenced by the instrument. By the same token, it will become clear who is rarely if ever selected for anything. This too can provide useful information when examining the intricacies of problem behavior.

Suicide

There are few issues prompted by human behavior that are as provocative as those arising from a child who is contemplating suicide. Although symptoms range from passive to aggressive, according to Paul and Epanchin (1986) there are five danger signs agreed upon as those most found among children who are thinking about suicide as a way of dealing with their unhappiness.

1. Marked changes in behavior and/or personality
2. Mental depression
3. A suicide threat/statement or behavior indicating a wish or intention to die
4. Making final arrangements (e.g., giving away prized possessions)
5. A previous suicide attempt

It would probably be safe to say that most if not all individuals have felt depressed at one time or another. But why do these feelings seem to persist with some people? Schloss (1983) poses three separate theories.

1. Learned helplessness—After having attempted to deal with their own problems and failed, individuals may come to perceive that they do not have control over their own lives. Their inability to cope with specific issues becomes generalized so that even when there are favorable adaptive behavior responses available to them, these responses are not used.
2. Social skills deficiency—Those who are depressed seem less able to gain positive reinforcement from social behavior and are less able to reinforce others, which in turn decreases the frequency with which they choose to engage in social exchanges.
3. Coercive consequences—Those who have chronic depression rely on coercive consequence patterns. This arises when anxious/withdrawn children receive positive reactions from others such as reassurance or sympathy, and then fail to develop the social skills that lead to more effective behavior.

ROLE OF THE TEACHER

The topic of student discipline has become a major issue in recent years (Covaleskie 1992). Gallup (1988) reports that beginning in 1986, management of conduct has been found to rank second only to drug abuse as a problem in schools. And as you might expect, managing conduct effectively requires the use of a variety of specific control techniques (Henkel 1991). What may work with one child may not work with another. Similarly what may work with one child on one day, may not work with that same child on another day. To bait the obvious, managing classroom behavior requires a great deal of insight, patience, and style.

When a teacher is confronted with behavior of the sort deemed unacceptable to the code of the group, it is important that this teacher first examine his/her own conduct.

Many teachers have been the cause of aberrant behavior among their students, if not by design, often by accident.

This impression should not come as any surprise, however, to those who have witnessed the way some teachers react to the young people within their classes. Many discipline problems would not exist if teachers treated students in a professional manner. Have you ever seen a student "put down" because he/she responded with an incorrect answer to a question? embarrassed because of the way he/she dressed? disenfranchised because of where his/her parents work or where he/she lives? ridiculed because of a classroom "accident..."?

In one first-grade class a student who wet his pants was told to remove his pants, hang them over a radiator, and go to the corner. When the other children laughed at the boy as he stood in his long underwear, the teacher had the child remove his underwear, place it alongside his pants on the radiator, and return to the corner to stand (nude from his waist down to his socks and shoes).

Is it any wonder that children develop emotional problems? Fortunately there are few teachers—or adults in any setting—who would act in such an irresponsible manner. Further it should be said that maladaptive behavior is not necessarily a product of a teacher's performance. The point is that teachers significantly influence student behavior. In many ways they are role models. Every behavior is caused. It is the function of those assuming responsibility for the care of children to exercise extreme care in the selection and delivery of content, methods, and materials.

The teacher sets the tone in the classroom or clinic. He/she arranges the equipment, decides on the methods of lesson presentation, and elects when to give a test. According to Purkey (1978) the teacher alone has the power to invite or not invite each student to learn. The teacher's behavior influences the behavior of students. To assess their potential influence, Wood (1992) offers fifteen questions teachers should ask themselves as they contemplate their approaches to the learning process.

1. Do I leave my personal problems at home?
2. Am I in good physical as well as emotional health?
3. Am I happy with my role in life?
4. Does my voice convey confidence?
5. Does my walk convey confidence?
6. Do I have a positive self-concept?
7. What is my attitude toward my peer group?
8. What is my attitude toward children?
9. Do I feel comfortable admitting a mistake?
10. Will I change my opinion when a valid reason for doing so is presented?
11. Do I have a sense of humor?
12. Can I laugh at myself?
13. Am I an attentive listener?
14. Do I teach subjects or children?
15. Do I accept the responsibility of mainstreaming students in an integrated environment most conducive to learning?

In an effort to help teachers select and develop behaviors that contribute to effective teaching, numerous rosters of ideas have been produced. Of the suggestions offered, the following list by Weber (1977) provides one of the most comprehensive available. Here it is suggested that a successful teacher will

1. encourage students to communicate openly.
2   address the situation rather than the character or personality of a student when handling a problem.
3. express true feelings and attitudes to students.
4. make expectations clear and explicit to students.
5. reinforce appropriate student behaviors.
6. train students to perform leadership functions and shares leadership with them.
7. listen attentively to students.
8. accept students as persons of worth.
9. not behave in a punitive or threatening manner.
10. display an awareness of what is going on in the classroom.
11. praise the accomplishments of the group.
12. use expressions indicating that the students constitute a group of which the teacher is a member.
13. elicit and accept student expressions of feelings.
14. clearly communicate appropriate standards for student behavior.
15. clarify the norms of the group.
16. provide students with opportunities to work cooperatively.
17. ignore inappropriate student behavior to the extent possible.
18. encourage the establishment of productive group norms.
19. not ridicule or belittle students.
20. communicate an awareness of how students feel.
21. respect the rights of students.
22. accept all student contributions.
23. guide students in practicing productive group norms.
24. encourage and support individual and group problem solving.
25. provide students with opportunities to succeed.
26. initiate, sustain, and terminate classroom activities with smoothness.
27. direct attention toward the group rather than toward the individual during general classroom activities.
28. allow students to experience the logical consequences of their behavior when physically safe to do so.
29. praise the accomplishments of students rather than the students themselves.
30. accept students and encourage them to be accepting of one another.
31. promote group morale by helping students engage in total-class activities.
32. make use of "time out" to extinguish inappropriate student behavior.
33. use nonverbal communication that supports and is congruent with verbal communication.
34. promote group unity.
35. encourage students to use time wisely.
36. train students to behave appropriately in the teacher's absence.
37. display the ability to attend to more than one issue at a time.
38. discuss issues with students rather than argue with them.
39. be nonjudgmental in discussing problem situations.
40. respect student privacy.

When trouble occurs in the class, teachers should first assess the environment and then themselves. Anticipating difficulty before it arises, however, will produce the best effects. Taylor (1978) describes eight procedures that, if followed, should go a long way in helping to curb discipline problems. The following list elaborates on Taylor's suggestions.

1. It is important to help students improve their self-esteem. Students who are reluctant to try new activities for fear of failing and who demonstrate lack of trust in themselves have low self-concept levels. These youngsters are in need of assistance. Give needed attention and offer enthusiasm for achievements, at all levels.*

2. Provide various learning procedures for each activity, such as field experiences, independent study, and individualized instruction. Some children are visual learners; others are auditory learners. Most children learn best from tactile, hands-on experiences. Match your teaching styles with the learning styles of the children in the class(es).

3. Include sport and recreation activities in the curriculum that will be carried over and reinforced by participation at local youth centers, neighborhood parks, and other recreational facilities within the community. To do this successfully requires familiarity with facilities and programs in various community settings.

4. Post lists of facilities, activities, and interesting persons to visit on strategically placed bulletin boards. This information will encourage students to explore meaningful program options.

5. Provide intramural programs and encourage student participation in after-school and weekend recreational activities. Give youngsters the opportunity to report their selections during show-and-tell periods. Be sure that children know that what they have to say in these sessions is valuable for others to hear.

6. Identify gifted athletes in the physical education class. Give students with above-average skills the opportunity to serve as class leaders or try out for varsity teams. Many exceptionally talented students with potential for interscholastic competition go unnoticed. Competition may be just the cure a youngster prone to discipline problems might need, Figure 10.1.

7. Procure group tickets so that students can attend sporting activities at nearby colleges and professional arenas. Many colleges provide tickets at no charge for such a purpose.

8. Provide experimental courses. Modify program offerings. Too many physical education curricula offer touch football in the fall, basketball in the winter, and softball in the spring.** Physical education class is often nothing more than organized recess. It is little wonder that students become bored and instigate discipline problems within the class.

---

* Help children to understand that they have the right to fail as well as the right to achieve.
**After learning that a basketball unit was taught each winter, grades seven to twelve, a member of the school board was heard saying, "If it takes you six years to teach basketball, you must be doing a terrible job with it." Indeed how much basketball should be taught in public school physical education classes when so many other exciting skills are never taught at all?

Figure 10.1. A gifted athlete might be recognized during a pickup game.

PROGRAMMATIC PROCEDURES

The structure of a class is very important to its successful management. Students must be instructed as to class rules and routines. Simply posting programmatic procedures will not ensure that they are understood. If students are going to be expected to act in certain ways, it is critical that expectations be made clear. One suggestion is to use a checklist, which the teacher can complete in advance and distribute, Table 10.6. While the contents of the document can be presented on the first day of class, by having the document in their hands, a ready reference is available.*

In addition to what is presented in Table 10.6, other information which could be considered for inclusion on such a checklist or memorandum would be

1. Procedures for class participation
   a) Asking for assistance
   b) Asking questions
   c) Responding to questions
   d) When talking is allowed
2. Procedures for going to the nurse
3. What to do when tardy in class
4. Policy for absences from class
5. Policy for making up work

---

* One could even provide a place for a student signature on the document which, if turned in, would indicate evidence of its receipt.

TABLE 10.6

Management Checklist

Class: _____ Section:_____ Time: _____

1. Uniform
   _____   Required
   _____   Not required

2. Lineup/seating arrangement
   _____   Assigned
   _____   Open

3. Behavior for entering class
   _____   Visiting with friends allowed
   _____   Visiting with friends not allowed
   _____   Note special directions on chalkboard

   _____   _____

4. Procedures for setting up equipment
   _____   Per individual assignment
   _____   Per group/squad assignment
   _____   Only when requested by teacher

5. Procedures for turning in written assignment
   _____   At the beginning of the class
   _____   At the end of the class
   _____   Only when requested by teacher

6. Behavior when leaving the class and locker room
   _____   Leave only when dismissed/excused by the teacher
   _____   Leave only when the bell is sounded

---

6. Policy on food or chewing gum
7. Policy on storage of clothes in locker room
8. Policy on showers/towels
9. Testing schedule
10. Grading policy

Most certainly there will be issues arising in class for which policies have not been prepared. Experience will help generate a more thorough list. Children need rules; they want rules. If they get rules that are thoughtful, fair, and consistently enforced, discipline problems will diminish in scope and intensity.

Because many children with behavioral problems will go to almost any length to get attention, it is important to be ready to provide alternative outlets. Make concerted efforts to arrange for cooperative activity. Since play can provide a forum for cooperation, it may also help facilitate positive social behavior. Experience has shown, however, that to expect a child to continue in unadapted cooperative play will likely lead to disappointment. When adapting play activities, consider the following:

1. Attempt to match the implements of play with the ability level of the child. Be certain that reasons for frustration are reduced. If the child is unable to "work the toy," an already unstable condition will be aggravated.
2. Attempt to improve skills that are practical and can be applied to life settings. For example, after seeing a ball game on film, in the play yard, or in a more formal arena, the child will find learning to throw a ball more meaningful. There is evidence that successful imitation breeds more imitation, and studies have shown the value of imitation in the acquisition of new behavior patterns (Buell et al. 1974).
3. Vary the geographical and social settings for play. The introduction of new facilities and friends, under controlled conditions, will help the autistic child become aware that alternatives to any single structure can be enjoyable. Ensure that the introduction of the unknown is tempered by access to the known.
4. Provide opportunities for success. All children need to have goals and specific objectives that are within reach. Many of these goals can be determined cooperatively by the teacher and the student through contracting. One such procedure is identified in the steps that follow (Wood 1992):
    a) Teacher identifies the target behavior.
    b) Teacher clearly identifies the behavior that will earn tokens for the student.
    c) Teacher posts appropriate behavior on a chart available to the student.
    d) Teacher and student select reinforcers to exchange for tokens.
    e) Teacher explains rules of token system to the student.
    f) Teacher requests the student to explain the system.
    g) Teacher initiates the token system.
    h) Teacher evaluates the token system.
    Other examples of behavior modification strategies are presented in the Developmental Activities.
5. Be consistent in the methods you use to correct the child. It is important that the youngster understand the ramifications of maladaptive behavior. If the consequences of poor behavior vary significantly, the child can become confused and frustrated, negating the principles of **reinforcement**.
6. Avoid a public display of annoyance when maladaptive behavior occurs. To belittle or berate the youngster in front of his/her peers will increase the probability of interpersonal friction between them. If students are cast in the role of problem children, there is a tendency for them to play out that part, particularly if they are seeking attention and there does not appear to be another way to get it.
7. Do not punish the group for the negative behavior of one under the assumption that peer pressure will force a reversal in conduct. There is evidence that increased hostility is likely to result between the students.
8. Make every effort to avoid exclusion of a child with a behavioral problem from play activity. Play helps the student adjust to the requirements of a classroom. Experiences with peer cooperation and following directions are too valuable to be denied to him/her (except as a last resort).
9. Use praise thoughtfully and often as a reward for achievement. A reward system of tokens or symbolism described previously has merit in classroom management, but intrinsic rewards are likely to be more enriching. The

satisfaction of having met agreed-upon objectives are longer lasting and have a greater chance for transfer to other tasks.

10. Make efforts to sequence activities when programing for those with behavioral disorders. The youngster should know the sequence, its rationale, and within reasonable limits move through the program step by step.

11. Make every effort to provide support for the student. As indicated earlier, there are many and assorted reasons for maladaptive behavior. We may be concerned about a child putting away his/her sneakers in a locker or hanging up his/her towel. At the same time, the child is concerned about the fact that his/her family is undergoing divorce, and he/she is concerned about his/her future. There may be no expression of love within the home. Given this scenario, suppose that a child expressed thoughts of suicide. Not knowing the private circumstances in the child's life, you might not take his/her feelings seriously. This could be a significant error. *Always take a person's feelings and thoughts seriously.* Other important points are:
    a) Listen. Do not leave the person alone without human support.
    b) Accept every complaint expressed by that person.
    c) Develop a plan that can be mutually worked out.
    d) If you cannot develop a plan, seek outside emergency intervention.

12. Assertiveness is an important tool for establishing interpersonal relationships between teachers and students. Facial expression, tone of voice, eye contact, body language, and persistence are fundamental—individually and collectively—to success in **behavior modification** (Fernandez-Balboa 1990).

BEHAVIOR MODIFICATION

Critical to dealing successfully with children who demonstrate maladaptive behavior is the ability to describe behavioral events objectively. As pointed out by Bijou, Peterson, and Ault (1974), however, accurate description of behavioral events rests with

> establishing a criterion or criteria in a way that two or more observers can agree on their occurences.

For example, to log the frequency with which a child hits other children, a definition of hitting must be established so that all evaluators can discriminate hitting from pushing or just patting. If the criteria are not completely understood, it is unreasonable to expect that an appropriate behavior-modification plan can emerge.

By definition, behavior modification is a discipline of psychotherapy. According to Watson (1973) and others it is concerned primarily with altering behavior that has been observed. Observing and objectively assessing behavior are the basis for the selection of treatment modalities. It is inappropriate to make treatment decisions upon the basis of medical diagnosis alone. Intelligent treatment decisions are based upon observable behavior. Behavior is characteristic of an individual, not of a medical diagnosis.

DEVELOPMENTAL ACTIVITIES

The behavior modification plan to be described is the operant conditioning method, which has two basic premises:

1. Voluntary behaviors can occur; that is behavior that is under the direct control of the child. These behaviors include such motor tasks as walking, skipping, hopping, running, and jumping.
2. Appropriately planned systems of reinforcement, successive approximation (**shaping**), and **stimulus control** influence a person's psycho-readiness to volunteer such behavior.

The systems of reinforcement, shaping, and stimulus control are outlined in the activities that follow:

I. Goal: Behavior Modifications

Major Objective	*Interim Performance Objective*
1. Reinforcement	1.1 Receive rewards for performing selected tasks, Figure 10.2. 1.1A Vocal applause 1.1B Pat on the head or back 1.1C A handshake 1.1D A drink of water 1.1E A longer period of play time

Figure 10.2. Rewards serve as motivators

Major Objective	*Interim Performance Objective*
2. Shaping	2.1 Succeed in skill components one at a time.
	2.1A Skip.
	2.1Aa Take step with one foot; receive reinforcement.
	2.1Ab Take small hop on same foot; receive reinforcement.
	2.1Ac Take step with other foot; receive reinforcement.
	2.1Ad Take small hop on that foot; receive reinforcement.
	2.2 Put skill components together to form the complete skill.
	2.2A Skip.
	2.2Aa Use balls of feet.
	2.2Ab Swing arms from shoulders in opposition to feet; receive reinforcement.
3. Stimulus Control	3.1 Volunteer selected movement patterns when appropriate.
	3.1A Skip when the group is asked to skip; receive reinforcement.
	3.1B Move using one of several techniques suggested by the instructor; receive reinforcement.

Although the principles of operant conditioning have been provided for a very basic skill, these same principles may be employed for virtually all physical education skills. The issue is having the child progress from a situation where he/she is singled out for praise to a situation where he/she senses gratification when the group receives praise. At this point, the child feels as though he/she is a bonafide member of the group. This is the essence of membership in a society.

SUMMARY

There are many factors contributing to behavioral dysfunctions in children. It appears that although these sources vary, most can be attributed to environmental circumstances. In this chapter, various classifications of disorders and defense mechanisms were presented.

Given the fact that behaviors can best be addressed at the level of prevention, a variety of formal and informal screening procedures were described. Further, accepting the fact that the teacher himself/herself has a great deal to do with the climate of the classroom, managerial techniques were presented. At this juncture, it should be realized that successful class control requires the teacher to acknowledge that his own persona can have significant impact on the types of behaviors that students will choose for themselves.

The chapter concluded with methods that teachers can employ in order to influence positive behavior. A merger of suitable management strategies with appropriately selected activities is at the foundation of classroom productivity. If teachers manage well, they can attain the order needed to facilitate learning. With the approaches presented in this chapter and the recommended laboratory and reading assignments ahead, you can manage to have that kind of order.

RECOMMENDED LABORATORY ASSIGNMENTS

1. Arrange to visit reputable sites where developmental programs for youngsters with behavioral problems are in operation. Observe classes in progress.
2. Interview successful practitioners to gain insight as to the techniques for behavior modification they find to be successful.
3. Administer the various informal and formal screening techniques that are described in this chapter. Become familiar with other assessment procedures.
4. Develop objectives for a sociometric assessment instrument; write items geared to measure the acquisition of stated objectives. Have a jury of specialists in the field assess the objectives and items for validity. Field test the instrument for item discrimination and test reliability.
5. Using the systems of behavior modification outlined in the "Developmental Activities," develop a plan of reinforcement, shaping, and stimulus control for various daily living and game skills. Supplement your roster of activities with those presented in other chapters of this book.
6. Read about the various behavior-modification plans that are described in the literature.
7. Review the recommended readings.

REFERENCES

Achenbach, T. M. 1982. *Developmental psychopathology.* 2d ed. New York: Wiley.

American Psychiatric Association. 1987. *Diagnostic and statistical manual of mental disorder.* 3d ed., Rev. Washington, DC: The Association.

Bijou, S. W., R. F. Peterson, and M. H. Ault. 1974. A method to integrate descriptive and experimental field studies at the level of data and empirical concepts. *Perspectives in Behavior Modification with Deviant Children.* Englewood Cliffs, NJ: Prentice-Hall.

Blanchard, B. E. 1936. A behavior frequency rating scale for the measurement of character and personality in physical education classroom situations. *Research Quarterly* 7: 56–66.,

Buell, J. 1974. Collateral social development accompanying reinforcement of outdoor play in a preschool child. *Perspectives in Behavior Modification with Deviant Children.* Englewood Cliffs, NJ: Prentice-Hall.

Children's Defense Fund. 1989. *A vision for America's future: An aqenda for the 1990s.* Washington, DC: The Fund.

Covaleskie, J. F. 1992. Discipline and morality: Beyond rules and consequences. *The Educational Forum* 56:(2): 173–83.

Cowell, C. C. 1958. Validating an index of social for high school use. *Research Quarterly* 29: 7–18.

Federal Register. 1977. *Rules and regulations for the implementation of part B of PL 94-142.* Washington, DC: U.S. Government Printing Office, 42474–42515.

Fernandez-Balboa, Juan-Miguel. 1990. Helping novice teachers handle discipline problems. *Journal of Physical Education, Recreation and Dance* 62(7): 50–54.

Gallup, G. 1988. The 20th annual Gallop poll of the public's attitudes toward the public schools. *The Gallup Report.* No. 276, 41–51.

Garrison, W. T., and F. J. Earls. 1987. *Temperament and child psychopatholoqy.* Newbury Park, CA: Sage Publications.

Gearheart, B. R., M. W. Weishahn, and C. J. Gearheart. 1992. *The exceptional student in the regular classroom.* 5th ed. New York: Macmillan Publishing Company.

Haring, N. G., and L. McCormick. 1990. *Exceptional children and youth.* 5th ed. Columbus, OH: Merrill.

Henkel, S. A. 1991. Teachers' conceptualization of pupil control in elementary school physical education. *Research Quarterly for Exercise and Sport* 62(1): 52–60.

Kanner, L. 1943. Autistic disturbances of affective contact. *Nervous Child* 2: 217–50.

Kauffman, J. M., and R. D. Kneedler. 1981. Behavior disorders. In *Handbook of Special Education,* edited by J. M. Kauffman and D. P. Hallahan. Englewood Cliffs, NJ: Prentice-Hall.

Maag, J. W., and K. W. Howell. 1991. Serving troubled youth or a troubled society? *Exceptional Children* 58(1): 74–76.

Meyen, E. L. 1990. *Exceptional children in today's schools.* 2d ed. Denver, CO: Love Publishing Company.

Nelson, D. O. 1966. Leadership in sports. *Research Quarterly* 37: 268–75.

Paul, J., and B. Epanchin, eds. 1986. *Emotional disturbances in children.* 3d ed. Columbus, OH: Merrill.

Purkey, W. 1978. *Inviting school success.* Belmont, CA: Wadsworth.

Schloss, P. 1983. Classroom-based intervention for students exhibiting depressive reactions. *Behavioral Disorder* 3: 231–36.

Taylor, J. L. 1978. Curbing discipline problems through physical education. *Journal of Physical Education and Recreation* 49: 38.

Thomas, A., and S. Chess. 1977. *Temperament and development.* New York: Brunner/Mazel.

U.S. Department of Education. 1988. *Tenth annual report to Congress on the implementation of the Education of the Handicapped Act.* Washington, DC: Author.

U.S. Department of Health, Education, and Welfare. 1977. Education of handicapped children (Implementation of Part B of the Education of the Handicapped Act). *Federal Register.* August 23, 1977 42478

Watson, L. S. 1973. *Child behavior modification: A manual for teachers, nurses, and parents.* New York: Pergamon Press.

Weber, W. A. 1977. Classroom management. In *Classroom Teaching Skills: A Workbook,* edited by J. M. Cooper. Lexington, MA: D. C. Heath.

Werry, J. S. 1986. Biological factors. In *Psychopathological Disorders of Childhood,* 3d ed., edited by H. C. Quay and J. S. Werry. New York: Wiley.

Wood, J. W. 1992. *Adapting instruction for mainstreamed and at-risk students.* 2d ed. New York: Macmillan Publishing Company.

RECOMMENDED READINGS

Abrams, B. J. 1992. Values clarification for students with emotional disabilities. *Teaching Exceptional Children* 24(3): 28–33.

Barkley, R. A. 1985. Attention deficit disorder. In *Handbook of Clinical Behavior Therapy with Children,* edited by P. H. Bornstein and A. E. Kazdin. Homewood, IL: Dorsey Press.

Beck, K. H., and T. G. Summons. 1990. Sources of information about drugs and alcohol for black and white suburban high school students. *Health Education* 21(2): 20–24, 49.

Belka, D. E. 1991. Let's manage to have some order. *Journal of Physical Education, Recreation and Dance* 62(9): 21–23.

Benson, D., L. Edwards, J. Roseel, and M. White. 1986. Inclusion of socially maladjusted children and youth in legal definition of the behaviorally disordered population: A debate. *Behavior Disorders* 11(3): 213–22.

Bower, E. M. 1981. *Early identification of emotionally handicapped children in the school.* 3d ed. Springfield, IL: Charles C. Thomas.

Center, D. B. 1986. Educational programming for children and youth with behavior disorders. *Behavior Disorders* 11(3): 208–11.

Chalke, F. C., and J. J. Day, ed. 1968. *Primary prevention of psychiatric disorders.* Toronto: University of Toronto Press.

Christof, K. J., and S. R. Kane. 1991. Relationship building for students with autism. *Teaching Exceptional Children* 23(2): 49–51.

Collingwood, T. R., R. Roynolds, B. Jester, and D. Debord. 1992. Enlisting physical education for the war on drugs. *Journal of Physical Education, Recreation and Dance,* 63(2): 25–28.

Crase, D., and M. Hamrick. 1990. Death education within health education: An update. *Health Education* 21(3): 44–48.

D'Alonzo, B. J. 1983. *Educating adolescents with learning and behavior problems.* Rockville, MD: Aspen.

Devoe, D., and B. McMillen. 1993. Teacher/student dyadic interaction with emotionally disturbed youth. *Research Quarterly for Exercise and Sport: Supplement* 64(1): A–115.

Dishman, R. K., and M. Steinhardt. 1990. Health locus of control predicts free-living, but not supervised, physical activity: A test of exercise-specific control and outcome-expectancy hypotheses. *Research Quarterly for Exercise and Sport* 61(4): 383–94.

Docheff, D. M. 1990. The feedback sandwich. *Journal of Physical Education, Recreation and Dance* 61(9): 17–8.

Dunlap, P., and L. A. Berne. 1991. Addressing competitive stress in junior tennis players. *Journal of Physical Education, Recreation, and Dance* 62(1): 59–63.

Ennis, C. D., J. Ross, and A. Chen. 1992. The role of value orientations in curricular decision making: A rationale for teachers' goals and expectations. *Research Quarterly for Exercise and Sport* 63(1): 38–47.

Evans, S. S., W. H. Evans, and R. A. Gable. 1989. An ecological survey of student behavior. *Teaching Exceptional Children* 21(4): 12–15.

Forness, S. R. 1988. Planning for the needs of children with serious emotional disturbance: The national special education and mental health coalition. *Behavior Disorders* 13(2): 27–33.

Fox, K. 1991. Motivating children for physical activity: Towards a healthier future. *Journal of Physical Education, Recreation and Dance* 62(7): 34–38.

Friman, P. C. 1990. Nonaversive treatment of high-rate disruption: Child and provider effects. *Exceptional Children* 57(1): 64–69.

Graziano, A. M., ed. 1979. *Behavior therapy with children.* Chicago: Aldine-Atherton.

Griffey, D. C., and L. D. Housner. 1991. Differences between experienced and inexperienced teachers' planning decisions, interactions, student engagement, and instructional climate. *Research Quarterly for Exercise and Sport* 62(2): 196–204.

Guerney, B. G. 1969. *New roles for professionals, parents, and teachers.* New York: Holt, Rinehart and Winston.

Hill, K. L. 1991. Pay attention! *Journal of Physical Education, Recreation and Dance* 62(9): 18–20.

Holleo, G. P., and W. H. Abrams. 1975. *Alternatives in community mental health.* Boston: Beacon Press.

Horine, L. 1990. The JOHARI window: Solving sport management communication problems. *Journal of Physical Education, Recreation and Dance* 61(6): 49–51.

Jackson, V. M., S. M. Dorman, L. K. Tennant, and W. W. Chen. 1989. Effects of teaching specific guidelines for alcohol consumption on alcohol knowledge and behavioral intent of college students. *Health Education* 20(6): 51–54, 62.

Jones, K. L., L. W. Shainberg, and C. O. Byer. 1975. *Emotional health.* San Francisco: Canfield Press.

Means, B., and M. S. Knapp. 1991. Cognitive approaches to teaching advanced skills to educationally disa !vantaged students. *Phi Delta Kappan* 73(4): 282–89.

Miller, S., and J. McCormick, eds. 1991. Stress: Teaching children to cope. *Journal of Physical Education, Recreation and Dance* 62(2): 53–70.

Moran, J. M. and L. H. Kalakian. 1977. *Movement experiences for the mentally retarded or emotionally disturbed child.* Minneapolis, MN: Burgess Publishing Company

Morgan, D. P., and W. R. Jenson. 1988. *Teaching behaviorally disordered students.* Columbus, OH: Merrill.

Mosston, M. 1992. Tug-o-war, no more: Meeting teaching-learning objectives using the spectrum of teaching styles. *Journal of Physical Education, Recreation and Dance,* 63(1): 27–31, 56.

Mustain, W. C. 1990. Are you the best teacher you can be? *Journal of Physical Education, Recreation and Dance* 61(2): 69–73.

Nelson, C. M., D. B. Center, R. B. Rutherford, and H. M. Walker. 1991. Serving troubled youth in a troubled society: A reply to Maag and Howell. *Exceptional Children* 58(1): 77–79.

Ostrosky, M. M., and A. P. Kaiser. 1991. Preschool classroom environments that promote communication. *Teaching Exceptional Children* 23(4): 6–10.

Page, R. M. 1990. Loneliness and adolescent health behavior. *Health Education* 23(5): 34–17.

Pate, J. E. 1963. Emotionally disturbed and socially maladjusted children. *Exceptional Children in the Schools.* New York: Holt, Rinehart and Winston.

Peterson, N. L. 1987. *Early intervention for handicapped and at-risk children: An introduction to early childhood special education.* Denver, CO: Love Publishing Company.

Ramsey, E., and H. M. Walker. 1988. Family management correlates of antisocial behavior among middle school boys. *Behavior Disorders* 13(3): 187–201.

Ratliffe, T., L. Ratliffe, and B. Bie. 1991. Creating a learning environment: Class management strategies for elelmentary PE teachers. Journal of Physical Education, Recreation and Dance 62(9): 24–27.

Rudisill, M. E. 1989. Influence of perceived competence and causal dimension orientation on expectations, persistence, snd performance during perceived failure. *Research Quarterly for Exercise and Sport,* 60(2): 166–75.

Rutter, M. 1975. *Helping troubled children.* NewYork: Plenum Press.

Rutter, M., and R. Schopler, eds. 1978. *Autism: A reappraisal of concepts and treatment.* New York: Plenum Press.

Self, H., A. Benning, D. Marston, and D. Magnusson. 1991. Cooperative teaching project: A model for students at risk. *Exceptional Children* 58(1): 26–34.

Shea, T. M., and A. M. Bauer. 1987. *Teaching children and youth with behavior disorders*. 2d ed. Englewood Cliffs, NJ: Prentice-Hall, Inc.

Simpson, R. L. 1987. Social interaction of behaviorally disordered children and youth: Where are we and where do we need to go? *Behavior Disorders* 12(4): 292–98.

Silverman, S. 1991. Research on teaching in physical education. Research Quarterly for Exercise and Sport 62(4): 352–64.

Sparks, W. G. 1993. Promoting self-responsibility and decision making with at-risk students. *Journal of Physical Education, Recreation and Dance* 64(2): 74–78.

Urey, J. R., and F. J. Biasini. 1989. Evaluating the 'difficult' child: Some practical suggestions. *Teaching Exceptional Children* 21(3): 10–13.

Weiner, B., and A. M. Mander. 1978. The effects of reward and perception of competency upon intrinsic motivation. *Motivation and Emotion* 2: 67–73.

Weiss, M. R., B. J. Bredemeier, and R. M. Shewchuk. 1985. An intrinsic/extrinsic motivation scale for the youth sport setting: A confirmatory factor analysis. *Journal of Sport Psychology* 7: 75–91.

Weiss, M. R., and T. S. Horn. 1990. The relation between children's accuracy estimates of their physical competence and achievement-related characteristics. *Research Quarterly for Exercise and Sport* 61(3): 250–58.

Wicks-Nelson, R., and A. C. Israel. 1984. *Behavior disorders of childhood*. Englewood Cliffs, NJ: Prentice-Hall, Inc.

Williams, G. J., and S. Gordon. 1974. *Clinical child psychology: Current practices and future perspectives*. New York: Behavioral Publications.

CHAPTER 11

The Gifted _____

Objectives

After reading this chapter, you should be able to

- **Identify various learning styles.**
- **Identify the gifted performer.**
- **Identify movements that have a major influence on successful performance of selected activities.**
- **Discuss various techniques for identifying levels of ability within a class.**
- **Describe the characteristics and uses of a cross-classification system.**
- **Identify a variety of organization al patterns that meet the needs, interests, and capabilities of above-average students.**

INTRODUCTION

While PL 94-142 has prompted attention for students with physical, cognitive, or behavioral disabilities, a group of exceptional children often subject to neglect within the classroom is the **gifted**. Often teachers are under the misguided impression that gifted students can and should be able to provide for themselves. It is not surprising that many of these talented students become bored with the curriculum in many of our schools. This boredom may lead to discipline problems. More importantly, gifted students are not provided with the opportunity to nurture whatever skills they have. Many of these skills are not even recognized as existing by those deemed to be experts in the field. As Champlin (1975) points out,

> Just as physical education activities must be modified and simplified for…[those with handicapping conditions]…, so must they be accelerated and intensified to provide motivation and opportunity for the more mature and skillful.…

It is also important to realize that motor ability tends to be specific. Children found to excel in one skill area may be but average or below in another. Like all students the gifted have relative strengths and weaknesses. Further, Sahagian (1988) notes that

---

KEY TERMS

categories of performance
cross-classification
diagnostic test activities
enrichment
field experiences
gifted
horizontal alignment
independent study
intramural programs

interscholastic athletic programs
leadership
round-robin tournament
squad leaders
student leaders
T-scores
vertical alignment
weighted scores

...some (are) well-adjusted, happy youngsters with lots of friends while others have low self-concepts and are under stress from high expectations from parents, teachers, peers, and even themselves.

Because a child is exceptional in basketball does not mean that he/she will be proficient in swimming. Consequently youngsters should be given a diagnostic skills test at the beginning of each unit in order to identify the gifted and those in other ability groups. Performance in previous years is not always a reliable indicator of current skill level.

In short we should organize and administer programs that are compatible with the capabilities and learning styles of our students. We should employ strategies that, according to Heitman and Kneer (1976), involve various delivery systems and practice opportunities designed to help the learners reach their physical education goals.

Kraft (1976) and others also stress the need to address student learning styles when choosing appropriate methods and materials, Table 11.1. Having the knowledge of how children learn can and should influence the teaching styles selected for employment.

According to Geiger and Kizer (1979) there are four factors that influence teaching success.

1. The teacher's personal philosophy concerning the role of physical education in the students' total development
2. The ability levels of the students
3. The selection and use of appropriate teaching strategies
4. The selection and use of supplies and equipment

Although cognitive potential may be found to be relatively homogeneous within a public school physical education class, psychomotor abilities may vary markedly. Clark (1992) argues that the needs of the gifted may be found in the areas of content, process, and **enrichment**. Once such needs are recognized, appropriate programs can be designed. In this chapter we will discuss gifted children and the screening procedures and program options suitable for them.

TABLE 11.1

Classification and Description of Selected Learning Styles

Classification	Description
Avoidant style	Not interested in learning within a traditional setting
Collaborative style	Cooperates with teachers and peers; enjoys sharing ideas and talent; sees classroom as a place for learning
Competitive style	Wants to perform better than others; in competition for grades and teacher approval
Dependent style	Interested in learning only what he/she has to; views teachers and peers as sources of support and guidance; demonstrates little intellectual curiosity
Independent style	Enjoys working independently; listens to ideas of others but works on content important to personal goals; confident of own abilities.
Participative style	Enjoys attending class; participates when prompted; interested in learning content cited on course outline

Source: Adapted from Grasha, A. F. (1972).

DEFINITION

A gifted performer is one who demonstrates skill at any point above one standard deviation of the average score for the group of which he/she is a part, Figure 11.1. The reference point for the probability curve is the student's group: An individual who may be an above-average performer in one school setting may only be average in another.

A ranking of students upon the basis of their performance on a skills test, without reference to the computation of a standard deviation value, will also indicate those with superior ability within a given group (assuming that the test is a valid one).*

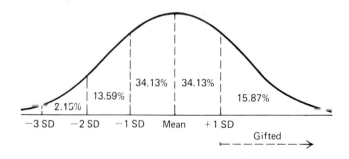

Figure 11.1. Probability curve showing standard deviation (SD) ordinate points from the mean of a distribution and percentages of students who earn scores to these points.

---

* See Chapter 18.

As noted previously, an individual who has above-average talent in one activity does not necessarily have above-average talent in another activity. It is particularly important to take this into account before deciding on program options for a class. Because certain activities involve similar skill components, there is no guarantee that skill in one activity will lead to success in another activity. Practice of specific skills required for success in an activity will, however, improve a student's potential for success in activities requiring similar skills.

Individuals who are exceptional performers in handball will probably be highly educable* in paddleball, racketball, squash, and perhaps badminton and tennis, Figure 11.2. This is because the movement patterns in the sports are similar.

On the other hand, a good tennis player will not necessarily be a good skier. These activities are different; their specific motor skill requirements are different.

To be effective, assessment must continue throughout the year. It is imperative that we assess each student's skill level at the outset of each unit of instruction. The youngster who has never demonstrated above-average skill in field hockey or basketball may have the qualities of an Olympian in track or field events.

SCREENING PROCEDURES

When attempting to diagnose the relative strengths of students within a given class, it is important that we first identify the major skills required for success in the activity about to be presented. While there may not be standardized testing instruments appropriate to your purpose, use your own criteria to create an assessment device that will satisfy your

Figure 11.2. Related movement patterns: *A,* handball; *B,* racketball.

---

* Educability refers to the ease with which new skills are learned.

own specific needs (Eby and Smutny 1990). If, for example, the activity to be presented is basketball, we would probably select shooting, passing, and dribbling as skills most critical to success. These three skills can also be called **categories of performance**.

Although activities taught in physical education classes ordinarily include more than three isolated skills or categories of performance, we must consider two important factors when deciding which skills to evaluate in a diagnostic test:

1. The skills most needed for success in a game situation
2. The amount of time needed to administer the **diagnostic test activities**

TABLE 11.2

Diagnostic Test Activities for Units of Instruction Typically Offered in Physical Education Classes

Unit of Instruction	Test Activities
Badminton and tennis	Service Forehand clear (high shot to back of court) Air or wall volley
Basketball	Lay-up shot Dribble (zigzag around pylons) Wall volley
Field hockey	Dribble (zigzag around pylons) Pass Shoot
Football	Pass Catch Kick
Golf	Drive Pitch Putt
Soccer	Dribble (zigzag around pylons) Pass Shoot
Softball	Throw for accuracy Catch Hit
Swimming	Water entry (adapted to disability) Bob Selected swimming stroke
Volleyball	Serve Setup Wall volley
Wrestling	Breakdown Escape Reversal

Note: Directions for administration of diagnostic test activities can be found in standard test and measurement physical education textbooks.

If we select three valid test items, administer them within a single class period, and proceed to organize and analyze the data appropriately, we can identify gifted students without sacrificing an inordinate amount of class time to do so. At the same time, students will gain some insight as to the skills they might practice in their leisure time. Table 11.2 identifies test activities appropriate for units commonly offered in physical education classes.

How can we identify gifted students using data from skills tests? The following section describes the testing and evaluative procedure that might precede a unit in basketball.

Basketball

To perform lay-up shots, the student stands with the ball under the basket. On command, the student attempts lay-up shots with either (usually dominant) hand for thirty seconds. The score is the number of lay-up shots made in that time.

The student must dribble around six pylons placed in a straight line. The first pylon is five feet from the starting line; the remaining pylons are eight feet apart. On command, the student dribbles the ball with his/her preferred hand around the right side of the first pylon, then to the left of the second pylon, and so on alternately around each pylon for thirty seconds. The score is the number of pylons traversed in the time limit, Figure 11.3.

To pass, the student stands with the ball behind a line six feet from an unobstructed wall. On command, the student volleys the ball at eye level against the wall for fifteen seconds. The score is the number of legal hand contacts that are made within that time. A legal contact is one that is made with both hands while standing behind the line.

Figure 11.3. Pylon zigzag dribble

Specifics such as time limits, distances between pylons, and the distance of the restraining line from the wall should be subject to modification depending on the age and grade level of the students, the number of students in the class, and the amount of time available for administering the test. Consider administering two trials for each item and counting the best of the two trials as the score.

The three scores for each student can be totaled, placed into a distribution, and analyzed by computing the mean and the standard deviation. (Computer programs are available for making such analyses.) Students who score at any point above one standard deviation of the mean are identified as gifted.*

If, on the other hand, the distributions for the three sets of scores were measured in different units (number of lay-ups performed in thirty seconds, amount of time it took [measured in tenths of a second] to traverse six pylons, and so forth), it would be inappropriate to add and average the raw scores. Instead compute mean, standard deviation, and **T-scores**** (or some other standard score). The T-scores for each student can then be totaled and averaged, Table 11.3.

Students earning a T-score of sixty or higher (an equivalent of one standard deviation above the mean) would be classified as gifted, Figure 11.4.

TABLE 11.3

T-Score Averages for Six Hypothetical Students

Student	T-Score				
	Test 1	Test 2	Test 3	Total	Average
A	30	40	50	120	40
B	45	65	55	165	55
C	35	40	50	125	42
D	65	72	85	222	74
E	70	70	70	210	70
Z	40	60	50	150	50

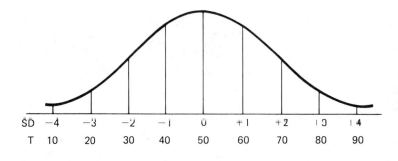

Figure 11.4. Comparison of T-score values to standard deviation units on a normally distributed probability curve.

---

* The number of students classified as gifted can be reduced markedly by using two standard deviations above the mean as the reference point.

** T-scores are standard scores in which the mean is 50 and the standard deviation is 10. (See Chapter 18.)

If we decide to add the raw scores together without reference to the mean, standard deviation, and standard scores, the raw scores can be ranked. If we perceive that one test activity is more predictive of success than the other test items, the scores for that particular distribution may be **weighted** in advance of summing the scores. In Table 11.4 the instructor has placed greater emphasis on success in making lay-up shots than in passing or dribbling.

After the totaled scores (weighted or unweighted) are ranked, assign the students to squads consisting of groups of students with similar rankings. The number of squads depends on the size of the class, the number of squads you decide to have, and the use to be made of the squad arrangement. Table 11.5 shows a typical class ranking into squads.

TABLE 11.4

Effect of Weighted Lay-up Shot Score on Total Score

Student	Diagnostic Basketball Skill Factors							
	2 (Lay-ups in 30 sec)	+	(Passes in 15 sec)	+	(Dribbles in 30 sec)		= Total
A	2 (25)	+	20	+	15		
	50	+	20	+	15		= 85
B	2 (15)	+	20	+	15		
	30	+	20	+	15		= 65
	(Layups in 30 sec)	+	(Passes in 15 sec)	+	(Dribbles in 30 sec)		= Total
C*	25	+	22	+	17		= 64

*Although student C earned higher scores in passing and dribbling, the total is lower because of the unweighted lay-up shots.

TABLE 11.5

Students ranked according to Test Scores

	Squad						
	A	B	C	D	E	Z	
Student with highest rank	1	10	11	20	21	30	Student with lowest rank
	2	9	12	19	22	29	
	3	8	13	18	23	28	
	4	7	14	17	24	27	
	5	6	15	16	25	26	

Note: As an alternative to squad letters, one might choose squad names such as colors, cities, animals, and so forth. This makes the ability ranking system less conspicuous.

CROSS-CLASSIFICATION

The ranking format in Table 11.6 is referred to as a **cross-classification system**. The students in squad *A* (the gifted students) would be used as **squad leaders** for the remaining squads.

TABLE 11.6

Members of Squad *A* Assigned to Lead Other Squads

			Squad		
A	**B**	**C**	**D**	**E**	**Z**
x	10	11	20	21	30
x	9	12	19	22	29
x	8	13	18	23	28
x	7	14	17	24	27
x	6	15	16	25	26
	(1)	(2)	(3)	(4)	(5)

Following the diagnostic skills test and before the second class period, meet with the squad leaders to discuss the prescription of activities for each of the squads. Squad *B*, for example, might work on outside shooting: squad *Z* might need to work on fundamental ball-handling skills. Each squad should be given an activity prescription that suits its needs. The squad leaders share their expertise with the squads they lead. The advantages of this arrangement are that the gifted will probably not become bored, each squad receives individualized instruction, and the instructor is free to move from squad to squad to deal with situations as they arise.

A squad leader may feel more comfortable working with one group than with another. The assignment of the squad leaders may be adjusted according to specific interests, needs, and leadership abilities.* Once adjustments are made, however, squad leaders ordinarily remain with their squads throughout the instruction phase of the unit.

Following each class, meet with the squad leaders to plan squad activities. Each squad should be given the opportunity to practice additional skills in accordance with its readiness level. Postclass sessions with leaders will help the instructor identify which skills should be addressed during the upcoming class(es).

For competition purposes the squad leaders return to their original places on the chart and serve as player coaches for their teams, Table 11.7. Table 11.6 emphasizes a **vertical alignment for instruction purposes, while Table 11.7 emphasizes horizontal alignment** for competition purposes.

---

* Squad members who have been assigned incorrectly because of (among other reasons) the less-than-perfect reliability of the diagnostic test should be reassigned.

TABLE 11.7

Members of Squad A Become Team Players and Captains

		Squad				
Team	A	B	C	D	E	Z
Astros	1	x	x	x	x	x
Bucks	2	x	x	x	x	x
Celtics	3	x	x	x	x	x
Jets	4	x	x	x	x	x
Knicks	5	x	x	x	x	x

A **round-robin tournament** could be arranged as a culminating activity in which the Astros would play the Bucks, the Celtics would play the Jets, and so on until each team had the opportunity to play every other team once. For round-robin competition with five teams it would be necessary to schedule ten games:

$$\frac{N(N-1)}{2} = \frac{5(4)}{2} = \frac{20}{2} = 10$$

Obviously the amount of time scheduled for competition purposes would govern the number of games that could be played and the length of time allotted for each game.

It can be seen from the alignment schemes in Tables 11.6 and 11.7 that squad membership is relatively homogenous and team membership is heterogeneous. This ensures fair competition.

LEADERSHIP DEVELOPMENT

The notion that all students have something to offer to the success of a class is an important one (Stainback, Stainback, and Wilkinson 1992). If one of the objectives of physical education is to nurture **leadership** skills and organizational acumen, it is important that we plan opportunities for such development and not leave it to chance. As Bucher (1975) points out,

> Leadership training programs...are a constructive answer to the often heard criticism that students are not given opportunities to assume independent responsibilities.

Further it is helpful to the entire class if we make use of the above-average skills that some students have, Figure 11.5.

In addition to providing these students with the opportunity to reinforce their knowledge and skill by planning explanations and demonstrations, leadership training programs provide the other members of the class (squad) with individualized plans.

Figure 11.5. Student leader teaching aquatic skills

All too often, physical education practitioners aim their teaching at the average students. Every student in class becomes subject to the same monologues and practice bouts regardless of background and skills. If programs of physical education are going to address the needs of all, we must do more to identify the ability levels of those in the class. Gifted students can then be provided with leadership challenges, and other class members will be challenged by individual and squad activity prescriptions.

Basic to the advancement of any leadership program is provision for planning and discussion sessions. In this regard, effective, proactive leadership implies having the skill, time, resources, and interest to be guided by the six P's.

Proper prior planning prevents poor performance (Grande, 1990).

It is important to provide opportunities for the **student leaders** identified to meet with us in order to review philosophy, objectives, and procedures related to their assignments. Among the factors to be discussed are

1. What leadership means
2. Characteristics of successful leaders
3. How the prospective leaders were selected
4. Why it is felt that their assistance is critical to the success of the instruction program
5. Specific responsibilities during instruction and competition sessions
6. Program and meeting schedule

To what extent will the student leaders be involved in the evaluation of the students within their squads? The role of the student leader is that of adviser. Student leaders can share in goal setting for their respective groups, give their impressions as to the level of group or individual readiness for any postinstruction testing program, and assist in the administration of these skill tests. The responsibility of grading students, however, always rests with the instructor.

How are the student leaders evaluated? This evaluation should not depend solely on the extent of achievement demonstrated by members of their squad. Equally important is the degree to which squad leaders are able to motivate their group members to maximum effort. It is our responsibility to suggest various motivational techniques, methods, and materials. The competence of the student leader can be assessed in terms of the following:

1. Ability to incorporate appropriate methods and materials into specific lessons
2. The squad's demonstrated effort to achieve
3. The squad's achievement of predetermined goals and objectives
4. Other factors, including
   a) Grooming
   b) Courtesy and tact
   c) Enthusiasm
   d) Patience
   e) Attendance at class and planning sessions
   f) Submission of reports as required

PROGRAM OPTIONS

Gifted students can benefit from programs besides leadership development. Some of these programs and special roles are listed in this section.

1. **Interscholastic athletic programs** include such activities as archery, badminton, baseball, basketball, bowling, cross-country, field hockey, football, golf, gymnastics, ice hockey, lacrosse, skiing, soccer, softball, swimming, diving, tennis, track and field, volleyball, and wrestling. Interscholastic athletic programs are expensive. Many support the thesis that resources should go into a variety of offerings rather than a few. This notion is particularly defensible if we are concerned with providing students who excel in different sport categories with the opportunity to compete at levels not ordinarily found within one's institution. Highly talented students within a school can benefit from competition with highly talented performers from other schools.

2. **Intramural programs** provide athletic competition within one school. Intramural activities are often an adjunct to classes in the sense that they provide laboratory experiences for those who have needs and interests not ordinarily satisfied within a typical physical education class. Intramural programs are not as expensive as interscholastic programs: Coaching, uniforms, and travel are not necessary. A greater variety of activities can therefore be offered in intramural programs than in interscholastic programs. Contrary to the opinions of many, intramural activities are not geared to accommodate only those who are insufficiently skilled to play on interscholastic teams.

3. **Independent study** provides students who are gifted with the opportunity to investigate topics not ordinarily covered within the class or not covered to the extent of a student's interest. Independent studies might involve research about such topics as aerobics; interval, repetition, Fartlek, or marathon training; and preventive medicine.

4. **Field experiences** provide selected students with the opportunity to engage in coaching and teaching within the community. Examples are coaching Little League teams; teaching swimming at a playground or camp; assisting with athletic programs at Young Women's Christian Associations (YWCAs), Young Men's Christian Associations (YMCAs), clubs, and camps.

5. Gifted students can demonstrate skills for the class. Many instructors avoid teaching certain activity units because they are unsure of their ability to demonstrate. Skilled students make good demonstrators, Figure 11.6.

6. A student leader can supervise the locker room, enabling the teacher to be in the gymnasium, swimming pool, athletic field, wrestling room, or where the majority of the students are gathered. Responsible supervision of the locker room is important because this area is a high-risk area with respect to injuries.*

7. A student leader can manage equipment and assist with inventories and laundry functions. Having dependable individuals in the equipment room is

Figure 11.6. Student leader demonstrating floor exercises

---

* Some high schools offer leadership certification programs for qualified students enabling them to perform selected supervisory functions.

extremely important. Supply and equipment security and maintenance is a basic ingredient of a successful program. A responsible student leader can also expedite the issue of supply items.

8. A student leader can assist school athletic trainers with first-aid duties in the training room or on the athletic field, Figure 11.7.

9. A student leader can assist with the measurement process during physical education testing sessions. This would include timing events, measuring distances, recording scores, spotting, and so forth.

10. A student leader can supervise bulletin board displays. Qualified and interested students can select and post materials that correspond with the units of instruction currently underway.

11. A student leader can serve as statistician for athletic events, class profiles, and so forth.

12. A student leader can act as special events coordinator for play days, sport days, exhibitions, and Special Olympics games. A qualified student can help attend to details that make the program run smoothly.

13. A student leader can assist with publicity, promotion, and public relations. Students who are gifted writers can prepare and submit approved articles about the physical education program to school and community newspapers and radio and television stations.

Consider granting physical education credit to students who successfully complete approved special activities. If these activities are not sufficiently worthwhile to justify giving credit, maybe they should be discontinued as an option for gifted students.

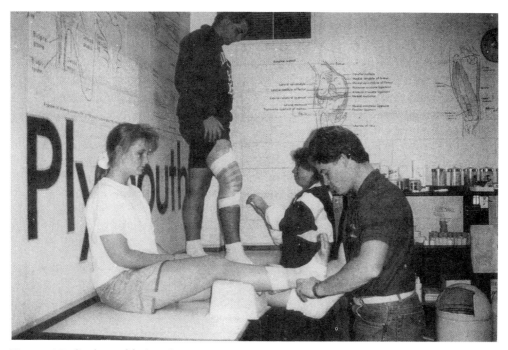

Figure 11.7. Student athletic trainers

Gifted individuals have special needs that must be met. Plan special experiences for students who would not be physically, mentally, and emotionally satisfied by the standard physical education session. Provide IEPs for the gifted. They too need adapted physical education.

SUMMARY

This chapter focused upon five issues pertinent to physical education programming for students who are gifted.

1. Presentation of definitions of the gifted and descriptions of various learning styles
2. Offering of strategies for screening students in order to reveal those with above-average abilities
3. Reviewing a cross-classification system as a way of promoting leadership opportunities
4. Examination of leadership development and its importance to the individual and to the group
5. Presentation of program options for those with above-average skills, interests, and motivation.

Gifted students for whom individualized opportunities are not provided are often those who remain handicapped within the physical education program. Practitioners must be alert to the needs requiring nurturing within their classes. This chapter was written to provide ideas as to how one might proceed and therefore increase the probability of meeting the expresssd or implied goals of all.

RECOMMENDED LABORATORY ASSIGNMENTS

1. Visit various schools to find out how gifted students are accommodated.
2. Interview successful practitioners to learn what screening procedures they use to identify gifted performers.
3. Review various test and measurement instruments to become familiar with the composition of approved standardized test batteries.
4. Add to the lists of skills suggested in this chapter that comprise diagnostic test batteries for commonly administered physical education activity units.
5. Practice administering diagnostic test batteries.
6. Gain practical experience with any five of the thirteen physical education program options for the gifted described in this chapter (e.g., offer services as an assistant coach within a community basketball or softball league).
7. Review the recommended readings.

REFERENCES

Bucher, C. A. 1975. *Administration of health and physical education programs.* St. Louis: C. V. Mosby.

Champlin, E. H. 1975. Is the program of high school athletics an integral part of physical education? In *Contemporary Readings in Physical Education*. Dubuque: William C. Brown.

Clark, B. 1992. *Growing up gifted: Developing the potential of children at home and at school*. 4th ed. New York: Merrill.

Eby, J. W., and J. F. Smutny. 1990. *A thoughtful overview of gifted education*. New York: Longman.

Geiger, W., and D. Kizer. 1979. Developing a teaching awareness. *Physical Educator* 36: 25–27.

Grande, P. C. 1990. The 1990s challenge: Leadership or survival. *Journal of Physical Education, Recreation and Dance* 61(5): 65–67.

Grasha, A. F. 1972. Observations on relating teaching goals to student response styles and classroom methods. *American Psychologist*, 27: 144–47.

Heitman, H. M., and M. Kneer. 1976. *Physical education instructional techniques*. Englewood Cliffs, NJ: Prentice-Hall.

Kraft, R.E. 1976. An analysis of student learning styles. *Physical Educator* 33: 140–42.

Sahagian, E. T. 1988. *Learning centers in your classroom: A way to provide for gifted learners*. Unpublished. Plymouth, NH: Plymouth State College.

Stainback, W., S. Stainback, and A. Wilkinson. 1992. Encouraging peer supports and friendships. *Teaching Exceptional Children* 24(2): 6–11.

RECOMMENDED READINGS

Adderholdt-Elliott, M., and S. H. Eller. 1989. Counseling students who are gifted through bibliotherapy. Teaching Exceptional Children 22(1): 26–31.

Balazs, E. K. 1974. Psycho-social study of outstanding female athletes. *Research Quarterly* 46: 267–73.

Brown-Mizuno, C. 1990. Success strategies for learners who are learning disabled as well as gifted. *Teaching Exceptional Children* 23(1): 10–12.

Casten, C. 1990. Put the Summer Olympics into your program with rhythmic gymnastics. *Journal of Physical Education, Recreation and Dance* 61(1): 6.

Cheffers, J., and L. Zaichkowsky. 1978. How do we help others by providing models of human movement? In *Introduction to Physical Education: Concepts of Human Movement*. Englewood Cliffs, NJ: Prentice-Hall.

Clumpner, R. A. 1979. Maximizing participation and enjoyment in the PE classrooms. *Journal of Physical Education and Recreation* 50: 60–62.

Davis, G. A., and S. B. Rimm. 1989. *Education of the gifted and talented*. 2d ed. Englewood Cliffs, NJ: Prentice-Hall.

Grogan, T. J., B. R. Wilson, and J. D. Camm. 1991. The relationship between age and optimal performance of elite athletes in endurance running events. *Research Quarterly for Exercise and Sport* 62(3): 333–39.

Hester, D, and D. Dunaway, eds. 1991. NAGWS: Paths to advocacy, recruitment, and enhancement. *Journal of Physical Education, Recreation and Dance* 62(3): 30–31.

Kew, F. C. 1978. Values in competitive games. *Quest* 29: 103–12.

Levy, C. 1992. Performing arts: An example of excellence in vocational arts education. *Journal of Physical Education, Recreation and Dance* 63(2): 36–38.

Michener, J. A. 1976. *Sports in America*. New York: Random House.

Miller, S. E. 1979. Do the nonhandicapped have a right to an individualized education program? *Journal of Physical Education and Recreation* 50: 19.

Murphy, W., and D. Smith. 1991. Expanding public opportunities through private partnerships. *Journal of Physical Education, Recreation and Dance* 62(8): 45–47.

Pendarvis, E. D., A. A. Howley, and C. B. Howley. 1990. *The abilities of gifted children*. Englewood Cliffs, NJ: Prentice-Hall.

Peterson, J. A., and H. R. Kroeten. 1973. Every man an athlete: The United States Military Academy's intramural program. In *Proceedings: Annual Meeting*. Minneapolis: National College Physical Education Association for Men.

Ribenest, R. S., ed. 1978. *Foundations of physical education*. Boston: Houghton Mifflin.

Sage, G. H., and S. Loudermilk. 1979. The female athlete and role conflict. *Research Quarterly* 50: 88–96.

Singer, R. N. 1979. Achievement motivation. *Journal of Physical Education and Recreation* 50: 37–38.

Singer, R. N., and W. Dick. 1974. *Teaching physical education: A systems approach*. Boston: Houghton Mifflin.

Stier, W. F. 1991. Women in the olympic movement: Advancing women's roles through education. *Journal of Physical Education, Recreation and Dance* 62(9): 62–66.

Wiggins, D. D. 1991. Prized performers, but frequently overlooked students. *Research Quarterly for Exercise and Sport* 62(2): 164–77.

Willard, D. E. 1989. Problem solving for students who are gifted. *Teaching Exceptional Children* 21(4): 30–33.

Wiseman, D. C. 1973. Athletics are not physical education. In *Proceedings: Annual Meeting*. Minneapolis: National College Physical Education Association for Men.

CHAPTER 12

Learning
Disabilities

Objectives

After reading this chapter, you should be able to

- Discuss what is meant by the term "specific learning disability".
- Know the incidence of learning disabilities among the school-age population.
- Describe gross motor, perceptual motor, and sensorimotor deficiencies often found within those who have learning disabilities.
- Explain the criteria that must be satisfied before a student can be coded as having a learning disability.
- Discuss the etiologies of learning disabilities.
- Identify and discuss teaching strategies appropriate for use with students with learning disabilities.
- Discuss examples of developmental activities appropriate for use with those who have gross motor, perceptual motor, and sensorimotor deficits.

INTRODUCTION

The term, **learning disability** has proven to be a very controversial one. Further, history as shown that it has generated more confusion and polarization among practitioners than any other category of exceptionality. This is due in large part to the fact that observers are making assessments from different professional orientations and personal biases. These orientations arise from such disciplines as education, medicine, and psychology—each contributing its own unique terminology. For example, education coined the phrase "specific learning disabilities"; medicine applies such labels as "brain damage" and "**minimum brain dysfunction**"; while psychology uses such expressions as "**hyperkinetic** behavior" and "perceptual disorders" to address the condition (Hardman et al. 1990).

KEY TERMS

asymmetry   minimum brain dysfunction
attention deficits   ocular control
auditory reception   part-whole method
biochemical factors   perseveration
body-spatial organization   proprioceptors (proprioceptive)
deficits in physical/motor skills   receptive aphasia
deficits in social skills   sensori-motor (integration)
diagnostic activity   special education criterion
discrepancy criterion   specific learning disability
dyslexia   stimuli
environmental factors   verbal expression
exclusion criterion   visual association
exteroceptors   visual closure
genetic   visual coordination and pursuit
gross motor development   whole-part-whole method
hyperkinetic   X chromosome
information processing   Y chromosome
learning disability

Although disagreement may exist as to the exact label to assign to children demonstrating characteristics of what we will call a **specific learning disability**, it is known that these children are a heterogeneous group with one feature in common: They have difficulty learning, and this difficulty is likely to occur in such areas as language arts, mathematics, or motor skills. This is why a multidisciplinary approach to assessment is so important if those responsible for preparing and implementing individual education plans are to be "tuned in" to the child's various needs.

The most widely accepted definition of learning disabilities was prepared by the National Advisory Committee on the Handicapped in 1968 and was subsequently adopted by Congress in 1975. With few changes it became part of PL 94-142.

"Specific learning disability" means a disorder in one or more of the basic psychological processes involved in understanding or in using language, spoken or written, which may manifest itself in an imperfect ability to listen, think, speak, read, write, spell, or to do mathematical calculation. The term includes such conditions as perceptual handicaps, brain injury, minimal brain dysfunction, dyslexia, and developmental aphasia. The term does not include students who have learning problems which are primarily the result of visual, hearing, or motor handicaps, of mental retardation, of emotional disturbance, or of environmental, cultural, or economic disadvantage (*New Hampshire Standards for the Education of Handicapped Students* 1988.)

While this definition satisfies most people, the National Joint Committee for Learning Disabilities (NJCLD) has continued to express some concerns about a number of its components—specifically:

1. The use of the word "children" is inappropriate in that a learning disability can occur at any age.
2. Clarification needs to be made that a learning disability can occur with other handicapping conditions.
3. Consideration should be given to deleting the phrase "a disorder in one or more of the basic psychological processes" and replacing it with "disorders that are intrinsic to the individual and presumed to be due to central nervous system dysfunction" (Hammill et al. 1981).

According to Kirk and Gallagher (1989) the last recommendation regarding the intrinsic nature of the condition is expressed or at the least implied in every current definition of learning disabilities. A large number of learning disabilities do not include those who may be performing poorly because of not having had the opportunity to learn, nor those who are sensory handicapped or mentally retarded.

INCIDENCE

Depending upon the perspective one chooses to employ, the estimates of prevalence of learning disabilities range from 3 percent to 20 percent of the population (Auxter and Pyfer 1989; Cratty 1980; Sherrill 1986). According to the U.S. Department of Education (1989), students with learning disabilities comprise about 5 percent of the school-age population, and according to Lerner (1989) there are about 2 1/2 times as many boys as girls.

While almost one-half of all children enrolled in special education programs have learning disabilities (Kirk and Gallagher 1989), most of them are mainstreamed in regular classes and receive part-time special education services in areas of need. For example, in 1986–1987, approximately 75 percent of students identified as learning disabled in the United States were served in regular classrooms (U.S. Department of Education 1989). This fact underscores the need for physical education practitioners to understand the various principles and practices appropriate to optimizing their learning opportunities.

CLASSIFICATIONS AND CHARACTERISTICS

Of the various problems associated with learning disabilities, the ones appearing to be most applicable to those responsible for the development of motor and physical fitness are in the areas of gross and perceptual motor skills and **sensori-motor integration**. In this regard, Valett (1969)* defined thirty-six learning behaviors that may appear in deficit form as a specific learning disability.

Gross Motor Development—the development and awareness of large muscle activity

1. Rolling: the ability to roll one's body in a controlled manner
2. Sitting: the ability to sit erect in a normal position without support or constant reminding

---

* Adapted from Programming Learning Disabilities by Robert Valett. Copyright 1969 by Fearon-Pitman Publishers, Inc., 6 Davis Drive, Belmont, CA 94002.

3. Crawling: the ability to crawl on hands and knees in a smooth and coordinated way
4. Walking: the ability to walk erect in a coordinated fashion without support
5. Running: the ability to run a track or obstacle course without a change of pace
6. Throwing: the ability to throw a ball with a reasonable degree of accuracy
7. Jumping: the ability to jump simple obstacles without falling
8. Skipping: the ability to skip in normal play
9. Dancing: the ability to move one's body in coordinated response to music
10. Self-identification: the ability to identify one's self
11. Body localization: the ability to locate parts of one's body
12. Body abstraction: the ability to transfer and generalize self-concepts and body localizations
13. Muscular strength: the ability to use one's muscles to perform physical tasks
14. General physical health: the ability to understand and apply principles of health and hygiene while demonstrating good general health

Perceptual-Motor Skills—the functional utilization of primary auditory, visual, and visual-motor skills

15. Auditory acuity: the ability to receive and differentiate auditory stimuli
16. Auditory decoding: the ability to understand sounds or spoken words
17. Auditory-vocal association: the ability to respond verbally in a meaningful way to auditory **stimuli**
18. Auditory memory: the ability to retain and recall general auditory information
19. Auditory sequencing: the ability to recall in correct sequence and detail prior auditory information
20. Visual acuity: the ability to see objects in one's visual field and to differentiate them meaningfully and accurately
21. **Visual coordination and pursuit**: the ability to follow and track objects and symbols with coordinated eye movements
22. Visual-form discrimination: the ability to differentiate visually the forms and symbols in one's environment
23. Visual figure-ground differentiation: the ability to perceive objects in foreground and background and to separate them meaningfully
24. Visual memory: the ability to recall accurately prior visual experiences
25. Visual-motor memory: the ability to reproduce motor-wise prior visual experiences
26. Visual-motor fine muscle coordination: the ability to coordinate fine muscles such as those required in eye-hand tasks
27. Visual-motor spatial-form manipulations: the ability to move in space and to manipulate three-dimensional materials
28. Visual-motor speed of learning: the ability to learn visual-motor skills from repetitive experience
29. Visual-motor integration: the ability to integrate total visual-motor skills in complex problem solving

Sensori-Motor Integration—the psychophysical integration of fine and gross motor activities.

30. Balance and rhythm: the ability to maintain gross and fine motor balance and to move rhythmically
31. **Body-spatial organization**: the ability to move one's body in an integrated way around and through objects in the spatial environment
32. Reaction speed-dexterity: the ability to respond efficiently to general directions or assignments
33. Tactile discrimination: the ability to identify and match objects by touching and feeling
34. Directionality: the ability to know right from left; up or down
35. Laterality: the ability to integrate one's sensory-motor contact with the environment through establishment of homolateral hand, eye, and foot dominance
36. Time orientation: the ability to judge lapses in time and to be aware of time concepts

The successful demonstration of the behaviors described are dependent upon the students' understanding of the directions. This may require a verbal step-by-step description as well as a physical demonstration of the task. A tactile "walk through" may also be helpful. Without a complete understanding of the requirements, one should not be surprised if a student falls short of teacher expectations. An examination of perceptual attributes important to refined motor performances will reveal that eyes, ears, and tactile receptors (called **exteroceptors**) and kinesthetic and vestibular (balance) receptors (called **proprioceptors**) are essential paths for receiving information. Other factors likely to hamper desired outcomes are: **attention deficits**, lack of suitable **information processing**, **receptive aphasia**, and **deficits in physical/motor** and **social skills**.

- Attention deficits—relate to the difficulty of the student to stay on task. This may be due to hyperactivity or simply having more of an interest in doing something else, particularly if he/she knows that he is more likely to be successful in the other activity.
- Information processing—refers to how information is received, stored, and retrieved for use. Although there are different views as to the etiology of this problem (Cermak 1983; Karr and Hughes 1987), one thing is certain: Students with learning disabilities often demonstrate skill levels that reflect deficiencies in the ways that they process information.
- Receptive **aphasia**—refers to the inability of the student to understand meanings of what is said. He/she may hear the words, but has difficulty translating these words into something that is meaningful to him/her.
- Deficits in physical/motor skills—are often revealed in a student's performance as compared to one of the same chronological age and/or grade level. While there are overlaps to be found in the physical and motor characteristics of children who are and are not coded as learning disabled, it is not unusual to find weaknesses in tasks requiring agility, balance, cardiovascular endurance, coordination, and strength. (Examples of related dysfunctions are displayed in Table 12.1.)
- Deficits in social skills—are found in many children with learning disabilities because of their apparent inability to accurately perceive the meanings of statements and actions of others. Like any other competency the acquisition of

TABLE 12.1

Selected Motor Characteristics of Some Children Who Have Learning Disabilities

Topic	Description
Asymmetry	A stabilizing of one of the limbs of the body (e.g., arm) when throwing a ball. Instead of assisting with the production of force, it is held in a rigid fashion.
Extraneous movements	Using unnecessary movements interfere with the normal motor pattern of a skill in that its execution no longer appears to be smooth and efficient. An example of such movement is flailing the arms laterally (instead of moving them forward and back in the sagittal plane) and simultaneously rotating the head in the transverse plane (when running for speed).
Falling after performance	Upon completing a task such as hopping, jumping, or throwing, the student will drop to the ground. This response does not appear to relate to the physical demands of the activity (such as fatigue).
Inability to control force	When dribbling a ball or jumping rope (for example), the student will tend to generate too much force in hitting the ball or moving the rope. On the other hand, too little force is often expressed on tasks that require power. (This appears to relate to inappropriate retrieval of information from prior experiences.)
Inability to maintain a rhythmic pattern	On tasks where the rhythm is self-imposed, such as performing a series of hops, some students may be unable to complete more than three or four hops before the movement is disrupted. The tendency is to accelerate the pace progressively so that their movements do not match those of the leader.
Inappropriate motor planning	This is one of the most distinguishable traits of children with learning disabilities. Appropriate motor responses depend on the proper integration of sensory input with past experiences. The lack of antecedent experiences and/or integrative ability may be evidenced by the misapplication of force, by the prematurity or delay of response, and by inappropriate responses to complex sequences of stimuli.
Inconsistency in performance	While performing motor tasks, vacillation in developmental levels becomes evident. On one occasion the student may be performing at one level of skill; on the next trial he/she may not do as well. (There is trial-to-trial variation.)
Loss of Dynamic Balance	The inability to maintain postural control of the body in relation to gravity may be a major reason why children with learning disabilities bump into objects and people and why they appear uncoordinated when performing gross motor tasks. (This appears to be particularly evident on skills requiring accuracy and control.)

TABLE 12.1 *continued*

Topic	Description
Mirroring	The inability to separate their directional movements from those of a leader. This dependency continues beyond the age when most children can respond independently to verbal cues, even in the presence of conflicting visual cues. (An example of this problem is when the teacher, while facing the class, raises his/her own right hand and asks that the students raise their right hands. The students may mirror the teacher by raising their left hands.)
Perseveration	This characteristic is revealed when the student continues the task or behavior when circumstances no longer require it. Once having achieved success in a skill such as bouncing a ball, he/she will continue to bounce it even though requested not to do so by the teacher. Other examples include the continuation of a dribbling motion with the arm though control of the ball has been lost.

Source: Adapted with permission from John L. Haubenstricker (May 1982). Motor development in children with learning disabilities. *Journal of Physical Education, Recreation and Dance*. American Alliance for Health, Physical Education, Recreation and Dance.

acceptable social skills is a function of acceptable practices and reinforcement. To that end, strategies for developing suitable behaviors merits inclusion in any physical education lesson plan. Certainly, team work is a worthy outcome for most classes.

In determining whether a child has a learning disability, the evaluation and placement team ordinarily rely on three criteria: an **exclusion criterion,** a discrepancy between potential and achievement, and a **special education criterion** (Kirk and Gallagher 1989).

- Exclusion criterion—Children whose difficulties can be attributed to auditory or visual impairments, emotional disturbances, mental retardation, or lack of ability to learn would normally be excluded from a learning disability designation. This does not imply, however, that children who are mentally retarded or who have visual or auditory impairments could not also have a learning disability. These students would require multiple services.

- **Discrepancy criterion**—Children with learning disabilities reveal differences in their performance levels between and within academic and/or developmental areas. A student with a developmental learning disability could express a significant disparity in linguistic, social, memory, perceptual-motor or sensori-motor abilities. It is this disparity between aptitude and actual performance within and between such areas that serves to identify a learning disability.

- Special education criterion—Children who are delayed educationally because they have not had the opportunity to learn can usually be accommodated within regular classes. Those with learning disabilities, however, require methods and materials not ordinarily used with the average child. When children require these special education services, another criterion for identification has been satisfied.

ETIOLOGY

Although a knowledge of the etiology of many conditions will not influence the curriculum in physical education, it is helpful for the practitioner to understand factors contributing to causes in that one might want to modify delivery strategies accordingly or perhaps alter the assignment. For example, an elementary school teacher had spent a considerable amount of time attempting to teach balance activities in gymnastics. Upon noticing that one of the students had particular difficulty when it came to skills requiring inverted positions (i.e., head balance), it was suggested that he work on the skill at home and that, perhaps, his dad would be able to help him. Later, it was discovered by that teacher that the boy's father also had problems in related areas. Apparently, the problem had a **genetic** base. As you can see, it is important for teachers of learning disabled children to know something about etiology in order to enable them to make more intelligent choices as to how they might best practice a particular or alternate skill (Gaddes 1985).

- Brain dysfunction—At present we have only partial knowledge of the relationship of behavior to central nervous system dysfunction. Yet we do know that since the brain is the control center of the body, it has at the minimum an indirect influence upon human capabilities and performance. This relationship has been the object of study by many neurologists and psychologists. *Psychopathology and Education in the Brain-Injured Child* (Strauss and Lehtinen 1947) is one such reference that attempts to describe the influence of brain injuries on hyperactivity, language, and perceptual disorders. The most recent work has been on hemispheric differences. While the left hemisphere deals primarily with linguistic and verbal tasks, the right hemisphere deals with auditory and visual-spatial activities and other non-verbal tasks (Wittrock, 1978; Gordon 1983). Galaburda (1983) hypothesized that the asymmetrical development of the cortex is responsible for the above-average number of dyslexic students who are left-handed, have musical talent, and superior visual-spatial skills. Since 1983, there is growing evidence that **dyslexia** and other learning disabilities are caused by a range of subtle brain abnormalities.

- Genetics—Hallgren (1950) Hallgren conducted an extensive study on Swedish families and found that the prevalence of communication disorders among the relatives of diagnosed dyslexics provided significant evidence of heredity as a contributing factor. Other findings by DeFries and Decker (1981) concur with those of Hallgren. Pennington and Smith (1983) reported evidence of chromosomal anomalies in students with learning disabilities. It appears that learning problems may be linked to an extra **Y chromosome** in boys or just one **X chromosome** in girls. Studies by Oliver, Cole, and Hollingsworth (1991) corroborate the findings of earlier investigators in suggesting the linkages of learning disabilities within families.

- **Biochemical factors**—It has been found that many children with learning disabilities do not have neurological or genetic problems of the type described previously.

Rather it is believed by some that there is an unknown biochemical imbalance which interferes with the student's ability to learn.*

- **Environmental factors**—A lack of stimulation in one's environment is believed to have an impact upon the ease with which children can learn. The same holds true for those who are malnourished, which according to Cruickshank and Hallahan (1973) may have an "immature" central nervous system leading to impaired development in general.

As the reader can observe, there are a variety of factors thought to cause learning disabilities in children. The teaching practitioner needs to be mindful of these issues in order to plan curriculum and delivery options suitable for these students. Although some of the differences between etiology and contributing factors remain obscure, it is necessary to ameliorate or remove threats to learning that are under our control. While it may not be within our influence to prevent the condition, we can still do what we can to understand its presence. In fact we can address exacerbating circumstances that, if unchecked, could add to the learning difficulties the student already has. The next section will include reference to such measures.

TEACHING STRATEGIES

The process of building successful remedial programs in physical education depends upon the behaviors (skills) the student is presenting at the present time and the identification of the behaviors (skills) the student must eventually be able to perform. To address present status, Johnson and Morasky (1980) and others suggest a number of procedures.

1. Examine various diagnostic instruments in order to determine their appropriateness for the individual(s) under consideration. This includes an examination of expressed purpose, type of validity (construct, predictive, etc.), type of reliability (internal consistency, stability, etc.), normative information, and administrative procedures.
2. Select for use those subtests within the chosen instrument(s) according to the criteria with which you are concerned. If you are interested in the assessment of occular control, it is important that the subtest measures that quality, Table 12.2.
3. For each area (quality) to be measured, list examples of the type of behavior (skill) the student must be able to demonstrate in order to score satisfactory in that area.
4. Note common examples of behaviors (skills) frequently observed in children who do not score well in these areas (e.g., cannot tell how many people are on the volleyball court by counting them).
5. Administer the instrument/subtests and record demonstrated behaviors (skills), Table 12.3.

Once the data are obtained and analyzed, the teacher is in a position to develop a program that will help the student move from where he/she is to where he/she should be.

---

* Phenylketonuria (PKU) is an example of a biochemical imbalance found in some children who are mentally retarded.

TABLE 12.2

Excerpts from the Remedial Materials Selection Chart for Purdue Perceptual Motor Survey*

Subtest Area	Criterion Example	Deficit Example
Balance and Posture	Subject is able to maintain balance while hopping in place.	Subject is generally awkward. He/she is shunned by other children in choosing sides for games demanding coordination.
Perceptual-Motor Match	When asked to do so, subject can draw a circle in correct size, shape, and direction.	Subject produces sloppy paperwork. He/she shows deficit art performance.
Ocular Control	Subject is able to establish eye contact and then follow a moving object with his/her eyes.	Subject gives poor performance when attempting to bat a pitched ball.
Form Perception	When shown a design, subject can reproduce it.	Subject reverses letters and has visual letter discrimination problems.

*Authored by E. G. Roach and N. C. Kephart, the instrument identifies children with perceptual-motor disabilities, tracing a child's development to the point where developmental dysfunction occurs. The entire survey is published by Charles E. Merrill Publishing Company, 1300 Alum Creek Drive, Box 508, Columbus, OH 43216.

Since most physical education teachers will be working with learning disabled children within mainstreamed or developmental classes, it is important that these practitioners be mindful of operational strategies found to be successful in these settings.

1. Select activities that include skills attainable by everyone. Although children have a right to fail, they also have a right to succeed.
2. Every **diagnostic activity** selected for presentation should be capable of being evaluated in an objective way.
3. Every task selected for the purpose of evaluation should be part of an ongoing program. Testing students in skills unrelated to what is or going to be taught will provide information of little consequence.
4. Assessing children on more than one occasion will provide more reliable information. On any given day a child may do better or worse than normal. One should not generalize about a student's basic skill level having administered a test on a single occasion.
5. Use a variety of activities to stimulate the senses. Too much time on an activity that emphasizes gross motor development will compromise the development of fine motor skills.
6. Make sure students understand the directions before they proceed. It may be helpful to have the students repeat the directions orally to you.

TABLE 12.3

**Excerpts from the Remedial Materials Selection Chart for the
Illinois Test of Psycholinguistic Abilities***

Subtest Area	Criterion Example	Deficit Example
Auditory Reception	Subject responds appropriately to an orally presented question (e.g., "Do trains swim?")	Failure to follow a simple auditory cue, such as "Run when I say go!"
Visual Association	Subject can choose the correct alternative to complete a visually presented analogy.	Subject fails to identify visual relationships, such as the "go to jail" square on the monopoly game.
Visual Closure	Subject can identify an object when only part of it is visible.	Subject needs to see an entire polysyllabic word before recognizing the word.
Verbal Expression	Subject can adequately describe an object shown to him.	Subject has difficulty describing an object he/she brings to "show and tell."

* Authored by S. Kirk, J. McCarthy, and W. Kirk (1968), the instrument assesses use and understanding of psycholinguistic abilities in young children; facilitates assessment of his/her abilities for purposes of remediation. The entire test is published by: University of Illinois Press, 54 E. Gregory Drive, Box 5081, Station A, Champaign, IL 61820.

7. When teaching skills, use more than one sensory modality. In this way, if a student has problems with auditory cues, he/she can access the information through visual or perhaps kinesthetic means.

8. Make explanations clear. Be prepared to use various examples in order to increase the chances for student understanding.

9. Allow ample time for tasks to be learned. Children with learning disabilities may take longer than ordinary to complete assignments.

10. Encourage students to complete the task even though it might not meet his/her or your expectations. Use positive reinforcers, as necessary.

11. Consider employing group leaders (see Chapter 11) in order to provide the teacher with the opportunity to work with the student with learning disabilities in a smaller group or one-on-one.

12. Use frequent praise for legitimate efforts made by the students. This helps to build self-confidence, Figure 12.1.

13. Control the teaching environment by stabilizing extraneous stimuli. This can be done by maintaining classroom order, both through the reduction of interruptions by others and by keeping supplies and equipment in designated spaces.

14. Teach by the **part-whole** or **whole-part-whole methods**. Always break activities down into their various skill components: then teach each component

Figure 12.1. Praise enhances self-confidence

one at a time. In this way focus is directed, the demands of a specific task are more easily understood, the student has the opportunity to be reinforced as elements are completed successfully, and the child is less likely to be overwhelmed.

15. If students with learning disabilities are on medications, be familiar with expected benefits and side effects. There are two problems associated with the use of medications.

    1. It is difficult to predict to which medication the student will best respond (Gualtieri, Golden, and Fahs 1983)

    2. The effects of dosages upon behavior and cognition vary. It has been estimated that dosages designated to elicit appropriate behavior may be 50—400 percent greater than what would be recommended to maximize cognitive performance (Pelham, 1983).

DEVELOPMENTAL ACTIVITIES

Earlier in this chapter, reference was made to the various classifications of disorders likely to arise in children with learning disabilities. Among these were crawling (under gross motor development); visual coordination and pursuit, sometimes referred to as ocular tracking (under perceptual-motor skills); and body-spatial organization (under sensory-motor integration). In an attempt to provide examples of the tasks appropriate to developmental programs for students with learning disabilities, I have chosen to present illustrations in these areas. An examination of the ideas presented should provide the reader with the basis for the development of tasks in related areas.

I. Goal: Gross Motor Development

Major Objective	*Interim Performance Objective*
1. Crawling	1.1 Crawl in a manner not deemed to be in a pattern, Figure 12.2.

Figure 12.2. Crawling

1.2 Crawl in accordance with a particular pattern.

1.2A Bilateral

1.2B Homolateral

1.2C Cross-lateral

1.3 Crawl in accordance with selected patterns.

1.3A Over distance

1.3B Over time

1.3C Over distance and time

1.4 Crawl in accordance with selected patterns, distance, time.

1.4A Over obstacles

II. Goal: Perceptual-Motor Skills

Major Objective	*Interim Performance Objective*
1. Visual Coordination and Pursuit	1.1 Tracking a moving ball on a trough.

Figure 12.3. Tracking a rolling ball

1.1A Moving slow

1.1B Moving fast

1.2 Tracking a rolling ball on the floor, Figure 12.3.

1.2A Moving slow

1.2B Moving fast

1.3 Stopping a rolling ball.

1.3A From a stationary position

1.3B Moving to the rolling ball

1.4 Tracking a ball in flight.

1.4A Thrown horizontally (low are)

1.4B Thrown vertically (high arc)

Major Objective	*Interim Performance Objective*
	1.5 Catching a ball thrown at him/her.
	1.6 Moving to catch a thrown ball.
	1.7 Bouncing a ball.
	1.7A While in a stationary position
	1.7B While moving in straight line
	1.7C While moving through pylons
	1.8 Hitting a ball with a bat.
	1.8A When ball is fixed on a tee
	1.8B When ball is swinging on a string
	1.8C When ball is thrown

III. Goal: Sensori-Motor Integration

Major Objective	*Interim Performance Objective*
1. Body-Spatial Organization	1.1 Move through hoops of various sizes.
	1.2 Move through mazes comprised of obstacles having various shapes and sizes.
	1.2A Over distance
	1.2B Over time
	1.2C Over distance and time
	1.3 Duplicate patterns.
	1.3A Shown on paper
	1.3B Shown on floor
	1.3C By mirroring teacher's posture
	1.3Ca Static
	1.3Cb Dynamic
	1.4 Drop pegs into receptacles having openings of various sizes.
	1.4A Selected distance
	1.4B Number at selected distances over time

SUMMARY

In this chapter, efforts were made to present issues and strategies appropriate for consideration when planning and delivering developmental and mainstreaming programs to those with learning disabilities. While researchers express differing views as to the incidence and etiology of these conditions, it is important to know the tendencies because of the impact that they may have on how a child might best be accommodated. These variances of opinion also help underscore the extent of the difficulty in arriving at a concensus on the very nature of the problem.

A thorough examination of the classifications, characteristics, and teaching strategies will arm the reader with a foundation for preparing meaningful lessons. Using appropriate assessment procedures will enable the teacher to identify the student's present status; using the suggested activities will help to bring that student to where he/she should be. Working with learning disabled children at the developmental level presents challenges of various dimensions. But the joy of seeing these children successfully integrated within regular activity programs makes the effort all the more rewarding—to the teacher, but most importantly to the child himself/herself.

RECOMMENDED LABORATORY ASSIGNMENTS

1. Arrange to meet with physical education teachers and clinicians who have experience working with children who have learning disabilities. Discuss the strategies that they employ to meet the diversified needs of these children.
2. Review textbooks, journals, and other print media in order to gain additional insights into curriculum and program delivery options.
3. Visit developmental and regular physical education classes where children with learning disabilities are enrolled. Observations of these classes can be of significant benefit as you contemplate program development within your own areas of responsibility.
4. Examine critical reviews of various instruments of assessment designed to measure sensori-motor behavior in order to determine those thought to be most valid for the specific purposes you have identified.
5. Obtain and practice using various assessment devices in order to increase your proficiency.
6. Meet with students with learning disabilities and their parents in order to learn of their insights as to methods and materials that they find beneficial.
7. Visit college preparatory programs where students are trained and certified to work with children who have learning disabilities. This will increase your understanding of program and delivery options.
8. Attend clinics, seminars, workshops, conferences, and conventions where topics are presented on such things as etiology, diagnosis, prognosis, assessment, curriculum methods, and materials.

REFERENCES

Auxter, D., and J. Pyfer. 1989. *Adapted physical education and recreation.* St. Louis: Times Mirror/Mosby College Publishing.

Cermak, L. S. 1983. Information processing deficits in children with learning disabilities. *Journal of Learning Disabilities* 16: 599–605.

Cratty, B. J. 1980. *Adapted physical education for handicapped children and youth.* Denver: Love Publishing Company.

Cruickshank, W., and D. Hallahan. 1973. *Psychoeducational foundations of learning disabilities.* Englewood Cliffs, NJ: Prentice-Hall.

DeFries, F., and S. Decker. 1981. Generic aspects of reading disability. In *Neuropsychological and neuropsycholinguistic aspects of reading disabilities,* edited by P. Aaron and M. Halatesha. New York: Academic Press.

Gaddas, W. 1985. *Learning disabilities and brain function: Neuropsychological approach.* 2d ed. New York: Springer-Verlag.

Galaburda, A. 1963. Developmental dyslexia: Current anatomical research. *Annals of Dyslexia* 33: 41–51.

Gordon, H. 1983. The learning disabled are cognitively right. Topics in *Learning Disabilities* 3:(1): 29–39.

Gualtieri, C. T., R. N. Golden, and J. J. Fahs. 1983. New developments in pediatric psychopharmacology. *Journal of Developmental and Behavioral Pediatrics* 4: 202–9.

Hallgren, B. 1950. Specific dyslexia (congenital word-blindness): A clinical and genetic study. *Acta Psychiatrica et Neurologica* 65: 1–287.

Hammill, D., L. Leigh, G. McNutt, and S. Larsen. 1981. A new definition of learning disabilities. *Learning Disability Quarterly* 4(Fall): 336–42.

Hardman, M. L., C. J. Drew, M. W. Egan, and B. Wolf. 1990. *Human exceptionality.* 3d ed. Boston: Allyn and Bacon.

Haubenstricker, J. L. 1982. Motor development in children with learning disabilities. *Journal of Physical Education, Recreation and Dance* 53: 41–43.

Johnson, S. T., and R. L. Marasky. 1980. *Learning disabilities* . 2d ed. Boston: Allyn and Bacon.

Karr, R., and K. Hughes. 1987. Movement difficulty and learning disabled children. *Adapted Physical Activity Quarterly* 5: 72–79.

Kirk, S. A., and J. J. Gallagher. 1989. *Educating exceptional children.* 6th ed. Boston: Houghton Mifflin Company.

Kirk, S., J. McCarthy, and W. Kirk. 1968. *Illinois Test of Psycholinguistic Abilities.* Urbana, IL: University of Illinois Press.

Lerner, J. W. 1989. *Learning disabilities.* 5th ed. Boston: Houghton Mifflin Company.

New Hampshire standards for the education of handicapped students (February 17, 1988). Concord, NH: State Board of Education.

Oliver, J. M., N. H. Cole, and H. H. Hollingsworth. 1991. Learning disabilities as functions of familial learning problems and developmental problems. *Exceptional Children* 57(5): 427–40.

Pelham, W. E. 1983. The effects of psychostimulants on academic achievement in hyperactive and learning disabled children. *Thalamus* 3: 1–49.

Pennington, B., and S. Smith. 1983. Genetic influences on learning disabilities and speech and language disorders. *Child Development* 54: 369–87.

Roach, E., and N. Kephart. 1966. *The Purdue Perceptual-Motor Survey.* Columbus, OH: Charles E. Merrill.

Sherrill, C. 1987. *Adapted physical education and recreation.* 3d ed. Dubuque, IO: William C. Brown.

Strauss, A., and L. Lehtinen. 1947. *Psychopathology and education of the brain-injured child.* New York: Grune and Stratton.

U. S. Department of Education. 1989. *Eleventh annual report to Congress on the implementation of the Education of the Handicapped Act.* Washington, DC: Division of Education Services, Special Education Programs.

Valett, R. 1969. *Programming learning disabilities.* Belmont, CA: Fearon-Pitman Publishers, Inc.

Wittrock, M. 1978. Education and the cognitive processes of the brain. In *Education and the Brain (Seventy-seventh Yearbook of the National Society of the Study of Education, Part 2),* edited by J. Chall and A. Mirsky. Chicago: University of Chicago Press.

RECOMMENDED READINGS

Baker, J. A. 1990. Overcoming Xenophobia: Learning to accept differences. *Health Education* 21(2): 55–56.

Bryan, T. H., R. Pearl, M. Donahue, J. H. Bryan, and S. Pflaum. 1983. The Chicago Institute for the Study of Learning Disabilities. *Exceptional Education Quarterly* 4(1): 1–22.

Carnine, D. 1989. Teaching complex content to learning disabled students: The role of technology. *Exceptional Children* 55(6): 524–33.

Cartledge, G., and J. F. Milburn, eds. *Teaching social skills to children: Innovative approaches.* 2d ed. New York: Pergamon Press.

Crews, D. J. 1993. Potential benefits of aerobic exercise for learning-disabled children. *Research Quarterly for Exercise and Sport: Supplement* 64(1): A–113.

Dunn, S. E., and R. Wilson. 1991. Cooperating learning in the physical education classroom. *Journal of Physical Education, Recreation and Dance* 62(6): 22–28.

Ennis, C. D., and W. Zhu. 1991. Value orientations: A description of teachers' goals for student learning. *Research Quarterly for Exercise and Sport* 62(2): 33–40.

Frostig, M., and P. Maslow. 1970. *Movement education: Theory and practice.* Chicago: Follett Publishing Company.

Gomez, N. 1992. Somarhythms—Developing somatic awareness with balls. *Journal of Physical Education, Recreation and Dance* 63(4): 71, 74–76.

Gonter-Gaustad, M., and T. Messenheimer-Young. 1991. Dialogue journals for students with learning disabilities. *Teaching Exceptional Children* 23(3): 28–32.

Graham, K. C. 1989. Paradigms for the study of teacher-student behavior: An alternative perspective. *Research Quarterly for Exercise and Sport* 60(2): 190–93.

Greenockle, K. M., A. A. Lee, and R. Lomax. 1990. The relationship between student characteristics and activity patterns in a required high school physical education class. *Research Quarterly for Exercise and Sport* 61(1): 59–69.

Gusthart, J. L. (1985). Variations in direct, indirect, and noncontributing teacher behavior. *Journal of Teaching in Physical Educaion* 4: 111–22.

Houck, C. K. 1984. *Learning disabilities: Understanding concepts, characteristics, and issues.* Englewood Cliffs, NJ: Prentice-Hall.

Jansma, P., and J. T. Decker. 1992. An analysis of least restrictive environment placement variables in physical education. *Research Quarterly for Exercise and Sport* 63(2): 171–78.

Keel, M. C., and D. L. Gast. 1992. Small-group instruction for students with learning disabilities: Observational and incidental learning. *Exceptional Children* 58(4): 357–68.

Keller, M. J., and S. D. Hudson. 1991. Creating play environments for therapeutic recreation experiences. *Journal of Physical Education, Recreation and Dance* 62(4): 42–44.

Kephart, N. 1971. *The slow learner in the classroom.* Columbus, OH: Charles E. Merrill.

Lochbaum, M. R. 1993. Psychological, behavioral, and academic characteristics of learning-disabled children in an aerobic exercise program. *Research Quarterly for Exercise and Sport: Supplement* 63(1): A–113.

McAuley, E., T. Duncan, and V. V. Tammen. 1989. Psychometric properties of the intrinsic motivation inventory in a competitive sport setting: A confirmatory factor analysis. *Research Quarterly for Exercise and Sport* 60(1): 48–58.

McLeskey, J., and K. L. Grizzle. 1992. Grade retention rates among students with learning disabilities. *Exceptional Children* 58(6): 548–54.

Meese, R. L. 1992. Adapting textbooks for children with learning disabilities in mainstreamed classrooms. *Teaching Exceptional Children* 24(3): 49–51.

National Joint Committee on Learning Disabilities. 1981. *Learning disabilities: Issues on definition.* Position paper of the National Joint Committee on Learning Disabilities. January 30, 1981.

Nelson, R., and B. Lignugaris/Kraft. 1989. Post-secondary education for students with learning disabilities. *Exceptional Children* 56(3): 246–65.

Osman, B. 1979. *Learning disabilities: A family affair.* New York: Random House.

Osman, B., and H. Blinder. 1982. *No one to play with: The social side of learning disabilities.* New York: Random House.

Patterson, P., and N. Faucette. 1990. Attitudes toward physical activity of fourth and fifth grade boys and girls. *Research Quarterly for Exercise and Sport* 61(4): 415–18.

Rey, P. D. 1989. Training and contextual interference effects on memory and transfer. *Research Quarterly for Exercise and Sport* 60(4): 342–47.

Sage, G. H. 1984. *Motor learning and control: A neuropsychological approach.* Dubuque, IA: William C. Brown.

Schumaker, J. B., and D. C. Deshler. 1988. Implementing the regular education initiative in secondary schools: A different ball game. *Journal of Learning Disabilities* 21: 36–42.

Shapiro, E. S., and F. E. Lentz. 1991. Vocational-technical programs: Follow-up of students with learning disabilities. *Exceptional Children* 58(1): 47–59.

Torgesen, J. K. 1980. Conceptual and educational implications of the use of efficient task strategies by learning disabled students. *Journal of Learning Disabilities* 13: 364–71.

Virgilio, S. J. 1990. A model for parental involvement in physical education. *Journal of Physical Education, Recreation and Dance* 61(8): 66–70.

Webb, P. 1983. Factors used to determine mainstreaming of mentally handicapped and learning disabled students into elementary school physical education programs. (Doctoral dissertation, University of Oregon, Eugene). *Dissertation Abstracts International* 44(7): 2087.

Weiss, M. R., B. J. Bredemeier, and R. M. Shewchuk. 1985. An intrinsic/extrinsic motivation scale for the youth sport setting: A confirmatory factor analysis. *Journal of Sport Psychology* 7: 75–91.

Wiig, E. H., and E. M. Semel. 1980. *Language assessment and intervention for the learning disabled.* Columbus, OH: Charles E. Merrill.

Woodward, J., and R. Gersten. 1992. Innovative technology for secondary students with learning disabilities. *Exceptional Children* 58(5): 407–21.

CHAPTER 13

Other Health Conditions

Objectives

After reading this chapter, you should be able to

- Identify and discuss causes, symptoms, high-risk behaviors, and implications as they relate to those with AIDS or the AIDS virus.
- Describe common causative factors related to anemia.
- Know the underlying characteristics of and developmental activities for children with asthma.
- Identify factors contributing to child abuse and its recognition.
- Describe cystic fibrosis: its characteristics, etiology, and implications.
- Describe the etiology and characteristics of diabetes mellitus and inguinal hernia.
- Discuss activities for the relief of dysmenorrhea.
- Describe the characteristics of those with Marfan Syndrome and the factors to be considered when planning physical education experiences.
- Discuss meningitis, pneumonia, streptococcal infections, and tuberculosis and their implications for the physical educator.
- Describe symptoms and treatments of panic attack.
- Know the implications inherent in the programming of physical education activities for those with "other health conditions."

INTRODUCTION

With the exception of Chapter 4, Chapter 11, and Chapter 12, Section II of this text has described anomalies that, for the most part have classic medical definitions. In this chapter, we will address other health conditions that have an impact upon normal functioning and, as a consequence, can influence program selection and delivery modalities.

KEY TERMS

allergy	immune system (deficiency)
anaerobic	inguinal hernia
aplastic anemia	Marfan's syndrome
asthma	meningitis
bronchospasm	migraine headache
child abuse	panic attack
cystic fibrosis	pernicious anemia
diabetes mellitus	physical abuse
dysmennorrhea	physical neglect
eczema	pneumonia
emotional maltreatment	pulmonary tuberculosis
erythroblastosis fetalis	sexual abuse
femoral hernia	streptoccal infections
gastrointestinal disturbance	urticaria
hay fever	virus
HIV	

When an existing condition interferes with affective, cognitive, and psychomotor performance, the individual quickly consults a physician. Unfortunately a cure is not always possible, sometimes because too great a delay has occurred between the onset of the symptoms and the procurement of medical assistance. Given the fact that an early diagnosis offers the greatest chance for an encouraging prognosis, a physical education teacher can provide a significant service by being alert to early signs and symptoms. Further, avenues of condition and disease treatment are becoming more accurately defined, increasing potential for rehabilitation or recovery.

ACQUIRED IMMUNODEFICIENCY SYNDROME (AIDS)

First diagnosed in 1981 (Yarber 1987), AIDS is caused by a **virus** that can destroy the body's **immune system,** leaving victims unable to fight off infection. As a result, they are susceptible to life-threatening opportunistic diseases—diseases that otherwise would have been destroyed. At present there is no vaccine or treatment available to reverse the underlying immune system deficiency.* Hence, persons with AIDS can acquire diseases that lead to death.

The virus has been given different names.

1. Human Immunodeficiency Virus (HIV)
2. Human T-Lymphotropic Virus Type III (HTLV-III)
3. Lymphadenopathy-Associated Virus (LAV)

Since **HIV** is considered the preferred term by many scientists, this is the term most of us will find employed throughout the literature.

---

* Though no treatment has yet been successful in restoring the immune system of AIDS patients, physicians have had some success in using drugs, radiation, and surgery to treat their various illnesses.

Etiology

The AIDS virus can be transmitted in three ways:

1. During intimate sexual contact
2. By intervenous drug needles, including transfusions
3. From an infected woman to her fetus/unborn child.

Although HIV has been isolated from blood, semen, tears, and saliva, there is no evidence to support the notion that the disease can be passed by casual contact or by air-, food-, or waterborne routes.

Most persons having the AIDS virus do not know they are infected until the disease symptoms develop. The HIV test detects antibodies to the virus; at present there is no test for the virus itself (King 1992). Antibodies appear about six weeks after exposure so one should wait at least that long before being tested.

Individuals may be at various stages of infection: incubating disease, mildly infected without symptoms, or chronic carriers of certain infectious agents. (Infection means having the AIDS virus in the body. Once the virus is acquired, a person is considered to be infected whether or not AIDS ever develops. Having AIDS means that the virus has done enough damage to allow some rare diseases to become established.) The most common illnesses of persons with AIDS are a lung infection called Pneumocystis Carinii Pneumonia (PCP) and a cancer called Kaposi's Sarcoma (KS), Figure 13.1.

Symptoms

Although many symptoms of infection may not be detected for many years (and individuals appear to be in good physical condition), others are similar to those of

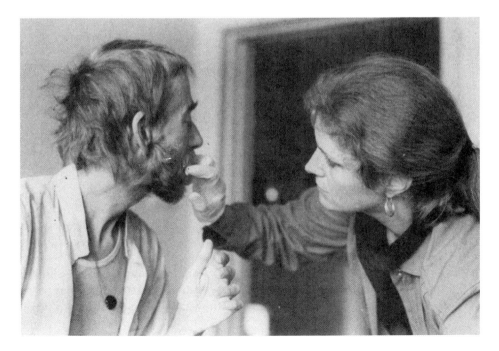

Figure 13.1. AIDS patient: Advanced stages

common minor illnesses, such as the cold or flu. The difference with the look-alike symptoms of minor illnesses, however, is that they may not go away or they may keep returning. These include diarrhea, fever, loss of appetite and weight, night sweats, and swollen lymph nodes. Anyone participating in high-risk activity should see a physician if AIDS symptoms are in place for more than two weeks. Only a physician can diagnose the condition.

Implications for Physical Education

Since ignorance of AIDS issues among school-age children appears to be the prevailing theme, it is extremely important that practitioners do what they can to instill greater knowledge and more favorable attitudes toward responsible behavior. AIDS is one of the foremost health concerns in the United States, and it has little chance of being eradicated in the immediate future. As of June 1991, 182,834 cases had been reported; of this number, 3,140 involved infants and children under the age of 13 (Centers for Disease Control 1991). According to Chu et al. (1991) it is likely that 20,000 children in the United States will be infected by the date of this book's publication.

The public's fear and lack of knowledge about the disease have impeded efforts to understand and control the epidemic (Keller 1992). Some parents have gone to great lengths in an effort to prohibit children with the AIDS virus from being in classes in which their own youngsters are enrolled. All teachers must do what they can to dispel untruths and rumors about how transmission takes place. Further, for a school to exclude a child with AIDS teaches all children the wrong lessons about tolerance and about community (Kirp and Epstein 1989).

However, this is not the entire problem. In a study by Anderson and King (1992) it was revealed that a high percentage of young people continue to practice high-risk behaviors in spite of knowing about HIV disease and safe-sex practices. The study concluded that

> HIV education programs that advise people to limit their number of sexual partners will have little or no impact on a sizeable minority of the population. For this group, the promotion of condoms and other safer-sex practices that do not limit sexual opportunities...[are likely to have more positive impact] (A-31).

In addition to enhancing knowledge and altering attitudes about participation in high-risk behavior, physical educators should do the following:

1. Stay up-to-date with regard to AIDS issues and integrate current findings into pertinent lessons, Table 13.1.
2. Practice approved first-aid procedures with injuries in which blood is a factor (e.g., guidelines produced by Centers for Disease Control, such as using gloves when treating broken-skin injuries or nose bleeds).
3. Have students avoid contact with the body fluids of others. These fluids often contain organisms of various sorts, some of which may cause disease.
4. Provide opportunities for students to shower thoroughly upon conclusion of activity sessions.
5. Encourage thorough laundering of uniforms and other clothing that may have been contaminated in play or instructional activity sessions.

6. Raise "comfort zones" of participants by removing the unknown. Disinfect all equipment, supply, and floor surfaces where children have been active.
7. Be aware of the physical limitations of your students so that conditioning and other activities requiring strength and cardiovascular endurance are designed appropriate to their tolerance and ability levels.

TABLE 13.1

AIDS Facts or Fallacies*

Answer Key			Items
True	*False*	1.	Everyone infected with the AIDS virus has developed AIDS.
True	False	2.	The AIDS virus itself usually does not kill the person.
True	False	3.	A person having the AIDS virus can pass it on even though there are no AIDS symptoms present.
True	False	4.	During sexual activity, exchange of body fluids is a way of transmitting the AIDS virus.
True	False	5.	Sharing IV drug needles and syringes puts a person at very high risk for getting the AIDS virus.
True	*False*	6.	A person can get the AIDS virus from giving blood.
True	*False*	7.	Only homosexual and bisexual men get AIDS.
True	False	8.	Women can transmit the AIDS virus to sex partners.
True	*False*	9.	A positive antibody test for the AIDS virus means that the person has or will develop AIDS.
True	False	10.	Students who have practiced high-risk behaviors, such as sex with high-risk persons or IV drug abuse, can get confidential AIDS testing and counseling.
True	*False*	11.	The AIDS virus can be spread through casual contact, such as touching or being near a person with AIDS.
True	False	12.	A person practicing sexual abstinence or partners practicing sexual fidelity who do not abuse IV drugs have almost no chance of getting the AIDS virus.
True	False	13.	The proper use of condoms is a good way to reduce the chance of getting the AIDS virus.
True	*False*	14.	Persons infected with the AIDS virus through IV drug abuse are not likely to pass the virus to sex partners unless the partner also abuses IV drugs.
True	False	15.	There is a national, toll-free, telephone hotline that provides AIDS information.

*Students can be given this test as a pre- or posttest assessment of current knowledge levels. Adapted from Yarber (1987). (The national, toll-free, telephone number for information on AIDS is l-800-342-AIDS.)

ALLERGIES

There are many kinds of **allergies**. Some are serious enough to impair sensorimotor performance—either despite or because of treatment. According to Wunderlich (1973),

> Neurologic and allergic dysfunction occur together with such regularity that one suspects on incidence factors alone that there is a relationship between the two.

On the other hand, there are others who believe that individuals with allergies do not have neurological impairments. Rather they suggest that it is adjustment to the allergy that may become temporary maladaptive behavior.

Further studies will help clarify the identification of any cause-and-effect relationship between an allergy and a neurological impairment. At present it is important to realize that only rarely does one form of allergy produce identical behavior patterns in different individuals.

Etiology

An allergy is a condition of hypersensitivity in which an individual experiences certain symptoms upon coming in contact with an allergen. The allergy-producing substances are often harmless—in similar doses—to others.

Many different substances have been found to cause allergic reactions in susceptible persons. For example, allergic reactions can be caused by any of the following:

1. Changes in temperature from cold to hot or vice versa in a relatively short period of time
2. Drug substances, including certain antibiotics, serums, and vaccines
3. Food items, including chocolate, eggs, milk, nuts, citrus fruits, strawberries, tomatoes, and wheat products
4. Infectious agents, including bacteria, fungi, and viruses
5. Substances that come in contact with the skin, including wool, dyes, animal fur or hair, feathers, poison sumac, and poison ivy
6. Substances transmitted through the air, including pollen, dust, smoke, and odors from deodorants, perfumes, and detergents

Symptoms

Symptoms may vary in intensity from exposure to exposure and from individual to individual. Among the more common symptoms are the following:

1. **Urticaria** (hives, nettle rash) is an inflammatory condition of the skin characterized by the eruption of pale, evanescent wheals (welts) that are associated with severe itching.
2. **Eczema** is an acute or chronic cutaneous inflammatory condition consisting of crusts, papules, scales, or vesicles alone or in combination. The condition may be dry or watery, and is accompanied by a burning and/or itching sensation, Figure 13.2.
3. **Hay fever** is an allergic condition of the mucus-covered air passages that is induced by external stimulation (e.g., pollen). Prevalent symptoms include watery discharges from the eyes and sneezing.

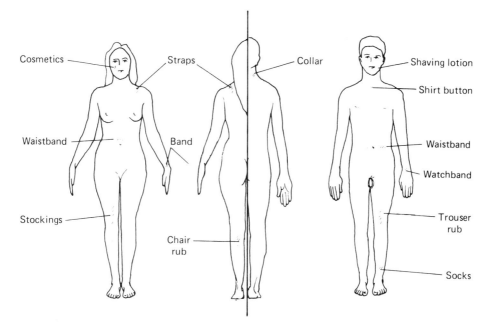

Figure 13.2. Exzema: Sites and contacts

4. **Migraine headache** is usually a severe pain on one side of the skull accompanied by disordered vision and nausea. Consistent findings emerging from research on causative factors of migraine headaches indicates that there are certain food substances that tend to trigger migraine headaches in some individuals. Food items found to be most causative are caffeine (found in coffee, tea), chocolate, monosodium glutamate (often found in servings of Chinese food), cheese products, nuts, and alcoholic beverages.
5. **Gastrointestinal disturbances** include diarrhea, nausea, and vomiting.
6. **Asthma** is a spasm of the bronchial tubes and/or swelling of mucuous membranes within the tube processes.

Implications for Physical Education

The physical education practitioner should know which students are susceptible to allergies and attempt to reduce their potential for exposure. We should help these youngsters avoid undue contact with aggravating substances (e.g., pollen, mat coverings, etc.). Class-time precautions can be valuable adjuncts to the treatment modes prescribed by the students' physicians. Keeping surface areas disinfected is one such method.

ANEMIA

Anemia is a deficiency of red corpuscles (erythrocytes), hemoglobin, or both within the blood. Frenay (1964) described three types.

1. **Aplastic anemia**—a condition in which the blood-forming organs do not produce erythrocytes. Aplastic anemia has been attributed to toxic drugs or exposure to X rays.

2. **Erythroblastosis fetalis**—an anemia of the newborn usually resulting from a helolytic reaction of the Rh-positive blood in the baby to the Rh-negative blood of the mother. (This condition will arise only when such Rh incompatibility exists.)

3. **Pernicious anemia**—referred to as a primary anemia. The condition is progressive and characterized by a deficiency of the antianemic principle vitamin B_{12}, a very low erythrocyte count, and general body weakness.

Implications for Physical Education

While anemic, the student should comply with the physician's prescriptions for diet and medication. Further since the youngster with anemia has a diminished capacity for sustained effort, de-emphasize activities requiring a great deal of stamina. Other activities are appropriate, however, and as approval is received from the child's physician, **anaerobic** activities can be resumed.

ASTHMA

Asthma, a term of Greek origin, is a condition characterized by wheezing respiration due to spasm or contraction of the bronchial tubes. Various intensities of asthma are described in Table 13.2.

TABLE 13.2

Classifications of Asthma

Classification	Description
Spasmodic asthma	Attacks are separated by long intervals of remission (freedom from symptoms).
Continuous asthma	Daily wheezing is present.*
Intractable asthma	Symptoms are continuous.
Status asthmaticus	Treatment renders little or no relief.

*Wheezing—A whistling or sighing sound resulting from narrowing of the respiratory passageway.

According to Hardman et al. (1990) the treatment of asthma requires a comprehensive diagnosis prior to applying intervention strategies. Differentiating asthma from other selected conditions can be very challenging. However, a skilled physician who conducts a comprehensive diagnostic examination can identify the asthmatic successfully. Some years ago Galton (1977) suggested that there appear to be stronger psychological factors in many instances of asthma than in other allergies, enough stronger so that asthma can be considered a psychosomatic as well as an allergic disorder. This view is still held today.

Whether its etiology is allergenic, psychosomatic, or both, asthma causes respiratory distress requiring attention. We must do everything possible to eliminate from the school environment factors that appear to be causative of asthma attacks. Approximately one-third of the illnesses suffered by school-age children are respiratory problems, including asthma. Suitable physical activities can build the student's tolerance and resistance mechanisms.

Implications for Physical Education

Begin each developmental physical education class with several minutes of breathing exercises. Sherrill (1976) suggests several procedures to follow when these exercises are presented.

1. Encourage each child to blow his/her nose and attempt to cough up phlegm into tissues that you have provided. Urge the students to avoid the habit of sniffling.
2. Emphasize long exhalations through the nose and short inhalations through gently pursed lips, Figure 13.3. Each exhalation should take nearly twice as long as each inhalation.
3. Advise the children that some coughing and wheezing is to be expected at the beginning of an exercise session. Regular training will help reduce one's period of discomfort.
4. Be sure that each student's chest and abdominal areas are free to move with each inhalation and exhalation. Loosening of tight waist belts will increase freedom.

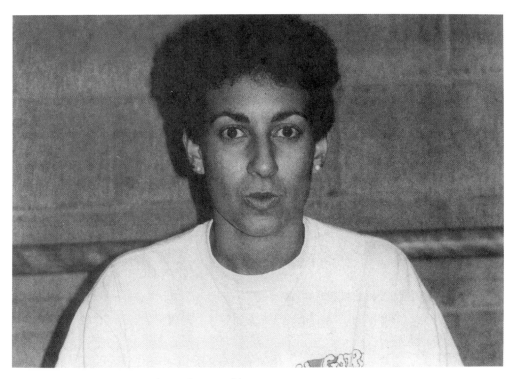

Figure 13.3. Inhaling through gently pursed lips

DEVELOPMENTAL ACTIVITIES

I. Goal: Reducing Bronchspasms

| *Major Objective* | *Interim Performance Objective* |

1. Breathing calisthenics

Figure 13.4. Inhaling while extending arms

Figure 13.5. Exhaling during lateral trunk flexion

1.1 Demonstrate three breathing phases while in the supine position, knees bent.

    1.1A Tighten abdominal muscles while exhaling slowly through the nose.

    1.1B Inhale through the lips while relaxing the abdominal muscles.

    1.1C Tighten abdominal muscles while exhaling through the nose.

    1.1D Repeat four times.

1.2 While in sitting position, legs straight, bottoms of feet resting against a wall.

    1.2A Inhale while expanding the chest.

    1.2B Exhale while reaching to touch the toes.

    1.2C Repeat four times.

1.3 While in standing position

    1.3A Inhale while extending the arms as high as possible, Figure 13.4.

    1.3B Lower the arms, bend extending arms forward while exhaling.

    1.3C Repeat four times.

1.4 While in standing position

    1.4A Inhale while extending the arms as high as possible.

    1.4B Lower the arms, bend to the side while exhaling, Figure 13.5.

    1.4C Repeat four times, alternating sides.

Major Objective	*InterimPerformance Objective*
2. Breathing games	2.1 Continue laughing for as long as object tossed by teacher or fellow student remains in the air.
	2.1A Ball
	2.1B Shuttlecock
	2.1C Handkerchief
	2.2 Blow up a balloon to a progressively greater circumference.
	2.3 Blow out a candle at progressively greater distances.
	2.4 Blow a ping pong ball across the floor to progressively greater distances.

Developmental activity programs that include relaxation techniques (Appendix E) are valuable for asthmatic children. Further Racaniello (1976) found that swimming or cycling may elicit fewer **bronchospasms** than running. This has been substantiated since that time by colleagues working in the field.

CHILD ABUSE

It has been reported that over 2 million children in the United States are the victims of **child abuse**. How much over is anyone's guess. Parents and other care givers are distressingly naive about the existence and/or elements of an abusive situation. Child abuse includes such things as

1. abandonment—in which the child has been left by his/her parent, guardian, or custodian without provision for care, supervision, or financial support (although financially able to provide such support).
2. neglect—including failure to keep the child and his/her surroundings clean; failure to procure standard or emergency medical care; failure to dress child in accordance with weather conditions; failure to provide regular meals.
3. trauma—including hitting the child with one's hands, fists, or other objects; kicking the child; burning the child; throwing the child so as to cause physical injury.
4. **sexual abuse**—including molestation up to intercourse itself; exploitation.
5. verbal abuse—including persistent scolding of the child for little or no reason; belittling of the child publicly or privately.

What causes child abuse? Historians claim that in the past, children were sometimes abused to expel evil spirits or please the gods. Causes today appear to be more in line with self-indulgence, greed, personal frustration, and/or the fact that abusers are modeling the behavior of their parents or guardians (in that abusers themselves were abused as children).

The characteristics of parents involved in the abuse of their children vary, but they do tend to share several of the following characteristics (Falk, Hill, and Ganem, undated):

1. They are isolated from family supports, such as friends, neighbors, and community groups.
2. They consistently fail to keep appointments, discourage social contact, rarely or never participate in school activities.
3. They seem to trust no one.
4. They are reluctant to give information about the child's injuries or condition. They are unable to explain the injuries or condition, or they give far fetched explanations of such injuries.
5. They respond inappropriately to the child's condition. They either overreact or seem hostile and antagonistic when questioned. Or they underreact, showing little concern or awareness and seem more occupied with their own problems than those of the the child.
6. They refuse to consent to diagnostic studies of the child.
7. They delay or fail to take the child for medical care—for routine checkups or for treatment of injury or illness; or they may choose a different physician or hospital each time.
8. They are overcritical of the child and seldom discuss the child in positive terms.
9. They have unrealistic expectations of the child, expecting or demanding behavior that is beyond the child's age or ability.
10. They believe in harsh punishment, often cruel or sadistic.
11. They seldom touch or look at the child in public.
12. They ignore the child's crying or react with impatience.
13. They keep the child confined—perhaps in a crib or playpen—for long periods of time.
14. They seem to lack understanding of the child's physical and emotional needs.
15. They are hard to locate.
16. They may be misusing drugs or alcohol.
17. They appear to lack control or fear that they may lose control.
18. Their behavior may generally be irrational. They seem incapable of child-rearing.

To be cared for and loved is a basic need of all children. If a child is deprived of loving care, the probability that he/she will reach adulthood with a healthy personality is reduced. A parent's emotional instability may be manifested in the negative treatment of his or her offspring. Where instability does exist in parents, they should be encouraged to attend group meetings such as those conducted by Parents Anonymous. Most states have local chapters of Parents Anonymous where people can go to share problems and nurture the hope that solutions will be found.*

Implications for Physical Education

The physical education practitioner should be alert to signs or abuse. Because many physical education programs require students to shower and change their clothes, the

---

* Specific addresses may be obtained by contacting Parents Anonymous Resource Office, c/o your state capital offices.

teacher is in a unique position to observe students for these signs (Bayless and Cutter 1986). In addition to characteristic signs of unusual tissue discoloration (such as injuries on a limb or trunk in various stages of healing) or withdrawal in a child who is typically outgoing and happy, there are other indicators of which one should be aware, Table 13.3.

TABLE 13.3

Indicators of a Child's Potential Need for Protection

Category of Abuse	Physical Indicators	Behavioral Indicators
Physical Abuse	• Unexplained bruises, welts, bite marks, bald spots • Unexplained burns, espicially cigarette burns or immersion burns (glove like) • Unexplained abrasions, lacerations, fractures	• Self-destructive • Withdrawn and aggressive • Uncomfortable with • physical contact • Arrives at school early or stays late as if afraid • to go home • Chronic runaway • Complains of soreness or moves uncomfortabnly • Wears clothing inappropriate to weather in order to cover body
Physical Neglect	• Abandonment • Unattended medical needs • Consistent lack of supervision • Consistent hunger, inappropriate dress, poor hygiene • Lice, distended stomach, emaciated	• Regularly displays fatigue or listlessness, falls asleep in class • Steels food, begs from classmates • Reports that no caregiver is at home • Frequently absent or tardy • Self -destructive • School dropout
Sexual Abuse	• Torn, stained, or bloody underclothing • Pain or itching in genital area • Difficulty walking or sitting • Bruises or bleeding in external genitalia • Venereal disease • Frequent urinary infections	• Withdrawal, chronic depression • Excessive seductiveness • Role reversal, overly concerned for siblings • Poor self -esteem, self-devaluation, lack of confidence • Lack of involvement with peers • Massive weight change • Suicide attempts

Table 13.3 *continued*

Category of Abuse	Physical Indicators	Behavioral Indicators
		• Hysteria, lack of emotional control • Sudden school difficulties • Inappropriate sex play or premature understanding of sex • Threatened by physical contact, closeness
Emotional Maltreatment	• Speech disorders • Delayed physical development • Substance abuse • Ulcers, asthma, severe allergies	• Habit disorders (rocking) • Antisocial, destructive • Neurotic traits (abnormal fears, sleeplessness) • Behavioral extremes passive and aggressive) • Delinquent behavior • Developmentally delayed

Adapted from Broadhurst, Edmunds, and MacDirken (1979).

Many cases of child abuse are not reported. Because of acts of omission on the part of teachers or other supervisors, many children will suffer the consequences. States have child protection laws, or their equivalent, that require teachers or other school employees who suspect that a child's physical or mental health or welfare may be adversely affected by abuse or neglect to report same to the principal or other designated personnel. These in turn are to call the proper child protection agency and give the following information:

1. Name, address, age, and gender of the student
2. Name and address of parent or caretaker
3. Name and address of the person allegedly responsible for the abuse and/or neglect (if known)
4. Name(s) of sibling(s) who may be in danger (if known)
5. Nature and extent of injuries or description of abuse

Learn the policy of your school, and act accordingly. When selecting physical education activities, consider the physical and emotional states of the abused child. Programs suited to students with temporary or permanent physical disabilities should be chosen and principles inherent in working with the emotionally disturbed should be kept in mind. Other guiding principles include the following:

1. Never underestimate the power that a positive adult relationship can have in a child's life. Children take their cues from adults.
2. Make your classroom as safe as it can be. Structure and routine can help children regain a sense of personal control.
3. Do not make promises you cannot keep. Be hopeful and honest, but promises not kept merely serve to break the child's trust—again.

4. Stay calm and open. Act nonjudgmentally toward a child's words or behavior. The child may interpret "anger" or "upset" as being directed at him/her. In this circumstance the child may think that what happened is his/her fault.

5. If a child tells you something, tell him/her that he/she did the right thing in telling. Children are often reluctant to tell for fear that they will get in trouble.

6. Do not speak badly of the offender to the child. That person is often known and loved by the child. Consider saying "What he did to you was wrong. I am sorry it happened to you." or "It was unfair of her to do that to you. I am sorry."

7. Never promise to keep something a secret. "I cannot promise to keep that a secret because we may have to tell someone to make it stop."

8. Do not act shocked, angry or upset at what a child may say or do. Remain open for more information. "I am wondering where you learned that." "I am wondering who taught you how to do that." "We need to tell someone so that (_____) can get help to stop doing that to you."

9. Consider integrating child abuse prevention education topics within your classroom. Health educators and school nurses are excellent sources of information.

10. Do not make a child feel strange or different, dirty, untouchable, or singled out. Treat him/her just like every other child, but with an extra dose of compassion. (Adapted from: National Committee for Prevention of Child Abuse, New Hampshire Chapter)

CYSTIC FIBROSIS

Cystic fibrosis is an inherited disease that causes a disorder of the secretory glands. With this condition, these glands produce abnormal amounts of mucous, saliva, and sweat. Three major organs are affected by the secretions: lungs, pancreas, and sweat glands.

In the lungs the thickened, gluelike substance obstructs functioning and raises the probability of infections. The pancreas is affected in a similar way. Excessive amounts of mucus prevents important enzymes from reaching the small intestine. Without these enzymes, fats and proteins are lost in frequent, greasy, and flatulent stools (Hardman et al 1990). Finally, those with cystic fibrosis produce sweat inordinately high in salt content. This feature emerges as significant to the diagnosis of the condition. With early diagnosis and quality care, most affected children can achieve growth gains approximating normal expectations. Cheney and Harwood (1985) report that more than 50 percent of those with the disease live beyond the age of twenty.

Etiology

While the causes of cystic fibrosis are unclear, it is known to be the most common life-threatening genetic disease among the caucasian population (Orenstein, Henke, and Cerny 1983). The incidence of the condition is at one out of two thousand live births and, of those affected, more than 90 percent die because of pulmonary dysfunction.

While exercise does not appear to have a positive influence on the pulmonary function of those with cystic fibrosis, recent studies have shown that it can increase the endurance of the respiratory muscles, thus enhancing exercise tolerance. Herein lies a major role for physical education.

Implications for Physical Education

The thoughtful planning and delivery of exercise and other activities will go a long way to improve the quality of life for those with cystic fibrosis. The advice for an active life has generally been based on the assumption that it would be better for them physically and emotionally. This is arguable given statements made by patients and their families that their condition improves when they are active. If we look at the extension of life without reference to its quality, important issues are being neglected.

Socialization is important for us all. Given the fact that having a life-threatening disease is likely to cause depression, those with cystic fibrosis are particularly in need of interactions with their peers. Physical educators should not leave this interaction to chance. Plan for activities requiring team solutions. Do all that you can to encourage group work.

Review the suggestions made in previous chapters regarding physical and motor fitness (Chapter 4) and social development (Chapter 10). Enter into dialogue with the child, the family, and the family physician in order to arrive at the best possible match between what is needed and what is delivered.

DIABETES MELLITUS

Diabetes mellitus is a disturbance in the metabolism of carbohydrates, fats, and proteins resulting from the inability of the pancreas (beta) cells to produce sufficient insulin. Without this hormone the body's ability to convert food components into the energy necessary to live and function is diminished. The diabetic child is often thin. He/she may have an unhealthy skin color and appear undernourished.

According to the American Diabetes Association one in ten thousand persons under the age of twenty will develop diabetes (Brothers 1976). The incidence figures for other age groups are presented in Table 13.4.

Etiology

It is not known why the pancreas fails to provide the necessary insulin, but there is some evidence that weight, in addition to age, is a contributing factor. While age and weight are influential factors, the most common form of diabetes is inherited. Brothers (1976) reports

The diabetic has inherited an abnormal set of those genes which confer the chemical capability for the metabolism of certain compounds that may be

TABLE 13.4

Diabetes Mellitus: Estimated Incidence per Ten Thousand Population

Incidence	Age Range
10	20–40
100	41–60
1000	Over 60

ingested or manufactured in the body. In diabetes, it is the metabolism of sugar that causes the primary problem.

According to some reports, diabetes is likely to reduce the optimum functioning of the kidneys. On the other hand Danowski (1974)—and others, since that time—have noted that for the vast majority of those with diabetes the kidneys remain entirely operational.

Implications for Physical Education

In addition to being alerted to the existence of a possible problem by virtue of a child who makes frequent requests to visit the restroom, Byrne (1981) and Lewis and Doorlag (1991) suggest other symptoms that may point to an undiagnosed diabetic.

1. Breath with a sweet, fruity odor (ketone breath)
2. Frequent thirst
3. Recurring nausea and vomiting
4. Panting without exercise (air hunger)
5. Dry skin and mucous membranes
6. Muscular weakness
7. Localized short recurring pain or general abdominal pain
8. Poor circulation, evidenced by cold feet and hands

Taken alone, each may not mean much. Observed in combination, however, they could be important indicators. If you observe these symptoms, mention your suspicions to the school nurse.

Although there is no known cure for diabetes mellitus, there is evidence that it can be controlled by either or all of the following:

1. Oral medication
2. Insulin
3. Diet

The attending physician will closely monitor the frequency and dose of the oral medication and insulin. The physical education teacher can help the student with regard to diet and exercise. Regular programs of exercise are valuable because they stimulate pancreatic secretions, control weight, and contribute to general health and physical fitness.

When planning program options for diabetic students, take the following into account:

1. The school nurse or physician should have a written record of the student's history and the most recent information regarding insulin dosage, diet, and urine tests.
2. Medications, including insulin, should be given only under the direction of a physician.
3. Written procedures should be obtained for treatment of hypoglycemia in each diabetic student. Each document should include:
   a) Name of the individual who is authorized to provide treatment
   b) Nature of the treatment modality that should be used in specific circumstances and the quantity of any substance to be administered

   c)   Whether the occurrence is to be documented.
4. Conditions for the implementation of treatment for hyperglycemia (with or without ketosis and acidosis) should be made clear.*
5. Written policies that cover the guidelines for emergency treatment of commonly encountered problems should be obtained.

DYSMENORRHEA

Dysmenorrhea is a term used to identify painful or difficult menstruation. The condition is reported to exist in approximately 25 percent of college-age women and in a slightly higher percentage of high school girls. Nearly seventy to eighty percent of these cases are reported to be functional in nature—i.e., they are due to fatigue, improper diet, insufficient exercise, and weak abdominal musculature (Wiseman 1982). Very few cases have been found to be of organic origin. If functional causes can be ruled out, however, it is important that a physician be contacted.

   If dysmenorrhea is diagnosed as functional, appropriately prescribed exercises can reduce the severity of cramps. These exercises should be performed on a regular basis, and should include the exercises described in the developmental activities that follow.

DEVELOPMENTAL ACTIVITIES

I. Goal: Reducing Dysmenorrhea

Major Objective	*Interim Performance Objective*
1. Promote blood circulation in abdominal and pelvic areas.	1.1 Perform the following exercise while in the supine position, knees bent, hands resting lightly upon abdomen, Figure 13.6.

Figure 13.6. Promoting blood circulation in abdominal and pelvic areas

1.1A Reduce arch in the small of the back by pulling in the abdominal muscles on count of "one" (second).

1.1B Relax abdominal muscles on count of "2" (seconds).

1.1C Perform cycle eight times. Repeat for three sets (one-minute rest period between each set).

> *Note:* Inhale during contraction phase; exhale during relaxation phase.

---

* Ketosis is the accumulation of such ketones as acetone and betahydroxybutyric acid within the body. Acidosis is a disturbance of the acid-base balance in the body. (Ketosis results from the incomplete combustion of fatty acids generally resulting from inadequate use of or deficiency in carbohydrates.)

Major Objective

2. Improve muscle tonus in abdominal area.

Figure 13.7. Hip flexion: Improving muscle tonus in abdomen

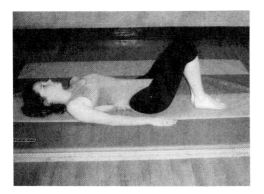

Figure 13.8. Hip extension: Returning to starting position, feet flat on floor

3. Stretching lumbar spine

Figure 13.9. Stretching lumbar spine: Starting position

Interim Performance Objective

2.1 Perform the following exercise while in the supine position, knees bent, hands resting lightly on the floor beside hips.

2.1A Flex hips and bring knees toward the chest, Figure 13.7.

2.1B Extend hips and return to starting position, Figure 13.8.

2.1C Perform cycle eight times. Repeat for three sets (one-minute rest period between each set).

Note: Inhale while returning feet and legs to starting position; exhale while hips are flexed.

3.1 Perform the following exercise while kneeling with body lowered so that the forearms and one side of the face are placed on mat, Figure 13.9.

3.1A Lower the chest toward the mat and hold this position eight seconds, Figure 13.10.

13.B Return to the starting position.

Major Objective   *Interim Performance Objective*

13.C Perform three eight-second sets with ten-second rest between each set.

> *Note:* Inhale and hold while lowering chest to the mat. Exhale and hold while returning to and maintaining starting position.

Figure 13.10. Stretching lumbar spine: lowering chest toward mat

Generally, there is no reason to excuse students from class during menstrual periods. Although some pain may exist, properly prescribed programs of activity conducted over a period of time can help to reduce discomfort.

INFECTIOUS DISEASES

As a consequence of classroom contact, school children are prime targets for infectious diseases. Some conditions are more serious than others. All conditions described in this section require the care and treatment of a medical practitioner before any rehabilitative or other activities can be undertaken.

Pneumonia
Pneumonia is an inflammation of one or both lungs. It is often accompanied by high temperature and an accumulation of fluid within the lungs.

Among the various types of pneumonia are

1. bronchopneumonia—inflammation within the bronchi and their divisions.
2. lobar pneumonia—inflammation of a single lobe of the lung. Only rarely are two or more lobes involved at one time.
3. Primary atypical pneumonia—characterized by patchy areas of inflammation in one or both lungs and caused by a viruslike organism.
4. Viral pneumonia—most common of the pneumonias in younger children and adolescents and caused by a virus strain. Virus is a term used to identify a number of infectious agents too small to be seen through a standard microscope.

Pulmonary Tuberculosis
Pulmonary tuberculosis is an inflammatory disease of the lungs caused by the tubercle bacillus. Tuberculosis occurs most frequently in persons between the ages of eighteen and thirty-five. No age group is exempt from the condition, however. Therefore the physical education practitioner should be aware of the typical symptoms so

that appropriate medical care can be procured during the initial stages of the disease. These symptoms are

1. Weakness and general fatigue following a work effort of low intensity
2. Failure to gain weight in accordance with normal expectancy tables
3. General reduction in appetite
4. Low-grade fever during the afternoon
5. Sweating at night
6. Coughing

Since there is significant variability in the type and severity of tuberculosis (Table 13.5), it is important that each individual be medically counseled in accordance with the complexity of his/her specific condition.

TABLE 13.5

Classes of Tuberculosis

Class	Description
Caseous pneumonic tuberculosis	Acute, inflammatory, ulceractive, progressive; frequently causes rupture of caseous lymph nodes
Endobronchial tuberculosis	Inflammation of the mucous membrane lining of the bronchi
Miliary tuberculosis	Distribution of minute tubercles in both lungs

Complete bed rest and proper diet are common treatment procedures until the disease can be brought under control. At that juncture progressive exercise programs can be provided to help the student regain normal strength and endurance levels. At the same time, the student should participate in activities such as archery, bowling, golf, and swimming—activities that can be performed at his/her own pace.

Meningitis

Meningitis is an inflammation of the membrane of the spinal cord. Nearly one-half of all meningitis patients are under the age of ten. The remaining half is largely comprised of young adults.

Among the symptoms of this acute, contagious, and serious condition are

1. Auditory and/or visual dysfunction
2. Fever
3. Loss of appetite
4. Constipation
5. Severe headache
6. Intolerance of light and sound
7. Lack of orientation with respect to time and space
8. Delirium and convulsions

TABLE 13.6

Classes of Meningitis

Class	Description
Choriomeningitis	A cerebral meningitis in which cellular infiltration of the meminges occurs
Influenzal meningitis	A form caused by a bacterium (hemophilus) that, in severe cases, can be seen under a microscope. (It is not related to epidemic influenza.)
Meningococcal meningitis	A classification in which the causative microorganism yields cerebrospinal type of meningitis

As is the case with many diseases, there may be complications with meningitis. Among these are: arthritis, endocarditis, mental retardation, pericarditis, and pneumonia.

Implications for physical education The student's physician will closely supervise the program of convalescence from meningitis. There are various classes of meningitis, Table 13.6; each generally requires a specific mode of treatment for optimum recovery.

Although meningitis is a serious condition, the rehabilitation period is not ordinarily as lengthy as it is with many other infectious diseases. Consequently, the physical education teacher can expect to involve these youngsters in progressive programs of activity within a relatively short period of time.

Streptococcal Infections

Streptococcal infections are caused by a genus of bacteria (streptococcus). Infections are readily transmitted through direct and indirect contact with already contaminated persons or objects. Common vehicles of contamination are discharges from the nose and mouth that travel through the air, or that land on objects that are subsequently touched by other people. Streptococcal infections commonly become manifest as tonsilitis and scarlet fever. Persons who have had rheumatic fever may sustain structural damage to the heart if they get streptococcal infections.

Implications for Physical Education Children who are recuperating from infectious diseases should participate in physical education activities of modified duration and intensity. The attending physician should judge the student's readiness for participation in a developmental or standard physical education class.

A child who returns to school after a bout with an infectious disease is a prime candidate for a relapse unless activity programs are prescribed cautiously. Cooperation between medical and physical education personnel can ensure that classes in physical education contribute to the child's rehabilitation. Physical education is one class that the student should not be without.

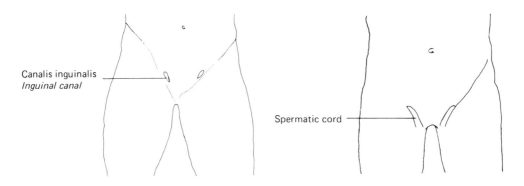

Figure 13.11. Inguinal canal: Site of inguinal hernia

Figure 13.12. Site of femoral hernia

INGUINAL HERNIA

Hernias are generally identified in accordance with their location. The **inguinal hernia**, the most common type, occurs at the inguinal canal, Figure 13.11.

Etiology

By the very nature of its structure the inguinal canal fosters weakness in the abdominal wall. If the abdominal muscles are weak, if there is an injury or surgical procedure in the area, or if a heavy load is lifted and pressure increased from within the abdominal cavity, there is a greater chance that an inguinal hernia will occur. The various classes of inguinal hernia are described in Table 13.7.

While the inguinal hernia is most prevalent in men, the **femoral hernia** is more common in women, Figure 13.12. In men the spermatic cords extend through the inguinal canals into the scrotum. In women the round ligaments of the uterus are in this location. The femoral rings are openings just below the inguinal ligaments. Since the diameter of the femoral rings is ordinarily larger in women than in men, women are more susceptible to femoral hernia.

TABLE 13.7

Classes of Inguinal Hernia

Class	Description
Congenital (direct) inguinal hernia	A loop of intestine protrudes directly through the muscles and along the external ring.
Acquired (indirect) inguinal hernia	The protrusion enters the canal at the internal ring and follows the course of the canal.
Incomplete inguinal hernia	The protrusion remains in the canal.
Complete inguinal hernia	A loop of intestine exits from the canal and enters the scrotum.

Implications for Physical Education

The only recognized cure for an inguinal hernia is a surgical procedure called a herniorrhaphy. Surgery should be performed as soon as possible following diagnosis of the hernia.

To help the student prepare for surgery, provide a program that includes deep breathing exercises, lower-limb movement,* and proper body mechanics. Activities that are contraindicated include: breath holding, gymnastics, track and field, weight lifting, and wrestling. Avoid activity prescriptions that cause intra-abdominal strain. Following surgery and convalescence, the student will gradually be able to participate in activities suited to his age, skill, and physical development.

MARFAN'S SYNDROME

Marfan's syndrome is a connective tissue disorder named after a French pediatrician, Antoine Marfan, who in 1896 identified characteristics unlike those found in other conditions. All organs contain connective tissue, but according to Pyeritz and Conant (1989), evidence of Marfan's syndrome appears primarily in the bones and ligaments (skeletal system), the eyes (ocular system), heart and blood vessels (cardiovascular system), and the lungs (respiratory system), Table 13.8.

TABLE 13.8

Common Characteristics of Marfan's Syndrome: By System

System	Characteristics
Skeletal	Arms, fingers, legs, and toes may be disportionately long as compared to the trunk. Rotolateral and lordotic curvatures of the spine are common. The sternum may either protrude (pigeon breast) or indent (funnel chest). The roof of the mouth is usually high arched, and the teeth can appear crowded in a long and narrow face.
Ocular	In about 50 percent of the cases the lens of the eye is off-center or dislocated. Nearsightedness (myopia) is common.
Cardiovascular	Mitral valve leaflets are often too large for the openings they need to cover. As a consequence they billow backward when the left ventricle contracts (called mitral valve prolapse). The aorta is often affected in that it enlarges and may cause a tear.
Respiratory	Diminished elasticity of tissue, which impacts upon the ease with which one can breathe. Spontaneous collapse of a lung may occur.

---

* Lower-limb exercises should be performed while the student is seated or lying down.

Of the conditions described, the most serious effect of this disorder is upon the cardiovascular system where an undiagnosed (or untreated) widening of the aorta could result in rupture and sudden death.*

Etiology

The syndrome is a heritable disorder of connective tissue arising in both genders and in all races. It is heritable because it has its basis in a genetic error (mutation), and because blood relatives have genes in common, more than one person in a family can be affected.

While some individuals may have many of the characteristics described earlier, others will have but a few. Critical to a successful diagnosis is the inclusion of the following evaluatory elements:

1. A complete family and medical history
2. A thorough physical examination
3. A thorough eye examination by an ophthalmologist (who uses a slit lamp to look for lens dislocation upon fully dilating the pupil)
4. An electrocardiogram (EKG) and an echocardiogram.

At present it is estimated that approximately forty thousand individuals are afflicted with the syndrome in the United States. This makes it nearly as prevalent as cystic fibrosis and muscular dystrophy (Romeo 1991). As with these and other conditions early diagnosis and intervention are important to long-term management, and the physical educator can play a major role in the process.

Implications for Physical Education

Before refining your activity program, it is necessary to consult with the child's family and physician(s) in order to determine the various dimensions of his/her disorder(s). Pursuant to these discussions, you will be ready to plan and deliver safe programs appropriate to individual needs. Cull pertinent ideas on developmental activities from Chapters 4–12, and consider the following:

1. Avoid contact activities that might cause trauma to the chest. Trauma from such activities as boxing, football, lacrosse, rugby, or wrestling could cause the sudden collapse of a lung or the rupture of a weakened (or enlarged) aorta.
2. Avoid activities in which there is a high risk of falling. Examples include the use of apparatus in gymnastics, horseback riding, or roller/ice skating. Again such a fall could affect the lungs or heart.
3. Avoid using isometric exercises. They can elevate blood pressure levels. This would not be good for the heart's valves or aorta.
4. Endurance/marathon running or high-impact aerobics would generally be contraindicated. These activities are designed to effect cardiovascular conditioning. These are excellent for a child with a healthy heart, but not for one who has a cardiovascular dysfunction.

---

* The reader may remember the sudden death of Flo Hyman, a former star of the United States Women's Olympic Volleyball Team.

5. Avoid activities in which there is the probability of rapid decompression. The trauma arising from diving could have serious consequences for the cardio-vascular system.
6. Activities placing excessive strain upon joints and ligaments should be avoided.
7. Use eye protection (goggles) for those with ocular system problems. Slow speed/flight of objects; they should be brightly colored and soft (foam, Nerf, rag).
8. Provide information to classmates regarding Marfan's syndrome so that they may better understand its effects upon the bodies of those involved (Romeo 1991).

PANIC ATTACK

Often thought to be of little medical significance, **panic attack** is surfacing as a major dysfunction for teenagers. Found to be more common in girls than in boys, the problem seems to emerge without observable causes. While more research needs to be done as to its etiology and prognosis, it is diagnosed when an unprovoked episode of at least four of the following symptoms occurs within a thirty-day period:*

1. Chest discomfort
2. Choking or smothering sensations
3. Faintness
4. Fears of losing control, going insane, dying
5. Feelings of unreality
6. Heart palpitations
7. Hot or cold flashes
8. Intense terror (the feeling you might have if you were surprised by a burglar with a gun in your own home)
9. Nausea
10. Numbness or tingling sensation, especially in the hands or feet
11. Shortness of breath
12. Sweating
13. Trembling

Although some suspect that genetics play a role in its existence, for many who have the condition there is no family history of such at all. There are physicians who believe that there is a link between panic disorders and mitral valve prolapse; others argue that the two events may coexist, but they do so by chance only.

Implications for Physical Education
Whatever the factors contributing to its presence, the physical educator must be observant to signs and symptoms. We might observe a child appearing to be afraid to

---

* For further information, contact:
  - The American Psychiatric Association, 1400 K Street, NW, Washington, DC. 20005.
  - The American Psychological Association, Public Affairs, 750 First St., NE, Washington, DC 20002.
  - The Anxiety Disorders Association of America, 6000 Executive Blvd., Suite 513, Rockville, MD 20852.
  - Panic Disorder, Pueblo, CO 81009.

engage in a competitive sport event or perhaps climb up onto a piece of gymnastics apparatus. It might be assumed that the task is the prompt, whereas there may be underlying panic disorder issues. The catalyst for the display of fear might be the request you have made.

Should you observe a student who is expressing the problem(s) associated with the symptoms, it would be appropriate to apply the referral policies of your school. There is medical treatment available, including medication (e.g., Ativan, Klonopin, Prozac, or Xanax) and behavioral/cognitive therapy. Medications can block or reduce the physical symptoms of panic attack, while therapy can help the person understand what is going on and can alert the person as to how he/she can help suppress frightening feelings and thoughts.

SUMMARY

General health impairments constitute a major source of concern among those conducting physical education classes. Further, it is not uncommon to find students seeking to be relieved from participating in scheduled activities. While a few of these youngsters may be manufacturing reasons for being excused, most do have legitimate health problems. As a consequence those charged with their instruction must be knowledgeable about the conditions they are likely to express.

Chapter 13 focused upon the health impairments not ordinarily classified with conditions described in earlier sections. Etiologies, characteristics, and implications for physical education were presented for these various problems. An understanding of the nature and ramifications of the selected problems will go a long way to reduce the anxiety often associated with their diagnosis—for the affected student, his/her classmates, and the teacher.

It has been suggested that physical education is for everyone. It is! Therefore practitioners have an obligation to do what they can to design and deliver programs that are in keeping with the needs of those enrolled. The careful study of this chapter and completing the recommended laboratory and reading assignments to follow will provide you with the tools to be successful.

RECOMMENDED LABORATORY ASSIGNMENTS

1. Make appointments with physicians to discuss the ramifications of activity for students with the conditions described in this chapter.
2. Arrange to visit schools in which children with "other health conditions" are participating in developmental or regular physical education programs.
3. Perform the developmental activities described in this chapter. List other activities that might help students who have asthma or dysmenorrhea.
4. Add to the roster of physical and behavioral indicators likely to be in place for those who are victims of child abuse.
5. Discuss issues related to panic attacks with those who are knowledgeable about pertinent symptoms. Get on the mailing list of professional organizations that provide materials on this disorder.

6. Meet with practitioners to discuss the various health conditions described in this book. Learn of the various programs and practices they employ that have been found to be successful.

7. Work with students who have been diagnosed as having conditions described in this chapter and help practitioners prescribe appropriate developmental physical education activities for them.

8. Read documents that describe conditions not discussed in this chapter that may be relevant to the kinds of activities prescribed for school-age children.

9. Arrange to receive regular physical examinations that screen for such conditions as diabetes mellitus and tuberculosis.

10. Review the recommended readings.

REFERENCES

Anderson, P. B., and B. M. King. 1992. Why HIV education sometimes fails to curtail high-risk sexual behaviors: Sex for some young adults can be more important than a long life. *Research Quarterly for Exercise and Sport: Supplement* 63(1): A–31.

Bayless, J., and M. Cutter. 1986. Teacher recognition of child abuse. Journal of Physical Education, Recreation and Dance 57(12): 73–74.

Broadhurst, D.D., M. Edmunds, and R. A. MacDirken. 1979. Early childhood programs and the prevention and treatment of child abuse and neglect. *The User Manual Series*. Washington, DC: U.S. Department of Health, Education and Welfare.

Brothers, M. J. 1976. *Diabetes: The new approach.* New York: Grosset and Dunlap.

Byrne, C. E. 1981. Diabetes in the classroom. *ECO*, Pp 5, 19. (Available from the National Education Association).

Centers for Disease Control. 1991. *HIV/AIDS surveillance report.* Atlanta, GA: Author.

Cheney, C., and I. R. Harwood. 1985. Cystic fibrosis. In *Current Diagnosis*, edited by R. B. Conn. Philadelphia: W. B. Saunders Company.

Chu, S. Y., J. W. Buehler, M. J. Oxtoby, and B. W. Kilbourne. 1991. Impact of the human immunodeficiency virus epidemic on mortality in children, United States. *Pediatrics* 87(6): 806–10.

Danowski, T. S. 1974. *Diabetes as a way of life.* New York: Coward, McCann and Geoghegan.

Falk, K. A., P. Hill, and S. Ganema. (Undated). *Child abuse and neglect: A handbook for New Hampshire educators.* Concord, NH: The New Hampshire Task Force on Child Abuse and Neglect.

Frenay, M. A. C. 1964. *Understanding medical terminology.* St. Louis, MO: Catholic Hospital Association.

Galton, L. 1977. *Medical advances.* New York: Crown Publishers.

Hardman, M. L., C. J. Drew, M. W. Egan, and B. Wolf. 1990. *Human exceptionality.* 3d ed. Boston: Allyn and Bacon.

Keller, M. J. 1992. Children and HIV/AIDS: A role for physical educators and recreation professionals. *Journal of Physical Education, Recreation and Dance* 63(4): 34–36.

King, M. 1992. What you should know about HIV testing. *Nursing 92* 22(3): 25.

Kirp, D. L., and S. Epstein. 1989. AIDS in America's schoolhouses: Learning the hard lessons. *Phi Delta Kappan* 70: 585–93.

Lewis, R. B., and D. H. Doorlag. 1991. *Teaching special students in the mainstream.* 3d ed. New York: Macmillan Publishing Company.

National Committee for Prevention of Child Abuse, New Hampshire Chapter. (Undated). *What can you, as a teacher, do in the classroom when dealing with an abused child?* Concord, NH: Author.

Orenstein, D. M., K. G. Henke, and F. J. Cerny. 1983). Exercise and cystic fibrosis. *The Physician and Sports Medicine* 11(1): 57–63.

Pyeritz, R. E., and J. Conant. 1989. *The Marfan syndrome.* 3d ed. Port Washington, NY: National Marfan Foundation.

Racaniello, A. F. 1976. *The effects of selected interval exercise routines on bronchospasm in asthmatics.* Master's thesis. Springfield College, Springfield, MA.

Romeo, T. J. 1991. *The Marfan syndrome: Physical activity guidelines for physical educators, coaches and physicians.* Port Washington, NY: National Marfan Foundation.

Sherrill, C. 1976. *Adapted physical education and recreation.* Dubuque: IA: William C. Brown.

Wunderlich, R. C. 1973. *Allergy, brains, and children coping.* St. Petersburg, FL: Johnny Reads.

Yarber, W. L. 1987. *AIDS: What young adults should know.* Reston, VA: American Alliance for Health, Physical Education, Recreation and Dance.

RECOMMENDED READINGS

American Diabetes Association. 1988. *Your child has diabetes...What you should know.* Alexandria, VA: Author.

Beck, K. H., and T. G. Simmons. 1990. Sources of information about drugs and alcohol for black and white suburban high school students. *Health Education* 21(2): 20–24, 49.

Bernhardt, B. A., P. Haul, J. Weiner, and J. O. Weiss. 1988. *The Marfan syndrome: A booklet for teenagers.* Port Washington, NY: National Marfan Foundation.

Boat, T. F., and D. G. Dearborn. 1984. Etiology and pathogenesis. In *Cystic Fibrosis,* edited by L. N. Taussig. New York: Thieme-Stratton, Inc.

Braasard, M. R., and L. E. McNeil. 1987. Child sexual abuse. In *Psychological Maltreatment of Children and Youth,* edited by M. R. Brassard, R. Germain, and S. N. Hart. New York: Pergamon Press.

Brainard, J. B. 1977. *Control of migraine.* New York: W. W. Norton.

Chng, C. L., and A. Moore. 1990. A study of steroid use among athletes: Knowledge, attitude and use. *Health Education* 21(6): 12–17, 11.

Clark, J. K., and W. L. Yarber. 1992. Two curricular settings of a HIV education unit related to secondary school students' HIV knowledge and attitude. *Research Quarterly for Exercise and Sport: Supplement* 63(1): A–33.

Conley, C. L. 1980. Sickle-cell anemia: The first molecular disease. In *Blood, pure and eloquent,* edited by M. W. Wintrobe. New York: MCGraw-Hill.

Dolger, H., and B. Seeman. 1977. *How to live with diabetes.* New York: W. W. Norton.

Falloon, J., J. Eddy, M. Roper, and P. Pizzo. 1988. AIDS in the pediatric population. In *AIDS: Diagnosis, Treatment, and Prevention,* edited by V. T. Devita, Jr., S. Hellman, and S. A. Rosenberg. Philadelphia: J. B. Lippincott.

Fejer, D., R. G. Smart, P. C. Whitehead, and L. Laforest. 1981. Sources of information about drugs among high school students. *Public Opinion Quarterly* 35(2): 235–41.

Ford, A. B., N. B. Rushford, and H. S. Sudak. 1984. The causes of suicide. In *Suicide in the Young,* edited by H. S. Sudak, A. B. Ford, and N. B. Rushforth. Boston: John Wright, PSG, Inc.

Franklin, J. C. 1971. *An experimental study of physical conditioning for asthmatic children.* Master's thesis, Texas Woman's University.

Gilliam, A., M. Scott, and J. Troup. 1989. AIDS education and risk reduction for homeless women and children: Implications for health education. *Health Education* 20(5): 44–47.

Goedert, J. J., and W. A. Blattner. 1989. The epidemiology and natural history of human immunodeficiency. In *AIDS: Diagnosis, Treatment, and Prevention*, edited by V. T. Devita, Jr., S. Hellman, and S. A. Rosenberg. Philadelphia: J. B. Lippincott Company.

Golub, L. J. 1959. A new exercise for dysmenorrhea. *American Journal of Obstetrics and Gynecoloqy* 78: 152–55.

Golub, L. J., and J. Christaldi. 1957. Reducing dysmenorrhea in young adolescents. *Journal of Health, Physical Education, and Recreation* 28: 24–25, 59.

Greenberg, R. E. 1987. Diabetes mellitus. In *Primary Pediatric Care*, edited by R. A. Hoekelman, S. Blatman, N. M. Nelson, and H. M. Seidel. St. Louis: C. V. Mosby.

Huntsman, R. G. 1987. *Sickle-cell anemia and thalassemia: A primer for health care professionals.* Ontario, Canada: The Canadian Sickle Cell Society.

Jackson, V. M., S. M. Dorman, K. Tennant, and W. W. Chen. 1989. Effects of teaching specific guidelines for alcohol consumption on alcohol knowledge and behavioral intent of college students. *Health Education* 20(6): 51–54, 62.

Kaufman, J., and E. Zigler. 1987. Do abused children become abusive parents? *American Journal of Orthopsychiatry* 57(2): 186–92.

Kempe, R. S. (1987). A developmental approach to treatment of the abused child. In *The Battered Child*, 4th ed., edited by R. E. Helfer and R. S. Kempe. Chicago: The University of Chicago Press.

King, M. J., T. D. Noakes, and E. G. Weinberg. 1989. Physiological effects of a physical training program in children with exercise-induced asthma. *Pediatric Exercise Science* 1: 127–44.

Kingery, P. M., and R. E. Glasgow. 1989. Self-efficacy and outcome expectations in the self-regulation of non- insulin dependent diabetes mellitus. Health Education 20(7): 3–9.

Leitschuh, C. A., and M. Brotons. 1991. Recreation and music therapy for adolescent victims of sexual abuse. *Journal of Physical Education, Recreation and Dance* 62(4): 52–54.

Lerner, E. A. 1987. *Understanding AIDS.* Minneapolis: Learner Publications Company.

McKusick, L., W. Horstman, and T. J. Coates. 1985. AIDS and sexual behavior reported by gay men in San Francisco. *American Journal of Public Health* 75(5): 493–96.

Mull, S. S. 1990. Help for the children of alcoholics. Health Education 21(5): 42–45.

Novick, J. 1984. Attempted suicide in adolescence: The suicide sequence. In *Suicide in the Young*, edited by H. S. Sudak, A. B. Ford, and N. B. Rushforth. Boston: John Wright, PSG, Inc.

Podolsky, S., L. P. Krall, and R. F. Bradley. 1980. Treatment of diabetes with oral hypoglycemic agents. In *Clinical Diabetes: Modern Management*, edited by S. Podolsky. New York: Appleton-Century-Crofts.

Powell, L., and S. L. Faherty. 1990. Treating sexually abused and latency age girls. *The Arts in Psychotherapy* 17(1): 5–48.

Radbill, S. X. 1987. Children in a world of violence. In *The Battered Child*, 4th ed., edited by R. E. Helfer and R. S. Kempe. Chicago: The University of Chicago Press.

Reichman, S. 1977. *Breathe easy: An asthmatic's guide to clean air.* New York: Thomas Y. Crowell.

Rimmer, J. H. 1989. A vigorous physical education program for children with exercise-induced asthma. *Journal of Physical Education, Recreation and Dance* 60(6): 91–95.

Roberts, L. 1988. Race for cystic fibrosis gene nears end. *Science* 240: 282–85.

Schlaadt, R. G. 1990. Prevention: The other war on drugs. *Health Education* 21(3): 58–60.

Summit, R. 1985. Causes, consequences, treatment, and prevention of sexual assault aginst children. In *Assault against Children*, edited by J. H. Meier. San Diego: College-Hill Press.

Vodola, T. M. 1978. *Diagnostic-prescriptive motor ability and physical fitness tasks and activities.* Bloomfield, NJ. C. F. Wood.

Williamson, R., B. Wanright, C. Cooper, P. Scambler, M. Farrall, X. Estivill, and P. Pedersen. 1987. The cystic fibrosis locus. *Enzyme* 38: 1–4, 8–13.

Wisniewski, J. F., G. R. Mohl, and D. M. Shedroff. 1990. Smokeless tobacco use by high school baseball players. *Health Education* 21(1): 10–15.

Young, M., C. Kersten, and C. Werch. 1992. Evaluation of a parent-child drug education program. *Research Quarterly for Exercise and Sport: Supplement* 63(1): A–48.

SECTION III

Programs in
Action

CHAPTER 14

*Adapted Games and Sports*_____

Objectives

After reading this chapter, you should be able to

- Discuss mainstreaming and factors influencing the least restrictive environment.
- Describe the Cascade System with respect to the placement of individuals with disabilities.
- Relate the mandates of Public Law 94-142 to physical education.
- Discuss recommended administrative and instructional strategies for implementing the concept of mainstreaming within individual/self-testing, rhythmic, dual, and team sport activities.
- Describe the general and specific rule, equipment and appliance modifications that can be used to accommodate optimum play experiences.
- Describe assistive devices used to aid persons with disabilities in performing selected motor activities.

INTRODUCTION

In Section II emphasis was placed on procedural techniques as they relate to physical education—i.e., on those measures recommended to use when children are in need of remedial services. You learned that these services can be extremely important to employ as a complement to what is ordinarily taught in a regular, mainstreamed class. As Ratliffe, Ratliffe, and Bie (1991) point out,

A major objective of...teachers is to improve children's learning readiness skills.

Developmental strategies can contribute to that purpose. In this chapter you will find information on how to plan for mainstreaming itself.

Over the years, the term *mainstreaming* has been subject to various connotations. On the one hand there are physical education teachers who believe that Public Law 94-142 is

---

KEY TERMS

adapted pushing device	forearm brace
anchor line	individual/self-testing activities
badminton racket extension	peer tutors (tutoring)
bihandled table tennis paddle	Putt-Putt golf
bow stringer	putter finger
bowling frame unit	rhythmic activities
bowling railing	right-angle footboards
cascade system	Section 504 of the Rehabilitation Act
criterion	spotters
dual activities	team sport activities
eligibility	vertical bow set

---

being complied with if they provide opportunities for students with disabilities to participate in an integrated class by having them keep time, keep score, chart offensive and defensive strategy, and hand out towels. If these tasks are important to the physical education experience, then all students should benefit by performing them. On the other hand some well-intentioned educators attempt to meet the needs of students with disabilities by modifying rules and adjusting commonly approved strategies for all class members. Game rules can be modified, but if the changes make games less physically challenging or less fun for the majority of the students in the class, little has been gained and much has been lost.

Practitioners who understand and practice the law as it is intended appreciate the benefit of mainstreaming insofar as it retains the least restrictive environment for all students. Physical education experiences should satisfy the needs of all. Where youngsters with disabilities can participate meaningfully in an integrated setting, opportunities must be provided for them to do so, Figure 14.1.

Mainstreaming may require support personnel. As Dunn (1976) points out, unfortunately,

> ...many school districts in their haste to integrate as many handicapped students as possible, have failed to provide the additional personnel which are necessary for a successful transition from special self-contained classes to regular classes. Both para-professionals and physical educators with special skills are required to assist the inexperienced and apprehensive teacher provide motor learning experiences for handicapped students.

Given the financial burden already being faced by schools throughout the nation, the procurement of additional revenues in the near future to provide additional personnel and services is unlikely (McCubbin and Zittel 1991). Nonetheless, quality programs can still be available. Quality is not necessarily a feature of unlimited resources. Rather it is a product of good people making good decisions. What is the criterion for making effective decisions? Adapt the classroom environment and teaching methodologies to accommodate individual learning styles (Brunner and Hill 1992). Know your students and focus on their abilities, not their disabilities.

Figure 14.1. Mainstreaming in physical education

MAINSTREAMING DEFINED

Public Law 94-142 specifies that students with disabilities are to be placed in the environment least restrictive to their optimum educational development.* The optimum learning environment for a child may be a regular class, a developmental physical education (special) class, or a combination of the two. The benefits and limitations of integrated and segregated programs must be assessed for each student. For the youngster with severe disabilities a special developmental program may be appropriate—at least for the initial stages of placement. After the student has reached selected sensorimotor objectives through developmental activities, he/she may be able to profit from gradual placement in integrated classes at selected times during the week—a combination-placement plan.**

Children with moderate disabilities are more likely candidates for mainstreaming than those with severe-to-profound disorders who might fare best in more supervised settings where a smaller ratio of students to staff is possible. As the necessary skills related to activities of daily living are acquired, these children may be able to transfer from a more- to less-protective environment, Figure 14.2—the **Cascade System**.

---

* While this author chooses to reference PL 94-142, the All Handicapped Children Act, the reader is reminded from Chapter 1 that in 1990, PL 101-476 was passed, which changed that terminology to the Individuals with Disabilities Education Act (IDEA).

** A combination-placement plan is one in which the student attends a special class at certain times during the day or week and an integrated class at other times.

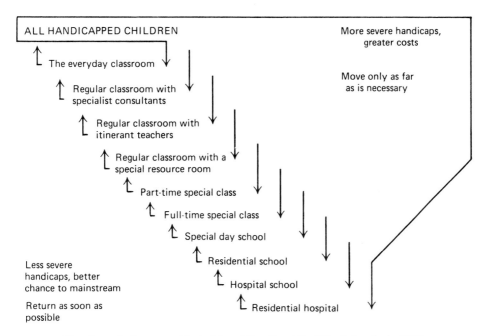

Figure 14.2. The Cascade System. *Adapted from Educational Facilities Laboratories 1974.*

In their quest to meet the requirements of Public Law 94-142, practitioners and theorists alike have raised numerous questions with respect to how the law should be interpreted. The American Alliance for Health, Physical Education, Recreation and Dance (AAHPERD) attempted to address frequently-asked questions by publishing reactions in *Update*, a monthly publication of the Alliance. Some of these questions and answers are presented next.

1. Physical education is defined in PL 94-142 as

the development of (a) physical and motor fitness, (b) fundamental motor skills and patterns, and (c) skills in aquatics, dance, and individual and group games and sports (including intramural and lifetime sports)...

The law states further that

...physical education services, specially designed if necessary, must be made available to every...child (with a disability) who is receiving a free appropriate education.

Does this mean that each child with a disability will receive instruction in each of the defined areas? What if the child is placed in a regular physical education class which does not cover an area—e.g., aquatics?
Answer: The PL 94-142 definition of physical education includes areas or elements considered to be physical education under the law. Several important points need emphasis.

a) To be considered physical education under the law, focus must be upon instruction and development of skills in one or more of the defined areas.

b) Valid assessments in these delineated areas provide a basis for determining whether specific physical and motor needs exist.

c) Children with no special physical and motor needs are placed in regular physical education programs and activities.

d) Children with special physical and motor needs are provided appropriate programs, activities, and placement according to their particular needs.

Therefore, a child for whom an individualized planning committee deems aquatic activities necessary cannot be placed only in a physical education program if that program does not provide opportunities in the prescribed area—aquatics in this instance (AAHPERD, October 1978).

2. Who is responsible for enforcing PL 94-142 in a school district?

Answer: The local education agency is responsible for enforcing PL 94-142 and abiding by educational provisions of **Section 504 of the Rehabilitation Act** throughout its district and in individual school buildings. The local education agency (LEA) is also responsible for monitoring programs and activities of its students who receive services on a contractual basis from other agencies and organizations, including private schools from whom such services are purchased. If an LEA chooses not to participate in its state special education program under PL 94-142, the state education agency must assume responsibility for students in that school system and see that all students receive a full, free, appropriate education as mandated under the law and through its rules and regulations (provided the state has accepted PL 94-142 funds). Local education agencies that do not participate actively in PL 94-142 still must be in compliance with educational provisions of Section 504. While PL 94-142 is basically compliance oriented, Section 504 is complaint oriented, since no action takes place for noncompliance unless complaints are entered with the Office of Civil Rights (AAHPERD, October 1978).

3. Is the secondary student in special education entitled to a four-year physical education program provided by the physical education department (our state only requires and provides one year of secondary physical education)?

Answer: Provisions of PL 94-142 include

instruction in physical education...as a defined part of special education.

Therefore physical and motor needs of every child for whom an individualized planning meeting is convened must deal with these areas. When valid assessment and evaluation procedures indicate that a child does have special physical and motor needs, annual goals, short-term instructional objectives, instructional strategies, and other provisions and requirements regarding individualized education programs must deal with his/her physical and motor needs. This process must be followed whether (or not) a state requires physical education for students without disabilities at grade levels in which a student with a disability is enrolled (the case in question) (AAHPERD, October 1978).

4. Will the regular classroom teacher be responsible for the disabled child's physical education if there is no physical education program in the school district?

Answer: Children with special physical and motor needs must be programmed in ways that ensure these needs are met. If a school district has no physical education program for nonhandicapped children, meeting special physical and motor needs of children with disabilities is still the responsibility of the local education agency. As such the classroom teacher can be the individual responsible for implementing this program and appropriate physical education activities. However, these services can also be contracted for from some other community agency such as parks and recreation departments, community agencies such as YM/YWCA, or private contractors. If nonhandicapped children are taught in physical education by a physical education specialist, Section 504 requires that children in special education receive the same services and opportunities (AAHPERD, October 1978).

5. Are gifted individuals covered under PL 94-142 and/or Section 504?

Answer: Definitions of disabled children in PL 94-142 and disabled persons in Section 504 do not include gifted students as individuals covered and protected under these legislative mandates. However, in some states gifted children are entitled to all basic provisions of PL 94-142 because of state statutes (AAHPERD, November 1978). Become familiar with the statutes of the states in which you are employed.

6. As increasing numbers of children with different disabling conditions are integrated into regular physical education, recreation, and sports programs, how is legal liability of local education agencies, personnel in specific schools, and individual teachers affected?*

Answer: While many variables and unpredictables exist regarding individual cases and situations, the key to liability is presence of negligence since students and their parents expect care from schools and their staff to save students from foreseeable harm. Could or should the teacher, in the exercise of reasonable prudence and foresight have anticipated danger under the particular circumstances? If the answer is *Yes*, the teacher is negligent if he or she failed to act so as to avoid such foreseeable danger (AAHPERD, November 1978).

7. May an entire special education class consisting of students homogeneously grouped according to a specific disabling condition be sent as a group to physical education?

Answer: Emphatically *NO*! In fact, this process by which children are placed and programmed categorically according to specific disabling conditions is exactly what PL 94-142 is designed to stop and prevent. Every child who fulfills the first **criterion** of **eligibility** under PL 94-142—i.e., possessing a specified handicapping condition as defined in the rules and regulations, is programmed and placed according to individual not group needs. Because an individual possesses a handicapping condition and has special needs in certain areas does not mean that he/she has special needs in all areas (AAHPERD, November 1978).

---

* Three books by Herb Appenzeller, entitled: *Physical Education and the Law*, *Athletics and the Law*, and *From the Gym to the Jury*—all published by The Mitchie Company, Charlottesville, VA—are excellent references with respect to legal liability.

8. What are the ways in which physical education teachers can get extra help to provide additional assistance in their classes to disabled children with special needs?

Answer: Several basic points need to be emphasized. Individualized education and one-to-one relationships are not synonymous. Many ways exist whereby a child's program can be individualized and personalized. For some individuals in certain activities at specific stages in the learning process, one-to-one attention may be the most appropriate approach. However, in other situations under different circumstances, small group, large class, squad, or other organizational approaches may be appropriate. Specially designed physical education programs, though not directly addressed in PL 94-142 rules and regulations, can be implemented in a regular class setting appropriate for a particular disabled child at a given time. This can be accomplished in many ways.

a) A buddy system that pairs a disabled child with an able-bodied partner for specific activities
b) Students as squad leaders
c) Circuit or station organizational patterns, Figure 14.3
d) **Peer tutoring**
e) Problem-solving, exploratory, and movement techniques at elementary school levels
f) Elective or selective program patterns at secondary school levels, especially senior high school
g) Flexible or optional unit scheduling, especially at middle, intermediate, and junior high school levels

Figure 14.3. A circuit organizational pattern in physical education

h) Contract techniques
i) Paraprofessional personnel, aids, volunteers, career education students, practicum or field work students
j) Team teaching involving regular classroom teachers, special education personnel, specially trained adapted physical education teachers, or resource/ resource room specialists
k) Preteaching certain activities to selected students with special needs
l) Developmental or adapted physical education classes to supplement not replace regular physical education classes (AAHPERD, November 1978).

9. If a child is referred by a local education agency for a medical evaluation, who is responsible for payment?

Answer: The local education agency is responsible for payment for evaluations of this type (AAHPERD, March 1979).

10. A student not in special education or disabled brings a note to be excused from physical education. How is this handled?

Answer: As presented, this student is not considered a student with a disability under definitions contained in PL 94-142 so that procedures and processes under this law do not apply (AAHPERD, December 1978).

11. What kind of adapted program can be run without a special facility of any kind?

Answer: PL 94-142 requires that children be programmed and placed according to each child's individual needs established through appropriate and valid assessment procedures. Both PL 94-142 and Section 504 require that each child with a disability be educated with able-bodied classmates to the maximum degree possible. When accommodations are needed, they can often be developed and provided in ways that enable students with disabilities to take part in regular programs and activities through equipment and device adaptations, modifications of rules, individualized instructional approaches, additional support and assistance for the student, and additional resources for the teacher. Major facility adaptations that enable a student to get into and use a physical education facility are no different from general accessibility provisions and standards. Special program needs must be justified on the basis of individualized education program planning for each child. Obviously many adapted physical education approaches can be carried out in regular programs in regular facilities. Legal, legislative, philosophical, and programmatic trends are away from segregated facilities and special programs except as needed to meet specific needs of individual children (AAHPERD, May 1978).

12. Will monies be available for facilities, staff, aides, and equipment?

Answer: Local education agencies receive PL 94-142 funds through state education agencies from the Bureau of Education for the Handicapped. However, there are specific conditions that must be met using these funds.
a) Direct services to children with disabilities not presently receiving educational services and to those not receiving full services must receive priority.
b) Funds are for excess costs incurred in providing a free appropriate education for children with disabilities.
c) Funds cannot be used to supplant or replace state and/or local funds allocated for educating children who have disabilities. Because of the relatively low per child amount currently received through federal funding, state and local education agencies must bear a large part of the financial

burden in providing necessary services. Courts have made it clear that lack of funds will not be accepted as an excuse for not meeting needs of populations covered by PL 94-142 and Section 504 (AAHPERD, May 1978).

The implications of mainstreaming for those dedicated to the principle that education is a right for all to enjoy are apparent. Continued efforts on behalf of the disabled will help to facilitate the selection of appropriate learning environments and programs for all.

STRATEGIES FOR MAINSTREAMING

The following general principles apply to mainstreaming students in physical education:

1. Be sure the student has been examined by a physician to determine whether special program modifications are needed.
2. Start with an activity the student can do. Base adaptations in activities upon the student's functional strengths rather than on diagnostic categories. Analyze the sensorimotor requirements of each activity in advance of its presentation.
3. Reduce the length of game periods, quarters, court size, etc., and allow for free substitutions.
4. Plan for rest periods. For those with cardiac deficiencies, for example, there should be as much rest time as activity time.
5. Create a buddy system in which two students function as one player. For example, one student can bat and the other student can run.
6. Adjust stances to accommodate student strengths. For example, in golf it might be easier for a student with leg braces to use the open rather than the closed stance.
7. Select activities that can be modified without ruining the game for others in the class. In general, individual activities of the carryover variety are best.
8. Change activities rather frequently so that students will have more opportunities to achieve success in things that they can do.
9. Involve students with disabilities in planning the modification of activities. Who would know better than the student himself/herself about what works.
10. Avoid excessive use of popular activities (e.g., basketball, baseball) where mindsets regarding specific rules are clearly established. Try new games (Rappa 1991).
11. Substitute walking and wheeling for running and skipping.
12. Have students bounce or roll a ball instead of throwing overhand.
13. Reduce distances in such games as quoit; shorten baselines in softball; lower basketball baskets and volleyball nets.
14. Substitute larger and lighter equipment when possible (e.g., plastic instead of hardwood lacrosse sticks).
15. Instead of playing three outs per one-half inning in softball, have each member of the up-to-bat team bat once. This allows each person to get up to bat in each inning because the team does not retire after the third out.
16. Reduce the swing radius of bats, rackets, and so forth by having students choke up on the handles.
17. Keep explanations and directions simple.
18. Attempt to maintain a slow tempo during competitive activities to reduce stress.

19. Encourage kinesthetics (e.g., body and spatial awareness, relationship of the body or prosthetic device to other body parts).
20. Stress safety.

Every activity, sport, and subject contains elements that can and often should be taught in a fashion that invites replication and/or discovery (Mosston 1992). Incorporate within your curriculum those activities that will establish skills fundamental to the learning of new activities, encourage practice for refinement of those skills (just for the joy of playing well), and allow for free and creative expression. Aquatics, dual and team sports, individual/self-testing activities, and rhythmics all have their unique contributions to make to one's total development. Plan and deliver them in a manner that will engage the interests of all for whom you have responsibility—the able-bodied and exceptional alike.

INDIVIDUAL/SELF-TESTING ACTIVITIES

In this section we will discuss specific adaptations for activities that are individualized in nature—i.e., activities that are performed without contributing teammates. Although aquatic sports (other than synchronized swimming or relays) represent an example of such an activity, they will not be presented here. Rather, they can be found in Chapter 15.

You will see to what extent adjustments may have to be made in rules and strategies. The information presented herein can be used as guidelines for adapting activities not included for presentation. Since these are **individual/self-testing activities**, the adjustments brought about will have little to no impact on other students who are enrolled in the class. You may remember from previous discussion that this is a relatively important consideration.

Archery

In archery the major adaptation needed by one with crutches is maintaining a balanced position while attempting to shoot. According to Cowart (1991) the approaches found to be most successful include kneeling on the ground, leaning against a high stable bench or chair, or sitting on a regular chair or wheelchair.

If you are going to have the student kneeling on the ground, be sure he/she is on a smooth, dry surface. (Using a mat can be helpful.) If you are going to have him lean against a chair or a bench, be sure it is stable. Other than these minor adjustments, the manner of teaching the skill remains the same as for able-bodied students (bow hold, nocking, draw, anchor point, aim, release, and follow-through).

For a student who is in a wheelchair it is the chair, not the foot position in relation to the firing line, that is important, Figure 14.4. Likewise, the 'extended shoulder' form with the bowarm is recommended in that it provides for a longer draw, thus helping to keep the bowstring away from the arm rest or wheel of the chair. Archery is an activity in which many individuals with disabilities can participate. Students in wheelchairs have been found to excell in archery competition.*

Although shooting techniques of nocking, drawing, aiming (other than for the visually impaired), and releasing are ordinarily not modified, the archer with disabilities may need some assistive devices. Among these are

---

* Archery competition for wheelchair participants is governed by the National Wheelchair Athletic Association. For more information contact this organization at 40–42 62nd St., Woodside, NY 11377.

Figure 14.4. Wheelchair archer

1. **Forearm brace** for those who do not have fingers for gripping the bow, Figure 14.5. The bow is affixed to the brace. Other than the grip, standard techniques are used.
2. **Bow stringer** for those who may lack the base leverage to string the bow, Figure 14.6. This device allows an archer, perhaps one who is in a wheelchair, to prepare the bow for use independently.
3. **Vertical bow set** and mouthpiece for those who lack the upper-body strength to draw the string in a standard way, Figure 14.7. The archer places a mouthpiece which has been affixed to the string in his mouth. The arrow is nocked by the instructor or a student partner. The string is drawn as the wheelchair is rolled back while the archer holds the mouthpiece tightly in the mouth. The archer reviews the angle of trajectory by raising or lowering the head. Release occurs when the archer lets the mouthpiece go.

Valuable aids for students who are visually impaired include:

1. **Right-angle foot boards**, which allow the archer to align himself/herself with the target, Figure 14.8.
2. Sounding devices (e.g., metronome, bell, voice command), which can assist the archer in perceiving the location of the target.

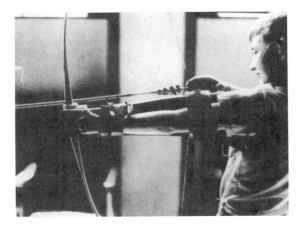

Figure 14.5. Forearm brace

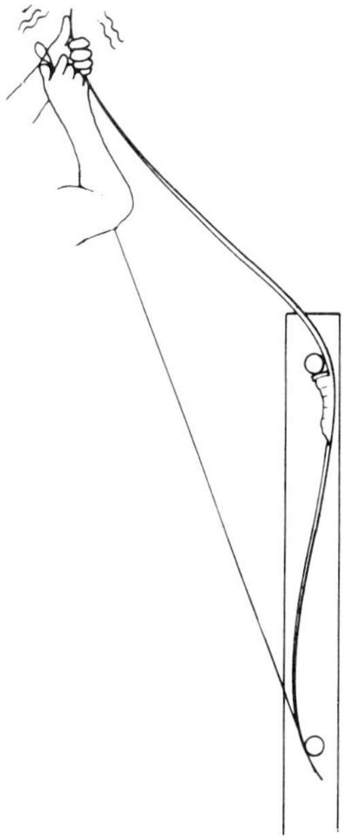

Figure 14.6. Bow stringer

Figure 14.7. Vertical bow set

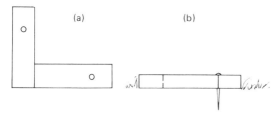

(a)   (b)

Figure 14.8. Right-angle footboard: *A*, top view; *B*, side view

3. **Anchor line**, which can run from the firing line to the center of the target, Figure 14.9. This can assist the archer in aligning the bow with the target as well as in moving to and from the target.

4. A knotted string running from the center to the periphery of the target or materials of different textures placed over the target scoring areas can help the visually impaired calculate their score.

5. Scoring sheets that permit the visually impaired to record their scores (raised line or braille) add to their sense of independence.

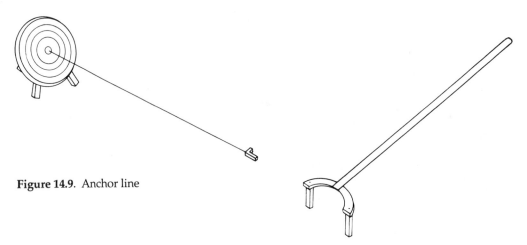

Figure 14.9. Anchor line

Figure 14.10. Adapted pushing device

Bowling

Bowling is another activity enjoyed by many persons with disabilities. For the most part, skills taught to those with disabilities are the same as for the able-bodied. Before commencing the instruction, however, it would be wise to conduct a preliminary evaluation in order to judge the student's capabilities. The Young American Bowling Alliance (1991) suggests that the instructor may need to be flexible in his/her approach to teaching. Some individuals may need to start at the foul line, rolling the ball with two hands; some may want to push the ball with the ball of the foot or other device while sitting in a wheelchair; others may choose to employ a four-step delivery.

A removable armrest would assist the wheelchair bowler with his/her pendulum swing. If this is not possible, a seat cushion can raise the bowler to a point where the pendulum swing can be made comfortably.

Among the various devices that can be used by a bowler with a disability are

1. An **adapted pushing device,** much like a shuffleboard cue, that can be used to deliver the ball down the lane, Figure 14.10. This device can be used when the bowler does not have the strength or sensorimotor control to hold and deliver the ball in a standard manner. This device can be used in front of or beside a wheelchair.

2. A **bowling frame unit** for a bowler who cannot control an adapted pushing device, Figure 14.11. The ball is placed on top of the unit by the student, bowling partner, or instructor. Once the unit is faced in the desired direction, the bowler need give but a slight lift or push to the unit lip to send the ball down the lane and on its way to the pins.

3. A **bowling railing** can help the visually impaired improve their perception of direction, Figure 14.12. The bowler holds onto the railing with one hand while moving toward the release point to increase the accuracy of the release.

4. Use appropriately weighted bowling balls. They are manufactured in sizes ranging from six to sixteen pounds. In general,

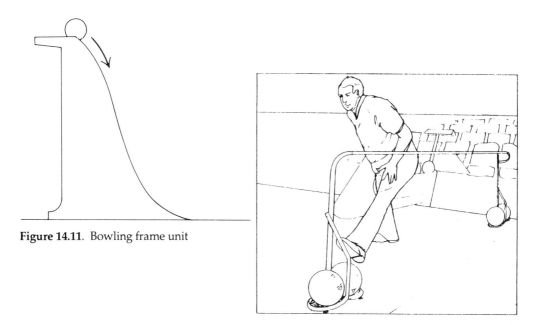

Figure 14.11. Bowling frame unit

Figure 14.12. Bowling railing

a) For children and those with more serious disabilities, consider using lighter-weight balls.

b) For the visually impaired and those who will be using the foot for ball delivery, use heavier balls.*

Golf

It can be expected that golf will provide more challenges than will archery and bowling because of the grip variations, swing, and distance between the holes. Golfers having difficulty with the grip can experiment with finger placement, shaping the club grip itself, and/or using special gloves. For a firmer grip, Pizarro (1984) suggests using a Velcro glove and sleeve. Velcro is sewn into the palm and fingers of the glove as well as on the sleeve (which fits over the grip of the golf club). This arrangement provides for a more secure club control.

Some students will want to use one arm when swinging. Through experimentation they will find the degree to which the length of the shaft, their 'choking up' on the shaft, and/or their grip(s) will have to be modified to provide the greatest power and efficiency. Those who need to use a crutch because of a leg impairment can do so while managing to swing the club with one arm. Of course a golfer can always use his wheelchair for playing golf. Removing the arm rests will make freer movement of the club possible.

---

* For more information on league and tournament rules and regulations contact the Young American Bowling Alliance, Greendale, WI.

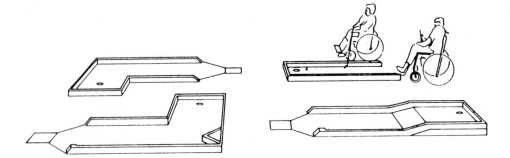

Figure 14.13. Four-hole Putt-Putt golf course

In general, golf is a more difficult game for wheelchair participants than archery or bowling primarily because the distance between holes and the terrain of a typical nine- or eighteen-hole golf course can make for a long and tedious experience. Moving from shot to shot along the course is so time-consuming that opportunities for actual play are limited. Until the golfer can drive the ball a reasonable distance, chip-and-putt and miniature (Putt-Putt) golf programs might be more enjoyable.

Putt-Putt golf has received increased attention from the physically disabled since late in 1960 when standardized courses were designed, Figure 14.13. Since then many golfers with disabilities have had the opportunity to improve their skills, self-esteem, and enjoyment of the game. Another development has been the standardization of the Putt-Putt course and rules, leading to the popularization of many regional and national tournaments.

Amateur and professional putters' associations have initiated tournaments and they lend support to many local programs. Putt-Putt golf is a growing phenomenon that can provide a source of enjoyment for countless numbers of persons with disabilities.

A rather recently developed device that helps a wheelchair golfer retrieve a golf ball is a **Putter Finger**—a soft molded-rubber suction cup that fits on the grip of virtually any putter, Figure 14.14. The golfer can reach out from his/her chair and procure the ball without having to depend on his partner.

Golf, chip-and-putt, and Putt-Putt can be played by monoplegics (disabled arm or leg), hemiplegics (disabled arm and leg on one side of the body), and the blind. Blind persons can use simple sounding devices, right-angle footboards, and cables indicating direction.

Figure 14.14. Putter Finger

Beginners should progress from larger cups and larger balls to smaller cups and regulation golf balls and from shorter to longer distances between holes. Hula hoops make good targets for chip shots.

Gymnastics

Gymnastics as an activity is not an unsafe one. It is the method of participation rather than the sport that can make it hazardous (Carpenter 1985). Therefore caution must be taken to ensure that

1. students have adequate strength levels to participate on the selected apparatus.
2. students are provided with adequate warm-up sessions in advance of performing activities requiring endurance, flexibility, and strength.
3. students are instructed properly with regard to techniques.
4. students are allowed to engage in only those activities that are found within their levels of physiological and psychological readiness.
5. **spotters** are trained properly in terms of understanding the skill and its common errors and that they are strong enough to catch someone should he/she fall.
6. equipment is secure in place with proper matting at its footings (and all other areas where performers could fall).
7. activities to be taught are not contraindicated because of individual medical/health problems.
8. the instructor understands all elements of the skill prior to teaching it. If the instructor cannot demonstrate the task himself/herself, it should be demonstrated by another teacher, a student, or by way of a video. In either case, the instructor should be sure that the skill is shown correctly.

While these guidelines are applicable to all elements of the gymnastics program, there are some recommendations appropriate to activities within the program. It is in this regard that the following suggestions are offered.

Balance Beam

1. Use line on the floor to introduce and practice new skills.
2. Elevate the beam to various heights allowing students to select the one that feels best for her.
3. Stack extra mats under the beam upon which the spotter can stand.
4. Allow the gymnast to hold the spotter's hand.
5. Teach the gymnast how to fall.

The student should learn that grabbing for the beam is likely to increase one's chances for injury. Pushing away from the beam is considered preferable (Allen 1991).

Horizontal Bar

1. Be sure the gymnast's hands are treated with a chalk substance in order to help resist blisters.
2. If no horizontal bar is available, use the higher bar of the assymetrical (uneven) bars to teach fundamental skills.
3. Start by having the students work with the bar at shoulder height.
4. Emphasize grip, arm, and shoulder strength development activities in the early stages of the horizontal bar program. Later the skills being practiced will in themselves develop these important fitness components, but at first one must have sufficient strength to learn and practice the skills being introduced.
5. Be sure that matting is provided at all possible falling zones.

Tumbling and Floor Exercise

1. Do not teach locomotor skills until stationary balances are secure.
2. When working on locomotor skills, be sure they are performed correctly. Emphasize accuracy before speed.
3. When working on routines, begin by having them of short duration. Gradually increase their length, adding skills previously learned as isolated activities.
4. Using marks (or checkpoints) on the mat will aid the student in developing his/her sense of direction and distance.
5. A simple routine that is well done should receive as much (or more) credit as a complex routine poorly done. Do *not* emphasize difficulty. Have the students concentrate on doing their best, no matter how simple the skill may be appear to be. Once confidence is built, more difficult skills can be encouraged. Using videotape is a useful way to provide useful feedback for your students.

Offered as examples, these suggestions should help set the stage for a safe, productive class. To find additional ideas for these and other gymnastic activities, refer to standard beginning- and/or intermediate-level gymnastics textbooks. But be sure to balance the skills and sequencing that are recommended by their authors against the exceptionalities of those who are enrolled in your classes. In short the assymetrical, horizontal, and parallel bars—as well as tumbling and floor exercise are all particularly suited to the visualy and hearing impaired, mildly and moderately mentally retarded, lower limb amputees, as well as many others who have the capacity for activities requiring physical fitness and kinesthesis.

Track and Field

Track and field is a valuable instructional unit because within it are varied opportunities to match students' skills with events. For example, wheelchair athletes can take part in the dash, distance events, putting, and throwing. Those with upper-limb disabilities can run and participate in the jumping events. Visually impaired youngsters can participate in sprint (with a buddy or guidewires) and endurance events. They can also learn jumping, putting, and throwing skills.

When teaching your students, be mindful of the capabilities they bring to the event(s). While many of the approaches the instructor will employ depend heavily on common sense, Gavron (1989) suggests five organizational strategies. Though useful in many activity settings, they are particularly pertinent within track and field.

1. Use of peer tutors. Track and field lends itself to small group approaches and buddy systems. Those with disabilities who are being introduced to new skills can learn a great deal from those who have been trained previously.
2. Adapt equipment. Field implements are available in junior weight sizes. They can also be found in foam and rubberized materials. Other examples of equipment modification include shorter poles for pole vaulting and lower standards for hurdling.
3. Adapt distances. It might be useful to reduce the length of track events. For example, a 40-yard dash instead of a 100-yard dash in elementary school would be very appropriate.

4. Modify techniques. Although there are models that characterize proper form, it may be necessary to allow, and in fact encourage, alternative postural and movement patterns. Some experimentation may be necessary to find the form style that works best.

5. Vary instructional approaches. Acknowledging that students have various styles and rates of learning, the instructor will want to vary approaches in order to better meet the diversified needs of students in the class. If the teacher relies heavily on oral presentation, and a student is a visual learner, it should not be surprising if the student has problems learning the intended skills. Other hints include simplifying directions, increasing opportunities for repetition, ensuring that each student practices the skills properly, giving specific and immediate feedback (in a ratio of 4 to 1, positive to negative), using poster boards displaying pictures of students performing their events, and organizing classes using squads, (per discussion in Chapter 11).

RHYTHMIC ACTIVITIES

Rhythmic activities can benefit everyone. Children and adults with disabilities can enjoy rhythmic activities whether they walk with crutches, use wheelchairs, or are visually or hearing impaired, Figure 14.15. Hearing impaired youngsters can sense the beat of a drum through sound vibrations in the floor. Other items that make helpful sound cues are bells, symbals, sticks, tambourines, and triangles.

Figure 14.15. Wheelchair dancing

An increasing number of those with disabilities are participating in folk, modern (interpretive), social, and square dancing. Why? Because rhythms can sooth the frustrated, stimulate the depressed, and provide a vehicle for expression not likely to occur in most activities of daily living. Rhythmics is one of the few activities in physical education in which creativity rather than imposed rules and strategies is the essence of participation and success.

DUAL ACTIVITIES

For the purposes of this text we will define **dual activities** as those in which one person (or couple) competes against another person (or couple). Dual activities have proved to be very suitable for mainstreamed classes. One major reason is that it is relatively easy for an instructor to unobtrusively select closely matched individuals or pairs for practice and competition. The dual activities presented in this section are badminton, handball, paddleball, racketball, squash, table tennis, and wrestling.

Badminton

For singles play, the dimensions of the badminton playing court should be reduced in size (depending on the extent of the player's disabilities), particularly in width. An individual in a wheelchair is not able to move quickly from side to side to return a shot. The wheelchair badminton player should be provided with a **badminton racket extension** for the handle of his racket, Figure 14.16. This adds to the player's reach, making the contest more competitive and enjoyable.

In doubles play, the player in a wheelchair is ordinarily assigned the front court as his/her area of responsibility. A partner (on foot) plays the back court.

Modification of the standard badminton rules can enhance the competition. Some suggestions for such modification follow.

1. Players should not alternate court positions. In doubles the more disabled player can be responsible for the front court, the less-disabled player can be responsible for the back court.
2. Players should not exchange their court positions during play. Doing so could be considered a fault.
3. Players should be allowed to choose whether they prefer to serve from the front court or the back court. (If they elect the front court, it might be necessary to reduce the dimensions of the receiving area.) All other standard badminton rules governing service should be enforced. A visually impaired student might participate in the game by performing all the serves for a doubles team.

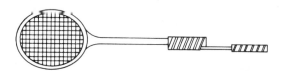

Figure 14.16. Badminton racket extension

Handball, Paddleball, Racketball, and Squash

Handball, paddleball, racketball, and squash are appropriate activities for those with disabilities, particularly if play is restricted to one wall. Among various possible rule modifications consider the following:

1. In singles play, reduce the width of the court for the disabled player so the opponent must direct his/her offense to a restricted portion of the front wall. This adjustment is reasonable because of the speed with which the ball moves and the difficulty an individual in a wheelchair, for example, might have in moving quickly to hit the ball.
2. In doubles play, the disabled player is best positioned so that his/her playing hand is toward the center of the court. Although coverage of the court depth is possible, he/she may lack the mobility to cover court width.
3. To provide greater opportunity for students with disabilities to return the ball, allow double bounces.

Table Tennis

Table tennis is well suited to those with disabilities because the playing area is relatively small and is in front of the player, Figure 14.17. Although the playing rules need not be modified to any great extent, assistive devices may be necessary for players with shoulder or arm dysfunction. A **bihandled table tennis paddle** can be used by those who lack strength in the shoulder, arm, wrist, or fingers, Figure 14.18. Use of both hands allows greater support and freedom of movement during volleys. For service, the ball can be either tossed with one hand (as in standard rules) or balanced on the paddle, hoisted into the air, and hit.

Figure 14.17. Table tennis

By having a string instead of a net splitting the surface of the table, a ball not going over the string will travel to the opponent's court allowing for easy retrieval for those in wheelchairs. A 1 1/2" rail on the two long sides of the table will also help to keep a rolling ball contained on the playing surface.*

Figure 14.18. Bihandled table tennis paddle

---

* See Chapter 17 for suggestions regarding the construction of a modified table tennis table (and other items).

Most individuals with disabilities can enjoy a table tennis game with very little in the way of rule or strategy modifications. With common sense and a little creativity the game can be enjoyed by anyone.

Wrestling

Wrestling is an outstanding activity for those with visual impairments. It helps develop agility, balance, coordination, and strength. In addition its potential for enhancing a student's self-esteem and self-reliance has been well documented. The only major rule modification necessary is that when opponents address each other for a take-down (at the beginning of a match or upon an escape), the action must be initiated (or resumed) from a touching position.

TEAM SPORT ACTIVITIES

Although there are obvious benefits to those activities in which achievement is based solely on individual effort, there is a place for **team sport activities** in the mainstreaming curriculum because of their contributions to the development of group (or team) inter-dependence. When teachers are able to develop a framework in which students can learn to work together for the attainment of a common goal, a laudable objective has been satisfied. Team sports provide that forum.

This section considers examples of activities likely to be found in the physical education curriculum. They are not selected for presentation as much because of their intrinsic value as they are because of the kinds of skills required for success. Upon examination of the suggestions it will become apparent that the principles can be transferred to virtually any team activity one would encounter. In this light, team activities to be covered are basketball, floor hockey, flag and touch football, soccer, and softball.

Basketball

Basketball can be enjoyed by most individuals if one pays attention to a few simple guidelines.*

1. If a youngster is in a wheelchair, have him/her concentrate on offense so that he/she need not chase opponents to their offensive end of the court.
2. When judging fouls, consider the chair as part of the body.
3. When the person in the wheelchair is attempting to pass, no one should stand within ten feet (or some other reasonable distance). A walking student cannot tie up a ball with a person who is in a wheelchair.
4. Allow two rolls of the wheels (while the ball is in the player's lap) before a dribble has to be made.
5. Use less-mobile or visually impaired players to take in out-of-bounds balls.
6. A player who is visually impaired can be positioned at a selected spot near the key on the offensive court. Contact paper (with rough side up) can be placed on the floor in an L-shape to provide orientation for a barefooted youngster.

---

* For more information about wheelchair basketball contact the National Wheelchair Basketball Association, 110 Seaton Building, University of Kentucky, Lexington, KY 40506.

Sounding devices can be placed on the center backside of the backboard to indicate basket location. Two or three small bells tied to the net of the basketball hoop can alert the blind player that the ball has passed through the rim following a successful shot. Most blind youngsters are not totally blind; they may be able to detect bright colors. Brightly painted court lines—orange, for example—can help many with visual impairments to locate boundary lines and other necessary markings. (These are also attractive to sighted individuals.) Brightly colored basketballs and basketballs in which sounding devices have been placed can be obtained.

7. Less-mobile players or an especially good shooter can be used as a front court player on a fast-break play.

8. Use a player in a wheelchair or on crutches at the head of the lane in zone defenses (e.g., diamond plus one). He/she will be able to block a clear route by making an excellent obstacle.

9. Provided a charging foul does not occur, consider allowing unlimited glide privileges during or immediately following a dribble. Do not be too quick to call a travel.

10. Consider a bounce pass mandatory for one who is passing to a student who is visually impaired. The bounce will give the person to whom the ball is thrown a greater opportunity to react to its height and direction.

11. The rules might be modified to state that the ball must be handled by each player at least once during an offensive series except perhaps during the execution of a fast break. Blocking a shot of one who is visually impaired could be considered a violation.

12. To stop play, use flashing lights or waving flags in addition to a whistle. This will aid those with auditory or visual impairments.

Floor Hockey

Floor hockey is gaining in popularity in mainstreamed classes. Youngsters in braces, with crutches, or in wheelchairs can enjoy the instruction and action of floor hockey competition. Among the suggestions to consider are

1. For those using crutches, attach a hockey blade to the bottom of one. This can also be done if the student is single-crutch dependent.

2. If a student is in a wheelchair, an option for securing the stick is to affix it to the foundation of the chair.

3. Do not allow the puck to rise above the floor on passes or shots on goal.

4. In order to slow down the game so that students can employ their own relative levels of ability, use a soft rubber puck (rather than a regular puck or plastic ball).

5. Consider having less-mobile players occupy goalie positions.

Flag Football and Touch Football

Flag football and touch football are possible when we take into account the kinds of things that the youngster with a disability can do. Again focus on abilities. If the student can throw, place him/her in a position that will afford the opportunity to do so. Single-arm amputees can throw and run down the field for one-hand and body catches. The visually-impaired can center the ball and block. Those who are hearing impaired can play any position. Additional suggestions are offered by Grosse (1991) in the following list:

1. Use players who are less-mobile in the offensive line to block for the quarterback.
2. For those in wheelchairs attach rip flags to the chair itself rather than to the person (where it might be less accessible and likely provoke excessive body contact).
3. Allow blocking from the front only.
4. On the opening play, substitute a throw for a kick. A throw can also replace a punt on fourth down. In general a throw is easier to place, easier to catch, and does not cover as much distance.
5. For the extra point following a touchdown, substitute a single play from the five-yard line. For example, two points can be awarded for a successful running play; one point can be granted for a successful passing play.

Soccer

Soccer is an outstanding game in which use of the arms—except by the goalie—is a violation of standard rules. As a consequence, students with little or no use of their arms are prime candidates for soccer instruction and competition. Among the recommendations made by successful soccer instructors are

1. Have players who are in wheelchairs serve as goalies (and/or make the throwins).
2. Athletes who are visually impaired can take the corner and penalty kicks (in addition to the throw-ins if you do not have a wheelchair athlete).
3. If wheelchair-bound athletes are playing positions other than goalie, they can be allowed to use their footrests to move the ball.
4. If students are using crutches, do not allow them to hit the ball with the crutches. They should be encouraged to use a swing-to or swing-through gait and kick the ball with their feet.

Softball

Unlike other activities presented in this chapter, situations arising in softball provide for partners to serve as single players. For example, a student who is in a wheelchair (or otherwise less mobile) can bat the ball, and his/her partner can do the running to first base. To carry this thesis further, those with arms can bat, those with legs can run. A student with one arm can catch the ball with his/her glove, tuck the glove into the opposite arm pit, retrieve the ball, and throw it. An example of a person who has mastered this skill is Jim Abbott, a professional pitcher in major league baseball. He/she can also bat by choking up on a lighter-weight bat. Other guidelines for the activity of softball are

1. Provide ample choices of bats having different sizes. One might even want to allow a plastic bat and ball to be used in certain situations.
2. Allow gloves of choice for defensive players. A student should be allowed to use a first baseman's mit at other positions if he/she feels more comfortable with it.

3. When judging base running, a crutch (or wheelchair) could make a legal touch of the base rather than having to use the foot, hand, or other part of the body.

4. Allow the batter the choice of slow or fast pitching.

5. Employ less-mobile players in positions where agility in moving laterally is not a dominant requirement in classroom softball competition (e.g., pitcher, catcher, first base, or third base).

6. A crutch should not be allowed for use as a bat. Have players either place both crutches under one arm while batting, or drop one and pick it up later (having had someone else do the running to first base).

7. Allow all players on a team to bat once through the batting order, then move to defense. This allows everyone on the team to hit once each inning. Therefore, no one causes the team to retire for the inning by making the third out.

8. When arranging competition for players who are visually impaired, a single can be made when a ball gets through the infield, but the batter cannot advance except on the next hit, and he/she can only advance one base at a time. A defender can make the out when he/she stops the ball from getting through the infield. Throwing the ball to first or another base for a force play is not a requirement. When the ball is stopped, the lead runner is the one who is out. An underhand pitch of the ball to approximately waist height is considered an ideal placement for the batter. Using a batting tee or rolling a ball in which a sounding device has been placed are other options.

9. Consider inserting the bases into the ground so that they will not be tripped over by those who are visually impaired or those who are in wheelchairs or using crutches.

10. At the onset of your instruction establish a routine of employing base coaches. This will help provide guidance to those who are more easily confused by emerging situations on the playing field.

Finally, arms and hands are required in most team sports. Should a student with crutches want to free his/her upper limbs by sitting in a wheelchair, this should be acceptable. Given the growth of wheelchair sports programs in this country, this option can represent a viable alternative. Do not, however, encourage his use of the wheelchair throughout the day. As indicated in previous chapters, it is important that the student use whatever residual leg strength there is in order to resist the progressive nature of some debilitating diseases. Walking on crutches will help do that. Staying in a wheelchair—without passive or active-assistive leg exercises—will not.

SUMMARY

Mainstreaming provides the basis for social exchanges so desperately needed by all children. These benefits, coupled with the skills gained through participating in diversified physical education programs, can help bridge the gap between idleness and fulfilling life experiences. The goal of reducing the barriers to participation is one we all share.

In this chapter I attempted to provide you with general and specific guidelines for mainstreaming students in selected individual/self-testing, rhythmic, and dual and team sport activities. Although we will find differences in learning styles among those who have disabilities, the same could be said of anyone. If we focus on abilities, take into account the laws of readiness and effect, and regulate our teaching styles in ways that match the ways children learn, the attainment of optimum achievement is within the reach of all who are fortunate enough to participate in the experience. It is the responsibility of all of us to see that this happens.

RECOMMENDED LABORATORY ASSIGNMENTS

1. Arrange for appointments with public school physical education program administrators to discuss procedures by which children with disabilities are mainstreamed within their schools.
2. Observe mainstreamed programs and record methods and materials used to accommodate students in these programs.
3. Meet with exceptional students in order to gain insights as to their perceptions of successful mainstreaming practices.
4. Place your name on the mailing lists of various agencies whose goals are to address program interests and needs of persons with disabilities. (See Appendix A for suggested agency titles and addresses.) Submit oral or written reports about new ideas presented in materials you receive over a period of time.
5. Complete a physical education practicum within classes where mainstreaming is being practiced.
6. List conditions not described in this chapter that could be accommodated within a mainstreamed class.
7. Describe physical activities not presented in this chapter that would be suitable for all students enrolled in mainstreamed class.
8. Make a list of methods and materials not described in this chapter that could be used to assist students with disabilities in meeting individualized education plan (IEP) objectives in a mainstreamed setting.
9. Become proficient in the use of methodology described in this chapter.
10. Review the recommended readings.

REFERENCES

Allen, K. 1991. Gymnastics instruction. In *Sport Instruction for Individuals with Disabilities*. Reston, VA: American Alliance for Health, Physical Education, Recreation and Dance.

American Alliance for Health, Physical Education, Recreation and Dance (May 1978). Questions and answers about PL 94-142 and Section 504. *Update*, p. 4.

American Alliance for Health, Physical Education, Recreation and Dance (October 1978). Questions and answers about PL 94-142 and Section 504. *Update*, p. 11.

American Alliance for Health, Physical Education, Recreation and Dance (November 1978). Questions and answers about PL 94-142 and Section 504. *Update*, Pp. 6–7

American Alliance for Health, Physical Education, Recreation and Dance (December 1978). Questions and answers about PL 94-142 and Section 504. *Update*, p. 10.

American Alliance for Health, Physical Education, Recreation and Dance (March 1979). Questions and answers about PL 94-142 and Section 504. *Update*, p. 6.

Brunner, R., and D. Hill. 1992. Using learning styles research in coaching. *Journal of Physical Education, Recreation and Dance* 63(4): 26–28, 61–62.

Carpenter, L. J. 1985. *Gymnastics for girls and women*. West Nyack, NY: Parker.

Cowart, J. 1991. Sport adaptations for students with crutches: Badminton, golf, archery, tennis. In *Sport Instruction for Individuals with Disabilities*. Reston, VA: American Alliance for Health, Physical Education, Recreation and Dance.

Dunn, J. M. 1976. Mainstreaming: Definition, rationale and implications for physical education. *Mainstreaming Physical Education: Briefings*. National Association for Physical Education of College Women and National College Physical Education Association for Men.

Educational Facilities Laboratories. 1974. *One out of ten*. New York: Author.

Gavron, S. J. 1991. Track and field for *all* persons. In *Sport Instruction for Individuals with Disabilities*. Reston, VA: American Alliance for Health, Physical Education, Recreation and Dance.

Grosse, S. J. 1991. Mainstreaming the physically handicapped student for team sports. In *Sport Instruction for Individuals with Disabilities*. Reston, VA: American Alliance for Health, Physical Education, Recreation and Dance.

McCubbin, J., and L. Zittel. 1991. PL 99-457: What the law is all about. *Journal of Physical Education, Recreation and Dance* 62(6): 35–7, 47.

Mosston, M. 1992. Tug-o-war, no more: Meeting teaching-learning objectives using the spectrum of teaching styles. *Journal of Physical Education, Recreation and Dance* 63(1): 27–31, 56.

Pizzaro, D. C. 1984. The Velcro golf glove and sleeve. *Able Bodies*, 4.

Ratliffe, T., L. Ratliffe, and B. Bie. 1991. Creating a learning environment: Class management strategies for elementary PE teachers. *Journal of Physical Education, Recreation and Dance* 62(9): 24–27.

Rappa, D., ed. 1991. *The NHAHPERD family cookbook: A favorite activities guide*. Bath, NH: New Hampshire Association for Health, Physical Education, Recreation and Dance.

Young American Bowling Alliance. 1991. Bowling for individuals with disabilities. In *Sport Instruction for Individuals with Disabilities*. Reston, VA: American Alliance for Health, Physical Education, Recreation and Dance.

RECOMMENDED READINGS

Adams, R. C., A. N. Daniel, and L. Rullman. 1972. *Games, sports and exercises for the physically handicapped*. Philadelphia: Lea and Febiger.

Anshel, M. H. 1990. An information processing approach to teaching motor skills. *Journal of Physical Education, Recreation and Dance* 61(5): 70–75.

Arlott, J., ed. 1975. *The Oxford companion to world sports and games*. London: Oxford University Press.

Baloche, L., and J. L. Blasko. 1992. Learning together—A new twist. *Journal of Physical Education, Recreation and Dance* 63(3): 26–28.

Clarkson, E. 1991. Partners in education. Journal of Physical Education, Recreation and Dance 62(8): 46–47.

Cowart, J. 1977. Badminton for the disabled. *GWS National Coaches Council Newsletter* 2.

———. 1978. Adapted Safe-T-Play handle bowling ball. *IRUC Briefings* 4.

Deline, J. 1991. Why can't they get along? *Journal of Physical Education, Recreation and Dance* 62(1): 21–26.

Docheff, D. M. 1990. The feedback sandwich. *Journal of Physical Education, Recreation and Dance* 61(9): 17–18.

Docherty, D. 1978. Heart rate response of badminton players relative to their skill level. *Canadian Journal of Applied Sports Sciences* 3(4): 220–222.

Docherty, D. 1982. A comparison of heart rate responses in racquet games. *British Journal of Sports Medicine* 16(2): 96–100.

Doolittle, S. A., and K. T. Girard. 1991. A dynamic approach to teaching games in elementary PE. *Journal of Physical Education, Recreation and Dance* 62(4): 57–62.

Dunn, J. M., J. W. Morehouse, and H. D. Fredericks. 1986. *Physical education for the severely handicapped: A systematic approach to a data-based gymnasium.* Austin, TX: Pro-Ed Publishers.

Ennis, C. C., J. Ross, and A. Chen. 1992. The role of value orientations in curricular decision making: A rationale for teachers' goals and expectations. *Research Quarterly for Exercise and Sport* 63(1): 38–47.

Eichstaedt, C. B., and B. W. Lavay. 1992. *Physical activity for individuals with mental retardation.* Champaign, IL: Human Kinetics, Inc.

Falvey, M.A. 1986. *Community-based curriculum: Instructional strategies for students with severe handicaps.* Baltimore: Paul H. Brookes Publishing Company.

Gray, G. R. 1990. Written lesson plans minimize the risk of injury. *Journal of Physical Education, Recreation and Dance* 62(7): 31–32.

Grosse, S. J. 1974. Wrestling for the handicapped: A cooperative program. *Journal of Health, Physical Education, Recreation and Dance* 45: 41–42.

Hamburg, J. 1992. Applying body therapy to dance and sport. *Journal of Physical Education, Recreation and Dance* 63(5): 48–50.

Hankin, T. 1992. Presenting creative dance activities to children: Guidelines for the nondancer. *Journal of Physical Education, Recreation and Dance* 63(2): 22–24.

Heer, J. 1984. Elements of archery. *Sports 'n Spokes.* Pp. 17–19.

Institute for Physical Education. 1975. *The handbook of physical education and activities for exceptional children.* Old Saybrook, CT: Author.

Jansma, P., and J. T. Decker. 1992. An analysis of least restrictive environment placement variables in physical education. *Research Quarterly for Exercise and Sport* 63(2): 171–78.

Kay, S. L., and W. A. Lewis. 1970. A bowling device for bilateral arm amputees. *Inter-Clinic Information Bulletin 9.*

Kegel, B. 1985. Golf. *Journal of Rehabilitation Research and Development, Clinical Supplement No. 1.* Pp. 18–21.

Lavay, B., and M. Horvat. 1991. Jump rope for heart for special populations. Journal of Physical Education, Recreation and Dance 62(3): 74–78.

Longo, P. 1989. Chair golf. *Sports 'n Spokes.* Pp. 35–38.

Metzler, M. W. 1990. Teaching in competitive games—Not just playin' around. *Journal of Physical Education, Recreation and Dance* 61(8): 57–61.

Morris, G. S., and J. Stiehl. 1989. *Changing kids' games.* Champaign, IL: Leisure Press.

Morris, L. R., and L. Schulz. 1989. *Creative play activities for children with disabilities.* Champaign, IL: Human Kinetics, Inc.

National wheelchair athletic association. (Annual). *Constitution and rules: Training techniques and records.* Woodside, NY: Author.

Nygaard, G. 1987. *Warnings: Current issues in sport law.* Reston, VA: National Association for Sport and Physical Education

O'Brien, E. F. 1991. Teaching dances of other cultures. *Journal of Physical Education, Recreation and Dance* 62(2): 40–41.

Orlick, T. 1978. *The cooperative sports and games book.* New York: Pantheon.

Parks, B. A. 1988. *Tennis in a wheelchair.* Princeton, NJ: United States Tennis Association.

Peddie, D., and T. Pennewell. 1991. A step in the right direction: Fitness and physical education for the '90s. *Journal of Physical Education, Recreation and Dance* 62(7): 64, 66.

Purcell, T. M. 1990. The use of imagery in childrens dance—Making it work. Journal of Physical Education, Recreation and Dance 61(2): 22–23.

Rich, S. M. 1990. Factors influencing the learning process. In *Adapted physical education and sport*, edited by J. P. Winnick. Champaign, IL: Human Kinetics, Inc.

Shea, E. J. 1986. Sport for life. *Journal of Physical Education, Recreation and Dance* 57(1): 52–54.

Weiss, R., and W. B. Karper. 1980. Teaching the handicapped child in the regular physical education class. *Journal of Physical Education and Recreation* 51: 32–35, 77.

CHAPTER 15

Outings, Camping, and Aquatics

Objectives

After reading this chapter, you should be able to

- Relate the value of recreational outings, camping, and aquatics to the total development of children, especially those who are physically, cognitively, emotionally, and/or socially challenged.
- Account for the emphasis placed on recreation programing by hospitals and county and community agencies.
- Describe the organizational structures of supervised camping programs.
- Identify factors that contribute to appropriate selection of camps for those with disabilities.
- Identify various agencies that conduct aquatic courses.
- Describe guidelines for selecting facilities, equipment, and supplies appropriate for use in aquatic programs.
- Discuss the physical and humanistic principles underlying the selection of skills to be learned by students who are enrolled in swimming classes.

INTRODUCTION

Recreation has long been considered an important avenue of expression for those who have disabilities. Anyone who has had the opportunity to see the glow of enthusiasm radiating from the face of a visually impaired teenager descending from a recent rock climb can well appreciate the value that a recreational experience can have. But there are critics, and these critics of recreational activities for persons with disabilities can generally be grouped into one of two categories:

1. Those who have never been witness to the joys experienced by those who have participated in these activities
2. Those who have observed (or read about) programs that are either mismanaged or poorly supervised.

KEY TERMS

acceleration	outings
action and reaction	private or commercial agencies
adipose	public camping programs
aquatics	quasi-public agencies
biological and behavioral idiosyncrasies	recreation
body positions: static and dynamic	resident camps
buoyancy	skill envelope
camping	special-purpose camps
day camps	stroke coordination
inertia	student achievement sheet
leisure-time activities	swimming readiness
leverage	water entry and adjustment skills

According to Etkes (1989) some recreation areas have been found to be hazardous and threatening for children with disabling conditions. Others argue that play areas can be very sterile. In short they have not always provided a positive experience (Schlein and Ray 1988).

When designing creative recreation or play environments, therapeutic specialists and other recreation leaders should first ask

What is the purpose of the...experience? (Keller and Hudson 1991). What in general terms can outdoor education do for the disabled? How can recreation help a youngster find his/her place in the real world? Pullias (1972) provides several responses.

1. It can establish a healing and growth-production relation with the natural world—the world to which man is so intimately related.
2. It can assist in the...habits of withdrawal and renewal which are fundamental to physical, mental, and spiritual health in modern life. Perhaps it can help to slow down and simplify the rushed confusion that characterizes so much of life.
3. It can offset the deadening effect upon the human mind of forever dealing with abstractions—with second, or third, or fourth-hand experience—with which modern life is encrusted. The human mind urgently needs direct experience, even if it is a very simple direct experience.
4. It can promote growth in sensitivity; that is, open the self up to the wide variety of experiences that nourish and bring to fruition the full richness of human nature.
5. At its best, outdoor experience may guide 'man' to find a renewed communion with the second...pole of his nature and the source of that nature: that spirit pole which makes 'man' truly 'man.'

The values listed can be pursued through a number of recreational activities. It has been said that "one man's pudding is another man's poison." Tillman (1973) said it better when he wrote,

Recreation program(ing) is like Russian roulette because it does not have a technique for measuring individual needs.

Indeed, the activity that satisfies the leisure requirements of one person may provide anxiety for another.

HUMAN NEEDS

All people need to express themselves in ways not ordinarily possible within the constraints of the home or school. **Leisure-time activities** can help youngsters with disabilities to form habits and attitudes that will contribute to their confident participation in other areas of their lives. Hiking, fishing, rock climbing, painting, skiing, scuba diving, parachute jumping, and other recreational activities can inspire the student with a disability to reduce the gap between his/her present lifestyle and what he/she wishes it was. As Bream (1964) pointed out, participation can help a child improve his/her morale and sustain it at more optimal levels; will channel his/her aggressive drives into appropriate outlets; and stimulate him/her to develop new interests as well as reestablish old ones.

But the attitudes of those in positions to advance recreation program opportunities for those with disabilities are critical. If recreation directors are of the opinion that such opportunities are important, the probability is high that program options will be made available. For example, Hoge (1990) conducted a doctoral dissertation in which the relationships between attitude and providing recreational services were examined. Within the limitations of the findings it was reported that a positive relationship does in fact exist. It is apparent, therefore, that recreation planners need to understand the importance of providing special recreation services. Favorable attitudes appear to be predictors of intentions to provide these opportunites. **Outings**, **camping**, and **aquatics** have the potential to contribute to the student's acquisition of physiological and sociological health and to self-esteem. They contribute much to "human ecology," Figure 15.1.

Program Brief

Prior to 1932 when the Bill of Rights for the Handicapped was drawn up at the White House Conference on Child Health and Protection, the recreation movement of those with disabilities was only intermittently successful. Most of the impact before 1932 was made through the efforts of the Association for the Aid of Crippled Children and other such agencies. The White House conference attracted specialists from various medical, therapeutic, recreational, and educational agencies, and a nationally unified movement began.

During World War II there was a significant increase in the number of hospital recreation programs available, Table 15.1. This trend has continued up to the present.

In 1969, Marston reported that an increasing number of communities were providing recreation for those with mental and physical disabilities. Nevertheless

...there has been a great lag in developing recreation services for the handicapped by community recreation departments (Marston 1969).

Figure 15.1. To be with nature and its boundless resources is to live

TABLE 15.1

Percentages of 3507 Institutions Providing Recreation

Classification	Percentage	Disability Served	Percentage
Veterans Administration	98.8	Mental illness	98.0
		Tuberculosis	90.7
State	89.3		
		Mental retardation	84.8
Military	81.7		
		Chronic disease	69.7
Public Health	49.0		
		Other	91.4
Voluntary (nonsectarian)	35.0		
Voluntary (sectarian)	32.4		
County	32.0		
Proprietary	27.0		
Miscellaneous	24.1		

Source: Courtesy of Silson, J. E., et al. 1959. *Recreation in hospitals: Report of a study of organized recreation programs in hospitals and the personnel conducting them.* New York: National Recreation Association. Pp 22–23.

In 1971, Berryman, Logan, and Lander reported that 94 percent of the county and municipal and recreation park departments under study were providing recreation for children and youth with disabilities, Table 15.2.

TABLE 15.2

**Percentage of Responding Agencies That Provided Recreation for
Children and Youth with Disabilities**

Agency	Percentage
Hospitals and residential schools	100
Private and parochial school districts	96
County and municipal recreation and park departments	94
United States Department of Agriculture, County Extension Service, 4-H clubs	92
Fraternal and service organizations and miscellaneous	87
All health organizations	87
Churches, libraries, and museums	82
Commercial and proprietary businesses	81

Note: Data based upon reports from a sampling of large metropolitan areas throughout the United States over a three-year period. This study was financed by the Children's Bureau of the United States Department of Health, Education and Welfare.

There have been positive changes in the amount and diversification of recreation services for those with disabilities. In no small way is this a concomitant outcome arising out of the laws enacted to serve impaired children within the schools (See Chapter l). We still have a ways to go if one can hope for a continued expansion of vital recreation services. In addition to continued "attitude adjustment" strategies this includes

1. developing more programs integrating the disabled with the able-bodied.
2. completely eliminating architectural barriers that keep those with disabilities from participating in selected community programs.

OUTINGS

What comprises risk recreation for those with disabilities? Picnics, visits to the zoo, or walks through the park are not sufficiently hazardous to preclude participation by anyone, and these outings are meaningful experiences. For some, however, these activities may not be as satisfying as riskier ones such as taking a canoe trip, hunting, horseback riding, snowmobiling or skiing, Figure 15.2. Peterson (1978) says,

> Recreation interests have always been individualistic. What turns one person on is total boredom to someone else. The issue remains that most people are free to choose their recreation interests. (Those with disabilities)...deserve that same

Figure 15.2. Slalom skiing

opportunity. If they select a risk recreation activity, their decision should be respected and their involvement facilitated. The right to risk belongs to everyone. The resulting joy and heightened emotional impact know no prejudice.

Canoeing to a campsite to picnic, hunt, or fish may provide more positive physiopsychic improvement than spending significantly more time in a office therapy session. At the very least doing so should be considered a viable alternative.

CAMPING

There are various types of supervised camping programs open to the disabled. These programs are sponsored by the following kinds of agencies.

1. **Private or commercial agencies**, in which fees for atteadance come from the clients. These fees vary in accordance with sophistication of the staff, program, facilities, and philanthropic tendencies of management. Examples are Boy Scouts, Girl Scouts, Young Men's Christian Association (YMCAs), Young Women's Christian Association (YWCAs), country clubs, and assorted privately managed organizations.
2. **Quasi-public agencies**, in which some of the funds for camp operation come from donations and endowments. The balance is paid by those enrolled in the program. The American Red Cross, Salvation Army, 4-H Clubs, and police and fire department athletic leagues are examples of quasi-public agencies.

3. **Public camping programs**, supported by tax funds. Public camping programs are usually sponsored by municipal park commissions, school systems, and town recreation departments.

The three types of programs just defined are ordinarily organized in accordance with one of the following four plans.

1. **Day camps** are located within or close enough to a community to allow the youngsters to be transported to camp from their homes daily. Generally the programs run on a two-week, five-days-per-week basis from 9:00 A.M. to 4:00 P.M. Although the number of buildings for use is usually quite small, day camps generally have lavatories, dressing rooms, supply and equipment storage rooms, an inclement weather station, and offices, Figure 15.3.

2. **Resident camps** usually have cabins, a dining hall, staff quarters, supply and equipment storage areas, nature and pioneering shelters, a recreation hall, an arts and crafts facility, and program offices, Figure 15.4. Although youngsters

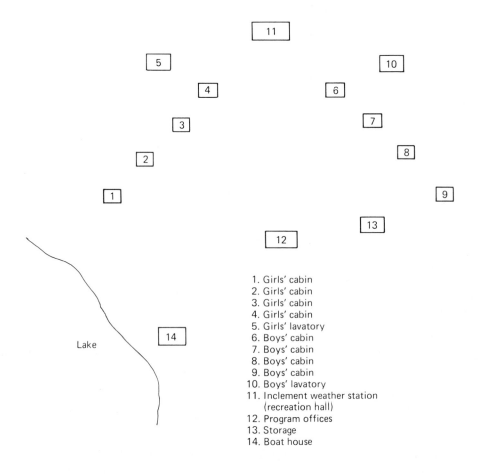

1. Girls' cabin
2. Girls' cabin
3. Girls' cabin
4. Girls' cabin
5. Girls' lavatory
6. Boys' cabin
7. Boys' cabin
8. Boys' cabin
9. Boys' cabin
10. Boys' lavatory
11. Inclement weather station
    (recreation hall)
12. Program offices
13. Storage
14. Boat house

Figure 15.3. A sample day camp facility

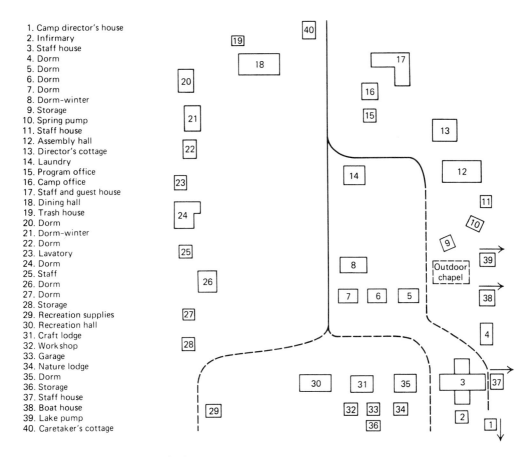

1. Camp director's house
2. Infirmary
3. Staff house
4. Dorm
5. Dorm
6. Dorm
7. Dorm
8. Dorm-winter
9. Storage
10. Spring pump
11. Staff house
12. Assembly hall
13. Director's cottage
14. Laundry
15. Program office
16. Camp office
17. Staff and guest house
18. Dining hall
19. Trash house
20. Dorm
21. Dorm-winter
22. Dorm
23. Lavatory
24. Dorm
25. Staff
26. Dorm
27. Dorm
28. Storage
29. Recreation supplies
30. Recreation hall
31. Craft lodge
32. Workshop
33. Garage
34. Nature lodge
35. Dorm
36. Storage
37. Staff house
38. Boat house
39. Lake pump
40. Caretaker's cottage

Figure 15.4. A resident camp facility

may enroll for an entire summer at some resident camps, most sessions are two weeks per camper so that more individuals can attend camp during the camping session. Fees include meals and lodging.*

3. Combination resident and day camps allow some campers to attend the program on a day-to-day basis, while other campers remain overnight. The choice usually depends on the nature of the program and the facilities available.

4. **Special-purpose camps** may be day, resident, or combination, and they promote a basic theme, e.g., aquatics, basketball, soccer, tennis, scouting.

How can we decide what camp is best for a particular youngster with disabilities? Consider these variables:

1. Nature of the disability
2. Reason the child is going to camp

---

* A greater number of program personnel is needed in a resident camp than in a day camp because of twenty-four supervisory responsibilities.

3. Philosophy of the camp
4. Facilities available (e.g., barrier-free access to waterfront area, recreation hall)
5. Location of camp
6. Size of the camp
7. Ratio of campers to staff
8. Topography of the campsite (e.g., flat, hilly)
9. Accreditation
10. Sponsoring agency
11. Organizational structure
12. Qualifications of the staff
13. Experience of the camp with individuals with disabilities
14. Camp program (activities, supplies, equipment)
15. Medical resources (e.g., permanent, on call)
16. Expense
17. Views of those who have attended the camp previously as campers or staff.

For Specific information regarding various camp programs and structure contact any or all of the following sources:

1. The community recreation department, whose director should have information as to the nature of the programs available. If the department has no permanent director, contact the selectperson, town manager, or mayor's office.
2. Local special interest groups. Parents, guardians, and friends may have had experience with specific camps and may be able to offer recommendations.
3. Specific agencies representing certain classifications of disabilities (see Appendix A). They can often identify accredited camping programs.
4. Public and private schools; colleges and universities. Camp administrators often contact physical education or recreation department faculty and supervisors to recruit campers or camp staff.
5. State office of parks and recreation. This department is usually located in the state capital and should be abreast of supervised camping opportunities within the region.
6. American Association for Leisure and Recreation, 1900 Association Drive, Reston, VA 22091
7. American Camping Association, Bradford Woods, 5000 S.R., 67N, Martinsville, IN 46151-7902
8. American Therapeutic Recreation Association, P.O. Box 15215, Hattiesburg, MS 39404-5215
9. Boy Scouts of America, 1325 Walnut Hill Lane, Irving, TX 75038-3096
10. National Handicapped Sports and Recreation Association, 4405 E. West Highway, #603, Bethesda, MD 20814
11. National Recreation and Parks Association, 2775 South Quincy Street, Suite 300, Arlington, VA 22206
12. YMCA of the U.S.A., 6083-A Oakbrook Parkway, Norcross, GA 30092
13. YWCA of the U.S.A., 726 Broadway, New York, NY 10003

An increasing number of high-quality camps are emerging on the local, regional, and national scenes. Individuals who work in the schools with students with disabilities should help those searching out good programs investigate the options available.

AQUATICS

Aquatics includes a variety of activities performed in or on the water. Through recent years, participation in these activities has swelled to the extent that the American Red Cross, United States Coast Guard Auxiliary, YMCA, YWCA as well as other organizations have embarked upon programs designed to increase the competence of prospective aquatic participants, guards, and instructors. Among these programs are

1. Infant and preschool aquatics
2. Basic water safety
3. Emergency water safety
4. Lifeguarding
5. Safety training for swim coaches
6. Basic sailing
7. Swimming and diving
8. Water safety instruction

Swimming ranks high among the most successful activities taught to persons with disabilities. Like any students, they may fear the water at first, but a competent and well-trained instructor can help them take to the swimming class in a manner rarely equaled in other programs.*

Swimming allows a freedom of movement that may not otherwise be possible for the child with a disability. Because of **buoyancy**, he/she can pay more attention to developing skills than resisting gravity. The child is free of crutches, wheelchair, or other device, and can participate in an activity that can lead to measurable physiologic growth. Very few programs offer such promise.

The physiological benefits of swimming are twofold.

1. The student has the opportunity to learn new skills while improving upon muscular strength and endurance, cardiovascular endurance, and range of motion.
2. Stress upon the nervous system is reduced as a result of appropriately programmed relaxation, enhancing the potential for attainment of emotional or psychological homeostasis.

The psychological benefit of swimming is that even moderately successful students will gain enhanced self-images and feel more comfortable interacting with other youngsters in and out of class. In the water the disability will be less restricting and less apparent to the student and his/her peers.

Facilities, Equipment, and Supplies

Very few schools have swimming pools of their own. On the other hand, public or private agencies within many communities do have swimming pools that can be used by school personnel to teach classes. Aquatics supervisors and instructors should know what constitutes a well-equipped facility.

---

* See Chapter 3 for examples of personal history program entry forms. These documents can help the instructor to understand the biological and behavioral tendencies of a child who is entering class.

Facilities It would be very difficult to find a swimming pool that had every desirable feature. Some features, however, are common to most successful pool facilities. These are listed as follows:

1. There should be no architectural barriers that exclude anyone from gaining access to locker rooms, shower rooms, restrooms, and the swimming pool itself. Ramps should be available where needed,* and handrails should be appropriately placed on ramps, on steps, in the shower room, and in toilet facilities. Doors should be at least thirty-three inches wide to allow wheelchairs to pass through. Decks on the pool side of each threshold should be the width of three wheelchairs so as to provide adequate space for negotiating a single wheelchair; all other decks should be wide enough to allow the passage of two wheelchairs.
2. Deck tiles should be small to reduce the chances of slipping.
3. There should be adequate deck space around the pool to allow for storage of wheelchairs and other equipment during class instruction. Cabinets and hooks should be available. Space should also be available for 'dry land' teaching.
4. It is helpful to those unfamiliar with the various pool depths to have horizontal lines on the walls that are as high as the water is deep. Such lines allow children to compare their heights with water depths so that they will know whether or not the water at each line would be over their heads.
5. Water in the shower room should be turned on and off by a master valve. If this alternative is not available, there should be buttons on the floor for use by students who have little or no use of their arms.
6. Steps, ladders (not recessed), ramps, and power and/or mechanical harness lifts should be available to assist paralyzed individuals into and out of the water. It is recommended that the decks should be no more than three inches above the surface of the water. They should be constructed with slightly raised edges to minimize the danger that wheelchairs might slip or roll in.
7. The pool should have an adequate instruction area where the depth of the water is no greater than three to four feet. Recessed handrails should be placed along the wall in the shallow end of the pool. A separate crib is helpful for very small children.
8. The depth of the pool should be recorded in braille along the pool walls. Letters, numbers, and geometric designs on the bottom of the pool aid academic reinforcement, Figure 15.5.
9. The temperature of the water should be approximately eighty to eighty-four degrees Fahrenheit during instruction periods. Higher temperatures may be necessary for those with neurological or musculoskeletal disorders. (Tissue viscosity can be reduced by higher water temperatures.) At higher temperatures, however, the chlorine and bacteria counts should be monitored more frequently.
10. The air temperature of the natatorium should be between four and six degrees Fahrenheit higher than that of the water. This minor variance helps to control condensation in the natatorium. More importantly it makes body adjustment to

---

* Ramps should not rise more than one foot for every twelve feet in length.

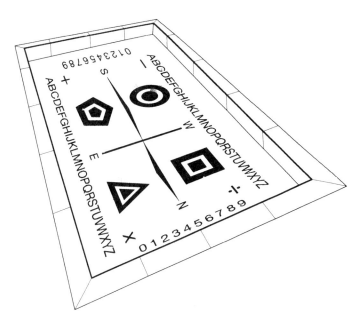

Figure 15.5. Swimming pool with academic reinforcement aids. *Adapted from the Yorktown Swimming Pool, Arlington, VA.*

different air and water temperatures less traumatic. At outdoor pools it may be necessary to postpone water work and perform land instruction and drills if the weather is cool.

Equipment Appropriate, easily accessible equipment is necessary for a program to function safely, Figure 15.6. Among the items that should be included at a well-stocked facility are

1. Telephone hot line to emergency stations
2. Backboard, sliding board, and surf board to assist swimmers into and out of the water. The backboard is also necessary for emergencies.
3. Safety lines, buoys, and area markers
4. Shepherd's crooks and reaching poles
5. Ring buoys, life rings, plastic jugs, and heaving lines
6. Benches and resting platforms
7. Underwater sound system, directional devices for students with visual impairments
8. One-meter diving board
9. Lifeguard stands.
10. Game equipment, such as basketball and water polo goals and volleyball standards.

Supplies Certain supplies are essential for swimming pool safety. Others are critical to the teaching of many skills. Among the more important items to have are

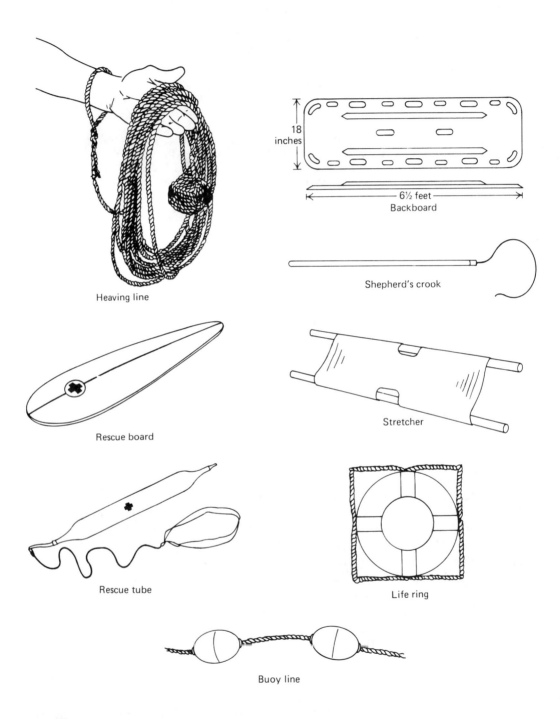

18 inches

6½ feet
Backboard

Heaving line

Shepherd's crook

Rescue board

Stretcher

Rescue tube

Life ring

Buoy line

Figure 15.6. Swimming pool safety aids

1. Personal flotation devices, including buoyant belts, inflatable arm and leg supports, inflatable vests and collars
2. Towels or small blankets that can be used to lower and raise smaller children into and out of the water
3. Swim fins, hand paddles, and pull buoys
4. Face masks and goggles
5. Pool caps, nose clips, and eardrum protectors
6. Flutter- or kickboards
7. Whistles
8. Academic reinforcement aids such as numbers, letters, geometric patterns, blocks of different colors, plastic or rubber animals.
9. Radio or metronome to use as a directional sounding device for those with visual impairments; green light at the shallow end of the pool, and red light at the deep end to orient those with hearing impairments.
10. Recreational aids such as various-sized special-purpose balls, hula hoops, diving or fetching rings, diving bricks, and sponges.

Program Organization

Many of the program suggestions described in Chapter 3 could be applied to a swimming class, provided that we take into account **biological and behavioral idiosyncrasies** that relate to water adjustment, Table 15.3.

TABLE 15.3

Factors to Consider When Teaching Swimming Skills to Children with Disabilities

Disabilities	Biological and Behavioral Considerations
Behavioral disorders	Provide opportunities for interpersonal teacher-student contacts; establish medium for positive reinforcement; structure for activities; keep activities of short duration and simple. Children are generally resistant to change and will demonstrate bizarre behavior and preoccupation with inanimate objects. Supervise drill periods carefully.
Musculoskeletal Disorders	
Muscular dystrophy	Cardiac and intercostal muscles may be involved. Avoid overexertion; emphasize relaxation techniques (e.g., floating).
Skeletal problems	If legs are involved, avoid weight bearing. Poor circulation may exist, so avoid chilling by monitoring length of time in water as well as differences between pool deck and water temperatures.
Spina bifida	Prevent contractures by emphasizing stretching, but do not force it. Understand use of bowel, bladder collection bags.
Neurological Disorders	
Cerebral palsy	Contractions hinder prone and supine recovery (return to vertical position in the water). Prone position leads to upward

TABLE 15.3 *continued*

Disabilities	Biological and Behavioral Considerations
	thrusting of head, supine position leads to hyperextension of head; hips are flexed. Encourage walking in pool; teach swimming skills while student is in vertical position. To help keep arms in extended position, child may clasp thumbs. Range of motion is limited, so modify strokes. Water temperature should approach eighty-six degrees.
Epilepsy	Have child wear identifying headband or cap; he/she should not dive or swim alone.
Multiple sclerosis	Water temperature should be eighty to eighty-four degrees; too high a temperature leads to neural innervation; too low a temperature leads to tension.
Organic Disorders	
Heart dysfunction	Provide frequent rest periods; use music for relaxation; hydrostatic (flat) position is best for most water activities.
Sensory Disorders	
Visual	Give student an opportunity to become oriented to the natatorium—to measure the environment. Child should not be encouraged to submerge early in the swimming experience as he/she must rely on hearing for orientation. Place a radio or metronome on deck table at shallow end of pool. Place rope across pool to separate shallow from deep end. Underwater swimming is not recommended for those with detached retinas because of water pressure.
Auditory	If lack of balance exists, child may be reluctant to float on back because orientation and recovery are affected. Child cannot ordinarily wear hearing aid in the water, and must rely on visual cues. Place a green light on deck table at shallow end of pool, a red light on deck table at deep end. Diving and underwater swimming may affect ears and orientation. Demonstration of swimming skills critical to success in view of problems associated with auditory learning.
Visual and auditory	To communicate, outline block letters in palm of child's hand or use manual alphabet that he/she can feel with his/her hands.
Mental Retardation	Presentation should be at a slow pace, and language should be simple. Demonstrations are important. Reinforce swimming skills through the use of assorted games and activities. Students need to develop strength and endurance.

Note: Preswimming mat work stressing unilateral and bilateral limb stretching may be extremely helpful for all children with disabilities. Use background music with relaxing tempo.

How can we identify, record, and keep track of students' skills as they are mastered? Whether we are responsible for one or six students, the procedure to be suggested provides an alternative for keeping track of each individual's progress. When a skill has been mastered, give the student an award and make an appropriate notation. You will then know exactly what skill is to be taught next when the student comes to class again. In sequence the procedure is as follows:

1. On a waterproof bulletin board place an envelope for each skill that can be taught to the children enrolled in class. On each **skill envelope** place a number representing the skill's order of sequence and a picture illustrating the skill. Within each envelope place more pictures that illustrate the skill, Figure 15.7.
2. Prepare a **student achievement sheet** for each child in the class. On the sheet put the student's name as well as numbers representing all the skills that can be taught to him/her, Figure 15.8. Attach the student achievement sheets to the bulletin board beneath the envelopes.
3. When the student arrives in class for the first time, test him/her in sequence on the skills that are to be taught. For each skill that the student can perform, draw a circle around the skill's number on the student's achievement sheet. For example, if a student can perform skills 1, 2, and 3, circle these numbers on the sheet, Figure 15.9.

Figure 15.7. Skill envelopes

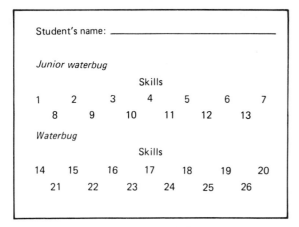

Figure 15.8. Student achievement sheet

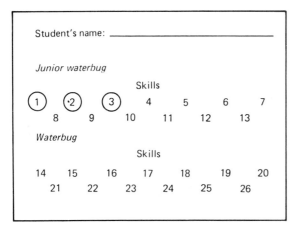

Figure 15.9. Student achievement sheet showing that the student has mastered skills 1, 2, and 3

4. When students return to class, refer to their student achievement sheets to see where each child's lesson should begin. Identify the skill number by looking at the picture on the numbered skill envelope. A student who has mastered skills 1, 2, and 3 will begin on skill number 4.

5. As each new skill is mastered, circle the appropriate number on the student achievement sheet and give the student a picture of the skill from the apppropriate envelope. (This represents an award that can be shared with friends and relatives.) This picture can then be displayed and retained with other pictures for subsequent 'recognition of achievement' ceremonies.

Unlike procedures in which lists are kept on clipboards or in rankbooks, this technique allows the students to see their progression, helps motivate them to improve, and enables a teacher who may be new to the student on a particular day to identify the skill to be addressed. Many swimming classes for students with disabilities have itinerant teachers. They may be students who are completing high school, college course practicums, or student teachers; service organization volunteers; or individuals who are seeking to enrich their own lives. New instructors will find it easier to organize class activities if the skill envelope procedure is in use.

Principles Related to Programming Swimming for Those with Disabilities

Teaching swimming is not unlike teaching many other activities within a physical education curriculum. Success depends on an intelligent application of general and specific educational principles. The supervisor of the aquatics program should be certain that each instructor complies with the following guidelines:

1. Access abilities rather than disabilities. Be wary of labels. Youngsters with similar disabilities may have very different abilities.

2. Adapt swimming strokes to accommodate the abilities of the child. The classic style of a particular swimming stroke may have to be modified if the child is to become proficient.

3. Understand the physical laws that influence swimming performance. This understanding may help a satisfactory teacher become better. The laws to consider are explained here.

   a) Buoyancy is the upward pressure of water on an immersed body. Buoyancy is affected by a person's muscle, bone, fatty tissue, and center of gravity. Since muscle and bone have a higher specific gravity* than **adipose** tissue, persons with little fat will tend to sink (negative buoyancy). A swimmer's center of gravity can be elevated if he/she raises his/her arms over the head. This brings the center of gravity into proximity with the center of buoyancy, which is the lungs.

   b) **Inertia** refers to the property of matter whereby any physical body will persist in its state of rest or uniform motion until acted upon by some external force. In swimming, the external force may be the movement of the person's arms through the water.

   c) **Acceleration** is the rate at which the velocity of a body will increase per unit of time. In swimming, it is important that the arm stroke be made close to and parallel with the midline of the body, and that this stroke be made at a constant rate. Altering the speed of the stroke affects acceleration and induces fatigue. While in competitive swimming a variance in intensity may be required, it is more efficient to swim at a steady rate. Energy is then conserved and strokes are more easily rehearsed.

   d) **Action and reaction** refers to the principle that for every action there is an equal and opposite reaction. In swimming, to propel the body forward the arms must be pulled backward, Figure 15.10. If, following the initial 'catch' of the water with the hand during the crawl stroke, that hand is pulled down instead of back (the action), the reaction will be elevation out of the water rather than forward movement.

   e) **Leverage** refers to the mechanical advantage that can be gained as a consequence of efficiently using one's resistance arm i.e., the arm that will be stroking. By flexing the elbow, the swimmer reduces the length of the resistance arm and, using less force, can generate propulsion equivalent to that possible had the arm been kept straight.

4. Encourage students with disabilities to participate in swimming programs. The potential for physical and social success is great. Those with disabilities are closer to being without handicaps in the water than anywhere else.

5. Encourage students with disabilities to participate regularly in all the activities of a swimming class, but take special precautions when necessary. Some factors that rule out participation on a particular occasion.

---

* Specific gravity is the ratio between the weight of the human body and the weight of an equal volume of water. The specific gravity of water is 1.0. If a person's specific gravity is greater than 1.0, he or she will sink.

Figure 15.10. Action and reaction: Moving the arm backward propels the body forward.

a) The chlorine count may be at a level that causes reactions in those who have allergies.

b) Children who have the following conditions should not swim: open sores such as ringworm or eczema; joint inflammations; ear infections; severe colds, including runny nose and frequent coughing; incisions; abrasions; and lacerations. Special care must be taken to look for wounds on paralyzed limbs (e.g., elbows, hands, knees, legs, and feet) because individuals with such conditions may not sense that injuries have occurred.

c) Water temperatures may be low enough to aggravate already tense striated or cardiac muscle tissue in children with cerebral palsy or heart conditions.

d) Some individuals with physical and/or cognitive disabilities will have psychological problems. Chapter 10 addresses methods and materials related to behavior modification.

DEVELOPMENTAL ACTIVITIES

Some adjustments will have to be made to the recommended sequence of swimming skills to accommodate children with certain disabilities. Getting into and out of the water may take more time for some students than for others. Flotation devices may have to be used. Demonstration methods may have to be emphasized for the hearing impaired and mentally retarded; auditory and tactile stimulation for those who are visually impaired.

Some skills will be mastered rapidly, while others may take several class periods. Whatever the circumstances, individualize methods and materials as much as possible.

I. Goal: Swimming Readiness

Major Objective	*Interim Performance Objective*
1. Locker room procedures	1.1 Undress, store clothes, shower, put on and remove bathing suit, dress.
	1.1A With assistance
	1.1B Without assistance as feasible
2. Preparation for pool entry	2.1 Get ready to enter the water by sitting on deck, in wheelchair, or in harness, Figure 15.11.
	2.1A With assistance
	2.1B Without assistance as feasible

Figure 15.11. Preparation for pool entry: Sitting on deck

3. Principles of safety	3.1 Learn rules governing safety in natatorium complex.
	3.1A Locker rooms
	3.1B Pool deck
	3.1C Water

II. Goal: Water Entry and Adjustment Skills

Major Objective	*Interim Performance Objective*
1. Safe water entries and exits	1.1 Enter water appropriately (off deck, wading, in wheelchair down ramp, in harness).
	1.1A With assistance
	1.1B With assistance as necessary

Major Objective	*Interim Performance Objective*
	1.2 Leave water appropriately (climbing onto deck, wading, in wheelchair up ramp, in harness).
	1.2A With assistance
	1.2B With assistance as necessary
2. Water adjustment	2.1 Move across shallow end of pool.
	2.1A With assistance
	2.1B Without assistance as feasible
	2.2 Demonstrate proper breathing.
	2.2A Inhale and exhale while raising and lowering self in chin-deep water
	2.3 Blow bubbles.
	2.3A In water with assistance
	2.3B In water without assistance
	2.3C While moving across pool
	2.4 Hold breath while under water.
	2.4A With assistance
	2.4B Without assistance
	2.5 Bob in water while hanging onto support.
	2.5A With eyes closed, three trials
	2.5B With eyes open, three trials
	2.6 Demonstrate rhythmic breathing.
	2.6A In chest-deep water, inhale above water surface and exhale through nose and mouth beneath water surface.
	2.6Aa With rhythm
	2.6Ab To twenty repetitions
	2.7 Imitate different animals while stationary or moving above and below water surface.
	2.8 Perform exercises while supported, sitting, or standing in waist- to chest-deep water.

Major Objective	*Interim Performance Objective*

Figure 15.12. Side bender

2.8A Side bender, Figure 15.12

2.8B Alternate toe touch

2.8C Side straddle hop
    2.8Ca Arms only
    2.8Cb With legs as feasible

2.8D Neck and limb curls

III. Goal: Body Positions: Static and Dynamic

Major Objective	*Interim Performance Objective*

1. Buoyancy

1.1 Float in prone position.
    1.1A With assistance
    1.1B Without assistance as feasible

1.2 Hold prone position while being pulled through water.

1.3 Move from prone position to vertical position.
    1.3A With assistance
    1.3B Without assistance as feasible

1.4 Float in supine position, adjusting overhead arm extension as necessary.
    1.4A With assistance, Figure 15.13
    1.4B Without assistance as feasible

1.5 Hold supine position while being pulled through water.

1.6 Move from supine position to vertical position.
    1.6A With assistance
    1.6B Without assistance as feasible

Figure 15.13. Buoyancy: Supine position

2. Propulsion

2.1 Demonstrate prone glide, kick, and recovery.
    2.1A With assistance
    2.1B Without assistance as feasible

Major Objective	*Interim Performance Objective*
	2.2 Demonstrate supine glide, kick, and recovery.
	2.2A With assistance
	2.2B Without assistance as feasible
	2.3 Recover object from bottom of the pool.
	2.3A With assistance as necessary

IV. Goal: Stroke Coordination

Major Objective	*Interim Performance Objective*
1. Crawl Stroke	1.1 Demonstrate combined stroke in following sequence:
	1.1A Arm stroke in chest-deep water
	1.1B Arm stroke and prone glide
	1.1C Arm stroke, prone glide, kick
	1.1D Arm stroke, prone glide, kick, rhythmic breathing
2. Elementary back stroke	2.1 Demonstrate combined stroke in following sequence:
	2.1A Fin in chest-deep water
	2.1B Back glide and fin
	2.1C Back glide, fin, and kick

After students complete the sequences of activities described in the "Developmental Activities," they are ready to learn more advanced entry and swimming techniques. As long as the basic skills are reinforced with periodic drills, students can be expected to progress in accordance with their physical, mental, and emotional readiness.

SOURCES OF AQUATIC INFORMATION

The following list is a sampling of sources from which aquatic information can be procured.

American Canoe Association
8580 Cinderbed Road, Suite 1900
P.O. Box 1190
Newington, VA 22122
(703) 550-7523

American Red Cross
17th and D Streets, N.W.
Washington, DC 20006
(202) 737-8300

American Swimming Coaches Association
1 Hall of Fame Drive
Ft. Lauderdale, FL 33316
(305) 462-6267

Council for National Cooperation in Aquatics
901 West New York Street
Indianapolis, IN 46223
(317) 638-4238

International Swim and Diving Federation
208-3540 West 41st Avenue
Vancouver, British Columbia
Canada V6N3E6

National Collegiate Athletic Association
P.O. Box 1906
Mission, KS 66201
(913) 384-3220

National Federation of State High School Associations
11724 Plaza Circle
P.O. Box 20626
Kansas City, MO 64195
(816) 464-5400

National Safety Council
444 North Michigan Avenue
Chicago, IL 60611
(312) 527-4800

National Spa and Pool Institute
2111 Eisenhower Avenue
Alexandria, VA 22314
(703) 838-0083

National Swimming Pool Foundation
10803 Gulfdal, Suite 300
San Antonio, TX 78216
(512) 525-1227

United States Coast Guard
Commandant (G-NAB)
2100 Second Street, S.W.
Washington, DC 20593-0001
(202) 267-1060

United States Coast Guard Auxiliary
3131 Abingdon Street
Arlington, VA 22207
(703) 538-4466

United States Diving, Inc.
Pan American Plaza
201 S. Capitol Avenue, Suite 430
Indianapolis, IN 46225
(317) 237-5252

United States Swimming, Inc.
1750 East Boulder Street
Colorado Springs, CO 80909
(719) 578-4578

United States Synchronized Swimming, Inc.
Pan American Plaza
201 S. Capitol Avenue, Suite 510
Indianapolis, IN 46225
(317) 237-5700

United States Water Polo, Inc.
1750 East Boulder Street
Colorado Springs, CO 80909
(719) 632-5551

United States Yacht Racing Union
P.O. Box 209
Newport, RI 02840
(401) 849-5200

U.S. Power Squadron
4104 Monument Avenue
Richmond, VA 23230
(804) 355-6588

SUMMARY

Outings, camping, and aquatics provide opportunities for exceptional children that are not often found within ordinary classrooms and clinics. As a consequence students might be deprived of many physical, psychological, and social benefits if such activities are not available to them.

In this chapter it has been shown that while a great deal of work has yet to be done, there have been advances in the number and quality of programs offered through public and private enterprises. It is incumbent upon those who are desirous of providing diversified alternatives to seek appropriate delivery systems, whether they be through day outings, camping, or aquatic programs. Examples of options available were discussed, as was instructional methodology. Contacting various organizations whose focus is on aquatics and/or outdoor education will add to the insights the reader can employ as he/she contemplates program and delivery alternatives.

RECOMMENDED LABORATORY ASSIGNMENTS

1. Arrange to visit camps that accommodate those with disabilities. Interview the directors, review camp philosophy, and examine barrier-free facility designs.

2. Complete a practicum at a camp where you will have primary responsibility for the care of a child who has a disability.

3. Visit with various officials of your local or state American Red Cross, United States Coast Guard Auxiliary, YMCA, and YWCA to find out more about the programs they offer for physically, cognitively, emotionally, and/or socially challenged citizens.

4. Go on a hiking trip with a colleague. Record activities that would have to be modified if one with a disability was to make the same trip.

5. Complete the progression of swimming skills described in the "Developmental Activities." List assorted games and activities that could be used to reinforce these skills.

6. Simulate various disabilities (e.g., become a visually impaired person by placing a cloth over your eyes; a paraplegic, monoplegic, or amputee by immobilizing arms or legs by splinting and wrapping). Have one who has experience in adapted aquatics teach you the progression of skills outlined in this chapter.

7. Complete prerequisite courses and become certified in aquatic instructor and lifeguarding programs.

8. Complete a practicum in a developmental or mainstreamed aquatics class. Work with children who have various types of disabilities. Summarize your impressions of physiological and behavioral idiosyncrasies that require special methods and materials.

9. Add to the list of aquatic and outdoor education sources described in this chapter.

10. Review the recommended reading.

REFERENCES

Berryman, D. L. A. Logan, and D. Lander. 1971. *Enhancement of recreation service to disabled children.* Mimeographed. New York: New York University School of Education Report of the Children's Bureau Project.

Bream, C. C. 1964. Rehabilitative recreation in V.A. hospitals. *Recreation* 57: 224–26.

Etkes, A. 1989. Designing a playground that fits. *Parks and Recreation* 24(3): 30–32.

Hoge, G. W. 1990. *Attitudes, subjective norms, perceived behavioral control, intentions, and behaviors toward providing special recreation.* Doctoral dissertation. Bloomington, IN: Indiana University.

Keller, M. J., and S. D. Hudson. 1991. Theory to practice: Creating play environments for therapeutic recreation experiences. *Journal of Physical Education, Recreation and Dance* 62(4): 42–44.

Marston, R. 1969. The status of recreation for the handicapped, as related to community and voluntary agencies. *Therapeutic Recreation Journal* 3(9): 23.

Peterson, C. A. 1978. The right to risk. *Journal of Physical Education and Recreation* 49: 48.

Pullias, E. V. 1972. Better education for modern man: Outdoor education—A ray of light. *Perspectives on Outdoor Education: Readings*. Dubuque: William C. Brown.

Schleien, S. J., and M. T. Ray. 1988. *Community recreation and persons with disabilities: Strategies for integration*. Baltimore, MD: Paul H. Brookes Publishing Company.

Silson, J. E. 1959. *Recreation in hospitals: Report of a study of organized recreation programs in hospitals and the personnel conducting them*. New York: National Recreation Association.

Tilman, A. 1973. *The program book for recreation professionals*. Palo Alto, CA: Mayfield.

RECOMMENDED READINGS

American Red Cross. 1988. *Basic/emergency water safety: Instructor's manual*. Washington, DC: Author.

———. 1988. *Basic water safety*. Washington, DC: Author.

———. 1988. *Emergency water safety*. Washington, DC: Author.

———. 1988. *Infant and preschool aquatics program: Instructor's manual*. Washington, DC: Author.

———. 1988. *Infant and preschool aquatics program: Participant's guide*. Washington, DC: Author.

———. 1988. *Safety training for swim coaches*. Washington, DC: Author.

———. 1988. *Safety training for swim coaches: Instructor's manual*. Washington, DC: Author.

———. 1988. *Start sailing right*. Washington, DC: Author.

———. 1990. *Lifeguarding*. Washington, DC: Author.

———. 1991. *Basic sailing: Instructor's manual*. Washington, DC: Author.

———. 1991. *Lifeguarding: Instructor's Manual*. Washington, DC: Author.

———. 1992. *Swimming and diving*. Washington, DC: Author.

———. 1992. *Waddles presents aquacktic safety*. Washington, DC: Author.

———. 1992. *Water safety instructor's manual*. Washington, DC: Author.

Amphlet, E. M. 1969. Blind horsemanship. *New Beacon* 53: 4–6.

Bedini, L. A. 1990. Separate but equal? Segregated programming for people with disabilities. *Journal of Physical Education, Recreation and Dance* 61(8): 40–44.

Bellinger, J. 1971. Skating for the sightless. *Rehabilitation Teacher* 3: 23–25.

Bisbee, M. 1974. Over the hills and far away. *Rehabilitation Teacher* 6: 19–28.

Brannan, S. 1975. Let's go learning in the outdoors. In *Proceedings: Our New Challenge: Recreation for the Deaf-Blind*. Seattle: Northwest Regional Center for the Deaf-Blind.

Carruthers, C. P., and C. D. Hood. 1992. Alcoholics and children of alcoholics: The role of leisure in recovery. *Journal of Physical Education, Recreation and Dance* 63(4): 48–51.

Colston, L. G. 1991. The expanding role of assistive technology in therapeutic recreation. *Journal of Physical Education, Recreation and Dance* 62(4): 39–41.

Cook, B. 1986. Handicapped give high marks to the parks: IAAPA members target facilities and assistance to this $30 billion market. *Funsworld*. Pp 5–9.

Cordellos, H. 1976. *Aquatic recreation for the blind*. Washington, DC: American Alliance for Health, Physical Education, Recreation and Dance.

Crase, N. 1987. The rowcycle. *Sports N' Spokes* 13(4): 16–19.

Curren, E. A. 1971. Teaching water safety skills to blind multi-handicapped children. *Education of the Visually Handicapped* 3: 29–32.

Della Fera, M. 1969. *More than recreation skiing and cycling for the visually handicapped*. Mimeographed. Boston: Graduate School of Special Education, Boston College.

Demers, G. E. 1991. Teach students to dive without fear. *Journal of Physical Education, Recreation and Dance* 62(5): 69–71, 79.

Deyoe, D. 1976. Spelunking and climbing: Experiences for the handicapped. *Quarterly Bulletin of the Association of Medical Rehabilitation Directors and Coordinators* 15: 6.

Dougherty, C. S. 1976. Community recreation for the handicapped. In *Proceedings: The Roles of Parents, Teachers, and Administrators in Programs for the Deaf-Blind*. Sacramento: Southwestern Region Deaf-Blind Center.

Dougherty, N. J. 1990. Risk management in aquatics. Journal of Physical Education, Recreation and Dance 61(5): 46–48.

Field, D. A. 1964. Blind on horseback? Why not! *Journal of Rehabilitation* 30: 17

Flatten,. K., and B. Wilhite. 1986. REACH: Recreation and exercise activities conducted at home. *Journal of Physical Education, Recreation and Dance* 57(1): 56–58.

Gorski, R. 1982. Opening up opportunities: Adaptive equipment for recreation. *Disabled USA*. Pp. 33–37.

Griffin, D. 1965. Teaching the blind to shoot. American Rifleman 113:.52–53.

Groseck, J. B. 1967. Blind golfer's tournament. *Seer* 37: 22–26.

Grossman, A. H. 1992. Inclusion, not exclusion: Recreation service delivery to lesbian, gay, and bisexual youth. *Journal of Physical Education, Recreation and Dance* 63(4): 45–47.

Hanneman, R. 1968. Bicycles provide recreation opportunities for the blind. *New Outlook for the Blind* 62: 57–59.

Henderson, K. A., and L A. Bedini. 1991. Using volunteers in therapeutic recreation. *Journal of Physical Education, Recreation and Dance* 62(4): 49–51.

Henderson, K., and M. D. Bialeschki. 1991. Girls' and women's recreation programming—Constraints and opportunities. *Journal of Physical Education, Recreation and Dance* 62(1): 55–58.

Henderson, L. A. 1990. Deep ecology and outdoor recreation—Incompatible? *Journal of Physical Education, Recreation and Dance* 61(3): 77–80.

Howard, G. 1975. National trends in recreation for the deaf-blind. In *Proceedings: Our New Challenge: Recreation for the Deaf-Blind*. Seattle: Northwest Regional Center for Deaf-Blind.

Hyman, D. 1969. Teaching the blind student archery skills. *Journal of Health, Physical Education, and Recreation* 40: 85–86.

Langendorfer, S. J. 1990. Contemporary trends in infant/preschool aquatics—Into the 1990s and beyond. *Journal of Physical Education, Recreation and Dance* 61(5): 36–39.

Lazarus, B. I. 1991. Franchising in a park and recreation setting. *Journal of Physical Education, Recreation and Dance* 62(8): 48–50.

Leonard, C. E. 1971. Sailing blind. *Yachting* 130: 62–63, 90, 92.

Midtlyng, J. 1990. Aquatic fitness—Waves of the future. *Journal of Physical Education, Recreation and Dance* 61:(5): 41–43.

———. 1992. Emergence of the aquatic profession in the year 2000. *Journal of Physical Education, Recreation and Dance* 63(5): 28–29.

Mitten, D. 1992. Empowering girls and women in the outdoors. *Journal of Physical Education, Recreation and Dance* 63(2): 56–60.

Reiser, V. C. 1991. Aquatic therapy: Wave of the past and the future. *Aqua Notes* 11:2, 5.

Robinson, J., and A. D. Fox. 1987. *Scuba diving with disabilities*. Champaign, IL: Human Kinetics.

Schleien, S. J., L. A. Heyne, J. E. Rynders, and L. H. McAvoy. 1990. Equity and excellence: Serving all children in community recreation. *Journal of Physical Education, Recreation and Dance* 61(8): 45–48.

Shirer, C. 1990. The whys and hows of a climbing conditioning class. *Journal of Physical Education, Recreation and Dance* 62(7): 33–37.

Smith, M. L. 1990. Swimming orientation for preschoolers. *Journal of Physical Education, Recreation and Dance* 61(1): 69–70.

Thompson, D. 1991. Safe playground surfaces: What should be used under playground equipment? *Journal of Physical Education, Recreation and Dance* 62(9): 74–75.

Weidow, G., and B. Kelly. 1991. A decision-making model for recreation program prioritization. *Journal of Physical Education, Recreation and Dance* 62(8): 50–51.

Young Men's Christian Association. 1987. *Aquatics for special populations*. Champaign: IL: Human Kinetics.

CHAPTER 16

Special Olympics and Wheelchair Athletic Programs

Objectives

After reading this chapter, you should be able to

- **Identify and discuss values intrinsic in athletic competition for those who are mentally or physically challenged.**
- **Discuss organizational structure of Special Olympics.**
- **Describe the *General Rules* and *Official Sports Rules* of Special Olympics International.**
- **Identify the sports sponsored by Special Olympics.**
- **Know the organizational structure underlying wheelchair athletic programs.**
- **Describe the system of medical classification recommended for use with wheelchair athletes when competing in formal contests against each other.**

INTRODUCTION

The value of competitive athletics has been affirmed and belittled throughout various periods of our history. Opposition to competitive sports has been based upon such things as:

1. Lack of concern for the physiopsychic readiness levels of those enticed to compete, particularly at the elementary and the junior high school levels
2. Expense, especially if there is a lack of dollars for other phases of the educational program within the school system
3. Exploitation of student athletes by the media and those with professional athletic interests

---

KEY TERMS

application for participation	paraplegia
cognitive development	physical development
General Rules	quadriplegia
hemiplegia	release form
medical classification	social development
monoplegia	Special Olymoics
National Wheelchair Games	Unified Sports
Official Sports Rules	volunteers
official summer sports	Wheelchair athletic programs
official winter sports	

---

4. Seasons that are too long preventing participants from engaging in a new sport interest at the start of its new season
5. Violence

While these arguments are sometimes valid, each can be eliminated if competitive programs are administered and supported with intelligence and integrity.

EDUCATIONAL VALUE

The educational value of competitive athletics is the contribution they can make to a student's physical, cognitive, social, and emotional growth and maintenance and to the spirit that can emerge in team members and supporters. Although each of these benefits can accrue from other academic experiences, healthy athletic competition can increase and enrich them.

Physical Development

Through regular participation in supervised practice and competitive sessions much improvement in basic body structure and function can occur. Agility, balance, coordination and (in particular) strength, muscular and cardiovascular endurance, and flexibility increase. The extent of improvement depends of course on the sport and the effort expended by the athlete. For example, among track and field events greater cardiovascular development and maintenance will result from participation in distance events than in shot put. Improvements in agility, balance, and coordination also depend on the requirements of the sport in which the student participates. Further the more the student practices correctly, the more he/she will improve.

Cognitive Development

As participation in athletic competition increases, greater opportunities occur for

...critical and constructive thinking in recognizing issues and making choices within a framework of social and moral standards (Shea and Wieman 1967).

Some time ago Oberteuffer (1952) offered the following reflection on competitive sports:

Depending upon the quality of leadership, opportunities are afforded to solve problems, to think for oneself, to reflect on past experiences, to reckon with consequences, to understand relationships, to act independently, to plan a course of action, to undertake a project, to summarize and conclude. Thus is aided the cultivation of a capacity to do reflective thinking.

Cognition skills are enhanced through repetition and transfer. By thinking out strategies and learning rules and nomenclature, processing abilities are being enriched.

Social Development
Participation in competitive athletic programs enables students to share in an effort toward a common goal. This is particularly so in team sports because team members must depend on each other to contribute skill and judgment toward the attainment of agreed-upon objectives. The understanding and acceptance of others for the uniqueness of the talents that they can offer is the basis for cooperation and constitutes the ultimate success of the group. In 1962 the American Alliance for Health, Physical Education and Recreation issued a platform statement which read in part,

> The participant in…athletics, in close association with others, gains the experiences which are identical with those required for an understanding of democracy and achieves the most important outcome which sports and games provides, namely, socialization.

Today and for whatever future exists, athletics can play a significant role in the socialization process.

Emotional Development
Through the avenue of competitive athletics, opportunities are provided for participants to learn a bit about self-actualization. As pointed out by Miller and McCormick (1991), the sport arena is well suited for educating participants on how to cope with their feelings. The ability to win and lose graciously is tested time and time again. Acceptance of the fact that one cannot win in every bout of competition will help the students to cope with the stresses of life. Participants will learn that the most that can be expected is that they give their maximum effort in whatever they attempt.

For these reasons and more, competitive athletic programs have a place in the education process. This is true for all students—"normal" or "exceptional."

COMPETITION FOR THE DISABLED

Despite some of the concerns expressed in the first paragraph of this chapter, I have found through coaching experiences in junior high school, high school, and college, as well as **Special Olympics** and **Wheelchair athletic programs**, that it is in competitive programs for those who are mentally or physically challenged that the organizational and administrative motives appear to be the purest. At no time have I been witness to a lack of concern for physiopsychic readiness, usage of funds so as to impede the progress of other programs, exploitation of participants, seasons that are too long, or violence among competitors or fans. In competitive sport programs for those with disabilities the participants are involved because of the values intrinsic to participation for its own sake—in particular the joy of making an effort. This also appears to be the essence of the attitudes held by those who are assuming responsibility for delivering these opportunities.

Special Olympics Programs

In 1968, the Joseph P. Kennedy, Jr. Foundation created Special Olympics—a sports training and athletic competition program for mentally challenged individuals. Now international in scope, athletes in over ninety nations are involved in competition. In 1991 the International Special Olympics Games in Minneapolis/St. Paul, Minnesota is said to have attracted approximately six thousand participants from around the world (New Hampshire Special Olympics 1991).

The Special Olympics program provides year-round training, competition, and recreation experiences for those who are eight years of age or older. Though there is no upper age limit, participants can have intelligence quotients no greater than 80. When classified for competition, both age and previous performance scores are used as criteria.

In order to provide the most beneficial experiences for athletes with mental retardation, Special Olympics (worldwide) functions in accordance with operating policies enforced by the **General Rules** and **Official Sports Rules** of the organization (Special Olympics International 1990).

1. Special Olympics incorporates universal values that transcend all boundaries of geography, nationality, political philosophy, gender, age, race, or religion.
2. Participation in Special Olympics training programs and competitive events is open to all people with mental retardation who are at least eight years old, regardless of the degree of their disability. Individuals with other disabilities are welcomed if they are also persons with mental retardation.
3. Special Olympics provides full participation for every athlete regardless of his/her economic circumstances.
4. Special Olympics believes that the athlete is all-important. Developing the physical, social, psychological, intellectual, and spiritual qualities of the participants underlies every effort made by the Special Olympics program.
5. Special Olympics encourages coaches and family members of athletes to make every effort to encourage Special Olympics athletes to reach their highest level of athletic achievement in a particular sport and to provide opportunities for them to do so.
6. Comprehensive, year-round sports training is available to every Special Olympics athlete, conducted by well-qualified coaches in accordance with the standardized sports rules formulated and adopted by Special Olympics International. Every athlete who competes in a Special Olympics sport will have been trained in that sport.*
7. Every Special Olympics program includes a variety of sports events and activities that are appropriate to the age and ability of each athlete. The program may also include **Unified Sports**** training and competition in which

---

* A minimum of eight weeks of training is recommended prior to competition.
** Comprised of equal numbers of Special Olympics Athletes and non-Special Olympians, Special Olympics Unified Sports Programs can be conducted in a variety of settings, including community or church sports programs, such as adult softball leagues or YMCA/YWCA bowling leagues; after school leagues at the junior or senior high school levels; independent leagues sponsored by business or civic groups.

individuals with and without mental retardation participate together on teams, and the Motor Activities Training Program for individuals with such severe mental retardation that they cannot benefit from standard Special Olympics training and competition programs.

8. Special Olympics encourages qualified athletes to participate in school and community programs where they can train and compete in regular sports activities. The athletes may at this point wish to leave Special Olympics or continue to take part in Special Olympics activities. The decision rests with the athlete.

9. Special Olympics fully supports the concept of integrating sports events for athletes with mental retardation with events conducted by sports organizations for individuals without mental retardation. The Special Olympics athletes may participate in the same heats as all athletes or in heats organized specifically for them. Such integration must offer realistic opportunities for athletes to train and successfully compete. Thus Special Olympics personnel should work to create a feasible format for these integrated activities.

10. Special Olympics organizes training and competition so as to have the highest possible quality in facilities, administration, training, coaching, officiating, events, equipment, athletic attire, etc.

11. Special Olympics believes that every athlete deserves an equal chance to excel during competition. Thus each competition division within a given event is structured so that every athlete/team in the division has a reasonable chance to win, Figure 16.1. This is done by placing athletes/teams in divisions according to accurate records of previous performance or trial heats and, when relevant, grouping by age and gender.

12. Special Olympics seeks to uphold the spirit of sportsmanship and love of participation for their own sake. Special Olympics believes that every athlete should participate to his/her fullest potential. This means that in team sports each coach will offer every athlete the opportunity to play in each game. This also means that each Games and Tournament should offer as many sports as possible, with events for athletes of all ability levels. Special Olympics promotes this philosophy in the training of its coaches and officials.

13. All Special Olympics Games and competitions—at the local, state, national and international levels—reflect the values, standards, traditions, ceremonies, and activities embodied in the ancient and modern Olympic movement, broadened and enriched to celebrate the moral and spiritual qualities of persons with mental retardation so as to enhance their dignity and self-esteem.

14. At every Awards Ceremony, in addition to the traditional medals for first, second and third places, athletes finishing from fourth place to eighth place are presented a suitable place ribbon with appropriate ceremony. An athlete who is disqualified or does not finish an event shall be given a participation ribbon.

15. Special Olympics training and competition activities take place in public, with every effort made to attract spectators and generate coverage by the news media, to enable athletes with mental retardation to demonstrate the special qualities of the human spirit in which they excel—skill, courage, sharing, and joy.

Figure 16.1. A proud Olympian displaying his silver medal. *Courtesy of New Hampshire Special Olympics.*

16. Special Olympics seeks to offer every athlete at least two opportunities annually to participate in locally-based competitions in each sport in which he/she is interested. These activities should include competitions with teams or individuals other than those with whom the athlete trains. In addition, in order to give athletes broader opportunities, area/provincial, regional, national, and international competitions as well as tournaments are organized within available resources. These types of competitions are open to athletes representing the full range of skill levels.

17. Special Olympics is not designed to train elite athletes exclusively, nor to bar athletes from competition if they are highly skilled. Fair and equitable methods are used to select athletes for participation in nonlocal competition so that every athlete has an equal opportunity to participate in each competition at his/her skill level.

18. In some countries with newly created Special Olympics programs it may not be possible, due to economic or other circumstances, to organize nationwide games. In this case Special Olympics International (SOI) may authorize such programs to focus on area or regional games with the goal of increasing public awareness of the capabilities of individuals with mental retardation.

19. Although Special Olympics is primarily and essentially a program of sports training and competition, efforts are made to offer or to cooperate with others who offer (as an integral part of Special Olympics Games) a full range of artistic, social, and cultural experiences. This includes dances, art exhibits, concerts, visits to historic sites, clinics, theatrical and motion picture performances, and similar activities.

20. All Special Olympics training and competition programs are to be conducted under the auspices of an organization specifically accredited and sanctioned by Special Olympics International (SOI) to conduct Special Olympics programs.

21. To the greatest extent possible, Special Olympics activities will be organized by and involve local **volunteers** (from school and college age individuals to senior citizens) in order to create opportunities for public understanding of and participation with people with mental retardation.

22. The families of Special Olympics athletes are encouraged to play an active role in their community Special Olympics program, to share in the training of their athletes, and to assist in the public education effort needed to create greater understanding of the emotional, physical, social, and spiritual needs of people with mental retardation and their families.

23. Special Olympics encourages community, state, and national sports programs—both professional and amateur—to include demonstrations by Special Olympics athletes as part of their major events.

24. Special Olympics recognizes the contributions and encourages the participation of other organizations—such as schools, parks and recreation departments and independent living centers—that conduct sports training for individuals with mental retardation. Accredited Special Olympics programs should encourage such organizations to train athletes in accordance with Special Olympics rules to facilitate the athletes' participation in Special Olympics competition.

A significant feature of Special Olympics is that there is a core of volunteers who, working under the guidance of a state director and his/her board, participate at various committee levels within the organization. Included among the groups that serve as the foundation for program operations are

1. Organization and administration
2. Training
3. Competition and games
4. Outreach
5. Family involvement
6. Finance
7. Fund raising
8. Public relations/Public education

While there is some variance between states as to the number of sports offered throughout the year, the following represents a roster of those most frequently made available (New Hampshire Special Olympics, 1992)

Official Summer Sports
Aquatics (swimming and diving)
Basketball

Candlepin bowling
Unified team candlepin bowling
Tenpin bowling
Unified team tenpin bowling
Cycling
Equestrian
Gymnastics
Team handball
Track and field
Powerlifting
Team soccer
Unified softball
Tennis
Unified volleyball

Official Winter Sports
Poly hockey
Freestyle skating
Speed skating
Alpine skiing (downhill)
Nordic skiing (cross country)

To access any of these programs, a completed **application for participation** must be submitted (Figure 16.2) along with a **release form** completed by the adult athlete or—in the case of a minor—his or her parent or guardian, Figure 16.3.

Special Olympics programs provide a very important service for many of our citizens, not only because of the benefits gained by the participating athletes themselves, but also because of the insights gained by the general public. There has been a raising of consciousness on the part of many who thought that those who were mentally challenged could not profit from sport participation. The successful experiences in Special Olympics do carry over into the classroom, home, and workplace. The research of Orelove, Wehman, and Wood (1982), Sherrill (1986) and Ballard and Calhoun (1991) attests to this fact.

Much of the success of these programs may rest with the principle that it is the effort, not winning, that represents the essence of competition.

The Special Olympics Oath
"Let Me Win, But If I Cannot Win, Let Me Be Brave In The Attempt."

Courtesy of New Hampshire Special Olympics, 603 El Street, Suite 101, Manchester, NH 03101-2508.

APPLICATION FOR PARTICIPATION IN SPECIAL OLYMPICS

_____
Agency/School

ATHLETE INFORMATION

NAME		SEX	DATE OF BIRTH
			Day / Month / Year
ADDRESS		☐ M ☐ F	
	PHONE NO. ( ) .		
NAME OF PARENT OR GUARDIAN			
ADDRESS			
	PHONE NO. ( ) .		

EMERGENCY INFORMATION

PERSON TO BE CONTACTED IN CASE OF EMERGENCY IF OTHER THAN PARENT OR GUARDIAN	
ADDRESS	
	PHONE NO. ( ) .

HEALTH AND ACCIDENT INSURANCE INFORMATION

COMPANY NAME	
POLICY NUMBER	

HEALTH INFORMATION

	CHECK ONE		COMMENTS
DOWN SYNDROME	☐ YES	☐ NO	
Atlanto-axial Instability by X-Ray Evaluation: If X-Ray positive check YES · If X-Ray negative check NO · If no X-Ray check (R)	☐ YES ☐ NO	☐ R	
HISTORY OF:			
DIABETES	☐ YES	☐ NO	
HEART PROBLEMS/BLOOD PRESSURE ELEVATION	☐ YES	☐ NO	
SEIZURES	☐ YES	☐ NO	
VISION PROBLEMS AND/OR VISION LESS THAN 20/20 IN ONE OR BOTH EYES	☐ YES	☐ NO	
HEARING AID/HEARING PROBLEMS	☐ YES	☐ NO	
MOTOR IMPAIRMENT REQUIRING SPECIAL EQUIPMENT	☐ YES	☐ NO	
BLEEDING PROBLEM	☐ YES	☐ NO	
HEAD INJURY/HISTORY OF CONCUSSION	☐ YES	☐ NO	
HEARING PROBLEMS	☐ YES	☐ NO	
FAINTING SPELLS	☐ YES	☐ NO	
HEAT ILLNESS OR COLD INJURY	☐ YES	☐ NO	
HERNIA OR ABSENCE OF 1 TESTICLE	☐ YES	☐ NO	
RECENT CONTAGIOUS DISEASE OR HEPATITIS	☐ YES	☐ NO	
KIDNEY PROBLEMS OR LOSS OF FUNCTION IN ONE KIDNEY	☐ YES	☐ NO	
PREGNANCY	☐ YES	☐ NO	
BONE OR JOINT PROBLEMS	☐ YES	☐ NO	
CONTACT LENS/GLASSES	☐ YES	☐ NO	
DENTURES/FALSE TEETH	☐ YES	☐ NO	
EMOTIONAL PROBLEMS	☐ YES	☐ NO	
SPECIAL DIET NEEDS	☐ YES	☐ NO	
OTHER	☐ YES	☐ NO	

MEDICATIONS

MEDICATION NAME	AMOUNT	TIME	DATE PRESCRIBED

ALLERGIES TO MEDICATION	

IMMUNIZATIONS

TETANUS	☐ YES	☐ NO	DATE OF LAST TETANUS SHOT / /	POLIO	☐ YES	☐ NO

SIGNATURE OF PERSON WHO COMPLETED HEALTH INFORMATION (NORMALLY SIGNED BY PARENT, GUARDIAN, OR ADULT ATHLETE)

SIGNATURE	DATE / /

IF THERE IS ANY SIGNIFICANT CHANGE IN THE ATHLETE'S HEALTH THE ATHLETE'S CONDITION SHOULD BE REVIEWED BY A PHYSICIAN BEFORE FURTHER PARTICIPATION.

MEDICAL CERTIFICATION

NOTICE TO PHYSICIAN: If the athlete has Down Syndrome, Special Olympics requires that the athlete have a full radiological examination establishing the absence of Atlanto-axial Instability before he/she may participate in sports or events which, by their nature, may result in hyper-extension, radical flexion or direct pressure on the neck or upper spine. The sports and events for which such a radiological examination is required are equestrian sports, gymnastics, diving, pentathlon, butterfly stroke, diving starts in swimming, high jump, alpine skiing and soccer.

CHECK ☐ I have reviewed the above health information on and examined the athlete named in the application, and certify there is no medical evidence available to me which would preclude the athlete's participation in Special Olympics.

RESTRICTIONS	
PHYSICIAN'S NAME	
PHYSICIAN'S SIGNATURE	DATE / /
ADDRESS	
	PHONE NO. ( ) .

Created by The Joseph P. Kennedy, Jr. Foundation for the Benefit of Citizens with Mental Retardation.

White Copy: STATE OFFICE   Yellow Copy: AREA DIRECTOR   Pink Copy: COACH

Figure 16.2. Special Olympics application form. *Courtesy of New Hampshire Special Olympics.*

OFFICIAL SPECIAL OLYMPICS RELEASE FORM

RELEASE TO BE COMPLETED BY
ADULT ATHLETE

I, _____ am at least 18 years old and have submitted the attached application for participation in Special Olympics.

I represent and warrant that, to the best of my knowledge and belief, I am physically and mentally able to participate in Special Olympics activities. I also represent that a licensed physician has reviewed the health information contained in my application and has certified, based on an independent medical examination, that there is no medical evidence which would preclude me from participating in Special Olympics. I understand that if I have Down Syndrome, I cannot participate in sports or events which by their nature result in hyper-extension, radical flexion or direct pressure on my neck or upper spine unless I have had a full radiological examination which establishes the absence of Atlanto-axial Instability. I am aware that I must have this radiological examination before I can participate in equestrian sports, gymnastics, diving, pentathlon, butterfly stroke, diving starts in swimming, high jump, alpine skiing, and soccer.

Special Olympics has my permission, (both during and anytime after), to use my likeness, name, voice, or words in either television, radio, film, newspapers, magazines, and other media, and in any form, for the purpose of advertising or communicating the purposes and activities of Special Olympics and/or applying for funds to support those purposes and activities.

If, during my participation in Special Olympics activities, I should need emergency medical treatment, and I am not able to give my consent or make my own arrangements for that treatment because of my injuries, I authorize Special Olympics to take whatever measures are necessary to protect my health and well-being, including, if necessary, hospitalization.

I, the athlete named above, have read this paper and fully understand the provisions of the release that I am signing. I understand that by signing this paper, I am saying that I agree to the provisions of this release.

_____   _____
Signature of Adult Athlete   Date

I hereby certify that I have reviewed this release with the athlete whose signature appears above. I am satisfied based on that review that the athlete understands this release and has agreed to its terms.

Name (Print): _____

Relationship to athlete: _____
                                        (e.g. family member, teacher, coach etc.)

RELEASE TO BE COMPLETED BY
PARENT OR GUARDIAN OF MINOR ATHLETE

I am the parent/guardian of_____ , the minor athlete, on whose behalf I have submitted the attached application for participation in Special Olympics. I hereby represent that the athlete has my permission to participate in Special Olympics activities.

I further represent and warrant that to the best of my knowledge and belief, the athlete is physically and mentally able to participate in Special Olympics. With my approval, a licensed physician has reviewed the health information set forth in the athlete's application, and has certified based on an independent medical examination that there is no medical evidence which would preclude the athlete's participation. I understand that if the athlete has Down Syndrome, he/she cannot participate in sports or events which by their nature result in hyper-extension, radical flexion or direct pressure on the neck or upper spine, unless a full radiological examination establishes the absence of Atlanto-axial Instability. I am aware that the sports and events for which this radiological examination is required are equestrian sports, gymnastics, diving, pentathlon, butterfly stroke, diving starts in swimming, high jump, alpine skiing, and soccer.

In permitting the athlete to participate, I am specifically granting my permission, (both during and anytime after), to Special Olympics to use the athlete's likeness, name, voice and words in television, radio, film, newspapers, magazines and other media, and in any form, for the purpose of advertising or communicating the purposes and activities of Special Olympics and/or applying for funds to support those purposes and activities.

If a medical emergency should arise during the athlete's participation in any Special Olympics activities, at a time when I am not personally present so as to be consulted regarding the athlete's care, I hereby authorize Special Olympics, on my behalf, to take whatever measures are necessary to ensure that the athlete is provided with any emergency medical treatment, including hospitalization, which Special Olympics deems advisable in order to protect the athlete's health and well-being.

I am the parent (guardian) of the athlete named in this application. I have read and fully understand the provisions of the above release, and have explained these provisions to the athlete. Through my signature on this release form, I am agreeing to the above provisions on my own behalf and on the behalf of the athlete named above.

I hereby give my permission for the athlete named above to participate in Special Olympics games, recreation programs, and physical activity programs.

_____   _____
Signature of Parent/Guardian   Date

Created by The Joseph P. Kennedy Foundation for the Benefit of Citizens with Mental Retardation.

White Copy: STATE OFFICE   Yellow Copy: AREA DIRECTOR   Pink Copy: COACH

Figure 16.3. Special Olympics release form. *Courtesy of New Hampshire Special Olympics.*

In addition to Special Olympic programs, there are other sport and training opportunities available for interested athletes.

Wheelchair Programs

The impetus for wheelchair sports in the United States came from paraplegic* veterans of World War II seeking an outlet for their restrained energies. In 1946, wheelchair basketball teams were formed that adapted the rules of regulation basketball to fit their own needs. These veterans were soon joined by persons disabled due to accidental leg amputations, poliomyelitis paralysis, spina bifida, and other assorted neurological and musculoskeletal disorders.

As a result of meetings between Dr. Ludwig Guttman, former Director of the Spinal Injuries Center in Stoke Mandeville, England (who was in the process of introducing new adaptations of sports for wheelchair competition) and Benjamin Lipton, Director of the Bulova School of Watchmaking (a vocationally oriented rehabilitation center in New York), the first **National Wheelchair Games** were organized (Boucher 1976). The year was 1957, and the events included archery, the javelin throw, the shot put, table tennis, 60- and 100-yard wheelchair dashes, and 240- and 400-yard relays. Since that time, basketball, bowling, discuss throwing, long-distance racing, shooting, snooker, swimming, weightlifting, the wheelchair slalom, the pentathlon, and other events have been added.

Although the first National Wheelchair Games had but sixty-three competitors, participants in regional and national events now number in the thousands. With the increase in interest and the resultant impossibility of accommodating these numbers during any single event, regional qualification meets were established. There are now ten regional sports groups under the auspices of the National Wheelchair Athletic Association (NWAA) that monitor regional competition.

1. Appalachian Wheelchair Athletic Association
2. Dixie Wheelchair Athletic Association
3. Far West Wheelchair Athletic Association
4. Hawaii Wheelchair Athletic Association
5. Michigan Wheelchair Athletic Association
6. Mid-Atlantic Wheelchair Athletic Association
7. New England Wheelchair Athletic Association
8. North Central Wheelchair Athletic Association
9. Southwest Wheelchair Athletic Association
10. Tri-State Wheelchair Athletic Association

In order to provide direction and influence over the many activities being endorsed by the NWAA, national sport governing bodies have emerged. At present, there are nine such groups.

1. American Wheelchair Archers Association
2. American Wheelchair Table Tennis Association

---

* **Paraplegia** means absence of complete function in parallel limbs, ordinarily both legs. **Hemiplegia** is impairment of two limbs on the same side of the body. **Monoplegia** is impairment of a single limb. **Quadriplegia** is the absence of complete function in all limbs.

3. National Federation for Wheelchair Tennis
4. National Wheelchair Basketball Association
5. National Wheelchair Shooting Federation
6. United States Quad Rugby Association
7. United States Wheelchair Swimming Association
8. United States Wheelchair Weightlifting Federation
9. Wheelchair Athletics of the USA

With interest growing at it is, it should be apparent to the reader that other sport governing bodies are likely to surface (National Wheelchair Athletic Association 1992).

In the quest to provide fairness in competition, it became necessary to classify the wheelchair athletes by the sites of their spinal cord lesions. Since existing systems of classification are based upon involvement of spinal cord levels or segmental nerve supply to muscles (Table 16.1), careful muscle examination should be made to determine the level of motor loss. Only then, according to McCann (1990), can a reliable assessment and an appropriate classification be made for each athlete.

While these **medical classifications** are helpful in establishing the point of motor loss, the demands of specific sport performance have not been generally taken into account when determining which group of athletes would be most equitably matched for competition. New international functional classification systems help to group athletes with similar function who may have varying physical anomalies. Since the Paralympic Games in 1988 many changes have been introduced, including making the classification of an athlete more sport specific (National Wheelchair Athletic Association 1992).

With regard to wheelchair basketball, for example, the following applies:

Player classification shall have point values as follows:

Class 1   1–1.5 points
Class 2   2–2.5 points
Class 3   3–3.5 points
Class 4   4 points

Definition of Classes:

Class 1   Functional potential corresponding to spinal lesion originating at T8 (eighth thoracic cord level) and above
Class 2   Functional potential corresponding to spinal cord lesion originating from T9 (ninth thoracic cord level) to L2 (second lumbar cord level)
Class 3   Functional potential corresponding to spinal cord lesion originating from L3 (third lumbar cord level) to L5 (fifth lumbar cord level)
Class 4   Functional potential corresponding to spinal cord lesion originating from S1 (first sacral cord level) to S2 (second sacralcord level).

At no time during a game shall a team have players participating whose total point value exceeds 13.5 points.

Although significant effort has been made to make the International Classification System precise, further study and experience will aid immeasurably in improving the criteria for competitive groupings. Fair competition dictates that the winner within a classification be the one who has demonstrated the greatest amount of skill and effort, not the one who has better use of muscle tissue. In addition caution should be exercised to ensure that the joy of competition is not sacrificed.

TABLE 16.1

Spinal Cord Simulation

The Spinal Cord	Cord Level
	Eight cervical (C) cord levels supply neck, shoulder girdle, arms, and diaphragm
	Twelve thoracic (T) (dorsal) cord levels supply upper trunk extension, intercostal muscles, and abdominal muscles
	Five lumbar (L) cord levels supply lower extremeties and lower back muscles
	Five sacral (S) cord levels supply leg muscles (S_1) and bladder muscles

Source: Adapted from McCann, B. C. Classification of the wheelchair athlete: A medical viewpoint (Mimeographed).

Note: Nerve roots emerge from each of these levels, supplying voluntary muscle power to muscles in the neck, trunk, and limbs in a clearly defined and consistent pattern. A careful muscle examination enables the examiner to determine the level of motor loss.

Local schools and communities interested in providing integrated opportunities for those with and without functional and structural disabilities need not be bound by the classification distinctions that have been presented in this section. These classification provisions are intended to serve physically challenged athletes when they are competing against each other in formal competition. At the same time, however, those charged with

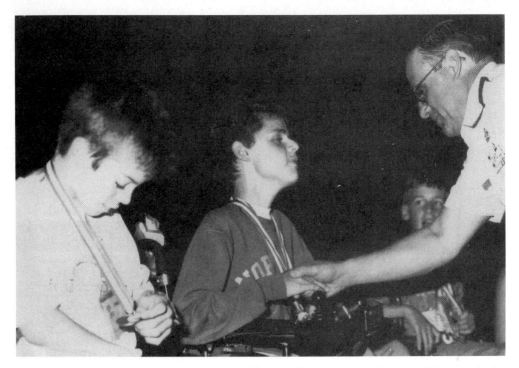

Figure 16.4. Winners of a competitive wheelchair athletic activity. *Courtesy of New Hampshire Special Olympics.*

organizing unified programs within local districts would be wise to consult sport rule references published by the National Wheelchair Athletic Association. Much of what is said about game rules themselves can be applied to mainstreamed settings.

As we read newspapers, listen to the radio, or watch television, we become increasingly aware that more and more wheelchair athletes are participating in competition for its own sake. Informal basketball leagues, wheelchair golf, and marathons are just a few of the sports in which wheelchair athletes are participating, Figure 16.4.

SUMMARY

Special Olympic and Wheelchair Athletic programs are viable adjuncts to developmental and general physical education programs currently underway within the public schools. They can also serve those who seek enrichment through recreational and competitive experiences within other settings. In this instance, there are classification systems designed to help ensure equitable competition.

The concept of providing educationally sound athletic and recreational programs is not new. To the mentally and physically challenged these programs can be a source of joy and fulfillment not attainable in most other circumstances. For this reason practitioners and theorists should do all they can to encourage athletic involvement by those in our society who have disabilities.

RECOMMENDED LABORATORY ASSIGNMENTS

1. Interview district and local school administrative officials to discover their perceptions of the educational value of competitive athletic programs.
2. Meet with personnel in local, state, and regional agencies who are responsible for wheelchair and Special Olympics programs. Find out how you might become involved as a volunteer.
3. Observe scheduled competitive and recreational activities for those who are mentally and physically and mentally disabled.
4. Play basketball and perform selected track and field activities in a wheelchair to find out what variables affect performance.
5. Arrange to be present when physicians are testing and classifying wheelchair athletes for participation in competition sponsored by the National Wheelchair Athletic Association.
6. Meet with wheelchair athletes to discuss their attitudes regarding participation in competitive athletics. Do the same with Special Olympians.
7. Visit a rehabilitation center to discuss with the staff the role that competitive and recreational activities can play in the overall rehabilitation process.
8. Serve as a volunteer coach or committee member for a local Special Olympics program.
9. Attend regional, state, national, or international competitive programs to see the skill and competitive spirit revealed by those who are mentally or physically challenged.
10. Write to the Joseph P. Kennedy, Jr. Foundation and the National Wheelchair Athletic Association and request information about their program offerings.
11. Review the recommended readings.

REFERENCES

American Alliance for Health, Physical Education, and Recreation. 1962. Athletics in education: A platform statement. *Journal of Health, Physical Education, and Recreation* 33: 24–27, 59.

Ballard, J. K., and M. L. Calhoun. 1991. Special Olympics: Opportunities to learn. *Teaching Exceptional Children* 24(1): 20–23.

Boucher, J. P. 1976. *Wheelchair athletics.* Paper presented before the Eastern District Association of the American Alliance for Health, Physical Education, and Recreation's 53rd Annual Convention, March 7–10, 1976, Mt. Pocono, PA.

McCann, B. C. (Undated). *Classification of the wheelchair athlete: A medical viewpoint.* (Mimeographed). Providence: Department of Rehabilitation Medicine, Rhode Island Hospital.

McCann, B. C. 1990. *Functional classification: The real scoop.* Colorado Springs, CO: National Wheelchair Athletic Association.

Miller, S., and J. McCormick. 1991. Stress: Teaching children to cope. *Journal of Physical Education, Recreation and Dance* 62(2): 53–54.

National Wheelchair Athletic Association. (Winter 1992). *Classification.* (Mimeographed). Colorado Springs, CO: Author.

National Wheelchair Athletic Association. (Summer 1992). National governing bodies. *National Wheelchair Athletic Association Newsletter.* P. 8.

New Hampshire Special Olympics. 1991. The 1991 international Special Olympics summer games. *New Hampshire Special Olympics Newsletter* 3(1): 1.

New Hampshire Special Olympics. 1992. NHSO Sports. *New Hampshire Special Olympics Newsletter* 4(1): 4.

Oberteuffer, D. 1952. Intercollegiate football. *College Physical Education Association Proceedings*. Pp. 12–18.

Ortlove, F. P., P. Wehman, and J. Wood. 1982. An evaluation review of Special Olympics: Implications for community integration. *Education and Training of the Mentally Retarded* 17: 325–329.

Shea, E. J., and E. Wieman. 1967. *Administrative policies for intercollegiate athletics.* Springfield, IL: Charles C. Thomas.

Sherrill, C. 1986. *Adapted physical education and recreation.* 3d ed. Dubuque, IA: William C. Brown.

Special Olympics International. 1990. *Official Special Olympics gneral rules.* Washington, DC: Author.

RECOMMENDED READINGS

American Alliance for Health, Physical Education, and Recreation; The Joseph P. Kennedy, Jr. Foundation; and Julian U. Stein. 1972. *Programs for the handicapped, Special Olympics Instructional Manual: From beginners to champions.* Washington, DC: The Alliance and the Kennedy Foundation.

Brunner, R., and D. Hill. 1992. Using learning styles research in coaching. *Journal of Physical Education, Recreation and Dance* 63(4): 26–28, 61–62.

Curtis, K. (Undated). *International functional classification systems.* (Mimeographed). Colorado Springs, CO; National Wheelchair Athletic Association.

Dahlgran, W. J., S. Boreskie, M. Dowds, J. B. Mactavish, and E. J. Watkinson. 1991. The medallion program: Using the generic sport model to train athletes with mental disabilities. *Journal of Physical Education, Recreation and Dance* 62(9): 67–73.

DePauw, K. P. 1990. PE and sport for disabled individuals in the United States. *Journal of Physical Education, Recreation and Dance* 61(2): 53–57.

Joseph P. Kennedy, Jr. Foundation. 1989. *Special Olympics motor activities: Training program.* Washington, DC: Special Olympics, Incorporated.

Lindstrom, H. 1992. Integration of sport for athletes with disabilities into sport programmes for abled-bodied athletes. *Palaestra* 8(3): 28–32, 58–59.

Luttrell, W. L., and J. M. Dunn. 1992. The level of happiness, satisfaction, and perceived importance of athletic competition of winners and losers in Special Olympics. *Research Quarterly for Exercise and Sport Supplement* 63(1): A-91–92.

Matthews, P. R. 1979. The frequency with which the mentally retarded participate in recreation activities. *Research Quarterly* 50: 71–79.

Michener, J. A. 1976. *Sports in America.* New York: Random House.

National Wheelchair Athletic Association. 1992. *Official rulebook.* Colorado Springs, CO: Author.

Paciorek, M. J. 1993. Technology only a part of the story as world records fall. *Palaestra* 9(2): 14–17.

Parker, A. W., R. Bronks, and C. W. Snyder. Walking patterns in Down's syndrome. *Journal of Mental Deficiency Research* 30(4): 317–30.

Perez, F. V., and T. Gutierrez. 1979. Participation for the handicapped. *Journal of Physical Education and Recreation* 50:101–2.

Poretta, D. L. , W. Moore, and C. Sappenfield. 1992. Situational anxiety in special olympics athletes. *Palaestra* 8(3): 46–50.

Weisz, J. R. 1981. Effects of the "mentally retarded label" on adult judgements about child failure. *Journal of Abnormal Psychology* 90(4): 371–74.

Wilkerson, M., and R. A. Dodder. 1979. What does sport do for people? *Journal of Physical Education and Recreation* 50: 50–51.

CHAPTER 17

Making Your Own Supplies and Equipment

Objectives

After reading this chapter, you should be able to

- Discuss the construction and use of assistive devices.
- Discuss the construction of low-cost game equipment.
- Describe procedures for constructing and using recreational and developmental equipment.
- Discuss recycling of selected throwaway items for use in general and developmental physical education activity programs.

INTRODUCTION

Because of limited budgets and the rising costs of supplies and equipment, physical education practitioners must consider alternative plans for providing items necessary for the conduct of developmental and general physical education programs. Most administrative decisions regarding physical education programs relate to financial considerations. If we do not plan alternative ways to acquire materials for classes and if it is claimed that some of these classes cannot be taught as they should be without these materials, administrators may be tempted, if not forced, to eliminate some valuable physical education experiences if money is not available.

The alternative to purchasing some of the high-cost supply and equipment items is to construct them yourself. This chapter will offer suggestions as to the methods and materials that can be used to construct assistive devices, low cost game equipment, and recreation and developmental equipment. I will also present techniques for recycling obsolete and discarded items. It is expected that construction can be accomplished within normal school hours and the low cost of supplies absorbed within the school budget.

442

KEY TERMS

abdominal exerciser	hoops
amputee's badminton serving tray	horizontal bar rack
badminton racket extension	lummi sticks
balance board	miniature trampoline
ball scoop	modified table tennis table
basketball retriever	multidirectional balance beam
beanbag board	newspaper ball
beanbags	paddle bat
bihandled table tennis paddle	posture grid
bowler's adaptive pushing device	pull-up bar
bowling frame unit	pylon crossbars
bowling pins	rhythm strips
bow stringer	right-angle footboard
buoy	scooter
can targets	sponge balls
crutch hockey stick	tapered balance beam
elevated sandbox	thermoplastic
flying saucers	vertical bow set
forearm archery brace	wooden blocks

CONSTRUCTING ASSISTIVE DEVICES

The major purpose of an assistive device is to help a person with a disability participate in activities that otherwise might be precluded because of functional or structural anomalies.

Amputee's Badminton Serving Tray

Materials

Wire coat hanger

Vegetable or soup can with a diameter of approximately 3 inches

Thermoplastic

Construction ideas Bend the wire coat hanger into a circle that fits around the can. (Leave the two parallel wires—about two inches apart—long enough to extend to within six inches of the elbow joint.) Cut off the top of the can, leaving a rim approximately one inch high. Bend the upper edge of the rim over the circular wire serving-tray frame, and solder.

The shaft of the tray (the two parallel wires) is firmly grasped with the terminal device of the amputee's prosthesis. Provide additional support by placing **thermoplastic** around the wire shaft and forming a molded cuff that will secure the shaft to the amputee's forearm, Figure 17.1.

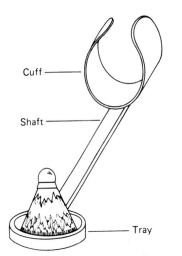

Figure 17.1. Amputee's badminton serving tray. *Courtesy of Adams, Daniel, and Rulman, 1972.*

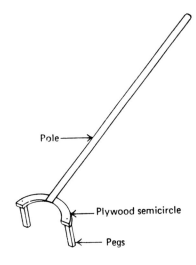

Figure 17.2. Bowler's adaptive pushing device

Use The amputee badminton serving tray makes it easier for a single-limb, above- or below-elbow amputee to use the prosthetic device to execute a serve in badminton. The player places the shuttlecock into the serving tray (feathers down), and lifts and slightly tips the tray so that the shuttlecock falls out and can be hit with the badminton racket held in the other hand.

Bowler's Adaptive Pushing Device

Materials

Hardwood pole 1–1-15/16 inches in circumference and 3–4-1/2 feet long

One 3/4-inch-wide semicircle cut from 1/2- or 3/4-inch plywood to fit up to one-half the circumference of the bowling ball

Two 1/2-inch-square pegs of hardwood whose length does not exceed the radius of the bowling ball

Glue

Nails

Construction ideas Affix the plywood semicircle to one end of the pole, Figure 17.2. Secure the pegs to the two open ends of the plywood semicircle on one of its 3/4-inch sides. The pegs elevate the plywood semicircle so that it fits around one side of the bowling ball. The device is used to push the ball down the lane.

Use The bowler's adaptive pushing device is used by wheelchair bowlers who for functional or structural reasons cannot hold the ball with the hand or perform the necessary pendulumlike swing with the shoulder. This device can also be used by someone with crutches or a walker.

Bihandled Table Tennis Paddle

Materials

One 1/4-inch piece of plywood, 6-3/4 inches long and 6-1/8 inches wide

Two l/2-inch pieces of plywood, 4-1/4 inches long and 1-1/8 inches wide

Piece of medium sandpaper, 6-3/4 inches long and 6-1/8 inches wide

Construction ideas Carefully glue the smooth side of the sandpaper to the surface of the piece of plywood. After the glue dries, attach the two plywood handles, Figure 17.3.

Use The bihandled table tennis paddle helps table tennis players with weak grip/arm strength initiate and maintain greater control of the paddle.

Bow Stringer

Materials

One 2-inch by 4-inch piece of hardwood, 5 feet long

Two carriage (or machine) bolts, 4 inches long and 3/8 to l/2-inch in diameter

Two strips of l/2-inch protective rubber tubing

Construction ideas Taper one end of the hardwood so that it can be sunk into the ground to a depth of 12–18 inches. Place the two bolts approximately 2 feet 6 inches apart on the wide side of the hardwood post. The bottom bolt should be about 9 inches above the ground. Put rubber tubing around each bolt in order to protect the surface of the bow, Figure 17.4.

Use The bow stringer helps the wheelchair archer string his/her own bow independently. A reasonable amount of upper-arm strength is necessary to use the apparatus successfully. Some caution and assistance may be necessary—particularly at the outset.

Bowling Frame Unit

Materials

Two pieces of 2-inch by 4-inch softwood (e.g., spruce), 32–36 inches long

One piece of 2-inch by 4-inch softwood (e.g., spruce), 48 inches long

Four pieces of 2-inch by 4-inch softwood (e.g., spruce), 5–6 inches long

Two pieces of 1/2-inch plywood, 32 inches long and 32 inches wide

Nails

Construction ideas Cut the softwood to desired lengths and construct the support system shown by dotted lines in Figure 17.5. Shape the two pieces of plywood to a curved 45-degree angle on the slope side and attach them to make a sandwich. When you cut the plywood, provide a lip at the top of the bowling frame unit so the bowler can start the ball rolling by lifting the lip. The lip can be supported by using one 2-inch by 4-inch piece of softwood. The remaining three pieces of 5–6-inch-long pieces of softwood should be nailed within the sandwich at strategic places along the slope side of the unit in order to provide additional support.

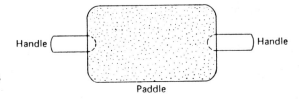

Figure 17.3. Bihandled table tennis paddle

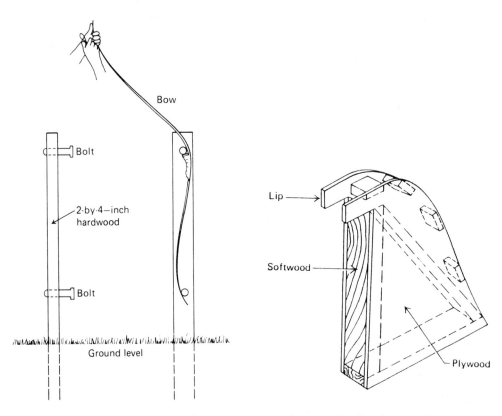

Figure 17.4. Bow stringer

Figure 17.5. Bowling frame unit

Use The bowling frame unit is centered at the top of the lane and the bowling ball is balanced on the lip. The bowler who has little arm strength can start the ball rolling by lifting the lip of the frame. The frame can then be moved and aligned with pins that may still be standing.

Crutch Hockey Stick

Materials

One standard crutch (the length depends on the size of the user)

One floor hockey blade

Stress or adhesive tape

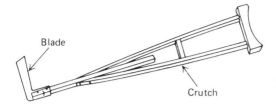

Figure 17.6. Crutch hockey stick

Construction ideas Remove the rubber stopper from the bottom of the crutch. Screw or tape a floor hockey blade to the base of the crutch, Figure 17.6. The blade is usually attached to the player's own crutch for the duration of play only.

Use The crutch hockey stick can be used as a crutch and as a hockey stick, enabling the student with a disability to use both crutches during scrimmage and hit the ball or puck with the converted crutch.

Forearm Archery Brace

Materials

One 3/4-inch by 6-inch board tapered to approximately 4 inches at one end, 3 or 4 inches longer than the archer's arm

One 3-inch by 4-inch block of wood

Two leather or cloth straps 2–3 inches wide and long enough to encircle the board and the student's arm

Screws

Construction ideas Attach the board to the inside of the archer's bow arm by encircling the arm and board with the straps, one slightly above the elbow joint and one in the area of the wrist and forearm. Once you have determined that the board is an appropriate length and that the straps will fit the user, attach an archery bow to the wrist (narrow) end of the board with screws. Screw the block of wood to the bow end of the board so that it touches the near end of the bow grip. This helps support the bow while the string is being drawn, Figure 17.7.

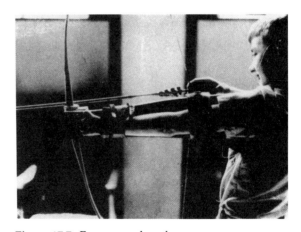

Figure 17.7. Forearm archery brace

Use The forearm archery brace is especially useful to an individual with a congenital or acquired amputation at the hand or the wrist area. Once the device is attached, the arrow can be nocked by the archer.

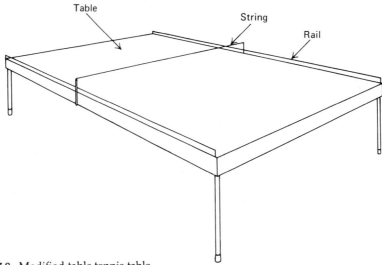

Figure 17.8. Modified table tennis table

Modified Table Tennis Table

Materials

Four 4-foot-6-inch pieces of softwood, 1 inch by 1-1/2 inches

One 6-foot-long piece of string

One standard 9-foot by 5-foot table tennis table

Construction ideas Nail the rails along the top edges of the two long sides of the table tennis table. (The rails should be 1-1/2 inches higher than the playing surface.) Attach the string, in place of a net, to the net clamps, Figure 17.8.

Use The modified table tennis table helps the wheelchair player to keep the ball in play. The rails keep the ball from rolling over the edges of the table and the string allows even poorly hit balls to reach the opponent. (A net would stop the ball in the middle of the table, where the player would have difficulty retrieving it.)

Posture Grid

Materials

Two 2-inch by 2-inch pieces of softwood 7 feet long

Two 2-inch by 2-inch pieces of softwood 3–3-1/2 feet long

Two support braces

String

Construction ideas Use the softwood boards to form a rectangular frame. Attach the two support braces to enable the frame to stand upright. Divide the rectangle in half by attaching a string to the two horizontal boards. (Use a plumb line for guidance.) Attach strings horizontally between the two perpendicular boards at 1-inch intervals, from approximately 2 to 6 feet above floor level, Figure 17.9.

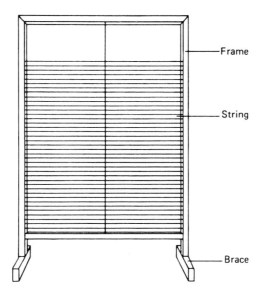

Figure 17.9. Posture grid

Use The posture grid is used to screen students for static postural anomalies from anterior, posterior, and lateral views. When a student is standing behind a grid, it is easier to detect deviations from what is considered to be normal alignment.

Badminton Racket Extension

Materials

One 9-inch to 12-inch pole with a diameter approximately the same as the shaft of a standard badminton racket

One standard badminton racket

One clamping device (or bracing material) tape

Tape

Construction ideas Overlap approximately one-third of the pole with the shaft of a standard badminton racket. Clamp the shaft and the pole together. Encircle tape around the handle area in order to increase the circumference of what will become the new grip, Figure 17.10. (You might use the handle of a previously broken racket head.)

Use The badminton racket extension is useful for a student who is in a wheelchair or who for some other reason has difficulty moving laterally. This device extends the performer's reach.

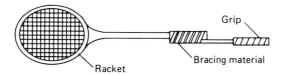

Figure 17.10. Badminton racket extension

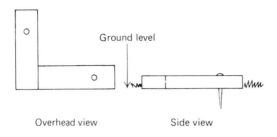

Overhead view   Side view   **Figure 17.11**. Right-angle footboard

Right-Angle Footboard

Materials

Two 2-inch by 4-inch pieces of softwood, 12–18 inches long

Anchoring material (spikes or tape)

Construction ideas Affix the two pieces of softwood at right angles to each other. Anchor the wood in place with spikes (if outdoors) or looped adhesive tape (if indoors), Figure 17.11. The boards should extend 2 inches above the playing surface.

Use The right-angle footboard helps the athlete who is visually impaired to align himself/herself with a target area (e.g., basketball goal, archery target). The toes of the preferred foot are placed where the two pieces of wood meet at the right angles.

Vertical Bow Set

Materials

One 1-1/2-inch by 5-inch piece of softwood, 10–12 feet long

One 1-1/2-inch by 5-inch piece of softwood, 3 feet long

Clamping devices

One archery bow and string

One mouthpiece

Figure 17.12. Vertical bow set

Construction ideas Affix the top portion of the long piece of softwood to the back of a basketball backboard (or some other supporting structure). Clamp the short piece of softwood to the back (out-of-bounds) side of piece A. The lower edge of piece B should be at approximately the mid-head height of the wheelchair archer. Clamp the archery bow in place parallel to the floor. Attach the mouthpiece (e.g., football mouthpiece) to the center of the bow string, Figure 17.12.

Use The **vertical bow set** will enable the wheelchair archer who does not have the use of his/her arms to participate in archery. Place the mouthpiece in the archer's mouth, nock the arrow, and pull the archer back by the shoulders, thus drawing the string. The archer aims by moving his or her head up or down (and/or laterally). The arrow is released when the archer releases the mouthpiece. Be sure that the pull needed to draw the string is not too great.

CONSTRUCTING LOW-COST GAME EQUIPMENT

If you construct your own game equipment, you can save a great deal of money in the physical education operating budget. The following represents a sampling of construction ideas that have proved to be successful.

Bean Bags

Materials

Heavy cloth material

Dry beans, corn, or peas

Construction ideas Cut the cloth into rectangular pieces approximately 6 by 12 inches or 8 by 16 inches. With the right sides together, fold the rectangle to form a square. Sew two adjacent sides together, then turn the cloth right side out. Put the dry beans, corn, or peas into the opening. (Use 1/2 cup for a small bag, 1 cup for a large bag.) Close the bag by sewing shut the opening, Figure 17.13.

Bean Bag Board

Materials

One 1/2-inch piece of plywood 4 feet long and 2 feet wide

One 3/4-inch by 5-inch piece of softwood, 4-1/2–5 feet long

Stain and paint

Construction idea Cut out four to six circles of various dimensions from the plywood. Stain the plywood and paint appropriate numbers under each of the circles. Attach the softwood brace to the back of the plywood at the center of the upper edge, Figure 17.14.

Bowling Pins

Materials

Ten plastic 1-quart or 1/2-gallon milk containers

Paint

Construction ideas Spray paint the ten plastic milk containers white, yellow, or orange (yellow and orange are generally more easily seen by bowlers with visual disabilities.) Paint a number (one through ten) on each of the containers, Figure 17.15. (Do not use a heavy ball for bowling activities.)

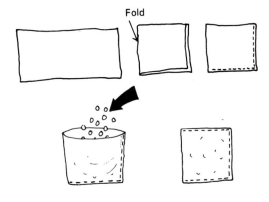

Figure 17.13. Steps in beanbag construction

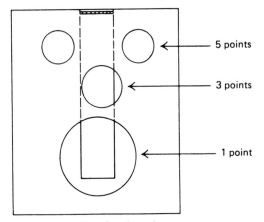

Figure 17.14. Beanbag board

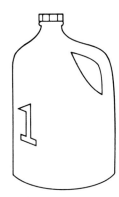

Figure 17.15. Milk container bowling pin

Hoops

Materials

Three-fourths-inch flexible plastic tubing, 8–8-1/2 feet long

Three-inch-long dowel rods that will fit inside the plastic tubing

Staple gun

Construction ideas Cut the plastic tubing to 6- to 8-foot lengths. Insert a dowel rod into the two open ends of the tubing to form a circle (hoop). Staple the tubing to the dowel rod, Figure 17.16. Be sure that the backs of the staples do not protrude or they will cut users.

Miniature Trampoline

Materials

Large truck (or commercial jet) inner tube

Canvas

Bootlaces

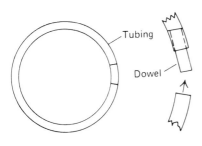

Figure 17.16. Hoop

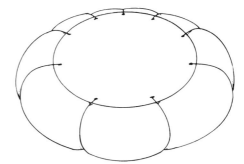

Figure 17.17. Miniature trampoline

Construction ideas Cut the piece of canvas into a circle a little smaller than the hole in the center of the inner tube. Make and reinforce small holes (to pass bootlaces through) at about 4-inch intervals around the edge of the canvas circle. Use the bootlaces to "sew" the canvas to one side of the inner tube, stretching the canvas across the hole and looping the laces around the tube, Figure 17.17.

Lummi Sticks

Materials

One-half- to 3/4-inch dowel rods or broom handles

Sandpaper

Stain or paint

Construction ideas Cut dowel rods into 8-inch lengths. Sand the edges to make them smooth. Stain or paint the lummi sticks, Figure 17.18.

Rhythm Strips

Materials

Crepe paper streamers, assorted colors

Lummi sticks

Construction ideas Cut crepe paper into 3-inch to 5-inch lengths. Affix two crepe paper streamers of the same color to each pair of lummi sticks, Figure 17.19.

Figure 17.18. Lummi sticks

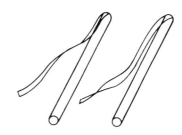

Figure 17.19. Rhythm strips

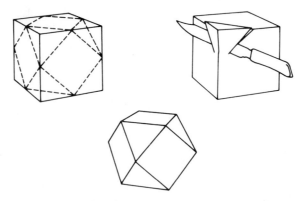

Figure 17.20. Sponge balls. *Courtesy of Corbin 1972.*

Sponge Balls

Materials

Six to 12-inch square pieces of sponge

Construction ideas Trim pieces of sponge into symmetrical geometric shapes, Figure 17.20.

CONSTRUCTING RECREATION AND DEVELOPMENTAL EQUIPMENT

Abdominal Exerciser

Materials

One wheel from a child's wagon

One 12- to 18-inch iron dowel that will fit through the wheel's axle hole

Two retainers with set screws (similar to those used to keep weights on a barbell)

          or

Old towels and adhesive tape

Construction ideas Put the dowel through the axle hole in the wheel and affix with retainers, one on each side, Figure 17.21.

If you use old towels as retainers, wrap the towels around the bar on each side of the wheel and wrap the towels with tape. The towels can be used as a grip, and they keep the wheel centered on the bar and rolling freely.

Figure 17.21. Abdominal exerciser

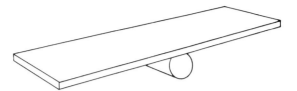

Figure 17.22. Balance board

Use To use the **abdominal exerciser**, the student kneels and grasps the dowel with both hands, then rolls the wheel (on the floor) as far forward as possible and back again while retaining balance. The exercise is continued through a prescribed series of repetitions.

Balance Board

Materials

One 32-inch by 9-1/2-inch piece of hardwood, 1–1-1/2 inches thick

One cylindrical hardwood post 5 inches in diameter and 8 inches long

Sandpaper

Stain or paint

Construction ideas Sand the surface areas and edges of each piece of wood. Stain or paint the piece of hardwood and the hardwood post.

Use Center the flat piece of stained hardwood on top of the cylindrical post (roller), Figure 17.22. The student steps onto the **balance board** and attempts to retain his/her balance.

Elevated Sandbox

Materials

One 48-inch by 24-inch piece of hardwood, 3/4–1 inch thick

Two 6-inch-wide pieces of hardwood 2 feet long

Two 6-inch-wide pieces of hardwood 4 feet long

Four 2-inch by 2-inch pieces of hardwood, 28–33 inches long

Four corner support braces

Four ball-bearing casters

Construction ideas Affix the 2-foot and 4-foot pieces of hardwood to the rectangular piece of hardwood to form a box. Attach the remaining four pieces of hardwood to the box, using the four corner support braces, to form a table, Figure 17.23. Place a caster on the bottom of each leg. Stain if desired.

A circle (2 inches in diameter) of very small holes can be drilled in the center of the box to allow for moisture drainage without loss of sand.

A heavy-duty 2-foot by 4-foot by 6-inch plastic tray (with a drain plug) can be placed into the box for supervised water-play activities.

Figure 17.23. Elevated sandbox

Use The **elevated sandbox** enables a student to roll his/her wheelchair under the table to get close enough to the table to enjoy sandbox play. A nonhandicapped child can use the sandbox at the same time.

Horizontal Bar Rack

Materials

Two 9-1/2 foot Pipes 1-1/2 inches in diameter

One 8-foot pipe 1-1/2 inches in diameter

One 7-foot pipe 1-1/2 inches in diameter

Three 3-foot pipes 1-1/2 inches in diameter

Pipe joints, four corner and two flat

Cement

Construction ideas Put together the pipes as shown in Figure 17.24, using the pipe joints. All perpendicular pipes should be set 2 1/2 feet into the ground and encased in concrete.

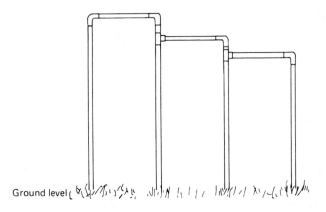

Ground level

Figure 17.24. Horizontal bar rack

Use The bars of the **horizontal bar rack** are wide enough so that a wheelchair can roll between them. One bar (the one at the right) is low enough to be reached while in a sitting position. The other two bars are designed for use by those who are not confined to wheelchairs.

Multidirectional Balance Beam

Materials

Three 2-inch by 4-inch pieces of hardwood 4 feet long

Four 2-inch by 4-inch pieces of hardwood 9 inches long

Eight hardwood dowels 1 inch in diameter and 2 inches long

Sandpaper

Stain

Construction ideas Sand and stain all pieces of hardwood. Implant and secure two dowels into each of the 9-inch pieces of hardwood. Sink the dowels 1 inch into the 9-inch by 4-inch side of the wood, 5 inches apart. Drill holes about 1 inch in diameter through each end of each long piece of hardwood on the 4-inch by 4-foot side. Assemble the balance beam by inserting dowels in hardwood bases through holes in long pieces, as shown in Figure 17.25.

Use Each of the three 4-foot-long pieces of hardwood can be pivoted on the dowels in different directions. The **multidirectional balance beam** helps students to develop balance, spatial relationships, and sensorimotor integration.

Scooter

Materials

One 12-inch by 12-inch piece of hardwood 1 inch thick

Four heavy-duty ball-bearing wheels 2 inches in diameter with attachments

Sandpaper

Stain or paint

Construction ideas Sand and stain or paint the piece of hardwood. Affix heavy-duty ball-bearing wheels to the hardwood square as shown in Figure 17.26.

Figure 17.25. Multidirectional balance beam (top view)

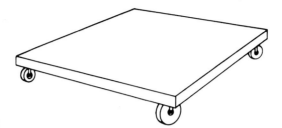

Figure 17.26. Scooter

Use Students sit or lie prone on **scooters** and propel themselves across the floor using arms or legs. This is fun and helps students to develop coordination, shoulder and arm strength, and endurance.

Tapered Balance Beam

Materials

One 2-inch by 4-inch piece of softwood, 14 feet long

Three 8-inch by 12-inch by 8-inch pieces of hardwood

Glue or screws (optional)

Sandpaper

Stain

Construction ideas Cut an opening 1 inch deep and 4 inches wide in the center of one 12-inch side of each block of hardwood, Figure 17.27. Firmly set the long piece of softwood into the openings of the support blocks, Figure 17.28. Space the blocks so that the beam will be stable and secure when someone walks on it. Sand the entire wood surface and mark the length of one side of the beam in inches. Stain the entire beam and its supporting blocks. Beginning 13 inches from one end of the beam, cut a gradual, beveled taper into the top of one end of the beam until it reaches a paper-thin edge at the other end, Figure 17.29.

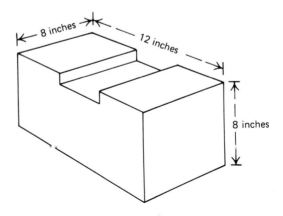

Figure 17.27. Tapered balance beam: supporting block

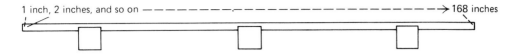

Figure 17.28. Tapered balance beam set in supporting blocks (side view)

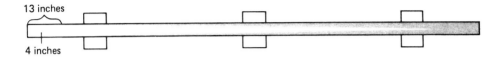

Figure 17.29. Tapered balance beam (top view)

Use The **tapered balance beam** is used to assess students' dynamic balance. The student being evaluated begins walking (heel-toe) on the widest (4-inch) portion of the beam and continues to walk until he/she loses balance. The distance covered to that point, in inches, is the student's score.

RECYCLING THROWAWAY ITEMS

Ball Scoop

Materials

One or l/2-gallon plastic bleach or milk container

Tape

Construction ideas Rinse the bottle thoroughly and cut out the bottom. Cover the cut edge with tape—inside and outside—to pad uneven and sharp edges, Figure 17.30).

Use The **ball scoop** is used for throwing and catching activities.

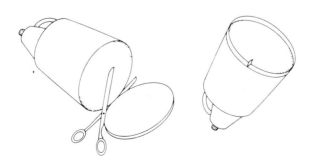

Figure 17.30. Ball scoop

Basketball Retriever

Materials

Old badminton or volleyball nets

Two 2-inch by 2-inch pieces of softwood 8 feet long

Two 2-inch by 2-inch pieces of softwood 4 feet long

Two 2-inch by 4-inch pieces of softwood 2-1/2 feet long

Connecting brackets

Rope

Construction ideas Form a rectangular frame by connecting the longer pieces of softwood together with brackets. Sew old netting together to form a piece 8-1/2 feet by 4-1/2 feet. Stretch the netting over the frame, leaving some slack. Attach the two remaining pieces of softwood to one end of the frame to form legs. Use rope to attach the other end of the completed frame to the supporting structure of a basketball backboard. Make this attachment up under but not touching the basketball net, Figure 17.31.

Use The **basketball retriever** enables the wheelchair basketball player to spend more time practicing his/her skills and less time chasing the ball because, following each shot at the basket, the ball will roll back to the player.

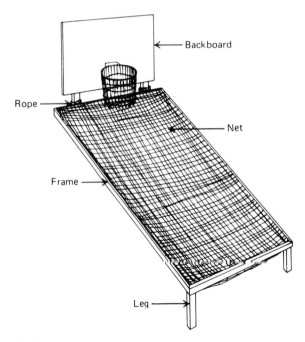

Figure 17.31. Basketball retriever

Can Targets

Materials

Fruit, juice, vegetable, and coffee cans

Tape

Construction ideas Rinse the cans thoroughly, cut out the bottoms, and remove the paper advertising from the exterior surfaces. Place tape around the rims—inside and outside—in order to cover uneven and sharp edges.

Use Have students throw beanbags or balls into the **can targets** set on the floor at various distances. Award points for successful throws according to can sizes. For example, a successful toss into a small can might be worth five points, while a successful throw into a large can might be worth one point.

Flying Saucers

Materials

Plastic lids from 1- and 2-pound coffee cans

Use Flying saucers (lids) can be thrown for distance and accuracy. Assign a point value to each lid color, and give each student, for example, a brown (one point), yellow (three points), and blue (five points) lid. If a student throws a blue lid farthest or most accurately, he/she is awarded five points. On the other hand, if the student's best throw is with the brown lid, one point is awarded.

Newspaper Balls

Materials

Newspapers

Masking tape

Construction ideas Mold several sheets of crumpled newspaper with your hands until it is the size and shape of a ball. Crisscross tape around the paper ball until all the paper is covered and the ball is firm.

Use The **newspaper ball** is useful for any game that does not require bounces or contact with a bat, hockey stick, or racket.

Paddle Bat

Materials

One wire coat hanger

One nylon stocking

Tape

Construction ideas Form a triangle with the wire coat hanger and straighten the hook. Stretch the nylon stocking tightly over the triangle. Wrap the end of the stocking around the straightened hook and cover with tape to form a handle, Figure 17.32.

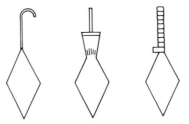

Figure 17.32. Paddle bat

Use The **paddle bat** can be used to hit a puff ball, newspaper ball, sponge ball, shuttlecock, hollow plastic ball, yarn ball, or similar lightweight ball.

Pull-up Bar

Materials

Broom handle

Sandpaper

Construction ideas Cut a discarded broom handle into 18-inch sections and sand the cut edges.

Use Pull-up bars can be used as batons, rhythm sticks, wands, and for modified pull-ups. When the bar is used for modified pull-ups, two students pair up according to size. One student stands, holds the bar, and straddles his/her partner, who is in the supine position on the floor. Instead of interlocking hands (as described in Chapter 4) the partner grasps the bar (forearms pronated) and pulls up until the lateral border of the chest contacts the medial portion of the standing partner's thighs.

Pylon Crossbars

Materials

Broom

Two pylon standards

Construction ideas Cut the broom off the stick so that as much of the handle can be used as possible.

Use When placed across two pylon standards, the broom handle makes a fine crossbar. Broom handles can also be used for

1. Balance sticks. A student attempts to balance the broom handle in the palm of the hand, on a finger, and so on. A student can also balance on the broom handle by placing it on the floor and standing on it with one foot or both feet along or across it.
2. Limbo sticks. The broom handle is held parallel to the floor at various heights by two students while a performer attempts to arch his/her back sufficiently to walk forward under the handle. (Limbo is a West Indian dance.)

3. Marker sticks. Broom handles can be used as restraining lines or distance markers for thrown balls, other broom handles, and other objects.

4. Stick throw. A student attempts to throw the broom stick, much like a javelin, into an open play area. The student who throws the broom handle the farthest distance wins.

5. Tinikling (pole dance). Two students kneel facing one another and hold the ends of two broom handles that lie parallel on the floor. These two youngsters move the sticks while two other youngsters hop in and out of the changing space between them. The sticks are moved to a *1-2-3* rhythm. On counts *1* and *2* the sticks are hit against the floor; on count *3* they are hit together approximately 3 inches above the floor. The *1-2-3* rhythmic pattern continues for the duration of the activity.

6. Tug-o-war. The broom handle is used instead of a rope to pull opponent(s) over a marker.

7. Wand wrestling. Two students face each other while holding the stick between them. Each student's hands are placed alternately so that neither youngster has both hands on the inside or the outside of the other's hands. On command, each student attempts to wrestle the stick free by twisting it back and forth.

Buoy

Materials

One or l/2-gallon plastic bleach or milk container with cap

Paint

Construction ideas Paint the container bright yellow or orange. Fill it about one-third full with water and replace cap.

Use Attach several **buoys** (at selected intervals) to a nylon rope and use it to mark off swimming areas. Attach a buoy to an anchor line and use it to mark the location of rocks or clusters of weeds in a swimming area. Connect a buoy to the end of a heaving line and use it to retrieve tired swimmers or nonswimmers. Connect two buoys with an elasticized cloth bandage (or other cloth strapping) and use this device as water wings.

Wooden Blocks

Materials

Wood scraps

Construction ideas Cut the wood scraps into assorted shapes, such as circles, rectangles, squares, and triangles.

Use The different geometric shapes of the **wooden blocks** can be used as bowling blocks, shuffleboard disks, targets for assorted throwing and tossing games, and the development of recognition skills.

SUMMARY

To construct some of the items that have been described within this chapter, you may want to seek technical assistance from school industrial arts departments and proprietors of hardware stores and lumber yards. With cooperation from colleagues and other professionals, there is little reason why you cannot embark on a low-cost supply and equipment construction program for your physical education program. Some of the projects can be adopted as projects to be carried out within industrial arts/woodworking classes.

RECOMMENDED LABORATORY ASSIGNMENTS

1. Construct some of the assistive devices described in this chapter.
2. Meet with physical education practitioners to discuss assistive devices successfully used in their programs.
3. Analyze the characteristics of those with physical impairments. Design assistive devices (not described in this chapter) that would increase their potential for successful participation in physical education activities.
4. Arrange to use selected assistive devices yourself in order to be able to demonstrate their use.
5. Construct the game, recreation, and developmental equipment that has been described in this chapter.
6. Arrange to visit schools and other facilities where developmental physical education equipment is being used by those who are physically impaired. Consult with these individuals in order to get ideas about improved design.
7. Examine equipment and identify items that might be constructed for less than their retail price.
8. List throwaway items not mentioned in this chapter that could be used in general and developmental physical education programs.

REFERENCES

Adams, R. C., A. N. Daniel, and L. Rullman. 1972. *Games, sports and exercises for the physically handicapped.* Philadelphia: Lea and Febiger.

Corbin, C. B. 1972. *Inexpensive equipment for games, play, and physical activity.* Dubuque: William C. Brown.

RECOMMENDED READINGS

Ball, M. 1969. Available resources. *Journal of Physical Education, Recreation and Dance* 57(1): 59–61.

Cowart, J., and M. Dresel. 1976. Sport adaptations for a student without fingers. *Journal of Physical Education and Recreation* 47: 46.

Huber, J. H., and J. Vercollone. 1976. Using aquatic mats with exceptional children. *Journal of Physical Education and Recreation* 47: 44, 46.

Institute for Educational Development, Inc. 1976. *Learning through activity program: Teachers utilization guide.* 143 Grove Road, South Orange, NJ: Author.

Isaacs, L. 1979. Life-size body awareness puzzles. *Journal of Physical Education and Recreation* 50: 66–67.

Kay, H. 1970. A bowling device for bilateral arm amputees. *Inter-Clinic Information Bulletin* IX: 7.

Klappholz, L., ed. 1977. Partner and individual wand exercises. *The Physical Activities Report, Issue #20*. Old Saybrook, CT: Institute for Learning, Division of Institute for Management, Inc.

Metzler, M. W. 1990. Teaching in competitive games—Not just playin' around. *Journal of Physical Education, Recreation and Dance* 61(8): 57–61.

Quackenbush, E. L. 1976. Maps and scooters. *Journal of Physical Education and Recreation*, 47: 47.

Wagner, P. A. 1976. Ball and tire activities. *Journal of Physical Education and Recreation* 47: 47–48.

Warrell, E. 1978. Equipment for indoor educational gymnastics. *Journal of Physical Education and Recreation* 49: 29, 61.

Werner, P., and L. Rini. 1975. *Perceptual motor equipment: Inexpensive ideas and activities*. New York: John Wiley and Sons, Inc.

Werner, P., and R. A. Simmons. 1990. *Homemade play equipment*. Reston: VA: American Alliance for Health, Physical Education, Recreation and Dance.

CHAPTER 18

Evaluation: Product and Process _____

Objectives

After reading this chapter, you should be able to

- Identify and discuss the role and components of evaluation in developmental and mainstreamed physical education programs.
- Describe criterion-referenced, norm-referenced, and probability-curve standards relative to evaluation.
- Define common test, measurement, and evaluation terms.
- Evaluate standardized tests in accordance with predetermined criteria.
- Know procedures for computing the mean, median, mode, standard deviation, T-scores, Z-scores, percentile ranks, and correlation.
- Identify and discuss general and specific classification procedures suitable for use within developmental and mainstreamed physical education classes.
- Identify and discuss category weighting.
- Discuss methods by which final grades may be determined for students enrolled in developmental and mainstreamed physical education programs.

INTRODUCTION

The success of any adapted physical education program is a product of the methods and materials used to affect learning. It is for this reason that we must be able to describe accurately the present status of our students. Once we know a student's ability level, we can select methods and materials that will maximize his/her potential for achievement.

Evaluation is an all-encompassing term that refers to the use of quantitative and qualitative information to determine the level and rate of student achievement, and the appropriateness of methods and materials used during the instruction process.

Physical education testing programs, assessment procedures, and evaluation strategies in general and those arising out of the Education for All Handicapped Children

---

KEY TERMS

accountability	percentile ranks
category weighting	practitioner-made instruments
central tendency	predictive validity
checklist	probability curve
concurrent validity	process
correlation	product
criterion-referenced standard	rating scale
curricular (face) validity	raw score
economy	real limits
evaluation	reliability
final grade	specific classification
frequency distribution	standard deviation
general classification	standard scores
grading scale	standardized test batteries
inclusionary	statistics
mean	T-score
measurement	teacher-made test
median	test
mode	utility
norm-referenced standard	validity
objectivity	Z-score

Act (Public Law 94-142) and Section 504 of the Rehabilitation Act of 1973 (Public Law 93-112) in particular are designed for

1. providing teachers, leaders, supervisors, parents, aides, attendants, and volunteers with information from which they can assess status of selected elements of motor development, physical fitness, and physical/motor proficiency for each child.
2. serving as one way to diagnose an individual's specific strengths and abilities, weaknesses, and deficiencies and to assess the individual's progress and development on selected elements of motor development, physical fitness, and physical/motor proficiency.
3. using test results for remedial grouping, diagnostic and prescriptive purposes; developing annual goals and short-term instructional objectives in selected elements of motor development, physical fitness, and physical/motor proficiency for each child; and assessing the degree to which provisions of individualized education programs have been accomplished.
4. giving students participating in specially designed physical education programs additional incentive to improve their levels of motor performance, physical fitness, and physical/motor proficiency.
5. stimulating teachers of students receiving special education and related services and agencies serving these populations to upgrade their physical education, recreation, and sports programs.

6. aiding in determining what comes next in instruction.
7. determining effectiveness of certain activities, approaches, and methods for each child.
8. providing a record of growth, development, performance, improvement, and progress for each child (American Alliance for Health, Physical Education, and Recreation 1978).

STANDARDS FOR EVALUATION

There are many ways to evaluate students. In most evaluative procedures the student's performance is compared to established standards. Different types of standards will be described in the sections that follow.

Criterion-referenced Standard

When using a **criterion-referenced standard**, the student is evaluated according to his/her ability to attain a specific objective that has been identified at the beginning of a unit of instruction (e.g., a behavioral objective on an individual education plan). An objective for a student in a wheelchair might be to negotiate an obstacle course that includes a ramp, curb, and corners within five minutes. If the student is able to achieve this objective, he/she has satisfied the requirements of this particular test activity.

Norm-referenced Standard

When using a **norm-referenced standard**, the student is compared with others of the same ability level, age, height, weight, grade level, geography, and/or gender. The norms (the standard) are ordinarily in percentile form (but they may also be found to be expressed in **Z-scores**, **T-scores**, ETS scores, grade equivalents, or stanines). If, for

TABLE 18.1

Percentile Norms of One Thousand Paraplegic Boys on a One-Minute Volleyball Wall-volley Skills Test (Three Foot Restraining Line).

Percentiles	Ages 13	14	15
100	40	45	50
99	39		49
98	38	44	48
97	37		47
96			46
95		43	45
94	36	42	
93	35	41	
92	34	40	44
91	33	39	43
90	32		42
10	4	5	5

example, a fourteen-year-old boy completes forty-one volleyball wall volleys in one minute, he would be at the 93d percentile according to the norms shown in Table 18.1. In other words, a score of 41 equals or exceeds 93% of the fourteen-year-old boys who take the test at the time norming occurred.

Probability Curve

Using a **probability** curve is a process of evaluation in which the student is compared with other students who have taken the **test** at the same time. The **mean** and **standard deviation** of the scores must be found. For example, if a student earns a score of 65 on your quiz on the rules and strategies of volleyball, his grade in the evaluation would be a C (if you use a full standard deviation technique) or a B (if you use a split standard deviation technique). For this illustration these grades are based on a mean of 60 and a standard deviation of 5 for the test scores, Table 18.2. Using the information in Table 18.2, one can see that in the split standard deviation technique, there is the probability of fewer C's than in the full standard deviation technique. At the same time the probability of earning an A, B, D, or F increases.*

TABLE 18.2

Probability Curve

Grade	Full Standard Deviation	Split Standard Deviation
A	71 – up	68 – up
B	66 – 70	63 – 67
C	55 – 65	58 – 62
D	50 – 54	53 – 57
F	below 49 – 49	below 52 – 52

The accurate assessment of skills and behavior pertinent to one's instructional objectives is one of the most difficult of tasks for the instructor. At the same time, the careful selection of valid instruments seems to have a low priority among many physical education teachers (Hensley, Morrow, and East 1990). One reason for this is that many knowledge and skills tests lack documented evidence of high **validity** ratings. As a consequence practitioners attempt to develop their own. This is fine, providing that **curricular validity** of these tests exists. In theory no one is better qualified to determine the relevance of testing instruments than the teacher who has taught the material to be tested. **Practitioner-made instruments** have the potential to be more valid than the standardized versions developed by those who have little or no knowledge of what was taught in individual classrooms.

---

*In the full standard deviation method the standard deviation is added to and subtracted from the mean in order to determine the score limits for a C. In the split standard deviation method, the standard deviation is divided in half by the mean of the distribution in order to determine the score limits for a C. The split standard deviation is more likely used when there is an extreme cluster of scores centered around the mean. This procedure provides the evaluator with the opportunity to discriminate between the upper and lower portions of that cluster.

Since many performances can be evaluated through **rating scale** observations, Verducci (1980) has suggested that the following guidelines be employed when developing such scales in order to make the task less threatening.

1. Determine the specific skills that are to be evaluated.
2. Identify traits that represent success for the performance being evaluated. (These may vary according to the group being rated.)
3. Determine the levels of success or ability for each skill. (A five-point rating scale is most common and generally provides adequate discrimination among ability levels.*)
4. Define each category or ability level in terms of observable behavior, Table 18.3.
5. Devise a form or system that permits the immediate recording of the rating of the observed behavior.

While well-constructed scales are critical to valid performance ratings, there are a number of other considerations to take into account when planning for their use.

TABLE 18.3

Sample Badminton Rating Scale

Circle the number that best represents the performance of the student.

5— significantly above average ability; considerably more skillful than the performance typical of the student's age and gender

4— above average ability; more skillful than the performance typical of the student's age and gender

3— average ability; typical performance for age and gender

2— below average ability; inferior to typical performance for age and gender.

1— significantly below average ability; considerably less skillful than the performance typical of the student's age and gender

Category	Rating
1. Serve	
a) Position of shuttlecock upon contact—racket head strikes shuttlecock below waist level.	5 4 3 2 1
b) Position of racket at end of serve—if long serve, racket head stops between shoulders and top of head at end of serve; if long serve, racket head does not rise above chest.	5 4 3 2 1
c) Height of serve relative to type of serve—clear serve is high and deep, drive serve is low over net and deep, short serve is low over net.	5 4 3 2 1
d) Placement of serve—well-placed relative to type of serve and position of opponent.	5 4 3 2 1
2. Strokes—consider placement and quality of each stroke.	
a) Clear—high and deep.	5 4 3 2 1

---

* A rating scale tends to be more reliable than a **checklist** (where only yes-or-no/agree-or-disagree responses are possible). This is because a rating scale provides for an assessment of quality on a continuum. A checklist generally provides for pass/fail assessments only.

TABLE 18.3 *continued*

Category	Rating				
b) Smash—hit from position above head and in front of body; path of shuttlecock is down.	5	4	3	2	1
c) Drive—sharp and low over net; hit from position about shoulder height; can be deep or midcourt, but not short.	5	4	3	2	1
d) Drop—hit from position waist-to-shoulder height; low over net; a hairpin type shot.	5	4	3	2	1
3. Strategy					
a) Places shots in different areas of the court.	5	4	3	2	1
b) Executes a variety of shots at opportune moments.	5	4	3	2	1
c) Takes advantage of opponent's weaknesses (e.g., poor net play, unreliable backhand).	5	4	3	2	1
d) Uses own best shots.	5	4	3	2	1
4. Footwork and Position					
a) Near center court position to respond to various shots and shot placements.	5	4	3	2	1
b) Has control of body at all times during play.	5	4	3	2	1
c) Body is in correct position when making each shot (usually determined by placement of the feet).	5	4	3	2	1
d) Racket is shoulder- to head-height and ready for use (wrist cocked) at all times; eyes are on the shuttlecock at all times	5	4	3	2	1

Note: While the four areas of badminton play may all be rated during competition, the areas of serve and strokes can be evaluated in noncompetitive situations. Area scores can be calculated, as can a total score. (Adapted from Baumgartner and Jackson (1991). *Measurement for Evaluation in Physical Education and Exercise Science.* Dubuque, IA: Wm. C. Brown. Suggested by Bill Landen, Indiana University)

1. The instructor should understand the limitations and sources of error associated with the use of rating scales, and strive to minimize their influence (e.g., previous ratings, halo effect, physical appearance, and personality of the student).
2. In order to increase the **reliability** of ratings, observe each student on more than one occasion. (Taking the average of the ratings is an option to consider.)
3. Ratings should be made while observing the performance of the student, not from memory.
4. When possible, use more than one person to rate student performances. This addresses the objectivity of the observations.
5. Focus on the task at hand. Allow adequate time to observe each student (Hensley, Morrow, and East 1990).

ESSENTIAL DEFINITIONS

1. The **product** is the student enrolled in the developmental or general (mainstreamed, **inclusionary**) physical education program.
2. The **process** represents the instructional procedures including all methods and materials used to affect the growth of the product.

3. **Measurement** refers to the procedures used to gather quantitative information regarding the present status or achievement level of the product.

4. The **test** is a measurement instrument used to collect quantitative information. Examples of test batteries are the *FITNESSGRAM* (Institute for Aerobic Research), *Fit Youth Today* (American Health and Fitness Foundation), and *Physical Best* (American Alliance for Health, Physical Education, Recreation and Dance) programs.

5. Validity refers to the degree to which a test measures what it purports to measure. Validity is the single most important characteristic of any test. A test may be reliable and objective, but if it lacks validity, it is a useless instrument of measurement.* Validity is also group and setting specific. What may be a valid test for ninth grade boys may be inappropriate for fifth grade boys.

6. Reliability is the degree to which a test measures whatever it measures in a consistent way. In general, the greater the number of parts (items) in a test, the more reliable it will be. The reason is that a test with greater item variety is more likely to touch upon qualities that the student is able to demonstrate. This advantage would be diminished, however, if the student became overly fatigued during the testing period. We have to exercise reasonable judgment when deciding what test or test battery will best assess the degree to which students have met selected objectives. As implied previously, a test can be reliable but not valid. For example, a student may perform a wheelchair 100-meter dash in fifteen and two-tenths seconds on one day, and perform in a like manner in the same event a few days later. The test for the 100-meter wheelchair event would be considered reliable because it measured a particular quality in a consistent way. The test would not be valid, however, if one selected the 100-meter event as a test for agility. What will the wheelchair 100-meter dash measure?

7. **Objectivity** (inter-rater reliability) refers to the degree to which two or more scorers agree as to the grade a student should receive for performance on a test. If the test is highly objective, all scorers will arrive at the same grade for each student. However, this statement holds true only if the scorers are equally competent judges of the ability being tested. (Review validity coefficients for **standardized test batteries** before you decide what test instrument to use.** It is unwise to consider using a test or test battery if its validity coefficient is less than 0.70. Reliability and objectivity coefficients should be no lower than 0.80 and 0.90 respectively.)

---

* Techniques for statistically computing the validity, reliability, and objectivity of measuring instruments are described in most test and measurement textbooks. See the recommended readings at the end of this chapter, for a list of such sources.

** Note: Curricular (or face) **validity** determinations will not yield a coefficient. This form of validity is determined by having a jury of individuals judge the proposed test items against the objectives of what is to be taught. If the test items appear to address these objectives, it would be reasonable to claim that the test has curricular validity. **Concurrent validity** is determined by correlating a test against another test (for which validity has already been established). Both tests would be administered to the same students at approximately the same time. **Predictive validity** is found by comparing the performance of students on a test (or test item) against a criterion (such as physical fitness). If a high correlation is found between the test item and physical fitness, it can be claimed that the item is a suitable predictor of physical fitness. Both concurrent and predictive validity procedures generate correlation coefficients.

8. **Utility** refers to the usefulness of the test; it should be able to serve a variety of functions. A test might
    a) identify achievement of the students being examined.
    b) provide scores for comparison with criterion-referenced, norm-referenced, and/or probability-referenced values.
    c) provide a basis for establishing one's status prior to a unit of instruction.
    d) provide data that would enable you to assess the student's growth against prior performance (a criterion-referenced value may be one's performance on a pretest).
    e) be a valuable learning instrument when reviewed by the students during and following its administration. It can help to clarify misconceptions.
    f) help to identify the relative strengths and weaknesses of instruction. If a large number of students all got the same question wrong, the fault is likely to rest with the instructor.
    g) serve as a basis for arriving at student grades.
    h) provide a basis for determining what should be taught next.
9. **Economy** refers to the dollar cost and the amount of time and/or equipment that it takes to administer a specific test. If you need expensive equipment to administer the test, or if the test takes an inordinate amount of class time to administer, it is wise to consider using another test. A test that requires expensive equipment or a lengthy administration period is not necessarily a valid test. Many valid, reliable, and objective tests require little equipment and can be administered within a typical class period.
10. A **teacher-made test** is one designed by you to measure the students' attainment of objectives related to such things as physical fitness, neuromuscular skills, knowledge, understanding, and attitudes. Ordinarily the teacher-made test has curricular (face) validity because the teacher who has constructed the test is the one who has conducted the class, and who is in the best position to address specific objectives developed for the class.
11. A standardized test has usually been administered to a sample group of typical students and evaluated by its designers as to the clarity of its directions and the validity of the test items with regard to the skills and knowledge it is supposed to measure. The standardized test usually comes with a manual that describes the procedures that were followed to establish validity. The manual should also include general and specific directions for test administration and norms with which the students' scores can be compared. Since there are many standardized tests on the market, the practitioner should exercise caution when considering the options available. There are many factors which should be taken into account. For an example of a form that can be used when comparing alternatives available, see Table 18.4.
12. **Statistics** is the science that deals with the collection, tabulation, and analysis of quantitative data. This analysis should allow you to draw conclusions and inferences regarding student status and achievement levels. However, the findings generated by the employment of statistics are only valid if the instruments selected for measurement are valid, the statistical treatment is appropriate to purpose, and errors are controlled.

TABLE 18.4

Standardized Test Evaluation Form

Title of test: _____

Purpose of test: _____

Author(s): _____

Publisher (and address): _____
_____

Date of publication: _____Date of last revision:_____

Target group(s): _____ Number of forms: _____ Norms _____

Type(s) of validity:_____ Evidence of validity according to:

   *Mental measurements yearbook:*_____
_____
_____

   Test critiques: _____
_____
_____

   *Other (Reference):*_____): _____
_____
_____

Type(s) of reliability: _____ Evidence of reliability according to:

   *Mental measurements yearbook:*_____
_____
_____

   Test critiques: _____
_____
_____

   *Other (Reference):*_____): _____
_____
_____

Standard error of measurement (or estimate):_____ Ease/cost of administration:
_____
_____

Durability of materials: _____
_____

Would you recommend the use of this instrument (why or why not)? _____
_____
_____
_____
_____

STATISTICAL TECHNIQUES

To be able to draw conclusions and make inferences regarding student performance, we have to be familiar with techniques for computing such statistics as the mean, **median, mode**, standard deviation, T-scores, Z-scores, **percentile ranks**, and **correlation**. These are the analytical procedures most often used by practitioners in the field. This section will address the computation of such values.

Frequency Distribution

Upon gathering scores generated by a test, a **frequency distribution** should be formed. Normally, they would be ordered in a column with the best (usually the highest of the earned scores) at the top and the poorest earned score at the bottom.* The data are then ready for statistical treatment.

Assume that a sitting softball-throw test item was administered to ten students, that the best score was 50', and that the low score was 35'. Table 18.5 shows a simple frequency distribution for these scores.

Mean

The most reliable measure of **central tendency** is the mean (common symbols: M, $\overline{X}$, M). The mean is the arithmetic average of a distribution of scores and takes into account the weighting of each and every score, which is why it is considered to be the most reliable of central tendency measures. Using a **raw score** formula, one can find the mean

TABLE 18.5

A Simple Frequency Distribution Representing the Scores Earned by Ten Students on a Sitting Softball Throw Measured to the Nearest Foot

Students	Variable X Scores	X^2	T-scores	Z-scores	Percentile Ranks
A	50	2500	66.80	1.68	100%
B	48	2304	62.55	1.25	90%
C	46	2116	58.29	.82	80%
D	44	1936	54.04	.40	70%
E	43	1849	51.93	.19	60%
F	41	1681	47.65	−.23	50%
G	39	1521	43.40	−.66	40%
H	38	1444	41.27	−.87	30%
I	37	1369	39.14	−1.08	20%
J	35	1225	34.89	−1.51	10%

---

* In some instances the lowest score is the best. An example of this would be where students have been timed to see how long it takes them to complete a task, such as a 100-meter wheelchair dash. Accordingly the lowest (or best) score would be placed at the top of the column.

by summing the scores (X) and dividing by their number (N): that is, $\Sigma X/N$. If the statistical analysis is to include more than finding the mean, use a frequency distribution of the type described. Otherwise, unordered scores can merely be added and averaged. For the distribution above, the mean would be calculated as

$$M \ = \ \frac{\Sigma X}{N} \ = \ \frac{421}{10} \ = \ 4.21$$

Median

The median (common symbols: Mdn, 50th percentile, Q_2, D_5) is the score at and below which 50 percent of the people being tested fell. Essentially the median is found through a counting process and is not affected by extreme scores (as the mean would be). To find the median, take 50 percent of N and count up that number from the lower end of the distribution. For the data in Table 18.5 the median is found by:

$$Mdn \ = \ .50(N) \ = \ .50(10) \ = \ 5$$

Count up from the bottom of the distribution until you get to the fifth number. This value is 41, the median. Fifty percent of the students earned a score of 41 or below.

Mode

The mode (common symbol: Mo) is the score earned by more persons than any other score. A distribution may be monomodal (one mode), bimodal (two modes), trimodal (three modes), or multimodal (four or more modes). There are also instances where no score was earned more than any other. This would be a non modal distribution, as in Table 18.5.

The mean, the median, and the mode are measures of central tendency. They provide us with indications as to the average, the midpoint, and the most frequently occurring scores within a distribution of values representing student performances. As you may surmize, the mode is the least stable in that it is subject to slight fluctuations. For example, if student E had thrown the softball one foot farther, there would be a mode and it would be 44.

Standard Deviation

The standard deviation (common symbols: SD, σ) represents the square root of the average of the deviations from the mean of the distribution. The raw score formula for computing the standard deviation is:

$$SD \ = \ \sqrt{\frac{\Sigma X^2}{N} \ - \ M^2}$$

For Table 18.5 the calculations for the standard deviation would be as follows:

1. Square each score (e.g., the square of the score 50 is 2500; the square of the score 48 is 2304, etc.).
2. Sum the squared scores and divide by N.
3. Square the mean (arithmetic average).
4. Subtract the squared mean value from the average of the squared scores.

5. Compute the square root. This will give you the standard deviation, which indicates the dispersion or spread of the scores. In a homogeneously grouped distribution, the standard deviation will be smaller than in a heterogeneous group of scores.*

For the distribution of scores in Table 18.5 the standard deviation is found as follows:

$$SD = \sqrt{\frac{\Sigma X^2}{N} - M^2}$$

$$= \sqrt{\frac{17945}{10} - 1772.41}$$

$$= \sqrt{1794.5 - 1772.41}$$

$$= \sqrt{22.09}$$

$$SD = 4.70$$

Standard Scores

Although there are a variety of **standard scores**, the ones most often used are T-scores, Z-scores, and percentile ranks. Standard scores allow you to total and average scores that have different denominators. For example, if you have administered a physical fitness test battery consisting of flexed-knee sit-ups (number accomplished in 30 seconds), the 100-meter dash (timed to the nearest tenth of a second—lowest being the best score), and the softball throw (measured to the nearest foot), it would be inappropriate to total and average the raw scores for each student and hope to arrive at a meaningful value. If on the other hand each score's distribution was converted to a standard value (T-score, for example), the resulting scores could be added and averaged. The result would be a meaningful answer that could be interpreted.

The formula for computing a T-score is

$$\frac{10(X - M)}{SD} + 50$$

Where

X = raw score for which a T-score is being computed

M = mean of the raw score distribution

SD = standard deviation of the raw score distribution

A short method for computing T-scores for a distribution would be to use a reciprocal—that is, the quotient of $10/SD$. The mean of the raw scores is always

---

* If you do not know or recall how to compute the square root, consult a table of square roots, which can be found in the appendixes of many statistics and educational measurement textbooks.

equivalent to a T-score of 50. Therefore the quotient of 10/SD is added to 50 and to each succeeding T-score value. These T-scores represent the equivalencies for the raw scores in the distribution. To compute T-scores below the mean, subtract the quotient from 50 and from each succeeding T-score value.

The formula for computing a Z-score is

$$\frac{X - M}{SD}$$

Where

X = raw score for which a Z-score is being computed

M = mean of the raw score distribution

SD = standard deviation of the raw score distribution

A short method for computing Z-scores for a distribution is to use a reciprocal—that is, the quotient of 1/SD. The mean of the raw scores is always equivalent to a Z-score of 0. Therefore the quotient of 1/SD is added to 0 and each succeeding Z-score value. These Z-scores represent the equivalencies for the raw scores in the distribution. To compute Z-scores below the mean, add the quotient to 0 and each succeeding Z-score value, and place a minus sign in front of each Z-score. (It may be remembered from Chapter 1, that Z-scores above the mean are positive and that Z-scores below the mean are negative.) You should also realize that if Z-scores are known, T-scores can be calculated directly by multiplying the Z-score by 10 and then add 50. How would you convert a known T-score to a Z-score?

The T-score and Z-score answers found through the use of a reciprocal may vary from those found using the standard formula to the extent that rounding off of numbers has occurred.

A T-score is more easily interpreted to students and parents than is a Z-score because each T-score is a positive number. In a Z-score distribution, values below the mean are all negative. Further it can be disconcerting to students and parents to be told that the arithmetic average of all the students in a selected test is zero. Z-scores are used primarily in sampling error theory.* Table 18.5 shows T- and Z-score values for equivalent sitting softball throw scores.

Percentile ranks are another type of standard score in which the value for each raw score is calculated by totaling the number of persons earning up to and including the score for which you desire the percentile rank. Divide this number by the total number of persons earning scores on the test, multiply the quotient by 100. Table 18.4 shows percentile rank values for equivalent sitting softball throw scores.

Correlation

Relationship studies enable the practitioner to determine whether performances on one test are related to performances on another test. These relationships are expressed as correlation coefficients. A perfect positive correlation is +1.00, a perfect negative correla-

---

* A discussion of sampling error theory is beyond the scope of this chapter. See the recommended readings for a selection of educational measurement and research design textbooks.

tion is −1.00, with gradations between those values and 0, which represents a finding that there is no relationship between the two tests. In general a high correlation is ±.70 and above, a medium correlation is ±.30–±.69, and a low correlation is between 0 and ±.29. A positive relationship implies that individuals who performed above the average of their peers on one test tended to do above average on the second test; students who performed below the average of their peers on one test tended to do below average on the second test. On the other hand a negative relationship implies that those who did well on one of the tests tended to do poorly on the second. A zero correlation indicates that there was no tendency for a relationship from one test to the other. The size of the correlation coefficient reveals the intensity of the relationship.

Should you be interested in determining the extent of relationship that exists between the sitting softball throw scores revealed earlier and extensor arm strength/endurance as measured by a push-up test (untimed), a correlation coefficient could be calculated using the Pearson-Product Moment Correlation technique.

$$r = \frac{\frac{\Sigma XY}{N} - [M_x \bullet M_y]}{SDx \bullet SDy}$$

Where:

1. The product of x and y are calculated for each student.
2. The products of x and y are summed and divided by the total number of students.
3. The product of the two means is subtracted from the answer in Step 2.
4. The product of the two standard deviations is divided into the answer found in Step 3.

Referring to Table 18.6, the computations would be as follows:

$$r = \frac{\frac{\Sigma XY}{N} - [M_x \bullet M_y]}{SDx \bullet SDy}$$

$$= \frac{\frac{17161}{10} - [42.1 \bullet 40.0]}{4.70 \bullet 7.62}$$

$$= \frac{1716.1 - 1684.0}{35.814}$$

$$\frac{32.1}{35.814}$$

$$r = .896$$

This finding indicates that there is a high positive relationship between the sitting softball throw and (untimed) push-ups. It appears that students who did above average in the softball throw also tended to do well in (untimed) push-ups. Likewise those

TABLE 18.6

**Data Representing the Scores of Ten Students on the
Sitting Softball Throw and (Untimed) Push-up Tests**

Students	Softball Throw (X)	(Untimed) Push-ups (Y)	XY
A	50	48	2400
B	48	48	2304
C	46	47	2162
D	44	42	1848
E	43	43	1849
F	41	43	1763
G	39	35	1365
H	38	36	1368
I	37	36	1332
J	35	22	770
	M = 42.1	M = 40.0	XY = 17161
	SD = 4.70	SD = 7.62	

students who performed below average in the softball throw tended to do below average in (untimed) push-ups. It is important to note, however, that this finding does not necessarily represent a cause-and-effect relationship.

While statistical software programs exist, it is prudent to be able to calculate pertinent statistics by hand before relying upon computer analysis. This fosters an understanding of processes and outcomes, which in turn provides for enlightened interpretations. Once the understanding of the process is in place, putting greater emphasis upon computers makes sense for many people.

The most important statistical procedures to know are how to calculate the mean and the standard deviation. That is because they serve as the basis for so many analyses.

1. Classification of students for physical fitness and/or skill instruction within a class
2. Grading of students on tests (see Chapter 4)
3. Computation of standard scores (e.g., T-scores and Z-scores)
4. Computation of product-moment correlation
5. Sampling error theory

CLASSIFICATION

There are two types of classification formats: general and specific. A **general classification** procedure does not group students according to their individual skill levels. General classification procedures are most often used for administrative purposes. For example, you might want to group students in squads alphabetically to expedite taking attendance at the beginning of each class period.

A **specific classification** scheme is used to group students according to their present abilities relevant to a unit of instruction. Classify students for a specific unit of instruction as follows:

1. Select two or three skills that are most representative of ability in a given activity. For example, if the unit to be taught is soccer, you might select passing, dribbling, and shooting.
2. Administer the three-item diagnostic test battery to the students during an introductory class period.
3. Rank the students according to their performances in the test battery. For example, if you use T-scores, the average T for each student could be ranked, providing a basis for placement into a squad, Table 18.7.

TABLE 18.7

Student Ranking Determined by Scores on Three-Item Test Battery

| | Squads | | | | | | |
	I	II	III	IV	V	VI	
Highest Rank	1	10	11	20	21	30	Lowest Rank
	2	9	12	19	22	29	
	3	8	13	18	23	28	
	4	7	14	17	24	27	
	5	6	15	16	25	26	

Note: Additional discussion of the use of ranking in classification systems is presented in Chapter 4.

Identify specific behavioral objectives for each person or squad. Set individualized objectives appropriate to each student's ability level at the beginning of the unit. If a student in a wheelchair can best benefit from instruction in squad VI—i.e., squad VI provides the least restrictive environment—provide this student with an individual education plan (IEP) that can be worked on in the squad context. This student's IEP might include skills related to the responsibilities of a soccer goalie—throwing and catching. If the objectives have been carefully prepared, and the students are able to meet these objectives, they should receive *A*s. As stated previously, not everyone should be required to meet the same objectives if their capabilities for achievement differ. Careful selection of behavioral objectives will put requirements into proper perspective for each student in a heterogeneous, mainstreamed physical education class.

CATEGORY WEIGHTING

Category weighting in physical education is largely a product of your personal philosophy. It is also based on the emphasis you have given to various general objectives during the course of a marking period. For example, in the first marking period the weighting of each category (general objective) toward the student's final grade might be:

Physical fitness	0%
Neuromuscular skills	50%
Knowledge and understanding	30%
Attitude	20%
	100%

Although a diagnostic physical fitness test might be given during the first marking period of an academic year, it would be inappropriate to grade students (for report card purposes) according to their performance on this test. In effect you would be assigning grades to students on the basis of what they had achieved prior to their enrolling in your class. Students should be evaluated on the degree of physical fitness achieved as a result of attending this particular class.

If the unit is soccer, the neuromuscular skills category will receive the greatest weighting. Knowledge of the history, rules, and strategy of soccer might receive the next highest weighting. Knowledge is weighted lower than neuromuscular skills if the development of neuromuscular skills has received the most emphasis during a particular marking period. In this soccer unit, attitude might receive the lowest of the three weightings. This is not to say that the development of proper attitudes is less important than other factors. In fact the development of positive attitudes toward other people, life, and the environment may be the most important benefit of a physical education class. The problem is that attitudes are the most difficult of variables to measure objectively. Further, favorable attitudes are likely integrated into the effort applied to practicing the skills or playing the game, thus making performances better.

An attitude questionnaire can be a useful tool for attitude assessment. Should it be filled out anonymously? If students have to identify themselves on an attitude questionnaire, they may be less inclined to express their true feelings. This is particularly so if the attitude is negative and the student feels that responses will affect his/her term grade. On the other hand if the questionnaire is filled out anonymously you will lack information that can help you address each student's individual needs.

The basis for attitude assessment in physical education classes is most often your observation and judgment. Because your observation and judgment can be subjective, you may find it difficult to defend heavy weighting of a category in which "impressions" have served as the basis for the grade. Needless to say, teachers must be able to demonstrate **accountability** for every decision they make.

In subsequent marking periods you might change the weightings of the categories. Whatever weightings you choose, evaluation of the students should be based upon what they have learned since the beginning of the developmental or mainstreamed physical education class.

FINAL GRADES

Grade thoughtfully. Each student's grade should reflect his/her attainment of objectives appropriate to himself/herself.

Assuming that the students have been (1) accurately pretested with respect to their physical fitness and neuromuscular skill levels, (2) provided with an IEP containing objectives that can be reached within a selected or reasonable period time, (3) taught in keeping with the most appropriate methods and materials, and (4) validly assessed with respect to their levels of achievement, the final grade will accurately describe performance.

Grading Scales

Two **grading scales** can be used to arrive at a final grade for a student: a five-point scale and a thirteen-point scale.

The five point scale A five-point scale is used when pluses and minuses are not to be considered. In this scheme an *A* is worth five points, a *B* is worth four points, a *C* is worth three points, a *D* is worth two points, and an *F* is worth one point. An *F* can also be worth zero points if no effort has been made by the student to take the test being graded. It is my belief that a person who has taken a test and failed it deserves a better grade than someone who has not made the effort to take the test at all. A five-point (rather than a four-point) scale provides for this distinction.

When computing a final grade, multiply the weight of the category by the weight of the grade in that particular category. Convert the total value to a letter grade (Table 18.8), taking into account the real limits of each number, Table 18.9.

TABLE 18.8

Computation of a Final Grade with the Five-Point Scale

Category	Category Weight (Percentage)	Grade Weight	Final Grade
Physical fitness	40	*B* (4)	1.60
Neuromuscular skills	30	*A* (5)	1.50
Knowledge and understanding	20	*C* (3)	0.60
Attitude	10	*B* (4)	0.40
Total:			4.10

TABLE 18.9

Real-Limit Equivalencies for the Letter Grades, Five-Point Scale

Letter Grade	Real Limits
A	4.50 –
B	3.50 – 4.49
C	2.50 – 3.49
D	1.50 – 2.49
F	0.50 – 1.49

TABLE 18.10

Letter Grade Values for the Thirteen-Point Scale

Letter Grade	Grade Weight
A+	13
A	12
A–	11
B+	10
B	9
B–	8
C+	7
C	6
C–	5
D+	4
D	3
D–	2
F	1

A total of 4.10—found in Table 18.8—is within the real limits of 3.50 and 4.49—found in Table 18.9. Consequently this student would receive a *B* for a final grade.

The thirteen-point scale A thirteen-point scale is used when pluses and minuses are to be attached to letter grades, Table 18.10.

Like the five-point scale, the thirteen-point scale allows you to use 0 to rate a student who has not made any attempt to take the test. The thirteen-point scale enables you to grade students within a letter grade range. Students who do C+ work can be distinguished from those who do C– work. In the five-point system, both of these students would receive Cs.

To compute a final grade, multiply the weight of the category by the weight of the student's grade in that particular category. Convert the total to a letter grade while taking into account the real limits of each number, Table 18.11. A 10.00 is within the real limits of 9.50 and 10.49, Table 18.12. As a consequence, this student would receive a *B+* for a final grade.

SUMMARY

A comprehensive evaluation program takes into account the many elements comprising the achievements of the student (product) and the appropriateness of methods and materials (process) used to facilitate instruction. It is concerned with the identification of a student's present status, the selection of appropriate evaluation criteria,

TABLE 18.11

Computation of a Final Grade with the Thirteen-Point Scale

Category	Category Weight (Percentage)	Grade Weight	Final Grade
Physical fitness	40	*B+* (10)	4.00
Neuromuscular skills	30	*A* (12)	3.60
Knowledge and understanding	20	*C+* (7)	1.40
Attitude	10	*B+* (10)	1.00
Total:			10.00

TABLE 18.12

Real Limit Equivalencies for the Letter Grades, Thirteen-Point Scale

Letter Grade	Real Limits
A+	12.50 –
A	11.50 – 12.49
A–	10.50 – 11.49
B+	9.50 – 10.49
B	8.50 – 9.49
B–	7.50 – 8.49
C+	6.50 – 7.49
C	5.50 – 6.49
C–	4.50 – 5.49
D+	3.50 – 4.49
D	2.50 – 3.49
D–	1.50 – 2.49
F	0.50 – 1.49

the selection and administration of appropriate instruments of measurement, the collection and analysis of scores, and the application of a grading technique that makes use of the best of professional insight.

Students with disabilities who are enrolled in developmental and mainstreamed classes are achieving at rates never before expected possible. We should make an effort to grade students on the attainment of reasonable and challenging objectives that can be reinforced by experiences that students will face after graduation.

RECOMMENDED LABORATORY ASSIGNMENTS

1. Arrange to meet with physical education teachers in order to discuss the programs of evaluation employed in their schools.

2. Administer a standardized physical fitness and/or neuromuscular skills test to students in an elementary and/or secondary school. Compute the mean, median, mode, standard deviation, T-scores, Z-scores, and percentile ranks for the scores earned. Correlate the scores of this test against scores of a second test taken by those students. Have the answers reviewed for accuracy. Interpret the results.

3. Make up a two- or three-item neuromuscular diagnostic skills test for at least one activity in each of the following general categories:
    a) Individual/self-testing activities
        (1) Archery
        (2) Bowling
        (3) Golf
        (4) Gymnastics
        (5) Track and Field
    b) Dual activities
        (1) Badminton
        (2) Handball
        (3) Paddleball, Racketball, Squash
        (4) Table tennis
        (5) Wrestling
    c) Team sport activities
        (1) Basketball
        (2) Floor Hockey
        (3) Flag football and Touch football
        (4) Soccer
        (5) Softball

4. Arrange to administer a three-item test battery designed to precede a volleyball unit to all students enrolled in an inclusionary physical education class. Compute the mean, standard deviation, and T-scores for each of the three distributions of scores, total and average these scores for all students, rank the averages of the T-scores; place (classify) the students into squads according to their rankings.

5. Review the abilities of students as identified in recommended laboratory assignment 4 and, as pertinent, arrange to sit in on the preparation of their IEPs.

6. Observe classes and assist squad members as they pursue behavioral objectives that have been indicated on their IEPs

7. Arrange to discuss with a physical education teacher how he/she selects and administers tests that measure the students' acquisition of individualized objectives.

8. Evaluate at least two standardized tests utilizing the form presented in this chapter.

9. Ask physical education teachers what procedures they use to grade students. Make every effort to relate this assignment to tasks described in laboratory assignments 4, 5, 6, and 7.
10. Attend conferences, clinics, seminars, and workshops about methods and materials related to the evaluation of the product and process of instruction.
11. Review the recommended readings.

REFERENCES

American Alliance for Health, Physical Education, and Recreation. 1978. *Practical pointers—Individual education programs: Assessment and evaluation in physical education* 1(9): 1.

Baumgartner, T. A., and A. S. Jackson. 1991. *Measurement for evaluation in physical education and exercise science.* Dubuque, IA: Wm. C. Brown.

Hensley, L., J. R. Morrow, and W. B. East. 1990. Practical measurement to solve practical problems. *Journal of Physical Education, Recreation and Dance* 61(3): 42–44.

Verducci, F. M. 1980. *Measurement concepts in physical education.* St. Louis: C. V. Mosby.

RECOMMENDED READINGS

Boyce, B. A. 1990. Grading practices —How do they influence student skill performance? *Journal of Physical Education, Recreation and Dance* 61(6): 46–48.

Byra, M. 1992. Measuring qualitative aspects of teaching in physical education. *Journal of Physical Education, Recreation and Dance* 63(3): 83–89.

Cureton, K. J., and G. L. Warren. 1990. Criterion-referenced standards for youth health-related fitness tests: A tutorial. *Research Quarterly for Exercise and Sport* 61(1): 7–19.

DiNucci, J., D. McCune, and D. Shows. 1990. Reliability of a modification of the health-related physical fitness test for use with physical education majors. *Research Quarterly for Exercise and Sport* 61(1): 20–25.

Fewell, R. R. 1991. Trends in the assessment of infants and toddlers with disabilities. *Exceptional Children* 58(2): 166–73.

Figueroa, R. A. 1989. Psychological testing of linguistic-minority students: Knowledge gaps and regulations. *Exceptional Children* 56(2): 145–52.

Fuchs, L. S., and S. L. Deno. 1992. Effects of curriculum within curriculum-based measurement. *Exceptional Children* 58(3): 232–43.

Gajria, M., and J. Salvia. 1992. The effects of summarization instruction on text comprehension of students with learning disabilities. *Exceptional Children* 58(6): 508–16.

Gay, L. R. 1992. *Educational research: Competencies for analysis and applications.* 4th ed. New York: Merrill.

Gross, L. D., J. F. Sallis, M. J. Buono, J. J. Roby, and J. A. Nelson. 1990. Reliability of interviewers using the seven-day physical activity recall. *Research Quarterly for Exercise and Sport* 61(4): 321–25.

Hopkins, W. G., and B. F. J. Manly. 1989. Errors in assigning grades based on tests of finite validity. *Research Quarterly for Exercise and Sport* 60(2): 180–82.

Kollath, J. A., M. J. Safrit, W. Zhu, and L. Gao. 1991. Measurement errors in modified pull-ups testing. *Research Quarterly for Exercise and Sport* 62(4): 432–35.

Kuzma, J. W. 1992. *Basic statistics for the health sciences.* Mountain View: CA: Mayfield Publishing Company.

Laughlin, N., and S. Laughlin. 1992. The myth of measurement in physical education. *Journal of Physical Education, Recreation and Dance* 63(4): 83–85.

Looney, M. A., and S. A. Plowman. 1990. Passing rates of American children and youth on the FITNESSGRAM criterion-referenced physical fitness standards. *Research Quarterly for Exercise and Sport* 61(3): 215–23.

Louie, L. H., and B. C. Chow. 1992. A factor analysis of selected badminton skill tests. *Research Quarterly for Exercise and Sport Supplement* 63(12): A–53.

McAuley, E., T. Duncan, and V. V. Tammen. 1989. Psychometric properties of the intrinsic motivation inventory in a competitive sport setting: A confirmatory factor analysis. *Research Quarterly for Exercise and Sport* 60(1): 48–58.

McLoughlin, J. A., and R. B. Lewis. 1990. *Assessing special students.* 3d ed. Columbus, OH: Merrill Publishing Company.

Noland, M., F. Dannier, M. McFadden, K. DeWalt, and J. M. Kotchen. 1990. The measurement of physical activity in young children. *Research Quarterly for Exercise and Sport* 61(2): 146–53.

Ocansey, R. T., and M. A. Kutame. 1991. Measuring soccer playing ability in natural settings. *Journal of Physical Education, Recreation and Dance* 62(7): 54–57, 77.

Osness, W. H. 1986. Physical assessment procedures. The use of functional profiles. *Journal of Physical Education, Recreation and Dance* 57(1): 35–38.

Puhl, J., K. Greaves, M. Hoyt, and T. Baranowski. 1990. Children's activity rating scale (CARS): Description and calibration. *Research Quarterly for Exercise and Sport* 61(1): 26–36.

Reaves, C. C. 1992. *Quantitative research for the behavioral sciences.* New York: John Wiley and Sons, Inc.

Safrit, M. J., A. S. Cohen, and M. G. Costa. 1989. Item response theory and the measurement of motor behavior. *Research Quarterly for Exercise and Sport* 60(4): 325–35.

Safrit, M. J., and M. A. Looney. 1992. Should the punishment fit the crime? A measurement dilemma. *Research Quarterly for Exercise and Sport* 63(2): 124–27.

Sainato, D. M., P. S. Strasin, D. Lefebvre, and N. Rapp. 1990. Effects of self-evaluation on the independent work skills of preschool children with disabilities. *Exceptional Children* 56(6): 540–49.

Silverman, S., R. Devillier, and T. Ramirez. 1991. The validity of academic learning time—Physical Education (ALT-PE) as a process measure of achievement. *Research Quarterly for Exercise and Sport* 62(3): 319–25.

Truesdell, L. A., and T. Abramson. 1992. Academic behavior and grades of mainstreamed students with mild disabilities. *Exceptional Children* 58(5): 392–98.

Urey, J. R., and F. J. Biasini. 1989. Evaluating the "difficult" child: Some practical suggestions. *Teaching Exceptional Children* 21(3): 10–13.

Veal, M. L. 1992. The role of assessment in secondary physical education—A pedagogical view. *Journal of Physical Education, Recreation and Dance* 63(7): 88–92.

Whitehead, J. R., and C. B. Corbin. 1991. Youth fitness testing: The effect of percentile-based evaluative feedback. *Research Quarterly for Exercise and Sport* 62(2): 225–31.

Willingham, W. W., M. Ragosta, R. E. Bennett, H. Braun, D. A. Rock, and D. E. Powers. 1988. *Testing handicapped people.* Boston: Allyn and Bacon, Inc.

Witt, J. C., S. N. Elliott, F. M. Gresham, and J. J. Dramer. 1988. *Assessment of special children: Tests and the problem-solving process.* Boston: Scott, Foresman and Company.

Zhu, W. 1992. Improving testing capability by applying multimedia technology. *Research Quarterly for Exercise and Sport Supplement* 63(1): A–55.

CHAPTER 19

Record Keeping and Public Relations

Objectives

After reading this chapter, you should be able to

- Identify and discuss basic strategies underlying effective office management.
- Know six business machines valuable to the efficient operation of an office.
- Describe commonly employed filing systems.
- Know the values of carefully managed inventory systems.
- Know basic guidelines to consider when selecting supplies and equipment.
- Describe supplies, equipment, and facilities common to a comprehensive physical education program—developmental and general.
- Know six audiovisual hardware items used in the teaching-learning process.
- Describe ways in which quality control can enhance the effectiveness of program operation.
- Discuss public relations.
- Identify and discuss the principles of public relations.
- Know the factors underlying the planning of a public relations program.
- Describe the alternative media and methods that can be used in a comprehensive public relations program.

INTRODUCTION

The importance of an accurate, efficient, orderly, complete, and secure record-keeping system cannot be overstated. This holds true whether you are keeping files on the students in developmental or regular physical education classes or for the school system as a whole. Without confidence in your ability to retrieve information when needed, you cannot function appropriately, and your colleagues or subordinates may begin to lose faith in your ability to be in control.

KEY TERMS

activity excuse form   inventories
advisory commitee   medical reports
alphabetical filing system   news story
annual report   numerical filing system
bid   office management
clinics   personal relationships
conventions   public relations
developmental program supplies   release forms
  and equipment   supply and equipment
efficiency control   checkout system
electronic data management   surveys
facility evaluation   tickle file
feature story   workshops

Unfortunately, proper record management is a subject that has often been neglected by those charged with its care. With the demands of day-to-day office routine, file folders may be misfiled or left on some desk not to be filed at all. Among the most important priorities of office management is appropriate record keeping.

OFFICE MANAGEMENT

Meeting visitors, answering and placing telephone calls, entering data on computer records, responding to and initiating correspondence, receiving and filing documents, and duplicating materials are tasks performed in all offices, large or small. Accurate record keeping lends order to all that has been attempted and accomplished.

To make the most efficient use of office time available, use a system. Incorporate into this system policies and procedures that will make office routine orderly and in keeping with sound office practice. Some basic policies and procedures of **office management** are the following:

1. Maintain office hours and keep these hours posted so that students, faculty, administrators, and others know when you are available for conferences. Once the hours have been established and posted, make every effort to honor them. It is extremely unfortunate when a visitor appears at a posted office hour and finds no one available. If meetings or emergencies call you away during office hours, post that information immediately. When individuals are unable to meet you during posted office hours, be prepared to make other times available. The person who needs to talk with you might have a class (or classes) at the time of your posted hours.

2. Be sure that each office employee greets visitors courteously; a first impression is often a lasting one. If a visitor arrives without appointment, an office employee should find out why the person has come. Should the greeter be unable to provide suitable answers to questions posed, an effort should be made to get them. If this is not possible, an appointment should be arranged for the

visitor to meet with someone who does have the answers. Provide a suitable waiting area for visitors who arrive early for appointments. Make every effort to keep your appointments on time. Be mindful of back-to-back appointments. Longer-than-expected sessions can impact on subsequent appointment times.

3. Limit use of the office telephone to professional calls. Incoming calls should be answered promptly and courteously, and referred appropriately. If the person being called is out of the office, the caller should be given the person's expected time of return. An invitation to leave a message should also be extended. The use of answering machines can provide a useful service when one's absence from the phone is required.

4. Respond to correspondence as soon as possible. One of the quickest ways for one to gain a poor reputation is to be negligent or careless about responding to letters or other memoranda. In addition to answering promptly (within twenty-four hours if possible), be sure that proper English is used. The letter that is mailed represents you and the institution you represent. The one impression the reader may have is the letter that has been received. It is a good policy to proofread all outgoing letters carefully. Many word processing progams have 'spell check' capabilities. Do not neglect to access that service. While checking spelling and grammar is important, be sure that the addressee's name is spelled correctly, that the address is accurate, and that a copy of the document is retained for the files. If a question posed in a letter to you would be answered best by someone else, reply that the question is being referred to another person and that the writer will be hearing from him/her. Give copies of the correspondence to the person who has the answer and request a copy of his/her response.

5. Index and file all documents that are received. Commonly received documentary materials are
    a) Sample textbooks
    b) School laws and policies
    c) Annual reports from the school, school system, school board, city, state, and federal governments
    d) Curriculum materials
    e) Magazines and periodicals
    f) Newspapers and newspaper clippings
    g) **Medical reports**, Figure 19.1
    h) **Activity excuse forms**, Figure 19.2
    i) Student participation forms
    j) Directories (e.g., school district employees, public officials, telephone)
    k) Bus schedules
    l) Other student activity forms (See Chapter 3)

6. Retain the original document from which duplicated materials were made. One curricular reference point for accountability in **public relations** efforts is the course outline. Have copies of outlines for each course on file. Since multiple sections of identical courses are often taught by more than one instructor, sharing "masters" avoids the effort and time it would take to create a document that already exists.

Parents or guardians – Mr. and Mrs. _____

Occupation of father _____ Occupation of mother _____

Family doctor _____ Family dentist _____

Name   Name

(Right margin, vertical: Last Name — First Name — Address — Telephone)

MEDICAL EXAMINATION		1	2	3	4
1. Date of examination					
2. Age					
3. Weight					
4. Height					
5. Hearing	Rt.				
	Lt.				
6. Eyes	Rt.				
	Lt.				
7. Test with glasses		Yes	Yes	Yes	Yes
		No	No	No	No
8. Ring worm					
9. Plantar warts					
10. Hair					
11. Personal hygiene					
12. Pulse before exercise					
13. Pulse after exercise					
14. Heart					
15. Lungs					
16. Tremor					
17. Abdomen					
18. Hernia					
19. Ears					
20. Nose					
21. Tonsils					
22. Adenoids					
23. Teeth					
24. Thyroid					
25. Glands					
26. Nutrition					
27. Skin					
28. PE classification					
Unrestricted (A or B)					
Partially restricted (C)					
Rest only (D)					
Permanent excuse					
Temporary excuse					
29. Swimming					
Permanent excuse					
Temporary excuse					
Doctor's initials					

HISTORY OF DISEASE

Columns: Chicken pox | St. Vitus dance | Diphtheria | Measles | Mumps | Pneumonia | Scarlet fever | Rheumatic fever | Whooping cough | Tonsillitis | Hay fever | Asthma | Date of vaccination for small pox | T. B. in family? | Date of skin test

Headaches:		Menstruation	
Never		Regular	
Occasionally		Irregular	
Frequently		Dysmenorrhea	
Operations:		Injuries	
Tonsils			
Others:			

Postural findings	L	R	L	R	L	R	L	R
Scoliosis	L	R	L	R	L	R	L	R
Shoulder high								
Hip high								
Feet:								
Pronation								
Long arch								
Transverse arch								
Head forward								
Round shoulders								
Hollow back								
Abdomen								
Body balance								
Posture grade								
Developmental PE								

COMMENTS:

Explanation of terms: 0 = normal; X = slight defect; XX = moderate; XXX = marked.

Figure 19.1. Medical form: Girl's health record

To: _____   Date: _____

Name of student: _____

Please excuse the student named above from physical
education activity class during period ____, _____,
because of: (Date)

_____

_____

_____

A physician has / has not examined this student
        (Circle one)

_____   _____
Name of physician   Signature of parent

Comments (Office use only):   _____
                               Home address

                               _____
                               Telephone number

Figure 19.2.
Activity excuse
form

Use a **tickle file** to remind you of the many details with which you must deal through the course of a school year. This calendar of events lists the specific things that should be done on or by certain dates.

A good secretary is indispensable to the efficient operation of a central office. The director needs a dependable person who can attend to basic procedures so that he/she will have time to administer the physical education programs and teach students. Business machines will help expedite paperwork and save hours of time. The following six items are recommended:

1. Computer/word processor/printer
2. Typewriter (standard or electric)
3. Photocopier, Figure 19.3
4. Calculator
5. Mimeograph machine *
6. Ditto machine *

FILING

As stated previously, an accurate, complete, efficient, orderly, and secure record-keeping system is basic to any efficient office operation. A major component of the record-

---

* While word processors and printers are efficient when initiating a master and reproducing relatively small numbers of materials, many consider the mimeograph and ditto machines less expensive when multiple copies of documents are necessary. A stencil, if stored properly, can be used for an indefinite period of time. Approximately two hundred clear copies can be made from a ditto master.

Figure 19.3. A program coordinator at work photocopying accreditation documents

keeping system is filing. All of the various records and reports must be filed so that you can retrieve them quickly when they are needed. Items that have been filed recently are ordinarily not too difficult to locate. On the other hand, materials that have been in the files for two or three years may be irretrievable unless a proper filing scheme is used.

There are two basic filing systems: alphabetical and numerical. The nature and intended use of the materials will help you to determine which system to use.

In the **alphabetical filing system**, papers are filed according to the first letter of the subject or person's name most relevant to the papers. For example, a topic beginning with the letter *D* would be filed with other topics beginning with the letter *D* and would be alphabetized to the second or third letter—for example, Daniels, Davies, Deck, Drugs, and so forth through the entire *D* file.

In the **numerical filing system**, code numbers are used to identify the file. For example, the number *14* might refer to medical records for students in the developmental physical education class; the number *24* might refer to Individual Education Plan (IEP) documents for these students; the number *34* might refer to records of term grades for these students. Items within each numbered file can be alphabetized.

Although in most smaller offices the alphabetical filing system is used, the numerical system may provide more security for confidential materials.

Whether an alphabetical or numerical filing system is used, the materials may be arranged vertically or horizontally. In the vertical arrangement, a folder serves as the basic filing unit. A letter or number may be placed on its tab. This will identify what classification of materials is in the folder. If materials are too large for easy placement in a vertical file, a horizontal (flat) arrangement can be used in which sections are separated by cardboard sheets. A tab can be placed on each sheet of cardboard to identify the documents that lie above or below it.

Another way to file horizontally is to place materials flat on the shelves of a bookcase. Each shelf can be labeled to identify its contents.

Another important filing procedure is cross-referencing. Many experienced office supervisors consider this procedure to be essential because some documents can be filed under separate headings. For example, a letter received from a school principal about a certain student's eligibility for participation in a mainstreamed class can be filed under the principal's name, under the letter (or number) representing the class to which the student will be assigned, or under the letter (or number) representing the student's name. The letter should be filed under the most logical heading (consistency is important) and the correspondent's name and the subject should be typed on colored typing paper for placement in the less logical files. This colored cross-reference form will help you find materials in a relatively short period of time. As you might guess, cross-referencing becomes more useful the longer items remain in the files.

Benefits of Electronic Data Management

Computers are able to store great amounts of information, and this information can be integrated relatively easily. Possibilities include computerizing the data now retained in file folders, index cards, on a Rolodex, or in an address book. However, Lockard, Abrams, and Many (1990) suggest that it requires some experience to judge the appropriateness of computerizing any specific set of data. Because a computer can do something does not mean that it is the best or even a better way of doing it. For example, having a computer file of phone numbers may sound good, but the probability is that using a telephone directory or Rolodex to find a number may require less time and effort. As with any process consider all the implications before making changes in your mode of operation. When appropriately implemented, **electronic data management** can do a great deal to increase the efficiency of office operations.

INVENTORIES

Proper management of supplies and equipment—inventories—is essential for any physical education program, whether developmental or general.

General Program Supplies

The following is a list of typical general program supplies:

Air pump with gauge

Archery supplies

Badminton rackets

Balance boards with rollers

Balls
    Baseballs
    Basketballs
    Cage balls

    Field hockey balls
    Footballs
    Golf balls
    Lacrosse balls
    Medicine balls
    Playground balls (assorted sizes)
    Soccer balls
    Softballs
    Table tennis balls
    Tennis balls
    Tether balls with lines
    Volleyballs
Baseball and softball supplies
    Bases
    Bats
    Chest protectors
    Gloves
    Masks
    Shin protectors

Beanbags

Blocks (wooden)

Chalk

Crossbars

Deck tennis rings

Discus

Eyeglass holders and protectors

Field hockey sticks

Floor hockey sticks and pucks

Frisbees

Golf clubs

Gym scooters

Hoops

Horseshoes (sets with pegs)

Indian clubs

Inner tubes

Jump ropes

Lacrosse sticks

Lummi sticks

Mats (multipurpose)

Measuring tape

Music/rhythm makers

Cymbals
Drums
Drumsticks
Tambourines
Triangles
Nets
Badminton
Basketball
Field hockey
Floor hockey
Lacrosse
Soccer
Table tennis
Tennis
Paddles

Parachute

Pegboard and pegs

Pinnies

Pitching targets

Pogo sticks

Pylons

Repair kit for balls

Scoops

Shuffleboard cues and disks

Shuttlecocks

Stilts

Table tennis paddles

Tees
Batting
Golf

Tennis rackets

Tote bags for balls

Track and field supplies
Batons
Crossbars
Discus
Hurdles (low and high)
Jump boards
Shots
Starter gun and blanks
Vaulting poles
Tug-of-war ropes

Wands

Whistles

Wire baskets to hold supplies

Yardsticks

General Program Equipment
The following is a list of typical general program equipment:

Asymmetrical bars

Backstop

Badminton standards

Balance beams (low and high)

Climbing ropes

Field markers

Goals
    Basketball (including backboards)
    Field hockey
    Floor hockey
    Lacrosse
    Soccer

Horizontal bar

Horizontal ladder

Jungle gym

Multipurpose (adjustable) chinning bar

Parallel bars

Piano

Pommel horse

Rebound boards

Screens (permanent wall and/or portable)

Stall bars

Table tennis tables and net standards

Tennis standards

Tetherball poles

Vaulting box

Vaulting standards

Volleyball standards

Weight training equipment
    Barbells
    Dumbbells
    Exercise boots and attachments

Inclined press bench
Neck weight collar and attachments
Squat rack and bench
Universal-type circuit-training unit

Developmental Program Supplies and Equipment
The following is a list of **developmental program supplies and equipment**:

Abdominal incline board

Ankle exerciser

Anthropemetric measuring tape

Balance boards and rollers

Barbell sets

Bean bags and targets

Bicycle exerciser

Calipers
Chest-depth
Shoulder-breadth-length
Skinfold

Chinning bar (adjustable)

Climbing ropes

Dry spirometer

Dumbbell set

Dynamometers
Back
Chest
Hand
Leg

Folding exercise mats

Foot inversion tread

Goniometer

Grip exercisers

Gym scooters

Heel stretcher

Hoops

Horizontal ladder

Indian clubs

Inner tubes

Isokinetic machinery

Jump ropes

Knee exercisers

Low balance beam

Medicine balls

Mobility aids
   Crutches
   Orthocanes
   Walkers
   Wheelchairs

Multiple hand (split-second) timer

Music makers
   Cymbals
   Drums
   Tambourines
   Triangles

Neck weight collar and attachments

Padded table

Parallel bars, wall mounted

Pegboards

Press bench (incline)

Posture rating station
   Fixed plumb line
   Three-section mirror

Quadriceps boots
   Bars
   Collars

Quadriceps table

Quoits
   Rubber, assorted colors
   Stand

Ramps and curbs

Rotary wrist machine

Rowing machine

Rubber-cable pull exerciser

Scale (weight)

Shoulder abduction machine

Snellen chart

Sphygmomanometer

Spirometer

Stadiometer

Staircase and railings

Stall-bar bench

Stall bars

Stethoscope

Tensiometer

Treadmill and railings

Wrist-roll machine.

Wrist pronator-supinator

Audiovisual equipment

In addition to having necessary supplies and equipment for use by students in their inclusionary, developmental, drilling, and demonstration sessions, it is important to have basic audiovisual equipment to enhance the teaching-learning process. The audiovisual equipment used most by physical education teachers is listed as follows.

1. Videocassette recorder/player with monitor for recording and displaying performances are useful for providing immediate feedback to students who are in the process of learning new skills. Players can also be used for showing skill modules. A distinct advantage of a VCR is that the tapes can be used over again for recording new events.

2. Sound film projectors: the sixteen-millimeter projector for showing films to large or small audiences; the eight-millimeter projector for showing films to small groups. Loop films are often available in cartridge form and ordinarily are designed to illustrate limited concepts such as the responsibilities of a soccer goalie, service in tennis, takedowns in wrestling, or the elementary backstroke in swimming. These limited concept films are also referred to as modules.

3. Thirty-five-millimeter slide projector for showing slides to large or small groups.

4. Overhead projector for projecting transparencies of tables or figures, teacher-made or commercial, on a screen. Large or small groups may be accommodated.

5. Opaque projector for projecting pictures or words directly from a book, picture, or other document onto a screen. Although the room in which the opaque projector is being used must be quite dark—which may prevent some students from taking notes—it is valuable because the instructor does not have to reproduce materials on paper, or prepare a transparency. Large or small groups may be accommodated.

6. Record and/or tape recorders and amplifiers (with a microphone). Again, these items are appropriate for use with large or small groups.

Purchasing

When selecting supplies and equipment for purchase, a variety of guidelines should be followed. Among the most critical are

1. Identify needs based upon inventory analysis.

2. Purchase items that cannot be constructed by you and/or your associates within the school system. Items can also be constructed by students in school industrial arts classes.

3. Be sure that selections are made by competent personnel.
4. Review design options as an ongoing process. Equipment styles or designs that were considered to be desirable at one time may not be appropriate now. This is a particularly important issue when considering safety factors.
5. Select standardized items as much as possible if doing so is practical from the standpoints of quality and cost. Standardized items are the simplest to replace or interchange.
6. Base selections upon economy without sacrificing quality.
7. State specifications clearly in writing for the vendor. Include code number designations, narrative descriptions, quantity, color, and size.
8. Entertain **bids**, Figure 19.4, with the lowest bid as a baseline figure. Consider item quality and vendor reputation regarding delivery and service.
9. Make purchases from reputable firms located near your school system. Good service is most likely from vendors that are not too far away.
10. Make purchases in advance of program needs. This is particularly true for major supply and equipment purchases. Orders rushed through at the last minute often lead to substitutions on the part of the manufacturer. This forces the school system to accept less-desirable items in order to have programs functioning on time. Sometimes late ordering means not being able to get the needed items at all. Consider centralized purchasing when various schools within the system need the same item(s). A considerable savings can be made when purchasing early and in large quantities.

Some time ago Bucher (1975) suggested a series of steps for a school system to follow when purchasing supplies and equipment. These procedures are still pertinent today.

1. Initiation. A request is made by the teacher for items to fulfill, augment, supplement, or improve the curriculum.
2. Review of request. The proper administrative personnel approve or disapprove the request after careful consideration of need (and budget parameters).
3. Review of budget allocation. A budget code number is assigned after availability of funds in that category has been determined.
4. Preparation of specifications. Specifications are prepared in detail, giving exact quality requirements, and made available to prospective contractors or vendors.
5. Receipt of bids. Contractors or vendors submit price quotations.
6. Comparison of bids to specifications. A careful evaluation is made to determine exact fulfillment of quality requirements.
7. Recommendations to the board of education. The business administrator prepares specific recommendations for approval.
8. Purchase order to supplier. After approval a purchase is made that fulfills the requirements at a competitive price.

The term **inventory** means an evaluation of supplies and equipment available for the program. Inventory procedures are used to identify and evaluate the following:

1. Quantity of items e.g., the number of badminton rackets, shuttlecocks, and so on.
2. Quality of items, e.g., whether the items are in good, fair, or poor condition.

PLYMOUTH   STATE   COLLEGE
Of the University System of New Hampshire
Purchasing Department
Facilities Services Building
Plymouth, NH   03264

603-535-2246 FAX 603-535-2711

V
E
N
D
O
R

REQUEST   FOR   QUOTATION

BID NUMBER: DATE: DUE DATE: DUE HOUR:

Quotes shall be returned in a sealed envelope plainly marked on the outside the BID NUMBER indicated below and returned to the Plymouth State College Purchasing Office or FAXed to the FAX number indicated above. At the appointed time and place the bids will be opened and publicly read aloud. Plymouth State College reserves the right to reject any of or all quotes and to waive any formalities in the bidding. All resulting mechanicals, designs for printed materials, and special tooling for other product, will become the property of Plymouth State College.

Quantity   Unit   Description   Unit Price   Extension

Please quote on this form and attach it to any additional information, brochures or descriptions of suggested alternatives. For any clarification of the specifications on this bid, the site contact at PSC is   at 603-535-

_____   _____   _____
Janice Lyman   Vendor Officer Signature   Date:
Purchasing Agent

Figure 19.4. Bid form. *Courtesy of Plymouth State College, Plymouth, NH.*

3. Usefulness to the program, i.e., whether the items should be stored for immediate use. If the items are not considered useful for the program currently under way, they can be stored in an "off-season" area, sold, or turned in for items more useful to the current program.

4. Storage location.

Various types of inventory forms can be used to record information. A form that has been found to be particularly useful is shown in Figure 19.5. The usefulness of any form, however, depends on the care that is taken in conducting the inventory evaluation. Supply and equipment items should be counted carefully and their condition rated. This information, along with specific program requirements, will serve as the basis for purchase requests. If budgets are being reduced, extreme care must be taken in determining priority requests.

Inventories are critical to instruction and learning. It is important to know the quantity and quality of the supplies and equipment available for use within the program, their relevance to the program, and where these items are stored. As Johnson (1977) pointed out,

Equipment (and supply) control begins and ends with a comprehensive inventory.

Inventories should be conducted at least three times during each school year: at the beginning of the year, at the completion of each unit of instruction or activity in which

Item	Storage area	Quantity	Condition			Number to order
			Excellent	Usable	Needs repair	

Figure 19.5. Inventory form

specific supply and equipment items are used, and at the end of the school year. The inventory taken at the beginning of the school year usually identifies supply and equipment needs. These needs often have to be communicated to the department chairperson by November, to the principal by December, and to the school board in January. Items that have been purchased the preceding spring or summer (with funds from the preceding year's budget) but not yet received should be included in the first inventory of the new school year.

Facility Evaluation

Through special or standard budgetary provisions it may be possible to renovate existing facilities or build new ones. Consequently an inventory should be made of existing facilities and a plan developed that includes priorities for renovation and expansion projects. Be prepared to make recommendations regarding **facility evaluation** should the opportunity arise.

Make an inventory of community facilities that might be used for school instructional and recreational programs.* Examples might include the Young Men's Christian Association (YMCA), Young Women's Christian Association (YWCA), athletic club facilities, and recreation centers (both public and private). With a knowledge of available resources outside of the school, administrators can make more intelligent decisions about building programs.

Facilities valuable for use within a comprehensive physical education program are

1. Athletic training room
2. Conditioning and development room
3. Dance room
4. Equipment storage rooms (for in-season and out-of-season items)
5. Field house (with indoor track, tennis courts, pole and jumping pits)
6. Gymnasia
7. Gymnastics room
8. Handball, paddleball, racketball, squash courts
9. Locker rooms and shower rooms for men and for women
10. Office space
11. Outdoor track
12. Playing fields
13. Practice fields
14. Supply storage rooms (for in-season and out-of-season items)
15. Swimming pool
16. Tennis room
17. Wrestling room

The list of renovation and construction priorities depends on a number of factors:

1. Current program offerings
2. Current school enrollment

---

* The use of community facilities should be explored. Gymnasia, conditioning rooms; handball, paddleball, racketball, squash courts; swimming pools; and outdoor playing areas might be available for rent, on a reciprocal basis, or free of charge.

3. Existing school facilities
4. Existing community facilities that can be used on a short- or long-term basis
5. Projected program and enrollment expansion or reduction for the next five, ten, or fifteen years.

Careful thought should go into the development of any list of activities. As priorities change through the years, be certain that evidence of the need for change can be documented and can support any new recommendations you might make. Any proposal for the construction and renovation of physical education facilities is only a part of the total master plan for a given school system. Changes are a necessary part of growth, but changes in what were well-thought-out proposals may have significant impact on the school system.

EFFICIENCY CONTROL

If an orderly scheme for supply, equipment, and facility use and care does not exist, institute a plan for periodic accounting. This **efficiency control** plan should include a system for checking items in and out.

It is desirable that supplies, equipment, and facilities be used by students during planned and unplanned sessions beyond the classroom. In fact use of these resources should be encouraged because it enables students to practice their skills and participate in open (drop-in) recreation. Establish an efficient **supply and equipment checkout system** to assess use. Daily monitoring can be facilitated by use of the form shown in Figure 19.6.

Name of student: _____ I.D. number: _____

Description of item: _____

Use to be made of item: ___Recreation___   ___Class___   ___Other___
                               (Circle one)

                                                                        A.M.
                                                                        P.M.
Checked out: _____   _____
                    (Date)   (Time)

                                                                        A.M.
                                                                        P.M.
Checked in: _____   _____
                    (Date)   (Time)

                                        _____
                                           (Signature of student)

Note to person on duty: Retain student identification card until item is returned to equipment room.

_____
   (Signature of staff member on duty)

Figure 19.6. Supply and equipment checkout form

At the conclusion of a specified period of time, the accumulated data can be recorded on a master form.

It is also worthwhile to record the use made of the facilities for classes, organized intramural activities, interscholastic team practices and competition, and drop-in recreation, Figure 19.7. When questions arise as to what use is made of supplies, equipment, and facilities within the physical education program, it may be helpful to be able to provide documentation of this use. Not only does this information offer testimony as to student interest in the program, but it also provides evidence of the need for essential expenditures for supplies, equipment, renovation, and construction.

Quality control encompasses inventories and checkout systems, use, cleaning and maintenance, storage, refinishing and renovation, and construction (see Appendix F).

PUBLIC RELATIONS

The activities and techniques used by individuals and organizations to establish favorable attitudes in their behalf on the part of the general public or of special groups is known as public relations. Often confused with the term publicity, public relations has much broader implications. Although publicity is its primary instrument, public relations should be concerned with all of the various impressions that are given to the public—not just those communicated through newspapers, radio, and television. Over fifty years ago Fine (1943) made this point by writing,

Room	Month _____			Week of _____			
	Sunday	Monday	Tuesday	Wednesday	Thursday	Friday	Saturday
Classroom number _____							
Classroom number _____							
Classroom number _____							
Dance room							
Exercise room							
Gymnasium							
Handball courts							
Indoor track							
Swimming pool							
Wrestling room							
_____							
_____							
_____							
_____							

Figure 19.7. Use of physical education/athletic facilities form

Public relations is more than a set of rules—it is a broad concept. It is the entire body of relationships that go to make up our impressions of an individual, an organization, or an idea.

Need for Public Relations

The advancement of educational materials and methodology is largely paid for by public tax dollars. Schools, therefore, have an obligation to give an accounting to the taxpayers who provide such funds. Adapting a marketing system can provide the framework and stimulation necessary to accomplish this task (Schneider, 1992).

Public support is needed when new programs are proposed. Unless a public relations plan has communicated to the public valid reasons for rendering support, the success of any new program is in jeopardy. Facility improvements, an increase in staff, or modification in curricular requirements for regular and/or developmental physical education programs may all require a greater expenditure of public funds. Information about the entire program is central to any public understanding of its value. A comprehensive public relations program disseminates information and can generate intelligent responses to questions regarding requests for additional dollars. The public is often unaware of what contemporary programs in physical education are able to accomplish. There has been a significant change in physical education programming within the last twenty years, but many people are plagued by memories of their own experiences.

Additional funds may be needed to underwrite program goals for children with disabilities who are enrolled in developmental and mainstreamed classes. Unless a public relations program is able to interpret successfully the values of programs in physical education for all children, administrators might decide to cut appropriations for general physical education programs in order to comply with the law without having to argue for increases in the total program budget.

The need to interpret the entire program to the public is apparent. A public that understands the values of physical education will be more sympathetic to requests by administrative officials for increases in financial support. Davis and Wallis (1961) clarified the purposes of a strong public relations program by offering the following twelve points:

1. Create good will with all pertinent publics (students, parents, school personnel).
2. Help pertinent publics understand the reasons for and values of physical education.
3. Inform pertinent publics of present programs and planned changes in programs, policies, etc.
4. Inform pertinent publics of services rendered by the department and of its willingness to serve.
5. Inform pertinent publics of events that have occurred and will occur.
6. Encourage participation in suitable activities related to the program and in the use of available facilities.
7. Inform the publics of the expenditure of funds (probably through the superintendent's annual report).
8. Enlist assistance in suitable projects and other help.
9. Encourage and publicize activities that are as self-supporting as possible.

10. Show reasons for greater financial support , if needed (and if approved by the school administration).

11. Rectify mistaken ideas, remove misunderstandings, erase negative attitudes.

12. Guide and promote public opinion in favor of worthy programs in physical education.

Principles of Public Relations

Various conditions underlie the effectiveness of a public relations program. Among these are the following:

1. The ability to identify immediate and long-range public relations needs and objectives.

2. Staff belief in the integrity of the program. If the staff is not united in support of existing and proposed programs, the probability of procuring public support is diminished significantly. The exhibition of silence or negative innuendoes by only a few staff members may do great harm. A unified staff is better able to portray an image that will promote public support.

3. It is important that the target population be defined before a public relations program is begun. Public relations techniques and strategies are governed in large part by a definition of the public to be addressed.

4. Public relations programs must be based upon truth. The public should expect and receive honest and accurate information. Misrepresentation will almost always be detected, and a single misrepresentation can discredit an organization more than any other factor. Further, the public will not soon forget the deception.

5. **News stories** should be well written. Poor news stories are worse than none and may not even get published. Scherer (1971) identified some common reasons why editors do not use material that has been submitted for publication.
   a) Limited local interest
   b) No reader interest
   c) Poor writing
   d) material obviously faked
   e) Inaccuracy
   f) Material stretched too thin.

6. Each staff person is directly or indirectly a spokesperson for the program. The principal, guidance counselor, nurse, department head, teacher, custodian, and bus driver all affect perceptions of the school. These individuals discuss many aspects of the overall school program with their families and friends. The impressions that are received through casual conversations may yield positive or negative reactions at the polls. Loyalty is an important ingredient of a successful public relations image. Students are also representatives of the school. A good program results in favorable unsolicited comments by students to any number of persons. A poor program results in negative comments.

7. Public relations should be an ongoing process. Campaigns for specific causes are often not effective because, to many within the public sector, campaign publicity has a taste of propaganda. Unfortunately, many school officials tend to neglect the public relations program until there is a crisis, at which time all-

out efforts are made to secure public support. A continuous public relations effort will keep the program image fresh in the minds of those who may ultimately be in a position to judge its destiny. In short—be proactive, not reactive.

8. The community should be involved in the public relations process. As Voltmer and Esslinger (1967) have pointed out,

The concept of public relations wherein everything originates within the schools and flows to the public is a limited one. The public is capable of providing more than mere financial support, as important as that is.

There is a trend in many communities to develop physical education **advisory committees**. These may be subcommittees of school boards, appointed committees of public officials, or committees appointed by school officials. Whoever assumes responsibilities for designating the composition of this advisory group should consider the following individuals for appointment:

a) Representative of the school administration
b) Special education teacher
c) Physical education teacher
d) Representative of the office of city or town government
e) Representative of the school board
f) High school senior
g) Representative of the alumni

A committee of school administrators made the following observation regarding public involvement in school affairs (Metropolitan School Study Council 1949):

The significance of public participation in educational planning is that it represents one of the most effective means of helping people talk through the problems of education. Citizens come together to explore, plan, and think through and solve educational problems in cooperation with the board of education and the professional staff. In this manner, by digging deeply into the rich strata that are basic to good education, the individual will grow in experience and knowledge. His view of education will be more complete. From these cooperative experiences will come understandings which lead to better support for the schools and an improved school program.

9. A good quality physical education program is the most important prerequisite for good public relations. The most sophisticated public relations plans will be unable to overshadow the the weaknesses of a poor program. A program that denies opportunity for all students to grow in behavioral, cognitive, and sensorimotor skills violates the principles of education. In 1950 the American Association of School Administrators offered its views on the matter by writing:

When the public relations program of a school system rests on a foundation of sound classroom accomplishment, it is like a house built upon a rock. Storms of ill-founded criticism and innuendo will not overwhelm it. Its foundations are sure. On the other hand, the most systematic and skillfully devised publicity cannot maintain the public's confidence or win its approval for a school program that is fundamentally unsound. No shoring up with "interpretation" can permanently conceal the shortcomings and failures of misdirected or ineffective teaching. Public relations, under such circumstances, is built on shifting sands. The public cannot hear what is said because it is so acutely aware of what the program is—or is not.

10. Public relations efforts must be evaluated. Public attitudes can generally be assessed by observation and polling.

Planning the Public Relations Program

An effective public relations program is dependent on the involvement of many interested and informed persons. It also has to do with knowing the community's political makeup, not so much in regard to those who occupy elected positions, but rather the power of special interest groups (Bedworth and Bedworth 1992). Students, teachers, administrators, school boards, advisory committees, and others can contribute much to the success of any public relations effort. McCloskey (1960) described a number of procedures that should be considered for adoption by those involved in planning for public relations. These procedures are still pertinent today.

1. Establish a sound public-communications policy.
2. Determine what educational services and developments benefit pupils.
3. Obtain facts about what citizens do and do not know and believe about educational values and needs.
4. Decide what facts and ideas will best enable citizens to understand the benefits children obtain from good schools and what improvements will increase these benefits.
5. Make full use of effective teacher-pupil planning techniques to generate understanding and appreciation.
6. Relate cost and tax facts more closely to opportunity for boys and girls to achieve.
7. Decide who is going to perform specific communication tasks at particular times.

Carrying out the Public Relations Program

While rising costs and fluctuating support from local communities have contributed to an atmosphere of uncertainty (Moore and Gray 1990), an ongoing public relations plan can provide evidence of good-quality school programs that can be reviewed objectively at any time. Unfortunately, many activities are perceived by school personnel as being so routine that they are neglected in the public relations effort. In addition, many teachers are so engrossed in their teaching assignments that they do not find or make time to engage in formal public relations activities. This is unfortunate because teachers know their programs best and can help to educate the public to make intelligent decisions regarding program support. According to Williams, Brownell, and Vernier (1964),

Notwithstanding the fact that a well-rounded program is of paramount importance, continuous efforts must be made to keep the public informed, especially concerning those aspects of greatest educational significance, or about which there is likely to be limited public understanding.

Those charged with the task of communication must be people who can express thoughts and ideas in ways that are easily understood. Speaking in this regard, Goldhaber (1990) wrote,

> To communicate, a person must be able to evolve a mental picture of something (create a concept), give it a name, and develop a feeling about it.

To help make possible the dissemination of information to the various publics regarding the physical education program and people associated with it, a multidimensional approach must be taken. The following sections describe procedures and tasks that can effect positive public relations.

Coordination of Effort Although every individual connected with the schools will directly or indirectly influence public relations by individual or collective behavior, it is important that one person (or office) coordinate the public relations effort. Duplication is important for emphasis—but is should occur by design, not by accident.

In addition to monitoring the ongoing public relations program, the coordinator—with a modest amount of clerical assistance—can address areas needing specific public relations attention. When several persons attempt to publicize given programs without direction and assistance from a coordinator, a number of problems may arise. Among these are:

1. Lack of consistency as to how topics are treated
2. Failure to reach the proper audiences
3. Unnecessary duplication
4. Use of valuable time to address topics better taken care of by someone else
5. Use of the wrong medium for the communication task at hand.

Personal Relationships As implied earlier in this chapter, every individual who is employed by a school system is its ambassador. **Personal relationships** can therefore be very important. For example, consider that statements made in casual conversations influence the perceptions that the many publics develop with respect to the schools. Therefore it is vitally important that criticisms of colleagues and programs be addressed within the school rather than in public. Loyalty is an important commodity. Successful public relations depends in large part on the attitudes employees portray about the school system for which they work.

Advisory Committees The public should be given the opportunity to share its insights regarding the strengths and weaknesses of a school program. An **advisory committee** can serve such a function. When representatives of the public sector are given the opportunity to interact with school personnel, they more readily understand the rationale behind some of the actions that have been taken. Further these representatives may be able to offer valuable suggestions as to how the public can best be apprised of ongoing, special, and proposed programs, as well as how to elicit its support.

Whether subconsciously or not, the public often divides the community into two groups—namely, school employees and others. If an advisory committee is formed, the public can affect programs and their development. This often changes the they-us syndrome to cooperation.

Articles for Publication There are three basic kinds of articles: advance stories, news stories, and **feature stories**. Advance stories alert the public that an event is to take place at a specific place and time. More than one advance story might be published before an important event.

News stories are written about an event that has occurred. These stories should include the basic elements common to all well-written newspaper articles: *who* did *what*, *when*, *where*, and *how*. A sixth component, *why*, may also be included depending on the nature of the event. A number of valuable suggestions for preparing news stories has been made by Harral (1952).

1. State facts only, not personal opinions.
2. Tell your story briefly in simple language, then stop.
3. Answer the questions *who*, *what*, *where*, *when*, and *why* (when appropriate) early in the story.
4. Make the report accurate and coherent.
5. Paragraph and punctuate properly.
6. Be especially careful about names, titles, hours, and subjects.
7. Avoid abbreviations, slang, adjectives, wordiness, and involved sentences.
8. Omit headlines.
9. Submit clean copy (word processed or typed), double spaced.
10. Always get your story in on time.

Feature stories usually discuss a theme. An example might be a story on a state Special Olympics program. An overview of the Special Olympics corporation, board of directors, goals, and program itinerary for the year could be a feature story. A feature story can be distinguished from a news story in that the latter ordinarily deals with a particular event at a particular time and place.

Annual Reports **Annual reports** provide an opportunity to describe physical education program highlights for the entire year. Curricular offerings, extracurricular activities, qualifications of staff, students served, and important needs and priorities of the department are ordinarily included in annual reports. Facts rather than opinions should be stated. For example, if there are specific structural barriers within the physical education plant that deny access to a number of students with disabilities, a simple statement of this fact is more likely to arouse favorable action than an emotional appeal.

Special Bulletins and Newsletters Bulletins and newsletters can be used to alert population segments to special events that have been scheduled for a particular period of time. They can also be used to inform an audience about events that have taken place. The principles of advance and news stories are appropriate, but can be applied on a less formal basis. Special bulletins and newsletters can, for example, inform parents about the criterion-referenced achievements of their children (see Chapter 18).

Radio Announcements An appealing radio announcement regarding an upcoming event can enlist the interest of the listening audience. Other than local newspapers the radio is the public's primary source of local information. Catchy phrases and gimmicks underlie many pleasing radio announcements.

The usual procedure is to prepare an audiotape that, after review by a news editor, is played at selected times. These tapes may use a monologue, skit, or question-answer format.

Television Television is another valuable medium for public relations. It can illustrate visually as well as tell about programs under way in physical education. The television presentation may be live or taped. Highlights of special physical education programs of the past provide valuable documentation that be referenced for programs being planned for the future.

Commercial television and radio stations are required by law to provide broadcast time in the interest of public service. A number of schools have regular programs on their local radio and television stations.

Public Speeches There are many opportunities for physical educators to speak before special interest groups. Through the course of an academic year many speaking invitations may be extended by civic and fraternal organizations, business and social service clubs, parent-teacher associations, and so on.

To promote positive public relations, speakers have to deliver high quality, carefully planned presentations. Slides and graphs can be used to enhance any discussion regarding physical education programs.

Because any one person may not be able to accept all invitations to speak, it is worthwhile to develop a speaker's bureau. This bureau can consist of specialists versed in various aspects of the program. For example, the nurse might speak on posture screening; the special education teacher might speak before a group interested in learning more about individual education plans (IEPs); the guidance counselor might address the history of vocational electives for graduates who have disabilities; the physical education teacher might speak on developmental physical education and the principles of inclusionary programs.

Student Publications Materials prepared by students can be very valuable in the promotion of various aspects of the physical education program. Other students, parents, school board members, faculty members, and administrative officials all have the opportunity to see these publications. Physical education teachers should cooperate as much as possible with students who are interested in writing news items about the physical education program. Incorrect information is less likely to appear in student publications if teachers and administrators take the time to provide the writers with accurate information.

Assembly Programs School assemblies provide an opportunity for special activities to be introduced, described, and demonstrated to the student body, faculty, and administration. Since it is unlikely that the general public will attend assemblies held during school hours, evening assemblies can be scheduled if the subject is of general interest.

Demonstrations Another way to show the activity options offered within the physical education program to the community is through formal demonstrations. Exhibitions offer the community visible accountability (Sizer 1992). The general public often equates physical education with interscholastic athletic activities. This is not surprising when we consider the sports topics usually addressed by newspapers, radio, and television. A demonstration of various developmental and general physical education activities can contribute a great deal to public awareness and support.

Many demonstrations are limited to gymnastics. Gymnastics is a valuable activity and is exciting to watch, but physical education includes many more program elements. To make the public aware of the scope of the physical education program, more than a single program component should be demonstrated, Figure 19.8.

Dauer and Pangrazi (1979) offer guidelines for planning physical education demonstrations.

1. The activities should illustrate the attainment of the objectives of physical education. They should grow out of, and be typical of, the program.
2. The activities should not require a long period of preparation so that the physical education period becomes a training period for the demonstration. However, sufficient rehearsal must be conducted.
3. Children should be properly dressed for the activity, but elaborate and intricate costuming should be avoided. Simple costumes that can be made by the children are most acceptable. No child should be left out because he or she does not have the right costume.
4. The demonstration should include a number of children. An attempt should be made to get all children in the groups involved in the program and to play fair by using typical groups. However, recognition can be given to children of superior ability by having them do specialty numbers.

Figure 19.8. Demonstration of a physical education activity

5. A printed program is desirable.
6. The principal or another administrative official should open the program with a word of welcome to the parents and other visitors. His or her remarks should include mention of the educational importance of physical education and the district's administrative support of the program.
7. A microphone should be available so running comment can be supplied as the activity unfolds. In this way attention can be directed to the crucial points to be observed.
8. The opening number should be an eye-opener and attention-getter. The program should end with some sort of grand finale.
9. The program should be fast moving and contain activities of good audience appeal. Music is indispensable; a well-balanced program contains several numbers with music.
10. The program should call attention to physical fitness, and some elements should be devoted to this area. A demonstration of physical fitness testing is always well received.
11. Some part of the program can include a demonstration of instructional procedures, rather than centering all attention on accomplishments.
12. It is important to avoid tests of strength and skill that might lead to the embarrassment of those defeated.
13. While a high degree of performance is not needed, the activities should be done reasonably well, within the level of the children's abilities.

Although demonstrations have not been as popular in recent years as they once were, a well-balanced public relations effort will have such programs on the agenda. Not only do they provide those in attendance with an awareness of program offerings, but they also provide those who are not necessarily gifted enough to serve as members of interscholastic teams with opportunities to demonstrate their achievements to the public. Further, coming together for an evening or weekend demonstration helps create another forum for school spirit and collegiality.

Clinics Clinics provide opportunities for colleagues and other interested persons to upgrade their skills. Usually clinics center around a specific theme within which practicing specialists are invited to present specific topics. Examples of programs suitable for clinics are given here.

1. A demonstration of how a developmental physical education class for those with neurological impairments can be organized and administered
2. A demonstration of procedures for including children with visual impairments in a standard physical education class
3. A demonstration of static and dynamic postural appraisal techniques

An advance story about the clinic will not only alert those who may be interested in attending, but indicate to the general public that in-service programs are being provided to upgrade teacher competencies. A news story that follows the principles of writing discussed previously will enhance public awareness of the event.

Workshops Workshops are more activity-oriented than clinics in that attendees are expected to participate in the program. For example, a workshop might be conducted on the occasion of a scheduled inclusionary program. A practicing specialist might begin the workshop by demonstrating selected methods and materials with the various children enrolled in the class, after which the attendees might work with the children themselves.

As is the case with clinics, public awareness of in-service workshops enhances public awareness of the whole program.

Convention Programs **Conventions** provide opportunities for theorists, researchers, administrators, and teachers to present topics in their respective areas of expertise. Conventioneers are exposed to different ways of addressing issues common to their professional assignments. State, district, and national conventions are extremely valuable sources of information. The sharing of professional experiences and ideas with others is an important part of public relations. It is one way that individuals (and their institutions) gain prestige among colleagues in their professions.

If someone in a school district has presented a topic at a convention, a news story should be written so that the public will be aware of the competencies of the teaching and administrative staff in the school system. The public should also be made aware of what individuals within the school district have served as presiders or attended as conventioneers. Teachers and administrators who demonstrate interest in improving their knowledge and skills are valuable to a school system and should be recognized as such.

Ideas brought back to the school system can be a source of revitalization for those who have not attended. Delegates should be encouraged to report the highlights of the sessions they have attended. In fact, a summary report suitable for distribution can be made a logical condition of receiving school district funds for attending the convention.

Videotapes and Films The medium of videotape provides immediate feedback for students and instructors interested in assessing present status and achievement. Videotape is also valuable for showing programs to special interest groups and to the general public. Public speaking sessions and television broadcasts are examples of public relations forums that make use of videotapes.

Films (movies) are more permanent and in the long run, more expensive than videotapes. Videotapes can be erased with succeeding programs; sixteen- or eight-millimeter motion picture film cannot have their images replaced easily. Both media, however, have their place in the total public relations effort.

Posters and Graphs Posters can be used to advertise activities that are under way or planned for the future. Art students can create posters for display in public places such as supermarkets, service stations, corridors of public buildings, and school bulletin boards. When done carefully and displayed appropriately, posters provide an attractive source of information for the public , Figure 19.9.

Graphs can be used to illustrate a number of things. For example, the relative growth status of students in a class can be averaged and portrayed by comparing such to other classes, other schools, and so forth. Expenditure emphases for the year can be displayed for school board members and other interested parties. Physical fitness test scores are often graphed. There are many computer software programs available that can provide outstanding graphic displays of data.* To a great extent the types of displays one uses are limited only by one's imagination.

---

* Examples of software programs providing graphic options are Microsoft Works and Lotus.

Figure 19.9. Poster display

Special-interest Mailings Key public relations news items should be sent to organizations to alert members to events under way or planned that may be of interest to them. Interorganization communications are valuable in any comprehensive public relations plan. Appendix B reveals a list of organizations that can be contacted.

School Alumni Alumni can assist in school public relations programs. Graduates can be asked to identify program needs according to their perspectives. An organized effort should be made to enlist the assistance of respected alumni when preparing documents that identify program needs. Supportive alumni living within the community can also serve as members of the speaker's bureau. Alumni might also help prepare news items for radio and television.

Photographs Clear photographs can portray children participating in physical education activities. Photographs can be submitted with news releases, posted on bulletin boards, and given to families and friends of the children. Copies of photographs should always be retained for filing. Oral presentations are often enhanced by photographs of students participating in past programs.

Accounting for institutional policies, releases must ordinarily be obtained from the parents or guardians of youngsters with disabilities before display of any photograph, videotape, or film (movie) of them. An example of a commonly used **release form** is shown in Figure 19.10.

Special Theme Weeks Special theme weeks help to promote selected phases of the physical education program and bring their existence to the attention of the public. Such themes as physical fitness and lifetime sports have been particularly successful in various

---

Department of Physical Education   Date:_____

I grant permission to use a picture of my child, _____
                                                                    (Student's Name)

for publicity purposes related to the implementation of physical education/
recreation programs.

Parent's Signature: _____   Date:_____

Figure 19.10. Photograph release form

communities. If endorsement of the town manager, mayor, governor, or other official can be procured additional public support is likely.

Surveys A valuable technique for assessing public interests in and awareness of various programs is the **survey**. Telephone calls, radio talk shows, questionnaires in newspapers, or bulletins brought home by students can help obtain public opinions. Data gathered can be used in the review and evaluation of public relations efforts. Lack of public awareness and endorsement is an indication that intensified public relations are necessary. The ultimate sign of public approval of the physical education program, and one that practitioners wholeheartedly believe in, is support at the polls, in town meetings, and other public forums where decisions regarding funding, faculty retention, and hiring are made. Do not underestimate the value of surveys. Garnering views from a population or random sample of school district taxpayers will provide useful information when planning public relations activities.

SUMMARY

Thoughtful teachers and administrators will adopt a system of office management, record keeping, and supply, equipment, and facility quality control that will maximize the usefulness and care of existing resources. At the same time, it is critical that they make serious efforts to describe their programs and needs to the public.

Public relations is an all-encompassing term. It represents what is done and not done to enhance public awareness intelligently regarding programs of physical education. Acts of commission and omission contribute greatly to the impressions many people have of physical education within the schools. I hope that the guidelines suggested in this chapter will aid all who are interested in increasing public awareness of and procuring support for programs of physical education that are underway and planned for the generations of young people to come.

RECOMMENDED LABORATORY ASSIGNMENTS

1. Arrange to meet with and interview office administrators with regard to their techniques of office management.

2. Arrange to interview department chairpersons, school principals, business managers, and school superintendents for the purpose of reviewing their record-keeping systems.

3. Meet with practitioners to discuss advantages and disadvantages of various facility styles in terms of their usefulness to general and developmental physical education programs.

4. Visit an elementary, junior high, or senior high school to discuss with teachers and administrators their perceptions of high-priority needs for facility renovation and expansion. Ask to examine the building master plans.

5. Visit various physical education facilities and take photographs of indoor and outdoor activity areas.

6. Review various inventory and checkout systems employed by physical education practitioners.

7. Examine supply and equipment catalogs to become aware of different costs and styles of the items advertised.

8. Sit in on school board meetings during discussions about budget proposals.

9. Become proficient in the use of business machines and audiovisual equipment described in this chapter.

10. Prepare a list of audiovisual and business machine equipment not described in this chapter that could add to administering, teaching and learning efficiency.

11. Arrange to meet with news editors of city newspapers and radio and television stations to discuss their perceptions as to how their respective media can contribute to public relations efforts.

12. Meet with public relations specialists in order to gain further insight into the principles of public relations.

13. Meet with public school administrative officials to discuss their formal public relations efforts.

14. Arrange to write an advance article on a special event that is scheduled for presentation in a local school. Submit the article to a local newspaper for publication.

15. Arrange to write a news story for a school program. Keep in mind the principles of good writing. Submit the story for publication.

16. Arrange to prepare a feature story on some phase of adapted physical education as programmed within a local school system. Submit it for publication.

17. Prepare a videotape that can be used to advertise an upcoming event in adapted physical education. Use a monologue, skit, or interview (question-answer) technique.

18. Review poster campaigns being sponsored or conducted by different agencies to gain insight into poster and graphic designs.

19. Arrange to design a poster for a Special Olympics or other program to be conducted within the community or state.

20. Attend physical education demonstrations in selected schools and observe the format being used. Attempt to assess public response to these programs.

21. Visit various schools to photograph or videotape selected components of their developmental and general physical education programs. Be certain to obtain permissions and releases in advance of collection and display.

22. Prepare a speech that describes a phase of adapted physical education that has not been formally promoted. Highlight the speech with slide photographs or videotapes.
23. Arrange to attend conferences, clinics, seminars, or workshops on methods and materials in public relations.
24. Review the recommended readings.

REFERENCES

American Association of School Administrators. 1950. *Public relations for America's schools: Twenty-eighth yearbook.* Washington, DC: The Association.

Bedworth, A. E., and D. A. Bedworth. 1992. *The profession and practice of health education.* Dubuque, IA: William C. Brown.

Bucher, C. A. 1975. *Administration of health and physical education programs.* St. Louis: C.V. Mosby Company.

Dauer, V. P., and R. P. Pangrazi. 1979. *Dynamic physical education for elementary school children.* Minneapolis: Burgess Publishing Company.

Davis, E. C., and E. L. Wallis. 1961. *Toward better teaching in physical education.* Englewood Cliffs, NJ: Prentice-Hall.

Fine, B. 1943. *Educational publicity.* New York: Harper and Row.

Goldhaber, G. M. 1990. *Organizational communication.* 5th ed. Dubuque, IA: William C. Brown.

Harral, S. 1952. *Tested public relations for schools.* Norman, OK: University of Oklahoma Press.

Johnson, M. L. 1977. *Functional administration in physical and health education.* Boston: Houghton Mifflin Company.

Lockard, J., P. D. Abrams, and W. A Many. 1990. *Microcomputers for educators.* 2d ed. Glenview, IL: Scott, Foresman/Little Brown Publishers.

McCloskey, G. 1960. Planning the public relations program. *National Education Association Journal* 49: 17–18.

Metropolitan School Study Council. Research Studies No. 3. 1949. *Public action for powerful schools.* New York: Teachers College Bureau of Publications.

Moore, D. B., and D. P. Gray. 1990. Marketing—The blueprint for successful physical education. *Journal of Physical Education, Recreation and Dance* 61(1): 23–26.

Scherer, D. J. 1971. How to keep your district in the public eye. In *Administrative Dimensions of Health and Physical Education Programs, Including Athletics.* St. Louis: C. V. Mosby Company.

Schneider, R. E. 1992. Don't just promote your profession—Market it! *Journal of Physical Education, Recreation and Dance* 63(5): 70–73.

Sizer, T. R. 1992. *Horace's school: Redesigning the American high school.* Boston: Houghton Mifflin Company.

Voltmer, E. F., and A. A. Esslinger. 1967. *Organization and administration of physical education.* New York: Appleton-Century-Crofts.

Williams, J. F., C. L. Brownell, and E. L. Vernier. 1964. *The administration of health education and physical education.* Philadelphia, PA: W. B. Saunders.

RECOMMENDED READINGS

Allen, C. A. 1988. Social interactions between a teacher and small group of students working with a microcomputer. *Computers in the Schools* 5(1/2): 271–84.

Alterio, M. J., J. Lazour. 1991. Directors of health and physical education—Developing a successful statewide organization. *Journal of Physical Education, Recreation and Dance* 62(1): 45–47.

American Alliance for Health, Physical Education and Recreation. 1979. Public relations. *Journal of Physical Education and Recreation* 50: 6.

Bates, B. G., and V. H. Trumball. 1987. There is software to motivate and teach the learning handicapped. *The Computing Teacher* 14: 27–29, 54.

Beld, G. G. 1971. School photos that get into the newspaper. In *Administrative Dimensions of Health and Physical Education Programs, Including Athletics.* St. Louis: C. V. Mosby Company.

Bell, J. A. 1990. A time to sow, a time to reap—Public relations. *Journal of Physical Education, Recreation and Dance* 61(3): 71.

Bronzan, R. T., and D. K. Stotlar. 1987. *Public relations and promotions in sport.* Daphne, AL: United States Sports Academy.

Brylinsky, J. 1991. Making a difference through support and leadership networks. *Journal of Physical Education, Recreation and Dance* 62(3): 55–59.

Caudillo, J. 1991. Essential elements of the grant proposal. *Journal of Physical Education, Recreation and Dance* 62(8): 33.

Collis, B. 1988. *Computers, curriculum, and whole-class instruction.* Belmont, CA: Wadsworth Publishing Company.

Crowe, W. C. 1950. *The use of audio-visual materials in developmental physical education.* Master's thesis. University of California at Los Angeles.

Dapper, G. 1962. *Public relations for educators.* New York: Macmillan.

Gallagher, J. D. 1976. Big buildings in small easy stages. *Journal of Physical Education and Recreation* 47: 26–27.

Gaskill, P. L., and G. E. Starr. 1991. Technical references. Their contribution to budget preparation and economic impact statements. *Journal of Physical Education, Recreation and Dance* 62(8): 43.

Glossbrenner, A. 1989. *Master guide to free software.* New York: St. Martin's Press.

Havitz, M. E., and C. Spigner. 1992. Access to public leisure services: A comparison of the unemployed with traditional target groups. *Journal of Physical Education, Recreation and Dance* 63(4): 41–44.

Hebbeler, K. M., B. J. Smith, and T. L. Black. 1991. Federal early childhood special education policy: A model for the improvement of services for children with disabilities. *Exceptional Children* 58(2): 104–12.

Hopper, C. A., M. B. Gruber, K. D. Munoz, and R. A. Herb. 1992. Effect of including parents in a school-based exercise and nutrition program for children. *Research Quarterly for Exercise and Sport* 63(3): 315–21.

Hutchins, K. 1991. Production and marketing. *Journal of Physical Education, Recreation and Dance* 62(5): 47–48.

Jones, A., and J. Loughton. 1991. Fund raising through foundations—Benefits to leisure service agencies. *Journal of Physical Education, Recreation and Dance* 62(8): 27–28, 30.

Jones, J. J. 1966. *School public relations.* New York: The Center for Applied Research in Education, Inc.

Karabetsos, J., and H. White. 1991. Fund-raising ideas for leisure services. *Journal of Physical Education, Recreation and Dance* 62(8): 29.

Kinzer, C., R. Sherwood, and J. Bransford. 1986. *Computer strategies for education: Foundations and content-area applications.* Columbus, OH: Merrill Publishing Company.

Lindsey, J. D., ed. 1987. *Computers and exceptional individuals.* Columbus, OH: Merrill Publishing Company.

McDermott-Griggs, S., and J. A. Card. 1992. Creating a successful fund-raising letter. *Journal of Physical Education, Recreation and Dance* 63(1): 57–59.

McLaughlin, J. 1990. Advocating for dance education in the nineties. *Journal of Physical Education, Recreation and Dance* 61(5): 62–63.

Nelson, W. T. 1984. *A comparison of selected undergraduate experiences of alumni who financially support their alma mater.* Unpublished doctoral dissertation. Indiana University.

Odden, A. 1992. School finance in the 1990s. *Phi Delta Kappan* 73(6): 455–61.

Pettine, A. M., and J. D. Nettleton. 1980. No money for new construction. *Journal of Physical Education and Recreation* 51: 26–27.

Raschke, D. B., C. V. Dedrick, and K. Hanus. 1991. Adaptive playgrounds for all children. *Teaching Exceptional Children* 24(1): 25–28.

Richey, D. L. 1991. The process and politics of advocacy. *Journal of Physical Education, Recreation and Dance* 62(3): 35–36.

Rowel, R. H., and R. T. Terry. 1989. Establishing interorganizational arrangements between volunteer community-based groups. *Health Education* 20(5): 52–55.

Seaward, B. L., and A. M. Snelling. 1990. A marketing strategy for a campus wellness program. *Health Education* 21(5): 4–8.

Shelton, C. 1991. Funding strategies for women's sports. *Journal of Physical Education, Recreation and Dance* 62(3): 51–54.

Theunissen, W. 1967. Turning complaints into compliments. *The Physical Educator* 24: 35.

Turner, E. T., and C. E. McDaniel. 1990. Designing a teaching/learning center. *Journal of Physical Education, Recreation and Dance* 62(7): 20–22.

Wiley, R. C. 1960. Physical education festival: A public relations device. *The Physical Educator* 17: 98–100.

CHAPTER 20

Epilogue

Objectives

After reading this chapter, you should be able to

- Distinguish between a disability and a handicap.
- Know the contributions of general and physical education in the adjustment of the disabled to society.
- Describe ways by which one can become certified in special education.
- Identify and discuss the principles that teaching practitioners should address with the disabled to enable them to adjust to learning and life.
- Identify barriers to and solutions for participating in leisure time activities.
- Know the role that society should play in assisting those with disabilities with their adjustments to life after graduation.
- Describe the value of sheltered workshops.
- Identify and discuss elements that should be included in a comprehensive vocational or career assessment program.
- Identify and describe basic human needs that must be satisfied for a meaningful and happy life.

INTRODUCTION

Schools have the responsibility to furnish important linkages between one's potential for and the acquisition of appropriate skills and behaviors. Not every child, however, has the physical, mental, and psychological capacity for total immersion in the programs that could foster optimum development in these areas. A child's view of his/her own disability may handicap the ability to meet certain needs and objectives.

Throughout the literature the terms **disability** and **handicap** are used to describe impairments. It is important for the reader to realize, however, that these expressions are not synonymous. While numerous writers have expressed their views on the distinction between the two, the essence of the difference has not been stated any more succinctly that in the words of Nesbitt (1975) when he wrote:

KEY TERMS

America 2000	handicap
barriers	intrinsic barriers
career assessment	leisure education
certification programs	modules
communication barriers	Pool Expansion Plan (PEP)
competency evaluation	restoration services
counselor	sheltered workshops
disability (disorder)	societal barriers
ecological barriers	training plan
environmental barriers	vocational assessment
exceptionality	

Disability is the actual dysfunction or limitation caused by the disease or injury. But the disability is a "handicap" only to the extent that a person is not able to function normally in employment, education, recreation, homemaking, and so on.

To carry the distinction a bit further, we can say that a handicap is the inability to live to the fullest extent of one's physical, mental, and psychological capacity. As Gunn and Peterson (1978) point out,

> The disabled person is considered to be someone who has found ways of coping with a dysfunction, while a handicapped person is someone who is blocked from participating.

One of the major contributions that the schools can make is to provide enabling opportunities—opportunities that will prove to the child that success is within reach, that he/she does not have to be handicapped because of a disability.

CONTRIBUTIONS OF EDUCATION

While a number of changes in educational programs for those with disabilities have evolved over the past fifteen to twenty years, there has remained a constant—the preparation of students with disabilities to be productive, contributing citizens of their communities (Meers 1992). Career development and transition to the workplace are related in a very significant way (Rau, Spooner, and Fimian 1989). Liebert, Lutsky, and Gottlieb (1990) also suggest that parents have a major role to play in helping their children plan for the future.

If the process of education is to be relevant, it must be geared to the learner as an individual. Each individual has needs that are unique to him/her. This individuality may vary from day to day, from activity to activity, and from minute to minute. We must be alert to these changes and be ready to adjust methods and materials in order to best address student idiosyncrasies.

It has been said by Logsdon and associates (1977) that teachers must accept responsibility for the education of the whole person. As a child's needs and interests are altered by either internal or external motivation, we must accept the fact that the human being is a unit— mind, body, and soul— and is not comprised of separate and distinct entities. In this regard, Piaget and Inhelder (1969) offered this thought:

> There is no behavior pattern, however intellectual, which does not involve affective factors as motives; but reciprocally there can be no affective states without the intervention of perceptions or comprehensions which constitute their cognitive structure....It is precisely this unity of behavior which makes the factors in development common to both the cognitive and the affective aspects.

In 1991, a two-day educational summit conference was called by President Bush, out of which arose six national goals—goals to be achieved by the year 2000 (*America 2000, An Education Strategy*). These goals are:

1. All children will start school ready to learn.
2. The high school graduation rate will increase to at least 90 percent.
3. All students will leave grades 4, 8, and 12 having demonstrated competency in challenging subject matter, including English, mathematics, science, history, and geography.
4. United States students will be first in the world in science and mathematics achievement.
5. Every adult American will be literate and will possess the knowledge and skills necessary to compete in a global economy and exercise the rights and responsibilities of citizenship.
6. All schools will be free of drugs and violence and will offer a safe, disciplined environment conducive to learning.

As we address an individual's capabilities and objectives, we must be aware that the child's disability is only a handicap to growth if the emphasis of instruction is toward what the child with a disability cannot do rather than toward what he/she can do. Stated directly and indirectly throughout the book, children with disabilities are able to accomplish significant and wonderful things. Many in fact have met or will meet the challenges implicit to the goals posed by the Secretary of Education. It is also important to note, however, that some of the goals may not be reasonable for all children who have disabilities. Do all the challenges implicit to the goals have to be met in order to be thought of as "totally educated"? Is there such a thing as being "totally" educated?

The question When is a person educated? is one for which there is no simple answer. When upon graduation, the student leaves the rather sheltered environment of the school setting, we hope that he/she has gained the necessary psychomotor, cognitive, and affective transition skills to effectively meet the requirements of daily living.

The graduate who leaves school to face the realities of society does so with the hope that; as Daniels and Davies (1965) have written, (a) there is a place for him or her, and (b) that he or she will 'make the grade.' At the same time, one of the greatest challenges facing school practitioners today is guiding those with disabilities in their move from the school to less-restrictive settings (George and Lewis 1991).

Each individual seeks and should find economic security and social acceptance, but there are obstacles to overcome. It is hoped that our schools are able to bring forth all the expertise at their disposal to help students with disabilities grow to their maximum potential and overcome these obstacles.

To serve this end, it is critical that teachers be as qualified as possible to work with children faced with the challenge of disabilities. While national and most state accreditation agencies require that teacher preparatory programs include a course (or its equivalent) in special education (e.g., Mainstreaming the Exceptional Child), it is doubtful that a single course (likely to be worth up to three academic credits) can do much more than cover the surface.

Some institutions provide opportunities for dual majors. A certifying major in physical education, complemented by special education, would be approaching the ideal. Other institutions may require a minor for graduation. In this instance special education would be a meaningful selection.

For those students who want to be certified in general special education or in a specific disability category, these options exist in some colleges and universities. At the same time, some institutions sponsor **certification programs** while teachers are on the job. One such program is coordinated by Plymouth State College of the University System of New Hampshire, which is described in the section that follows.

Like many states, New Hampshire has an insufficient number of institutions graduating certified special educators to meet the needs of local schools. Meanwhile, there are those in the schools who are certified and teaching other subjects, and who would like to get certified in a second area—special education. The **Pool Expansion Plan (PEP)** is Plymouth State College's response to this interest. It involves the following steps (Boggess 1992):

1. Application/Admission. The PEP process permits the identification of each applicant's training needs. An applicant provides documentation of prior learning in the competency areas. This information is reviewed by an admissions committee. Traineeships are awarded each month, based upon an individual's potential for success within PEP's supervised independent study format. A field site for the internship component is identified and approved, and the appropriate certification alternative is determined.

2. **Competency Evaluation.** If admitted, the candidate has the opportunity to orally validate mastery of competency areas with a board of experienced educators. The training plan of modules is established through the Competency Evaluation Board.

3. **Training Plan.** With the regional coordinator, the training plan is then translated into a timeline for implementation. In addition the arrangements for supervision by a PEP-trained field supervisor within an approved field site are finalized to permit each trainee to begin module work.

4. **Modules.** Module study guides correspond to the competency areas. For each module, the trainee completes readings in textbooks and hands-on activities, which are in turn documented in a notebook. This notebook, which is evaluated by field supervisors and coordinators, will continue to serve as a valuable resource when the training program is completed.

5. Completion/Certification. A certificate of completion is earned for each module successfully completed. When all modules have been completed, a certificate of completion for the entire training plan is issued. Then procedures for the appropriate certification (referenced in #1 above) take effect.* For Alternative IV certification, completion of the Individual Professional Development Plan is verified by the employing district, and the graduate is endorsed by PEP for certification. For Alternative III, there is an additional step: The graduate completes a board examination for certification through the Bureau of Teacher Education and Professional Standards.

In addition to qualifying oneself for public and private school service within the United States, there are also an increasing number of opportunities for overseas assignments with the Peace Corps. Such assignments include working with children who are mentally retarded, learning disabled, blind and visually impaired, deaf and hard of hearing, or emotionally disturbed.** For those with disabilities, teaching can provide numerous opportunities for lifelong careers. In addition to teaching topics within fields of specialization, a teacher with a disability provides an outstanding role model for children and others within the school system.

The more experiences one can garner, the better prepared one will be to meet the challenges posed by working with diversified student populations. In addition to possessing the skills necessary to facilitate the learning of the many activities intrinsic to a comprehensive program of studies, education practitioners should also be able to provide guidance in resolving the many questions a student with a disability might have about societal services. Among the questions asked most frequently are

1. Where do I find information on benefits, exemptions, and social services?
2. What are the opportunities to acquire a post-high school education? Do all colleges and universities have academic support services should they be needed?
3. How do I gain the opportunity to demonstrate competence in selected work skills? What companies provide training opportunities for those with disabilities?***
4. How do I find information as to the availability of suitable housing?
5. Whom do I contact in order to learn of the community's transportation alternatives should I need to avail myself of them?

Although a teacher cannot be expected to know the answers to all possible questions one might ask, at the very least he/she should know where answers can be found. Appendix A provides a roster of organizations available for assistance to individuals/ groups seeking their services.

---

* In New Hampshire, Alternative I certification arises out of graduating from an accredited teacher-education program within the state. Alternative II certification is possible when one graduates from an accredited teacher-education program in another state.

** Additional information regarding overseas opportunities can be obtained by writing to Peace Corps of the United States, Public Response Unit, 9th Floor, Washington, DC 20277-3741.

*** The Office of Special Education and Rehabilitation Services (OSERS) of the Department of Education has directed policy and funding initiatives to support the development of supported employment service opportunities in all fifty states (Wehman 1991).

CONTRIBUTIONS OF PHYSICAL EDUCATION

As we enter the twenty-first century, the importance of regular activity has been recognized as never before (National Association for Sport and Physical Education 1992). With this in mind I have attempted to identify and describe, throughout this text, procedures by which we as physical education practitioners can address the principles of education in general and the objectives of physical education in particular in order to optimize conditions for learning. Our discussion has been presented in three phases:

1. Foundations of Adapted Physical Education, which presented the scope of adapted physical education including types and incidences of disabilities, anatomical and physiological considerations, and principles of program organization.
2. Introduction to Disabilities, which addressed specific characteristics of anomalies likely to be found among the school-age population, including physical, motor, and postural fitness disorders; sensory disabilities; cardiovascular disorders; musculoskeletal and neurological disorders; mental, behavioral, and learning disabilities; behavioral disorders; the gifted and talented, and other health conditions.
3. Programs in Action, which included reference to inclusionary programs; adapted games and sports; outings, camping, and aquatics; Special Olympics and Wheelchair athletic programs; guidelines for making and/or recycling supplies and equipment; evaluation; record keeping and public relations.

If you conscientiously read the text material while keeping chapter behavioral objectives in focus, complete the recommended laboratory assignments, and review the recommended readings, you should have the knowledge required to prescribe appropriate developmental and general activities for your students.

Over thirty years ago Ashcroft (1963) examined numerous factors contributing to the effective preparation of children with disabilities for integration in society. Since then many others have corroborated his findings reported here.

1. Exceptional children need information, knowledge, and skills that will enable them to cope adequately with life in their unique circumstances. Competence to deal with the vocational and social tasks of life will promote adjustment by enabling the individual to elicit positive attitudes from those with whom he/she lives and works.
2. Educational programs have one ultimate goal—the optimum adjustment and integration of the exceptional child. The physical placement of an exceptional child in a normal setting guarantees neither acceptance nor integration with his/her classmates. The child must be helped to develop the attitudes and skills that will promote his/her acceptance and integration.
3. Theory and research primarily provide information about exceptional children as groups. Ultimately we must deal with the exceptional child as an individual. Knowledge from theory and research must supplement the experiences derived from personal contacts in individual work with children to promote good adjustment.

4. The exceptional individual, like all others, is sensitive to the attitudes he/she perceives as existing in those with whom he/she lives and works. His/her own attitudes toward himself/herself and others are built and shaped in response to the treatment accorded him/her.

5. Since behavior and adjustment can be so profoundly affected by environmental factors, the teacher must systematically strive to create an emotionally accepting school environment for each child.

6. The exceptional child can be cruelly rejected or can feel thus rejected as much or more as a result of the ignorance (stereotyped attitudes and prejudices) of others as from malice. Information about exceptional individuals must be widely available to dispel such ignorance. The teacher must be accurately informed and disseminate accurate and objective information.

7. The exceptional child needs to grow in independence. The teacher should not do for the child anything the child can do for himself/herself to promote growth toward a reasonable degree of independent functioning.

8. Open channels of communication and clarity of understanding among parents, faculty, and administration are important to the adjustment of the exceptional child. The teacher should facilitate such communication as a means of promoting the child's adjustment.

9. The teacher should examine his/her own motives in working with exceptional children. Teachers who are motivated to work with exceptional children to fill their own unmet needs are unlikely to be effective in working with such children.

10. The temptation to exploit exceptional children for the admiration of the public must be resisted. This is often difficult because of the natural appeal of the unusual or exceptional child.

11. The teacher must attempt to differentiate the realistic or irreducible limitations of the impairment from those associated effects that may result from overprotection, overindulgence, or excessive sympathy.

12. Since **exceptionality** has different meanings and values to different people, the teacher should attempt to clarify its meaning for himself/herself, for the child, and for others in the child's environment.

13. The teacher's role is primarily that of educator rather than therapist. The teacher must operate within the limits of his/her own understanding and seek specialized help from those specialists in other disciplines who have unique complementary and supplementary assisting roles to play.

14. The exceptional child needs the security of clearly defined behavioral limits. Neither extreme permissiveness nor rigid autocracy provides an optimum learning climate for these children.

15. The exceptional child must be treated attitudinally in terms of what he/she has, not in terms of what he/she lacks. This is in contrast to traditional educational treatment and planning that does need to be in terms of what the child lacks with regard to information, knowledge and skills. Again, however, educational planning should capitalize on what the youngster has to work with.

The physical education practitioner is in an enviable position to address these issues. It is the acquisition of skills germane to the developmental and mainstreamed program of physical education and presented for practice within an appropriate learning environment that will add significantly to the child's chances of success when meeting the various challenges of life.

Moucha (1991) affirmed the value of physical activity to her development as a sportswomen by writing,

> Sports for the disabled allows me to compete with others of my equal functional ability. It is good to know that there are other hemiplegics out there who want to do things with their lives.*

The intelligent use of leisure time is in large part a product of how effective schools have been in preparing students with disabilities for the **barriers** they might face. Successful daily living includes the right and ability to access the options available. Lessons about barriers may be important to the curriculum.

Bammel and Bammel (1992) suggest that barriers to participation fall into three categories.

1. **Environmental** (those factors that are imposed on the individual by external conditions), **ecological**, and **societal barriers**
   a) Ecological barriers are those existing in the natural environment, such as hills and sand.
   b) Societal barriers include architecture, attitudes of others, barriers of omission, economic factors, rules/regulations, and transportation.
2. **Intrinsic barriers**—those barriers that arise in the individual himself/herself, such as lack of knowledge about services available, tendency to be dependent upon others to make recreation decisions for one, deficiencies in social skills due to previous deprivation of opportunities.
3. **Communication barriers**—those barriers that occur when individuals have difficulty expressing their needs and/or when others are just not receiving the message

Much has been written about the role of the schools in preparing students for worthy use of leisure time. The American Alliance for Health, Physical Education, Recreation and Dance, the National Recreation and Park Association (1969), and others have offered the following suggestions with respect to **leisure education**:

1. Ascertain and evaluate carryover of activities from physical education in the school setting to the community recreational setting and carryover of childhood recreational skills into adulthood.
2. Fear is a dominant factor when one is deciding whether or not to participate in a recreational activity. Since ignorance is usually the cause of fear, the physical educator needs to teach those things that will increase the confidence a student has in himself/herself.
3. Determine basic recreation and physical education skills needed by children with disabilities.

---

* See Chapter 2 for other reflections of Susan Ann Moucha.

Figure 20.1. Experiencing one of many recreational activities suitable for children with exceptionalities.

4. Ascertain to what extent new skills are retained and incorporated into recreation patterns. According to Ford and Blanchard (1985) an increasing number of children with disabilities are being programmed into recreational activities for the purpose of developing self-confidence, learning to adjust to new situations, experiencing group problem solving, and experiencing success, Figure 20.1.

5. Evaluate relationships between leisure time skills and vocational-social-emotional adjustments of those with different disabling conditions.

6. Determine how to counsel individuals to match activities with abilities and disabling conditions with opportunities.

7. Devise techniques and methods to assist individuals locate and use community resources.

8. Devise methods and model programs to assist those with disabilities to become more recreationally independent and literate.

9. Examine the recreation experience itself in terms of variables that influence activities and how they exert this influence, how these variables can be manipulated to alter the recreation experience to bring about behavioral changes, and benefits and/or detrimental effects of specific recreation activities.

10. Determine how those with disabilities use their leisure time and provide programs to prepare them for active participation in a wide variety of recreational activities.

Children do not automatically develop the skills, knowledge, and behaviors suitable to success. They need guidance; they need instruction. The National Association of Sport and Physical Education (1992) points out that in recent years a growing body of evidence has heightened our understanding of the benefits of developmentally appropriate physical education.

CONTRIBUTIONS OF SOCIETY

In the not-too-far distant past, rejection and ridicule were commonplace for those with disabilities within many segments of our so-called civilized society. Unfortunately evidence exists to show that some people still exhibit ignorant attitudes, particularly as it relates to the workplace. An interesting development has been the participation of business and industry in recommendations for education reform (Yates 1987). Although much discussion has focused on the school's responsibility to business, there are indications that future emphasis will shift more to business and industry's responsibilities to schools (Meyen 1990). School and business partnerships are succeeding in efforts to provide valuable resources while decreasing the isolation of the schools in their quest to prepare students for the work force (McLoughlin, Bennett, and Verity 1988). As a consequence, increased employment opportunities for those with disabilities can be expected.

Sheltered Workshops.

One significant contribution to the preparation of the more seriously disabled for society's work force is the **sheltered workshop**. Not a new phenomenon it is an alternative to a competitive employment model, where persons with disabilities are supervised in work settings with nondisabled employees.

The majority of these workshops are operated privately as charitable or other nonprofit institutions. Largely geared to the adult the major objective of the training program is to help those with disabilities acquire sufficient social and work skills to function successfully in a limited or regular work setting or, at the very minimum, become self-sufficient in a permanent sheltered setting while contributing financially toward his/her own support. Goldman and Soloff (1961) suggested fours basic purposes of a sheltered workshop. These purposes are still considered valid today.

1. Workshops provide a concrete work experience. A situation simulating actual job conditions provides opportunities for clients to participate in a realistic work setting. In such a setting a client can see for himself/herself how he/she functions on various jobs, what it feels like to work, or how he/she feels about taking orders. The client can begin to see and feel what it means to say that a work situation is different from a school situation or other social situations. Actually being in the setting provides its own kinds of learning. The work atmosphere as a social situation is as important in this respect as the specific learning of manual or social skills. This is the milieu therapy aspect of the workshop. The atmosphere helps provide learning, goals, and emotional

support for clients and helps them adjust to work and to job relationships. The **counselor** is also aided by the concreteness of the experience, for the workshop provides specific answers to some questions about clients. The counselor is likely to discover what kinds of work his/her client relates to best, what levels of productivity the client reaches, whether productivity problems are related to relationship problems, and how the client relates to coworkers. By having available the observations of the workshop staff, the counselor can compare what is actually happening in the work setting to the client's own statements about his/her abilities, goals, and problems.

2. The workshop provides a sheltered setting. While attempting to simulate work conditions as closely as possible, we are usually gradual in our imposition of controls and standards on individual clients. Thus a young man without work experience may test various ways of dealing with his superiors without fear of being fired before he settles on what is most appropriate for himself. Again, a client learns that he can test himself without fear of suffering from the consequences of his actions. He may experiment with different methods of doing a job, with the amount of talking he can do while working, or with the necessity of keeping regular hours. He can test these activities and relationships in a setting in which he learns that he is respected and given time to learn what is most appropriate.

3. The workshop provides a therapeutic setting for some. This area must be approached cautiously. We suggest, however, that the reality functioning of the ego is often strengthened in a positive workshop experience and that the defenses which are preventing adequate adaptations to work demands can be modified. On the other hand we question whether there are any radical changes in personality organization of clients or any major changes in the defense systems. There are likely to be therapeutic results for some clients, but the extent of therapy is limited.

4. Workshops provide a group setting. Clients are working together under supervision. Each person is able to compare his/her own work with that of others. He is able to see that his/her problems are not unique. He/she can develop friendships and compare notes on work experiences. He/she is not trying to overcome problems on his/her own.

If successful counseling and placement have occurred, those with disabilities can profit immeasurably from training in a sheltered workshop. It is anticipated that, pursuant to a period of training, those who have participated in the program will respect punctuality, reliability, and responsibility and feel pride in a job well done (Zaetz 1971). These are among the goals of successful employees at all work settings.

In order for those responsible for delivering services to plan intelligent program alternatives, there are a number of procedures that should be in place. The types of information generally required in **vocational assessment** (**career assessment**) programs include

1. finding those who are at risk for employment early.
2. conducting medical examinations, personal interviews, and tests of aptitudes and interests.

3. ascertaining degrees of awareness and knowledge of careers and the world of work.
4. determining work/study habits and skills for specific occupations.
5. providing prevocational and vocational instruction that is directed toward a definite job goal.
6. offering restoration services for those in need, e.g., surgical, psychiatric, and prosthetic assistance.
7. placing the individual in job settings (e.g., competitive employment or sheltered workshop) appropriate to his/her interests and abilities.
8. establishing goals and objectives against which frequent evaluations can be made.
9. arranging for necessary transportation, training apparatus, books, and materials to support the placement.
10. developing a program of follow-up to make sure that the training is/has been adequate and that placements are proper.

Vocational or career assessment is an ongoing process of identifying individual student characteristics, strengths and weaknesses, and interests as well as education, training, and placement needs (Illinois State Board of Education 1987). As with all assessments, however, the information gathered is only as good as the validity of the questions and/or observations (McLoughlin and Lewis 1990).

Playing fair with respect to vocational counseling and placement for those with acquired or congenital disabilities is only part of society's responsibility. Society can also help to enhance the person's zest for (and quality of) life. It is important that we all live life to its fullest (keeping in mind that this is not a rehearsal for life, this is it). This requires that basic human needs be met. These needs are

1. The need to acquire skills and become proficient in activities of daily living. Activities of daily living include dressing, personal grooming, self-feeding, and communication and mobility skills. Acquisition of these skills will meet not only physical needs, but psychological needs. While many of these skills can be taught in the schools, they must be reinforced elsewhere.
2. The need to share confidences with someone. All of us have concerns that we need to share. We need to have someone in whom we can confide when things are bothering us. We need to know someone who is concerned about our feelings, our interests, and our wants. Providing opportunities for people to meet increases one's network of contacts and friends. From these events very special confidants can emerge.
3. The need to have sufficient nourishment and rest, a secure home, a spiritual source, and faith in the future.
4. The need to enjoy leisure (through recreation and sport) at home, the community, or beyond.
5. The need to be accepted by the group of which one is a part. In this regard, Wright (1960) stated,

One of man's basic strivings is for acceptance by the group, for being important in the lives of others, and for having others count positively in his life.

(When)...a disability is linked with...inferiority, realistic acceptance of one's position and one's self is precluded.

6. The need to be loved—perhaps the greatest of all human needs. It is more than having someone in whom one can share confidences. Love is the warmest and most intense regard one person can have for another. It does not imply sexual intimacy. Rather love is a deep and thoughtful regard (without condition) for the well-being and happiness of another.

SUMMARY

While there are such unresolved issues as the type of training that will best prepare one to work with diversified student populations, the degree to which mainstreaming represents a least restrictive environment for all students, or the extent to which technology can (or should) go in assisting those with disabilities in classroom or clinical settings, the fact that education and society can make positive contributions to fulfilled lives for the disabled is without question. Underlying these contributions is interest on the part of us all. Reading, writing, researching, listening, watching, and thinking are ways we express interest. The truly interested person will find ways to help improve the quality of life for others. I hope that this text has contributed in some way to enhancing the interest levels of all who read it.

RECOMMENDED LABORATORY ASSIGNMENTS

1. Interview high school administrative officials about how their schools familiarize students with information as to where they can get answers to questions regarding architectural barriers; post-high-school educational options; exemptions, benefits, and social services; housing; transportation; and vocational and career training and placement.
2. Interview high school guidance counselors about their perceptions of the vocational and career opportunities for graduates who have disabilities and about their placement success.
3. Meet with high school students who have disabilities to find out about their vocational and/or career aspirations.
4. Meet with high school graduates to talk about problems they have encountered in seeking post-high-school job training and/or college admission.
5. Visit sheltered workshops to find out about programs and practices therein.
6. Interview employment managers to gain insight as to prevalent attitudes regarding the training and hiring of those with disabilities.
7. Meet with community recreation directors and review their programs for the disabled.
8. Write to representatives of federal and state governments and ask about legislation or the need for legislation regarding services for those with disabilities.
9. Read laws on the accessibility of buildings and facilities. Become familiar with state building codes.

10. Visit public buildings and make a list of architectural barriers. Write a letter to appropriate government officials regarding your findings.

11. Become familiar with local ordinances and state rules and regulations pertaining to persons with disabilities. Your research should include the topics mentioned in recommended laboratory assignment 1.

12. Investigate the protection or lack of protection of those with disabilities under current housing laws. Explore alternative housing plans.

13. Write your own proposed legislation and submit it to state representatives for consideration.

14. Add to the list of basic human needs cited within this chapter. Analyze ways in which these needs can best be met.

15. Review the recommended readings.

REFERENCES

America 2000, An education strategy. 1991. Washington, DC: U.S. Government Printing Office.

American Alliance for Health, Physical Education, Recreation and Dance, and the National Recreation and Park Association. 1969. *Physical education and recreation for handicapped children.* Washington, DC: The Associations.

Ashcroft, S. C. 1963. Exceptionality and adjustment. In *Exceptional Children in the Schools.* New York: Holt, Rinehart and Winston.

Bammel, G, and L. L. Bammel. 1992. *Leisure and human behavior.* 2d ed. Dubuque, IA: William C. Brown.

Boggess, B., ed. 1992. *PEP talk.* Plymouth, NH: NH Special Education Teacher Training.

Daniels, A. S., and E. A. Davies. 1965. *Adapted physical education.* New York: Harper and Row.

Ford, P., and J. Blanchard. 1985. *Leadership and administration of outdoor pursuits.* State College, PA: Venture Publishing, Inc.

George, N. L., and T. J. Lewis. 1991. Exit assistance for special educators—Helping students make the transition. *Teaching Exceptional Children* 23(2): 35–39.

Goldman, E., and S. Soloff. 1961. Issues in rehabilitation workshops. *Journal of Personnel and Guidance* 40: 169–73.

Gunn, S. L., and C. A. Peterson. 1978. *Therapeutic recreation program design: Principles and procedures.* Englewood Cliffs, NJ: Prentice-Hall.

Illinois State Board of Education. 1987. *Vocational assessment of secondary special needs students.* Springfield, IL: Illinois State Board of Education.

Liebert, D., L. Lutsky, and A. Gottlieb. 1990. Postsecondary experiences of young adults with severe physical disabilities. *Exceptional Children* 57(1): 56–63.

Logsdon, B. J. 1977. *Physical education for children: A focus on the teaching process.* Philadelphia: Lea and Febiger.

McLoughlin, A., W. J. Bennett, and C. W. Verity. 1988. *Building a quality workforce.* Washington, DC: Joint Initiative of the U.S.. Department of Labor, Education, and Commerce.

McLoughlin, J. A., and R. B. Lewis. 1990. *Assessing special students.* 3d ed. Columbus, OH: Merrill Publishing Company.

Meers, G. D. 1992. Getting ready for the next century: Vocational preparation of students with disabilities. *Teaching exceptional children* 24(4): 36–39.

Meyen, E. L. 1990. *Exceptional children in today's schools.* 2d ed. Denver, CO: Love Publishing Company.

Moucha, S. A. 1991. The disabled female athlete as a role model. *Journal of Physical Education, Recreation and Dance* 62(3): 37–38.

National Association for Sport and Physical Education. 1992. Developmentally appropriate physical education practices for children: Position paper. *Update.* Pp. 1–2.

Nesbitt, J. A. 1975. Special community education for the handicapped: A proposal model to meet the total life and leisure needs of the handicapped child and adult. In *Common-Unity in the Community: A Forward-Looking Program of Recreation and Leisure Services for the Handicapped.* Eugene, OR: Center of Leisure Studies, University of Oregon.

Piaget, J., and B. Inhelder. 1969. *The Psychology of the child.* New York: Basic Books.

Rau, D., F. Spooner, and M. J. Fimian. 1989. Career education needs of students with exceptionalities: One state's case. *Exceptional Children* 55(6): 501–07.

Wehman, P. (principal investigator). 1991. *A national analysis of supported employment implementation: Fiscal years 1986–1989.* Richmond, VA: Virginia Commonwealth University.

Wright, B. 1960. *Physical disability: A psychological approach.* New York: Harper and Row.

Yates, J. R. 1987. Current and emerging forces impacting special education, Part I. *Counterpoint* 8(4): 4–6.

Zaetz, J. L. 1971. *Organization of sheltered workshop programs for the mentally retarded adult.* Springfield, IL: Charles C. Thomas.

RECOMMENDED READINGS

Anthony, W. 1972. Societal rehabilitation: Changing society's attitudes toward the physically and mentally disabled. *Rehabilitation Psychology* 19: 117–26.

Ashworth, S. 1992. The spectrum and teacher education. *Journal of Physical Education, Recreation and Dance* 63(1): 32–35, 53.

Attarian, A., and L. Gault. 1992. Treatment of Vietnam veterans with post-traumatic stress disorder: A model program. *Journal of Physical Education, Recreation and Dance* 63(4): 56–59

Boyd, W., and F. Hartnett. 1975. Normalization and its implications for recreation services. *Leisurability* 2: 22.

Bullock, C. C., and M. J. Mahon. 1992. Decision making in leisure: Empowerment for people with mental retardation. *Journal of Physical Education, Recreation and Dance* 63(8): 36–40.

Chase, N. K. 1981. *Outward bound as adjunct to therapy.* Unpublished manuscript. Denver, CO: Colorado Outward Bound School.

Crase, D. 1990. Aligning the professoriate for the 21st century. *Journal of Physical Education, Recreation and Dance* 61(9): 41–43.

deBettencourt, L. U., N Zigmond, and H. Thornton. 1989. Follow-up of postsecondary-age rural learning disabled graduates and dropouts. *Exceptional Children* 56(12): 40–49.

Dunlap, L. K., G. Dunlop, L. K. Koegel, and R. L. Koegel. 1991. Using self-monitoring to increase independence. *Teaching Exceptional Children* 23(3): 17–22.

Dunn, J. M., ed. 1991. PL 99-457: Challenges and opportunities for physical education. *Journal of Physical Education, Recreation and Dance* 62(6): 33–34, 47.

Dutton, D., and M. Male. 1992. *Technology for students with special needs.* Wilsonville, OR: Franklin, Beedle and Associates, Inc.

Getzel, E. E. 1990. Entering postsecondary programs: Early individualized planning. *Teaching Exceptional Children* 23(1): 51–53.

Goodman, N. 1963. Variant reactions to physical disabilities. *American Sociological Review* 28: 429–35.

Grande, P. C. 1990. The 1990s challenge—Leadership or survival. *Journal of Physical Education, Recreation and Dance* 61:(5): 65–67.

Hicks, N. (14 September 1969). Life of disabled is tied to family. *New York Times*, p. 73.

Hunt, J. 1969. A decade of progress. *Journal of Rehabilitation* 35: 9.

Hunter, R. I. 1987. The impact of an outdoor rehabilitation program for adjudicated youth. *Therapeutic Recreation Journal* 21(2): 30–34.

Kearney, C. A., and V. M. Durand. 1992. How prepared are our teachers for mainstreamed classroom settings? A survey of postsecondary schools of education in New York State. *Exceptional Children* 59)(1): 6–11.

Kortering, L., N. Haring, and A. Klockars. 1992. The identification of high-school dropouts identified as learning disabled: Evaluating the utility of a discriminant analysis function. *Exceptional Children* 58(5): 422–35.

McGrew, K. S., R. H. Bruininks, and M. L. Thurlow. 1992. Relationship between measures of adaptive functioning and community adjustment for adults with mental retardation. *Exceptional Children* 58(6): 517–29.

Nadolsky, J. M. 1971. *Development of a model for vocational education of the disadvantaged.* Washington, DC: Department of Health, Education and Welfare.

Nelson, R., and B. Lignugaris-Kraft. 1989. Postsecondary education for students with learning disabilities. *Exceptional Children* 56(3): 246–65.

Pease, P. C. 1985. Assessment of a teacher education program based on student intern performance. *Journal of Teaching in Physical Education* 5(1): 52–58.

Petrofsky, J. S., S. W. Brown, and H. Cerrel-Bazo. 1992. Active physical therapy and its benefits in rehabilitation. *Palaestra* 8(3): 23–27, 61–62.

Petrofsky, J. S., and J. Smith. 1988. Computer-aided rehabilitation. *Aviation, Space and Environmental Medicine* 59: 670–79.

Rehabilitation and Research Center. 1967. *Testing orientation and work evaluation in rehabilitation: Evaluator's manual.* 340 East 24th Street, New York, NY: Institute for the crippled and disabled.

Rosen, M., G. R. Clark, and M. S. Kivitz. 1977. *Habilitation of the handicapped.* Baltimore: University Park Press.

Rubin, S. E., and R. T. Roessler. 1978. *Foundations of the vocational rehabilitation process.* Baltimore, MD: University Park Press.

Sears, J., A. Bishop, and E. Stevens. 1989. Teaching Miranda rights to students who have mental retardation. *Teaching Exceptional Children* 21(3): 38–42.

Shapiro, E. S., and F. E. Lentz, Jr. 1991. Vocational-technical programs: Follow-up of students with learning disabilities. *Exceptional Children* 58(2): 47–59.

Sharpe, T. 1992. Teacher preparation—A Professional development school approach. *Journal of Physical Education, Recreation and Dance* 63(5): 82–87.

Shea, E. J. 1986. Sport for life. *Journal of Physical Education, Recreation and Dance* 57(1): 52–54.

Sutter, P., T. Mayeda, T. Call, G. Yanagi, and S. Yee. 1980. Comparison of successful and unsuccessful community placed mentally retarded persons. *American Journal of Mental Deficiency* 85: 262–67.

Swanson, D. P. 1992. I Can: An acronym for success. Teaching Exceptional Children 24(2): 22–26.

United States Department of Labor. 1967. Sheltered workshops: A pathway to regular employment. *Manpower Research Bulletin Number 15.* Washington, DC: United States Government Printing Office.

Wehlage, G. 1986. At-risk students and the need for high school reform. *Education* 107(2): 321–42.

Wehman, P. 1990. School-to-work: Elements of successful programs. *Teaching Exceptional Children* 23(1): 40–43.

Wickett, M., (speaker). 1988. *It's all within your reach.* [Audio cassette program]. Chicago: Nightingale-Conant.

Wilkerson, M., and R. A. Dodder. 1979. What does sport do for people? *Journal of Physical Education and Recreation* 50: 50–51.

Will, M. 1984. Bridges from school to work life. *Programs for the Handicapped.* Washington, DC: U.S. Department of Education, Office of Special Education and Rehabilitative Services.

Ysseldyke, J. E., M. L. Thurlow, and J. G. Shriner. 1992. Outcomes are for special educators too. *Teaching Exceptional Children* 25(1): 36–50.

APPENDIX A

Agencies and Organizations _____

Adapted Physical Education Council
American Alliance for Health, Physical Education, Recreation and Dance
1900 Association Drive
Reston, VA 22091

Administration on Developmental Disabilities
200 Independence Avenue, S.W.
Washington, DC 20201

Alexander Graham Bell Association for the Deaf, Inc.
3417 Volta Place, N.W.
Washington, DC 20007

Amateur Athletic Union
3400 W. 86th Street; P.O. Box 68207
Indianapolis, IN 46268

American Academy for Cerebral Palsy and Developmental Medicine
2405 Westwood Avenue; P.O. Box 11083
Richmond, VA 23230

American Alliance for Health, Physical Education, Recreation and Dance
1900 Association Drive
Reston, VA 22091

American Annals of the Deaf
P.O. Box 55369
Little Rock, AR 72225

American Association on Mental Retardation
1719 Kalorama Road, N.W.
Washington, DC 20009

American Association of Psychiatric Services for Children
1133 Fifteenth Street, N.W.; Suite 1000
Washington, DC 20005

American Association of School Administrators
1801 North Moore Street
Arlington, VA 22209

American Athletic Association for the Deaf
1134 Davenport Drive
Burton, MI 48529

American Bar Association Child Advocacy Center
800 M Street, N.W.; Suite 200
Washington, DC 20036

American Cancer Society
777 Third Avenue
New York, NY 10017

American Council for the Blind
1010 Vermont Avenue, N.W.; Suite 1100
Washington, DC 20005

American Diabetes Association
1819 H Street, N.W.; Suite 1200
Washington, DC 20006

American Epilepsy Society
179 Allyn Street; Suite 304
Hartford, CT 06103

American Foundation for the Blind
15 West 16th Street
New York, NY 10011

American Juvenile Arthritis Organization
1314 Spring Street, N.W.
Atlanta, GA 30309

American Occupational Therapy Association
1383 Piccard Drive; P.O. Box 1725
Rockville, MD 20850

American Physical Therapy Association
1111 N. Fairfax Street
Alexandria, VA 22314

American Printing House for the Blind
1839 Frankfort Avenue
Louisville, KY 40206

American Psychiatric Association
1400 K Street, N.W.
Washington, DC 20005

American Psychological Association
1200 Seventeenth Street, N.W.
Washington, DC 20036

American Speech-Language-Hearing Association
10801 Rockville Pike
Rockville, MD 20852

Anxiety Disorders Association of America
6000 Executive Blvd; Suite 513
Rockville, MD 20852

Apple Computer's Office of Special Education Programs
20525 Mariani Avenue
Cupertino, CA 95014

Association for the Advancement of Health Education
1900 Association Drive
Reston, VA 22091

Association for Research, Administration, Professional Councils and Societies
1900 Association Drive
Reston, VA 22091

Association for the Education and Rehabilitation of the Blind and Visually Impaired
206 North Washington Street; Suite 320
Alexandria, VA 22314

Autism Society of America
1234 Massachusetts Avenue, N.W.; Suite 1017
Washington, DC 20005

Boys Club of America
771 First Avenue
New York, NY 10017

Braille Circulating Library
2700 Stuart Avenue
Richmond, VA 23220

Clearinghouse and Research in Child Abuse and Neglect
P.O. Box 1182
Washington, DC 20013

Clearinghouse on Disability Information
Office of Special Education and Rehabilitative Services
Room 3132, Switzer Building, 330 C Street, S.W.
Washington, DC 20202

Committee on Sports for the Disabled
United States Olympic Committee
1750 E. Boulder Street
Colorado Springs, CO 80909

Council for Disability Rights
343 South Dearborn, #318
Chicago, IL 60604

Council for Exceptional Children
1920 Association Drive
Reston, VA 22091

Cystic Fibrosis Foundation
6931 Arlington Road
Bethesda, MD 20814

Disability Law Center, Inc.
11 Beacon Street; Suite 925
Boston, MA 01108

Disability Rights Center, Inc.
1616 P Street, N.W.; Suite 435
Washington, DC 20036

Epilepsy Foundation of America
4351 Garden City Drive; Suite 406
Landover, MD 20785

ERIC Clearinghouse on Handicapped and Gifted Children
Council for Exceptional Children
1920 Association Drive
Reston, VA 22091

Fearon Teaching Aids
P.O. Box 280
Cathage, IL 62321

Gallaudet University Press
800 Florida Avenue, N.E.
Washington, DC 20002

Gifted Child Society, Inc.
190 Rock Road
Glenrock, NJ 07452

IBM National Support Center for Persons with Disabilities
P.O. Box 2150
Atlanta, GA 30055

Jewish Welfare Board
15 E. 26th Street
New York, NY 10010

Juvenile Diabetes Foundation International
60 Madison Avenue
New York, NY 10010

Learning Disabilities Association of America
4156 Library Road
Pittsburgh, PA 15234

Leukemia Society of America
733 Third Avenue; 14th Floor
New York, NY 10017

Muscular Dystrophy Association
810 Seventh Avenue
New York, NY 10019

National Aid to the Visually Handicapped
3201 Balboa Street
San Francisco, CA 94121

National Association for Down Syndrome
P. O. Box 4542
Oak Brook, IL 60521

National Association for Girls and Women in Sport
1900 Association Drive
Reston, VA 22091

National Association for Parents of the Visually Impaired
P. O. Box 180806
Austin, TX 78718

National Association for Retarded Citizens
2501 Avenue J
Arlington, TX 76006

National Association for Sickle Cell Disease
3460 Wilshire Boulevard; Suite 1012
Los Angeles, CA 90010

National Association for Sport and Physical Education
1900 Association Drive
Reston, VA 22091

National Association for the Deaf-Blind
12573 S.E. 53rd Street
Bellevue, WA 98006

National Association for the Visually Handicapped
305 East 24th Street
New York, NY 10010

National Association of Parents of the Deaf
814 Thayer Avenue
Silver Spring, MD 20910

National Association of School Psychologists
1511 K Street, N.W.; Suite 716
Washington, DC 20005

National Association of State Directors of Special Education
2021 K Street, N.W.; Suite 315
Washington, DC 20006

National Association of the Deaf
814 Thayer Avenue
Silver Spring, MD 20910

National Braille Press
86 St. Stephen Street
Boston, MA 02115

National Center for Stuttering
200 East 33rd Street
New York, NY 10016

National Center for Youth with Disabilities
University of Minnesota; P.O. Box 721
Minneapolis, MN 55455

National Clearinghouse for Bilingual Education
1118 22nd Street, N.W.
Washington, DC 20037

National Clearinghouse on Family Support and Children's Mental Health
Portland State University; P.O. Box 751
Portland, OR 97207

National Clearinghouse on Postsecondary Education for Individuals with Disabilities
One Dupont Circle, N.W.; Suite 800
Washington, DC 20036

National Collegiate Athletic Association
P.O. Box 1906
Mission, KS 66201

National Council on Disability
800 Independence Avenue, S.W.
Washington, DC 20591

National Dance Association
1900 Association Drive
Reston, VA 22091

National Down Syndrome Congress
1640 West Roosevelt Road
Chicago, IL 60608

National Easter Seal Society for Crippled Children and Adults
2023 West Ogden Avenue
Chicago, IL 60612

National Exploring Division, Boy Scouts of America
325 Walnut Hill Lane
Irving, TX 75038

National Federation of State High School Associations
P.O. Box 20262
Kansas City, MO 64195

National Foundation for Ileitis and Colitis
444 Park Avenue South
New York, NY 10016

National Handicapped Sports and Recreation Association
1145 19th Street, N.W.; Suite 717
Washington, DC 20036

National Hemophilia Association
The Soho Building
110 Green Street; Room 406
New York, NY 10012

National Information Center for Handicapped Children and Youth
P.O. Box 1492
Washington, DC 20013

National Information Center on Deafness
800 Florida Avenue, N.E.
Washington, DC 20002

National Kidney Foundation
2 Park Avenue; Suite 908
New York, NY 10016

National Marfan Foundation
382 Main Street
Port Washington, NY 11050

National Maternal and Child Health Clearinghouse
38th and R Streets, N.W.
Washington, DC 20057

National Multiple Sclerosis Society
205 East 42nd Street
New York, NY 10017

National Retinitis Pigmentosa Foundation, Inc.
1401 Mount Royal Avenue
Baltimore, MD 21217

National Tay-Sachs and Allied Diseases Association
92 Washington Avenue
Cedarhurst, NY 11516

National Wheelchair Athletic Association
3595 East Fountain Boulevard; Suite L-1
Colorado Springs, CO 80901

Office for Civil Rights, U.S. Department of Education
Operations Support Service and Technical Assistance Branch
Switzer Building; Room 5431
330 C Street, S.W.
Washington, DC 20202

Office of Indian Education Programs, Bureau of Indian Affairs
MS 3512-MIB
18th and C Streets, N.W.
Washington, DC 20245

Office of Vocational and Adult Education, U.S. Department of Education
Policy Analysis Staff
Switzer Building; Room 4525
330 C Street, S.W.
Washington, DC 20202

Orton Society (Dyslexia)
724 York Road
Baltimore, MD 21204

Palaestra
P.O. Box 508
Macomb, IL 61455

Panic Disorder
Pueblo, CO 81009

President's Committee on Employment of People with Disabilities
1111 20th Street, N.W.
Washington, DC 20036

President's Committee on Mental Retardation
330 Independence Avenue, S.W.
Washington, DC 20201

Recording for the Blind, Inc.
215 East 58th Street
New York, NY 10022

Scoliosis Research Society
444 North Michigan Avenue
Chicago, IL 60611

Special Olympics International, Inc.
1350 New York Avenue, N.W.; Suite 500
Washington, DC 20005

Speech Foundation of America
P.O. Box 11749
Memphis, TN 38111

Telecommunications for the Deaf, Inc.
814 Thayer Avenue
Silver Spring, MD 20910

United Cerebral Palsy Association, Inc.
66 East 34th Street
New York, NY 10016

United States Amputee Athletic Association
P.O. Box 210709
Nashville, TN 37221

United States Armed Forces Sports
Hoffman Building #1; Room 1416
2461 Eisenhower Avenue
Alexandria, VA 22331

United States Association for Blind Athletes
33 North Institute
Brown Hall; Suite 015
Colorado Springs, CO 80903

United States Cerebral Palsy Athletic Association
34518 Warren Road; Suite 264
Westland, MI 48185

United States Department of Justice, Civil Rights Division, Coordination and Review
    Section
P.O. Box 66118
Washington, DC 20035

Winter Games of the Disabled
3701 Connecticut Avenue, N.W.; Suite 236
Washington, DC 20008

YMCA of the USA
101 North Wacker Drive
Chicago, IL 60606

YWCA of the USA
726 Broadway; Fifth Floor
New York, NY 10003

Checklist for Braces and Wheelchairs _____

Short Leg (Ankle-Foot) Brace

A. With the brace off the student
1. Do joints work easily?
2. Can shoes be easily removed?
3. Is the workmanship good?
   a) No rough edges
   b) Straps secure
   c) Leather work stitched properly

B. Student standing with brace on
1. Are the sole and heel flat on the floor?
2. Are the ankle joints aligned so that they coincide with the anatomical joints?
3. Is there ample clearance between the leg and the brace (one finger width)?
4. Does the T strap exert enough force for correction without causing deformity?
5. Do the uprights coincide with the midline of the leg when viewed from the side?
6. Do the uprights conform to the contour of the leg?
7. Is the brace long enough?
   a) It should be below the bend of the knee so the student can bend the knee comfortably to 120°.
   b) It should not be lower than the bulky part of the calf muscle.

C. Student walking with brace on
1. Is there clearance between the uprights and the leg?
2. Are there any gait deviations?
3. Is the brace quiet?

Long Leg (Knee-Ankle-Foot) Brace

A. With the brace off the student:
1. Do joints work easily?

2. Can shoes be easily removed?
3. Is the workmanship good?
   a) No rough edges
   b) Straps secure
   c) Leather work stitched properly

B. Student standing with brace on
   1. Are the knee joints aligned at the approximate anatomical joints?
      a) There should be no pressure from the thigh band when knee is bent. (If there is, joints are too high).
      b) There should be no pressure from calf band when knee is bent. (If there is, joints are too low).
      c) There should be no pressure on calf. (If there is, joints are too far forward).
      d) There should be no pressure on shin or knee cap. (If there is, joints are too far backward).
   2. Are locks secure and easy to work?
   3. Is the brace long enough?
      a) Medial upright should be up into groin region but should not cause pain.
      b) Lateral upright should be one inch longer.
   4. Are the thigh bands and calf bands about equal distance from the knee?

Long Leg Brace with Pelvic Band (Hip-Knee-Ankle-Foot Orthosis)

A. With the brace off the student
   1. Do joints work easily?
   2. Can shoes be easily removed?
   3. Is the workmanship good?
      a) No rough edges
      b) Straps secure
      c) Leather work stitched properly

B. Student with brace on
   1. Is the pelvic band located below the waist?
   2. Is the student comfortable sitting and standing?
   3. Are the hip joints in the right place and do the locks work easily?

Other Points to Check

A. Do the shoes fit and are they in good repair?
B. Do reddened areas go away after the brace has been off twenty minutes?
C. Is the student comfortable?
D. Is the brace helping the student?

Plastic Braces

A. Does the brace conform to and contact the extremity?
B. Is the student wearing a sock between foot and brace?
C. Does the brace pull away from the leg excessively when the student walks?
D. Do reddened areas go away after the brace has been off twenty minutes?

Lower Extremity Prosthetics

A. Is the student wearing prosthesis (frequency)?
B. Does the student use assistive devices with prosthesis (crutches, canes, one cane, other)? If so, what does he/she use and how often?
C. Is the prosthesis on correctly?
   1. Is the toe turned out about the same as the other foot?
   2. When the student sits is the knee in alignment?
D. Does the leg appear the same length as the normal leg?
   1. Does the student stand straight when bearing weight on the prosthesis?
   2. Are the shoulders even when leg is bearing weight (one shoulder does not drop)?
   3. When the student walks, does the knee stay straight without turning out or in?

Gait Deviations

A. Does the student stand straight when bearing weight on the prosthesis?
B. Does the artificial leg swing forward without turning in or out?
C. Does the student swing the artificial leg through without rising up on the foot of the normal leg?
D. When the student walks, does the leg swing straight forward? (It should not swing in an arc.)
E. When the student stands, are the feet a normal distance apart? (The stance should not be too wide.)
F. Does the knee bend and straighten like a normal leg?

Condition of the Prosthesis

A. Do the suspension joints appear to be in good condition (leather, joint, band)?
B. Does the leg stay in place when the student is standing and sitting?
C. Does the knee bend appropriately?
D. Are the joints quiet when moved?
E. Do the foot and ankle appear to be in one piece?
F. Is the shoe in good condition (heel, sole)?

Wheelchair

A. Arms
   1. Are the armrests and side panels secure and free of sharp edges and cracks?
   2. Do the arm locks function properly?
B. Back
   1. Is the upholstery free of rips and tears?
   2. Is the back taut from top to bottom?
   3. Is the safety belt attached tightly and not frayed?
C. Seat and frame
   1. Is the upholstery free of rips and tears?
   2. Does the chair fold easily without sticking?
   3. When the chair is folded fully, are the front post slides straight and round?

D. Wheel locks
   1. Do the wheel locks securely engage the tire surfaces and prevent the wheel from turning?
E. Large wheels
   1. Are the wheels free from wobble or sideplay when spun?
   2. Are the spokes equally tight and without any missing spokes?
   3. Are the tires free from excessive wear and gaps at the joined section?
F. Casters
   1. Is the stem firmly attached to the fork?
   2. Are the forks straight on sides and stem so that the caster swivels easily?
   3. Is the caster assembly free of excessive play, both upward and downward as well as backward and forward?
   4. Are the wheels free of excessive play and wabble?
   5. Are the tires in good condition?
G. Footrest/Legrest
   1. Does the lock mechanism fit securely?
   2. Are the heel loops secure and correctly installed?
   3. Do the foot plates fold easily and hold in any position?
   4. Are the legrest panels free of cracks and sharp edges?

With Student Sitting in Wheelchair

A Seat width
   1. When your palms are placed between the student's hip and the side of the chair (skirtguard), do the hands contact the hip and the skirtguard at the same time without pressure?
   2. Or, is the clearance between the student's widest point of either hips or thigh and the skirtguard approximately one inch on either side?
B. Seat depth
   1. Can you place your hand, with fingers extended, between the front edge of the seat upholstery and to the rear of the knee with a clearance of three or four fingers?
   2. Or, is the seat upholstery approximately two to three inches less than the student's thigh measurement?
C. Seat height and footrest
   1. Is the lowest part of the step plates no closer than two inches from the floor?
   2. Or, is the student's thigh elevated slightly above the front edge of the seat upholstery?
D. Arm height
   1. Does the arm height not force the shoulders up or allow them to drop significantly when the student is in a normal sitting position?
   2. Is the elbow positioned slightly forward of the trunk midline when the student is in a normal sitting position?
E. Back height
   1. Can you insert four or five fingers between the student's armpit area and the top of the back upholstery touching both at the same time?
   2. Is the top of the back upholstery approximately four inches below the armpit for the student who needs only minimum trunk support?

With Student Pushing or Riding in Wheelchair

    A.   Is the wheelchair free from squeaks or rattles?

    B.   Does the chair roll easily without pulling to either side?

    C.   Are the large wheels and casters free of play and wobble?

Adapted from V. J. Morganstern and M. K. Dykes. 1979. *Teaching exceptional children.* Reston, VA: Council for Exceptional Children. Pp. 51–56. Reprinted with permission.

APPENDIX C

*Developmental Exercises without Apparatus*_____

Isotonic Exercises

General Note: The number of repetitions and sets should be determined by the readiness level of the students and the stress caused by the exercise.

1. Side straddle hops, Figure C.1

Purpose: Accelerate heart rate, stretch major muscle groups.

Starting position: Feet together, arms at sides

Count 1: Swing arms over head, spread feet apart.

Count 2: Return to starting position.

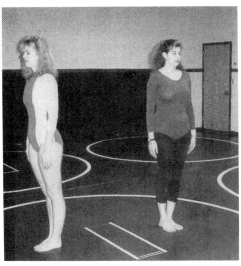 

Figure C.1. Side straddle hops (jumping jacks). A-start position B-end position

2. Thighs-toes-thighs-up, Figure C.2

Purpose: Stretch hamstring muscle group.

Figure C.2. Thighs-toes-thighs-up

Starting position: Feet together, arms extended over head.

Count 1: Bring arms forward and touch knees with hands.

Count 2: Continue flexing at the hips to touch the toes.

Count 3: Begin extension at the hips to touch knees.

Count 4: Return to starting position.

   3.   Four-count toe touch, Figure C.3

Purpose: Stretch medial thigh muscles, hamstrings, external oblique muscles.

Starting position: Arms extended straight forward, thumbs interlocked, feet wide apart.

Count 1: Flex at hips, touch fingers to left foot.

Count 2: Touch floor between feet with the hands.

Count 3: Touch fingers to right foot.

Count 4: Return to starting position.

   4.   Front leg stretch, Figure C.4*

Purpose: Stretch muscles in backs of thighs.

Starting position: Prone, right knee flexed, right hand around right ankle.

Count 1: Slowly pull ankle to hip, hold three-to-five seconds, return leg to floor.

Starting position: Prone, left knee flexed, left hand around left ankle.

Count 1: Slowly pull ankle to hip, hold three-to-five seconds, return leg to floor.

---

* Movement to the most flexed position of the knee would be an isotonic exercise. Once the leg is being held in position under resistance, the exercise is isometric.

Figure C.3. Four-count toe touch

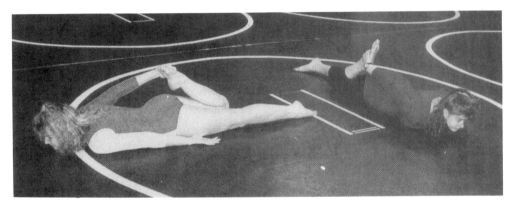

Figure C.4. Front leg stretch

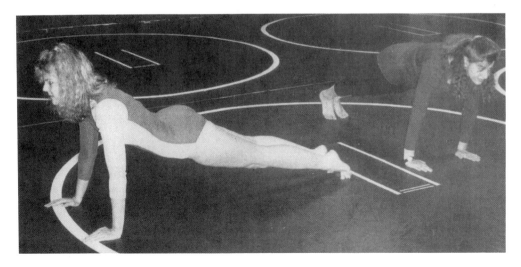

Figure C.5. Push-ups

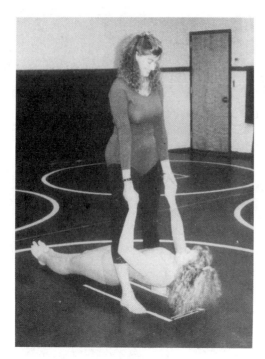

Figure C.6. Partner pull-ups

5.   Push-ups, Figure C.5

Purpose: Strengthen muscles of the arms and shoulders

Starting position: Front leaning rest, chest on floor between the hands.

Count 1: Push body up by extending elbows.

Count 2: Return to starting position.

6.   Partner pull-ups, Figure C.6

Purpose: Strengthen muscles of the arms and shoulders.

Starting position: Performer supine, arms extended, palms away, fingers interlaced with partner's fingers; partner standing, straddling performer over performer's chest (toes at armpits).

Count 1: Pull self up until lateral borders of chest contact medial portions of partner's thighs (keep body in straight line from heel contact on floor to head).

Count 2: Return to starting position.

Figure C.7. Trunk rotation

7. Trunk rotation, Figure C.7

Purpose: Stretch muscles in the shoulder girdle and sides of the trunk.

Starting position: Arms extended to the side at shoulder level, feet wide apart.

Count 1: Twist trunk to the left, continue with arms as far as possible.

Count 2: Return to starting position.

Count 3: Twist trunk to the right, continue with arms as far as possible.

Count 4: Return to starting position.

8. Flexed-knee sit-ups, Figure C.8

Purpose: Strengthen abdominal muscles.

Starting position: Supine, fingers interlocked behind head, hips and knees flexed (partner may assist by holding down performer's feet), elbows straight to sides.

Count 1: Sit up, touch chest to knees.

Count 2: Return to starting position.

Note: Exercise can be modified by alternating the touching of right elbow to left knee, left elbow to right knee, and so on with each alternating sit-up.

Figure C.8. Flexed-knee sit-ups

Figure C.9. Leg adductions

   9.   Leg adductions, Figure C.9

Purpose: Stretch and strengthen leg and external oblique muscles.

Starting position: Side rest, top leg raised in the air approximately eighteen inches, hand of top arm placed on floor in front of the chest for leverage.

Count 1: While keeping top leg in the air, raise bottom leg until it touches the medial side of top leg.

Count 2: Return to starting position.

Note: Repeat through selected number of repetitions and then switch sides to exercise the other side of the body.

   10.   Body twist, Figure C.10

Purpose: Stretch and strengthen muscles of the trunk.

Starting position: Supine, arms at the side, palms down, legs extended at 90° angle to floor.

Count 1: While keeping legs straight, slowly lower them to the floor toward the left hand.

Count 2: Return to starting position.

Count 3: While keeping legs straight, slowly lower them to the floor toward the right hand.

Count 4: Return to starting position.

Note: The knees may be flexed if necessary in order to reduce the radius of rotation and reduce stress in the abdominal area.

   11.   Heel raises, Figure C.11

Purpose: Stretch and strengthen calf muscles.

Starting position: Feet approximately shoulder-width apart, arms positioned for balance.

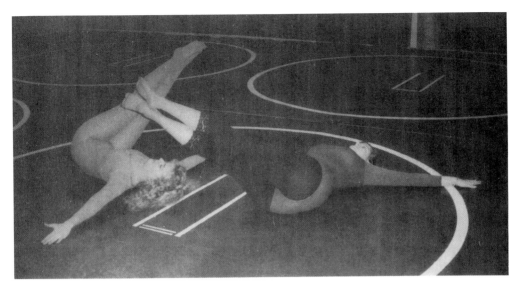

Figure C.10. Body twist

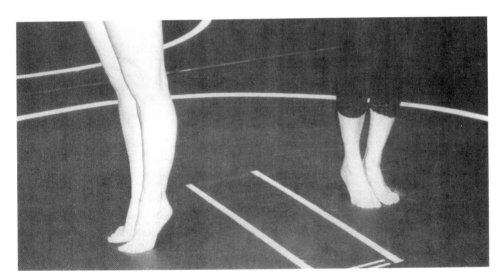

Figure C.11. Heel raises

Count 1: Raise heels off the floor to maximum point.

Count 2: Return to starting position.

Note: A board can be placed under the toes to increase the range of motion.

12. Small arm circles, Figure C.12

Purpose: Stretch and strengthen shoulder muscles.

Starting position: Arms extended to the side at shoulder level, feet positioned for balance.

Figure C.12. Small arm circles

Count 1: Circumduct shoulder so that arms describe small forward circles in succession.

Count 2: Reverse the direction of the arms so that they describe small backward circles in succession.

Isometric Exercises

General note: Performers should attempt to isolate the isometric contraction to the specific muscle group identified in the purpose of the exercise. It is very easy to tighten up the entire body. This can be avoided by continuing inhalations and exhalations through the stress period. Further an isometric contraction should be held no longer than eight seconds. As muscles are tightened, blood vessels that supply nutrients to muscle tissue constrict. To maintain circulation, a brief period of relaxation or muscle movement should follow each isometric exercise.

    1.   One-hand lateral neck flexion, Figure C.13

Purpose: Strengthen lateral muscles of neck.

Starting position: Sitting, heel of the right hand placed upon the right side of the head above the ear.

Count 1: While resisting with the neck muscles, apply moderate pressure with the hand, hold eight seconds, relax ten seconds, repeat two additional times.

Starting position: Sitting, heel of the left hand placed upon the left side of the head above the ear.

Figure C.13. One-hand lateral neck flexion

Count 1: While resisting with the neck muscles, apply moderate pressure with the hand, hold eight seconds, relax ten seconds, repeat two additional times.

Note: In order to flex the lateral neck muscles through a complete range of motion, the performer may begin the exercise by completing three sets while the head is in a vertical position, then follow with three sets at 30° and 60° on each side.

2. Two-hand neck extension, Figure C.14

Purpose: Strengthen muscles of the neck.

Starting position: Sitting, fingers interlaced and placed behind the neck.

Count 1: While resisting with the neck muscles, apply moderate presure forward with the hands, hold eight seconds, relax ten seconds, repeat two additional times.

Note: Strength may be developed through a complete range of motion by applying resistance while the head is placed at various angles from the vertical.

3. Medial-to-lateral straight-arm press, Figure C.15

Purpose: Strengthen shoulder and arm muscles.

Starting position: Standing, fingers of the left hand placed around the wrist of the right hand (behind the back).

Count 1: While resisting with the left hand, attempt to move the straight right arm laterally, hold eight seconds, relax ten seconds, repeat two additional times.

Starting position: Standing, fingers of the right hand placed around the wrist of the left hand (behind the back).

Count 1: While resisting with the right hand, attempt to move the straight left arm laterally, hold eight seconds, relax ten seconds, repeat two additional times.

Figure C.14. Two-hand neck extension

Figure C.15. Medial-to-lateral straight-arm press

4. Push up and hold, Figure C.16

Purpose: Strengthen muscles of the arms and shoulders.

Starting position: Front leaning rest, chest on floor between the hands.

Count 1: Push up with the hands until the arms are approximately one-fourth extended, hold eight seconds, relax ten seconds by lowering self to floor, repeat two additional times.

Count 2: Push up with the hands until the arms are approximately one-half extended, hold eight seconds, relax ten seconds by lowering self to floor, repeat two additional times.

Count 3: Push up with the hands until the arms are approximately three-fourths extended, hold eight seconds, relax ten seconds by lowering self to floor, repeat two additional times.

Note: Effort should be made to keep the body straight during the push-ups.

5. Arm flexor press, Figure C.17

Purpose: Strengthen muscles of the arms.

Starting position: Right arm extended, palm up, to 45°; left hand, palm down, placed around wrist of right hand.

Count 1: While resisting with the left hand, attempt to flex the right arm, hold eight seconds, relax ten seconds, repeat two additional times.

Starting position: Left arm extended, palm up, to 45°; right hand, palm down, placed around wrist of left hand.

Count 1: While resisting with the right hand, attempt to flex the left arm, hold eight seconds, relax ten seconds, repeat two additional times.

Note: To flex the arm muscles through a complete range of motion, the performer may apply resistance at various angles from 45° (e.g., 90° and 135°).

Figure C.16. Push up and hold

Figure C.17. Arm flexor press

6.   Sit up and hold, Figure C.18

Purpose: Strengthen abdominal muscles.

Starting position: Supine, knees flexed and fingers interlaced behind neck, back straight, elbows out to side (partner may hold performer's feet down).

Count 1: Flex the hips to raise the trunk 30° from floor, hold eight seconds, relax ten seconds by lowering self to floor, repeat two additional times.

Count 2: Flex the hips to raise the trunk to 60° from floor, hold eight seconds, relax ten seconds by lowering self to floor, repeat two additional times.

7.   Straight-arm abduction/adduction, Figure C.19

Purpose: Strengthen shoulder muscles.

Starting position: Sitting, legs extended to the front and apart 30° from midline; hands, palms out, on medial surfaces of knees (arms straight).

Count 1: While resisting with the legs, attempt to push arms "through the knees," hold eight seconds, relax ten seconds, repeat two additional times.

Starting position: Sitting, legs extended to the front and apart 45° from the midline; hands, palms in, on lateral surfaces of knees (arms straight).

Count 1: While resisting with the legs, attempt to pull arms "through the knees," hold eight seconds, relax ten seconds, repeat two additional times.

Figure C.18. Sit up and hold

Figure C.19. Straight-arm abduction

8.   Leg flexion and extension, Figure C.20

Purpose: Strengthen leg muscles.

Starting position: Standing, hands on hips, feet shoulder-width apart and flat on floor
    (toes forward).

Count 1: While keeping back straight, flex knees to 10° angle, hold eight seconds; flex knees to 20° angle, hold eight seconds; continue procedure through 30°, 40°, and so on to 90°. (Do not flex knees more than 90°.)

Count 2: While keeping back straight, extend knees from 90° to 80° angle, hold eight seconds; extend knees to 70°, hold eight seconds; continue procedure through 60°, 50°, and so on to complete extension.

Figure C.20. Leg flexion and extension

APPENDIX D

Developmental Exercises with Apparatus

Weights, Benches, and Bars

General note: Although strength is increased as a result of weight training, muscular endurance can be increased also if increasing numbers of repetitions are performed. Generally, increase in resistance (the weight load) improves strength, while increase in the number of repetitions improves endurance.

1. Curls, Figure D.1

Purpose: Strengthen muscles of the arms.

Equipment: Barbell, dumbbells, universal gym.

Starting position: Standing, feet comfortable distance apart, arms extended downward, underhand grip on weight bar.

Count 1: Flex elbows while inhaling.

Count 2: Return to starting position while exhaling.

2. Chin-ups, Figure D.2

Purpose: Strengthen muscles of arms and shoulders.

Figure D.1. Curls

Equipment: Horizontal bar.

Starting position: Hanging from horizontal bar, arms extended, underhand grip.

Count 1: Pull chin above bar while inhaling.

Count 2: Return to starting position while exhaling.

Note: Chin-ups are performed with underhand grip (palms facing one's face) pullups are performed with overhand grip (palms facing away from one's face).

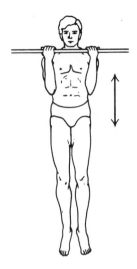

Figure D.2. Chin-ups

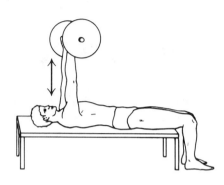

Figure D.3. Bench press

3. Bench press, Figure D.3

Purpose: Strenghen musculus deltoideus and musculus pectoralis major.

Equipment: Barbell, dumbbells, universal gym, bench.

Starting position: Supine on exercise bench, feet on floor, arms extended supporting weight with overhand grip.

Count 1: Lower weight to chest while inhaling.

Count 2: Return to starting position while exhaling.

4. L Seat dips, Figure D.4

Purpose: Strengthen muscles of arms and shoulders.

Equipment: Two exercise benches.

Starting position: Hands shoulder-width apart on one bench; heels of feet on the other bench; arms extended, body in L position.

Count 1: While inhaling, lower body by flexing elbows as much as possible.

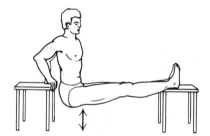

Figure D.4. L Seat dips

Count 2: Return to starting position while exhaling.

5. Dips, Figure D.5

Purpose: Strengthen muscles of arms and shoulders.

Equipment: Parallel bars.

Starting position: Cross rest with arms extended, feet off floor.

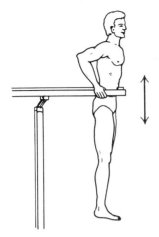

Figure D.5. Dips

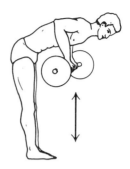

Figure D.6. Bent-over rowing

Count 1: While inhaling, lower body until elbows are bent to 90° angle.

Count 2: Return to starting position while exhaling.

6. Bent-over rowing, Figure D.6

Purpose: Strengthen musculus latissimus dorsi.

Equipment: Barbell, dumbbells

Starting position: Standing, hips flexed to 90° angle, arms extended toward floor with hands supporting weights in overhand grip. Forehead can be placed on padded table for added stability and balance.

Count 1: While inhaling, pull weight up until it touches chest.

Count 2: Return to starting position while exhaling.

7. Side lateral raises, Figure D.7

Purpose: Strengthen deltoid muscles.

Equipment: Dumbbells

Starting position: Standing, feet comfortable distance apart, arms extended down at sides while supporting dumbbells with overhand grip.

Count 1: Raise dumbbells sideways by abducting at shoulder joint, arms fully extended, until arms are parallel with floor; inhale while raising arms.

Count 2: Return to starting position while exhaling.

8. Seated press, Figure D.8

Purpose: Strengthen musculus deltoideus and muscles of arms.

Equipment: Barbell, dumbbells, universal gym, bench.

Starting position: Sitting, body facing one end of the bench, weight held in overhand grip and placed on shoulders.*

---

* If using barbell, it can be placed at shoulder level in front or behind neck (for variation).

Figure D.7. Side lateral raises

Figure D.8. Seated press

Count 1: While exhaling, raise weight until arms are fully extended overhead.

Count 2: Return to starting position while inhaling.

9. Decline sit-ups, Figure D.9

Purpose: Strengthen abdominal muscles

Equipment: Inclined bench.

Starting position: Supine on inclined bench with head at end, feet secured by ankles at upper edge, fingers interlaced behind neck, hips flexed.

Count 1: While exhaling, sit up until elbows touch knees.*

Count 2: Return to starting position while inhaling.

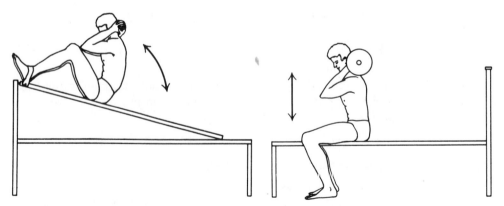

Figure D.9. Decline sit-ups

Figure D.10. One-half squats

---

* As a variation, touch chest to knees with elbows out to side.

10.   One-half squats, Figure D.10

Purpose: Strengthen muscles of legs.

Equipment: Barbell, universal gym, squat bench.

Starting position: Straddle seat of squat bench with weight resting on shoulder behind neck, secure weight with overhand grip.*

Count 1: Stand while exhaling.

Count 2: Return to starting position while inhaling.

Pulley Weights

Progressive resistance exercises are easily done with pulley weights. In the following figures, various exercises are illustrated.

Standing position, facing wall

1.   Overhand grip, arms extended and parallel to floor. Pull in sagittal plane. Return to starting position, Figure D.11.
2.   Overhand grip, arms extended sideways and parallel to floor. Pull in transverse plane. Return to starting position, Figure D.12.

Standing position, facing away from wall

1.   Overhand grip, arms extended to sides. Pull in transverse plane. Return to starting position, Figure D.13.

Standing position, one side to wall

1.   Overhand grip, right arm extended toward wall. Pull in frontal plane. Return to starting position, Figure D.14. When appropriate number of repetititons is completed, exercise with left arm.

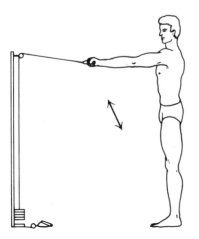

Figure D.11. Pulling in sagittal plane, facing pulley.

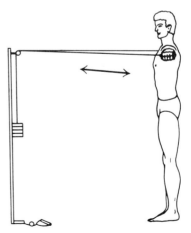

Figure D.12. Pulling in transverse plane, facing pulley.

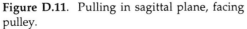

* As a variation, weight can rest on shoulders in front of the neck.

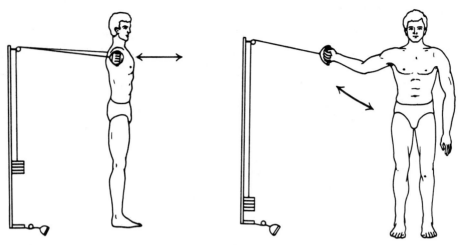

Figure D.13. Pulling in transverse plane, with   **Figure D.14**. Pulling in frontal plane.
back to pulley.

Supine position feet toward wall

1. Overhand grip with arms down at the sides. Abduct at shoulders. Return to starting position, Figure D.15.
2. Overhand grip with arms down at the sides. Raise arms until hands are above the face. Return to starting position, Figure D.16.

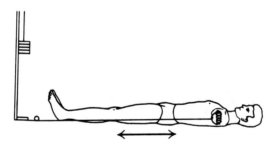

Figure D.15. Abducting at shoulders, feet toward pulley.

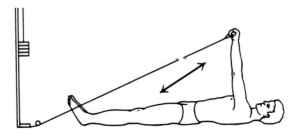

Figure D.16. Raising arms, feet toward pulley.

Supine position head toward wall

1. Overhand grip with arms extended on the floor overhead. While keeping arms straight, pull weights to the side until hands are parallel with shoulders. Return to starting position, Figure D.17.
2. Overhand grip with arms extended on the floor over head. While keeping arms straight, pull weights up until hands are above the face. Return to starting position, Figure D.18.

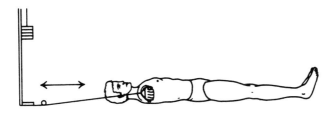

Figure D.17. Pulling to the sides, head toward pulley.

Figure D.18. Raising arms, head toward pulley.

Stall Bars

Stall bars are equipment common to developmental physical education classes. The exercises that can be performed on them are limited only by the imagination. In the following figures a sampling of exercises is illustrated.

Facing away from bars with underhand grip on uppermost bar

1. Flex hips while rotating legs in circular pattern, Figure D.19.

Figure D.19. Flexing hips while rotating legs.   **Figure D.20**. Flexing knees to chest.

**Facing away from bars with over-
hand grip on uppermost bar**

    1. Flex knees and bring them up
        toward the chest. Return to
        starting position, Figure D.20.

**Facing bar with overhand grip on
uppermost bar**

    1. Perform pull-ups, Figure D.21.

**Facing away from bars with insteps
of feet placed on rungs, assume
push-up position, hands on floor**

    1. Perform push-ups. Increase re-
        sistance, when ready, by placing
        insteps on progressively higher
        bars, Figure D.22.

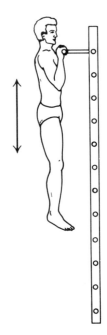

Figure D.21. Pull-ups

Supine position with insteps of feet tucked under lower rung, knees flexed, fingers interlaced behind neck

1. Perform sit-ups, Figure D.23.

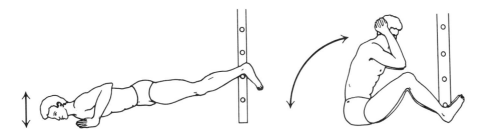

Figure D.22. Push-ups   **Figure D.23**. Sit-ups

APPENDIX E

Suggested Exercises for Relaxation

Because of the extent of the stresses and anxieties of everyday life, the ability to relax is important. Unfortunately, not enough time is spent teaching relaxation techniques in most developmental and general physical education classes. The following general rules should be applied to relaxation exercises taught in physical education programs.

1. Be sure that the room is a comfortable temperature. It is recommended that the thermostat be set at approximately seventy-five degrees.
2. Lower the lights to reduce visual stimulation. Post a sign outside the door to reduce if not prevent interruption.
3. Encourage students to wear comfortable and loose-fitting clothing and to remove shoes and socks.
4. Select soft music with slow tempo to enhance the mood of relaxation. If the music appears to stir the students, turn it off.
5. During the period of relaxation give directions in a soft, comforting tone.
6. Encourage students to breathe slowly and rhythmically.

Exercises that promote relaxation are as follows:

1. Supine position, arms and legs extended in most comfortable manner, Figure E.1. (Rolled up towels placed under the neck, small of the back, forearms, and knees may help.) Tense major muscle groups as instructed for eight seconds each, relax.
2. Front leaning rest position, chest on floor between the hands. Without lifting the stomach from contact with the floor, lift the head and shoulders as far as possible, Figure E.2. Hold eight seconds, relax.
3. Prone position, arms down sides, palms down, knees and ankles together. Lift the legs as far as possible, Figure E.3. Hold eight seconds, relax.
4. Supine position, legs as straight as possible, arms extended for balance. Lift the legs over the head until the toes touch the floor, Figure E.4. Hold thirty seconds. Be sure that breathing is continued in a slow and even cadence.

Figure E.1. Supine position

Figure E.2. Lifting head and shoulders

Figure E.3. Lifting legs as far as possible

Figure E.4. Touching toes to the floor

5. Supine position, legs extended into the air as far as possible ("bicycling" position) hands on hips, elbows on floor, Figure E.5. Stretch and hold thirty seconds. Be sure that breathing is continued in a slow and even cadence.

6. Prone position, knees flexed so that feet can be grasped with hands behind back. Arch the back as much as possible, Figure E.6. Hold eight seconds, relax.

7. Lotus position, knees flexed, feet supinated, hands on knees, back straight, Figure E.7. Hold thirty seconds. Be sure that breathing is continued in a slow and even cadence.

Figure E.5. Stretching legs into the air

Figure E.6. Arching back

Figure E.7. Lotus position

8. Sitting hurdler's position, left leg extended, bottom of right foot on inside of left thigh, hands on hips, back straight, Figure E.8. Be sure that breathing is continued in a slow and even cadence. Repeat with right leg extended, left leg bent.

Figure E.8. Sitting hurdler's position

APPENDIX F

Architectural Barrier-Free Design Codes

(Adapted from Office of Facilities Engineering/Office of the Assistant Secretary for Management and Budget. Revised August 1978. *Technical handbook for facilities engineering and construction manual, Section 4.12: Design of barrier-free facilities.* 330 Independence Avenue, S.W., Washington, DC: OFE/HEW).

Ramps

- Ramps shall have a maximum gradient of 8.33 percent, or 1 foot rise in 12 feet of run, Figure F.1.
- Ramps shall have non-slip surfaces.
- Each ramp shall be provided with a level platform at the top at least 60 inches by 60 inches if a door swings out toward the platform or the ramp. If the door does not swing toward the platform or the ramp, there shall be a level platform at least 36 inches deep and 60 inches wide. All platforms shall extend at least 12 inches beyond each side of a door.
- There shall be a straight clearance of at least 72 inches at the bottom of each ramp.

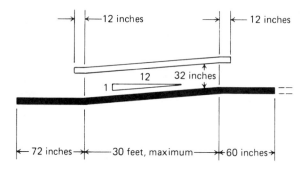

Figure F.1. Ramps. *From Technical Handbook, Office of Facilities and Engineering, U.S. Government.*

- Ramps shall be provided with level landings at 30-foot intervals and at all changes in direction.
- Ramps shall be provided with handrails 32 inches in height on at least one side and preferably both sides. The rails must be smooth and extend at least 12 inches beyond the top and bottom of the ramp.

Corridors, Public Spaces, and Work Areas

- All public spaces in a building shall be designed to accommodate those with physical disabilities.
- Corridor width must be a minimum of 60 inches for wheelchair maneuverability, Figure F.2.
- Doors opening into corridors from habitable areas shall be recessed so as not to reduce corridor width.

Doors (Exterior and Interior)

Automatic doors are desirable if they otherwise conform to the requirements of this section, Figure F.3. Manually operated sliding doors are acceptable if they meet the requirements given in this section and if careful attention is paid to the operating hardware. Recessed handles should be avoided.

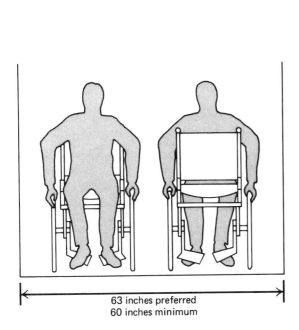

Figure F.2. Corridors. From *Technical Handbook, Office of Facilities and Engineering, U.S. Government.*

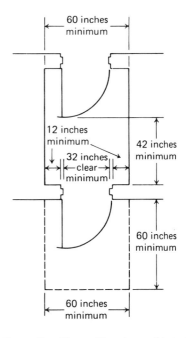

Figure F.3. Doors: Exterior and interior. From *Technical Handbook, Office of Facilities and Engineering, U.S. Government.*

- Doors must have a clear opening of at least 32 inches when open and must be operable by a single effort. The force required to open a door shall not exceed eight pounds (five pounds is preferable). (*Note:* A 32-inch clear opening requires a door wider than 32 inches. Two leaf doors are not acceptable unless they open with a single effort or unless one of the leaves provides a minimum clear opening of 32 inches.
- The floor on both the inside and outside of each door must be level for at least 60 inches from the door. The floor must extend at least 12 inches beyond each side of the door.
- The inner and outer doors of a vestibule must be separated by at least 42 inches in addition to the door swing area (see Figure F.3). Both doors shall swing in the same direction.
- Thresholds shall be flush with the floor if possible. Where a raised threshold is necessary, it must be beveled gradually from both sides.
- Kickplates at least 16 inches high are recommended for all doors.
- Door closers with a 4- to 6-second time-delay are recommended.
- Handles shall be mounted at a maximum height of 42 inches. (Panic devices should be 32 inches above the floor.) Hardware on doors leading to hazardous areas should be knurled as a warning to the blind, Figure F.4.
- Vision panels are desirable in all swinging doors. Where provided, glass must be safety-type and the bottom of the glass should be 36 inches maximum above the floor. (*Note:* A narrow vertical vision panel 6 to 8 inches wide at the latch side of the door is effective.)

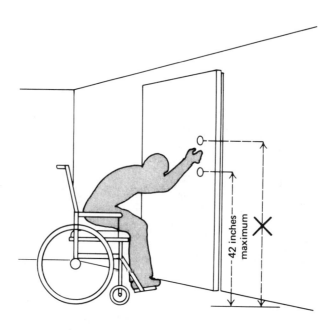

Figure F.4. Door handles. From *Technical Handbook, Office of Facilities and Engineering, U.S. Government.*

Stairs (Exterior and Interior)

The following provisions apply to all stairs that are required in order to meet building exit requirements, Figure F.5.

- Width should be 44 inches minimum.

- Risers should not exceed 7 inches in height.

- Steps shall not have square or abrupt nosings. Splayed risers with nonprojecting nosings are preferred.

- Treads shall be of a nonslip material.

- Approaches and landings should be level and differentiated from the steps by contrasting color or texture. (*Note*: Unenclosed stairs should be provided with a means of warning the blind of their existence, such as abrasive strips imbedded in the floor at the approaches.)

- Handrails 32 inches high (measured vertically from the stair nosing) are required on both sides of each stair. They should be circular or oval in section, 1 1/2 inches to 2 inches in diameter, and have a nonslip finish. At least one handrail must extend a minimum of 18 inches beyond both the top and the bottom step, Figure F.6.

- Stairs should be adequately illuminated at all times (5 footcandles at a recommended minimum).

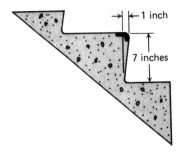

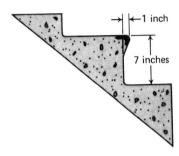

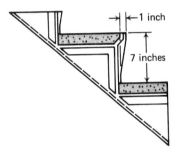

Figure F.5. Stairs: Exterior and interior. From *Technical Handbook, Office of Facilities and Engineering, U.S. Government.*

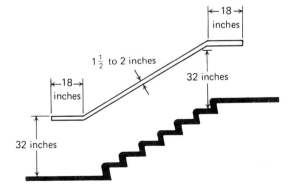

Figure F.6. Stair handrails. From *Technical Handbook, Office of Facilities and Engineering, U.S. Government.*

Toilet Facilities

- An appropriate number of toilet rooms shall be accessible to and usable by those with physical disabilities.
- Accessible toilet rooms shall have sufficient space to allow for wheelchair traffic.
- At least one toilet stall in each toilet room serving those with disabilities shall have
  1. a minimum width of 36 inches and a depth of at least 56 (and preferably 60) inches.
  2. a door (where doors are used) 32 inches wide that swings out.
  3. wall-mounted grab bars on each side, 1 1/2 inches in diameter, 1 1/2 inches clear of the wall, and mounted securely at ends and center 33 inches high and parallel to the floor.
  4. a water closet with seat 20 inches above the floor, Figure F.7.
- At least one basin in each toilet room serving those with disabilities shall be mounted with a 29-inch minimum clearance underneath the apron of the fixture, Figure F.8.

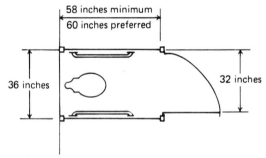

Figure F.7. Toilet stall. From *Technical Handbook, Office of Facilities and Engineering, U.S. Government.*

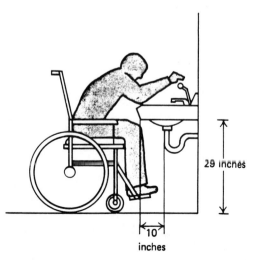

Figure F.8. Basin Fixture. From *Technical Handbook, Office of Facilities and Engineering, U.S. Government.*

- Men's toilet rooms shall have wall-mounted urinals with the rim 19 inches above the floor, or shall have floor-mounted urinals that are at the same level as the main floor of the toilet room.
- Mirrors and shelves shall be mounted above accessible basins at as low a height as possible, but not to exceed 40 inches from the bottom of the mirror to the floor.
- At least one towel dispenser or towel rack and one each of other dispensers and disposal units shall be mounted no higher than 40 inches above the floor, Figure F.9.

Drinking Fountains and Table Surfaces

- At least one drinking fountain usable by those with physical disabilities shall be provided at an accessible location on each floor.
- The fountain shall be hand operated or hand-and-foot operated with up-front water jet and controls.
- A wall-mounted model with a 12-inch projecting basin is preferred. The rim of the basin should be from 30 inches to 36 inches above the floor. Fully recessed models are not acceptable, Figure F.10.

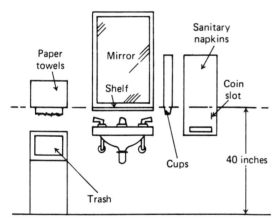

Figure F.9. Arrangement of basin and accessory fixtures. From *Technical Handbook, Office of Facilities and Engineering, U.S. Government.*

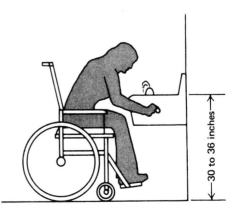

Figure F.10. Drinking fountain. From *Technical Handbook, Office of Facilities and Engineering, U.S. Government.*

- Work surfaces, storage units, keyboard tables, and conference tables should be capable of being adjusted incrementally in height. Work surface units (other than keyboard tables) should have a clear height to the underside of the work surface, which can be adjusted from 25 inches to 30 inches, Figure F.11.
- Fixed tables (dining surfaces) should provide clear space under the tabletop not less than 30 inches wide per seating space, nor less than 27 inches clear height to a minimum depth of 12 inches from the edge of the table, Figure F.12.

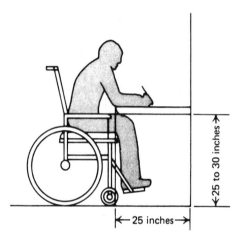

Figure F.11. Work surface. From *Technical Handbook, Office of Facilities and Engineering, U.S. Government.*

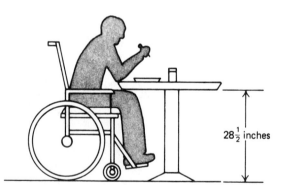

Figure F.12. Fixed eating table. From *Technical Handbook, Office of Facilities and Engineering, U.S. Government.*

Name Index

Williams, J.F., 511
Wiseman, , 354
Wittrock, M., 326
Wong, D.L., 228
Wood, J., 432

Wood, J.W., 288, 293
Woods, N.F., 188, 165, 233, 239
Wright, B., 535
Wunderlich, R.C., 342

Yarber, W.L., 338, 341
Yates, J.R., 533

Zaetz, J.L., 534
Zittel, L., 369

Subject Index